MODERN COMMUNITY
MENTAL HEALTH

MODERN COMMUNITY MENTAL HEALTH

An Interdisciplinary Approach

Kenneth R. Yeager, PhD, LISW
David L. Cutler, MD
Dale Svendsen, MD, MS
Grayce M. Sills, PhD, RN, FAAN

OXFORD
UNIVERSITY PRESS

Oxford University Press is a department of the University of Oxford. It furthers the University's objective of excellence in research, scholarship, and education by publishing worldwide.

Oxford   New York
Auckland   Cape Town   Dar es Salaam   Hong Kong   Karachi
Kuala Lumpur   Madrid   Melbourne   Mexico City   Nairobi
New Delhi   Shanghai   Taipei   Toronto

With offices in
Argentina   Austria   Brazil   Chile   Czech Republic   France   Greece
Guatemala   Hungary   Italy   Japan   Poland   Portugal   Singapore
South Korea   Switzerland   Thailand   Turkey   Ukraine   Vietnam

Oxford is a registered trademark of Oxford University Press in the
UK and certain other countries.

Published in the United States of America by
Oxford University Press
198 Madison Avenue, New York, NY 10016

Library of Congress Cataloging-in-Publication Data
Modern community mental health : an interdisciplinary approach / [edited by]
   Kenneth R. Yeager, PhD, LISW, David L. Cutler, MD, Dale Svendsen, MD, MS,
   Grayce M. Sills, PhD, RN, FAAN.
   pages cm
   Includes bibliographical references and index.
   ISBN 978–0–19–979806–3 (hardcover : alk. paper)   1. Community mental health
   services – Administration.   2. Mental health – Social aspects.   I. Yeager, Kenneth.
   II. Cutler, David L.   III. Svendsen, Dale.   IV. Sills, Grayce M.
   RA790.5.M57 2013
   362.2'2—dc23
   2012029881

ISBN 978–0–19–979806–3

9 8 7 6 5 4 3 2 1
Printed in the United States of America
on acid-free paper

CONTENTS

SECTION IV
LEADERSHIP, ADMINISTRATION, MANAGEMENT

ACKNOWLEDGMENTS

First and foremost, our deepest gratitude goes to our editors: —all Oxford University Press Staff who supported and assisted us with the conceptual development of this text; and Nicholas Liu, who saw this book to its conclusion. We are fortunate to have had their inspiration, support, and dedication through the cumbersome and tedious process of this book's development. It was their support, guidance, encouragement and editorial suggestions that improved the book proposal and the final manuscript. Additionally, we would like to thank Jessica Levy Auslander, who kept the book manuscript on schedule and organized as we struggled through the various chapter drafts and seemingly endless papers of revisions, and for organizing the glossary of terms and electronic resources.

Most importantly, this book was made possible by the talented group of chapter authors, who were charged with the difficult task of writing very readable, practical chapters that captured the essence of their topic within a concise format. It is our belief that each of these chapters represents the future of community mental health practice. We would also like to thank John Campo and Amanda Lucas for supporting the Division of Public and Community Psychiatry within the Department of Psychiatry of Ohio State University. Their vision has set the stage for transition into the next phase of community mental health practice. Finally, we would like to thank our families for supporting us in taking the time away from them necessary to complete this book—without the support and understanding of our loved ones, this book would not have been written.

CONTRIBUTORS

EDITORS

Kenneth R. Yeager, PhD, LISW

Kenneth R. Yeager, PhD, is an associate professor, clinical, in the College of Medicine, Department of Psychiatry of The Ohio State University, and director of quality improvement for OSU Harding Hospital. Dr. Yeager has numerous publications in the following areas: Treating co-morbid substance abuse and mental illness; quality improvement and developing quality metrics; and evidence-based practice, including the Oxford University Press book titled "*Evidence-Based Practice Manual: Research and Outcome Measures in Health and Human Services.*" He is a member of Oxford Bibliographies Online editorial board and a treating clinician for the National Football League Program for Substances of Abuse.

David L. Cutler, MD

Dr. Cutler has served since late 2004 as the medical director of the Mental Health and Addiction Services Division of the Multnomah County, Oregon, Department of Human Services. He is an auxiliary professor at The Ohio State University Department of Psychiatry, where, in 2005 and 2006, he was the visiting "professor of public psychiatry." Before that, he was professor of psychiatry at the Oregon Health and Sciences University from 1977 to 2004, and director of the Public Psychiatry Training Program in the department of psychiatry (1985–2004). Dr. Cutler trained in psychiatry at the University of Washington and the University of California, Irvine. He served in the U.S. Air Force from 1971 to 1973 and was director of outpatient services at Southern Arizona Mental Health Center from 1973 to 1977.

He has published extensively on subjects ranging from training in public psychiatry, rural psychiatry, forensic psychiatry, and ethical issues in community mental health to the treatment of persons with severe mental illnesses. Between 1987 and 2005, he was editor in chief of the *Community Mental Health Journal.* Dr. Cutler's career also includes stints on numerous editorial review boards, consultation posts, memberships on national and local task forces, and advisory boards and committees. Dr. Cutler was an early board member of the American Association of Community Psychiatrists (AACP) and has remained a board member since 1989. He is a

Distinguished Life Fellow of the American Psychiatric Association and has received numerous awards from the National Alliance on Mental Illness (NAMI), the American Board of Psychiatry and Neurology (ABPN), and other national organizations.

Dale Svendsen, MD, MS

Dale Svendsen is currently the director of the Division of Public and Community Psychiatry at The Ohio State University Department of Psychiatry. Svendsen joined Ohio State after retiring as the medical director of the Ohio Department of Mental Health, where he worked diligently to build and implement best practices in public mental health across the state of Ohio. Svendsen has a particular interest in the integration of physical health and mental health care. He has served in numerous leadership positions and has completed publications in areas of comorbid health and mental health, and the implementation of best practices and evidence-based practices. Dr. Svendsen has received multiple awards for his leadership at the state and national levels.

Grayce M. Sills, PhD, RN, FAAN

Sills joined the Ohio State University faculty in 1964 as an assistant professor. By retirement in 1991, she had held a number of administrative positions, including director of the Advanced Psychiatric Mental Health Nursing Program, chair of the Department of Family and Community Nursing, director of graduate studies, and acting dean of the College of Nursing. Sills was a leader in shaping Ohio State's College of Nursing, including the development of the master's and doctoral programs and its acquisition of college status. Her commitment and skill as a teacher earned her a teaching and service award from the College of Medicine, and the Alumni Award for Distinguished Teaching, the university's highest honor for teaching. Sills is a nationally acclaimed scholar in the field of psychiatric nursing and has served on a number of local and state committees to improve services for the mentally ill. In 1988, Governor Richard Celeste appointed her to chair the Study Committee on Mental Health Services for the State of Ohio. A registered nurse, Sills holds a bachelor's degree from the University of Dayton. She earned her MS and PhD at Ohio State. She holds an honorary doctorate from Indiana University and is a fellow of the American Academy of Nursing.

CONTRIBUTORS

Robert W. Ahern, PhD, LISW-S
Clinical Director
Chief of Staff
Juvenile and Probate Court
Union County, OH
Instructor
College of Social Work
The Ohio State University
Private Practitioner
New Reflections Counseling Center
Marysville, OH

Anthony O. Ahmed, PhD
Assistant Professor
Department of Psychiatry and Health
  Behavior
Georgia Health Sciences University
Augusta, GA

Elaine Alberti, MN, RN
Clinical Nurse Specialist
Eastern State Hospital
Medical Lake, WA

Jessica Levy Auslander, MA, NCC/NCSC, DCC
Instructional Development Specialist
Department of Psychiatry
College of Medicine
The Ohio State University Wexner Medical
  Center
Columbus, OH

Carl C. Bell, MD
President & CEO
Community Mental Health Council &
  Foundation, Inc.
Director
Institute for Juvenile Research
Director
Public and Community Psychiatry
Clinical Professor of Psychiatry and Public
  Health
Department of Psychiatry
College of Medicine
University of Illinois at Chicago
Chicago, IL

Loretta Berti, PhD
Research Assistant
Section of Psychiatry and Clinical Psychology
Department of Public Health and
  Community Medicine
University of Verona
Verona, Italy

David E. Biegel, PhD
Henry L. Zucker Professor of Social Work
  Practice
Co-Director
Center of Substance Abuse and Mental
  Illness
Mandel School of Applied Social Sciences
Case Western Reserve University
Cleveland, OH

Christopher D. Bowling, MSEd, CLEE
Lieutenant
Crisis Intervention Team (CIT) Coordinator
Columbus, Ohio Division of Police
Columbus, OH

Daniel W. Bradford, MD, MPH
Director, Psychosocial Rehabilitation and
    Recovery Center &
Inter-professional Fellowship on Psychosocial
    Rehabilitation
Durham VA Medical Center
Assistant Professor
Department of Psychiatry and Behavioral
    Sciences
Duke University Medical Center
Durham, NC

Peter F. Buckley, MD
Professor of Psychiatry and Health Behavior
Dean of the Medical College of Georgia
Georgia Health Sciences University
Augusta, GA

Joyce Burland, PhD
Clinical Psychologist
Author of the NAMI Family-to-Family
    Education Program
Sante Fe, NM

Lorenzo Burti, MD
Professor of Psychiatry
Section of Psychiatry and Clinical Psychology
Department of Public Health and
    Community Medicine
University of Verona
Verona, Italy

Elisabetta Canova, MA
Psychiatric Rehabilitation Specialist
Community Mental Health Service of
    South-Verona
Verona, Italy

Philip Cass, PhD
Chief Executive Officer
Columbus Medical Association
Columbus, OH

Kevin Corcoran, PhD, JD
Professor
School of Social Work
Portland State University
Portland, OR

Christy Daron, MSW, LSW
Program Manager
Woman's SMD Residential Home
Southeast, Inc
Columbus, OH

Jean Dentinger, MPA
Diversion Courts Manager
Multnomah County Department of Human
    Services
Portland, OR

Robert E. Drake, MD, PhD
Professor
Psychiatry, Community and Family
    Medicine
The Dartmouth Institute
Dartmouth Medical School
Lebanon, NH

Benjamin G. Druss, MD, MPH
Rosalynn Carter Chair in Mental Health
Department of Health Policy and
    Management
Behavioral Sciences and Health Education
Rollins School of Public Health
Emory University
Atlanta, GA

Ken Duckworth, MD
Medical Director
NAMI
Assistant Clinical Professor of Psychiatry
Harvard Medical School
Cambridge, MA

Hon. Charlotte Coleman-Eufinger
Juvenile and Probate Court
Union County, OH

Anita Everett, MD, DFAPA
Section Director
Community Psychiatry
Johns Hopkins School of Medicine
Johns Hopkins Bayview Medical Center
Baltimore, MD

Neil Falk, MD
Associate Medical Director
Cascadia Behavioral Healthcare, Inc.
Portland, OR

Marianne Farkas, ScD
Director of Training, Dissemination,
   Technical Assistance
Clinical Professor
Center for Psychiatric Rehabilitation
Boston University
Boston, MA

Daniel B. Fisher, MD, PhD
Executive Director
National Empowerment Center
Cambridge, MA

Kamal Floura, MD
Medical Director
Eastern State Hospital
Medical Lake, WA

Rick Forbess, MSSW
Associate Director of Training,
   Dissemination, Technical Assistance
Center for Psychiatric Rehabilitation
Boston University
Boston, MA

Michele Fornari, MA
Psychiatric Rehabilitation Specialist
Community Mental Health Service of
   South-Verona
Verona, Italy

Fred Frese, PhD
Associate Professor of Psychiatry
Northeast Ohio Medical University
Rootstown, OH

Buddy Garfinkle, MA, MSW
Associate Executive Director
Bridgeway Rehabilitation Services, Inc.
Elizabeth, NJ

Julie P. Gentile, MD
Associate Professor
Wright State University
Dayton, OH

Rupert R. Goetz, MD, DFAPA
Chief Medical Officer
Oregon State Hospital
Salem, OR

Darcy Haag Granello, PhD, LPCC
Professor
Counselor Education
The Ohio State University
Columbus, OH

Patricia A. Griffin, PhD
Senior Consultant
SAMHSA GAINS Center
Pennsylvania Mental Health and Justice
   Center of Excellence
Philadelphia Department of Behavioral
   Health and Intellectual disAbility Services
Philadelphia, PA

Will Hall, MA, Dipl.PW
Director, Portland Hearing Voices
Host, Madness Radio
Co-Founder, Freedom Center
Portland, OR

Lisa Halpern, MPP, CPRP, CPS
Director of Recovery Services
Vinfen
Cambridge, MA

Michael Hogan, PhD
Commissioner
New York State Office of Mental Health
Albany, NY

Kevin Huckshorn, RN, MSN, CADC
Delaware Director
Division of Substance Abuse and Mental
　Health
New Castle, DE

Carroll S. Jackson, LISW-S
Montgomery County Board of
　Developmental Disabilities
Mental Health Clinic
Dayton, OH

David P. Kasick, MD
Assistant Professor of Clinical Psychiatry
College of Medicine
Director of Consultation-Liaison Psychiatry
The Ohio State University Wexner Medical
　Center
Columbus, OH

Holly Kastan, MSW, LSW
Director of Planning, Development and
　Outreach-OSU STAR Program
Department of Psychiatry
The Ohio State University Wexner Medical
　Center
Columbus, OH

Kathleen Kemp, PhD
Postdoctoral Fellow
Institute of Law, Psychiatry and Public Policy
　(ILPPP)
University of Virginia
Western State Hospital
Charlottesville, VA

Lenore A. Kola, PhD
Associate Professor of Social Work
Co-Director, Center for Evidence Based
　Practices at Case
Mandel School of Applied Social Sciences
Case Western Reserve University
Cleveland, OH

Carol Kottwitz, MN, PMHCNS, BC
Clinical Nurse Specialist
Eastern State Hospital
Medical Lake, WA

Janice L. LeBel, EdD
Director of Program Management
Commonwealth of Massachusetts
　Department of Mental Health
Boston, MA

Harriet P. Lefley, PhD
Professor
Department of Psychiatry and Behavioral
　Sciences
University of Miami Miller School of
　Medicine
Miami, FL

Jayme Lynch, CPS
Director
Peer Support and Wellness Center
Decatur, GA

Christopher T. Manetta, DO
Kirtland Air Force Base Medical Facility
Kirtland AFB, NM

Shané P. Marshall, LISW, LCDCIII
Readjustment Counseling Therapist
Department of Veterans Affairs, Vet Center
　Consultant
Shé Petite Management & Consulting
Columbus, OH

Dominica F. McBride, PhD
President
The HELP Institute, Inc
Director of Research
Community Mental Health Council, Inc
Chicago, IL

Bentson McFarland, MD, PhD
Professor of Psychiatry
Professor of Public Health and Preventive
　Medicine
Oregon Health and Science University
Portland, OR

Patrick D. McGorry, AO, MD, BS, PhD, FRCP, FRANZCP
Executive Director
Orygen Youth Health Research Centre
Professor
Centre for Youth Mental Health
The University of Melbourne
Director of Clinical Services
Orygen Youth Health
Melbourne, Australia

Ryan P. Melton, PhD, LPC, ACS
EASA State Clinical Coordinator
Mid-Valley Behavioral Care Network
Salem, OR

Kenneth Minkoff, MD
Senior System Consultant
ZiaPartners, Inc
San Rafael, California
Clinical Assistant Professor of Psychiatry
Cambridge Health Alliance Department of
   Psychiatry
Harvard Medical School
Cambridge, MA

Mark R. Munetz, MD
The Margaret Clark Morgan Foundation
   Chair
Professor of Psychiatry
Northeast Ohio Medical University
Rootstown, OH
Chief Clinical Officer
Summit County Alcohol, Drug Addiction
   and Mental Health Services Board
Akron, OH

Julie Niedermier, MD
Associate Professor of Clinical Psychiatry
Director of Education
Department of Psychiatry
The Ohio State University Wexner Medical
   Center
Columbus, OH

Bernadette Nunley, JD
Assistant County Attorney
Multnomah County, OR

William Nunley, MD, MPH
Associate Medical Director
CareOregon
Corrections Health Consulting Psychiatrist
Multnomah County Health Department
Project Coordinator
Bazelon Center for Mental Health Law
Cascadia Behavioral Health Care
Portland, OR

Donata Pavani, MA
Psychiatric Rehabilitation Specialist
Community Mental Health Service of
   South-Verona
Verona, Italy

Narsimha R. Pinninti, MD
Professor of Psychiatry
UMDNJ School of Osteopathic Medicine
Chief Medical Officer
Twin Oaks Community Services
Cherry Hill, NJ

David A. Pollack, MD
Professor for Public Policy
Department of Psychiatry
Division of Management
Oregon Health and Science University
Portland, OR

Alan Q. Radke, MD, MPH
Medical Director
Department of Human Services
State of Minnesota
St. Paul, MN

Mark Ragins, MD
Medical Director
Mental Health America-Los Angeles
The Village
Long Beach, CA

Jeffrey L. Ramirez, PhD, PMHNP, BC
Assistant Professor
Gonzaga University
Spokane, WA
Clinical Nurse Specialist
Eastern State Hospital
Medical Lake, WA

Christina L. Rodriguez, MSW
Counselor
EASA Marion County
Salem, OR

Robert J. Ronis, MD, MPH
Douglas Danford Bond Professor and
    Chairman
Department of Psychiatry
Case Western Reserve University School
    of Medicine
Cleveland, OH

Sean N. Roush, OTD, OTR/L
Assistant Professor
School of Occupational Therapy
Pacific University
Hillsboro, OR

Tamara G. Sale, MA
EASA State Program Coordinator
Mid-Valley Behavioral Care Network
Salem, OR

Lisa T. Schmidt, PhD, CPRP
Associate Clinical Professor/Associate
    Director
Department of Behavioral Health Counseling
College of Nursing and Health Professions
Drexel University
Philadelphia, PA

Phil Shapiro, MD, MPH
Medical Director
Central City Concern
Old Town Recovery Center
Portland, OR

James Sizemore, MDiv
Readjustment Counseling Therapist
Department of Veterans Affairs, Vet Center
Columbus, OH

Phyllis Solomon, PhD
Professor of Social Work
School of Social Policy & Practice
Professor of Social Work in Psychiatry
Department of Psychiatry, Medical School
University of Pennsylvania
Philadelphia, PA

Margaret A. Swarbrick, PhD, OT, CPRP
Director
CSPNJ Institute for Wellness and Recovery
    Initiatives
Clinical Assistant Professor
School of Health Related Professions
University of Medicine and Dentistry of New
    Jersey
Freehold, NJ

Gregory B. Teague, PhD
Associate Professor
Department of Mental Health Law & Policy
College of Behavioral and Community
    Sciences
University of South Florida
Tampa, FL

Sharon Jenkins Tucker, MA, ITE, CPS
Executive Director
Georgia Mental Health Consumer Network
Decatur, GA

Craigan T. Usher, MD
Assistant Professor of Psychiatry
Director, Child & Adolescent Psychiatry
    Residency Training Program
Oregon Health & Science University
Portland, OR

Vikki L. Vandiver, Dr.PH, MSW
Professor
School of Social Work
Portland State University
Affiliate Professor
Department of Psychiatry
Oregon Health and Science University
Portland, OR

**Suzanne Elizabeth Vogel-Scibilia, MD,
DFAPA**
Assistant Clinical Professor
University of Pittsburgh
Beaver, PA

Elizabeth Reisinger Walker, MAT, MPH
Doctoral Candidate
Department of Behavioral Sciences and
    Health Education
Rollins School of Public Health
Emory University
Atlanta, GA

Laura Weisel, PhD
CEO, Clinical Director
TLP Group
Columbus, OH

Leslie A. Winters, JD
Assistant General Counsel
The Ohio State University Wexner Medical
    Center
Columbus, OH

Robert M. Wolf, MD
Medical Director
Early Assessment and Support Team
Mid-Valley Behavioral Care Network
Salem, OR

Judy Wortham-Wood, MA
Executive Director
The Mental Health and Recovery Board of
Wayne and Holmes Counties
Wooster, OH

SECTION I

COMMUNITY MENTAL HEALTH

Progress and Principles

C H A P T E R 1

INTRODUCTION

KENNETH R. YEAGER, DAVID L. CUTLER, DALE SVENDSEN,
AND GRAYCE M. SILLS

odern Community Mental Health: An Interdisciplinary Approach is being released on the heels of the fiftieth anniversary of the Eisenhower Commission Report (1961) and on the cusp of the same anniversary of the Community Mental Health Act (1963). Both reports set the stage for the recognition of the broad scope of mental illness within the United States, and the launch of the community mental health movement. The first presidential commission on mental illness and health "Action for Mental Health" (1961) recommended a new national mental health program. This report also recognized the fortieth anniversary of the Rehabilitation Act (1973) which established major funding resources for those with debilitating mental illness. Rehabilitation is still a topic and focus of much debate in mental health policy. When this book was first conceptualized it was near the tenth anniversary of the Presidents New Freedom Commission (2003) which outlined the importance of the integration of physical and mental health and stressed the importance of the actualization of the principles of "recovery." Each of these earlier reports represents the evolutionary concepts which undergird the development of the current community mental health system in the United States. We believe we have crafted this book to incorporate most of those key concepts contained within the presidential reports and landmark legislation into the context of today's community service delivery system. We have done so with the intent of honoring those original reports and legislation while providing a current context for application in today's challenging service delivery system.

Working together in the mental health system 50 years ago most often meant "doing to or doing for" patients as opposed to "working with" in a collaborative relationship. Back then, traditionally, there were four core professional mental health disciplines within community mental health. At present there are almost too many varied types of workers to count. Yet the central fact remains that working together across disciplines is the key to achieving a clinically competent, culturally competent, outcomes effective workforce. Now 50 years later community mental health practice means working together *with* recovering people, whose talents and skills are uniquely targeted for work in community mental health practice. We have changed our perception of what is important in providing care within the community setting. Some 50 years ago, mental health workers thought those with mental illness had little to offer; their perceptions or thought processes were often considered to be blunted by the illness. Yet it is the experience of the illness that makes this group of often very capable individuals very effective and skilled in providing empathic, inspirational support to others who struggle at various stages and crisis points with these illnesses.

Perhaps more than any other country, in the United States the workforce is hampered in becoming fully effective by many barriers. Not the least of which is the myriad of licensing, titling, and credentialing policies and procedures, combined with twisted and confusing funding streams, that serve to make service delivery to needing and deserving populations difficult, and to say the least, frustrating, as well as incredibly challenging and complex. The day-to-day challenges can at times be overwhelming. These challenges can provide an overwhelming sense of accomplishment or failure and certainly almost every emotion in between. At times navigating the system itself can be daunting for both consumers and professionals within the system. By definition, community mental health practice is ever-changing. As communities change, the professions change and in recent years, changes in funding have drastically affected the system of care. A call for empirically supported interventions has spurred dramatic changes in care delivery that have been intended to improve the level of safety and quality of care provided. The integration of the voice of the consumer and needs of family members is being improved. Often now, these voices are responded to, leading to many changes in the system of care as well as the composition of the teams providing care. Given the complexities of community mental health practice and the increasing time pressures of day-to-day practice, most students and practitioners need a roadmap to provide direction in working together through the complex, ever-changing, and at times treacherous terrain of the community system. Our hope is that this book will help provide some direction and guidance for those who travel this terrain.

Today, the core four mental health disciplines still exist, but they exist within a matrix that is much larger and one that is much more diverse and complex. Now one finds a workforce comprised of job coaches, case managers, professional counselors, couple and family therapists, consumer advocates, patient's rights advocates, payees, brokers, pharmacists, clergy, administrators, risk managers, and many, many others. As diversity emerged in those providing care, lines of care responsibilities blurred. While some saw and supported this divergence from what was perceived as stagnant approaches to practice, others dug in, attempting to redraw lines of role definition, using legislation and licensure to define scopes of practice, in an effort to assure payment within existing payor structures. Amidst all of the confusion, a simple concept was lost: the concept of working together. Yet, even as confusion grew about how services would be delivered, clarity began to emerge regarding a new and evolving approach to mental health care and "service delivery."

DO YOU REMEMBER WHEN COLLABORATION MEANT WORKING WITH THE ENEMY?

Our editor Dr. Sills is quick to quote an African American spiritual in which one of the lines sings, "Everybody talkin' 'bout heav'n that ain't goin' there…." In the same sense today, everybody talking about collaboration may not be going there. Community mental health care is difficult. We are on the verge of a transformation in community mental health practice. The practices are about to change. Funding streams are about to change, and most important, there may be an opportunity to finally reunite the mind and the body within a framework of community mental health practice.

This book will present new ways of doing mental health practice that are collaborative and interdisciplinary or even *transdisciplinary*, a term that will be defined later in this book in Vandiver and Corcoran's chapter (Chapter 36). We found very early in our interdisciplinary efforts and collaborations exactly how difficult this work can be to do effectively. We all have our own concepts regarding this process. We all have our own approaches to interdisciplinary collaboration. In fact, it was not until well into the process of developing this text that we realized what interdisciplinary mental health practice had become, and it was different from what any of us had conceived of within our own discipline-limited views. Our early efforts were focused on balancing the number of nurses, social workers, physicians, and psychologists, seeking exactly the right mix, being careful not to leave any single discipline out of the carefully constructed proposal of chapters to be included in the text.

You will see when reading this text that we quickly moved away from this concept, as it was not only difficult to find exactly the right mix, but more importantly because to do so would leave out the opportunity to bring forward important concepts of community mental health that far transcend any selected set of disciplines. Most important, building this text around disciplines completely left out consumers, an unacceptable option! We have made a conscious decision to bring forward a constellation of concepts: some unique, some complex, some simple and to the point, but all specifically designed to point to the future of community and public psychiatry. Your particular discipline may be missing. If it is, we apologize. It is not because we chose not to highlight your specific discipline's work. Rather, it is because we have limited space and opportunities to highlight every approach that is representative of a single discipline.

ORGANIZATION OF THIS BOOK

This work contains 37 original chapters written by a diverse group of experienced and cutting-edge practitioners: each chapter represents the changing face of community mental health. All chapters present current practices by leaders in the field of community mental health, covering a diverse span of mental health and associated professionals and consumers to address the current challenges in mental health service delivery. This book seeks to integrate a diverse group of perceptions in regard to mental health treatment, and we believe it is the first to take a truly interdisciplinary approach incorporating evidence-based approaches and best-practice approaches while intertwining consumer and family needs within a framework of what can best be described as the ever-changing faces and definitions of community mental health providers. Our focus is on core competencies, not all aspects of community mental health, as taking that on would require multiple volumes of text that, in the end, would not be helpful to the reader of this book. Our overarching goal is to provide the best knowledge within a realistic format to inform a current model of community mental health practice.

SECTION 1: COMMUNITY MENTAL HEALTH: PROGRESS AND PRINCIPLES

This section represents our strong commitment to community. It begins with an overview of what was intended to be, what has happened, and where we are today. Within this section, you will find content that is intended to highlight system responses to current challenges. We selected topics that cover current challenges—some new and some familiar—that are relevant and necessary to understand when defining community mental health practice. In a world in which new research and knowledge development continues to shape and transform the way services are provided.

SECTION 2: PREPARATION FOR COMMUNITY WORK

In this section, we provide an overview of the core competencies necessary to practice within the community mental health setting. We have taken a hard look at what comprises the critical knowledge base for community mental health practice. We have closely examined the literature, including criticism of America's higher education system, and have summarized findings and a potential demonstration model for interdisciplinary education. Yeager, Sills, and Kastan explored the work of the Annapolis Coalition and others when examining core competencies needed for comprehensive behavioral education. Within this chapter, gaps in learning are identified, and potential explanations for identified gaps are provided. You will find here the only chapter in this book that singles out any one discipline. Dr. Julie Niedermier examines the specific need for training medical students in preparation for the diverse presentation of mental health needs and the synergistic impact of mental health on physical health. As mentioned above, some topics are familiar challenges; for example, Lefley and Shapiro explore "The Power of Groups in the Treatment of Serious Mental Illness," an important concept for sustained recovery and a practice that has roots in community mental health. Bell and McBride define and describe "cultural competency," a key skill in working with diverse populations in community mental health. Some concepts take the familiar and link it to new knowledge, such as Cutler and Everett's chapter examining "interdisciplinary mental health consultation and collaboration." And Walker, Tucker, Lynch, and Druss examine "physical and mental health care." You will also find chapters that should have been included since the onset of community mental health practice, but have not, such as the "consumer–professional partnership during the recovery era," by Vogel-Scibilia and Frese. The unfortunate reality is there simply was not enough space to cover all topics.

SECTION 3: BEST PRACTICES AND CURRENT EVIDENCE FOR CLINICAL PRACTICE

The largest section of this book, the best-practices section is designed to provide students and practitioners with current knowledge and best practices. In selecting topical areas for chapters, we made every attempt to include cutting-edge areas of concern to community mental health practice, with a keen eye toward authors who would provide a realistic view of the challenges faced within the changing environment of care. The challenge that emerged was to provide a balanced viewpoint of community mental health practice from the standpoint of providers, consumers, families, and diverse populations.

Beginning with an overview of "evidence-based practice in community mental health" by Kola, Biegel, and Ronis, this section continues the exploration of familiar topics within a current conceptual interdisciplinary framework of practice. For example, Gentile, Manetta, and Jackson explore new and emerging best practices in working with combined "mental illness and intellectual disability." In a similar vein, Halpern, Duckworth, and Lefley apply "family psychoeducation," providing an exemplary outline of best practices in working to build support for families. Chaplain Jim Sizemore and Shané Marshall expand care-provider diversity and take us into the world of working with military veterans and their families, a population recognized as changing in numerous areas, including but not limited to risk, diversity, and need. In keeping with the foundation of community mental health, Schmidt, Pinniniti, Garfinkle, and Solomon provide a comprehensive examination of best practices with "assertive community treatment teams." To round out this section, Ragins and Pollack provide a current view of "recovery and community mental health" which they believe will revolutionize and transform the mental health system.

SECTION 4: LEADERSHIP, ADMINISTRATION, AND MANAGEMENT

In the closing section of this book, we turn to leadership and management. Svendsen, Hogan, and Coleman-Eufinger walk readers through the model that led Ohio's mental health transformation of examining processes and practices that led to innovative changes within the state's mental health leadership processes. A critical issue that is on the mind of all in community mental health practice is how processes are funded, and questions of what the future will hold. Frank and Ignolia examine the "economics of behavioral healthcare." In keeping with the theme of concepts that have emerged and evolved is the topic of "co-occurring disorders": Yeager and Minkoff examine the establishment of systems of care for managing persons with co-occurring disorders. Another question on the minds of the editors of this book is how we know we are headed in the right direction. To answer this question we turn to Vandiver and Corcoran for the final word on "quality management and program evaluation." We hope our readers will find the material and web based resources useful in their studies and in their work.

CHAPTER 2

PUBLIC MENTAL HEALTH IN AMERICA

"Enlightenment" to Accountable Care

DAVID L. CUTLER, GRAYCE M. SILLS, DALE SVENDSEN, AND
KENNETH R. YEAGER

The history of society's efforts to deal with mentally ill persons has been punctuated by a variety of dramatic events that have shaped public opinion and at times formed a nexus of ethical and political debates. This chapter examines the history of community mental health policy from its earliest voices in antiquity, to the Enlightenment, to nineteenth-century asylums, and all the way to twenty-first-century service models and perhaps a bit beyond. We will shed light on the evolution of some of these early public mental health ideas, philosophies, and practices, and on how they have adapted, changed form, and continue to influence current models of community-based funding and programs.

INTRODUCTION

To discuss the history of mental health care is a somewhat daunting task from the perspective of the second decade of the twenty-first century. Too much has occurred in too short of a time to adequately do it justice. Nevertheless, we agreed to undertake this "mission impossible," so our job is to give it a try. If we overlook your favorite historical moment, please accept our apologies in advance for leaving it unnoticed. That said, we need to start somewhere, and a good starting place might be with the Greeks' and the Romans' medical healing centers out in the countryside. Equipped with hot- and cold-water spas, these Asklepian colonies are a likely, pleasantly anti-quarian, classical spot to begin. By analogy to modern times, the Greek colony of Epidavros could be viewed perhaps as the "Cleveland Clinic" of antiquity. There, patients suffering from various agonizing ailments were hoping that the opportunity to be near *Asklepios*, the god of medicine and healing, would be curative. But even in Epidavros, just like in a modern emergency room, they often waited substantial amounts of time in order to be assessed by a sort of combination priest-physician specialist, and then were sent to the *Avaton* to sleep and then to dream. Ah, but "what dreams may have come?" (*Hamlet*). A diagnosis would have been made by dream interpretation, and then certain treatments prescribed. At the time, the only treatments available were things like diet, exercise, and hydrotherapy. To this day, the Epidavros site still contains ruins of ancient baths, lodgings, and dwellings for priests. There was also a round *tholos* building (the medical school), other temples, stoas, a gymnasium, and a stadium (Ehrenwald, 1976). Today, patients might go to Cleveland, Ohio, to get their diet, exercise, and surgery, and once cured, perhaps to visit the Rock and Roll Hall of Fame when they were feeling a little better.

Rather than dwell too long with the ancient world, let us move forward a few centuries to the religious sanctuaries of the Middle Ages, such as the colony at Geel, Belgium, which was rooted in an eighth-century tragedy. The story begins with the death of an Irish queen. Her husband, the king, was grief-stricken until it occurred to him that he had a young daughter, Dymphna, who could take her mother's place. Not surprisingly, Dymphna was not interested in being her father's wife and managed to flee, with the help of a priest, across the North Sea to Belgium. Sadly, her father, as he was the king with great resources available, had little trouble finding her there. He gave her one more ultimatum, which she refused in public, and then, as the legend goes, he chopped off her head. But as so often was the case in those days, a miracle occurred. Dymphna did not get her head back, but according to legend, the mentally ill people in the town who were watching this gruesome event got their sanity back. It sounds unlikely, but people suffering from various sorts of mental illnesses began coming to Geel for a cure. The town housed them in the church until there was no more room in the sanctuary, then they began building wings on the back of the church to house them (perhaps this was the first mental hospital) (Goldstein and Godemont, 2003). To this day, under the auspices of Saint Dymphna (the patron saint of the mentally ill) long-stay hospital patients at Geel are still discharged to foster homes in the surrounding farms where they become contributing members of the hardworking Flemish farm families (perhaps the first community mental health program). This re-socialization sort of treatment was revolutionary and spread throughout the Netherlands and to other parts of Europe. According to Aldana and colleagues (2010), the very first European mental hospital (*Spital Dels Folls, Orats, e Ignocents* [Hospital of Lunatics, Insane, and Innocents]) was erected in Valencia, Spain, in 1410 after Friar Jofre preached a sermon regarding the mistreatment of the mentally ill. This was repeated in Spanish South America in the sixteenth century. But such places were not established in North America until much later (although the Geel idea was noticed by Dr. John Galt of Williamsburg State Hospital in the early nineteenth century, who tried his best to get the people of tidewater Virginia to adopt it). Such humanistic, social support, and stress reduction schemes in the form of asylums have worked in the past and have been replicated and reinvented successfully over and over in other times and places.

But the Church was not always so tolerant of the mentally ill. During the Roman Catholic Inquisition, thousands faced a different sort of treatment. The *Malleus Maleficarum*, published in 1487 by two monks, Heinrich Kramer and James Sprenger, provided a framework (sort of an early *Diagnostic and Statistical Manual* [DSM]) for identifying witches. One symptom for the diagnosis of "witch" included having sex with the Devil. Unfortunately, many mentally ill women seemed to match the criteria and became fuel for the bonfires instead of being sent for rest and rehabilitation to Valencia or Geel.

In 1637, Rene Descartes, a Frenchman living in Leiden, the Netherlands, published his *Discourse on Method*. In it he proposed the famous maxim "I think therefore I am" ("*Cogito ergo sum*"). This idea became fuel for the Enlightenment and was eventually perhaps the single most unifying concept behind the American Revolution. But, although he was a scientist and a scientific philosopher, Descartes was also a good Catholic, and although he was usually in trouble with his church for being too much of a "thinker" for the Inquisition-oriented conservatives, nonetheless, he was a good pious Catholic. In fact, near the end of his life, in 1650, he actually helped Queen Christina of Sweden convert to Catholicism, which meant that by law in Protestant Sweden she had to give up her throne and quit being a queen. How did Descartes manage to justify his religious and scientific beliefs? He was able to sustain his beliefs largely because of the so-called Cartesian dualism he is now famous for. He believed the soul is located in the brain (to be specific, the pineal gland), and from that crucial anatomical point, it controls the body. The body is like a stage in the life of a moth, which, when all used up, returns to the earth. The soul, on the other hand, is eternal and travels upward (hopefully) into the heavens.

"Going to heaven" really meant a lot to people back then. Actually, it is still very understandable and sensible to think this way. After all, can thoughts be physical things? Do they exist like bones and muscle, or are they something else, something more than just electric impulses in the brain? And also, do we not still think of ourselves as separate from a mechanical and vulnerable, often painful body, which we control from the position of the mind (inside the head)? Indeed, the body can break down at any moment for any reason, necessitating a trip to the emergency room or the Cleveland Clinic. Yet, are we not still thinking and therefore being who we are, and does who we are include a soul or are we just a pineal gland full of hormones? Thomas Moore (2010) in a recent book argues that modern medicine should return to caring for the soul instead of trying to cure it or medicate it.

THE ENLIGHTENMENT

The so-called era of moral treatment also did not begin in the Americas either. It was an eighteenth-century movement that drew its inspiration from the seventeenth-century philosophers of the Enlightenment like Descartes and Spinoza, and culminated with the actions of revolutionary physicians like Philippe Pinel and Vincenzo Charugi. The latter, from 1785 to 1788, was director of the Santa Dorotea hospital in Florence, Italy, where he outlawed chains as a means of restraint for psychiatric patients. Generally, we think of the Frenchman Pinel unchaining the mental patients, but, in fact, not only was this a decade later than Charugi, it was actually Pinel's assistant, Jean Pussin, who replaced the iron shackles (with straitjackets) in 1797 at Bicêtre hospital in Paris, after Pinel had moved to the Salpêtrière Hospital. So, perhaps the Italians were first to usher in the "moral treatment" idea of humane treatment for the mentally ill (100 years before they invented pizza with mozzarella for Queen Margherita). Later, the French and then the British adopted the idea. In 1796, William Tuke, a Quaker and a layman, founded the Retreat at York, England, for insane members of the Society of Friends (Quakers). It soon became famous for its humane treatment of mentally ill persons; so much so, that eventually the Americans became interested in his ideas.

The early days of this "moral treatment" mental health care in America began with what was essentially integrated psychiatry and medicine (something we are hoping for now). All doctors in those days did a bit of mental health work. At Pennsylvania Hospital in 1752, a separate ward for psychiatry was established, the first of its kind in the new world. Francis Fauquier (b. 1703–d. March 1768), was sent to the colony of Virginia after a successful career in England, where he had become a sort of Enlightenment man, a scientist member of the Royal Society, and was for a time a governor of the London Foundling Hospital for Street Waifs and Orphans. He had been born in England the son of Dr. John Fauquier, a French Huguenot (who had been recruited from France to England to work with Sir Isaac Newton at the London Mint). Francis Fauquier was appointed Royal Governor (1758–1768), and a member of the Virginia House of Burgesses. In 1766, he proposed that Virginia build its own public hospital for the insane. Although Fauquier died before it was built, Williamsburg, Virginia, opened the first American public mental hospital entirely devoted to the care and treatment of the mentally ill, in 1773.

Dr. Benjamin Rush (a signer of the Declaration of Independence) had a most serious interest in the mentally ill. He joined the staff of Pennsylvania Hospital in Philadelphia in 1783, just before this new country was to draw up its new Constitution. In 1812, Rush published the first American book on mental illness, *Medical Inquiries and Observations upon Diseases of the Mind*, which for most of the nineteenth century was the only American book on such matters. Unfortunately, we no longer cherish much of Rush's work, because most of it involved such treatments as purgatives, bleedings, and odd gadgets such as a "Gyrator" device designed to shock people into their senses. By 1817, with the founding of Friends Hospital in Pennsylvania and the 1818 opening of the McLean Asylum in Charlestown, Massachusetts, the ideas of William Tuke began taking root in America (Bragg & Cohen, 2007). Five years later, the Hartford Retreat was established in Connecticut by Samuel Woodward, and social, milieu, and "kindness" therapy became fashionable.

THE NINETEENTH CENTURY: "FROM SHINE TO SHAME"

Thomas Kirkbride (1809–1883), superintendant of the New Pennsylvania Hospital, became famous as an asylum architect after he published an article in 1847 on hospital construction that resulted in the construction of hundreds of giant, long buildings with towers between wings, some of which stand even today, nearly two centuries later. In 1838, Wilson Awl (1799–1876) started the Ohio State Asylum in Columbus, Ohio. He was also one of the first thirteen members of the American Association of Medical Superintendents, which later became the American Psychiatric Association (13 original founders of the APA, 1844). Dr. Awl is said to have become famous for his statement that he was able to cure 100 percent of the patients he had at that facility. He became known as "Dr. Cure Awl." Pliney Earle (1809–1892), superintendant of the Bloomingdale Asylum in New York, was skeptical of some of these early treatments and their apparently spectacular results. He published in the *American Journal of Insanity* in 1854 a paper on the misuse of "bloodletting in mental disorders" (Garrick, 2010), and in 1877, he issued a statistical treatise, "The Curability of Insanity," refuting many of the claims of cures by pointing out that "cured people" were in fact often later readmitted (via the original revolving door).

Another important leader in the fight for humane treatment of the mentally was John Galt, who graduated from the University of Pennsylvania Medical School in 1841 and became the superintendant of the Virginia State Hospital at Williamsburg. Galt believed in treating patients with kindness and involving them in recreational and work activities. He also advocated (unsuccessfully) for the Geel plan at Williamsburg, where patients could live on surrounding farms. He called it the "third Revolution," one that would result in the "elimination of all badges of degrading inferiority" for the patients. Unfortunately, the people of Virginia, and all the other states for that matter, wanted more distance, not less, from the "insane" (Zwelling, 1985).

These early pioneers were noticed by a Boston Sunday school teacher, Dorothea Dix, who observed and was appalled by the conditions in the jails of Boston for mentally ill persons, whom she found chained to the walls there. Her ensuing crusade for "moral treatment," from the 1840s to the 1870s, spread these humane-treatment ideas across the country and brought mentally ill persons out of jails and prisons and into free-standing mental hospitals managed by doctors who were called "alienists." Some of the most historical highlights of those years had to do with her visits to various states' legislatures delivering her "memorials," in which she argued that the number of beds in the existing state hospitals were inadequate to look after all those mentally ill people she was finding in various poorhouses and prisons (Dix, 1848). It is interesting to note that Mrs. Dix, in her memorial of 1848, documented the population of each hospital that existed at the time. She pointed out that McClain Hospital in Charlestown, Massachusetts, "second to none in the United States," had 180 patients; that Friends Hospital at Frankfort, Pennsylvania, had 95 patients; but that Blackwell Island Hospital in New York City had over 400, "under the most terrible of all privations." Indeed, the American era of moral treatment of the insane was already showing signs of ending right in the middle of the nineteenth century.

One of the last gasps of the moral treatment era occurred in 1854, when Dorothea Dix and former president Millard Fillmore were able to get both houses of Congress to pass a national mental health act: "An Act making a grant of public lands to the several States for the benefit of indigent insane persons." But in his veto message to the Senate of the United States on May 3, 1854, President Franklin Pierce cited Jackson, Jefferson, and in particular Madison (in his *Federalist Papers*): "The powers delegated by the proposed Constitution are few and defined. Those which are to remain in the state governments are numerous and infinite." It was thought that Pierce was trying to avert the looming civil war. Had it become the law of the land, the federal government would have acquired a big role in mental health care. So there was no federal mental health act for another century, and the Civil War, of course, happened anyway.

But here is one more little-known moral-treatment moment. In the 1840s, masses of people had begun to leave the East Coast and travel through the Midwest in groups of horse-drawn wagon trains heading westward, over the Rocky Mountains, to the California and Oregon territories, the land bordering the Pacific, and the Columbia River region. Dorothea Dix herself also went west, speaking to legislatures along the way, and she visited Oregon in 1869, ten years after it became a state. She came because the state was trying to decide whether to keep the private hospital it had been contracting with since 1862, or to build a state-run public hospital like those in big Eastern states. By 1869, treatment was not looking so moral in those places. Many more "Blackwell Islands" had already exceeded the 250-census limit that Dr. Kirkbride had recommended, and milieu therapy had become difficult to carry out. Hawthorne Hospital for most of its existence, on the other hand, had fewer than 200 patients, and Dr. Hawthorne knew them all. The hospital held dances on the weekend to which the public was invited, and when patients were better, Dr. Hawthorne gave them money so they could return by stagecoach or sailing ship to their families in California or back east. In a report to the Oregon legislature, he wrote, "To turn these poor people out without money, employment, or any way of reaching their homes is to expose them to the danger of a relapse to their former mental condition." Mrs. Dix, after visiting the Hawthorne hospital, advised the state not to build a state hospital in Oregon but to continue to fund Dr. Hawthorne's hospital (Cutler, 2001). Unfortunately, after Dr. Hawthorne died, in 1883, the state went ahead and built a "Kirkbride"-style Oregon State Hospital, which remained in use until 2011, some of which retains landmark status and still stands today.

The movement to build state hospitals was massive in the nineteenth century, but unfortunately the advice of Dorothea Dix, Pliny Earle, and Thomas Kirkbride was seldom heeded. The hospitals kept growing in number and in size. In the late nineteenth century, Emil Kraepelin (1856–1926), a German psychiatrist coined the term *dementia praecox* (early dementia) in his 1883 book *Psychiatrie*; and later, Eugene Bleuler (1857–1939) expanded the concept to include symptoms such as autistic thinking, associational difficulties, ambivalence, and affect inappropriateness: the so-called Four A's of schizophrenia (Bleuler, 1950). These men saw these conditions in the institutions where they worked and studied, but had no idea what could be done about it. So these advancements in nosology did not necessarily produce a similar advancement in treatment. Rather, they foreshadowed what was to become a grim prognosis for those people entering large public hospitals in that era.

A GREAT NEW CENTURY (BUT OLD INSTITUTIONS DID NOT GO AWAY)

The twentieth century began much like the nineteenth century finished: with growing numbers and sizes of Kirkbride-type mental hospitals. By this time, most were huge and unmanageable. But there were new thoughts about the etiology of mental illness, both in the psychological and the social paradigms. Sigmund Freud (1856–1939) was first a neurologist, like his European colleagues Kraepelin and Bleuler, but he became interested in psychological phenomena like hypnosis, as opposed to biological reductionism, which seemed to stem from Kraepelin. He offered hope at a time when things looked very bad for persons with mental illness, and caused something of a sensation in the United States following his visit to Clark University in Worcester, Massachusetts. Although Freud is not known for his interest in psychosis, he did write a very interesting psychoanalytic analysis of the psychotic delusions of a certain German Supreme Court judge, Daniel Paul Shreber (first published in German in 1911). The Freudian psychoanalysts led a new movement to listen more carefully to patients, albeit for evidence of deep-seated psychosexual conflict. These original concepts have become ubiquitous and continue to permeate our thinking about mental illness, but, as we shall see, they did not provide an appropriate basis for developing effective treatment models for persons suffering with severe mental illnesses. Luckily, the contributions of another European-born psychiatrist, Adolph Meyer, far less well-known than Freud, did provide such a basis. Meyer (1866–1950) was born near Zurich, Switzerland, received a medical degree from the University of Zurich, and studied psychiatry with Auguste-Henri Forel. But in 1892 he was forced to come to the United States in order to secure a teaching post. This he attained at the University of Chicago, which stationed him at the mental hospital in Kankakee, Illinois, where he made observations about patients' case histories. From these experiences, he wrote extensively and developed a theory of psychobiology, which held that stress could induce mental illness. Meyer used a diagram he called a "life chart" and pointed out that if one takes a careful history one can observe the temporal relationship between stressful life events and the advent of psychiatric disorders. These observations proved to be key to the development of a theory of epidemiology regarding mental illness and ultimately to ideas about prevention. He was promoted to professor of psychiatry, first at Cornell University (Ithaca, New York) from 1904 to 1909, and then after he moved to Johns Hopkins University (Baltimore, Maryland), from 1910 to 1941 he continued to publish papers but wrote no books, nor spawned any psychotherapy movements. He had little interest in psychoanalysis, but he became quite famous as the "modern founder of American psychiatry." Meyer, for his part, credited Benjamin Rush as the "father of American psychiatry."

In 1909, Clifford Beers, a recovered mental patient, established the National Committee for Mental Hygiene. Adolf Meyer and William Alanson White (superintendent of St. Elizabeth's Hospital, in Washington, D.C.) both supported the goals of the National Committee to prevent mental illness and to improve institutional conditions for the mentally ill. Through their leadership in academic medicine, they were also able to shape the reformation of psychiatric training during the first half of the twentieth century.

In 1941, Dr. Robert Felix of Baltimore (later to become the first director of National Institute of Mental Health [NIMH]) was working on a Master's in Public Health (MPH) at the Johns Hopkins School of Hygiene and Public Health. He was already steeped in ideas about the importance of the community in mental health care, at least in part because he had received his residency training in psychiatry under a former student of Adolph Meyer's at Hopkins. He and another student of Meyer's had prepared a paper titled "The Organization of a National Mental Health Program," which would be afterwards described as "more ego than thesis". Despite the war, Felix was able to keep his dream alive, and in 1944 he presented to the Surgeon General a draft of what in 1946 became the National Mental Health Act. On April 15, 1949, Robert Felix became the first director of the NIMH: this marked the beginning of the federal government's research efforts to determine the causes of mental illness. In the following years, with the aid of a coalition of like-minded people, Felix continued to push vigorously the idea of extramural services, shaping the terms of the future system of community mental health centers throughout the United States. In this effort he was also successful, so that in 1963, the Community Mental Health Centers (CMHC) Act was passed by Congress. Many of us were inspired by that original definition of a CMHC and are reluctant to accept that things have changed, in some cases quite spectacularly.

THE SIXTIES AND SEVENTIES: REVOLUTION AND CONSOLIDATION

The model was ahead of its time. It was a response by the John F. Kennedy administration to the first presidential (Eisenhower) commission report, "Action For Mental Health," published in 1961, which recommended, among other things, that: "a national mental health program should set as an objective one fully staffed, full time mental health clinic available to each 50,000 of population. Greater efforts should be made to induce more psychiatrists in private practice to devote a substantial part of their working hours to community clinic services, both as consultants and as therapists." Those were lofty ideas, as were many other ideas that did not make it into the 1963 Mental Health Centers Act. In all, 750 of these things (out of a possible 1,500 catchment areas) were funded nationwide before the Reagan Administration put an end to it in

1981, and since then the Feds have never seemed to be able figure what sort of leadership they ought to be providing for mental health. Instead, there has been a series of failures to capitalize on a great idea before its time.

To be fair, back in 1963, hardly anyone had any idea how to implement such programs. There was a huge lack of professionals in all the disciplines, and those who existed did not have the sort of evidence-based skills that have been shown to be effective today. On the other hand, the idea of deinstitutionalization was already well established. The discovery of antipsychotic medications (Delay & Deniker, 1952) in the early Fifties, coupled with a revival of a sort of "moral treatment" then known as "therapeutic communities," resulted in large numbers of individuals' becoming capable of being discharged from those old, overcrowded state hospitals. From a historical perspective, it is not clear to this day whether it was the pills or the community meetings that made the crucial difference, but some are now arguing deinstitutionalization was mostly made possible by the latter. Maxwell Jones was a British psychiatrist who first treated war neurosis during World War II and later invented a sort of group therapy after the war for hospitalized patients in London. He called it "therapeutic community." Jones (1953) argued that hospitals were obsolete and dehumanizing, and that the way to get patients out was to first form therapeutic community groups inside, then patient governments inside, then draw up discharge plans to get them outside. Once out, though, many patients came back because of lack of after-care (Cutler, 1983). But state hospital populations continued to drop dramatically: from a high of almost 600,000 in the mid-Fifties to fewer than 200,000 by 1980.

It is also important to note that during this period, nearly all training in psychiatry occurred in these large public hospitals. Psychiatry, despite the advent of psychoanalysis, was still a hospital-based public-oriented profession, just as it was in 1844 when the original 13 founders formed the Association of Mental Hospital Superintendants. That was about to change. After World War II, psychiatry departments began their inexorable move into university hospitals and general hospitals. By the late 1950s, this was becoming the rule. In the 1960s these departments began getting quite large, and today they have evolved into massive and eclectic institutions (Goetz et al., 1998; Svendsen et al., 2005). This evolution first took a decidedly Freudian path; consequently, by the 1960s, most academic departments were led by psychoanalysts, not Kraeplenian nosologists or biologically oriented organicists. However, the Freudian era faded quickly into what now seems a perpetual "decade of the brain" phase, which has on one hand de-Freudianed, but on the other, medicalized American psychiatry.

In spite of the move to university-based training, most programs were not really equipped to provide relevant training to various professionals on how to perform in community mental health centers. An exception to this was the Laboratory of Community Psychiatry started by Gerald Caplan (1963) at the Harvard School of Public Health, where an interdisciplinary training program focusing on consultation skills was devised for interested professionals in order to help them to go out and develop innovative mental health programs. In *Support Systems and Mental Health* (1974), Caplan outlined the roles of nurses, primary care physicians, and social workers in preventing mental health problems and developing community mental health models. He strongly emphasized the importance of natural support systems and how professionals needed to understand how to find, relate to, and support these naturally occurring groups in order for them to be effective in preventing relapse. Similar interdisciplinary training schemes sprang up and spread across the country in the Sixties and Seventies, based on Caplan's teachings (Cutler & Huffine, 2004) and nurtured by training grants from the NIMH (Goetz et al., 1998). These grants were extremely important in developing human resources to cope skillfully and effectively with large numbers of people no longer hospitalized but still needing enormous amounts of assistance to remain symptom-free and find pensions, health insurance, and housing in order to be able to stay out of the hospital, jail, or the streets.

Another aspect important to understanding this era is that, even though mental health was not a high priority during the Nixon and Ford years, it also did not become a major target, either. In fact, in 1974 the Democrat-controlled Congress passed a series of amendments to the Community Mental Health Centers Act that actually increased the comprehensiveness of the array of services provided by federally funded centers. In addition to the basic grouping of inpatient, outpatient, partial hospitalization, emergency services and consultation; services to children and the elderly were added. At this point, mental health centers were also expected to screen for hospitalization and provide follow-up services as well, functions that for some reason were left out of the original Act. It is interesting that these schemes were left out, because the whole purpose of the legislation was supposed to be a response to the call to "provide treatment without hospitalization." All of this was initially vetoed by President Ford in 1974 but the veto was subsequently overridden in 1975 by the heavily Democratic Congress (Cutler et al., 2003).

As a result, federal grants for mental health centers proliferated throughout the rest of decade and across the country from east to west. Many states failed to get grants before 1975 when funds for construction ran out, but scrambled and succeeded later in the decade in getting staffing grants for their local catchment areas to be included in existing outpatient facilities. In Multnomah County in Oregon, for example, several grants were written in the late Seventies, but were never submitted because no one was sure where the money would come from to pay for staff in these centers after the eight years of federal funding were finished. At the end of the decade, the county finally submitted four staffing grants, three of which were funded, thereby establishing mental health centers across the county and covering all of its catchment areas.

Unfortunately, there were multiple problems associated with implementing these grants. For one thing, community mental health centers were the "new kids on the block" and as such clashed with existing entities already run by states or counties and charged with similar functions. The centers were actually in direct competition with state hospitals, many of which operated their own outpatient aftercare programs. Some of these programs were actually quite superior and more relevant to the state hospital population than the mental health centers were. Some examples of these programs are the Assertive Community Treatment (ACT) program of Madison, Wisconsin, run by Mendota State Hospital, and the LINK program of Pendleton, Oregon, run by the Eastern Oregon State Hospital. These programs began with federal HIP (hospital improvement) grants and were staffed by hospital staff who knew the patients and their disabilities and they were able to tailor service to the needs of the clients.

Unfortunately, community mental health centers were not really prepared for the great wave of deinstitutionalization. In most places, even though patients were being discharged from the hospitals, the staffs of these new centers (mostly psychodynamic therapists) had no idea what to do with them. They simply lacked the right skills. The movement was highly criticized for this (Langsley, 1980). Most of the centers did eventually succeed in developing crisis and emergency services and, ultimately, hotlines, mobile crisis teams, and walk-in clinics. Ironically, the really disabled and hard–to-treat clients wound up using these new services instead of traditional therapy services, which were available to them on an appointment basis, but which they may have been too disorganized to take advantage of, or which they did not find useful.

Some lawsuits that were brought in the Seventies also had profound effects. For instance, the 1971 Willowbrook scandal in New York and the 1972 *Wyatt vs. Stickney* case in Alabama highlighted the lack of adequate treatment for people suffering from mental illness and mental retardation living in state institutions. These lawsuits established the fact that people in the custody of the state needed to be treated. It gave momentum to the forces of deinstitutionalization, which were based on the idea that if people were not in the custody of the states, they could be served by less-expensive community mental health services. Also around that time (1972), Supplemental Security Income (SSI) for the disabled was established, along with the Rehabilitation Act of 1973, which identified mental illness as a disability that was eligible for funding to help individuals have an income or help them in acquiring gainful employment.

THE MENTAL HEALTH SYSTEMS ACT OF 1980

The middle years of the decade of the Seventies were perhaps the most "miraculous" period in the history of mental health since Saint Dymphna. A certain governor of Georgia had a spouse who was very interested in mental health and mental illness. She traveled the state during those years performing minor "miracles." One story about her was when she showed up in a small town in Northern Georgia to visit a group home for mentally ill ladies. Apparently, the mayor of the town did not want the facility to remain there, was blocking funding for it, and instead was lobbying the state for a municipal water project. Rosalind Carter called the mayor and arranged to meet him at the group home for afternoon tea. That morning she went to the home, gathered up the ladies, and took them all downtown and bought them new dresses. When the mayor arrived, they were cheerfully unpacking their presents. Mrs. Carter looked at the mayor and in her most charming Southern drawl said something like this: "Why, Mr. Mayor, I'm sure you're going to love how nice these ladies look in their new dresses. I'm so impressed with what a lovely home you have for them here." He agreed. "Perhaps my husband will also be interested in your water project?" The mayor smiled and declared how much he loved that group home. That mental health program in Northeast Georgia went on to develop a program they called "The Balanced Service System," which was eventually published (Melville et al., 1977) and later adopted as a model to survey mental health centers by the Joint Commission on Accreditation of Hospitals (JCAH).

The Carters wasted no time after the election of 1976 in setting up a second presidential commission. In 1977 Rosalind Carter and her commission toured the country to assess the state of the mental health system after the 14 years of community mental centers. One stop was Tucson, Arizona, where a member of the commission was in charge of much of the system there. Several agencies testified to the continued lack of funding to serve people with severe mental illness. One organization called COPE (Community Organization for Personal Enrichment) told Mrs. Carter that they operated a group of free, church-based drop-in day centers staffed entirely by volunteers, most of whom were either persons who recovered from mental illness (like Clifford Beers, the founder of the American mental health hygiene movement) or family members of people who were suffering with mental health disabilities and also that, as a social model, did not need any federal money to do what they were doing. Mrs. Carter smiled, perhaps because they were the only ones who did not seem to need money. That program still exists, and is now the biggest behavioral health program in southern Arizona (they now get a lot of federal Medicaid dollars to do what they do). The commission (Bryant, 1978) found that despite a massive increase in community-based agencies over the previous 15 years, many groups were largely left unserved or underserved. These included racial and ethnic minorities, the urban poor, migrant workers, Vietnam veterans, children and adolescents, and of course, persons suffering from chronic psychiatric disorders. The commission recommended, among other things, that 75 million dollars be appropriated in the first year and 100 million in each of the next two years to serve these groups. All of this was in line with the NIMH Community Support Program, which began in 1977 to push for community mental health centers to provide these new community support services for the chronic and severely mentally ill. Another big boost, this time in the area of advocacy, occurred in 1979, when a group of families of people with mental illnesses met in Madison, Wisconsin, to form the National Alliance for the Mentally Ill (NAMI). Very soon every state had its own chapter, and NAMI members got busy advocating with federal, state, and local governments to increase funding and services to those suffering with severe mental illnesses. The culmination of all this work at the end of the decade was the passage by Congress of the Mental Health Systems Act in 1980.

THE DISCOVERY OF MEDICAID: 1981–1992

The Mental Health Systems Act had barely come alive when the new president (Ronald Reagan) did what he could to kill it (Cutler et al., 2003). No money was allocated for it. In January of 1981, he also recommended a cut of 25 percent immediately from the old CHMC revolving fund used for the previous 15 years to start federal CMHCs. After that it was supposed to be cut another 25 percent per year until it disappeared entirely. What was left was later converted into block grants to the states and no longer went to the catchment areas that had written the grants unless the individual states chose to send the money that way. In addition, the Omnibus Budget Reconciliation Act of August 1981 eliminated all of the ten federal regional offices for mental health and all the federal mental health initiatives that had been implemented since the 1963 CMHC Act.

These cuts removed 400 federal jobs and destroyed the federal government's ability to process, supervise, and provide training and technical assistance to the surviving federal community mental health centers. Between 1980 and 1982, funding support for mental health centers dropped from $293 million down to $203 million (Foley & Sharfstein, 1983). CMHCs had to find new ways to get money and technical support in order to survive. One way to do it was to increase fees and copays. Another way was to figure out how to bill the emerging fee-for-service federal Medicaid program, which by the 1980s most if not all states were participating in. States had individually tailored matching schemes with the federal government for these dollars. If you happened to be a high-poverty state, you could get something close to a 70 percent/30 percent match of federal to local funds. If your state was not so high in poverty, the ratio was more like 60/40. Although many states had initially been leery of accepting this money for fear it would go away like the CMHC money, they soon realized this would turn out to be even a bigger cash cow for them than CMHC dollars, and they did not have to watch local jurisdictions go around them and get money directly from the federal government without the state having a say in how it was spent. But as it turned out, they were not surprised to discover that the feds were considerably more interested in how the states were spending their money than they were about local catchment areas, so instead of local control, states wound up having to invent plans that would pass federal muster (exactly what President Franklin Pierce was worried about back in the nineteenth century).

The Medicaid program essentially medicalized community mental health. What had been conceived of as a psychosocial model had to be turned into a medical model for all intents and purposes. But ironically, psychiatrists became less and less prominent as leaders in the management of these entities, prompting a spate of articles highlighting reasons for their exodus (Winslow, 1979; Diamond et al., 1985; Clark & Vaccaro, 1987). Instead, their services became more and more important as direct service providers, primarily of medications. In 1985, during the Reagan administration and at the request of the pharmaceutical industry, the Food and Drug Administration (FDA) quietly published a notice in the federal registry allowing direct-to-consumer advertising of drugs. This set off a race to the airwaves to talk patients into talking doctors into prescribing new (and more expensive) drugs. Medicaid costs resulting from this and other deregulation maneuvers reduced the federal budget at the time, but in the long run, direct advertising has increased the cost of health care dramatically because of the resultant increase in the use of expensive medications, which did not necessarily work better than the older medications (Lehrer, 2010), but were appealing due to powerful advertising. Medicaid costs for case-management programs for persons with severe mental illnesses also became greater when it became clear that just discharging patients from state hospitals was not enough for them to survive in the community. They needed help from professionals in navigating the arcane system of entitlement programs, housing programs, and rehabilitation programs in order to benefit from their new freedom (Cutler & Manderscheid, 1987).

RESPONSE TO THE MEDICALIZATION OF MENTAL HEALTH

At the center of the convergence of medicalized treatment, payment systems, and newly developed recovery and self-help programming, stood the patient. In no small part due to the changes outlined above, the domain for biologically based mental health services expanded greatly. Psychological distress became a legitimate problem requiring treatment. Helping people to develop coping mechanisms to address the fast-changing conditions around them, thereby enhancing their self-esteem and emotional well-being, was the goal.

But the biological revolution in psychiatry over the past three decades did more than move mental health forward. Advances in psychopharmacology have slowly morphed into a driving force in mental health treatment, changing the approach to mental health treatment to take advantage of a funding stream of Medicaid dollars. And this increased access to care was not without consequences. It led us to an era of expectations of "miraculous cures." This cure-all mentality can almost be dated to January of 1988, when Prozac was introduced to the American market. Within a couple of years this pill was able to gain "most prescribed" status. The added effect of legal marketing by drug companies directly to consumers gave Prozac and other selective serotonin reuptake inhibitor (SSRI) antidepressants a most-favored status among persons who were not seriously mentally ill but just wanted to "feel better." Many were able to meet criteria for major depressive disorder but were not actually disabled by it. This, combined with broader insurance payment systems, led to a considerable expansion of access to treatment via a variety of prescribers. As a result, the clientele of mental health services also began shifting back to less seriously ill persons. Before long, the public mental health system was in danger of catering to the "worried well" rather than providing treatment for severely mentally ill and disabled persons. At the same time, lawmakers and policy developers began to focus attention on cost-containment, and very quickly, care providers discovered the power of the managed-care network to dictate who received care and for how long. The major question of the day became how to meet the needs of the individual in a system where costs were soaring while major social, medical, and emotional needs were not being met.

As state Medicaid budgets rose, fiscal crises developed for some state governments. States needed a way to contain costs. The generic term "managed care" is used to describe health care delivery that incorporates mechanisms to monitor and authorize service utilization. The previous decade had witnessed a groundswell of public skepticism of government spending and a related decrease in state and federal funding for human services. As Medicaid-based programs grew rapidly, increasing costs, many states began developing behavioral health managed-care schemes for Medicaid and indigent clients with severe mental illness, substance-use disorders, or both (Ballit & Burgess, 1999). In the mid-1980s, the federal government had approved waivers for states to develop new market arrangements for Medicaid. Some states actually farmed out their entire Medicaid programs to private-sector managed-care companies.

By January of 1999, a total of 47 states were redesigning their Medicaid programs, up from 14 in 1996 (SAMHSA, 1999). In 1998, 54 percent of Medicaid recipients were enrolled in some form of managed behavioral health care (Findlay, 1999). Unfortunately, this led to the moral dilemma of for-profit managed-care organizations thriving while services to the neediest were being rationed. The program also did not contain costs and continued to raise concerns over escalating expenditures for health care as a portion of government and employer costs. A specific focus of this concern was the expansion of mental health and substance abuse benefits in proportion to national health expenditures. By 1990, health care expenditures constituted about 12 percent of the gross national product (McKusick et al., 1998). Between 1987 and 1992, Medicaid spending rose 12 percent annually—five times the rate of inflation. Expenditures for Medicaid increased from 8.1 percent of state budgets in 1987 (Ross & Croze, 1997) to 20 percent in 1993 (Ridgely, Giard, & Shern, 1999), a proportion larger than that typically spent on higher education or law enforcement (Sullivan, 1995). The Clinton administration's plan to fix all this somehow never got off the ground. The failure of that administration to pass comprehensive health reform, combined with the overwhelming desire to contain costs that were consuming an inordinate proportion of the U.S. gross "national health product," left plenty of room for the continued development of "innovative" managed approaches to health care cost containment. These approaches have grown and multiplied in complexity, remain in effect as routine practice, and are still evolving.

The U.S. Surgeon General's 1999 report on mental health was a collaborative effort of the National Institute of Mental Health, which supports and conducts research on mental illness and mental health, and SAMHSA. The report reviews scientific advances in the nation's understanding of mental health and mental illness. The result was a comprehensive examination of the way mental health services were provided in this country. This was followed by a series of recommendations for improvement. Central to the Surgeon General's report was the critical gap—lasting about 15 to 20 years—between knowledge and practice, between what is known through research and what is actually implemented in many public mental health systems across the country (David Satcher, Surgeon General).

A NEW MILLENNIUM AND A NEW FREEDOM COMMISSION, 2001–2009

Reform continued to be a topic of the new George W. Bush presidency. In 2002, a commission appointed by President Bush examined the provision of mental health services in this country. Required by executive order to complete its work in one year, the President's New Freedom Commission on Mental Health published in 2003 both an interim and a final report that once again critiqued the massive fragmentation in the nation's system of mental health care for both adults and children, as well as high unemployment among those with mental illnesses, lack of care for older persons with mental illnesses, and a continuing low priority for mental health and suicide prevention in our nation. These findings were not surprising to anyone and not all that different from those of the two previous presidential commissions, both of which outlined all of this in even greater detail (Appel & Bartemeier, 1961; Bryant, 1978). The Commission's report also provided a vision for mental health services in this country:

> We envision a future when everyone with a mental illness will recover, a future when mental illnesses can be prevented or cured, a future when mental illnesses are detected early, and a future when everyone with a mental illness at any stage of life has access to effective treatment and supports—essentials for living, working, learning, and participating fully in the community.

This vision included six goals marked by an understanding that recovery is possible and that access to effective treatments and supports brings a life in the community within range of most people affected by mental disorders:

> *In a Transformed Mental Health System . . .*
> > *GOAL 1: Americans Understand That Mental Health Is Essential to Overall Health.*
> > *GOAL 2: Mental Health Care Is Consumer and Family Driven.*
> > *GOAL 3: Disparities in Mental Health Services Are Eliminated.*
> > *GOAL 4: Early Mental Health Screening, Assessment, and Referral to Services Are Common Practice.*
> > *GOAL 5: Excellent Mental Health Care Is Delivered and Research Is Accelerated.*
> > *GOAL 6: Technology Is Used to Access Mental Health Care and Information.*
>
> (Hogan et al., 2003)

The work of the President's Commission provided some good ideas along with a set of guidelines for policymakers and advocates interested in improving the mental health system at the local, state, and federal levels. But it was not accompanied with funding; resulting, in essence, in another unfunded government mandate for the already strapped and fragmented mental health system to cope with. In fact there was a recession in the early 2000s, and community mental health providers continued to see and deal with increasing cuts in funding for the provisions of mental health services. The federal initiative was directed toward transformation of the current mental health service delivery system without increasing funding. The Commission itself was charged from the onset not to recommend funding increases. Consequently, many felt the result of this Commission was essentially nothing;

President Carter's mental health commission made similar points 25 years ago. In fact, the 2003 report, reflecting the misguided thinking of Washington's mental health establishment, fails to gauge the full extent of the mental health system's crisis, and its 19 recommendations are a hodge-podge of boilerplate and evasion. All that saves the report from being a total waste is a hint that suggests a better way forward. Read through the report and you quickly discover just how many of its recommendations are mere platitudes, crafted to patch over disagreements within Washington's fractious mental health community over such controversies as compulsory treatment and the legitimate purview of "mental health." We must "promote the mental health of young children," the report declares, as if anybody would object to such a goal. Or: we need to "create a comprehensive state mental health plan"—neglecting to mention that states already must have such plans in place in order to qualify for federal mental health grants. (Torrey, 2003)

Transformation of the mental health care was supposed to: incorporate evidence-based practices as part of routine practice, and by doing so, resolve workforce shortage issues, ensure access to care by removing financial barriers, coordinate mental health care with general health care and social services, and develop a way to systematically measure and improve the quality of care delivered. The combined knowledge of each action enumerated above continued a movement in the field toward evidence-based practice (EBP), which had the potential to improve the quality of care provided by applying the current best evidence in accordance with patients' preferences for care. It was assumed that EBP would reduce cost by applying best approaches, therefore developing better outcomes in care. Additionally, when combined with growing concerns raised by the Institute of Medicine, EBPs appeared to have the potential to reduce numerous avoidable deaths or injuries in health and mental health care delivery (Roberts & Yeager, 2004).

Beginning in 2006, cuts under the leadership of President Bush delivered blows to the mental health budget that stalled transformation efforts. The budget plan moved forward a total of $45 billion in federal share reductions over the next decade, primarily through tightening of rules on state matching funds. While the budget demonstrated $60 billion in cuts, this was countered by about $15 billion in "modest new spending," for a resulting net reduction of $45 billion. The budget cut was just the first of several planned steps to reduce Medicaid spending: the Bush Administration forecast included proposals to cap federal Medicaid spending. The result of efforts to cut the budget resulted in states facing heavy losses to their mental health funding, with the top five states demonstrating cuts as high as 47.5 percent in Kentucky, 35 percent in Alaska, 22.7 percent in South Carolina and Arizona, and 22.4 percent in Wisconsin. What began as an era of hope closed as the decade of decline for our nation's community mental health system.

THE OBAMA ERA

While it is still early to declare victory, one thing is for certain; with the passage of the Patient Protection and Affordable Care Act, the Democrat-led U.S. Congress made a bold, but certainly not definitive step. This legislation followed on the heels of the long-awaited passage of the Mental Health Parity and Addiction Equity Act (MHPAEA), provisions within MHPAEA function as baseline requirements for the newer healthcare reform legislation. Thus, passage of healthcare reform meant that MHPAEA's parity definitions will soon apply to virtually all

Americans, even as Medicaid is expanded, new health insurance exchanges are established, and new coverage mandates and penalties are created for employers and individuals. But conservatives quickly labeled the plan "Obamacare" and pronounced it too expensive, even though many of its features were estimated to save billions. The government's figures predict a savings total of 120 billion dollars just in Medicare over five years.

Health Care Delivery System Reforms Savings through 2015
Reforming provider payments—rewarding quality and efficiency...$55 billion
Investing in patient safety—lowering hospital readmissions and hospital-acquired conditions...$10 billion through 2013
Cracking down on fraud and abuse in the Medicare system...$1.8 billion
Getting the best value for Medicare beneficiaries and taxpayers for durable medical equipment...$2.9 billion ($17 billion over ten years)
Reducing excessive Medicare payments to insurance companies...$50 billion

In 2010, a Republican victory turned the House of Representatives over to conservative Republicans who immediately announced they would repeal this overly ambitious, costly scheme. So far that has not happened, because the Senate remains in the control of the Democrats and President Obama was re-elected for a second term in November 2012. But, at the moment this chapter is being written, it is yet unclear what form the new healthcare system will take. Indeed, many questions remain unanswered regarding the new law's effects on the behavioral healthcare industry. Approaches to care, regulatory requirements, system approaches, and service structures remain undefined as dozens of government agencies have yet to draft regulations. The battle of the budget is far from over, and arguments that label the changes too expensive may or may not be based in science but still have plenty of political traction. In addition, given that many of the requirements of this bill will not be implemented until 2014 or later, all we can do, at best, is speculate regarding the upcoming integrated and accountable service delivery system.

SOME CHALLENGES

One complication that appears to be inevitable will be communication of benefits and service structures. Some accounts estimate that the combination of expanded Medicaid coverage and new health information exchange (HIE) insurance options will provide coverage for an additional six million to 10 million people seeking mental health and substance use disorder treatment. The implementation of new HIE insurance options will expand access to insurance. While this is necessary, it will not be sufficient to improve behavioral health outcomes. Improved outcomes will not occur unless behavioral healthcare consumers are informed of how to access and use their insurance benefits. For consumers of mental health and addiction treatment services, this is a significant challenge. Without clearly articulated processes of how consumers of behavioral health services will access benefits, many will be unable to enroll themselves in new insurance and Medicaid programs. And, once enrolled, they are likely to need help to access and utilize benefits within the expanded healthcare coverage plan. Consumers and their families will need help understanding exactly what reform can mean for them, how their benefits may change, and what new coverage options are available. It is probable that the burden of helping these individuals to secure their benefits will once again fall on care providers. Undoubtedly this will further strain an already overtaxed workforce.

Let us revisit the expanded coverage for an additional six to ten million people seeking mental health and substance use disorder services. Doing so will lead to the third logical question, which is one of capacity. When we ask the question "Do we have the capacity to meet the demand for substance use and mental health services?" the answer appears to be no. Currently, many behavioral health facilities are understaffed and face problems in recruiting and training new employees, due to both funding limitations and a limited pool of candidates. Emergency departments are seeing unprecedented numbers of behavioral health emergencies, and abuse of opiates and prescription pain medications approach epidemic proportions across the nation.

Colleges and universities are behind in education to meet the demands of this ever-changing and evolving field, with recently graduated mental health care providers being under-prepared to meet the demands of day-to-day practice. The Annapolis Coalition has clearly outlined core competencies to meet the demands of today's mental health treatment delivery system; however, many universities are not up to this challenge. It is clear that challenges for future care providers are not being met.

Then there is the issue of human resources. How many graduates will it take to meet the demand for services? Will the role of mental health providers need to be reexamined? Will there be a need to develop entirely new types of positions to meet the requirements laid out in the reform statutes? It is, or at this time appears, true that the current reform law establishes a national Health Care Workforce Commission, as well as several workforce development grants and healthcare workforce loan repayment programs. Only time will tell if these make a difference.

Next, one must consider the structure of the service delivery system. The establishment of new health and medical homes and accountable care organizations (ACOs) are the heart of this new care delivery system. Both health/medical homes and accountable care organizations seek to coordinate care and reduce the cost of treating patients with chronic and comorbid conditions, including severe mental illness. Effective since 2011, under the new Medicaid rules, patients with chronic conditions can designate a provider as a "health home" to provide comprehensive care and services, with a 90 percent subsidy in federal matching dollars for two years. This is a prospect that has many behavioral healthcare organizations scrambling to qualify as medical "home" providers. However, to do so, they must compete with general practitioners and others for status as the "hub" in this collaborative model. The prospect of competing against the general practitioner offices has the potential to reshape the mental health care delivery system.

There are questions that will need to be answered. For example: what is the best model, is a model of co-location of services more cost effective than providing collaborative services? Choosing one model over the other will eventually determine if the course of care remains task-centered or returns to a person-centered model of care. In co-located care delivery systems, one can almost visualize an assembly line where hypertension is treated at one station and depression is treated at the next. While this may be more efficient, it certainly will not address the interaction of the illnesses. Collaborative care will address the interactions of the illness, but may not provide a patient-centered approach that is holistic in nature. While it is possible to accomplish the same end, it is unclear which approach will be adopted, how it will be applied, and what the impact will be on community mental health as it is known today. The good news is that there will be grant funding included in reform legislation and managed by SAMHSA to support the co-location of mental health and primary care providers. Additionally, seed dollars are earmarked to support new wellness and prevention programs, although the role of behavioral health in those programs has yet to be defined.

ACOs are to be structured as a bundled risk model (under Medicare). In this model, providers create a care network that addresses the 80/20 effect of managing the 20 percent of the population that uses 80 percent of services provided. In this model, providers will apply a proactive approach that seeks to manage care, improve quality, and reduce spending for "at-risk" patients. ACOs typically involve hospitals or multi-specialty physician practices working with additional outpatient providers to form a safety net for high-risk populations. The goal is to move from a reactive to more proactive treatment model, while reducing costs.

CONCLUSIONS: "WHERE ARE YOU GOING, WHERE HAVE YOU BEEN?" JOYCE CAROL OATES

At this moment, we are all waiting to see the final product. As regulations are being written, the White House, the Department of Health and Human Services, and other government agencies are striving to plan and launch a new series of healthcare reform communications that will help drive the healthcare industry. At present, states and local jurisdictions as well as behavioral healthcare providers are waiting for the many detailed rules, procedures, and new accountable care organizations needed to fill out the nation's plan for a reformed healthcare system. Consumer advocacy groups and consumers alike are waiting to test and refine the effectiveness of this new system. As we write this, we want to emphasize that we feel that it cannot be overstated how important it is to understand that all disciplines will need to work together in whatever this new model becomes. That is why we have talked so much about where we have come from—in order to see where we may be going. Working together we can find the roadmap for the future, in education of new mental healthcare providers who can work in new healthcare organizations, establishing effective approaches across new integrated systems of care, and serving as a theoretical springboard for progress.

REFERENCES

Aldana, L. L., San Miguel, P. S. and Moreno, L. R. (2010). The foundation of the first western mental asylum. *American Journal of Psychiatry,* 167(3): 260.

Appel, K. E. and Bartemeier, L. H. (1961). *Action for Mental Health: The Report of the Joint Commission on Mental Illness and Health.* New York: Basic Books.

Ballit, M. H., Burgess, L. L. (1999). Competing interests: Public-sector managed behavioral health care. *Health Affairs, 18*(5): 112–115.

Beers, C. (1921). *A Mind That Found Itself.* New York: Doubleday.

Blueler, E. (1950). *Dementia praecox or the group of schizophrenias.* Oxford, England: International Universities Press.

Bragg, M. A. and Cohen, B. M. *From asylum to hospital to psychiatric health system. American Journal of Psychiatry,* 164(6): 883.

Bryant, T. E. (1978). *Report to the President from the President's Commission on Mental Health,* Vol. I. Washington, D.C.: U.S. Government Printing Office.

Caplan, G. (1963). *Principles of Preventive* Psychiatry. New York: Basic Books.

Caplan, G: (1974). *Support Systems and Community Mental Health.* New York: Behavioral Publications.

Clark, G. and Vaccaro, J. (1987). Burnout among CMHC psychiatrists and the struggle to survive. Hospital and Community Psychiatry, 38(8): 843–847.

Cutler, D. L. (1983). *Effective Aftercare for the 1980s. New Directions for Mental Health Services*, Vol. 19. San Francisco: Jossey-Bass.

Cutler D. L., Manderscheid, R. (1987). Epidemiology of Chronic Mental Disorder: Reactions and Recommendations. In *The Chronic Mental Patient*. Washington, D.C.: APA Press.

Cutler, D. L. (2001). Moral treatment at the end of the Oregon Trail: Dr. James Hawthorne, 1819–1881. *American Journal of Psychiatry,* 158(6): 871.

Cutler, D. L., Bevilacqua, J., and McFarland, B. H. (2003): Four decades of community mental health: A symphony in four movements. *Community Mental Health Journal,* 38(5):

Cutler, D. L. and Huffine, C. (2004): Heroes in community psychiatry: Gerald Caplan Community. *Mental Health Journal,* 40(3):

Delay, J., Deniker, P., Harl, J. M., et al. (1952). Traitements d'états confusionnels par l'chlorhydrate de diméthylaminopropyl—N-chlorophénothiazine (4560 RP). *Annales Médico-psychologiques,* 110, 112–117.

Diamond, H., Cutler, D. L., Langsley, D. G., Barter, J. T. (1985). Training, Recruitment, and Retention of Psychiatrists in Community Mental Health Centers: Issues and Answers. In *Community Mental Health Centers and Psychiatrists*. Joint Standing Committee, American Psychiatric Association and National Council of Community Mental Health Centers, Washington, D.C.

Dix, D. L. (1848). *Memorial: A Grant of Land for the Relief and Support of the Indigent Curable and Incurable Insane in the United States.* Presented to the 30th Congress, United States Senate.

Ehrenwald, J. (1976). *Healing magic in sleep and dream. Chapter 4 in The History of Psychotherapy*. New York: Jason Aronson.

Findlay, S . (1999). Managed behavioral health care in 1999: An industry at a crossroads. *Health Affairs,* 18(5): 116–124.

Foley, H . A., & Sharfstein, S. S. (1983). *Madness and government: Who cares for the mentally ill?* Washington, DC: American Psychiatric Press.

Garrick, M. L. (2010) . Bloodletting: 1854. *American Journal of Psychiatry, 167*, 1435–1436.

Goetz, R. et al. (1998). A three-decade perspective on community and public psychiatry training in Oregon. *Psychiatric Services*, 49(9), 1208–1211.

Goldstein, J. L. and Godemont, M. M. (2003). The legend and lessons of Geel, Belgium: A 1500-year-old legend, a twenty-first century model. *Community Mental Health Journal,* 39(5): 441–458.

Hawthorne, J. C. (1872). *Report of the Superintendent of the Oregon Hospital for the Insane. Messages and Documents,* Oregon Legislative Assembly, 7th Regular Session.

Hogan, M. F. et al (2003) The President's New Freedom Commission on Mental Health.

Joint Commission on Hospital Accreditation (1979): Program Review Document. Chicago: Community Mental Health Service Programs.

Jones, M, (1853). *The Therapeutic Community.* New York: Basic Books.

Langsley, D. G. . (1980). The community mental health center: Does it treat patients? *Hospital and Community Psychiatry, 31*, 815–819.

Larsell, O. (1945), History of the care of the insane in the State of Oregon. *Oregon Historical Quarterly,* 56, 295–326.

Leff, J. (2001). Can we manage without the mental hospital? *Australia and New Zealand Journal of Psychiatry,* 35, 421–427.

Lehrer, Jonah, (2010). The truth wears off. *The New Yorker Magazine,* Dec. 10, pp. 52–57.

Masuda, M., Cutler, D., Hein, L., Holmes, T . (1978). Life events and prisoners: A study of the relationship of life events to prison incarceration. *Archives of General Psychiatry*, 35(2): 197–203.

McKusick, Mark, T., King D, E, et al. (1998). *National Expenditures for Mental Health, Alcohol, and Other Drug Abuse Treatment,* 1996. Rockville, MD: Substance Abuse and Mental Health Services Administration.

Melville, C. (ed.) (1977). *The balanced service system: An approach to the delivery of mental health services.* Atlanta: Georgia Mental Health Institute.

Moore, T. (2010). *Care of the Soul in Medicine.* New York: Hay House Publishers.

Olson, R. Paul (2006). *Mental Health Systems Compared; Great Britain, Norway, Canada, and the United States.* Springfield, IL: Charles Thomas Publisher.

Pollack, D. A., and Cutler, D. L. (1992): Changing roles: Psychiatry in community mental health centers. In: *Innovations in Mental Health*, S. Cooper and T. Lentner (eds.), Sarasota, FL: Professional Resource Exchange.

Resnick, E. V. (1876). Mental health care in America (1976). *Hospital and Community Psychiatry*, 27, 519–521.

Richardson, J. D. (1899). Franklin Pierce Veto Message to the Senate of the United States, May 3rd, 1854. In *Messages and Papers of the Presidents 1789–1897,* Published by Authority of Congress, Vol. V, pp. 247–256.

Ridgely, M. S., Giard, J, Shern, D. (1999). Florida's Medicaid mental health carve-out: Lessons from the first years of implementation. *Journal of Behavioral Health Services and Research,* 26, 400–415.

Roberts, A. R., and Yeager, K. R. (2004). *Evidenced Based Practice Manual.* New York: Oxford University Press.

Ross, E. C., Croze, C . (1997). Mental health service delivery in the age of managed care. In *Mental Health Policy and Practice Today*, Atkins, T., Callicutt, J. W. (Eds .). Thousand Oaks, CA: Sage.

Satcher, D. (1999). United States Public Health Service Office of the Surgeon General. *Mental Health: A Report of the Surgeon General.* Rockville, MD: Department of Health and Human Services, U.S. Public Health Service.

State Profiles (1999): *On Public Sector Managed Behavioral Health Care.* Rockville, MD: Substance Abuse and Mental Health Services Administration, Office of Managed Care, 2000.

Sullivan, M. J. (1995). Medicaid's quiet revolution: Merging the public and private sectors of care. *Professional Psychology: Research and Practice,* 26, 229–234.

Svendsen, D. P., Cutler, D. L., Ronis, R. J., Herman, L. C., Morrison, M. A., Smith, M. K., and Munetz, M. (2005). The professor of public psychiatry model in Ohio: The impact on training program innovation and the quality of mental health care. *Community Mental Health Journal*, 41(6): 775–784.

Torrey, E. T. (2003). Leaving the mentally ill out in the cold. *City Journal.*

Warner, R. (1994). *Recovery from Schizophrenia.* New York: Routledge,.

Winslow, W. W. (1979). The changing role of psychiatrists in community mental health centers. *American Journal of Psychiatry*, 136, 24–27.

Zwelling, S. S. (1985): *Quest for a Cure: The Public Hospital in Williamsburg,* Virginia. The Colonial Williamsburg Foundation.

STATE PSYCHIATRIC HOSPITALS IN THE TWENTY-FIRST CENTURY

RUPERT R. GOETZ AND ALAN RADKE

For a long time, state psychiatric hospitals *were* the mental health system. Derived from Europe's insane asylums, psychiatric hospitals in this country began as a refuge for a mix of people, including those suffering from mental illness, with developmental disabilities, and the poor. When President Franklin Pierce vetoed the National Mental Health Act in 1854, the responsibility for these facilities was by default thrust firmly on the states (Cutler et al. 2012). These "state psychiatric hospitals" (state hospitals) gradually clarified their role as serving persons with severe and persistent mental illness, and with deinstitutionalization in the later twentieth century, former steady resident growth turned into downsizing and enormous change. Unfortunately, the community mental health system did not grow in proportion to the need of those discharged, and neglect also found the hospitals, bringing back the most deplorable conditions.

This period of neglect has more recently been followed by a period of relative attention and stabilization, but also a time of searching for state hospitals' futures. And "futures" is intentionally plural. While state hospitals have large commonalities, their current and certainly their future roles will differ significantly, driven by national, state, and regional forces that dictate their evolution (Garfield 2009). Thus, change has been the main theme for state hospitals for decades.

It then comes as no surprise that a view of these facilities since the 1980s must be a dynamic, not a static, one. We will present an overview; then point to clinical, administrative, and financial forces driving change; and finally look ahead with only one certainty: namely, that change is likely to increase in pace and scope. One place to begin our story is with two prototypical patients—the first admitted to the Oregon State Hospital (OSH) in the early 1980s, and the second admitted in the early 2010s.

In the early 1980s, "Jane Doe" was a common sight in Portland's parks, and community merchants tolerated her sleeping on their doorsteps. Community Assertive Community Treatment (ACT) Team providers were unable to connect with her and get her to stay on her medications.

Often drunk, she deteriorated to the point where a visit to the University Hospital's emergency room resulted in civil commitment to OSH. Once detoxified from alcohol, Jane still refused medication and remained severely disorganized, so she was started on involuntary medications. A first-generation antipsychotic and benzodiazepines limited her acute episodes of agitation. Over a period of three months, she settled in to a pattern of marginal engagement. She half-heartedly participated in groups, and began orienting back to the community. After six months, social workers found her a group home, and she was discharged into the care of a local community mental health center. Jane appeared to manage her life in the community over the next decade, supported by targeted and at times intensive community case management.

In the 2010s, "John Doe" was also a familiar figure downtown. Generally avoided because of his bizarre behavior, his physical features spoke of the ravages of methamphetamine. When he tried to break into a store's garage for a place to sleep, he wound up in jail. Found unfit to stand trial, John was admitted to the OSH for fitness restoration. His extensive history of legal involvement and frequent admissions there painted a more detailed picture. Adopted early, he had grown up in an abusive home and never finished high school, because of schizoid behavior and early drug involvement. Cycles of frequent hospitalizations and incarceration for violence followed, leading up to this admission. After being restored to legal fitness, he was found "guilty except for insanity" and returned to OSH, where he remained for over a year. Tenuously stabilized on two antipsychotics, two mood stabilizers, and a benzodiazepine (together with side-effect medication), John is only partially able to sit through group treatment sessions. His participation is minimal and his future-orientation is absent, despite peer specialists' trying to engage with him. John's violence makes his future placement problematic, even with further stabilization. Skeptical community providers are unlikely to accept him, and the conditional-release board is unlikely to consider such a release any time soon.

Without delving into all the forces driving changes over the last thirty years, these composite cases are probably replicated in many state hospitals. So, it may be useful to briefly look back at OSH.

Completed in 1883 as the Oregon Insane Asylum, this abbreviated version of a Kirkbride plan formed a "J" along Salem's Center Street, then in the outskirts of the state's capitol city. In 1958, the hospital's census peaked at over 3,500 patients, then gradually decreased, to somewhat over 650 now. Featured in the 1975 drama film, *One Flew Over the Cuckoo's Nest*, it shared the ups and downs of many facilities. Great clinical leaders such as Maxwell Jones and Dean Brooks helped develop strong therapeutic communities, with their open, voluntary wards.

But the facility came under stress. The psychiatric residency had to be given up when the state was unable to keep up the necessary financial commitments. Ultimately, the decline led to involvement of the U.S. Department of Justice (USDOJ), alleging civil rights violations. Significant attention and reinvestments followed. Now, as of this writing, patients and staff completed the last of three moves into the completely rebuilt facility, the newest state hospital in the country. It retains its historical center building, but its future remains a challenge, with state budget shortfalls and a stretched community mental health system.

Without delving into the history of Oregon's community mental health system, the state's patients have also changed. The "typical" severely and persistently mentally ill (SPMI) person presenting with one or two diagnoses in the 1980s seems to belong to the past. Most people admitted to the OSH now show three common characteristics: they present with complex, co-occurring illnesses; they are often forensically involved; and acute-care, community hospitals have been unable to adequately address their needs. In many cases, little distinguishes current

OSH patients from the mentally ill prisoners across the parking lot in the state's correctional facility. While a number of medically compromised and elderly patients in a medical unit and a civil commitment branch in urban Portland are exceptions, roughly 75 percent of the patients in Salem are involved in the criminal justice system.

The OSH story mirrors that of many state hospitals. Overcrowding and lack of treatment resources are common. While some state hospitals found their own path into sustainability and even excellence, many others drew the attention of the USDOJ for violations, before investments allowed change. All are part of stretched community mental health systems, and the large budgets state hospitals command often drive what is possible elsewhere.

We begin this chapter with an overview; followed by a section on special clinical, administrative, and financial issues; before we look forward to what the future might hold. Where possible, we will identify common elements; where not, we will focus on specific examples within the authors' experience.

OVERVIEW OF STATE HOSPITALS

In 2007, every state mental health authority (SMHA) operated psychiatric inpatient beds that provided care to individuals who were unable to care for themselves or were a danger to themselves or others. During that year, state hospitals served approximately 3% of all mental health consumers served by the system, at an expenditure of approximately $8 billion (27% of total SMHA expenditures). Forty-nine states and the District of Columbia operated a total of 232 states hospitals that served approximately 175,500 persons, with approximately 43,500 patients residing in them at the end of 2006. In over half the states there were fewer than three psychiatric hospitals. Thirteen states had only one state psychiatric hospital, and 11 states, mostly in the eastern and southern regions of the country, had six or more. This represented a huge change from 1950, when there were over 512,500 patients in state and county psychiatric hospitals. By 2005, that number had declined to somewhat less than 50,000 patients, and the number of hospitals had declined by 37% to 204 (note that Center for Medicare and Medicaid Services [CMS] numbers and National Association of State Mental Health Program Directors [NASMHPD] National Research Institute [NRI] numbers differ) (Lutterman et al. 2009).

Often built between 1850 and 1900, the average state hospital now serves roughly 500 adult patients with about 1,700 staff organized into clinical and administrative departments. Primarily forensic institutions, patients are admitted there either because they are unfit to stand trial, or as "guilty except for insanity" (or the state's equivalent) until they can be conditionally released. Most state hospitals also accept civilly committed patients and in rare instances, guardian-directed or voluntary admissions.

Even looking only at the type of person served, state hospitals across the country vary significantly. Patient age groups range from children to the elderly. Almost all hospitals (over 80%) serve both adults and the elderly; significantly fewer (around 50%) serve adolescents, while only 30% to 40% serve children (Lutterman et al. 2009).

Over three-quarters of admittees are forensic commitments. The length of stay varies broadly; with only a few of the facilities focused on providing acute, short-term care (fewer than 30 days). Most consider themselves tertiary care facilities, serving intermediate-range (30–90 days) and long-term state patients (Lutterman et al. 2009). The average length of stay for state hospital patients is roughly 120 days, but the range is enormous, with facilities having some patients who have been there over 20 years and are unlikely to ever be released. Discharge for the mostly forensic patients requires both a court order and the availability of step-down residential treatment facilities or always-staffed group homes, something that is often difficult to obtain together, making many states vulnerable to not serving patients in the most integrated community environment (Salzer et al. 2006). Such placement in most integrated settings is demanded by the U.S. Supreme Court decision in *Olmsted v. L.C. and E.W.* (1999).

So, how do these state hospitals work? There are few organizations of the size of state hospitals that do not begin their web pages with a mission, vision, and values statement. Common missions and visions include hope, recovery, safety, quality, and evidence-based care; values include patient-focus, teamwork, respect, dedication, and compassion. Some hospitals emphasize their role in the community more; others, their innovation.

It might seem logical to clinicians reading this chapter that our next topic would be the clinical practices that have been shown to achieve such goals, followed by administrative structures to support them, and finally, the cost of such care. Unfortunately, state hospitals must always struggle to live within their means. The reality is that administrations have had to become adept at balancing the inherent tension between funding and clinical care. Thus, our overview will first describe administrative practices, then clinical ones, with a last comment about funding.

While originally built as asylums or refuges where the directing physician dictated both clinical and administrative practices, today's state hospitals are at their heart hospitals, with such structures separated. Statutes, administrative rules, and hospital policies and procedures generally guide the organization. Following these, administrative departments support clinical ones, maintaining (for example) the physical plant, food and nutrition, personnel practices, and budget management.

The chief executive officer (CEO or superintendent) these days is generally not a physician: the administrative complexity requires special skills. Various chiefs, such as a chief of operations (COO) and chief financial officer (CFO), make up the next layer of administrative positions, which also includes a chief medical officer (CMO) or medical director. In some cases, this position serves as the chief of psychiatry and chief of medicine, with nursing answering through its own director of nursing (DON), and other clinical disciplines operating under a distinct director of clinical operations (DCO). In others, the CMO administratively leads all clinical disciplines. Some or all of these positions usually make up the executive committee or CEO cabinet. Depending on the institution's size, numerous additional layers may follow.

An inherent tension that each organization must solve is how vertical or horizontal (narrow or broad) this pyramid of positions should be. Sometimes, a more vertical organization with fewer positions supervised by each leader allows for better implementation of new strategies and less administrative silos. There is no best answer.

Besides administrative structures, it might be argued that state hospitals run on workgroups and committees. Where the administrative structures can be identified through job descriptions, job assignments, performance appraisals, and personnel hiring and firing, much of the day-to-day work of state hospitals occurs in an alternate system. Committees and subcommittees tend to be responsible for a hospital's activities, including the development and updating of policies and procedures, and examining data whether such practices are followed. These groups generally answer to a single executive committee.

Variations are numerous, so a new staff member entering a state hospital and trying to understand how the organization functions could do significantly worse than looking at an organizational chart that lays out the administrative lines of authority, a committee chart that lays out how various appointed groups interrelate, and scanning the hospital's policies and procedures, which are usually clearly and centrally posted.

Common to all state hospitals are professional departments that organize their clinical staff according to their disciplines. Psychiatry, medicine, nursing, psychology, and social work departments are almost universally present. How rehabilitative disciplines are organized and combined tends to vary more. In some cases, vocational and educational services, as well as pastoral care and peer-delivered services, find themselves together with occupational and recreational therapy.

No matter its organization, an essential dynamic for each state hospital is how practices across different clinical disciplines are aligned into a cohesive whole. A key tension must always be resolved: Clinical authority in a hospital ultimately rests in a physician's order and their independent license. Medical staffs usually function under their own set of bylaws, answering directly to the hospital's governing body. Where administrative controls are executed through job descriptions and assignments, the clinical practices of individually licensed, professional staff are generally governed by their peers. How does an administration direct such independent practice? For example, the hospital administrator may like the reported effectiveness and cost savings of a medication algorithm. However, if a medical staff refuses to buy in, tensions emerge. Whatever the processes, resolving such tensions is critical to state hospital governance.

Another dynamic may equally challenge a hospital's organization. Few physicians maintain that they run the units on which they practice: unit function and its milieu are clearly the purview of nurses. Who, then, ultimately decides (for example) on transferring a patient between two units? In some organizations, physician-to-physician communication negotiates such moves. In others, a senior nurse serves as transfer manager and assigns patients to units. When there are disagreements, friction results. Much can be learned about how a state hospital functions by examining its physician–nurse relationships.

Yet, administrative structures alone cannot run state hospitals. It might be argued that it is "leadership" that in fact extends the organization's vision from the superintendent to each direct care staff. This is not leadership as in "command and control," it is leading by personal responsibility. This has both administrative and clinical importance: how will a person suffering from mental illness find their personal path of recovery to a meaningful life without every staff member taking responsibility for what they control?

Dean Brooks, the superintendent of the OSH, told the following story. Visiting a superintendent friend on the night after President John F. Kennedy was buried, the two decided to make 11:00 p.m. rounds. The first wards were peaceful, but in another building the lights burned brightly. Some women had pillows over their faces, and others had pulled up the covers. Dr. Brooks asked an aide, "When do you turn the lights out?" The response was startling: "Oh, we don't, Doctor." "Why?" "It's the law." The superintendent-friend changed the law then and there, and the lights were turned out for the first time in perhaps 25 to 50 years. On the next unit, the two friends almost stumbled over several bushel baskets full of women's shoes. They were of all sizes—some new, some old, some over-at-the-heels as though they had been worn by feet four sizes too large. When they asked about the baskets, the superintendents were told that these were "shoe baskets": Every night, patients put their shoes in one of the baskets, and the following morning, it was first come, first served. Needless to say, Dr. Brooks' anxiety ran high when he returned to his own hospital. Did he have bushels of shoes, too? Meeting with his superintendent's committee, an elected patient representative group from every ward, it was not hard to identify the first similar issue: A patient asked, "How come we don't have any place to hang our towels in the bathroom?" Supplying towel racks seemed easy enough, but identifying and changing all of the areas where dehumanization had crept in over the years in the hospital proved a much harder, sustained task. Leadership could be seen as counteracting the inevitable dehumanization that occurs when institutional rules evolve without being challenged by "seeing the human face directly" (Brooks 1969).

Leadership thus ties the mission, vision, and values of a state hospital through its structures and disciplines to the treatment processes and programs to give these facilities their unique therapeutic nature. What is it, then, that state hospitals do clinically? They combine both the capacity to accept the most severely ill people and the opportunity for extended stays into a critical safety-net service for the mental health system of care as a whole.

State hospital admissions units tend to see people from the community or correctional settings in their severest distress. Generally expert at psychopharmacology and behavior management, they focus on stabilization from these severe symptoms of mental illness. In some hospitals, separate units exist for the admission of persons found unfit to stand trial, and they therefore add fitness-restoration to this acute-stabilization role. Away from the front and looking toward the back door, transition or discharge units tend to focus on preparing patients for returning into community settings. Their expertise often includes rehabilitation and helping patients avoid the revolving door of readmissions (30-day readmissions have tended downward from 9% to somewhat below 8% in the last decade [Schacht 2010]). Significant understanding of community resources, as well as the legal process associated with conditional release, is required here.

Over the past decades, the view of treatment has become a more dynamic than static one, considering discharge options from the beginning of admission. Yet, most state hospitals still have a core set of patients for whom discharge into the community is unlikely. In the not-too-distant past, this was much more common. Lengths of stay were such that one new CMO received the following incredulous response from the unit nurse when asking for a patient's discharge plan: "What do you mean, discharge? This is his home!" Now, discharge into a community setting is the expectation, and extremely long-stay patients significantly challenge the discharge-oriented milieu. In fact, balancing the needs of active clinical treatment toward discharge with measures designed to enhance a patient's quality of life while in the hospital long-term is a common clinical dilemma.

No matter the length of stay or purpose of the unit, the process of planning and implementing treatment is often remarkably similar. On admission, a comprehensive set of assessments is undertaken, augmented as a patient stabilizes and more information becomes available. Responsibilities are frequently divided by clinical disciplines and supported by the standardized instruments or approaches. Too numerous to mention here, standard assessments of violence risk and suicidality, as well as clinical symptoms (such as depression or anxiety) are often part of the initial assessment. Then, usually within the first few hours, an initial treatment plan is developed. It later becomes the comprehensive treatment plan, which is regularly updated, driving interventions throughout the hospital stay. Numerous published and locally developed treatment planning methods exist, generally involving translation of a patient's problems, strengths, and goals into specific objectives and interventions to be carried out by identified staff, at an identified frequency, and with measurable outcomes. Treatment planning is generally done in interdisciplinary meetings, often with a psychiatrist considered the treatment team leader. In recent years, significant emphasis has been placed on assuring that this treatment planning includes the patient at its center. All too often in the past, treatment planning occurred in small, closed-door sessions, and the patient was merely asked to acknowledge the plan upon its presentation to him or her. This movement from a physician-centered to a person-centered approach is one hallmark of change in treatment planning during the last decade.

Treatment delivery has seen equally enormous change. It would be well beyond the scope of this overview to describe the broad array of biological, psychological, and social therapies that are currently available in state hospitals. Biological therapies tend to revolve around pharmacotherapy and in some cases electroconvulsive treatment (some states do not allow the latter in state hospitals, despite the need for it by persons so severely ill). Antipsychotics are the prototypical medication. In recent years, second-generation drugs have largely replaced first-generation, with approximately 90% of patients on antipsychotics receiving them (Schacht 2010). Given the cost of medications, particularly newer antipsychotics, some states have tried to implement restrictions or algorithms that spell out what they consider to be best pharmacotherapy practices. For example, they may recommend the use of second-generation antipsychotic medications only after a first-generation medication has failed, or may make the use of mono-pharmacy (medications from one class) the rule, with poly-pharmacy reserved as a last resort. Overall, however, changes in the available medications are so rapid that few generalizations can be made about the practices and individual facilities.

Individual and group psychotherapies, such as cognitive behavioral therapy (CBT) or dialectic behavioral therapy (DBT) have also emerged as treatment mainstays. As state hospitals are generally stretched for staff, group modalities tend to outweigh the use of individual psychotherapy. Rehabilitative services, ranging from occupational and recreational therapy to vocational and educational supports, have also expanded enormously, becoming particularly important as a recovery model takes hold nationwide.

One particular method of delivering such services deserves mention: "Treatment malls" have often replaced ward-based treatment. Similar in concept to community colleges, these malls offer opportunities to leverage both staff capabilities and patient needs into an integrated, central location (Bopp et al. 1996). Particularly important in the current environment, it appears that mixing both civil and forensic patients in such malls is the realistic practice (Webster et al. 2009).

One critical topic that is easily overlooked when describing treatment in state hospitals is supervision and consultation. Clinical staff working in these facilities vary enormously in their training and experience. Invariably, patients spend most of their time interacting with staff who have a high school diploma or bachelor's degree. Yet their training and mentoring is easily neglected. Then they learn from their peers, where bad habits are picked up with the good as "the way things really work around here."

For example: Mr. Smith was a familiar face around the unit. Always loud and intrusive, his schizoaffective disorder had been hard to treat, and he was on multiple medications. He rarely slept through the night. Shortly after several new mental health technicians joined the team, his pattern gradually changed. He became more withdrawn and isolative, though during the day this change was barely noticeable. New junior staff teased the old-timers about their "difficult nights," remarking on how calm things seemed. Thankfully, nighttime rounds were done faithfully, and one early morning Mr. Smith was found unconscious with a loop of torn bedding around his neck. Alarms went off, and the treatment plan was changed to address his worsening depression. Junior staff had in fact been aware from relatively early that the patient's mood had changed. However, the changes were gradual and appeared to them to be an improvement, instead of a worsening.

How is particularly junior staff to develop an understanding of their role in assessment, monitoring, and treatment without ongoing systematic training, supervision, and easy access to consultation? Just as leadership was earlier characterized as counteracting the inevitable dehumanization in large state hospitals, so, too, supervision and consultation might in this context be characterized as counteracting the inevitable accommodation to the clinically commonplace. But supervision and consultation is not only important for junior staff. Clinical treatment teams consisting of professional staff plan and implement treatment interventions for their patients. They also become stuck in a complex case or miss gradually emerging problems. Clinical supervision—for example, through discipline chiefs—assures that teams can step back to see the forest where they earlier saw only trees. Ready access to consultation is practically the same thing. Rather than allowing individuals or teams to struggle with patients or situations that repeatedly turn up in the morning report, the offer of consultative support can ensure that clinical problems, even if only recognized by a sense of discomfort on the part of the consultee, receive expeditious attention.

SPECIAL STATE HOSPITAL ISSUES

Of necessity, this overview had to be brief. To augment it, we offer a more detailed look at a few special clinical, administrative, and financial issues that seem important. We begin with state hospital culture.

Where state hospitals began as asylums (Geller & Morrissey 2004), many unfortunately soon became facilities to house those unwanted by their communities. Over time, hastened by a lack of resources, it is not surprising that their culture became one of containment rather than treatment. As long as problems from within their walls did not spill out into the surrounding communities, public neglect was balanced by lack of treatment on the inside. Seclusion and restraint is a typical example, with state hospitals nationwide seeing a gradual decline in combined restraint, though not seclusion, numbers. From 2002 through 2009, restraint hours fell from roughly 1:1000 to roughly 2:1000 patient hours, while the ratio of patients restrained remained steady, between roughly 3.5 and 4.0%. At the same time, seclusion hours remained relatively steady at 1:2000 patient hours, while the percent of patients secluded also remained relatively steady around roughly 2.5% (Schacht 2010).

What happened? From the perspective of one of the authors, the movement to reduce the use of seclusion and restraint is an exemplary cultural shift, one from coercion to an understanding of the role of "trauma informed care" in state hospitals. Such trauma-informed care consists in its most simple definition of understanding that persons seeking care in mental health settings have histories of physical and/or emotional trauma; that organizations must know how this trauma affects these people; and must provide trauma-specific interventions to address the consequences of the trauma. Efforts in the state of Pennsylvania (Smith et al. 2005) to reduce the use of seclusion and restraint served as a backdrop when NASMHPD convened a series of meetings to develop a response to the landmark Hartford *Courant's* articles. What ultimately emerged were the National Executive Training Institute's six core strategies. As efforts were underway nationally to implement these, evidence emerged that reducing seclusion and restraint reduced injuries and costs (LeBel & Goldstein 2005). However, evidence also emerged that successful initiatives proved much broader than alone implementing the six strategies. State hospitals that moved significantly toward the elimination of seclusion and restraint were in fact engaged in a significant cultural change. The cultural change was one of moving from reactive, coercive strategies to proactive, person-centered ones. Key to successfully making this shift appeared to be an understanding of how traumatized both patients and staff in these hospitals were. While there has been a more formal review of the evidence base for the six core strategies, attention has shifted toward the implementation of "trauma-informed care" strategies (Murphy, 2005), which required the culture of care to change.

For state hospitals to fulfill their mission, they must create a therapeutic environment. Without delving into the extensive literature on culture and culture change, several dynamics specific to state hospitals must be understood. The first is that the clinical model of tertiary inpatient psychiatry is rapidly evolving. Where in the past a medical model meant that physicians dictated care, expecting staff to implement that care and patients to accept it, lessons first from the substance abuse and now the mental health communities challenged hospitals to shift to a more recovery-oriented, person-centered model of care. This is a significant shift, which has yet to be fully reflected in training programs, including psychiatric residencies across the country.

The second dynamic is the evolution of evidence-based practices in these state hospital settings. Whereas in the past, psychopharmacology was the main consideration, now the increasing use of behavioral supports shortly after admission and rehabilitative techniques closer to discharge, together with motivational enhancement and peer specialist services (services provided by persons with a lived experience of mental illness [Daniels et al. 2010]) along the way, all emerged. This increasing differentiation of services challenges each organization's capacity to motivate, train, and supervise its staff uniformly across all disciplines.

Even if managing these two dynamics were straightforward, significant countervailing factors exist. In some instances, staff have developed the perspective that state employment assures them stability and absence of change. Engaging such individuals in the necessarily dynamic process of improving care can rise to the level of a cultural shift. Also, as hospitals attempt to implement facility-wide improvements, the special populations it serves dictate an individualized approach; the desire for uniform practice challenges an individualized, person-centered decision. Staff may become confused: "If it took 30 days to reinstate John's off-grounds privileges, why are you considering the same privilege for Mary after only two weeks?" Maintaining accountability by standardized criteria is a much simpler organizational task than training individuals to anticipate individual problems early and take personal responsibility to see them addressed—again a cultural shift of major proportions. In many ways, changes in hiring, assigning, training, and supervising staff reflect the evolving understanding of person-centered care.

One such evolution is facilities' understanding of *recovery*, not only in its prevailing sense in the community, but from their perspective as an increasingly forensic organization that is part of the community. People today are most often admitted to state hospitals through the civil commitment or a forensic (criminal justice) process. This means they are forced to be there. The community may care only that, on average, state hospitals report one elopement per 5000 inpatient days (Schacht 2010). What does person-centeredness and recovery mean in this context? Does it mean that patients who must expect discharge back into prison or a secure facility should progress toward open community outings? A frank discussion of such realities between all parties, staff and people served alike, will be required for a state hospital to arrive at shared expectations. Considering all these dynamics, alignment between the facilities' philosophy of care and the philosophy of staff and patient management is at the heart of the culture shift that state hospitals face.

One product of the forensic process is that it imposes legally binding requirements on both the person whose case was heard and the system as a whole. A court order in a forensic case generally leads to immediate admission. Civil commitment tends not to have the same imperative force. In some states, changes in the threshold for civil commitment toward requiring increased acuity make use of this process harder, while lack of state hospital beds available to admit patients through the civil process further amplifies the lack of access to this tertiary resource. State hospitals are becoming even more forensic (Bloom 2006).

The increasingly forensic nature of state hospitals makes it particularly important to consider a second special issue: patient treatment rights. Even under civil commitment, a person's civil rights are preserved by stipulations in the law. Since these are mostly state laws, the details of a person's treatment rights vary. In general, civil commitment laws encourage voluntary treatment over involuntary if the person is capable of giving informed consent and is accepting of treatment. Furthermore, if a person is committed, the laws require supervision and treatment in a least-restrictive alternative; i.e., a treatment level of care appropriate to the person's treatment needs. The duration is also limited, usually to the time necessary to restore the person's mental health. Under indeterminate commitments such as "mentally ill and dangerous," the length of commitment is determined primarily by the risk to public safety. In these cases, a protracted court monitoring process is used to assure that the person's behavioral condition remains stable and public safety is preserved.

Voluntary versus involuntary treatment is generally determined by the person's level of competence and willingness to accept treatment. If the person is a competent consenter—i.e., able to give informed consent and accepting of treatment—then the person can determine their treatment course. If the person is a competent refuser (i.e., capable of giving informed consent but rejecting treatment), then unless otherwise ordered, the person can refuse to be involved in treatment. If the person in an incompetent consenter (i.e., accepting of treatment but unable to give informed consent), then the person will generally require a substitute decision maker or guardian appointed by the court to make treatment decisions. In such cases, the court must take steps to determine need for treatment and establish the legal authority for the treatment provider to make treatment decisions in the best interest of the person. Some states have more restrictive legal stipulations for intrusive treatment, most often understood to be somatic psychiatric therapies, such as psychotropic medications and electroconvulsive therapy. These commitment laws usually require a second court hearing to authorize such treatment.

Consent to physical health care is a separate matter, generally addressed differently than by civil commitment laws. Laws usually preserve the person's rights to determine treatment of physical health conditions by assuming that the person is competent to give informed consent unless adjudicated by the court as incompetent. Only in cases of emergency or urgent care wherein the person is unable to give informed consent because their decision making (executive functioning) is impaired does the law grant the treating provider or facility director the right to make a substitute decision. In some cases, when a person has a life-threatening condition, is capable of making his/her own treatment decisions, and is refusing treatment, an ethics issue may arise for the treating facility or provider. In these instances an ethics committee review is warranted.

The patient rights discussed so far pertain to treatment itself. Closely related is the state hospital's role in controlling unhealthy behavior. Smoking has become a significant rights and treatment concern for both provider and patient. A majority of state hospitals no longer permit smoking in the hospital or on the hospital grounds. The decision to go smoke-free is based on the findings that people with serious mental illness live on average 25 years less than the general population (Parks et al. 2006). The years lost are thought to be due to preventable risk factors, including smoking. Thus, smoking is increasingly considered a health problem that trumps a person's right to engage in unhealthy behavior, at least while hospitalized, where smoking also provides endless opportunities for patient-to-patient and staff-to-patient coercion. A smoke-free state hospital has two obligations to the smoking patient. First, the hospital must provide nicotine-replacement therapies to avoid nicotine-withdrawal syndromes, and second, the hospital must have a voluntary smoking cessation program for the patients who want to quit. The experiences of smoke-free state hospitals have been quite positive, with reduction in patient-to-patient aggression, less seclusion and restraints, fewer patient injuries, and fewer staff injuries, as well as less damage to the treatment environment. In some facilities that have gone smoke-free, it is ironic that the change appeared much more difficult for staff than for patients.

Over the last 20 years, state hospital staffs have become more cognizant that the people they serve are made up of special populations; that is, people with multiple disabilities and multiple diagnoses. It is important to recognize these special populations so that services can be customized to their needs. For this discussion, we will designate three special populations: people with complex/co-occurring behavioral health conditions, people with serious mental illnesses (SMI) and a history of aggressive behaviors, and people with SMI and chronic physical health conditions.

People with complex/co-occurring behavioral health conditions commonly cause diagnostic and treatment dilemmas for state hospital staffs. People with SMI and substance use disorders should be treated using an "integrated dual diagnosis treatment" (Mueser et al. 2003) approach, starting with a determination of their readiness for treatment. People with SMI and acquired or traumatic brain injuries must be assessed using neuropsychiatric and neuropsychological evaluations to clarify what the possible etiologies of their behavioral dysregulation are in order to guide treatment. Likewise, people with SMI and developmental or intellectual disabilities must undergo full neuropsychological and functional assessments to structure person-centered therapies to meet their treatment needs. People with co-occurring SMI and personality disorders should have their underlying personality structure evaluated to determine whether specialized cognitive/behavioral therapies, such as dialectical behavioral therapy, would be of benefit.

People with SMI and a history of aggressive and violent behaviors who are currently having an acute exacerbation of their mental illness and demonstrating aggressive behavior are particularly disconcerting for state hospital staffs. The risk of harm to other patients, staff, and the person creates urgency to expeditiously evaluate and stabilize the person. Once this is done, interventions can be considered. Usually, a combination of medications and focused behavioral supports is required. State hospitals have developed intensive care and high observation units to treat this special population. Even so, many of these units are constantly full, resulting in milieu disruptions on their units.

Special subgroups within the category just discussed might be those with the severest antisocial or borderline personality disorders. When very destabilized, such patients significantly challenge a state hospital's usual therapeutic reflexes. In antisocial personality disorder or even outright psychopathy, intentional premeditated violence becomes especially dangerous for staff, who are often incapable of distinguishing volitional behavior from the behavior due to the patient's psychiatric illness. Particular attention must be paid to assuring an environment of safety for both staff and other patients. Quite different, though equally challenging, are people with borderline personality disorder who are distressed to the point of severe self-harm that has become nearly constant. Engagement and management of boundaries with such patients is often a particular challenge for less-prepared staff. Long-term, tertiary state hospitalization often does little for such individuals, unless a strong focus on trauma is maintained. Both subpopulations require highly skilled clinical leaders to assure a milieu becomes and remains therapeutic. All too often, staff derail into punitive techniques or splitting between "rescuers" and "confronters," a problem that tears at the therapeutic fabric of a unit.

Another significant subpopulation for state hospitals are people with SMI who have chronic medical conditions that have been untreated or poorly treated. They are at high risk for medical morbidity or mortality. Common medical conditions, such as cardiovascular disease, diabetes, smoking related conditions, and infections, would be treatable, but may have been neglected. Many state hospitals have developed units to evaluate and appropriately treat the co-occurring medical conditions. This issue is even more common in geriatric, because as people with SMI age, they become more susceptible to dementias and chronic deliria. Such co-occurrence of mental illness symptoms, medical problems, and behavioral dysregulation due to organic brain factors quickly exceed a community nursing home's capabilities, prompting attempts to gain state hospital admission for these patients.

With growth in these special populations, state hospitals have had to adapt their general psychiatric units to better serve them. This has put the spotlight on recruiting and retaining mental health professionals with specialized training and experience. As the U.S. population increases and ages, there will only be more demand for specialized behavioral health services. Unfortunately, at the same time, we see a decreasing work force because of retirements of the "baby boomers" and a flat number of new trainees. To avert a crisis, state hospitals will need to develop action plans (Hoge et al. 2007) and adopt collaboration strategies, including the use of telemedicine to fill their specialized services needs.

One final special population deserves particular mention: namely, sexual offenders. The practice of civilly committing persons to state mental health agencies for treatment under "sexually violent predator" statutes following completion of their criminal sentences was upheld by the 1997 U.S. Supreme Court decision in *Kansas v. Hendricks*. A number of states created such programs, and case law (e.g., *Turay v. Seling*) clarified the mandates to provide "adequate" treatment, to define terms and conditions for their continuing confinement, and to make thoughtful release decisions. Given the clinical experience in treating such persons, this seemed difficult to do, so caution in developing the programs was advised (NASMHPD 1999). State forensic hospitals that have people with sexually violent predator commitments have experienced significant negative consequences. Most prominent seems to be the reinforcement of the idea that all people in state forensic hospitals should be considered by the public, courts, and legislators as extremely dangerous and difficult to treat. Programming in some facilities became more correction-like, with the expectation of antisocial behavior and the use of punitive interventions. Commitments also increased for sociopathic and psychopathic persons who had mild to moderate mental illnesses and who formerly were criminally adjudicated and went to prison. Even people with serious mental illnesses and a history of aggressive behavior due to their mental illnesses have seen an increase in forensic commitments. Some states now segregate their state-operated sex offender programs from their mental illness forensics programs. But the damage is done. Even in these states, the negative impact of developing "sexually violent predator" statutes that commit sex offenders to forensic state hospitals will linger for years.

While public pressure seems to be pushing more dangerous persons suffering from less severe mental illness out of the community and into the state hospitals, the community still is where most mental health care occurs and where state hospital patients return. The interface between both deserves much more attention than it has generally received.

Among the unsung heroes of the public mental health system are local community hospitals. Not only do community hospitals usually serve as emergency departments for state hospital patients and provide medical inpatient services for patients who have exceeded the facility's capacities to provide care, they also often serve as the acute psychiatric inpatient units in their communities. State hospitals commonly restrict themselves to long-term, tertiary psychiatric care of people with serious mental illness. This leads to complex, at times even contentious, relationships. An example may illustrate this.

While on the inpatient unit Friday night, patient Mary Doe suddenly seizes and drops to the floor unconscious. She is at OSH for treatment of her schizophrenia, but also suffers from diabetes mellitus and has been known to ingest a variety of materials. Staff trained in CPR rush to her aid and monitor her vital signs, but can do little else; 911 is called. Waiting for the EMTs to arrive takes some time. Despite arriving at the hospital within minutes of the call, they must enter through a sally port where metal-detection and remote camera monitoring create difficulties sorting out the stretcher, supplies, and personnel. Then, unfamiliar with the hospital, they have to be guided to the scene. Following their protocols, the EMTs take over, pushing aside an on-call physician who just arrived. The patient is transported back to the local ER, where medical assessment fails to give a clear answer, so the patient is admitted, requiring two "sitters" from OSH to stay with her. Twenty-four hours later, after more extensive tests, she is released back to the state hospital with a presumptive diagnosis of medication-induced seizure. The attending psychiatrist has little understanding of what transpired until he arrives on Monday morning.

Obviously contrived, this example illustrates a variety of limitations of the state hospital–community relationship. State hospitals may not have Advanced Cardiac Life Support (ACLS)-certified staff, may have a psychiatrist on call who is uncomfortable with emergency medical procedures, and may have limited emergency medical supplies like a crash cart. Especially in forensic settings, sally ports and scene control—absent frequent drills—present many further challenges to emergency personnel. Thankfully, EMTs are generally expert at adapting to adverse conditions. Agreements between the state hospital, local emergency services, and the community hospital can anticipate such issues and strengthen the collaboration. Shared training, development of staging areas where a transportable emergency patient can be taken for easy access by EMTs, and ER-physician to state-hospital-physician communication protocols are all important elements of such coordination.

It usually falls to the community hospital to support the state hospital with extensive medical workups and complex treatment, including surgery. This relationship is often well delineated through contractual relationships. However, complex cases present challenges to the collaboration between the state hospital psychiatrists, community hospital treating physicians, and nurses. For example, the community hospital may have seen only rarely a case of severe neuroleptic malignant syndrome, yet they are called upon to provide ICU services for just such a case. Ongoing psychiatric consultation becomes critical. Another aspect is staffing. The community hospital may have no difficulty with an urgent surgery; however, when the patient is psychiatrically unstable (and in many instances as a matter of routine or of state hospital custody), additional nursing staff supplied by the state hospital is required.

Where many state hospitals have medical units with a higher level of nursing and medical expertise, these are frequently full and reserved for committed people who meet the state's criteria. The situation can become much more contentious when community resources are also stretched to their limit.

Another brief story: The OSH chief medical officer (CMO) receives an urgent call from his counterpart at the community hospital. It seems that a patient suffering from episodes of major depression and PTSD, with an underlying borderline personality disorder, was admitted through their ER many weeks ago. She has been referred to the state hospital, ostensibly for long-term psychiatric rehabilitation following self-injury, but has been turned down as not meeting inpatient criteria. The patient had been shuffled from group home to group home, making herself *persona non grata* at all of the area residential treatment facilities with her self-harm. Desperate after being told she was being "kicked out" again, she jumped off a local parking structure and was admitted from the community ER with multiple traumas to her legs and pelvis. Surgical stabilization and rehabilitation proceeded relatively smoothly, and psychiatric consultation kept her mental illness symptoms under fair control. Now, weeks later, the community hospital social workers are at their wit's end about finding her a residential placement: no community-based program will even look at her. The community hospital has long since ceased being paid for her care and can find no way to discharge her. The community hospital social workers have fixed on the patient's multi-year history in the state hospital and see this as the only remaining solution, prompting the CMO's call. Review by the CMO shows that she in fact does not meet state hospital admission criteria, so the case is appealed to the state's mental health division to consider administratively admitting her anyway.

There are no easy answers here. If state hospital admission criteria are not met, such a case would present *Olmstead* problems for the mental health administration if admitted anyway. Community hospitals all too often hold cases who symbolize the limits of the public mental health system. Whether it is too few beds of a certain type or too few providers of specialty services such as DBT, the issues reach far beyond the scope of state hospitals alone. While the details of such cases vary by area, they all emphasize the need for local collaboration between state, county, and community stakeholders of the public mental health system. There is probably no clearer and more urgent administrative issue than linking the state hospital with its community. With state variables so high, it is unlikely that large, national solutions can be found to guide necessary local work, though recent federal initiatives, such as the Accountable Care Act, will need to play out.

When the federal government created Institutions for Mental Disorders (IMD) in the mid-1960s disallowing Medicaid money to fund state hospital services appropriation of monies through state legislatures became the single most important financial issue. This is not to say that the cost of care, cost effectiveness, and billing and accounting for care provided are not critical. It is only that state hospitals usually represent the single largest state budget item. Accordingly, scrutiny is usually intense.

In fact, some irony can be found in the story that Dorothea Dix, who visited the hospital in 1869, approved of the care at Oregon's Private Hawthorne Hospital, yet the state still went ahead with the decision to build its own Kirkbride hospital. The fact that Dr. Hawthorne was charging $6.00 per patient per week (an early model of capitation) and that the total constituted over half of the legislature's budget doubtless led to this effort to control costs by building a public hospital (Cutler 2001). Unfortunately, costs were not contained.

Cost remains the central problem. Private billing of patients, depending on their ability to pay, and billing of federal entitlement programs cannot distract from the fact that states must bear the lion's share of the burden. This requires that state hospital administrations be expert at working with their legislators. It is a complex case to make that the state hospital provides the necessary care and does so cost-effectively. Are the right patients able to get into the hospital? Are they receiving expeditious care? Is the care effective, and are discharges timely? All of this must be presented within the larger context of the local legal and community system of care.

State hospitals have moved from consuming over 60% of the state mental health authorities' (SMHA) total expenditures in the 1980s to somewhat over 25% by 2010. This has occurred while overall SMHA expenditures remained relatively steady in constant dollars, though growing significantly in current dollars, from overall roughly $6 billion to over $35 billion during the same timeframe. In 2010, SMHA-controlled revenues were made up of roughly 40% state general funds with an additional 20% state Medicaid match, drawing in roughly 30% of Medicaid, Medicare, and block grant and other federal funding (NRI 2011).

Such costs require champions within the state hospital, the administration, the legislature, and the community, if they are to be regularly covered. Legal pressure has at times and in various locations helped turn such funding into a necessity, but anti–mental illness stigma and lack of integration of state hospitals within the overall health care system remained potent barriers.

FUTURE TRENDS FOR STATE HOSPITALS

As noted earlier, change has been a constant in past years for state hospitals. In the following section, we will build on the past changes and first explore some of the current driving forces, then offer an example to illustrate where these forces might lead us.

Similar to other areas of healthcare, one of the driving forces in the evolution of state hospitals has been the progression of evidence-based clinical practices and an understanding of their translation into practice. Not only has pharmacotherapy evolved from first-generation antipsychotic medications, guided (for example) by the Texas Medication Algorithm Project (Miller et al. 2004), but there has been a clearer understanding of the role of recovery (Onken et al. 2002) and the need for psychosocial rehabilitative services. This ongoing clinical evolution is clearly going to remain a major driver in the future of state hospitals.

Yet the possibly most powerful factor is the financial forces shaping state hospitals. These facilities can only operate within the budgets they are given. While in some locations these budgets are relatively stable, overall financial stress on states' revenues has driven many hospitals into particularly lean times. Improvements in clinically effective treatments have in many places become difficult to implement, hindered by the downturn in the economy. There is clearly precedent. As noted earlier, state mental health authorities' expenditures are generally rising steadily in current dollars, remaining roughly steady in constant dollars. The recession in 2002–2004 led to steep reduction in this rise by roughly half of its percent change. It comes as no surprise, then, that the current recession has caused a dip in such change by almost three-fourths (NRI 2011). A major contravening force has been the involvement of the U.S. Department of Justice's pressing states under the Civil Rights of Institutionalized Persons Act of 1980 (CRIPA). Where hospital conditions have deteriorated to the point that civil rights violations could be found, such federal action has led to investments by more than 35 states.

In this context, changes in administrative practices might be seen as updating the link between clinical and financial forces affecting state hospitals. Specific practices are too numerous to mention, particularly in light of the differences from one state to another. However, a few deserve special mention. In these tight financial times, Centers for Medicare and Medicaid Services (CMS) accreditation, which opens the door to federal funds, has become increasingly important. More broadly, hospital accreditation by bodies such as The Joint Commission (TJC) is often seen as setting a floor under administrative practices. A second administrative practice is the development of electronic health records. To date, many state facilities struggle with largely outdated paper records wherein it is not only extremely hard to find important information, but which complicate the collection of meaningful data that can be aggregated into useful information. In part due to federal requirements, electronic health records are becoming increasingly common. A third example might be the emphasis on continuous quality improvement using quality-management techniques imported from industry into health care and now into state hospital facilities. Performance improvement methodologies such as Six Sigma and LEAN (Kim et al. 2006) are becoming increasingly common in state hospital management. They help move organizations from simply reporting metrics for national comparison, such as TJC's ORYX system, to becoming more information-driven organizations. Finally, physical plant management and electronic improvements, such as swipe-card timekeeping, electronic gate controls, and ongoing camera monitoring, contribute to significant improvement in state hospital environments.

So, where might these clinical, financial and administrative forces lead state hospitals' futures? One future may be better integration between state hospitals and the community. Rather than speculating about possible models, we will look to one state's efforts in this regard.

INSTITUTION TO COMMUNITY:
THE MINNESOTA EXPERIENCE

In 1987, the state legislature passed the Minnesota Comprehensive Mental Health Act. The intention of the law was to improve the public mental health system, which had fallen in its ranking with other states to the lowest quartile. Part of the Act focused on state hospitals to improve mental health professional staffing and allow people served to return to the community. Over the next few years, the regional treatment centers (state hospitals) hired psychiatrists, psychologists, and social workers who were licensed and board-certified. Psychiatric units on the campuses were specialized, including admission, high observation/intensive care, Mental Illness and Chemical Dependency (MI/CD), behavioral treatment, geriatric psychiatry, child/adolescent psychiatry, and community transition. The effect of hiring well-trained mental health professionals and reconfiguring the general psychiatric units into specialty units resulted in shorter lengths of stay. Add to that the new generation antipsychotics and antidepressants as well as anticonvulsants being used as mood stabilizers, and the censuses at the state hospitals began to decrease.

In Minnesota, as in many states, any unused appropriation dollars at the end of the fiscal year are to be returned to the general fund. As the state hospital units were closing, the associated appropriation was to be given up. With every unit closed, twenty full-time equivalent staff members were to be laid off. As a result of these possibilities, a new initiative was proposed to reinvest the appropriation funds made available when a state hospital unit was closed. The Adult Mental Health Initiative was passed in 1993. It allowed for state staff to be reassigned to the community. Regional planning groups determined the community infrastructure needs of the regions. The counties negotiated with the Department of Human Services, State-Operated Services (SOS) for needed staff, including psychiatrists, psychologists, social workers, and psychiatric nurses. Two hundred SOS staff members were placed in the community by contracting with SOS. As a result of these shared services contracts, the community infrastructure evolved. Intensive residential treatment units, assertive community treatment services, adult rehabilitative mental health services, and crisis services were developed using best-practice models. Length of stays at the state hospitals continued to shorten; censuses continued to drop.

There came a point when in rural Greater Minnesota, the state hospital censuses were so low that maintaining the large state hospital buildings and grounds was cost-prohibitive. One example is the state hospital in Northwest Minnesota. Designed for 3000 people, it only had 30 people on an average daily census. As closures were being considered, each region became concerned about losing their regional treatment center. A three-year-long planning process resulted in the development of the community behavioral health hospital (CBHH) model. A CBHH is a 16-bed mental health unit designed to serve people in need of acute inpatient psychiatric services. Ten of these CBHHs were proposed, to be placed throughout Greater Minnesota as determined by the regional planning groups. They were to have short lengths of stay with the intention of returning the hospitalized person to their own community.

To complement the new hospital system, SOS developed the Central Preadmission Office (CPA). CPA is a single point of access to all state-operated hospitals. The CPA officer gathers information to determine if the referred person's required hospital level of care, medical stability, and behavioral treatment. An attending provider or doctor on call makes the final admission authorization decision based on the information provided.

The first CBHH opened in March 2006, and the last opened in August 2008. Aggressive utilization review and utilization management were used to gather data on the utilization patterns of the CBHHs as well as the referral patterns with CPA. Admission denials and diversions were tracked. Outliers of people who did not meet hospital-level-of-care criteria on admission or on continued stay were analyzed. Findings resulted in a services gap-needs analysis. The analysis demonstrated a number of gaps. Although gaps were expected after the closure of the former state hospitals, who admitted anyone the community could not or would not serve, the findings were remarkable. People with severe mental illness and co-occurring chronic medical conditions that were unmanaged or mismanaged were having problems finding integrated treatment. People with severe mental illness and substance use disorders in need of detoxification could not get into community detox programs. People with complex, co-occurring conditions and low functioning with behavioral crises could not find crisis beds. People with serious mental illness and violent histories who were currently aggressive could not get into psychiatric inpatient units. And people with serious mental illness and co-occurring conditions who had histories of community treatment failures got stuck in hospital beds even though they no longer needed the hospital level of care.

Up until spring of 2008, the metropolitan regional treatment center remained a long-term general state hospital program. Because it was the only non-forensic state hospital in the state, it was getting admissions from across the state of people who could not readily return to the community or who had co-occurring medical conditions or had significant behavioral disturbances. As a result, the hospital was becoming a catch-all for people who had nowhere else to go. SOS leadership made a decision to specialize the metro hospital into a tertiary care psychiatric hospital. Three services were developed: medicine/psychology, complex/co-occurring disabilities, and intense behavioral treatment service. The med/psych service provides services to people with SMI and chronic medical conditions that are unmanaged or poorly managed, with one unit specifically designed for people with significant co-occurring dementia or chronic delirium. The complex/co-occurring service has one unit for people with co-occurring substance use disorders and another for people with co-occurring personality disorders. The intense behavioral treatment service has a unit for intensive care and high observation and the other unit as a step–down (less intensive level of care). This redesign has allowed for the system of care to be more responsive to some of the unmet needs, although there is a waiting list to get into the specialty hospital.

Additional utilization-management studies determined that the specialty hospital should develop a unit for people with severe mental illness and co-occurring intellectual or developmental disabilities. As this unit is a psychiatric program, the person must meet inpatient psychiatric level-of-care criteria. Also, an assessment and triage team was developed to complement Central Preadmission for people who have complex conditions that require a joint effort to serve, or for people who are stuck in hospital beds no longer needing the hospital level of care but having no placement in the community.

Next steps for state-operated services are the development of specialized intensive residential treatment (IRT) programs and ambulatory services. Three of the CBHHs have been closed because of underutilization. Two have been converted to specialized IRTs serving people with co-occurring conditions. Two other IRTs have been developed: one for people with SMI and the other for developmental disabilities, SMI, and traumatic or acquired brain injuries. Ambulatory services include around-the-clock assessment and triage; around-the-clock consultation and liaison; care coordination; a call center for access to all SOS services; and psychiatric transition clinics. The future of the SOS hospital system is integration with community providers. Network discussions with community health care organizations are underway. They focus on becoming part of integrated service networks to serve people who use the public mental health system closer to their home communities with the goal of returning the person as soon as possible to the home of their choice. Even a brief glance at the example shows how sustained and purposeful efforts need to be to arrive at a fully integrated service system. Another possible future is the development of a "shared safety net."

As state hospitals closed beds and units in the era of deinstitutionalization, some states reinvested appropriation dollars into community infrastructure. With appropriations, communities developed crisis beds, residential treatment programs, assertive community treatment teams, and psychosocial rehabilitation programs. Therefore, in states that reinvested appropriation dollars, the state hospitals no longer have sole responsibility to be the safety net.

The concept of a shared safety net was addressed in the Surgeon General's 1999 *Report on Mental Health* and the 2003 *President's New Freedom Commission on Mental Health Report*. Assumptions of a shared safety net are that the state is transitioning from an institutional model of care to a community-based service model. That said, transformation is ongoing, and the services are being optimized to meet persons' service needs. Shared safety-net principles are recovery-informed; wellness, care coordination, and accountability. Providers and services embrace a person's recovery efforts and support shared decision-making. Wellness as a whole-person approach to the person's medical as well as behavioral needs is facilitated. Care is coordinated with all providers by a care coordinator who is embedded in the treatment team. Accountability is assured by sharing structural, process, and person-centered outcome information with all involved in the person's treatment.

How each state should define the "shared safety net" remains an unanswered question. To clearly understand the concept, one must define each element of the term. "Shared" suggests that all stakeholders in the person's care and treatment, including the person himself or herself, must communicate, coordinate, and collaborate to assure that the person-served needs are being met. "Safety" indicates that the person being served and the public are protected from catastrophic events stemming from the person's mental illness that could be reasonably prevented. "Net" is best interpreted as a comprehensive, integrated system of services that is accessible to the person served and can meet his or her needs. A shared safety net fits well with health care reform. It promotes integration of behavioral health services with primary care services. It assures accountability. And it suggests that funding is directed to the needs of the person served at the right time, in the right place, and with the right amount of services.

Public mental health resources are limited and do not match the demand for services. Reinvesting appropriation funding from state hospital beds to community infrastructure makes sense in this context. However, it is critical that states carefully examine the possible uses of freed-up funding before returning the money to general funds, if such a safety net is to be created.

SUMMARY

While some forces press for the completion of deinstitutionalization and hospital closure, state psychiatric hospitals are likely to remain an essential part of the community mental health system of care in most areas, particularly as community-based care comes under pressure (Manderscheid et al. 2009). However, as the most expensive part of that system, and largely supported by state budgets that are under pressure, they are likely to continue to evolve in locally relevant, but nationally divergent ways.

A major, ubiquitous force is the state's role in sustaining its own safety net, including assuring treatment and custody for persons with forensic status. There is much work to be done in state hospitals if we are to move from the stagnant grade of "D" given our states in the National Alliance on Mental Illness's "Grading the State" report (Aaron et al. 2009).

In the meantime, it will be critical at all levels of state and local leadership to understand the historical and the current clinical, administrative, and financial practices of the facilities in their areas. What leadership and supports are necessary to assure that they cost-effectively provide largely tertiary, longer-term psychiatric inpatient care to an increasingly diverse patient population? Guiding the local and national forces into synergy seems to be the next pressing frontier in their ongoing evolution as part of healthcare reform.

REFERENCES

Aaron L, Honberg R, Duckworth K, et al.: *Grading the States 2009: A Report on America's Health Care System for Adults with Serious Mental Illness.* National Alliance on Mental Illness, Arlington, VA, 2009.

Bloom JD: Civil Commitment Is Disappearing in Oregon. *Journal of the American Academy of Psychiatry and Law.* 34(4):534–537, 2006.

Bopp JH, Ribble DJ, Cassidy JJ, Markoff RA: Re-engineering the State Hospital to Promote Rehabilitation and Recovery. *Psychiatric Services*, 47(7):697–701, 1996.

Brooks DK.: A Bushel of Shoes. *Hospital and Community Psychiatry* 20(12):371–375, 1996.

Cutler D: Moral Treatment at the End of the Oregon Trail: Dr James C. Hawthorne, 1819–1881. *American Journal of Psychiatry* 158(6):871, 2001.

Cutler DL; Sils G; Svendsen D; Yaeger K: Public Mental Health in America: "Enlightenment" to Accountable Care. In: *Textbook of Modern Community Mental Health Work: AN Interdisciplinary Approach.* New York: Oxford University Press, 2012.

Daniels A, Grant E, Filson B, Powell I, Fricks L, Goodale L (Eds.): Pillars of Peer Support: Transforming Mental Health Systems of Care Through Peer Support Services. www.pillarsofpeersupport.org; January, 2010.

Garfield RL: Mental Health Policy Development in the States: The Piecemeal Nature of Transformational Change. *Psychiatric Services* 60(10):1329–1335, 2009.

Geller JL, Morrissey JP: Asylum Within and Without Asylum. *Psychiatric Services,* 55(10):1128–1130, 2004.

Hoge MA, Morris JA, Daniels AS, Stuart GW, Huey LY, Adams N: *An Action Plan for Behavioral Health Workforce Development: A Framework for Discussion. The Annapolis Coalition on the Behavioral Health Workforce,* Cincinnati, OH, 2007. (Under Contract No.: 280-02-0302, the Substance Abuse and Mental Health Services Administration, U.S. Department of Health and Human Services).

Kim CS, Spahlinger DA, Kin JM, Bili JE: Lean Health Care: What Can Hospitals Learn from a World-Class Automaker. *Journal of Hospital Medicine,* 1(3):191–199, May/June 2006.

LeBel J, Goldstein R: The Economic Cost of Using Restraint and the Value Added by Restraint Reduction or Elimination. *Psychiatric Services,* 56(9):1109–1114, 2005.

Lutterman T, Berhane A, Phelan B, Shaw R, Rana V: Funding and Characteristics of State Mental Health Agencies 2007. HHS Publication No. (SMA) 09-4424, Center for Mental Health Services, Substance Abuse and Mental Health Services Administration, Rockville, MD, 2009.

Manderscheid RW; Atay JE; Crider RA.: Changing Trends in State Psychiatric Hospital Use from 2002 to 2005. *Psychiatric Services* 60(1):29–34, 2009.

Miller AL, Hall CS, Buchanan RW, Buckley PF, Chiles JA, Conley RR, et al.: The Texas Medication Algorithm Project Antipsychotic Algorithm for Schizophrenia: 2003 Update. *Journal of Clinical Psychiatry,* 65(4):500–508, 2004.

Mueser KT, Noordsy DL, Drake RE, Fox L: *Integrated Treatment for Dual Disorders: A Guide to Effective Practices.* New York: The Guilford Press, 2003.

Murphy T, Bennington-Davis M: *Restraint and Seclusion: The Model for Eliminating Use in Health Care.* Arlington, VA: American Psychiatric Publishing, 2005.

National Association of State Mental Health Program Directors: *Issues Pertaining to the Development and Implementation of Programs for Persons Civilly Committed for Treatment Under Sexually Violent Predator Statutes.* Third Medical Director's Council Technical Report, National Association of State Mental Health Program Directors, Alexandria VA, 1999.

NASMHPD Research Institute: *State Mental Health Agency Revenues and Expenditures for Mental Health Services.* National Association of State Mental Health Program Directors (NASMHPD) Research Institute, Alexandria VA, 2011.

Onken SJ, Dumont JM, Ridgway P, Dornan DH, Ralph RO: *Mental Health Recovery: What Helps and What Hinders? A National Research Project for the Development of Recovery Facilitating System Performance Indicators.* Phase One Research Report; National Technical Assistance Center of the National Association of State Mental Health Program Directors, Alexandria VA, 2002.

Parks J, Svendsen D, Singer P, Foti ME: *Morbidity and Mortality in People with Serious Mental Illness.* 13th in a Series of Technical Reports, the National Association of State Mental Health Program Directors, Alexandria VA, 2006.

Salzer MS, Kaplan K, Atay J: State Psychiatric Hospital Census After the 1999 Olmsted Decision: Evidence of Decelerating Deinstitutionalization. *Psychiatric Services* 57(10):1501–1504, 2006.

Schacht LM: *National Public Rates: Behavioral HealthCare Performance Measurement System.* National Association of State Mental Health Program Directors Research Institute, Alexandria VA, 2010.

Smith GM, Davis RH, Bixler EO, Lin HM, Altenor A, Altenor RJ, et al.: Pennsylvania State Hospital System's Seclusion and Restraint Reduction Program. *Psychiatric Services*, 56(9):1115–1122, 2005.

Webster SL, Sheitman BB, Barboriak PN, Harmon SH, Paesler PT, Gordon PA, et al.: Integrating Forensically and Civilly Committed Adult Inpatients in a Treatment Mall Program at a State Hospital. *Psychiatric Services*, 60(2):262–265, 2009.

CHAPTER 4

INVOLUNTARY CIVIL COMMITMENT

Applying Evolving Policy and Legal Determination in Community Mental Health

WILLIAM NUNLEY, BERNADETTE NUNLEY, DAVID L. CUTLER, JEAN DENTINGER, AND BENTSON MCFARLAND

INTRODUCTION

Involuntary civil commitment is the legal procedure used by the courts to require mentally ill and dangerous individuals to accept psychiatric treatment. It is a process that is basic to all mental health systems, yet most mental health professionals know little about it. Its coercive nature is to a large extent what causes much of the avoidance and perhaps explains the lack of attention paid to it in academic course work. However, understanding this process is really quite important for anyone working in the field.

The policies and procedures referred to here as "civil commitment" have significantly changed during the past forty years in the United States (Faulkner et al. 1985). These changes are based to a large extent on a series of judicial decisions within civil (non-criminal) law and have tended to narrow the criteria of commitment (with a few significant exceptions). Like all legal procedures, the commitment process continues to evolve into more complex and detailed forms based on a continuing accumulation of interrelated clinical, legislative, and legal decisions. As a result, the process, which used to be fairly simple and based mostly on medical opinion, has moved much more into a formal legal framework argued by lawyers, not doctors. As such, some would say the issue of civil rights has gained ascendancy over that of clinical necessity (Bloom 2006). This civil/legal procedure must occur in an extremely short time period in the midst of a psychiatric crisis, a period vulnerable to disparate views of events and intentions. We will present in this chapter first a contextual case example, then an overview of the legal and policy basis of civil commitment, and finally, stratified intervention considerations for the various stages of the civil commitment process.

CASE EXAMPLE

"DT" is a 20-year-old junior at a local state university in the state of Oregon, where, until one month ago, he was studying product design. DT began seeing the first of two *licensed clinical social workers* two years ago for counseling, a few months prior to beginning cannabis (marijuana) use, which he now smokes daily.[1] His counselors have provided engagement, treatment, and recovery recommendations in part based on a diagnosis of obsessive compulsive disorder (OCD). Following a six-week progression of paranoia, *his parents* take DT to an urgent walk-in clinic where he is assessed by *a licensed clinical social worker* and *a psychiatric nurse practitioner* who recommend acute hospitalization and psychiatric medication for psychosis. A few hours after DT declines voluntary hospitalization, DT pushes *his father* in the chest, causing him to stumble, but not hard enough to bruise him. Following a call to 911, *police* arrive at the family house, administer a temporary mental health custody hold, and escort DT to a local hospital emergency room. In the emergency room, DT briefly discusses the event in his home. *His mother* describes him becoming increasingly aggressive and threatening during the previous week (he left his college dorm and was sleeping at his parents' home). The *emergency medicine physician* briefly interviews DT and administers a "Notice of Mental Illness," detaining him for evaluation.

Following a two-day evaluation in the emergency room (staying in a locked room with a single mattress on the floor), DT is transferred to an inpatient psychiatric unit and meets an *acute psychiatric team*. Both parents talk to the acute care providers and explain that, about a month ago, DT reported hearing the voice of God, made bizarre statements, had difficulty maintaining a regular sleep and eating schedule, and became increasingly irritable—marked departures from his normal polite demeanor. DT tells the clinical social worker that he hears God's voice daily, follows the instructions provided for most activities, and is not bothered by this experience. He declines psychiatric medication and cannot explain his physical attack on his father.

During the first day on the unit, a *court investigator* (a licensed clinician appointed by the court to establish any necessity for involuntary hospitalization) interviews DT and explains four options for resolving the involuntary hold: 1) Discontinuation of the hold by the court investigator if there is insufficient evidence to demonstrate imminent safety concerns; 2) Continuation toward a commitment hearing where the "allegedly mentally ill person" presents his or her story to a *civil judge* with aid of *legal counsel*, whereby the judge decides the person has a right to refuse treatment; or, 3) The civil judge civilly commits the person to involuntary treatment based on criteria, duration, and terms set by state statutes (in Oregon, mandated treatment can be for up to 180 days in acute care, a state hospital, or a community program.); or 4) Acceptance of voluntary, conditional treatment. On the second day of care, DT begins taking medication and states that he prefers not to present his case before a judge. On the third day of treatment, his involuntary hold is discontinued, and his request to be released from the hospital is granted with an expedited effort for coordination of clinical care.

LEGAL HISTORY AND CONTEXT FOR CIVIL COMMITMENT

OVERVIEW

Providing clinical service or social support during experiences like DT's presents conceptual challenges. On one hand, holding him in a facility against his will can be framed as unlawful incarceration—he has not been accused or convicted of a crime. On the other hand, if he is not detained to receive treatment, he may cause serious harm to his father (or himself or someone else). The coupling of medical intervention with forced detention is a complex balance. In the United States, this balance of rights and safety risks arises in civil commitment and is based on two basic legal concepts, an individual's right to "liberty" and the right to "due process." The Fourteenth Amendment of the U.S. Constitution states, "No State…shall…deprive any person of life, liberty, or property, without due process of law…." In other words, prior to civil commitment and curtailing an individual's "liberty," the government must follow a series of mandated steps.

Since the 1960s and the Civil Rights era, state and federal courts have codified the process used to restrict an individual's liberty through civil commitment. Over time, what was predominantly a physician's decision and one based on a government's *parens patriae* responsibility has changed into a legal decision based on "police power," made by a judge, with clinical evidence presented in an adversarial proceeding. Institutionalized individuals' lawsuits for release from mental hospitals illustrate the tension between this government *parens patriae* responsibility and power. For example, in *Lake v. Cameron,* the court not only reviewed a woman's commitment to a mental hospital and her request for release, but also commanded the lower court to inquire into "alternative courses of [mental health] treatment" (*Lake v. Cameron,* 364 F. 2d 657, 661 [D.C. Cir. 1967]). Even today, courts struggle to decide cases based on an individual's right to liberty—the legal question generally set before a court in a civil commitment hearing—when an individual is clearly in mental health crisis and needing treatment, yet not at a level of being an "imminent danger" to self or others.

Generally, a citizen may only be confined in the "least restrictive" treatment setting required for the individual's safety. The "least restrictive" concept was established in *Lake v. Cameron,* when the court stated that the "state may restrict the exercise of fundamental liberties only to the extent necessary to effectuate the state's interest" (*Lake v. Cameron,* 364 F. 2d. 657, 661 [D.C. Cir 1966]). The "least restrictive" standard was further established in 1975, when the U.S. Supreme Court said, "A state cannot constitutionally confine, without more, a non-dangerous individual who is capable of surviving safely in freedom by himself or with the help of willing and responsible family members or friends" (*O'Connor v. Donaldson,* 422 U.S. 563 [1975]). In other words, an individual's need for treatment is insufficient evidence for civil commitment. Today, a state must prove "more" than a need for treatment to civilly commitment someone who is mentally ill.

In parallel to cases defining the level of restriction in treatment settings, courts clarified the legal process and proceedings used to civilly commit individuals; again, based on due process rights. In 1972, a Wisconsin court held the state civil commitment law unconstitutional because of its failure to meet due process requirements. In *Lessard,* a woman was detained on an emergency basis and then committed to a hospital without being given notice of her hearing, without assistance of legal counsel, and based on hearsay evidence. In essence, the woman was committed without any attention to her due process rights. As a result of the government's failure to follow due process, the court determined and clarified that individuals facing civil commitment must be given 1) a hearing prior to a deprivation of liberty, 2) notice of the scheduled hearing, 3) right to legal counsel, 4) notice of the right to avoid self-incrimination, and 5) protection through the rules of evidence. (See, generally, *Lessard v. Schmidt,* 349 F. Supp. 1078 [E.D. Wis. 1972]). Additionally, the court advised the State to present 1) available alternatives to civil commitment, 2) alternatives the State investigated, and 3) why the investigated alternatives were not suitable. *Id.* at 1096. In effect, the State had to prove why a person should be civilly committed if adequate treatment were available in a community setting.

FEDERAL AND STATE POLICIES DEFINING INVOLUNTARY CIVIL COMMITMENT PRACTICES

DEINSTITUTIONALIZATION

If DT's case occurred prior to the Civil Rights era, he would have been much more likely to be admitted for long-term institutionalization, rather than briefly hospitalized. The lawsuit-driven movement away from institution-based care has contributed to a large reduction in long-term psychiatric care in the United States. As context, the population of American asylums was more than 500,000 during the 1950s. Concepts of person-centered care and individual decision-making were rare. For example, psychiatric hospitalizations did not distinguish voluntary from involuntary status (all were involuntary); and wealthy families commonly institutionalized unwanted mentally ill relatives (Grob 1994).

The decrease in psychiatric hospital care in favor of community-based opportunities for care is referred to as *deinstitutionalization*. In the United States, two waves of deinstitutionalization policy and program changes have been experienced (Stroman 2003). The first wave began in the 1950s and significantly reduced the number of people with severe mental illness in state hospital settings. The second wave began in the mid-1960s, with a focus on individuals diagnosed with a developmental disability (e.g., mental retardation). Six main factors led this wave of decreased institutional care: criticisms of public mental hospitals; advances in psychopharmacological and additional treatments; federal policy changes in the treatment for those with mental illnesses, including social security and disability (with significant focus on President Kennedy's community-based health care and mental health care redesign that abruptly ended, mid-development, following his assassination); a shift to less restrictive and more flexible community based care; change in the public's opinion about those with mental disabilities; and states' desires to reduce the cost of mental hospitals (Stroman 2003). Unfortunately for clients today, the reduction in hospital-based care was made with a political commitment to provide corresponding increases in community-based mental health care. The increased community-based mental health care has never been fully developed.

The large social and service delivery changes during deinstitutionalization resulted in dramatic reductions in the rate of hospital-based psychiatric care. Deinstitutionalization resulted in loss of psychiatric beds (both acute and long-term beds), such that between 1955 and 2005, the number of state hospital beds in the United States declined from an average of 340 beds (state and county) per 100,000 residents to 17 beds per 100,000 (Torrey et al. 2006). This is a 95% decrease in the number of available beds in the nation's public mental hospitals, following a peak of 559,000 in 1953 (19 of 20 beds are no longer available compared to the mid-1950s: Torrey et al. 2006).

ADVOCACY LEADERSHIP SHAPING PREVIOUS AND CURRENT COMMITMENT LAWS AND PRACTICE

Two primary agencies largely shaped the national discourse concerning civil commitment. The Bazelon Center for Mental Health Law is a national leader in civil rights–based mental health law reform. Since its inception in 1972 as the Mental Health Law Project, the organization employed specialized attorneys and mental disability program and policy leaders to effect improvements in individual rights to treatment choices. In 1993, the organization changed its name to The Judge David L. Bazelon Center for Mental Health Law in honor of Judge David L. Bazelon, whose decisions as Chief Judge of the United States Court of Appeals for the District of Columbia Circuit pioneered the field of mental health law. The Bazelon Center has effectively argued for limitations to civil commitment within their national efforts for specific standards in mental health and disability services and protections. In addition to the historical injustices of individuals' being committed to treatment for reasons other than safety or provision of care (such as cases of women and under-represented racial minorities being held in psychiatric hospitals against their will), Bazelon argues that civil commitment is the result of failures in the community mental health system to provide responsive detection and intervention during mental health crisis escalation.

The Treatment Advocacy Center (TAC) is a United States national nonprofit organization founded in 1998 by E. Fuller Torrey, a psychiatrist and schizophrenia researcher. TAC began as a part of the National Alliance on Mental Illness (NAMI), with a focus on psychiatric provider and family perspectives on civil commitment. According to their mission statement, TAC advocates the "elimination of legal and clinical barriers to timely and humane treatment for Americans diagnosed with severe psychiatric disorders who refuse care." TAC has two goals. First, to expedite involuntary treatment for people with severe mental disorders who refuse treatment. Second, to reform current federal and state policies that hinder treatment for individuals with mental illness at risk for personal harm due to homelessness, victimization from violence, or adverse health and social consequences from the natural history of untreated mental illness, including suicide. Additionally, TAC advocates for acute services expansion and awareness of anosognosia, the concept that a person may lack awareness regarding his or her illness. TAC used an expert panel to determine the number of public hospital beds needed for a "minimum level of care" for each state. The panel recommended that 50 public hospital beds per 100,000 population are needed for a minimum level of care (Torrey et al. 2006).

Advocacy efforts concerning civil commitment can be viewed as covering a continuum between individual autonomy and medical-legal decision-making based on individual and public safety during periods of psychiatric symptomotology. Figure 4.1 illustrates a balance of values, decision-making reference, and problem definition during determination of state statutes defining commitment laws and procedural terms and conditions.

Multiple national and local individuals and groups articulate thoughtful arguments and position statements along this continuum. Proponents of restricting or eliminating involuntary

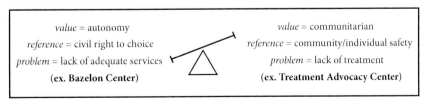

FIGURE 4.1 Conceptual Values Model.

civil commitment include MindFreedom; multiple religious groups, including Scientology; and psychiatrist Thomas Szasz. The effort to define and advance a lower threshold includes the National Alliance on Mental Illness, the American Psychiatric Association, the American Psychological Association, and the National Association of Social Workers. Ideally, the spectrum of personal beliefs and understanding about the professional roles and responsibilities of involuntary civil commitment would be defined and discussed within an interdisciplinary team providing evidence-based assessment and recommendations within a person-centered recovery plan. In practice, it is not unusual for clinicians, peer specialists, and the person in recovery to discover they hold a different or similar place on the commitment continuum during emergent or urgent mental health need.

INVOLUNTARY CIVIL COMMITMENT BEYOND INSTITUTIONAL CARE

The evolving role and legal basis of civil commitment can best be understood as one of many factors shaping current rights and requirements for community mental health treatment. One of the essential additional systemic elements related to outpatient and inpatient commitment are the policies and procedures related to institutional mental health care. In more recent years, mental health advocacy groups pushed for stronger protections for the institutionalized mentally ill, most recently through the Americans with Disabilities Act (ADA) and the Civil Rights of Institutionalized Persons Act (CRIPA). [CRIPA 42 USC Section1997][2]

The ADA requires that the State provide services to qualified individuals with disabilities in the most integrated setting appropriate to their needs. (See 42 U.S.C. Section 12132, and implementing regulations 28 C.F.R. Section 35.130[d] [individuals committed to hospitals are considered "qualified individuals with disabilities" under the ADA]). If a State fails to provide appropriate services, an individual harmed by this failure may sue based on discrimination due to the individual's disability. In the civil commitment context, the ADA requires the State to consistently review the placement of persons with disabilities in institutions, to determine if placement in community settings meets this "nondiscriminatory" standard (*Olmstead v. L.C.* 527 U.S. 58, 1999). Lawsuits brought under CRIPA and the ADA seek to protect individuals from being civilly committed beyond medically appropriate lengths of time, and require states to place people in settings integrated into their communities.

Under the ADA and *Olmstead*, a hospital is considered the most segregated setting in which an individual may be placed for treatment (*Olmstead* 527 U.S. at 600–601). To prevent discrimination against a person who has been institutionalized, a government must follow a series of steps: 1) determine via treatment professionals if community placement is medically appropriate, 2) determine that the transfer is not opposed by the individuals, and 3) determine that the placement can be "reasonably accommodated taking into account the resources available to the state and the needs of others with mental disabilities" (*Olmstead* at 601–603).

In attempt to balance the aims of individual and community safety while meeting federal requirements for provision of care in the least restrictive setting, many states have turned to mental health care treatment through alternative channels like court-ordered assisted outpatient treatment (AOT). At the time of this publication, forty-four states have AOT laws, which include court-ordered treatment. Some, but not all, include medication requirements for individuals who have a history of adverse events and non-adherence. The concept behind the laws is to require treatment before a mental health crisis results in harm to the mentally ill individual or to another person.

AOT laws allow courts to order a diversion from civil commitment so that certain individuals with serious mental illness will accept treatment as a condition for living in the community. The laws require civil commitment (for a limited period of time) if the individual refuses the diversion treatment. Each AOT law sets forth a list of criteria that must be met before an individual is subject to the law, such as specific incidents of recent need for hospitalization or acts of serious violent behavior, an unlikeliness to voluntarily participate in recommended treatment, and a determination that the patient will relapse or deteriorate to the point of serious harm to the patient or others. Prominent examples of AOT laws include Kendra's Law (New York) and Laura's Law (California).

As with other areas of community mental health, the policies and practices of AOT vary substantially between states and communities. Additionally, AOT programs are especially vulnerable to funding reductions due to fiscal policy related to blended federal, state, and local funding. Evidence in support of AOT includes improvement in psychiatric symptoms, reduction in adverse social factors such as homelessness and incarceration, improvements in cost-effectiveness and utilization, and reduction in the number of arrests (Segal & Burgess 2006; Gilbert 2010; Swartz et al. 2010).

AOT encounters a fundamental challenge for those who lose decision-making capacity as a result of the natural history of their medical (psychiatric) condition. One must have threatened or committed a previous, serious if not violent act (a criminal offense), and the act must have been in the context of mental illness, in order to receive care. Limiting an individual's liberty based on a *prediction* of serious violent behavior is ripe for legal challenge if a collaborative legal approach informed of clinical assessment and recovery is not established in the person's legal community. Additionally, the role of dangerousness as the fulcrum implementing involuntary emergent treatment can exacerbate public perceptions and stigma concerning the risk of harm from other community members who have serious mental health conditions. This stigma can be a primary barrier for seeking effective treatment and initiating person-centered recovery earlier in the natural history of mental illness.

STRATIFIED INTERVENTIONS DURING STAGES OF THE INVOLUNTARY CIVIL COMMITMENT PROCESS

STAKEHOLDERS

The civil commitment process in each community is based on local implementation of state criteria and procedures. Legislatures frequently update state statutes based on advocacy for further interpretation of case law precedent. The resulting civil commitment practice is designed to prevent a community member with acute psychiatric symptoms from harming themselves or someone else, while avoiding unnecessary detention. As with DT, assessing the need and providing effective intervention for individual or public safety requires timely contributions by multiple people. The roles and responsibilities vary from jurisdiction to jurisdiction. In general, the following five roles are essential: 1) the person with emergent mental health needs, 2) social supports and primary relationships, 3) mental health providers, 4) associated medical staff, and 5) legal providers.

The scope of challenges and recovery opportunities are defined throughout this text. People with mental illness face significant obstacles to care, evidence-based assessments and treatment recommendations, and coordinated approaches to person-centered care. The process of civil commitment evaluation and detention can aggravate symptoms and a sense of being stigmatized for the person in recovery. In communities where family or treatment providers testify in support of involuntary commitment, the person may withdraw from or end long-term relationships based on disclosures during testimony. With DT, intervention is warranted based on the desire for his safety and safety of those around him and avoidance of stigmatization and potential incarceration if a violent or tragic event occurred. When a person does not believe intervention is necessary, it is essential for others to provide support and expertise to help make a safe determination.

Additional support hopefully comes from primary and social relationships as well. These may include significant others, family members, friends, co-workers, and other community members (such as fellow students, members of the same religious community, or peers in recovery). Depending on the relevant statutes and local practice, social supports and concerned citizens may provide a primary, secondary, or peripheral role in the evaluation and determination of commitment. As demonstrated in DT's case, the role of family as primary support is a fundamental component of public mental health and person-centered recovery. Definition of family rights to serve as information sources has been a significant focus of civil commitment advocacy (see the National Alliance on Mental Illness website listed in the reference section for further information).

Clinicians fill a broad range of roles and responsibilities prior to, during, and after civil commitment. Before the Civil Rights era, involuntary commitment was almost exclusively based on psychiatrists' decisions. Now, state statutes delineate civil courts as the arbiter of commitment, and clinicians provide evaluation, provision of care, engagement, and contingent coordination of options in cases where judicial review does not result in commitment. As with all of community mental health, effective fulfillment of these roles requires integration by licensed clinical social workers, psychologists, substance abuse counselors, peer support, psychiatrists, and/or psychiatric nurse practitioners, depending on the staffing and statutory requirements of the community. Due to practice patterns and limitations in access, physical medical staff perform many of the initial screens and legal detention requirements. Emergency physicians, primary care or (non-psychiatric subspecialty) physicians, nurses, and in some communities alternative medicine providers and pharmacists have legal authority to initiate or provide assessment supporting or refuting the need for commitment.

Changes in civil law and the deinstitutionalization of those with severe mental illness without corresponding provision of community mental health resources has resulted in a fundamental shift in first-response to mental health and behavioral crisis. In many communities, law enforcement and public safety emergency communication (such as 9–1-1) are the default first-responders in the mental health crisis system. The civil legal system has evolved to meet the demands of involuntary civil commitment. However, it is important for those outside of the legal system to be aware that the criminal justice system has significantly expanded in a way that arguably corresponds with deinstitutionalization. People with mental illness are disproportionately represented in the 9 million arrests each year in the United States, and this overrepresentation has grown significantly, with current estimates of 15% of men in jail and 31% of women in jail having a severe mental illness (Cutler et al. 2002; James & Glaze 2006; Steadman et al. 2009). In the majority of cases, the criminal justice system (served by police, sheriff, criminal judges, district and defense attorneys, and probation and parole officers) evaluate and make civil and criminal determinations without mental health evaluation or coordination. Entry into the civil legal system occurs at different stages of engagement with providers.

CRISIS PRIOR TO ENGAGEMENT WITH
MENTAL HEALTH PROVIDERS

Significant challenges and limitations exist when urgent or emergent symptoms are the catalyst for seeking professional service or peer support. Someone's mood, thought, and behavior in crisis are managed exclusively through individual effort and primary social supports prior to engagement with clinicians. In crisis, vital information about the person's values, strengths, and preferences may not be included in an assessment and therefore is omitted from a person-centered recovery plan. Behavioral dysregulation and psychosis often lead to significant deviations from expectations and community norms. The risk of engagement with police and the criminal justice system is high. In most jurisdictions, once a person's crisis is identified as a criminal case, assessment and adjudication is limited to the more formal criminal procedures.

Clinicians introduced to or working with family members or friends not yet engaged in professional recovery services will do well to remember the limitations of acute assessments. Prioritizing safety and advocating collaborative problem-solving with public safety (and criminal justice leaders) is important. Understanding local civil commitment procedures, the essential documentation for custodial, evaluation, and civil commitment determination, and the required and discretionary participation in commitment determinations is essential. Significant variation between jurisdictions exists—some community practices require clinical documentation but exclude participation from the process (legal and social supports are the primary contributors), while some communities include a collaborative model where acute and longitudinal providers are the central arbiters for the legal decision. The National Alliance on Mental Illness is an excellent resource for family information about the civil commitment process, options for local support groups, and potential advocacy efforts to improve the state legislative rules and local practices. Significant differences exist between relevant state codes defining who and how emergency detention for evaluation can be initiated. The list includes:

- Family members (some states stipulate age and certain family roles)
- Peace officers
- Certain clinicians (some states restrict the power only to physicians)
- Administrators of mental health facilities
- County health officers
- Court magistrates
- Probation and parole officers
- Any concerned person

CRISIS WHEN PREVIOUSLY ENGAGED WITH
MENTAL HEALTH PROVIDERS

Initial assessment and introductory clinical work should begin with definition of a safe, legal, and tenable crisis plan. Person-centered, proactive planning in the event of mood, thought, or behavior dysregulation is key for reducing the risk of involuntary hospitalization and potential adverse events, including arrest. The Substance Abuse and Mental Health Services Administration's *Practice Guidelines: Core Elements for Responding to Mental Health Crises* provides a helpful overview accessible to all stakeholders in understanding effective mental health crisis intervention (Health and Human Services 2009).

The recovery movement has developed several processes and methods of empowering people receiving behavioral health service. These should be translated into a crisis plan during the inductive phase of treatment and recovery planning. A good crisis plan should be specific, succinct, and include contingent personal, social, and professional supports. Borrowing from a parallel process in physical health, the introduction of psychiatric advance directives (instruments developed prior to crises that define recovery and intervention preferences if crises occur) can be a useful format for establishing a tenable plan for clients desiring a medical model–based approach. An alternative approach to crisis planning includes use of a checklist for targeted symptoms, implementation of supports for decision-making (and a potential proxy), and preferences for safe and effective choices including location of urgent or emergency evaluation. Pragmatic and simple plans are usually best. Independent of the format, clinical and social supports providing proactive discussion of partial or complete loss of decision-making capacity (and necessity of civil commitment) reduce the risk of uncoordinated, reactive crisis intervention.

A proactive crisis plan allows someone in recovery to identify personal strengths and strategies for safety (and interventions prior to emergent symptoms and need). A proactive plan also allows clinical and social supports to establish collaborative approaches for engaging police officers. Police officers often respond well to predictable algorithms that prioritize safety, absence of weapons, and options when someone is partially or minimally responsive to verbal commands. While no substitute for clinical assessment and collaborative planning, police assessment and public interventions as first responders have advanced through crisis intervention training (CIT) and mental health first aid (See websites in References).

THE DETERMINATION PHASES OF INVOLUNTARY CIVIL COMMITMENT

Involuntary detainment prior to a commitment hearing is relatively brief. Emergency evaluation and preliminary hearing requirements range from under 12 hours to 20 days (with 72 hours serving as the most common timeframe) and formal judicial hearing requirements range from two to 20 days depending on the state. (Treatment Advocacy Center 2011). Despite the expedited determination phase, the process of evaluation and implementation of involuntary commitment can have a significant effect on mental health symptoms and recovery. Women and men with interpersonal violence histories may have a debilitating increase in trauma-related mood and behavioral dysregulation. People with paranoia or persecutory delusions related to authority figures may incorporate the detainment experience into their belief system.

Family members and others with close relationships to someone being evaluated for civil commitment can face difficult decisions about their degree of participation during evaluation. On one hand, full and objective disclosure about the events and concerns for safety of the person potentially committed may be the necessary intervention to avoid harm or incarceration. On the other hand, the rates of civil commitment in many communities are extremely low. For example, if our case, DT, were to be involuntarily committed to treatment, he would be one of fewer than 10% of those who are placed on 72 hour holds in Oregon to be so adjudicated.

Effective participation by family members and additional close relationships should include the following:

- Objective, detailed information about events with concerns for safety
- A working knowledge of the mental health symptoms
- Identification of pragmatic consequences if involuntary treatment is not provided
- Additional information such as treatments that have been helpful

Treatment providers must maintain a proper humility concerning family members' participation and coping strategies. Unsuccessful commitment almost always ends with a client leaving the hospital. After the legal and mental health professionals have provided their services, for many families, the difficult and necessary decisions about how to translate the commitment process and concerns begin. Connection to support groups, other families with similar lived experiences, and effective outpatient providers is essential.

The requirements for legal evaluation are fairly proscriptive. In some jurisdictions, the active treatment team (either acute-care-based or longitudinal providers) serves as the primary source of civil court information, and appointed clinical evaluators present the current clinical presentation, likely risks, and tenable options. In other communities, court-appointed or local mental health authority–appointed investigators gather clinical, legal, and additional collateral information. This information is then presented and defended via legal counsel. The information may be presented in a process similar to that of criminal court (with a state attorney and a public defender), but in most states the process is less formal and includes court-designees. Based on state statutes, a civil judge, arbitrator, or court-appointed official decides if enough information is present to warrant continued involuntary detention.

INVOLUNTARY CIVIL COMMITMENT IMPLEMENTATION

Evaluation and final determination of involuntary civil commitment is based on state legal statutes (See Treatment Advocacy Center website in References). In general, civil commitment includes a definition of "mental illness" (with inclusion or exclusion criteria for substance abuse and sexual offenses), a defined time frame (commonly up to 180 days), and inclusion and exclusion criteria based on clinical judgment of resolution of danger and clinical stability. In cases requiring longer terms of evaluation and treatment, state statutes define terms for subsequent judicial review.

FINAL THOUGHTS

Involuntary civil commitment can have a significant impact on the subject's recovery. Extended periods of biopsychosocial evaluation, active treatment, and development of social supports can change the trajectory of the person's recovery. Through commitment, people stuck in extended periods of sub-acute and acute crises may engage in meaningful, effective person-centered recovery and medication optimization that allows for their safety and the safety of those in their community. However, as with other severe medical conditions and intervention, civil commitment can result in significant social consequences. These can include the following:

- Financial (individuals can be and usually are financially responsible for treatment)
- Limitations or exclusion from insurance eligibility
- Firearms-possession limitations or exclusions
- Limitations on professional or personal licensure
- Social stigma (portions of court records may be sealed, but civil commitment hearings and records may be public)
- Difficulties retaining or reinstating child custody

As in other areas of care, establishing the foundational knowledge of involuntary civil commitment allows clinicians and social supports to help determine the risks and benefits of intervention.

NOTES

1. Italics are used to highlight the number of roles involved in the civil commitment process.
2. CRIPA is a federal act that authorizes the U.S. Attorney General and the U.S. Department of Justice to investigate violations of federal rights in state-run mental health institutions.

REFERENCES

Bloom, J.D. (2006). Civil Commitment Is Disappearing in Oregon. *Journal of the American Academy of Psychiatry and the Law,* 36(4): December, 534–537.

Cutler, D.L., Bigelow, D., Collins, V., Jackson, C., and Field, G. (2002). Why Are Mentally Ill Persons in Jails and Prisons? in: P. Backlar & D.L. Cutler (Eds.), *Ethics in Community Mental Health Care; Commonplace Concerns,* pp. 137–156. New York: Kluwer Academic.

Faulkner, L. R., Bloom, J.D., McFarland, B.H. et al. (1985). The Effect of Mental Health System Changes on Civil Commitment. *Bulletin of the American Academy of Psychiatry and the Law,* 13: 345–359.

Gilbert, A.R. Mosser L.L., Van Dorn, R.A., et al. (2010). "Reductions in Arrest Under Assisted Outpatient Treatment in New York." *Psychiatric Services,* 61: 996–999.

Grob, G.N. (1994). *The Mad Among Us: A History of the Care of America's Mentally Ill.* New York: Free Press.

Health and Human Services. (2009). *Practice Guidelines: Core Elements for Responding to Mental Health Crises.* SMA-09-4427. Rockville, MD: Center for Mental Health Services, Substance Abuse and Mental Health Services Administration.

James., D.J., and Glaze, L.E. (2006). *Mental Health Problems of Prison and Jail Inmates.* NCJ 213600. Washington, D.C.: U.S. Department of Justice, Bureau of Justice Statistics.

Segal, S.P., and Burgess, P.M. (2006). The Utility of Extended Outpatient Civil Commitment. *International Journal of Law and Psychiatry,* 29(6): 525–534.

Steadman, H.J., Osher, F.C., Robbins, P.C., et al. (2009). "Prevalence of Serious Mental Illness Among Jail Inmates." *Psychiatric Services,* 60: 762–765.

Stroman, D. (2003). *The Disability Rights Movement: From Deinstitutionalization to Self-determination.* Lanham, MD: University Press of America.

Swartz, M.S., Wilder, C.M., Swanson, J.W., et al. (2010). "Assessing Outcomes for Consumers in New York's Assisted Outpatient Treatment Program." *Psychiatric Services,* 61: 976–981.

Torrey, E.F., Entsminger, K., Geller, J., et al. (2006). *The Shortage of Public Hospital Beds for Mentally Ill Persons: A Report by the Treatment Advocacy Center.* Retrieved April 2011 from http://www.treatmentadvocacycenter.org/reportbedshortage.htm.

Treatment Advocacy Center. (2011). *Initiating Court-Ordered Assisted Treatment Inpatient, Outpatient and Emergency Hospitalization Standards by State.* Retrieved April 2011 from http://treatmentadvocacycenter.org/storage/documents/Initiating_Court-Ordered_Treatment.pdf.

TRAUMA-INFORMED CARE

KEVIN HUCKSHORN AND JANICE L. LEBEL

INTRODUCTION

The acknowledgment of traumatic life experiences in the lives of people is widely ignored and "shrouded in secrecy and denial" (Hodas, 2006; National Association of State Mental Health Program Directors [NASMHPD], 1998, p. 5). The concept of "trauma" does not fit well within the traditional medical model, with its focus on biological causes of illness (NASMHPD, 1998). Therefore, the application of trauma knowledge and principles to service delivery is sorely lacking. Even though the experience of trauma cuts across many service systems and requires an organized approach, the fragmented linkages among mental health, substance abuse, primary care, criminal justice, homelessness, and domestic violence agencies has frustrated attempts to develop an integrated conceptual framework in human service systems (NASMHPD, 1998).

The single most compelling reason to understand trauma, its impact, and the importance of trauma-informed care is the prevalence of trauma and post-traumatic stress disorder (PTSD), which is higher than was previously estimated and is associated with high rates of medical and mental health services; making it one of the costliest under-diagnosed problems in American healthcare today (Cusack, Frueh, Hiers, Suffoletta-Maierle, & Bennett, 2003; Felitti, Anda, Nordenberg, Williamson, Spitz, Edwards, et al., 1998; Nemeroff, 2004). Traumatic life experiences are common, demanding of health-care resources, and particularly pronounced in mental health care where some estimates indicate that nearly all consumers, particularly those served in the public sector, have experienced trauma (NASMHPD, 2010).

It is the authors' intent in this chapter to discuss the importance of traumatic life experiences in persons with behavioral health disorders *for individuals who work in human service systems*. Traumatic life experiences are ubiquitous, often undisclosed, and can greatly affect the trajectory of a person's illness, treatment, and recovery. Professionals working in care-providing settings, regardless of their discipline, must be aware of the pernicious impact of trauma and the pragmatic treatment tenets of trauma-informed care. Moreover, clinical and service support for trauma survivors should be done collaboratively and in an integrated fashion. Without this grounding, the best-intentioned health care professionals can find their most prudent clinical analysis and interventions minimally effective.

WHAT IS TRAUMA?

Traumatic events are defined as those that involve a direct threat of death, severe bodily harm, or psychological injury that the person, at the time, finds intensely distressing (American Psychiatric Association [APA], 1994; Rosenberg et al., 2001, p. 2). The most common traumatic events reported are witnessing someone being badly injured or killed, being involved in a natural disaster or a life-threatening incident, molestation, rape, combat exposure, physical assault, and physical abuse (Solomon & Davidson, 1997). For the purpose of this chapter, trauma and traumatic events will be defined as the personal experience of interpersonal violence, including sexual abuse, physical abuse, severe neglect, loss and/or the witnessing of violence (Jennings, 2004a; Moses, Reed, Mazelis, & D'Ambrosio, 2003; NASMHPD, 2004).

TRAUMA EXPOSURE AND PREVALENCE

Exposure to trauma is a significant factor in the lives of many people who enter the behavioral health system (NASMHPD, 2010). Psychiatric manifestations related to trauma exposure include but are not limited to: mood, anxiety, behavioral, identity, eating, and substance abuse disorders, many of which can be co-occurring (van der Kolk, 2001).

Epidemiological studies estimate that between 36% and 81% of the general population has experienced a significant traumatic event in their lives, and the rates are even higher for subpopulations of persons who seek clinical services from public mental health and substance abuse providers (Cusack, Frueh, & Brady, 2004; Frueh et al., 2000; Mueser et al., 1998; Rosenberg, Mueser, Jankowski, & Hamblen, 2002). Kessler and colleagues (1995) conducted the only nationally representative study of the general population in the United States to date. Face-to-face interviews with nearly 6000 people aged 15 to 54 demonstrated that 60% of men and 51% of women reported experiencing at least one traumatic event at some time in their lives, and 17% of men and 13% of women had experienced more than three such events (Kessler, Sonnega, Bromet, Hughes, & Nelson, 1995; Solomon & Davidson, 1997).

Traumatic life events are not limited to persons with behavioral health disorders. In the landmark *Origins of Addiction: Evidence from the Adverse Childhood Experiences Study*, Felitti and colleagues (1998) found that the "compulsive use of nicotine, alcohol and injected street drugs increases proportionally in a strong, graded, dose-response manner that closely parallels the intensity of adverse childhood experiences" in a population-based study of over 17,000 middle-class American adults.

POST-TRAUMATIC STRESS DISORDER

The most recognized and clearly defined trauma-related diagnosis is post-traumatic stress disorder (PTSD). The disorder is characterized by one or all of the following symptoms: 1) re-experiencing the traumatic event in nightmares, flashbacks, intrusive memories, bodily sensations; 2) avoidance behavior such as numbing, dissociation, and withdrawal; and 3) hyperarousal symptoms including heightened reactivity to triggers, and extreme anxiety and fearfulness (APA, 2000).

According to the President's New Freedom Commission on Mental Health Care subcommittee on trauma (2003):

"The syndrome of PTSD is associated with significant social maladjustment, poor quality of life, medical comorbidity, physiological arousal, general symptom severity, and psychiatric comorbidity. There are neurobiological markers, such as dysregulation of the hypothalamic-pituitary-adrenal axis, that differentiate PTSD from other mood and anxiety disorders. There is also strong evidence that trauma victimization is associated with increased levels of HIV- related risk behaviors, substance abuse and homelessness. Taken together, data indicate that PTSD is a complex psychiatric disorder resulting in considerable emotional distress, disability and a wide range of adverse consequences." (Cusack, Frueh, Hiers, Keane & Mueser, 2003, p. 2)

Despite some improvement in the assessment of trauma, PTSD and co-occurring trauma-related disorders continue to be missed and trauma symptoms are often misunderstood and inadequately treated (Mueser, Rosenberg, Goodman, & Trumbetta, 2002; NASMHPD, 2010; Rosenberg et al., 2001). Proper diagnostic tools and trained staff who understand trauma prevalence and how it can be expressed by trauma survivors are essential to identifying and effectively treating this large segment of the mental health population (Carmen et al., 1996; NASMHPD, 2010).

THE PHYSIOLOGICAL, PSYCHOLOGICAL, AND SOCIAL IMPACT OF TRAUMA

Research has demonstrated that exposure to trauma can negatively affect the mind and the body. Traumatic experience can adversely impact normative functioning, cognition, social and emotional well-being, and the experience of sensation (Kardiner, 1941; Saporta, 2003). A meta-analysis of the literature indicates several neurological structures and functions can be compromised by PTSD (Karl et al., 2006). Childhood trauma can adversely impact the hippocampus, a part of the brain involved in learning and memory, as well as multiple frontal-limbic system structures that help regulate emotional responses to stress and fear (Karl et al., 2006). Research also indicates that traumatic experience has an untoward impact on the hypothalamic-pituitary-adrenal axis which is a major part of the neuroendocrine system that controls reactions to stress and regulates many body processes (Bremner, 1997; Bremner et al., 2003; Caffo, Forresi, & Lievers, 2005; Lipschitz, Rasmusson, & Southwick, 1998; Rasmusson & Friedman, 2002; Sala et al., 2004).

The physical impact of childhood abuse can include brain injury, physical disabilities, sexually transmitted diseases (including HIV infection), chronic pelvic pain, headaches, stomach pain, sleep disturbances, eating disorders, asthma and other respiratory problems (Jennings, 2004a). Adverse childhood experiences appear to be related to the presence of diseases later in life, including ischemic heart disease, cancer, chronic lung disease, and liver disease (Felitti et al., 1998). Adults who experience multiple types of abuse in childhood have a two- to fourfold increase in smoking, multiple sexual partners, and severe obesity (1998). Similarly, exposure to multiple traumas in childhood increases the risk of experiencing psychosis in adulthood (Galletley, Van Hooff, & McFarlane, 2011).

The perception of, effect of, and response to trauma are unique to each trauma survivor (Aldwin & Yancura, 2004; NASMHPD, 2010; Olff, Langeland, & Gersons, 2005; Pine, 2003). Because there is a considerable range of response to trauma at the physical and experiential level, treatment must be individualized. The reader is directed to the websites identified at the end of this chapter for additional information.

TRAUMA-INFORMED CARE AND SERVICE IMPLICATIONS

As the behavioral manifestations or "survival strategies" of trauma are recognized, it is important for staff working in behavioral health settings to have a thorough understanding of a trauma-informed care (TIC) approach. This is a framework which recognizes the profound multidimensional impact of trauma and incorporates that understanding into services and treatment approaches. Recently, researchers conducted a review of the literature and identified key principles of TIC: 1) trauma awareness, 2) emphasis on safety, 3) opportunities to rebuild control, and 4) use of a strengths-based approach (Hopper, Bassuk, & Olivet, 2010, pp. 81–82). These researchers also developed a consensus-based definition of TIC:

> Trauma-Informed Care is a strengths-based framework that is grounded in an understanding of and responsiveness to the impact of trauma, that emphasizes physical, psychological, and emotional safety for both providers and survivors, and that creates opportunities for survivors to rebuild a sense of control and empowerment (Hopper et al., 2010, pp. 81–82).

Trauma-informed care is a universal precautions approach that is designed to be both preventative and rehabilitative in nature. This approach addresses the relationship between environmental or subjective triggers, the perception of danger, and the neurobiological activation that leads to a distressed physical state and resulting problematic behavior (Harris & Fallot, 2001; NASMHPD, 2010). In addition, it acknowledges the centrality of trauma and its profound impact on a person's perception of emotional and physical safety, behaviors, relationships, and medical status (Jennings, 2004b; NASMHPD, 2010). Central to effective TIC practice, whether at the organizational or the individual practitioner level, is the need to continually review the professional literature on trauma against existing policies, procedures, and practices within the mental health treatment setting (NASMHPD, 2010).

Developing a trauma-informed system of care requires sustained leadership and action over time. Trauma experts Maxine Harris and Roger Fallot identified five essential elements to achieve a trauma-informed system of care (2001). These include: 1) administrative

commitment to change, 2) universal screening, 3) staff training and education, 4) hiring practices, and 5) review of policies and procedures. There is need to determine if any policies
or procedures are damaging and replicate past abusive practices. There is special need for
alertness to "traumatic reenactments masquerading as benign practice," and policies and procedures that may inadvertently permit and rationalize abusive responses and relationships
(Harris & Fallot, 2001, p. 9). Such practices are damaging at the moment and also reactivate
past experiences of abuse.

"Trauma-informed care" differs from "trauma-specific services" (Hopper et al., 2010).
The goal of TIC is to impart a philosophy, culture, and understanding about trauma at
a systemic, organizational, and service level. Trauma-specific services are designed to
"directly address the impact of trauma, with the goals of decreasing symptoms and facilitating recovery" (Hopper et al., 2010, p. 81). Trauma-specific services are intended for
individuals who develop mental disorders resulting from traumatic exposure. Functionally,
trauma-specific services help traumatized individuals regain a sense of personal control
and balance through the implementation of tailored strategies to minimize emotional distress and attain a calmer, safer state (Champagne & Stromberg, 2004; Hopper et al., 2010;
LeBel & Champagne, 2010). Trauma-specific treatment services are beyond the scope of
this chapter, however: the reader is directed to the Web Resources section of this chapter
for additional information.

RECOGNIZING TRAUMA-INFORMED CARE

A multidimensional application of trauma-informed principles is provided in Table 5.1.

Table 5.1 A Multi-dimensional Application of Trauma-informed Principles:
Translating Theory into Practice

Trauma-Informed	Not Trauma-Informed
The Environment of Care	
Clean and well maintained	Dirty; environmental neglect
Décor/paint in soothing colors	Décor/paint in harsh colors
Sound is quiet, soft music	Loud sounds, yelling, raucous music
Aroma is neutral or pleasant	Foul odors: cleaning products, urine, smoke
Individual chairs, discrete seating areas	Group seating, large sofas, rows
Seating is clean and comfortable, plastic/wood seating minimized	Seating is stained/soiled, hard seating, institutional furniture
Individual chairs, discrete seating areas	Group seating, large sofas, rows
Entry signage is clear, welcoming	Missing or no Welcome signage
Signage is instructive/minimal	Signage is rule-laden/restrictive
Artwork is calming, attractive	No artwork or staff-oriented postings
Art with human forms minimized	Art with human forms displayed
Flooring is clean/damage-free	Flooring is stained/scuffed/damaged
Environment is organized, clutter is avoided	Environment is disorganized and cluttered

Trauma-Informed	Not Trauma-Informed
Overcrowding does not occur	No attention to crowding/room "density"
Individual bathroom options	Group bathrooms
Staff Appearance	
Good hygiene, clean	Poor hygiene, unkempt
Attire connotes professionalism and respect; easy to identify staff	Unprofessional attire, clothing disrepair, curlers, not easy to identify who is staff
Clothing is not sexually provocative	Cleavage shown, tight pants/shirts, short skirts worn
Power symbols removed/minimized	Keys, badges, uniforms, gloves are displayed
No religious icons, jewelry is discreet	Appearance of religious objects is not considered
Staff Behavior	
Manners and respect are clear	Discourteous, disrespectful behavior
Solicitous of consumer needs	Ignore consumers' physical/emotional state
Respond to requests for help	Minimize or fail to respond to requests for help
Timely, minimize delay/unpredictability	Often late, off-schedule without apology
Sincere apology offered as needed	No/poor apology offered for service problems
Actively engaged in their role	Absent, in staff office, not engaged in their role
Speak in clear, normal tones	Yell, curse, mutter
Make eye contact	Look away, eye-rolling
Smile, pleasant demeanor	Negative attitude, chip on shoulder, uninterested
Open physical stance, nodding	Arms folded, legs akimbo, shaking head
Staff initiate greeting/conversation	Staff ignore/wait for consumer to initiate dialogue
Sincere engagement demonstrated: eye contact, smile, and a handshake are offered upon meeting/greeting	Poor greeting/initial introduction/acknowledgement
Staff attuned to consumer mood/needs	Staff ignore consumer mood/needs
Staff attuned to environment's condition, pick up trash, throw away empty coffee cups, old newspaper, ripped magazine, etc.; reading materials are current	Staff oblivious to environment, walk past trash, ignore disarray, inattentive to old materials in consumer areas
Staff offer water/beverage if available. Staff do not eat/drink in front of consumer unless able to offer the same.	Staff eat or drink beverages without offering the same, without apology or consideration
Recognition that stressful work conditions and supporting consumers with challenging behavior can lead to a negative internal reactions ("counter-transference"), and supervision/supervisory support to manage this is important	Failure to recognize problematic internal responses to stressful situations and/or receive regular supervision
Open to change, thinking creatively, problem-solving with others, capable of hearing concerns/criticism and learning	Prevailing sense of "We already do all of that" and failure to recognize or be open to service gaps/consumer experience and service-user reality

(continued)

Trauma-Informed	Not Trauma-Informed
Organizational Understanding	
Agency has trauma policy/philosophy statement	No statements about trauma
Agency articulates commitment to TIC	No TIC statement exists
Trauma/impact is taught to staff/consumers/family	Trauma/impact is not taught
Staff are taught "person-first" language, avoiding judgmental phrases, not labeling; and document with this understanding	"Person-first" language is not understood/ taught, people are referred to by their diagnosis, documentation is judgmental and blaming (e.g., use of words like *manipulative, attention seeking, non-compliant*)
Universal trauma screening occurs for all, including staff	No trauma screening
Trauma is continually assessed for staff/consumers	Trauma is not continually assessed
Staff/consumer triggers/calming strategies identified	Triggers/strategies are not identified
Clear organization plan for behavioral crises	No organizational plan
Discrete areas for calming/crisis management identified	No discrete areas identified; everything occurs in full view
Active supervision occurs to develop/support staff	No or rare staff supervision
Agency has after-hours support protocols	No after-hours support
Agency values consumer feedback and makes concerted outreach efforts beyond simple satisfaction surveys to obtain consumer input, and responds to feedback obtained	No or minimal efforts to obtain consumer satisfaction
Consumer consent protocols are written, clear, known by all staff, and routinely revisited	Consent is not solicited, or only a cursory practice of getting it is followed
Services include strength-based, wellness-oriented skill development such as healthy living, relationships, nutrition/exercise	Services are deficit-pathology-based, focused on symptom management and treatment compliance
Mental Health Practices	
Medication and Administration	
Consumers are educated, provided choices	No or minimal education or choice
Processes are explained (e.g., med. admin).	No process is explained
Consumers have choice over med. route	No med. route choice is offered
Intramuscular medication is avoided at all costs	Intramuscular medication is routine
Side-effects are explained and tracked	Side-effects are not followed up on
Physical Examination	
The process is explained beforehand	The process is not explained
Asking if they want a support person present	Not asking if support would help
Permission to touch the person's body is obtained	No permission is obtained
The examination is explained as it occurs	No explanation during the examination
Treatment Considerations	
Treatment goals reflect consumer preferences	Treatment goals do not include the consumer's preferences
Treatment is integrated across disciplines, with physical health and other service providers	Treatment is fragmented

Trauma-Informed	Not Trauma-Informed
Consent for treatment is explained, obtained and revisited routinely, particularly as treatment changes. A copy of all consent documentation is also provided to the consumer	Consent is minimally discussed/reviewed, not revisited and not copied for the consumer
Preferred gender of treater is solicited and respected if at all possible	Gender preference is not solicited or respected
Choice of treater is offered as possible	Treater choice is not offered
Consumer's wish to have a peer/family/support person present during treatment planning/reviews is honored	Consumer's wish to have a peer/family/support person present during treatment planning/reviews is not acknowledged
Everyday language is used	Much jargon, clinical verbiage & "psychobabble" is used
Evening treatment/groups minimized	Time of day is not considered
Non-coed, gender specific groups offered	Gender dynamic is not considered
Group collaborative decision making occurs	No group decision making
Safety/WRAP plans are developed	No Safety/WRAP planning
All statements of abuse are responded to	Abuse allegations are ignored or minimized
Focus of treatment is education/skills	Focus of treatment is on diagnosis, illness, medication management
Housing services conduct trauma assessment	Housing service ignores trauma
Transitions include safety plans/communication	No continuity to service/approaches
Peers are on-staff and available	Peers are not part of the service
Consumer choice of door being open/closed is respected	Door position not considered
Choice of seating in clinician's office is provided	No seating options are available
Sensitivity to seating configuration and proximity of seating options	Office seating arrangement is not considered or seating options are close together, or large sofas
Sensory experience/education is incorporated	Sensory experience is not considered or addressed
Consumer culture of origin is respected and incorporated into service planning	Consumer culture is ignored or not meaningfully incorporated into care
Co-occurring treatment needs are assessed and incorporated into service provision as indicated	Co-occurring treatment needs are not considered, assessed or integrated into treatment
Recognition of the importance of physical boundaries and that touch, sometimes even a handshake, can be triggering	Lack of awareness of physical boundaries and failure to see that any casual touch (e.g. pat on back, guiding the arm, brushing up against while passing) can be problematic
Recognition of the importance of social boundaries and that jokes, story-telling, innuendo, and double-entendres can convey risk or threat	Lack of awareness of social boundaries and failure to see that jokes, stories, innuendo, double-entendres can compromise a consumer's sense of personal safety

Conceptually adapted and expanded from Harris & Fallot, 2001 and NASMHPD, 2010.

APPLICATION OF TRAUMA-INFORMED CARE PRINCIPLE

Peer Supports

The concept of peer support has been developing for decades, since consumers of services realized that alternatives to formal mental health treatment were necessary and that people in recovery could help others get there. As early as 1989, the National Association of State Mental Health Program Director's issued a statement that "consumers have a unique contribution to make improvements to the quality of mental health services" (NASMHPD, 1989). The President's New Freedom Commission report (2003) made recommendations that the mental health system be more consumer- and family-focused and identified their lack of involvement as a major weakness.

Peer support is provided by people who self-identify as recovering from a mental health or co-occurring disorder to other consumers of behavioral health services who are generally much earlier in their recovery process (Bluebird, 2008). Peer support services are now provided by individuals in both inpatient and outpatient settings who fill a myriad of different roles. Some of these roles include "peer specialists" who can be certified in some states and work in inpatient, crisis, and community programs alongside more traditional staff; "peer bridgers" who often work with individuals in transition between hospital and community settings, and peers who work in peer-run wellness centers, employment programs, and crisis alternatives that provide social, financial, and educational resources to persons seeking help to manage their disorders and lives (Bluebird, 2008).

The principles that provide the foundation for peer support services are tied closely to the principles of trauma-informed care. This is because the addition of peers to the mental health workplace changes the culture of that workplace (NASMHPD, 2010) by helping "transform systems into environments that replace historically rule-based treatment with treatment and environments that promote empowerment, hope, respect, and healing" (Bluebird, 2008, p. 6). Peers serve as role models for providing services in new and creative ways, serve to help individuals in care find their voice, and help demonstrate empowerment, respect, and individualized care (Bluebird, 2008).

Recovery Planning

Current research and reports by past service recipients who are successfully recovering from serious mental and substance-use disorders note that the *direct involvement* of the individual in the development of their own recovery plan is critical to creating better outcomes (Adams & Grieder, 2005). Also critical is a primary focus on the person's strengths and assets, rather than on problems and a deficit-based care model (Adams & Grieder, 2005). These fundamental principles that support person-centered, recovery-oriented treatment planning are cornerstones in a trauma-informed environment. These principles honor the client's own life experiences and spend time finding out "what happened to you" in a way that is individualized and compassionate.

This approach requires a fundamental revision in most agency's treatment planning processes; which historically have been "run and written by professionals," based on problems, weaknesses, and diagnoses, and rarely include the client in any meaningful manner. In fact, in many agencies, the treatment planning process is poorly understood by the clientele who are being served and, as such, are relatively meaningless to them.

An agency informed about trauma will seek the full inclusion of the people they serve in order to engage them in their own recovery process no matter how long that may take. Trauma-informed agencies understand that treatment planning processes are key to recovery-oriented care and outcomes and that, if the client does not participate in own their recovery (treatment) plan, then the treatment has been a failure and the plan will not be followed.

It is not possible to cover all the specific issues related to person-centered, trauma-informed recovery planning in this chapter. The reader is directed to the work of Adams and Grieder titled *Treatment Planning for Person-Centered Care* (2005).

Treatment Services

Trauma screening and assessment services include the universal use of a standardized screening and assessment tool soon after admission for all adults and children who enter the system of care, regardless of which "door" they enter (NASMHPD, 2010). Positive responses to "screening" would result in a more robust trauma assessment, be revisited periodically, and be used as a part of all treatment, rehabilitation, and discharge planning (NASMHPD, 2010).

Trauma-informed services and service systems are evidenced when all components of the system have been reconsidered and evaluated in the light of a basic understanding of the role that violence plays in the lives of people seeking behavioral health services; are capable of supporting and sustaining "trauma-specific" services as needed; and when all staff demonstrate a basic understanding of trauma that accommodates the vulnerabilities of trauma survivors and allows services to be delivered in a way that avoids re-traumatization and facilitates consumer participation in treatment.

Trauma-specific services, including emerging best-practice treatment models, are in place when services designed specifically to treat the actual sequelae of sexual or physical abuse and other psychological traumas are available in adequate numbers to serve the need Jennings, 2004b). The reader will find more information about trauma-specific treatment, systems development, and research in Web Resources section of this chapter.

SENSORY-BASED TREATMENT

Sensory-based treatment targets the intense physical manifestations of traumatic sequelae and has been found to be helpful to survivors of trauma who find it challenging to maintain self-control when under duress (Champagne & Stromberg, 2004). These strategies offer a different treatment experience and method, beyond the realm of conventional trauma approaches such as exposure interventions, cognitive restructuring, didactic psycho-education, or other talk-based therapies that have no evidence base of effectiveness with traumatized individuals (Rosenberg et al., 2001).

Sensory modulation and integration offers another treatment opportunity for trauma survivors and brings with it a growing evidence base from occupational therapy research (Koenig & Kinnealey, 2005; Moore & Henry, 2002; Smith, Press, Koenig & Kinnealey, 2005). Sensory interventions can help survivors recognize and regulate sensory experience and sensory preferences, and begin to heal the mind through the physical sensations of the body (Champagne & Stromberg, 2004; Fisher, 2006; LeBel & Champagne, 2010; Schabner, 2005). As explained by van der Kolk (2004, p. 336), "simply talking about the traumatic experiences is usually not enough to help people put their emotional responses behind them. Traumatized individuals need to have experiences that directly contradict the emotional helplessness and physical paralysis that accompany traumatic experiences."

Environment of Care

An essential sensory experience key to creating a trauma-informed care service is the comfort of the physical environment. This is the first sensory experience a consumer will have when they arrive at the clinical service setting, whether is it an inpatient, outpatient, or private practitioner's office. This is the first impression and first opportunity to convey care and respect. It is also the very beginning of the effective therapeutic relationship. It is no wonder that a major health care supply firm with its international headquarters in New Zealand invested significant resources in creating a beautiful entry and waiting area and elevated the role of "receptionist" to "The Director of First Impressions." The first person to greet clients must understand the importance of their role; it is key to beginning of an effective relationship and successful service delivery.

Another environmental change that is becoming more common is the development of special rooms called "Comfort Rooms" or other similar names. Usually starting out with a vacant office or a little-used seclusion room, staff and consumers plan together to create a respite space that includes calming colors, wall murals with a theme like beach scenes, comfortable furniture, music or calming sounds, rugs, and any other normalizing accoutrements (Bluebird, 2004; Bluebird, 2008).

Also important in TIC is to pay attention to signage, informal and formal messaging on walls (even jokes), paint colors, noise levels, tone of voice, lighting, cleanliness, space, staff use/display of keys, wall art, reduction in the use of the overhead announcement system, and normalized unit names (from, e.g., "K3 Unit" to the "Magnolia Unit"). A recent study found that enhancing the physical environment was uniquely and significantly correlated with reducing these institutional practices—even more than teaching staff about the impact of trauma and trauma-informed care principles (Borckardt et al., 2011).

Coercive Practices

The use of coercive, dangerous, and violent interventions such as seclusion, restraint, the use of involuntary medications, rigid rules and level systems can easily traumatize the individual in care, the staff expected to use these interventions, and all the observers of these events. Current best practices are readily available that facilitate great reductions in these practices, and systems of care that are trauma-informed implement these practices as a number-one priority (Huckshorn, 2004; Huckshorn & LeBel, 2009; NASMHPD, 2010).

HYPOTHETICAL CASE EXAMPLE

Mary P. is a 31-year–old, single Euro-American female with a long history of multiple contacts with the mental health systems in several states. She was referred to a local community mental health agency by the regional public state hospital (APH) where she had been a patient for four years. The reason for the referral was to ask the community mental health center to identify an Assertive Community Team (ACT) care manager to begin to develop a relationship with her in order to help the state hospital recovery team develop a discharge plan. The care manager was assigned ("TM") and as a first step, went to the facility to meet Mary and review her records.

Mary was born to two heterosexual parents. Neither parent had stable employment. The parents abused substances, and early social work documentation reported that Mary's father was physically abusive to her mother, but she refused to press charges. He abandoned the family when Mary was two years old. Mary's mother became addicted to crack cocaine and was hospitalized several times in psychiatric facilities. When Mary was four years old, the children were removed from the home, placed in state custody, separated, and put into foster care. Mary was placed in at least three foster care homes. By age eight, she was adopted by a couple who tried to provide a safe and loving environment for her, but she immediately started having trouble in school, would either withdraw or throw tantrums with little provocation. At the age of ten, Mary experienced her first hospitalization in what would become a long pattern of hospitalizations lasting from months to years at a time. She was variably diagnosed with oppositional defiant disorder, childhood schizophrenia, psychosis not otherwise specified (NOS), night terrors, antisocial personality disorder, depressions, bipolar disorder, as developmentally disabled, and finally with borderline personality disorder, for the last 15 years. During these years of repeated hospitalization, Mary received multiple medications of all classes and routes and experienced multiple events of seclusion, restraint, and involuntary medication administration. When Mary was 27 years old, her adoptive parents moved to a northeastern state and had Mary transferred from the state hospital in the home state to APH. Since this move, Mary has lived in APH since that time, four years, except for one failed discharge attempt to a local group home where she tore up the home and ran away. She returned to APH on her own in a few days post event and has remained at APH since.

The ACT care manager, TM, found that Mary's course of hospitalization at APH has been typical of a long-term care-oriented, custodial care facility that was most comfortable with relying on diagnoses and medication to treat clients. While Mary had a therapist, she was provided traditional one-to-one therapy designed to help her to improve her behaviors based on a program of levels, privileges, and consequences for bad behavior. Mary's behaviors included frequent attacks on staff and other clients that included kicking, biting, spitting, and striking. About one year ago, Mary seriously hurt two staff member and charges were pressed. During the arrest proceedings Mary assaulted a police officer and was charged with a felony. She spent six months in prison, mostly in solitary confinement due to her behaviors. Upon release from prison she came back to APH and continued to display the same kind of aggressive behavior and was kept on 2:1 observations throughout. Even with this intervention, she managed to swallow two batteries, bang her head multiple times, and was routinely restrained up to four hours at a time for aggression and refusing to calm down. TM also noted that Mary's extensive trauma history was noted, but not addressed.

Four months into this admission, Mary's situation came to the attention of several hospital leadership staff, including two new peer specialists, who had been trained in the principles of trauma-informed care. They carefully reviewed the literature and medical record, interviewed staff, and reviewed video of a sample of Mary's aggressive episodes. They determined that Mary always demonstrated "warning signs," and that Mary's triggers were most often being ignored, and she was demeaned, treated like a child, and told "no," and that most of all she was bored and had lost hope. These staff decided that Mary required a special treatment program at the hospital on a different unit (where staff did not know her well) and a different recovery team, including a new attending psychiatrist.

Two of these staff started to visit Mary daily: the director of psychology and a peer specialist. They were successful in developing a relationship with her and working with her to develop a treatment schedule that she actively created. It was at this point that TM was brought in to work directly with Mary's new recovery team as TM also had been trained in trauma-informed care principles and represented an agency known to take some risks and to be very creative. When TM joined the hospital team, her first assignment was to meet with Mary and ask her to describe her daily schedule. TM was amazed that Mary had moved on, in just two months, from being "a violent, impulsive patient" to one who was now engaged daily in getting her GED with a personal instructor, taking art lessons, learning to type and to use a computer with internet access, and working five hours a week passing mail and cleaning administrative offices. Notably, the new attending psychiatrist had weaned her off all psychotropic medications but prn Ativan for anxiety to get a better picture of Mary's "real self."

TM continued to work with the hospital recovery team and brought that information back to her agency to help design a discharge plan for Mary—a client who had lived in institutions for most of her adult life. It was decided that a supported apartment with wraparound ACT services would be the best option as long as Mary had access to full services of her choice during the daytime. Later, TM discovered that Mary had a friendship with another client at APH who had been similarly institutionalized but was a bit ahead of Mary in her recovery. TM, working with the hospital and the community service program, spent two months exploring whether these two could be roommates; starting on Mary's hospital unit. As such, both were discharged to the community in a supervised apartment but with two different primary care managers and two different peer specialists to work with them. TM worked with Mary to replicate many of her activities at the hospital to the community and included Mary in interviews with a GED and art teacher as well as a number of job coaches; all of whom Mary helped to choose.

Over the next year, Mary came back to the hospital three times for four to five days each. She came back due to overwhelming feelings of anxiety or feeling like she had failed at something, resulting in tearing up her apartment. Each time she was able to work through these issues, though it was difficult due to her propensity to ruminate and insist that she "could not do this." She also swallowed a AAA battery one time, but the community team decided to not make a big deal about that and just watched her.

The specific recovery/treatment team changes that are needed to promote trauma-informed care, as discussed in this hypothetical case example, are listed in Table 5.2.

Table 5.2 An Example of Recovery/Treatment Team Changes Needed to Promote Trauma-Informed Care

Practice Issue	Trauma-Informed Approach by Team	Change Needed
The State Hospital Recovery Team is developing Mary's discharge plan Understanding Mary's life story. "TM" is the primary source of information about Mary's life experience.	Mary should be leading the development of her discharge plan. What is Mary's goal? What does she want? Mary should be a key informant about her life story and constructing the narrative of her life	Recovery team must actively engage Mary and support her inclusion, decision-making, and preferences Treatment and recovery teams must look beyond often-inaccurate second- or third-hand, outdated reports and reexamine information with the person-served
Trauma assessment	Part of understanding Mary's life story involves conducting a careful trauma assessment, probably over several sessions, with someone she trusts who can sit with her and listen to what has happened to her	A trauma assessment tool is needed and must be used and revisited as trust develops over time
The description of Mary's life lacks any discussion of her strengths, talents, hobbies, personal interests, where she finds meaning, whom she feels close to, spirituality and pleasure	All dimensions of meaning-making would be assessed and amplified. Recognizing Mary for the person she is requires creating a "healthy" identity—not one based on being a "patient," not a diagnosis, or a placement problem	Strengths, interests, talents, and activities that create meaning are the pathway to recovery. This must be assessed and be an active part of treatment and recovery plan
Loss of hope	Successfully starting and maintaining a path toward recovery requires hope. With such a painful life course—does Mary have any hope? Does her Treatment/Recovery Team?	Consider implementing a hope-assessment scale, such those used in Ohio treatment programs.

(continued)

Practice Issue	Trauma-Informed Approach by Team	Change Needed
Attribution that Mary "tore up" the group home she was previously placed at "failed"	Staff should use person-first language and avoid damaging shaming/blaming language and attributions.	Deconstruct the event and analyze all the contributing factors that led to the alleged event, understand the triggers and what the system missed in its work with Mary, to support her transition to the next service. Review the circumstance with Mary to ensure her perspective is incorporated into the current transition planning process. Document this information in non-judgmental language
Mary has clear triggers that upset her, such as points-levels and being told "no," which are being ignored	Practices that take away personal power, autonomy, choice and decision making are contrary to trauma-informed care	Treatment and recovery teams should continually assess all decision-making methods and procedures to be sure consumer inclusion is central to their protocols
Traditional, consequence-based talk-oriented treatment has been provided, with little success	Trauma-informed care requires clinical/support staff to learn what works or has worked in the past. If traditional approaches do not work—methods must be changed, otherwise active treatment is not being delivered.	Continually assess methods to ensure consumers are attaining the skills they need to further their recovery is essential. Treatment/recovery teams should continually solicit what consumers want, include it in treatment programming and measure the effectiveness of the same
It was decided a supported apartment with wraparound services would be best	As written, this implies Mary was not part of the decision making or given the power to choose her services.	Treatment/recovery teams must collaborate in full partnership with persons-served. Decisions made about another's life must include the consumer
TM discovered Mary had a friendship with another patient	Relationships whether therapeutic or social are important social supports to be recognized	TM and all members of the treatment/recovery teams should be as vigilant about strengths and interests as they are with symptoms and side effects
Mary came back to the hospital, feeling overwhelmed, like she failed	Given the volatility of Mary's life experience and difficulty with community-living, it is important to *forecast* the possibility of challenges in the community and develop a safety-net of interim service with Mary and other service providers. Giving Mary control—before the fact—gives her a margin of comfort, allays some fear, and normalizes the "uneven" path toward recovery	Treatment/recovery teams must think flexibly and ensure that service transitions are well planned, the plans are tested/verified/realistic, and revisited as circumstances change

RECOVERY/TREATMENT TEAM COHESION AND DISCIPLINE-SPECIFIC CONSIDERATIONS

Implementing TIC can present challenges for treatment providers, regardless of discipline and service setting. These challenges are separate and distinct from day-to-day obstacles of working in health care today such as time demands, funding constraints, multiple layers of authorization, and differing clinical approaches. The implementation of trauma-informed care principles requires a shared understanding and philosophical agreement about the role trauma plays in etiology, treatment, and recovery trajectory. In addition to a synchronous framework, TIC demands effective communication among and between the treatment team members. Without a cohesive team approach, treaters run the risk of confounding synergistic care and becoming unwitting "actors" in traumatic "re-enactment"—that is, re-creating the essence of the survivor's traumatizing circumstance. Paradoxically, recapitulating the traumatic scenario can create a margin of familiar comfort to the consumer-survivor, but ultimately this process can damage and dilute treatment efficacy (Hodas, 2006).

In general, all mental health practitioners must understand and work to uphold their ethics codes with respect to individual dignity; the unwavering provision of respect and dignity to all service recipients; a thorough understanding of cultural competency and social justice; and the importance of individual empowerment and provision of choice (Koocher & Keith-Spiegel, 2007). Some basic tenets apply to all disciplines.

- *Having clear values and principles*: An organizational *"values and principles" template that directs professional decisions* is a critical tool that helps assure ethical and trauma-informed practice for any behavioral health practitioner. These values and principles should be based on professional ethics codes, and any dilemmas need to be discussed and reviewed with colleagues and supervisors. However, each practitioner is responsible for their own practice, and "group-think" is never a reason to make an unprofessional decision. Professionals who understand the principles of trauma-informed care work from a clear vision imbued by their ethics codes; introspection; and an understanding about what coercion, discrimination, disrespect, and a lack of choice does to other human beings.
- *Assuring informed consent*: Human rights law includes the doctrine of informed consent, and many ethical standards exist to protect these rights, including but not limited to the Nuremberg Code, the Declaration of Helsinki, and the Guidelines of the Council of International Organisations of Medical Sciences (Gostin, Hodge, Valentine, & Nygren-Krug, 2003). However, the informed-consent rights of persons who are competent to make their own decisions are commonly violated (Mental Health America, 2010). True informed-consent procedures include providing a service recipient all of the information he or she needs to make an informed decision about whether to agree to a proposed treatment. This includes an explanation in lay language that is written; that explains the risks, benefits, side effects, and adverse effects of the proposed treatments; as well as information on alternative treatments and an informed statement about prognosis regarding each treatment. Trauma-informed care principles not only support the use of adequate informed consent but specifically guard against any overt

or covert pressure from any behavioral staff member to influence a client's decisions. Informed-consent statutes and trauma-informed care principles guard the health care goal to "do no harm."

- *Staying current*: An implicit expectation of all healthcare providers is that they should stay current on best and promising practices through continued education throughout their career. It is disturbing to note the number of behavioral health staff working in a variety of inpatient and outpatient settings who get a degree and then stop pursuing quality continuing education to stay current. State boards of professional regulation are not positioned to monitor or enforce the professional expectation that all clinicians stay current and competent. Efforts are made through the mandatory recording of an individual clinician's annual continuing education credits, but there is little oversight of quality or standards regarding this education. Therefore, many practitioners currently do not even have basic information on trauma-informed care or other emerging best practices.

SOME DISCIPLINE-SPECIFIC CONSIDERATIONS

Mental health practitioners, by and large, rely on the "therapeutic use of self" to facilitate treatment. Treatment dilemmas can occur for the practitioner when the clinical imprimatur to "treat" in the best interest of the consumer collides with the consumer's wishes. The cost of imposing treatment against the consumer's will ushers in the use of coercion and force, which can create an immediate breach in the therapeutic relationship.

NURSING

Nurses by role are directly responsible for medication administration and have identified a specific ethical dilemma in fulfilling this task when trying to implement TIC (Regan, 2010). In a report using case illustrations, nursing leadership described the dynamic tension with colleagues that resulted during their efforts to bring about this change (Regan, 2010). Each involved medication being court-ordered or imposed through a substituted judgment process that would force the consumer to take the medication against her or his wishes. Nursing staff recognized that administering the medication involuntarily would thwart their capacity to leverage their personal relationship with the consumer to eventually take the medication voluntarily, and would create a breach in the therapeutic alliance. Physician colleagues were unhappy that their orders to administer the medication intramuscularly and involuntarily were not being honored. According to the author, "One of the most uncomfor issues that surfaced was that of power inequities and the assumption that the physician's decision would preempt the nurses' concerns. Moreover, in this instance, the nurses were being expected to carry out an order that would involve coercion and a practice that they believed would cause the patient harm" (Regan, 2010, p. 221). In each case, time and better relationships led to the consumers' decisions to take the medication voluntarily; however, the tension between colleagues—both working from a best-interest imperative—highlighted the issues in implementing TIC.

PSYCHIATRY

It is reasonable to assume that psychiatrists would be likely to face similar ethical dilemmas in promoting TIC when faced with decisions about proceeding with coercive practices such as involuntary commitment, forced medication, and restraint or seclusion use. In these circumstances, the consumer's will, choice, and personal freedom are eclipsed by physician decision-making. This typically results in consumers' feeling explicit coercion, which some consumers have likened to being tortured or feeling like a criminal (LeBel, 2011). Coercive practices violate a basic principle of TIC: restoring a sense of personal control to the person served (Saks, 2002). Most medical schools do not address these issues, and physicians are left to follow their personal philosophies to make these decisions. As such it is important that organizational policies address these issues.

PSYCHOLOGY

Psychologists, too, run the risk of having some of their discipline's practices contribute to a consumer's feeling traumatized or re-traumatized while receiving service. Specific practices include diagnostic assessments and issuing reports on evaluation findings that can influence important decisions affecting the consumer's life, such as: guardianship, special-education eligibility, civil/psychiatric commitment, forensic evaluation of competency to stand trial and criminal responsibility, and retaining parental rights. Failing to adequately explain the purposes and procedures associated with the assessment process and obtaining informed consent can mimic the loss of control previously experienced by some trauma survivors. If trust is not established at the outset of an evaluation process, fear of disclosure can also result in information being withheld (Harris & Fallot, 2001), which could impact the findings.

In addition, psychologists are mental health practitioners who study and analyze behavior. When a psychologist uses applied behavioral analysis and functional behavior assessment, an incomplete understanding of the consumer's challenges may result if the analysis sidesteps etiology—how and why the behavior developed in the first place. By focusing only on immediate antecedents to problematic behavior and responses that maintain or reinforce the behavior without the greater context of trauma experience—the efficacy of treatment can be adversely impacted (Mohr, Martin, Olson, Pumariega, & Branca, 2009).

SOCIAL WORK

The field of social work is involved daily in decisions that are often coercive to the people they are trying to serve. Social workers are often expected to label parents "abusers and neglectors" in the public welfare system. These actions often attack groups of impoverished families experiencing difficulties and become punitive and coercive, instead of fighting to find resources to help families to cope (Pelton, 2001, p. 438). Social workers in psychiatry or developmental disabilities are often involved in removing clients' rights to make decisions and/or assigning others as representative payees to manage the clients' funds with little attention paid to individual assessments that would support these actions (Pelton, 2001). The use of blanket measures that reduce a group of people's rights is coercive, paternalistic, discriminatory, and is the opposite of social justice (Pelton, 2001). Social workers and their colleagues must learn to make decisions based on a template of values and ethical principles (U.S. Department of Health and Human Services, 1999).

REFERENCES

Adams, N. & Grieder, D. (2005). *Treatment Planning for Person-Centered Care.* Maryland Heights, MO: Elsevier.

Aldwin, C.M., & Yancura, L.A. (2004). Coping and health: A comparison of the stress and trauma literatures. In: Schnurr, P.P., & Green, B.L. (Eds.), *Trauma and Health. Physical Health Consequences of Exposure to Extreme Stress,* pp. 99–125. Washington, DC: American Psychological Association.

American Psychiatric Association. (1994). *Diagnostic and Statistical Manual of Mental Disorders.* (fourth edition). Washington, DC: APA.

American Psychiatric Association. (2000). *Diagnostic and Statistical Manual of Mental Disorders* (text revision edition). Washington, DC: APA.

Bluebird, G. (2004). Redefining consumer roles: Changing culture and practice in mental health settings. *Journal of Psychosocial Nursing and Mental Health Services, 42*(9): 46–53

Bluebird, G. (2008). *Paving new ground: Peers working in in-patient settings.* Alexandria, VA: National Technical Assistance Center, National Association of State Mental Health Program Directors.

Borckardt, J.J., Adan, M., Grubaugh, A.L., Danielson, C.K., Pelic, C.G., Hardesty, S.J., et al. (2011). Systematic investigation of initiatives to reduce seclusion and restraint in a state psychiatric hospital. *Psychiatric Services 62*: 477–483.

Bremner, J.D. (1997). Neuroimaging studies in PTSD. *NCP Clinical Quarterly, 7*(4): 70–73.

Bremner, J.D., Vythilingam, M., Vermetten, E., Adil, J., Khan, S., Nazeer, A. et al. (2003). Cortisol response to a cognitive stress challenge in posttraumatic stress disorder (PTSD) related to childhood abuse. *Psychoneuroendocrinology, 28,* 773–750.

Caffo, E., Forresi, B., & Lievers, L.S. (2005). Impact, psychological sequelae and management of trauma affecting children and adolescents. *Current Opinion in Psychiatry, 18*(4): 422–428. Retrieved on January 3, 2006, from http://www.medscape.com/viewarticle/507657.

Carmen, E., Crane, B., Dunnicliff, M., Holochuck, S., Prescott, L., Reiker, P., et al., (1996). *Massachusetts Department of Mental Health, Task Force on the Restraint and Seclusion of Persons Who Have Been Physically or Sexually Abused: Report and recommendations.* Boston, MA: Massachusetts Department of Mental Health.

Champagne, T., & Stromberg, N. (2004, September). Sensory approaches in inpatient psychiatric settings: Innovative alternatives to seclusion and restraint. *Journal of Psychosocial Nursing, 42*(9): 35–44.

Cusack, K.J., Frueh, B.C., Hiers, T., Suffoletta-Maierle, S. & Bennett, S. (2003). Trauma within the psychiatric setting: A preliminary empirical report. *Administration and Policy in Mental Health. 30*(5): 453–460.

Cusack, K.J., Frueh, B.C., Hiers, T.G., Keane, T.M. & Mueser, K.T. (2003). The impact of trauma and posttraumatic stress disorder upon American society. Report to the President's Commission on Mental Health. Unpublished subcommittee report. Washington, DC.

Cusack, K.J., Frueh, B.C., Brady, K.T. (2004). Trauma history screening in a community mental health center. *Psychiatric Services, 155,* 157–162.

Felitti, V.J., Anda, R.F., Nordenberg, D., Williamson, D.F., Spitz, A.M., Edwards, V., et al. (1998). Relationship of childhood abuse and household dysfunction to many of the leading causes of death in adults: The adverse childhood experiences (ACE) study. *American Journal of Preventive Medicine, 14*, 245–258.

Fisher, J. (2006, January). *Working with the neurobiological legacy of early trauma.* Lecture series presentation. Boston, MA: The Trauma Center.

Frueh, B.C., Dalton, M.E., Johnson, M.R., Hiers, T.G., Gold, P.B., Magruder, K.M., et al. (November 2000). Trauma within the psychiatric setting: Conceptual framework, research directions, and policy implications. *Administration and Policy in Mental Health, 28*(2): 147–154.

Galletley, C., Van Hooff, M., & McFarlane, A. (2011, April). Psychotic symptoms in young adults exposed to childhood trauma—A 20-year follow-up study. *Schizophrenia Research, 127*(1–3): 76–82.

Gostin, L, Hodge, J.G., Valentine, N.B., Nygren-Krug, H. (2003). The domains of health responsiveness: A human rights analysis. EIP Discussion Paper No. 53. World Health Organization. Retrieved on June 12, 2011, from http://www.law.asu.edu/publichealthlaw/PublicHealthLaw/Resources.aspx.

Harris, M., & Fallot, R.D. (2001). *Using Trauma Theory to Design Service Systems.* San Francisco: Jossey-Bass.

Hodas, G.R. (2006). Responding to trauma: The promise and practice of trauma informed care. Retrieved on May 23, 2011, from http://www.nasmhpd.org/general_files/publications/ntac_pubs/Responding%20to%20Childhood%20Trauma%20-%20Hodas.pdf.

Hopper, E.K., Bassuk, E.L. & Olivet, J. (2010). Shelter from the storm: Trauma-informed care in homelessness services settings. *The Open Health Policy and Services Journal, 3*: 80–100.

Huckshorn, K.A. (2004). Reducing seclusion and restraint use in mental health settings. Core strategies for prevention. *Journal of Psychosocial Nursing and Mental Health Services, 42*, 22–23.

Huckshorn, K.A. & LeBel, J. (2009). Improving Safety in Mental Health Treatment Settings: Preventing Conflict, Violence, and the Use of Seclusion and Restraint in Sharfstein S, Dickerson F, & Oldham J (Eds.): *The Textbook of Hospital Psychiatry* (pp. 253–266). Arlington, VA: American Psychiatric Publishing.

Jennings, A.F. (2004a). The Damaging Consequences of Violence and Trauma: Facts, Discussion points, and Recommendations for the Behavioral Health System. Alexandria, VA. National Association of State Mental Health Program Directors (NASMHPD)/National Technical Assistance Center (NTAC).

Jennings, A. (2004b). Criteria for building a trauma-informed mental health service system. Unpublished papers in draft. Rockville, ME.

Kardiner, A. (1941). *The Traumatic Neuroses of War.* New York: Hoeber.

Karl, A., Schaefer, M., Malta, L.S., Dörfel, D., Roleder, N., & Werner, A. (2006). A meta-analysis of structural brain abnormalities in PTSD. *Neuroscience and Biobehavioral Reviews, 30*, 1004–1031.

Kessler, R.C., Sonnega, A., Bromet, E., Hughes, M., & Nelson, C.B. (1995). Posttraumatic stress disorder in the National Comorbidity Survey. *Arch Gen Psychiatry, 52*, 1048–1060.

Koenig, K., & Kinnealey, M. (2005, May 13). *Comparative outcomes of children with ADHD: Treatment versus delayed treatment control condition.* Presentation at the American Occupational Therapy Association meeting in Long Beach, CA, Retrieved on July 21, 2005, from http://www.sciencedaily.com/print.php?url=/releases/2005/05/050513103548.htm.

Koocher, G.P. & Keith-Spiegel, P. (2007). *Ethics in Psychology and the Mental Health Professions: Standards and Cases.* New York: Oxford University Press.

LeBel, J., & Champagne, T. (2010, June) Integrating sensory and trauma-informed interventions: A Massachusetts state initiative, part 2. *American Occupational Therapy Association Mental Health Special Interest Section Quarterly, 33*(2): 1–4.

LeBel, J. (2011). Taking issue: Coercion is not mental health care (Part II). Psychiatric Services, *62*(7), 806–807.

Lipschitz, D.S., Rasmusson, A.M., & Southwick, S.M. (1998). Childhood posttraumatic stress disorder: A review of neurobiological sequelae. *Psychiatric Annals, 28*(8): 452–457.

Mental Health America (2010, March 5). Position statement 22: Involuntary mental health treatment. Retrieved on June 22, 2011, from http://www.nmha.org/go/position-statements/p-36.

Mohr, W.K., Martin, A., Olson, J.N., Pumariega, A.J., & Branca, N. (2009). Beyond point and level systems: Moving toward child-centered programming. *American Journal of Orthopsychiatry, 79*(1): 8–18.

Moore, K.M., & Henry, A.D. (2002). Treatment of adult psychiatric patients using the Wilbarger protocol. *Occupational Therapy in Mental Health, 18*(1): 43–63.

Moses, D.J., Reed, B.G. Mazelis. R. & D'Ambrosio, B. (2003). *Creating Trauma Services for Women with Co-occurring Disorders: Experiences from the SAMHSA Women with Alcohol, Drug Abuse and Mental Health Disorders Who Have Histories of Violence Study.* Delmar, NY: Policy Research Associates.

Mueser, K.T., Goodman, L.B., Trumbetta, S.L., Rosenberg, S.D., Osher, F.C., Vidaver, R., et al. (1998). Trauma and posttraumatic stress disorder in severe mental illness. *Journal of Consulting and Clinical Psychology, 66*, 493–499.

Mueser, K.T., Rosenberg, S.D., Goodman, L.A., & Trumbetta, S.L. (2002). Trauma, PTSD, and the course of schizophrenia: An interactive model. *Schizophrenia Research, 53*, 123–143.

National Association of Mental Health Program Directors (NASMHPD). (1989). *Position Statement on Consumer Contributions to Mental Health Service Delivery Systems.* Alexandria, VA: NASMHPD.

National Association of Mental Health Program Directors (NASMHPD). (1998). Responding to the behavioral healthcare issue of persons with histories of physical and sexual abuse. National Trauma Experts Meeting. April 2–3. Alexandria, VA: National Technical Assistance Center.

National Association of State Mental Health Program Directors (NASMHPD). (2004, in draft) Position Statement on Services and Supports to Trauma Survivors. Alexandria, VA: NASMHPD.

National Association of State Mental Health Program Directors (NASMHPD). (2010). *National Executive Training Institute Curriculum for the Creation of Violence-Free, Coercion-Free Treatment Settings and the Reduction of Seclusion and Restraint, 8th edition.* Alexandria, VA: National Association of State Mental Health Program Directors, Office of Technical Assistance.

Nemeroff, C.B. (2004). Neurobiological consequences of childhood trauma. *Journal of Clinical Psychiatry, 65*(suppl 1): 18–28.

Olff, M., Langeland, W., & Gersons, B.P.R. (2005). The psychobiology of PTSD: coping with trauma. *Psychoneuroendocrinology, 30*, 974–982.

Pelton, L.H. (2001). Social justice and social work. *Journal of Social Work Education. 37*(3): 433–439.

President's New Freedom Commission on Mental Health, (2003). *Achieving the Promise: Transforming Mental Health Care in America. Executive Summary.* DHHS Pub. No. SMA-03–3832. Rockville, MD.

Pine, D.S. (2003). Developmental psychobiology and response to threats: Relevance to trauma in children and adolescents. *Biological Psychiatry, 53*, 796–808.

Rasmusson, A.M., & Friedman, M.J. (2002). The neurobiology of PTSD in women. In R. Kimerling, P.C. Ouimette, & J. Wolfe (Eds.), *Gender and PTSD,* pp. 43–75. New York: Guilford Press.

Regan, K. (2010). Trauma informed care on an inpatient pediatric psychiatric unit and the emergence of ethical dilemmas as nurses evolved their practice. *Issues in Mental Health Nursing, 31*, 216–222.

Rosenberg, S.D., Mueser, K.T., Friedman, M.J., Gorman, P.G., Drake, R.E., Vidaver, R.M., et al. (2001). Developing effective treatments for posttraumatic disorders among people with severe mental illness. *Psychiatric Services, 52*(11): 1453–1461.

Rosenberg, S.D., Mueser, K.T., Jankowski, M.K., & Hamblen, J. (2002). Trauma exposure and PTSD in people with severe mental illness. PTSD Research Quarterly, Summer 1–8.

Saks, E.R. (2002). *Refusing Care: Forced Treatment and the Rights of the Mentally Ill.* The Chicago: University of Chicago Press.

Sala, M., Perez, J., Soloff, P., Ucelli di Nemi, S. Caverzasi, E., Soares, J.C., et al. (2004). Stress and hippocampal abnormalities in psychiatric disorders. *European Neuropsychopharmacology, 14,* 393–405.

Saporta, J. (2003). Synthesizing psychoanalytic and biologic approaches to trauma: Some theoretical proposals. *Neuro-psychoanalysis, 5*(1): 97–110.

Schabner, D. (2005, May 13). Studies debunk stigma of "It's All in Your Head." ABC News Internet Ventures, Retrieved on November 2, 2005, from www.abcnews.go.com/Health/print?id=720963.

Smith, S.A., Press, B., Koenig, K.P., & Kinnealey, M. (2005). Effects of sensory integration intervention on self-stimulating and self-injurious behaviors. *American Journal of Occupational Therapy, 59*(4): 418–425.

Solomon, S.D. & Davidson, J.R.T. (1997) Trauma: Prevalence, impairment, service use and cost. *Journal of Clinical Psychiatry, 58*(Suppl 1): 5–11.

U.S. Department of Health and Human Services (US DHHS). (1999). Mental health: A report of the Surgeon General. Rockville, MD: U.S. Department of Health and Human Services, Substance Abuse and Mental Health Services Administration, Center for Mental Health Services, National Institutes of Health, National Institute of Mental Health.

van der Kolk, B.A. (2001). The assessment and treatment of complex PTSD. In R. Yehuda (Ed.), *Traumatic Stress* (pp. 1–29). Washington, DC: American Psychiatric Press. Retrieved on October 20, 2005, from http://www.traumacenter.org/van_der_Kolk_Complex_PTSD.pdf.

van der Kolk, B.A. (2004). Psychobiology of posttraumatic stress disorder (pp. 319–344). In J. Panksepp (Ed.), *Textbook of Biological Psychiatry,* New York: Wiley & Sons, Inc.

AN APPROACH TO INTERDISCIPLINARY MENTAL HEALTH WORK IN SOUTH-VERONA, ITALY

LORENZO BURTI, LORETTA BERTI, ELISABETTA CANOVA, MICHELE FORNARI, AND DONATA PAVANI

INTRODUCTION

This chapter presents a model of intervention that is the rule of law in Italy, where public interdisciplinary mental health teams, consumers' families, other health and social bodies, and voluntary and consumers' organizations cooperate to sustain a stable-over-time, mixed formal and informal network for the care of the mentally ill, including the severest cases, in the community. This model was made possible by, in essence, a radical revolution in the whole national health system, which definitively phased out all state mental hospitals and replaced them with a community-based system of care.

THE SETTING: THE ITALIAN 1978 PSYCHIATRIC REFORM

In 1978, a new psychiatric reform law, No. 180, was passed by the Italian parliament. Its principal characteristics were the following:

- The phasing out of state mental hospitals by blocking all admissions, including readmissions, to prevent institutionalization rather than mass-discharging inpatients to the community.

- The development of a comprehensive network of community-based services with each local entity taking responsibility for a specific catchment area.
- Psychiatric hospitalization, when deemed necessary, was directed to small units (no more than 15 beds, as prescribed by law, to avoid the construction of new mass institutions) located in general hospitals.

The Italian reform is not the only innovative one in the Western world, but it was, and probably still is, perceived as the most radical one, because it *replaced* the state mental hospital with alternative community services. About seven hundred community mental health services were established, corresponding to the number of catchment areas into which Italy was divided. These services must by law include a gamut of intra- and extramural programs to provide all the necessary psychiatric supports and interventions for the population of persons with severe mental illnesses. The complete lack of a state hospital backup makes community services entirely responsible for comprehensive care rather than balancing or supplementing the mental hospital. This clinical community-based action could not have happened without the support of the new law and administrative regulations that allow for a different structural organization of services, and concomitant strategies for intervention.

The reform law replaced the previous one, Law No. 36 of 1904. Typical for its times, Law 36 addressed social control rather than patients' health and emphasized the dangerousness of patients. Criticism of Law 36 increased after World War II, parallel to the criticism to the mental hospital in all the Western world. In 1968, as an effect of the *movement for deinstitutionalization*, some notable amendments were approved by the parliament.

The deinstitutionalization movement had its leader in Franco Basaglia, a psychiatrist with a phenomenological orientation who, after an academic career, was appointed director of the state hospital of Gorizia, a small city in northeastern Italy, in 1961. With his charisma he attracted dedicated colleagues who shared his ideas, both idealistic and pragmatic. They managed to completely transform the hospital in a relatively short period of time. Grates were removed, wards opened, and patients were allowed to move freely within the hospital and, subsequently, in town. Traditional institutional practices like ECT, isolation, and restraints were proscribed, and discharges were prepared for and encouraged. Other colleagues and students were attracted by the novelty of the model and then exported it to other cities, so achieving the critical mass that was instrumental in paving the road for the 1978 psychiatric reform.

THE ITALIAN NATIONAL HEALTH SERVICE

In December 1978, Law No. 180 was incorporated in the act that initiated the Italian National Health Service, Law No. 833. The Italian National Health Service made health care available to *all* citizens free of charge, or with a minimal contribution from the individual, for minor ailments and related interventions and medication.

This set up a national health insurance scheme similar to the British and Scandinavian ones. The plan is paid for by a payroll tax, and the state distributes the funds per capita (with ad hoc adjustments taking into account specific disadvantages of some areas) to the regions, which, in turn, redistribute them to local health authorities following the same criteria. The framing of the mental health system within the public national health service provided a stable and predictable source of financial support based on capitation payment.

More than thirty years have passed since the 1978 reform; during all those years, opposition to the reform and proposals to repeal it abounded, especially in the first decade, because of some discontent with the delays in developing residential community service alternatives to the mental hospital, due to insufficient funding. All the proposals, though, failed for exactly the same reason: lack of funds to develop the hospital-based services for medium-to-long stays, as required by those who opposed the reform. However, in the mid-1990s, a comprehensive set of services, including residential communities for the long-term disabled, was made available in the nation. While some areas are less served than others, even they offer at least the basic ingredients of community care (general hospital beds, day care, ambulatory care, community teams, and residential communities).

THE CASE OF GIOVANNI: THE ASYLUM VS. COMMUNITY CARE—THE PATIENT'S PERSPECTIVE

Giovanni is an older gentleman who has a diagnosis of paranoid schizophrenia. He spent twelve years in the state hospital, and after the 1978 reform, he was referred to our community service. In the beginning he was very resistant to treatment and had to be involuntarily committed due to his lack of adherence to pharmacological treatment, occasional threats of violence, and his hobby of collecting knives. But over time we began to develop a reciprocally trusting relationship, and he gradually became easier to manage in the community. Currently, he lives in his apartment, takes the medication prescribed, and attends our day center. When a WHO delegation came to visit our service, we brought them to visit Giovanni. He considered this an honor, and, to our utmost surprise, instead of embarking on his habitual tale of his being a descendant of Julius Caesar, he gave a precise and detailed description of the unhealthy and degrading environment of the asylum, illustrating in his own words the perceived advantages and satisfactions of the new, community-based approach and expressing a touching and thoughtful appreciation of our work. The WHO officers took notes.

THE SOUTH-VERONA COMMUNITY MENTAL HEALTH SYSTEM: COMMUNITY TEAMS, FACILITIES, ORGANIZATION, AND STAFF ATTITUDES

The Institute of Psychiatry of Verona was the first Italian university institute to assume direct responsibility for a defined catchment area (South-Verona: pop. 100,000) by establishing the South-Verona Community Mental Health Service (CMHS) according to the directives of the Italian psychiatric reform law.

In South-Verona, direct responsibility for the catchment area has resulted in a close connection between research, teaching, and clinical work. The evaluative research has been primarily dedicated to monitoring the South Verona CMHS, using an epidemiological framework and setting up a psychiatric case register, which is still in operation. The clinical approach responds to public-health principles and provides continuity of care through different times and sites of intervention. All faculty members are involved in research, teaching, and clinical work, and provide the example and the encouragement to their students, in particular to post-graduate ones, to operate in the same way and to take advantage of the opportunity to be trained in real community work under supervision. The combination of clinical care, research, and teaching facilitates the transfer of this new knowledge to clinical practice and to the education of students and of residents who can work in a setting that is similar to what they expect to find in their future job.

As we previously noted, South-Verona community mental health staff are divided into three multidisciplinary teams, each of which serves a portion of the whole catchment area. The members of each team include a psychiatrist, a psychologist, social workers, residents, nurses, rehabilitation therapists, counselors, and students of the corresponding professions doing their internship. The teams operate according to a "single staff module" to ensure continuity of care, both longitudinally (through the different steps of treatment) and crosswise (through the different components of the service): the team remains in charge of the patient wherever he is at any given time. Within each team, patients are assigned to one particular member of the staff, the *therapeutic case manager*, who is also supported by two or three colleagues so that someone who knows the patient can be available at any given time if the patient appears unexpectedly in crisis. Patients, in fact, are welcome to drop by without an appointment whenever they are in need. Thanks to the organization of our work, it is likely that a patient will find one of the workers he or she knows and trusts, which is a definite advantage in a crisis.

VIRGINIA IS ANGRY

This lady is a long-term recipient of our services. She attends the day center and has developed a good relationship with all the staff, especially Domenico, a senior nurse. From time to time, she has had a relapse into psychotic symptoms accompanied by tantrums. On one occasion, she threw a rock and broke the neighbor's window, who then called our service. The community team on duty went to her home, but Virginia refused to open the door. The team remained and upon their insistence she agreed to talk, but only with Domenico. The negotiator was then summoned, and when he arrived, Virginia opened the door without further resistance and accepted appropriate treatment without objections. Without the home visit it is possible that she could have been either arrested for her destructive behavior or rehospitalized.

The attitudes of the team described above have continued over the past thirty years and have preserved the values of relationships in mental health treatment during an era of profound evolution in psychiatry that may make it more difficult to match technological specialization and organizational efficiency with a human orientation in the therapeutic relationship. It is considered fundamental that scientific, up-to-date knowledge matches a humanistic psychosocial clinical approach: both are considered equally important and complementary.

Over the years, the turnover of mental health workers has been low in South-Verona, with the exception of retirements. Workers are fond of their service and of this style of work that has its roots far in the past, in the Italian deinstitutionalization movement. The young residents, social workers, and nursing students may be unaware of the efforts and political struggles that were necessary to build the present system of community care, but they are rapidly absorbed into the atmosphere that facilitates the transmission of expertise in the model and respond enthusiastically to it.

Psychiatry's need to be soundly scientific in order to maintain the pace with the rest of neuroscience carries the risk that psychological distress, emotional upset, and disturbed and disturbing behaviors will come to be viewed as brain diseases beyond reach of even the best psychosocial interventions. Modern psychiatrists who receive only biologically oriented training also risk losing experience and expertise in establishing therapeutic relationships in their work with patients and may also unknowingly undermine the work of other professionals whose therapeutic tools are strictly relational. Recovery and rehabilitation are difficult to pursue in such a context (Mosher & Burti, 1994). We have tried to make sure this does not happen at the Institute of Psychiatry of Verona, where research, teaching, and clinical work have remained closely interconnected for many years. New lines of study have been developed in basic research with an increase in scope and intensity over time, without compromising these traditional values. In addition, new research units have been developed in the fields of psychosocial studies, such as "communication in medicine" and "integrating physical health, mental health, and human rights." The Institute of Psychiatry of Verona and the South-Verona CMHS were designated by WHO as Collaborating Centers for Research and Training in Mental Health in 1987. Since then, the designation of our center has been confirmed every four years.

The South Verona Community Mental Health Service offers the following programs (Tansella et al., 2006):

- *Community Mental Health Center* (CMHC): Open six days a week, from 8:00 a.m. to 8:00 p.m., this is the hub of the system. A 15- to 30-minute case-centered meeting takes place every morning with the participation of all the service staff, including the chief nurse of the hospital ward. The doctor on duty reports the events that occurred during his shift, and urgent decisions and referrals are decided on the spot. The CMHC is used in different ways: as an outpatient facility, a crisis intervention center, a post-admission treatment center, and a day center for patients in rehabilitation where a number of different psychosocial groups are held. However, while participation in groups is decided according to a set treatment plan, the CMHC serves also as a walk-in center where all patients willing to spend some time or the whole day are welcome, and formalities are reduced to a minimum. Lunch is served at noon for those remaining all day. The staff believes that dependency is rather something to work through rather than a risk to be afraid of, and is well aware that many patients actually do not have *any* alternative for socialization where they can be accepted with respect and dignity in spite of their disability. As a result, some long-term patients are accepted without a time limit, but over time they become active members of the day center and find useful roles in daily activities; if they are elderly, it is unrealistic to expect that their improvement can be effectively used in society at large and a discharge is not stressed. However, one cannot ever say: some actually find their own external activities while maintaining a friendly relationship with the center they visit from time to time. On the other side, the day center offers time-limited programs specifically for young patients for whom detailed personal treatment plans are drawn up, with specific attainable goals. The programs take place in the mid-afternoon, when the elderly patients leave the center to go home. This is in order to take into consideration youngsters' unwillingness to mix with the veterans who, in their eyes, represent depressing models. The CMHC is also the headquarters where staff meet and extramural interventions are planned and coordinated. It was recently restored and enlarged, so it looks attractive to patients, who come with pleasure. It also houses the offices of the professional members of the community teams, those of the residents, and large meeting and conference rooms that are used for various purposes.

- *Psychiatric unit*: An open ward of 15 beds located in the university medical center (about 800 beds total). In a sense, it is a traditional hospital ward, and not particularly attractive. However, admitted patients have free access, or are accompanied by the staff, to other nodes of the network of services, typically the CMHC, where patients who are at the end of their acute phase are invited to attend during the day. In the ward, besides all medical activities, individual and group treatment is provided by psychologists. Since there are only acute hospital-based psychiatric beds, it is consequential that the service has to work hard to assure the treatment of all patients, including the most severely afflicted ones in the community, without the backup of a hospital-based long-term accommodation. Besides the clinical advantage for the patients, this allows also a powerful training of the providers' ingenuity in using community resources that are already available, both the natural and the professional ones.
- *Outpatient department*: Provides consultations, individual and family therapy. Offices are located in the general hospital and in the mental health center.
- *Home visits and other extramural interventions*: These are provided by community teams and can take place as an emergency intervention or on a scheduled basis to monitor a case at home and to provide support to the family. A main goal is the prevention of an emergency possibly leading to hospitalization. Home visits are valued by the service because they provide much more relevant information than in-office consultations and are well-accepted by patients and caregivers, who perceive them as helpful and supportive.
- *Psychiatric emergency room*: It is manned by the psychiatrists on duty 24 hours a day, seven days a week, who are usually assisted during working hours by the treatment team members who are (or will be) in charge of the patient requiring the urgent intervention. An emergency night and weekend service, coordinated by the psychiatrist on duty and run by two psychiatric nurses, is available—they are on call to provide care in the supported apartments and hostel, as well as at the homes of patients already in the charge of the service.
- *Psychiatric and psychological consultation-liaison service*: For other medical and surgical departments (run by the Department of Psychosomatics and Clinical Psychology), this service maintains psychiatric integration with other hospital-based medical activities and ensures continuing contact with our patients when they are hospitalized for medical reasons.
- *Residential facilities*: Two group homes are available for up to six people who do not need supervision overnight. Four other apartments (with a total number of 18 beds) offer different levels of staff supervision (in terms of hours of presence per day) according to the degree of competence of the patients. One hostel (with 12 beds, supervised 24 hours a day by nurses, rehabilitators, and counselors), is also available to accommodate patients who are particularly disabled, usually after a hospital admission.

- *Clinical psychology and psychosomatics unit*: Offers the liaison service mentioned above and outpatient interventions specialized for anxiety, depressive, and somatoform disorders.
- *Psychotherapy and eating disorders unit*: An outpatient service offering individual, group, and family psychotherapy. The eating disorders section, recently established, is part of a regional network of services and is staffed by a multidisciplinary team including an internist, a dietician, a psychiatrist, and a psychologist.
- *The Verona psychiatric self-help group*: For more than twenty years, a psychiatric consumer, ex-user, survivor, self-help group has collaborated with the CMHS to supplement the needs of housing, work, socialization, and evening and holiday leisure activities using the collaborative self-help model (users are supported by a part-time psychiatrist and a few counselors). The group is able to find about a hundred regular job positions per year and runs twenty group homes plus five more networked apartments to offer hospitality to patient-members of the group, with 35,000 days of hospitality per year.
- *The research project on early treatment of psychosis*: Recently, a multi-center study on the early treatment of psychosis has started; its results will be transferred to routine clinical practice.

This connected network of services and programs facilitates an easy and prompt offer of different treatment modalities of intervention and the referral of the patient to the most appropriate node. This assures the cross-sectional integration of different programs and interventions. In addition, the patient is allowed to move, or is accompanied, through the network to find the needed treatment in the appropriate node of the system. The promotion of circulation of the patient in the whole network is of particular importance because it offers him the opportunity to experiment with various solutions to his problems and introduces the goal of moving along the network in the direction of personal and social enrichment and growth. However, a patient is welcome to drop by and informally attend the day centre, as mentioned before.

MARIO: A WELCOME LONG-TIME MEMBER OF THE DAY CENTER

Mario is now 65; he was admitted with an acute psychotic episode some twenty-five years ago and suffered of several relapses afterward that made him lose his job and become socially marginal. Instead, he found relief and a sense of belonging at the day center, where he could recover some active roles in helping with the personnel in daytime chores. Attempts to transfer his acquired skills to the outside world failed while he was getting older. So we decided that it was okay for him to be a senior attendant of the day center, where his active presence is respected and appreciated. He has a family, where he also helps, so that he does not attend daily, but the center remains a secure point of reference for him. Other elderly patients like him attend the center in much the same way.

The team usually chooses home treatment as first option to support people during an acute episode, rather than admission, even in the presence of severe symptoms and of the need for initiating an antipsychotic treatment, because, whenever possible, non-hospital treatment is preferable, especially in a first episode (NICE, 2012). The experience accrued over the years in responding to all psychiatric needs on a community basis, without the backup of a state mental hospital, after the Italian reform, has contributed to a sparing use of general hospital beds as well. As an effect, psychiatric general-hospital admissions have slightly, but consistently, decreased over the years up to present time (de Girolamo & Cozza, 2000; de Girolamo et al., 2007). In the following vignette, further important reasons for avoiding admission included the fact that this was patient's first contact with the psychiatric system, she was young, and there was an offer of family support.

SILVIA: A SPARING USE OF THE HOSPITAL

Silvia is an attractive 20-year-old brunette, who at the time of first contact appeared shabby and neglected. In the initial interview she displayed disorganized thoughts and behaviors, social withdrawal, depressed mood, very low self-esteem and moments of anger. But she also gave the impression that she had adequate control of her behavior as well as supportive relatives, so an emergency admission was not deemed necessary and home treatment was indicated. Home visits were begun to monitor Silvia's response to the antipsychotic medication at moderate dosage. In addition, a series of individual therapeutic sessions were provided by a senior resident under the supervision of an expert faculty clinical psychologist. Silvia's parents were invited to participate in the psycho-educational group of caregivers. Unfortunately, three months later, symptoms had not improved as expected. Silvia continued to abuse street drugs, and managing her within the household became difficult. An agreement with the patient and the family was obtained for a brief hospitalization in order to provide respite for the family, to titrate the psychopharmacological treatment, and also stop her use of street drugs. At discharge Silvia was accommodated in a transitional residence setting: the "service hostel." There the goals were to offer a surrogate family as an alternative to the natural one, which home visiting had determined was less ideal than it appeared to be at the beginning. Other goals included providing Silvia with more autonomy within a structured residential setting. The latter seemed necessary considering Silvia's risky behaviors, including poor adherence to pharmacological treatment, substance misuse, self-hurting, the risk that she would run away. Later Silvia moved into a residence with a lower level of staff supervision and, eventually, to a group home. Now she is fairly well organized and has a part-time job.

The informal and flexible setting of the self-help group has revealed unexpected possibilities with cases that are intolerant towards the formal setting of psychiatric facilities.

PROSPERO: A VERY DIFFICULT CASE FINDING HIS WAY IN THE SELF-HELP GROUP

Prospero, 26, has a diagnosis of antisocial personality disorder along with substance abuse, and he has an extensive list of criminal trials, convictions, and substantial periods of time spent in jail. Whenever he is without support in the community, such as when mother is hospitalized for physical illness, he comes to the emergency room late at night, drunk and violent, destroying property, and gets admitted to the psychiatric ward, where he also is destructive. Backup nurses have to be summoned, and he has to be heavily medicated. Next morning, once sober, he is amenable and requests discharge, which is generally accorded along with (temporary) staff relief. Attempts to keep him involuntarily committed, in fact, result in nightmare stays with continuous fights and physical confrontations with the hospital personnel. Ward leadership is at a loss as to how to solve the case, when the psychiatrist of the self-help group initiative suggests they admit Prospero into one of their group apartments. Management of him in that setting is also not easy, requiring intense monitoring by the psychiatrist and apartment staff, especially at night, often involving the ejection of drug dealers and pushers who are friends of Prospero's. On the other hand, something unexpectedly positive happens: Prospero begins to make friends with other residents of the apartment, and reciprocal respectful relationships develop with folks not involved in criminal activity. After all, they identify with one another as similarly deprived and marginalized. As time passes, Prospero develops a feeling of belonging and self-esteem as he participates in and contributes to the group spirit, with corresponding appropriate behavior. To us, this case is one of the miracles that our health and social workers witness from time to time.

MISSION OF THE SERVICE AND STYLE OF INTERVENTION

The mission of the South Verona community service is that of assuming and maintaining full responsibility for the psychiatric needs of the population served, with a special commitment to the more disturbed and disturbing individuals. The term *needs* is intended in a broad sense, in that it includes also all the basic needs that are common in the severely mentally ill, besides the clinically relevant ones. Patients' needs for been treated with dignity and respect are highly valued. Special needs, even if apparently whimsical, are also taken into consideration, when meeting them is beneficial.

ROBERTO IS A VETERAN: HE DESERVES SPECIAL ATTENTION

Roberto is 35, with multiple diagnoses: bipolar disorder, personality disorder, and poly-substance abuse in the past. He was in and out of touch with the service for several years, developing a sort of roller-coaster rapport. In the last couple of years, though, he settled into a trusting relationship with his doctor, became adherent to treatment, and managed to settle down. He also began a cordial and friendly relationship with one of the authors (senior professor Lorenzo Burti). By mutual agreement he gained the privilege to drop in any time, without having to be announced and wait. This accommodation was aimed at coping with Roberto's impulsiveness and vulnerability to frustration. Roberto has reciprocated this privilege with kindness and tact of his own. He stays only for brief moments, asking for "the wise suggestion of the day" and then leaves, satisfied. This response is what was expected by Professor Burti, who believes that within Italian culture, meeting the needs and even indulging the whims of veterans who have suffered every kind of frustration is an appropriate supportive and empowerment intervention.

In the multi-professional team there is a close integration of the medical, psychological, and social components, and professional specificity comes second in deciding who becomes the key person directly in charge of a certain patient. The intensity and quality of the therapeutic relationship come first. As a consequence, there may be a certain overlapping of roles among the different professionals who participate in the team.

MARCO: NO PSYCHIATRIST, PLEASE; SOCIAL WORKER IS OK

Marco denies being sick. Therefore, he does not want to have anything to do with a physician. But he has no house, no job, no money at all. So, he needs the social worker[1]. Day after day, the two build a good relationship, and the social worker becomes the team member of reference, getting more and more influential. Marco starts trusting her and eventually accepts treatment prescriptions, collectively decided by the team, through her.

Another important characteristic of the team style of work is that all clinical decisions are collegially discussed and agreed upon. Clinically oriented meetings abound to give everybody in the team the opportunity to provide his opinion, which is highly appreciated and taken into account to mold the final decision.

MARTA: THE REBEL

Marta is a rebellious young woman intolerant of authority. So she is opposing the administration of drugs by the personnel and, when she is at home, by the parents. A specific program is negotiated with her regarding the psychopharmacological treatment, which she often refuses. Various modalities are employed, all entailing Marta's active involvement, since she feels too much controlled if drugs are directly administered to her by others. Different intervals of time are tried and different doses of drugs given to her at the mental health center she attends daily for self-administration. These choices are taken by the team after long discussions, with a frequent division of the team members into "hawks" and "doves." Eventually, though, Marta reciprocates the team's trust with the desired compliance.

Hierarchy in the center is substantially flat, and experience, rather than authority and academic or career credentials, is valued. The postgraduate students learn a lot from senior nurses, who love to "teach the doctors". There is a great passing on of responsibility; that is, of power. Senior staff professionals are unobtrusive but always available for suggestions and backup support. Workers have the necessary freedom and power to make decisions on their own but do not feel alone: supervision is always available. These characteristics of the work are important for operating in a timely and effective way and also to prevent burnout, which may be an unwanted side-effect of a sense of impotence and the lack of support, in combination with difficult and often unrewarding work.

TAILORING INTERVENTIONS IN A MULTI-PROFESSIONAL TEAM

The team adopts specific, tailored strategies in the light of the observed characteristics of each case, also adapting the style of intervention to the needs expressed by the patient. A comprehensive multidisciplinary assessment (psychiatric, psychological, and medical) is used, but substantial importance is also accorded to a phenomenological approach. Many clinical histories and courses suggest that taking the patient's preferences into account is crucial: their cultural and personal characteristics and lifestyles must be carefully addressed, as well as their interests and expectations. A phenomenological approach helps the team frame a psychotic breakdown within the patient's personal history and look for normalizing meanings in the symptoms rather than simply defining them as "illness."

ELISA: A DIFFICULT PATH TO DISCOVER HER REAL SELF

Elisa, 22, an art student in another town, away from her parents' home, develops a friendship with a colleague who is a member of an urban tribe of extremist punks that she soon joins. Elisa decreases the frequency of visits to her family and finally completely stops them, while she is initiated into the use of various street drugs and stealing in order to buy them. The group is evicted and moves to an abandoned and rotten building. Since she does not even answer the phone, her worried parents go and find her in a state of severe physical neglect and psychological derangement. She shows bizarre ideas and behaviors, like speaking of herself in the third person, rejecting the use and possession of money and objecting to consumerism, seriously decreasing her food intake, and vomiting. She also develops ideas of thought-transmission and attributes magical meanings to objects of common use. The parents bring her back home and then to our service.

Elisa's clinical history and present status are interpreted by the team not only according to her psychopathology, but also in the light of her personal and family history (too complex to be reported here), characterized by a profound contradiction between compliance and defiance. Elisa's behavior is interpreted as a search for her own path, which unfortunately leads her to an unhealthy and disorganized lifestyle. In the management of the case, the team then decides to accept Elisa's unconventional orientation as far as possible, siding with her in the search for individualization while containing her tendency toward inappropriate behaviors.

Home visits usually involve a mini-team of two or three workers, including a nurse and a psychiatrist. As previously said, these visits are also considered a more efficient assessment tool than in-office interviews because they frame the patient, his story, and his behavior in the whole context. The causes, or precipitants, of a problem, and possible solutions are often obvious in the patient's natural context.

MARINA: TOO RESPONSIBLE FOR THE FAMILY TO STAY IN HOSPITAL

Marina, 25, became severely psychotic and needed hospitalization. Once admitted, she continued to remain grossly agitated in spite of sedatives: she repeated over and over that she had to go home, while shaking the ward door. A home visit revealed a family in miserable conditions: the father was blind and paraplegic after an occupational accident, and the mother was disabled with an early dementia. The house was a mess. It was clear that Marina was the only competent member of the family and that her agitation was due to her preoccupation and stress associated with caring for her family. The team reassured Marina that the social worker would quickly provide a housemaid to help the family during her admission. She was also accompanied home to show her that the housemaid took good care of the house and the parents. Marina's agitation disappeared and she was effectively treated and discharged soon afterwards.

Home visits are also an effective ingredient in increasing camaraderie, motivation, and staff ingenuity in finding alternative solutions for crisis resolution. Once again, the lack of the backup of the institution, in this case the office, increases the staff's creativity. Home visits are also used to follow up patients already known to the service and their caregivers routinely. In a catchmented community service, in fact, most patients are already known to the staff, and these patients may be provided with long-term, community-based monitoring and support, which may prevent or at least identify the exacerbation of symptoms and allow the staff to promptly take appropriate measures. This practice is common in all community-based services and is cited here just to highlight its importance in even its generic form. In fact, over time, home visits may be considered too non-specific and too generic and be replaced by more specific programs. A great heterogeneity of models is represented in the field. We are convinced that the basic ingredients of a mixture of monitoring and support, within the framework of a long-term, trusting relationship with the family, make *generic* home visiting an effective intervention. As reported in an in-depth review (Burns et al., 2001): *it seems that home treatment services that visit patients at home regularly and those that take responsibility for both health and social care are more effective in reducing the number of days spent in hospital.*

CONCLUSION

Deinstitutionalization, with the shift from institutional to community care ordered by a national legislation, and policies that prescribe the development of a comprehensive array of accessible services to respond to the different needs of the population of reference, is the foundation on which all the work described above can solidly stand. Community teams have the appropriate legal, organizational, and procedural instruments in support of their clinical actions.

The integration of mental health into general health services, actually into the National Health Service, is fundamental in confronting the additional stigma attaching to mental patients when they are treated in a separate, often discriminated-against sector of medicine, and facilitates service accessibility and integration through primary health care. Financing based on capitation payment, typical of the public national health service, provides a secure source of economic support. The phasing out of mental hospitals produced the desired shifting of funds from institutions to community care: money, in fact, must follow the services.

At the service level, the organizational structure facilitates continuity of care, a wide range of accessible services, the networking between the various nodes of the service and with the natural support system, especially the families that are valued as partners, which is just and effective since they live in close contact with their ill relative and carry most of the burden of the relationship.

All in all, these aspects reflect nothing but the recommendations of WHO that for half a century has adopted, developed, and disseminated the principles of deinstitutionalization and of a public health approach (World Health Organization 2001a; World Health Organization 2001b). In recent years, the shift away from the institutions, which were often associated with human rights violations and substandard living conditions, has been refueled by a novel emphasis on the human rights of the mental and other disadvantaged patients by the United Nations, whose most recent and specific document is the Convention on the Rights of Persons with Disabilities (CRPD: see http://www.un.org/disabilities/default. asp?navid=13&pid=162).

In conclusion: the treatment ingredients of the service herein described and further illustrated with some clinical vignettes are typical of a community service that has been developed according to the principles of the Italian psychiatric reform and resulting community care. We wish to stress again that clinical decisions, especially the critical ones, are always carefully pondered by the community team acting as a whole, and extensively discussed with all the workers involved in the case in the various phases of the treatment plan. Outcomes are carefully monitored in a similar way. We wish finally to express that we do not assume this to be *the* model of community work—that any model must be framed in its specific setting and that the transfer to other settings may need minor, or even major, appropriate adjustments.

NOTE

1. In the Italian system, the social worker is specifically in charge of the practicalities of the social problems of the case, and has fewer managerial duties and almost no treatment role compared to analogous American colleagues.

REFERENCES

Burns T, Knapp M, Catty J, Healey A, Henderson J, Watt H, Wright C. (2001). Home treatment for mental health problems: A systematic review. *Health Technol Assess,* 5(15):1–139.

de Girolamo G, Cozza M. (2000). The Italian psychiatric reform: A 20-year perspective. *Int J Law Psychiatry,* 23:197–214.

de Girolamo G, Barbato A, Bracco R, Gaddini A, Miglio R, Morosini P, et al. (2007). PROGRES-Acute group. Characteristics and activities of acute psychiatric in-patient facilities: national survey in Italy. *Br J Psychiatry,* August; 191:170–177.

Mosher LR, Burti L. (1994). *Community Mental Health: A Practical Guide.* New York: Norton.

NICE (2012) www.nice.org.uk.

Tansella M, Amaddeo F, Burti L, Lasalvia A, Ruggeri M. (2006). Evaluating a community-based mental health service focusing on severe mental illness: The Verona experience. *Acta Psychiatr Scand* (Copenhagen), *113*(Suppl. 429):90–94.

World Health Organization. (2001a). *The World Health Report 2001: Mental Health—New Understanding, New Hope.* Geneva: World Health Organization.

World Health Organization. (2001b). *Mental Health Policy Project: Policy and Service Guidance Package. Executive Summary.* Geneva: World Health Organization.

BRIDGING THE INTERDISCIPLINARY EDUCATION TRAINING GAP

KENNETH R. YEAGER, GRAYCE M. SILLS, AND HOLLY KASTAN

INTRODUCTION

For many working in behavioral health, it is a time of both excitement and frustration. The profession's advancements in pharmacology and therapeutic interventions are growing at a breathtaking pace. New, promising and intriguing therapeutic processes such as deep brain stimulation for the treatment of depression and obsessive compulsive disorder hold both promise and fears – promise in hope of an effective treatment, and fear from memories of past cutting-edge treatments in psychiatry that did not stand the test of time, such as ocular lobotomy. One of today's most rewarding aspects of community mental health is working in teams together with clients in a collaborative effort toward recovery. It is a time for working with, rather than doing for.

It is a time that is both promising and frustrating, as awareness of potential treatment advancements stands juxtaposed to a growing body of evidence that America's graduate education programs are not keeping up with current advances in mental health treatment. In this chapter we will explore the driving forces behind transformations in care-delivery systems in mental health. We will discuss advances, changes, and challenges in payment structures; advances in evidence-based practices and current best practices; and movements to improve both the safety of care processes and the overall quality of care provided; and we will examine consumer, family, and recovery efforts, all aimed at transforming the mental health service delivery system. Next we will discuss the graduate education system structure to identify barriers to developing parallel academic structures designed to meet changing education demands. We will discuss the findings and recommendations of the Annapolis Coalition to align graduate behavioral health education structures with current practice structures. Finally, we will provide an overview of the demonstration project of The Ohio State University that is an effort to provide interdisciplinary behavioral health education to graduate students across disciplines.

THREE DECADES ESTABLISHING A FOUNDATION FOR TRANSFORMATION

EFFORTS TOWARD COST CONTAINMENT

Healthcare began to change drastically nearly three decades ago. Soaring healthcare costs combined with a lack of progress toward improving outcomes led to challenges of the assumptions of the treatment programs of the day (specifically, long-term inpatient treatment programming). Managed care emerged as a leader in the charge against traditional treatment approaches. Everything in behavioral healthcare was under scrutiny: lengths of stay, levels of care, location and intensity of care were all challenged with regard to their effectiveness and cost.

Cost, however, was not the only focus during these times of changes. Effectiveness became a major point of contention, with some arguing that brief, solution-focused approaches would provide similar outcomes to those of long-term traditional approaches to treatment like psychotherapy. Many clinicians argued that traditional treatment approaches provided a quality of care superior to that of emerging brief treatment approaches designed to contain costs. The argument between quality of care and quantity of care surrounding issues of cost-containment raised serious and challenging questions; questions that would not be answered rapidly or easily. Out of this debate emerged the need to turn to research findings to determine the *most effective* approaches to care. The examination of research evidence to determine the appropriateness, effectiveness, and cost benefit of any given treatment led to the emergence of evidence-based approaches to care.

EVIDENCE-BASED APPROACHES

Evidence-based practice has been defined as "the conscientious, explicit and judicious use of the best available scientific evidence in professional decision making" (Sackett, Richardson, Rosenberg, & Haynes, 1997). More simply defined, it is the use of treatments for which there is sufficiently persuasive evidence to support their effectiveness in attaining the desired outcome. Proctor and Rosen (2004) suggest that evidence-based practice comprises three assertions: (a) intervention decisions based on empirical, research-based support; (b) critical assessment of empirically supported interventions to determine their fit to and appropriateness for the practice situation at hand; and (c) regular monitoring and revision of the course of treatment based on outcome evaluation. In general, decision making using evidence-based or evidence-informed methods is achieved through a series of steps beginning with evaluating the problem to be addressed and developing an answerable question. The next step is to gather and critically evaluate available evidence, which is followed by applying the results of the assessment and evaluation to practice or policy, and then continuously monitoring patient progress to the point of reaching the desired outcome.

QUALITY AND SAFETY

As evidence-based or evidence-informed practice grew, a parallel priority emerged requiring that effective treatment is also considered in light of the degree of safety involved for the patient.

This question was highlighted by the Institute of Medicine's (IOM) report and publication *To Err Is Human* (Kohn et al., 2000) Most notable in this report is the attention given to medical errors in the American healthcare system, which have resulted in up to 98,000 deaths annually. The IOM report states:

> *Medical errors can be defined as the failure of a planned action to be completed as intended or the use of a wrong plan to achieve an aim. Among the problems that commonly occur during the course of providing healthcare are adverse drug events and improper transfusions, surgical injuries and wrong-site surgery, suicides, restraint-related injuries or death, falls, burns, pressure ulcers, and mistaken patient identities.* (IOM, 2001, p. 130)

This report launched new safety standards calling on providers to incorporate safety plans and programming throughout all of the healthcare industry. In behavioral health, safety was called to the forefront following the report of the death of a young boy placed in restraints by a treatment aide who had been inadequately trained in the application of restraint. This event resulted in a number of investigative reports on injuries and deaths that occurred from the use of restraint and seclusion (Busch & Shore, 2000).

Examination of safety within the environment of care became a focus of care standards and best practices, all designed to maintain the safety of the patient within the care environment and through prescribing and treatment efforts. A new focus was put on the application of improvement science as a method of measuring and assessing the degree of safety within any given level of care or care environment. Today, many of these measures are publicly reported in efforts to increase transparency in order to improve patient safety and enhance patient outcomes (Kohn et al., 2000).

CONSUMERISM

Beyond calls for improved cost and safety, a third voice was heard. The voice of the consumer emerged as a remarkable force in behavioral healthcare and community mental health. The voice of the consumer has become an important factor in refining information provided to families regarding the care of their loved ones. Increasingly, the National Alliance on Mental Illness (NAMI) and other consumer and family organizations have called for information and education on treatment options, exploring what options are available for care, and what treatments have the best outcomes for particular diagnostic categories; also medication options, asking questions related to medication cost, effectiveness and side-effect profiles. Actions like the call for increased information from NAMI has led to an increasingly important attention to the voice of the consumer. Today, consumer organizations are actively seeking a voice in treatment, policies, and practice alternatives specifically to meet individualized needs based on gender, race, culture, and age. All of this is being built under a new and ever-evolving understanding of recovery and empowerment. The consumer movement has led to a growing acknowledgment of unmet needs for treatment, resulting in improved access to care, collaborative interactions with family and community support organizations, and the integration of ongoing mental-illness management with primary care needs (Rees & Young, 1981).

HEALTHCARE REFORM

The Patient Protection and Affordable Care Act (PPACA) is a United States federal statute signed into law by President Barack Obama on March 23, 2010. The law (along with the Healthcare and Education Reconciliation Act of 2010) is the principal healthcare reform legislation of the 111th United States Congress. This legislation reforms certain aspects of the private health insurance industry and public health insurance programs, increases insurance coverage of pre-existing conditions, expands access to insurance for over 30 million Americans. The PPACA is leading to the emergence of greater integration of mental illness within primary healthcare in what is being described as "medical homes." A medical home, also known as "the patient-centered medical home" (PCMH), is "a healthcare setting that facilitates partnerships between the individual, their personal care provider and when appropriate, the patient's family." It is believed by many that the provision of medical homes may allow better access to healthcare, increase satisfaction with care, and improve health. Provider organizations are now facing greater accountability with the emergence of publicly available data outlining performance metrics, which will soon be tied to reimbursement for services based on performance rather than a set amount for a specific diagnostic group. In turn, this "pay for performance" approach will lead to greater challenges in management of difficult populations. This may be accomplished through accountable care organizations. An accountable care organization (ACO) is a type of payment-and-delivery reform model that seeks to tie provider reimbursements to quality metrics and reductions in the total cost of care for an assigned population of patients, frequently groups of "at-risk" populations (Commonwealth Fund Resources, 2011).

A group of coordinated healthcare providers form an ACO, which then provides care to a group of patients in an effort to use quality-metrics to monitor and reduce patient care cost through proactive care models specifically designed to manage the patient risk profile. For example, populations with severe and persistent mental illness, who are known to have a remarkable history of trauma, are known to utilize greater levels of healthcare as they age. This concept has been demonstrated through a project known as the ACE Study, which examined the impact of "adverse childhood events" on long-term healthcare utilization patterns. The ACE Study is an ongoing collaboration between the Centers for Disease Control and Prevention and Kaiser Permanente. Led by co-principal investigators Robert F. Anda, M.D., M.S., and Vincent J. Felitti, M.D., the ACE Study is perhaps the largest scientific research study of its kind, analyzing the relationship between multiple categories of childhood trauma (ACEs), and health and behavioral outcomes later in life. The database of greater than 17,000 ACE scores has shown e positive correlations to a great number of chronic physical and behavioral health conditions, including, but not limited to: autoimmune disorders; heart, lung, and liver diseases; cancer; hepatitis or jaundice; diabetes; bone fractures; and sexually transmitted diseases (Commonwealth Fund Resources, 2011).

All of this leads back to the publication of President George W. Bush's New Freedom Commission Report (2003), which suggests "there can be no such thing as good physical health without good mental health." Knowing the impact of adverse life experiences on physical health, the obvious approach to proactively managing disease is to proactively manage behavioral health. But how are our educational institutions keeping up with the massive reforms currently under way within America's healthcare system? And how effective are graduate education programs in preparing students for a career within the newly emerging healthcare model?

A WIDENING TRAINING GAP

While some inroads have been made in graduate education, there is still a visible gap between the dramatic changes in America's healthcare system and the graduate education training programs; in part, because of the bureaucratized system of universities leading to systems in which change is often a cumbersome and slow process. Those in positions with the greatest ability to effect change in the education process are more invested in research than in revolutionizing graduate education. This reality exists because within the university system, changes in the clinical environment are frequently overlooked. An unfortunate reality is many of university professors are not interested in the evolution and revolution occurring in healthcare. While a fascinating thing to watch from a distance, the actual integration of graduate education with current healthcare advancements does little to lead to faculty advancement within the university. Incentives for promotion and tenure are based on research, not clinical care (Hoge, 2002; Hoge, Jacobs, Belitsky, & Migdole, 2002).

Additionally, teaching does little to support one's advancement within the university system. Frequently, those with the most clinical experience are able to "buy time," enabling them to spend more time in research than in teaching activities. In reality this may not be a bad thing, as many of the most experienced faculty are the most distant from clinical practice, current evidence-based approaches, and current state-of-the-art practices. They have been protected within the large academic institutions, which have, by and large, been insulated from the changing environment. Theory, then, becomes the basis of graduate education, taught from a perspective that often wishes to return to a less complex time of clinical practice, and certainly is not based in the reality of today's evolving clinical experience. When one is removed from clinical practice, one's approach becomes theoretical, and one may examine the literature rather than grapple with the challenges faced by many within the community-practice setting. Rarely is the academic's focus on the challenges of practice in an environment of dwindling resources where complex competing patient needs and demands are shaping approaches to practice (Hoge, 2002).

There have been some disciplines that have embraced evidence-based approaches at the time of this chapter: a simple online search for a specific discipline combined with evidence-based practice, such as "nursing" and "evidence-based practice," can demonstrate the divergence among disciplines in their adoption of evidence-based approaches; the following search result numbers, while not scientific, are interesting indicators of the amount of interest, whether positive or negative, in evidence-based practice within a variety of disciplines.

- Nursing = 11,800,000
- Psychology = 32,300,000
- Social Work = 117,000,000
- Counseling = 9,040,000
- Psychiatry = 6,380,000

While evidence-based practice and the use of guideline-based practice is not the be-all and end-all, certainly it is essential to understanding the concepts associated with improvement science, translational research, and integrated practice approaches associated with interacting with managed-care companies, and being current with best practices and outcome research, which will be a driving factor within emerging accountable care organizations as well as those involved in publicly reporting outcome data. All are essential skills to be developed for any practice in today's complex healthcare environment.

One explanation for varying interest levels in different disciplines is that training continues to occur within "silos" dedicated to each unique discipline, regardless of the long standing clinical practice approaches occurring within interdisciplinary, multi-specialty, co-located practice sites, despite growing evidence of the efficacy of team-based approaches like assertive community treatment approaches. It is not unusual to have multiple disciplines using the same text with a very similar syllabus, teaching the same topics such as group or individual therapy, DSM-IV-TR diagnostic criteria, or similar topics. The question remains, why are we not integrating disciplines at the graduate education level?

WHAT IS THE CURRENT STATUS OF PROFESSIONAL GRADUATE EDUCATION?

While healthcare has experienced a boom in growth in both technology and theory, including daily integration of best practices, checklists, and evidence-based approaches, there is considerably less discussion about the structure, process, and content of how best to educate healthcare providers within the academic arena. The process of how we educate future healthcare professionals has changed very little over the past three decades; decidedly, the application of even emerging advances in technology has been overlooked as many in the academic realm have become slaves to academic traditions and married to self-serving, narrow topics that drive research funding but actually contribute very little toward translation of evidence to application at the bedside (Hoge, 2002; Hoge et al., 2002).

All too often, educators emphasize to clinicians the need to evaluate and align care-giving processes with the strongest evidence of effectiveness, yet as this is being completed in the clinical arena, where is the ear of the research to hear the feedback provided? For the past decade, clinicians in the health and mental health fields have provided feedback indicating that certain elements of current research and the resulting evidence-base are less effective than originally believed, or impractical to apply in the field, but the feedback loop has been broken. Unfortunately, there is evidence that some academic institutions have failed to function as role models of the advice they have provided. Don't get us wrong, this is not the case with all institutions of higher learning. Many educational best practices are influencing the field within nonacademic and nontraditional settings. There are pockets of remarkable learning based in practicum and demonstration projects across the nation, working to build educational best practices derived from families, professional settings for clinical practices, professional organizations, and yes, from the failings of evidence-based findings (Hoge, 2002; Hoge et al., 2002)

HOW WIDE IS THE GAP?

When comparing the distance between current practice approaches based on healthcare reform when compared with current educational approaches, we see that there are multiple gaps in America's graduate training system, such as: Theory vs. Practice, Education vs. Practice, Training Setting vs. Practice Setting, Past Focus vs. Future Focus, Discipline-Driven vs. Interdisciplinary – the list goes on and on. This is not new – calls for medical education reform can be traced back to the early 1900s – yet what appears to be a chronic problem of not keeping current with healthcare practice is now acute and reaching epidemic proportions. The cure for this is not immediate, nor is it simple, nor is the change in process to be tied solely to the university structure (Hoge, 2002; Hoge et al., 2002).

The barriers to change are many: for example, there are competing views of illness, treatment, and recovery. Examination of the challenges and ongoing debates regarding healthcare reform make this clear. "Turf" issues exist in the form of "scope of practice"; that is to say, what is the work of one discipline may at times overlap and be at odds with other disciplines examining the same or similar areas of practice. University and discipline-specific accreditation bodies have rules and standards that frequently function as a barrier to interdisciplinary education practices. Additionally, state licensing requirements frequently erect barriers to integrated education. Last but not least, educational financing systems may be barriers to integrated educational processes. Any of the above can be a barrier to transformation in training: when they are combined, it becomes easier to understand why graduate education programs are not going to be able to "turn on a dime."

It has been suggested that areas targeted for improvement should include educating graduate students on the dynamics of healthcare systems, focusing on best practices associated with the disorders, and populations served within the health and behavioral healthcare system (Hoge, 2002). Curricula must be based on emerging evidence-based approaches within health and behavioral healthcare, so that students have an awareness of the most current approaches to challenges that will be faced within the delivery of health and behavioral health services. Thus students must be educated to translate the scientific findings into the services. One of the barriers to accomplishment of this goal is that graduate school training programs still take place, for the most part, within discipline specific academic silos. This structure leaves students unprepared for multidisciplinary practice as they enter the workforce (Hoge, 2002). Moreover, they are unlikely to appreciate the value-added benefit of collaborative practice.

THE DEMONSTRATION PROJECT

HOW DID THE PROJECT ACHIEVE ITS OBJECTIVES?

In 2008, the Ohio State University Collaborative for Interdisciplinary Behavioral Healthcare Education was established to facilitate recognition of and respond to the interdisciplinary behavioral healthcare training recommendations put forth by the New Freedom Commission Report and the Annapolis Coalition. Two measures were continued during the reporting period. The first measure was a pre- and post-seminar student assessment of competency in key areas. The second measure was interdisciplinary collaboration using the Index of Interdisciplinary Collaboration (IIC).

The Objective: Provide and measure education designed to meet recommended core competencies.

THE COLLABORATIVE FOR INTERDISCIPLINARY BEHAVIORAL HEALTHCARE EDUCATION

STRUCTURE

The Collaborative for Interdisciplinary Behavioral Healthcare Education (the Collaborative) was developed in response to the education recommendations of the Annapolis Coalition and the President's New Freedom Commission. The Collaborative is supported through funds provided by the Ohio Department of Mental Health, the Columbus Medical Association, the Ohio State University Department of Psychiatry, and in-kind support from the John Glenn Institute of Ohio State University.

Participating in the Collaborative are faculty and graduate students from the areas of primary care medicine, psychiatry, psychology, psychiatric nursing, advanced practice nursing, social work, couples and family therapy, and counseling. All share a desire to work collaboratively with colleagues in the field to improve their competency in providing consumer-driven care. The core competencies recommended by the Annapolis Coalition have been adopted as the foundation of the curricula (Hoge, 2002). Core competencies are applied both in the classroom and in what is more broadly defined as a "workforce" setting. Workforce settings, for these purposes, are defined as the locations where the various providers deliver care within the healthcare system, including members of the general and specialty medical healthcare system and human service system providers who routinely encounter mental health issues.

THE CURRICULUM AND ASSUMPTIONS

The curriculum includes weekly clinical seminars and clinical placements in both traditional and nontraditional sites (see Table 7.1). This dual focus enables participants to integrate and apply new skills based on the following core competencies outlined by the Annapolis Coalition:

- Healthcare regulation and reform
- Economics of behavioral healthcare
- Overview of managed care
- Organizational structures
- Medical necessity
- Practice standards, guidelines, pathways
- Quality management
- Integration of primary and behavioral healthcare
- Consumerism in clinical practice
- Evidence-based approaches
- Goal-focused treatment planning
- Continuum of care
- Documentation of care
- Practice models and settings
- Professional roles
- Interdisciplinary relations
- Medical/legal issues
- Clinical skill base
- Professionalism

The clinical seminars in the Collaborative are based on a set of six guiding assumptions. First, knowledge obtained in the graduate experience is likely to affect one's future practice and relationships. Currently, graduate training emphasizes that students be grounded in the perspective of a single discipline. This is a fundamental principle for the "guild" aspects of the discipline,

Table 7.1 The Curricula

Clinical Seminars Topic Overview

Summer 2005

- President's New Freedom Commission
- Hydraulics of the Healthcare and Mental Health Care System
- Evidence-Based Practice and "recovery"
- Cultural Competence – Best Practices
- Collaboration from Systems to Dyads: Relationship to Best Practice
- Trauma, treatment, and prevention
- Interprofessional ethics and challenges
- Evaluation and feedback

Fall 2005

- Challenges to and barriers in interdisciplinary practice
- Orchestrating interdisciplinary school-based mental health services
- Consumer and Family-Based Recovery Panel
- Intensive Outpatient Program Proposal
- Evaluation and feedback

Winter 2006

- System Pragmatics
- U-Concept/Process of Change
- Health Care Systems (2-part)
- Health and Mental Health Systems (2-part)
- Policy and Planning at the State Level
- Managed Care
- Mental Health Systems (agency)
- Evaluation and feedback

Spring 2006

- Legal Systems
- Mental Health and Drug Courts
- Mental Health in Corrections
- Primary Care
- Child Welfare Policy
- Evaluation and feedback

Summer 2006

Faculty and students met informally on a weekly basis over the summer to jointly plan clinical seminars and programs for the 2006–2007 academic year.

Fall 2006

Weekly coverage of the represented disciplines, including history, important dates, etiology of problem behaviors (including assessment and diagnosis), treatment of problem behaviors, education and licensure requirements, ethical considerations, third-party reimbursement, prescriptive authority, and case studies:

- Primary care
- Social work
- Psychology
- Psychiatry
- Family Nurse Practitioner (FNP)
- Psychiatric Mental Health Advanced Practice Register Nurse (PMH-APRN)

(continued)

Table 7.1 Continued

- Couple and Family Therapy
- Addictions

Winter 2007
- Community Mental Health – Public Policy (Don Wood)
- Mental Health is Essential to Overall Health (Mike Hogan)
- Schools Proposal-Demonstration wellness project
- Review of East Fifth Model and Kellogg Proposal
- Pediatric integrated model (John W. Campo, MD)
- Hydraulics of the Healthcare System (Jeff Biehl and Reed Fraley)
- Polarity Therapy/Mind-body connection (Mary Jo Ruggieri)
- Cultural Competence (Multiethnic Advocates for Cultural Competency)

such as meeting curricular standards while in school as well as the licensing and board certification requirements upon graduation. It became apparent through the Collaborative that many programs teach in the same topic areas. The difference is that each has a discipline-specific focus. For example, the curricula of nursing, social work, psychology, psychiatry, and couples and family therapy all provide classes on group therapy, all use similar course outlines, and all use the Yalom text a classic textbook for teaching group therapy methods . As a result, when students become practitioners, they can only offer a client their discipline-specific perspective, which may or may not be in the client's best interest. Hoge (2002) indicated that the usual course of treatment occurs in discipline-specific silos, without regard to the benefits integrative programming can provide. Hence the insistence in the work of the Collaborative that the clinical experience be of such a nature that the collaboration becomes integral to the experience. It is this type of experience that will produce the next generation of talent for the healthcare workforce.

The second assumption is that students and faculty learn together. In the Collaborative, we have observed that interdisciplinary behavioral education transforms theory into knowledge through experience. The faculty and staff endeavor to set the stage for lifelong learning by challenging students and each other to examine current practice within the framework of the best existing evidence, and to develop an understanding of, and appreciation for, the power of collaborative, integrative care.

The third assumption is that a systems perspective will serve as an overarching theoretical framework. Students and faculty in the Collaborative know in advance that problems are going to be examined from various perspectives. Consequently, they demonstrate great openness to feedback and are quite adaptable to the developmental chaos that sometimes presents itself within the model of interdisciplinary education. It is also thought that this provides good exposure to the kind of clinical situations they will encounter in the current practice environment.

The fourth assumption of the clinical seminars is that students should be exposed to and learn how to engage and influence persons in local, state, and national leadership positions. Offered as a student/faculty seminar, this experiential and didactically facilitated process provides a focus on common concepts and emergent themes within and among disciplines that is used to conceptualize interdisciplinary practice.

The fifth assumption frames the current reality of the practice environment by asserting that behavioral healthcare problems are not only encountered in traditional behavioral healthcare settings, but that more than 50 percent of these problems are encountered in other settings. The clinical seminars strive to help students master the skills of the core competencies in a wide range of settings, with an emphasis on vulnerable populations.

The sixth and final assumption has been stated in part above – that is, the concept that experience transforms information into knowledge. The Collaborative encourages students to recognize and embrace the concept of interdisciplinary behavioral healthcare as a catalytic, transformational concept with components that represent a major departure from traditional approaches to graduate professional training.

LESSONS LEARNED

PRACTICE SETTINGS

Over the past decade, a new paradigm in behavioral health has emerged that emphasizes issues like cost control, evidence-based practice, patient safety, access to care, treatment relevance for diverse populations, quality management, and consumerism. All are critical components of clinical care. However, these issues are process measures that are most easily captured through clinically based data-collection processes. Unfortunately, they do little to improve key elements of customer satisfaction. For example, a hospital may measure access to service by determining how high the hospital's rate of acceptance is of the clients who present for care. However, this measure does not capture the number of patients who never present for care because they do not have the means, either physical or financial, to come to hospital in the first place. In this case, a better measure might be how easy it is for patients, regardless of their circumstances, to obtain the services they need through a variety of community avenues.

In developing an interdisciplinary approach to behavioral healthcare, the Collaborative is working to establish a model by way of a pilot project within the community and working with a vulnerable population that incorporates the following elements:

1. culturally sensitive/competent;
2. trauma-informed;
3. collaborative/integrative;
4. community-based;
5. consumer driven; and,
6. are found in traditional and nontraditional treatment sites.

The experience to date suggests that traditional training sites tend to be more restrictive than nontraditional sites in terms of being able to offer an integrative care system. Figure 7.1 demonstrates this paradigm shift.

While the distinction is subtle, there are remarkable differences in practice approaches. The organizational charts of many mental health practices at traditional sites suggest that the typical program is set up, at least on paper, as a collaborative or team practice model. However, upon closer inspection, it is often found that the work of the team is less than collaborative and is simply more co-located. The determining factor of the level of collaboration in an organization

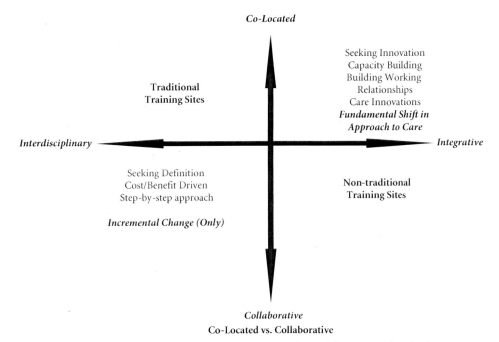

Co-Located vs. Collaborative

FIGURE 7.1 When training sites are based on co-location, traditional decision-making is the common approach. This approach includes great efforts to define problems, application of cost/benefit analysis and a systematic approach to care provision changes. When non-traditional sites are developed using an integrative collaborative process, care delivery focused on innovation, capacity building, establishing working relationships and innovative care structure. This leads, in turn, to fundamental shifts in care models.

is both the quality and the quantity of interaction between and among team members and the clients/patients. In the typical traditional program, the team meets to discuss or review the case, and from that point on, the team collaboration is minimal at best. Team members from each discipline scatter to accomplish their assigned tasks. While it is true that team members must work independently of each other, there is an opportunity for continued integrated decision-making and discussion processes to facilitate collaborative integrative care.

A similar process seems to exist in the area of multidisciplinary approaches. Staff meets initially to develop care planning. However, as time progresses, team members become focused on tasks unique to their individual disciplines, without collaborative interaction with other disciplines. It seems likely that many programs that describe themselves as providing interdisciplinary, collaborative care are in reality providing care with many disciplines that are simply co-located.

However, when developing nontraditional care sites for training, the Collaborative identified remarkable differences in approaches to program development. The nontraditional sites apply integrative and collaborative processes that seek primarily to identify and establish relationships with the population being served and to meet the greatest need. Efforts toward modification of care delivery focus on concepts of innovation, capacity building, and establishing working relationships, as well as on designing innovative care structures. This process leads to fundamental shifts in care. Team members interact with the client population based on individualized treatment needs that utilize a team approach throughout the care of the individual.

THE INTERDISCIPLINARY MODEL — "AN ACTIVE PARTNERSHIP"

The work in the development of the Collaborative has led to the awareness that collaborative, integrative care is a highly consumer-focused activity. Their experience suggests that the most successful efforts are those that include the patient as a partner in the development of their care plan, which is sometimes referred to as "the interdisciplinary model of care."

The interdisciplinary model of care takes collaboration to another level, incorporating ongoing cross-disciplinary education and regulated overlapping roles. This approach explicitly includes the patient and the family at all stages as active team members, setting it apart from other models of care (Rhee & Ruddy, 2005). In the interdisciplinary approach to healthcare, members of the team offer unconditional respect not only to their colleagues, but also to their patients for their life experiences and knowledge. Russell suggests that, especially in working with the poor and underserved, interdisciplinary care above all else is what is needed in those medically underserved communities (Russell, 2006).

This approach is also recommended by the second goal of the President's New Freedom Commission, which envisions a transformed mental health system where consumers, along with service providers, will actively participate in designing and developing the systems of care in which they are involved (President's New Freedom Commission on Mental Health, 2003, p. 7).

Also, recommendation number six of the Annapolis Coalition Conference on Behavioral Workforce Competencies states that persons with mental health problems or illnesses and substance use disorders and the families of these individuals should play a central role in building a competent workforce by having formal input both into the identification of essential competencies and into the competency assessments of individual providers, treatment teams, service organizations, and systems of care (Hoge et al, 2005). Treatment approaches are consumer-driven and focus on the needs and viewpoint of the consumer and the consumer system. Thus, the consumer is valued as an active partner, and those needs are the priority in the treatment planning process.

CULTURALLY COMPETENT CARE

Professionals must also be trained in cultural competency (Hoge et al, 2005). Both the New Freedom Commission (2003) and the Annapolis Coalition (2004) emphasize the importance of cultural competence as a practice of care givers across disciplines. The Pew Health Professions Commission reports "cultural sensitivity must be a part of the educational experiences that touches the life of every student" (Murray-Garcia & Tervalon, 1998). Furthermore, the Institute of Medicine defines *optimal primary care* in a broad sense, stating that it includes "an understanding of the cultural, nutritional, and belief systems of patients and communities that may assist or hinder effective healthcare delivery" (Murray-Garcia & Tervalon, 1998). *Cultural competence* is "a commitment and active engagement in a lifelong process that individuals enter into on an ongoing basis with patients, communities, colleagues, and with themselves" (Brown et al., 2003).

TRAUMA-INFORMED CARE

Providing trauma-informed care is also critically important to the optimal treatment of consumers. Trauma-informed services recognize the impact of violence and victimization on the person's development and coping strategies. A trauma-informed approach is one that uses an empowerment model. Within the trauma-informed framework, staff and students work with the individual and the agency to solicit consumer input and involve consumers in designing and evaluating services. The goal of trauma-informed services is to minimize the possibilities of re-traumatization (Elliot, Bjelajac, Fallot, Markoff, & Reed, 2005). It has been the experience of the Collaborative that this information is largely absent in many graduate training programs. The introduction of a trauma-informed approach has been a remarkable challenge, but it has also provided great yields in progress made by those served in the nontraditional training sites.

INTERDISCIPLINARY PROCESS

Recently, healthcare leaders and policy makers, most notable among them the Pew Health Professions Commission and the Institute of Medicine (IOM), have recommended an interdisciplinary team approach to care (IOM, 2000, 2001, 2003; PEW Health Professions Commissions, 1998). This approach, should be mastered during the years of professional education and training. In fact, recent IOM reports (2001, 2003) single out "competency to practice as part of an interdisciplinary team" as one of the five core competencies (Cashman, Reidy, Cody, & Lemay, 2004). The Institute of Medicine's vision for health professions education specifies working together across professions and schools to provide patient-centered care. Improvement in the collaborative preparation of health professionals is seen as central to achieving substantial improvement in the quality of healthcare (Mitchell et al., 2006). Through seminars and clinical work at placement sites, efforts are made to improve collaborative interactions among all disciplines, creating an environment of open and honest dialogue. The disciplines work together to develop the curriculum, which includes an exploration of the origins of the different disciplines in an effort to identify possible root causes of historic conflicts between professionals. Relationship-building between faculties from different disciplines is a critical piece of this training model in collaboration (Edwards, Patterson, Grauf-Grounds, & Groban, 2001). In order for a paradigm shift to occur toward a more collaborative approach, faculty will need to be vigorous advocates with their academic colleagues.

TIMING OF TRAINING

The model used by the Collaborative is to provide the experience before the student's entry into the workforce, thus influencing the student's approach to treatment, attitude toward interdisciplinary collaboration, and competencies. The intention is to preempt the powerful model presented by the typical workforce setting, which is more often than not a "same-old-same-old" culture. In a report of a successful collaborative model that included a psychiatrist, a family therapist, a family therapist intern, and a family practice resident,

Edwards et al. (2001) concurred that it is critical that students receive training prior to their entry into the workforce: and that residency training is a critical period for development of these skills. It is during residency that young professionals develop their skills in assessing patients' needs, and their capacity and the capacity of other professionals to meet those needs. Edwards and colleagues further suggest that those initial impressions about the skills and the value of other professions' skills can lead to lifelong attitudes of appreciation (Edwards et al., 2001).

EVIDENCE-BASED APPROACH

Clearly, it is time for the field to look in new directions for innovations and leadership to support an evidence-based approach for educational best practices (Roberts and Yeager, 2004). The Collaborative seminars and treatment sites strive to keep pace with the constantly changing demands of the workplace. All aspects of the clinical seminar and practical experience are designed to inform practice and to enhance clinical competencies as outlined by the work of the Annapolis Coalition and the President's New Freedom Commission. Educational experiences are evidence-based and designed to transform theory into practical knowledge through clinical experience. Faculty and students examine and rate applicable levels of evidence available for programming provided by the nontraditional training sites. The application of evidence-based practice is utilized to influence learning as well as to serve as future measures of outcome.

PROGRAM, STUDENT, AND FACULTY EVALUATION

While the establishment of interdisciplinary education may be regarded as an ambitious undertaking, the results of the feedback and evaluations from the first 18 months of the Collaborative are promising. As of Spring Quarter 2007, 25 students and eight faculty members had participated in the program. Both quantitative and qualitative evaluations had been conducted to determine gains made by the members of the Collaborative. In order to assess participant understanding and application of 24 identified core competencies, the Collaborative utilized a five-point rating scale based on the core competencies to determine progress toward increased knowledge. Students participating in the Collaborative demonstrated a 1.8-point improvement on a five-point scale in their understanding of identified core competencies (see Table 7.2). A randomized sample of students from traditional graduate programs remained at baseline scores.

Both faculty and students acknowledged that they now had an enhanced understanding of collaboration in the following five key areas identified as part of Bronstein's model for interdisciplinary collaboration (Bronstein, 2003): interdependence, number of newly created professional approaches/activities, flexibility, collective ownership of goals, and working relationships within and between diverse populations.

Analysis of variance was utilized to document changes in levels of interaction between interdependence, number of newly created professional approaches/activities, flexibility, collective ownership of goals, and working relationships of participants of the Collaborative study all were measured at a 95 percent level of confidence. Results were as follows:

For interdependence: $f = 3.24$;
Number of newly created professional approaches: $f = 3.04$;
Flexibility: participants demonstrated: $f = 2.32$;
In collective ownership of goals: $f = 3.14$; and,
Working relationships; $f = 2.67$.

As with the previously listed self-ratings of skill level of competency, students demonstrated significant improvement in all levels of interdisciplinary interaction.

Table 7.2 Evaluation of the Collaborative for Interdisciplinary Education

Topics	Average Level of Competency	
	Pre-Seminar	Enhancement
Health Care Regulation and Reform	2.2	4.2
Economics of Behavioral Health Care	2.4	4.4
Overview of Managed Care	2.4	4.7
Organizational Structures	2.2	4.2
Utilization Management Process	2.0	4.4
Medical Necessity	2.2	4.6
Levels of Care Criteria	2.6	4.8
Practice Standards, Guidelines, and Options	3.0	4.1
Working with Managed Care Organizations	2.6	4.2
Quality Management	2.6	4.4
Behavioral Health and Primary Medical Care	3.2	4.7
Consumerism in Clinical Practice	3.4	4.8
Historical Overview of Service Delivery	2.4	4.7
Basic Facts About Behavioral Disorders and Their Treatment	3.4	4.8
The Continuum of Care	2.4	4.3
Goal-Focused Treatment Planning	3.2	4.6
Documentation of Care	3.4	4.4
Practice Models, Settings, and Economics	2.8	3.8
Professional Roles and Interdisciplinary Relationships	3.6	4.8
Legal Issues	2.0	4.8
Ethical Issues	3.0	4.2
Clinical Skills	3.2	4.7
Clinical Management Skills	2.8	4.5
Administrative Skills	2.7	3.8
ALL TOPICS	2.7	4.5
Not Very Competent	1.0–2.4	none
Somewhat Competent	2.5–3.9	some
Very Competent	4.0–5.0	a great deal

CONCLUSION

Interdisciplinary health and behavioral healthcare education is a catalytic, transformative concept with components that represent a dramatic departure from traditional approaches to graduate professional training. The Collaborative for Interdisciplinary Behavioral Healthcare Education at the Ohio State University is not the first, nor will it be the last, to address this topic. This chapter is intended to serve as a springboard for thought in the areas of interdisciplinary education by:

1. discussing the current challenges for graduate education
2. examining the core competencies needed to prepare graduate students for the workforce
3. detailing the processes needed to work toward integrating core competencies into health and behavioral health medicine, and
4. stressing the importance of establishing nontraditional training sites for graduate students in health and behavioral health

This chapter serves only as preliminary data. However, there is clear evidence that interdisciplinary education processes, while challenging, can provide remarkable outcomes in shaping and informing practice for the future. Both students and faculty participating in the Collaborative reported remarkable growth in the area of interdisciplinary education, in both teaching and learning. Additionally, the project has served to establish a level of trust between disciplines that clearly indicates that ongoing process measures can be applied to this topic.

Barriers exist in areas such as funding streams generated by service activities. Access to grant dollars is also a tricky aspect when examined within an interdisciplinary framework. Academic revenue-generation and productivity models are currently under development and will need to be refined prior to full implementation of the interdisciplinary program within the curriculum of each college participating. Additionally, integration of interdisciplinary education into the curricula faces external barriers by the accreditation entities for each program. Research that focuses on effectiveness in the areas of teaching, learning, and economies of scale is yet to be explored at even a cursory level.

The Collaborative intends to continue to develop, apply, and demonstrate academic and service delivery models that can be replicated in nontraditional settings. It is our belief that this work will lead to advances in health and behavioral healthcare services provided to at-risk populations within an interdisciplinary training model. We think that this model has the potential to be replicated across the nation within a variety of community service organizations as well as in graduate training programs settings. It is exciting to think about the far-reaching implications or exactly what kind of social, economic, and medical progress is possible under this new paradigm.

REFERENCES

Bronstein, L. R. (2003). A model for interdisciplinary collaboration. *Social Work*, 48(3), 297–306.

Brown, D., Behringer, B., Smith, P., Townsend, T., Wachs, J., & Stanifer, L., et al. (2003). Graduate health professions education: An interdisciplinary university–community partnership model 1996–2001.

[Electronic version]. http://www.ingentaconnect.com/content/apl/cefh/2003/00000016/00000002/art00006 *Education for Health: Change in Learning & Practice*, 16(2), 176–188.

Busch, A. B., & Shore, M. F. (2000). Seclusion and restraint: A review of recent literature. *Harvard Review of Psychiatry*, 8(5), 261–270. Cashman, S., Reidy, P., Cody, K., & Lemay, C. (2004). Developing and measuring progress toward collaborative, integrated, interdisciplinary health care teams. [Electronic version]. *Journal of Interprofessional Care*, 18(2), 183–196. www.ncbi.nlm.nih.gov/pubmed/15203676

Commonwealth Fund Resources on Accountable Care Organizations, The Commonwealth Fund, December 2011. Downloaded December 14, 2011, from http://www.commonwealthfund.org/Publications/Other/2011/Accountable-Care-Organizations.aspx.

Edwards, Todd M., Patterson, J. E., Grauf-Grounds, C., & Groban, S. (2001). Psychiatry, MFT, and family medicine collaboration: The Sharp behavioral health *clinic. Families, Systems, and Health,* 19(1), 25–35.

Elliot, D. E., Bjelajac, P., Fallot, R. D., Markoff, L. S., Reed, B. G. (2005). Trauma-informed or trauma-denied: Principles and implementation of trauma-informed services for women. *Journal of Community Psychology*, 33(4), 461–477.

Hoge, M. A. (2002) The training gap: An acute crisis in behavioral health education. Administration and Policy in Mental Health, 29(4/5), 305–317.

Hoge, M. A., Jacobs, S., Belitsky, R., & Migdole, S. (2002). Graduate education and training for contemporary behavioral health practice. *Administration and Policy in Mental Health*, 29, 4–5.

Hoge, M. A., Morris, J. A., Daniels, A. S., Huey, L. Y., Stuart, G. W., & Adams, N., et al. (2005). Report of recommendations: The Annapolis Coalition Conference on Behavioral Health Work Force Competencies. [Electronic version]. *Administration & Policy in Mental Health*, 32(5–6), 651–663.

Institute of Medicine. (2001). *Crossing the Quality Chasm: A New Health System for the 21st Century* (pp. 130–133). Washington, DC: National Academy Press.

Institute of Medicine. (2003). *Health Professions Educations: A Bridge to Quality*. Washington, DC: National Academy press.

Kohn, L. T., Corrigan, J., & Donaldson, M. S. (2000). *To Err Is Human: Building a Safer Health System*. Washington, DC: National Academy Press.

Mitchell, P. H., Belza, B., Schaad, D. C., Robins, L. S., Gianola, F., & Odegard, P. S., et al. (2006). Working across the boundaries of health professions disciplines in education, research, and service: The University of Washington experience. [Electronic version]. *Academic Medicine*, 81(10), 891–896. www.ncbi.nlm.nih.gov/pmc/articles/PMC2720359

Murray-Garcia, J., & Tervalon, M. (1998). Cultural humility versus cultural competence: A critical distinction in defining physician training outcomes in multicultural education. *Journal of Health Care for the Poor & Underserved*, 9(2), 117–125.

New Freedom Commission on Mental Health. (2003). *Achieving the Promise: Transforming Mental Health Care in America. Final Report*. DHHS pub no SMA-03 – 3832. Rockville MD: Department of Health and Human Services.

Pew Health Profession Commission. *Recreating Health Professional Practice for a New Century*. San Francisco, Calif, USA: Pew Health Professions Commission; 1998

Proctor, E. K., & Rosen, A. (2004). Concise standards for developing evidence-based practice guidelines. In A. R. Roberts & K. Yeager (Eds.) (2004). *Evidence-based practice manual: Research and outcome measures in health and human services* (pp. 193–199). New York: Oxford University Press.

Rhee, K., Ruddy, G., (2005). Transdisciplinary teams in primary care for the underserved: A literature review. [Electronic version]. *Journal of Health Care for the Poor & Underserved*, 16(2), pp. 248–256. www.ncbi.nlm.nih.gov/pubmed/15937389

Rees, A. M., & Young, B. A. (1981). *The Consumer Health Information Source Book*. New York: R.R. Bowker Co.

Roberts, A. R., & Yeager, K. R. (Eds.). (2004). *Evidence-based practice manual: Research and outcome measures in health and human services.* Oxford; New York: Oxford University Press.

Russell, L. D. (2006). Revolutionizing the training of clinicians for the poor and underserved. [Electronic version]. *Journal of Health Care for the Poor & Underserved, 17*(1), 6–11. academic.research.microsoft.com/Author/46261256/latonya-d-russell

Sackett, D. L., Richardson, W. S., Rosenberg, W., & Haynes, R. B. (1997). *Evidence-based medicine: How to practice & teach EBM.* New York: Churchill-Livingstone.

SECTION II

CORE COMPETENCIES

Preparation for Public and Community Work

RECOVERY AND RESILIENCY

Transitioning from the Hospital to the Community

JEFFERY L. RAMIREZ, ELAINE ALBERTI, CAROL KOTTWITZ, AND KAMAL FLOURA

CASE STUDY

Lori is a 35-year-old female with a history of bipolar affective disorder with psychotic features and an Axis II disorder of mixed personality disorder (histrionic and narcissistic with antisocial traits). She has been married twice, the first marriage ending when her husband died in a highly publicized car accident. She met and married her second husband within a year of her first husband's death. She has two sons. She was originally hospitalized when she was 28 years old. She had attempted to leave her second husband due to his "explosive" anger problems. She took her sons and went to stay with her mother, who lived in a different city. She claimed that her husband followed her and "snatched" the sons. She was found wandering the streets, distraught, paranoid, and delusional. When the police were called, they stated that she was uncooperative and belligerent. She was civilly committed to the state hospital. Lori's main course of treatment in the hospital was medication, which was dictated by the psychiatrist. Milieu therapy was loosely structured, and there was minimal group and individual treatment offered. Lori was discharged back to the community within three weeks.

Lori was hospitalized five times over four years. Once discharged into the community, she would become noncompliant with taking her medication and refuse to meet with her outpatient Program of Assertive Community Treatment (PACT) team. She would quickly decompensate and become labile, grandiose, and delusional, resulting in hospitalization.

Prior to her last hospitalization, a treatment mall model was implemented in a vacant building at the hospital. She was evaluated by her treatment team and assigned to groups at the Treatment Mall. For several months, Ms. L refused to leave the ward to attend the Treatment Mall. On her ward she was anxious, labile, and easily angered. When redirected by staff, she would become hostile, belligerent, and verbally abusive. Several medications and combinations of medications were tried, with minimal success.

Five months into this hospitalization, a new treatment mall program was developed. This program was developed for acute patients with problems of emotional dysregulation, cognitive impairment, and/or behavioral issues that were a safety risk. The group size is smaller, which lowers the environmental stimulus, allows for cognitive differences, and allows staff to give more assistance or make allowances when patients' symptoms of their mental illness interfere with attending to group material or completing tasks. The foundation of the program is to provide a safe, nurturing environment that promotes recovery at each patient's level. This program runs Monday through Friday from 9:00 a.m. to 2:00 p.m. All patients are expected to attend their mall programming.

Lori's treatment team arranged meetings with the hospital's clinical pharmacist, the unit clinical director, and the Treatment Mall manager. Her medications were changed, and she was transferred from the main Treatment Mall program to the Connections/Preparations program. Her groups were low-stimulus and focused on mindfulness and emotional regulation. She developed a positive relationship with one of the group leaders and was assigned to more groups. As Lori was able to demonstrate her ability to concentrate on group tasks and manage her anxiety and anger, process and psychoeducational groups were gradually added to her schedule. These groups included: Women's Process Group, Medication Education, Depression and Anxiety Management, Journaling, and Community Toolbox (a discharge-readiness group). Lori started talking about the trauma she experienced regarding the death of her first husband and her relationship with her ex-husband. After being hospitalized for seven months, Ms. L and her treatment team met with her PACT team, and a discharge plan was developed. She was discharged back into the community to live with her family.

INTRODUCTION

The purpose of this chapter is to provide an historical overview of changes in mental health hospitals by moving from the asylum era to a recovery-oriented environment. Mental health hospitals must have structured systems in place to assist the patients in obtaining the skills needed to begin their own recovery journey through personal empowerment, resilience, and transitioning from the hospital to the community.

There have been several attempts to reform the system that have not been in the best interests of the patients. In this chapter, the term *patient* will be used in the context of referring to people who are receiving inpatient care, and the term *consumer* will be used when referring to people receiving treatment outside of the hospital.

It will take several system changes to improve the delivery of mental health services. Both hospitals and communities must work together with a shared vision focusing on the needs of the patient and how the system can support them in the journey of recovery. In addition, it is essential for teams made up of several different disciplines to work together in a collaborative fashion and truly become interprofessional.

HISTORICAL OVERVIEW OF THE MENTAL HEALTH SYSTEM

Attempts to reform the care and treatment of people with mental illness date back to the 1800s. Many of these attempts had good intentions, but the impact on the consumers of mental health services was sometimes disastrous and continues to challenge the mental health system.

The first asylums were created in the 1800s during the "moral treatment" era (Linhorst, 2006). Moral treatment was considered the best approach to help people develop internal controls so they could learn to self-regulate their illness. The hospital staff focused on providing structured daily living environments, providing a kind, and gentle approach instead of the punishment and coercion that were often used in other settings such as jails (Linhorst, 2006).

The asylums quickly became overcrowded with patients and had untrained and unprofessional staff caring for this population with very complex needs. There were reports of horrible abuse and the use of unconventional treatments such as mechanical restraints. These asylums quickly became places to house the mentally ill and provide custodial care. "Custodial care" is a model of treatment that only meets the basic needs of the patient for survival, and no other rehabilitative treatment is delivered (Linhorst, 2006; Geller, 2000).

Dorothea Dix was a women who came from a wealthy and educated family. Her goal in life was to be a schoolteacher. Later in her career, she taught women inmates in a local jail and was appalled at the living conditions. She went to several states and toured various jails, private asylums, and almshouses, and found deplorable conditions (Linhorst, 2006). She became an activist for people with mental illness. Her political achievements eventually involved the care and treatment of people with mental illness, and she worked on legislative bills to transform the mental health system (Linhorst, 2006). Dix argued that the federal government should be responsible and care for this population but President Franklin Pierce vetoed the bill she proposed in 1854 (Linhorst, 2006).

Psychiatry was a specialty in medicine that was not well respected and had to fight to be accepted as a specialty in medicine (Linhorst, 2006). The medical community, utilizing the medical model, tried to cure the mental illnesses. There continued to be all kinds of experimental cures such as frontal lobe lobotomy. There were some psychiatrists who believed people with mental illness could recover and improve the quality of their lives.

From 1900 to the 1950s, there was tremendous growth in the state hospitals. According to Geller (2000), there were 322 state and county hospitals serving people with mental illness, and 512,501 patients at the end of the year 1950. There continued to be reports of overcrowding, underfunding, and disgusting living environments. One of the most impactful changes in mental health treatment took place in 1963, when President John F. Kennedy called on Congress to reform the mental health system by "dehospitalizing" patients (Geller, 2000). The goal of this Act was to respond to the deplorable conditions of state hospitals and to provide services in the community. However, the number of hospitals was reduced to 232 and fewer than 60,000 beds for people with chronic mental illness. The deinstitutionalization of people with psychiatric disabilities occurred over 30 years ago, and treatment in the community has to cope with a new set of challenges in order to meet the needs of this population. The communities do not have the resources to care for the number of people with chronic mental illness, and these people are now filling the streets as homeless individuals or ending up in jail or prison. Due to these consequences, the consumers became intolerant of the limited treatment options and began to become more vocal, active, and demanding of better conditions and treatment. This was the beginning of the self-advocacy and consumer survivor movement. The consumer movement was actually initiated early in 1900, by Clifford Beers, who was a patient in a state hospital and was so dissatisfied with the care and treatment in the hospital that he started the National Committee on Mental Hygiene, which is now known as the National Mental Health Association (Pratt, Gill, Barrett, & Roberts, 2007).

CONSUMER SURVIVOR MOVEMENT

The civil rights movement in the 1960s was a time that helped mental health consumers reflect on how they were treated and drew more consumers together so they could organize. The civil rights movement stimulated all disadvantaged populations to seek equality and justice for all. Consumers became empowered and wanted the same rights as their fellow human beings and citizens of the United States (Linhorst, 2006; Pratt et al., 2007). This was also the time when several thousand patients were being released to the communities that were ill equipped to meet their needs. Patients who were already traumatized from the abuse in state hospitals did not receive any better treatment from the communities. In the community they were over medicated, stigmatized, labeled by their diagnosis, and had limited services available for their very complex mental health needs (Linhorst, 2006; Pratt et al., 2007).

The pivotal moment for consumers came when the National Institute of Mental Health (NIMH) requested that consumers speak at their conference about the services they needed in the community after being discharged from a hospital (Pratt, et al., 2007). During the 1980s, more consumers began to share their stories and speak out about the failures in the mental health system. One of the activists and consumers at this time was Judi Chamberlin, who was the author of a book titled *On Our Own*. In addition, consumers were attending national conferences as speakers and getting the attention of the legislature (Pratt, et al., 2007). Another attempt to transform the mental health system soon followed in the 1990s, known as the "recovery movement."

RECOVERY MOVEMENT

In 2001, President George W. Bush released his strategic plan to promote access to educational and employment opportunities for people with disabilities. President Bush appointed a committee to research, study, and identify the service gaps to make recommendations to improve the mental health system. The President released this pivotal report titled *Achieving the Promise: Transforming Mental Health Care in America* (2003). The goal of The President's New Freedom Commission on Mental Health (2003) was to transform the mental health system and integrate recovery into every aspect of the plan. This would ensure that people with mental illness would be able to achieve in-community living and have easy access to current treatments.

In addition, the commission's report pointed out that in order for the system to be transformed, the mental health system must address the issue of stigma. The commission defined *stigma* as follows:

> [Stigma] refers to a cluster of negative attitudes and beliefs that motivate the general public to fear, reject, avoid and discriminate against people with mental illness. Stigma is widespread in the United States and other Western nations. Stigma leads others to avoid living, socializing or working with, renting to, or employing people with mental disorders—especially severe disorders such as schizophrenia. It leads to low self-esteem, isolation, and hopelessness. It deters the pubic from seeking and wanting to pay for care. Responding to stigma, people with mental health problems internalize public attitudes and become so embarrassed or ashamed that they often conceal symptoms and fail to seek treatment (New Freedom Commission on Mental Health, 2003).

The recovery movement has been discussed and debated in the literature for the last two decades (Ranz & Mancini, 2008; Ralph, 2000).The concept of recovery continues to be ambiguous and without a clear definition to most mental health professionals (Davidson, O'Connell, Tondora, Styron, & Kangas, 2006). Transforming the mental health system using the recovery concept has made an impact on shifting the paradigm of the professionals from using the top-down, medical model to empowering the consumer and collaborating with them in their recovery process. The recovery movement is making an impact on the practice of psychiatry because it involves the patient in shared decisions and respects their rights. In addition, recovery is seen as a self-care and self-determination framework so that the consumer/patient is the one driving the treatment (Fardella, 2008).

Patricia Deegan, a psychologist and a mental health activist, continues to conceptualize recovery for the professionals in the mental health system. Dr. Deegan was diagnosed with schizophrenia during her teen years. She required hospitalization at times and felt the system was dehumanizing, stigmatizing, and instilling dependency and hopelessness in the consumers. Dr. Deegan realized that people with psychiatric disabilities were capable of achieving life goals, but the barriers in the system had low expectations and used well-meaning but coercive interventions that prevented people from achieving recovery (Pratt et al. 2007). Dr. Deegan argues that just because a person has a mental illness, this does not mean they cannot live a full and rich life.

Recovery has many different definitions. Dr. Deegan defines *recovery* thus:

> Recovery is a process, a way of life, an attitude, and a way of approaching the day's challenges. It is not a perfectly linear process. At times our course is erratic and we falter, slide back, and regroup and start again. The need is to meet the challenge of the disability and to reestablish a new and valued sense of integrity and purpose within and beyond the limits of the disability; the aspiration is to live, work and love in a community in which one makes significant contributions (Ralph, 2000).

Mental health communities and hospitals struggle with the implementation of strategies in the President's New Freedom Commission on Mental Health (2003). One of the ways to transition a person from the hospital to the community is by using a psychosocial rehabilitation framework to guide the care and treatment of the person. This approach can begin in the hospital and continue in the community until the person is able to fully recover.

Hospital staff must provide the foundation to begin the recovery process at the point of admission. This may be the first time that the person has been exposed to recovery concepts and therefore, begins the recovery journey. The goal during this hospitalization is to reconnect in relationships to other people: someone needs to believe in the person, engage the person in such a way that their symptoms are minimized, and instill hope. In essence, the hospital staff need to find the person inside the illness and treat them with respect and compassion. This will allow the person to adapt to their symptoms and set out on the path to recovery.

THE DEPARTMENT OF JUSTICE AND THE MENTAL HEALTH SYSTEM

In recent years, the Department of Justice (DOJ) has brought legal action against a number of state psychiatric facilities under the Civil Rights of Institutionalized Persons Act (CRIPA). They have forced transformation on systems that were not progressing in this direction adequately of their own accord. DOJ indicated that "The State must also provide persons committed to psychiatric hospitals for an indefinite term with mental health treatment that gives them a realistic opportunity to be cured and released" (*DOJ vs. Napa*, 2008). DOJ lawsuits have also noted that "residents of state-operated facilities have a right to live in reasonable safety and to receive adequate health care, along with habilitation to ensure their safety and freedom from unreasonable restraint, prevent regression, and facilitate their ability to exercise their liberty interests" (*DOJ vs. North Carolina*; March, 2004). The state is further obliged to provide services in the most integrated setting appropriate to individuals' needs (See *Olmstead vs. L.C.*, 527 U.S. 58, 1999).

Recovery is cited in *Achieving the Promise: Transforming Mental Health Care in America, Federal Action Agenda: First Steps* as the "single most important goal" for the mental health service delivery system. Recovery is variously described by a number of concepts, but has been boiled down to three components: Each patient must be assisted in (a) finding his/her own individual pathway to hope, (b) taking personal responsibility for illness management and wellness, and (c) "getting on with life" beyond his/her illness.

Unfortunately, current state systems are not designed to maximize recovery. Recovery embodies the concept that people with mental disorders are in charge of their own health and well-being. Historically, hospitals of all sorts place responsibility for treatment on the shoulders of doctors, nurses, professional treatment teams, and hospital administrators. Transformation requires that patients and hospital staff work together, but emphasizes that patients must feel they have a stake in their own recovery process and know that their voices will be heard. When people with mental illnesses do not receive treatment, or when they receive expensive or ineffective treatment that does not promote recovery, they frequently suffer from physical health problems as well as a variety of other deleterious effects, including failure in school, separation from family and friends, unemployment, homelessness, incarceration, premature death, and suicide. On the other hand, when recovery programs are successfully implemented, they can be very cost-effective.

INTERPROFESSIONAL TEAM COLLABORATION

The importance of highly functioning interprofessional or interdisciplinary teams has gained substantial attention over the past ten years. *Interprofessional practice* is defined as working with individuals of other professions to maintain a climate of mutual respect and shared values. The Institute of Medicine (IOM) highlighted the importance of team-based care in its 2001 report, *Crossing the Quality Chasm: A New Health System for the Twenty-first Century*. At about the same time, the Agency for Healthcare Research and Quality and the Department of Defense formed a partnership focusing on a patient-safety initiative aimed at improving teamwork in healthcare settings. Since that time, healthcare literature reflects the positive patient outcomes from improving interdisciplinary collaboration. The study of interdisciplinary team collaboration in palliative care, oncology, geriatrics, inpatient intensive care units, and inpatient orthopedic units all support improved responses to complex patient needs.

The elements and dynamics of interprofessional collaboration have also been studied, culminating in a report by the Interprofessional Education Collaborative Expert Panel in 2011. The panel identified four interprofessional competency domains, each containing a set of more specific competency statements.

Domain 1: Values/ethics for interprofessional practice
Statement: Work with other professions to maintain a climate of mutual respect and shared values.
Domain 2: Roles/responsibilities
Statement: Use the knowledge of one's own role and those of other professions to appropriately assess and address the healthcare needs of the patients and populations served.
Domain 3: Interprofessional communication
Statement: Communicate with patients, families, communities, and other health professionals in a responsive and responsible manner that supports a team approach to the maintenance of health and the treatment of disease.
Domain 4: Teams and teamwork
Statement: Apply relationship-building values and the principles of team dynamics to perform effectively in different team roles to plan and deliver patient/population-centered care that is safe, timely, efficient, effective, and equitable.

So what would interprofessional team collaboration look like in a psychiatric setting where rehabilitation and recovery principles guide the care? Core team members typically consist of the psychiatrist, registered nurse, social worker, and a representative from rehabilitation services (occupational therapist, recreational therapist, activities therapist) and the patient. Each team member, keeping the patient's goals at the center, would work toward assisting the patient with stabilization of symptoms, learning or relearning skills to achieve discharge, reintegration into the community, and improved quality of life. The team would come together, with their individual discipline assessments, to put together an interdisciplinary formulation. This interdisciplinary clinical formulation documents how the team makes sense of who the patient is, where they are in their life now, and where they want to be (McLoughlin & Geller, 2010). This process transcends a typical disciplinary approach to reach a broader understanding of the person and their needs. This requires team members to work across disciplinary boundaries, to be open to different perspectives, to be willing to engage in the effort to collaborate with others with meeting the patient's needs as the common value. It also requires being able to articulate one's own role and expertise in relation to the team and to understand and navigate issues around hierarchies, group processes, and power dynamics (Young et al., 2011).

With the patient's goals at the center, nursing and social work professionals may offer a group to build skills around illness and self-management, recreational therapists may offer budgeting and money management, the psychologist may provide individual therapy, the psychiatrist and pharmacist may provide group education about medications, and nurses provide education on nutrition and healthily living. All treatment, regardless of modality or discipline, is offered keeping the elements of recovery and the principles of psychosocial rehabilitation as a framework.

PSYCHOSOCIAL REHABILITATION

Promoting recovery is a process that can begin in the hospital and must continue in the community. The key to recovery is the management and control of symptoms to allow the person to function in meaningful activities such as school, work, hobbies, and any other activity that brings fulfillment to the person. A person with a serious mental illness can recover even though the illness is not "cured" (Anthony, 1993). Psychosocial rehabilitation is sometimes referred to as "psychiatric rehabilitation," a strategy assisting the person to attain optimal functioning in everyday living. The level of functioning a person achieves is based on the individual's skills, abilities, and competencies he has or is able to achieve (Pratt, 2007; Anthony et al. 2002).

There have been various definitions of psychosocial rehabilitation (PSR). As PSR began to gain more creditability in the 1990s, the International Association of Psychosocial Rehabilitation Services (IAPSRS) provided the following definition:

> *The goal of psychiatric rehabilitation is to enable individuals to compensate for, or eliminate the functional deficits. Interpersonal barriers and environmental barriers created by the disability, and to restore ability for independent living, socialization and effective life management (in Pratt, 2007).*

The PSR principles are aligned with recovery and make it a logical strategy to use for people who are suffering from serious persistent mental illness. PSR provides the support and framework to guide both providers and consumers of mental health treatment. The National Consensus Statement on Mental Health Recovery (Substance Abuse and Mental Health Services Administration, 2004) published the definitions and fundamental elements of recovery. Recovery should be:

- Self-directed—Consumers lead, control, exercise choice over, and determine their own path of recovery by optimizing autonomy, independence, and control of resources to achieve a self-determined life. By definition, the recovery process must be self-directed by the individual, who defines his or her own life goals and designs a unique path toward those goal.
- Individualized and person-centered—There are multiple pathways to recovery based on an individual's unique strengths and resiliencies as well as his or her needs, preferences, experiences (including past trauma), and cultural background in all of its diverse representations. Individuals also identify recovery as being an ongoing journey and an end result as well as an overall paradigm for achieving wellness and optimal mental health.
- Empowering—Consumers have the authority to choose from a range of options and to participate in all decisions—including the allocation of resources—that will affect their lives, and are educated and supported in so doing. They have the ability to join with other

consumers to collectively and effectively speak for themselves about their needs, wants, desires, and aspirations. Through empowerment, an individual gains control of his or her own destiny and influences the organizational and societal structures in his or her life.

- Holistic—Recovery encompasses an individual's whole life, including mind, body, spirit, and community. Recovery embraces all aspects of life, including housing, employment, education, mental health and healthcare treatment and services, complementary and naturalistic services, addictions treatment, spirituality, creativity, social networks, community participation and family support as determined by the person. Families, providers, organizations, systems, community, and society play crucial roles in creating and maintaining meaningful opportunities for consumer's access to these supports.

- Non-linear—Recovery is not a step-by-step process but one based on continual growth, occasional setbacks, and learning from experience. Recovery begins with an initial stage of awareness in which a person recognizes that positive change is possible. This awareness enables the consumer to move on to fully engage in the work of recovery.

- Strength-based—Recovery focuses on valuing and building on the multiple capacities, resiliencies, talents, coping, abilities, and inherent worth of individuals. By building on these strengths, consumers leave stymied life roles behind and engage in new life roles (e.g., partner, caregiver, friend, student, employee). The process of recovery moves forward through interaction with others in supportive, trust-based relationships.

- Peer supported—Mutual support, including the sharing of experiential knowledge and skills and social learning, plays an invaluable role in recovery. Consumers encourage and engage other consumers in recovery and provide each other with a sense of belonging, supportive relationships, valued roles, and community.

- Respectful—Community, systems, and societal acceptance and appreciation of consumers, including protecting their rights and eliminating discrimination and stigma, are crucial in achieving recovery. Self-acceptance and regaining belief in one's self are particularly vital. Respect ensures the inclusion and full participation of consumers in all aspects of their lives.

- Responsible—Consumers have a personal responsibility for their own self-care and journeys of recovery. Taking steps toward their goals may require great courage. Consumers must strive to understand and give meaning to their experience and identify coping strategies and health processes to promote their own wellness.

- Hopeful—Recovery provides the essential and motivating message of a better future, that people can and do overcome the barriers and obstacles that confront them. Hope is internalized; but can be fostered by peers, families, friends, providers, and others. Hope is the catalyst of the recovery process.

THE IAPSRS GOALS, VALUES AND GUIDING PRINCIPLES OF PSR

GOALS

- Recovery
- Community integration
- Quality of life

VALUES

- Self-determination
- Dignity and worth of every individual
- Optimism
- Capacity of every individual to learn and grow
- Cultural sensitivity

GUIDING PRINCIPLES

- Individualization of all services
- Maximum client involvement, preference, and choice
- Partnership between services provider and service recipient
- Normalized and community-based services
- Strengths focus
- Ongoing, accessible, coordinated services
- Skills training
- Partnership with family

(Pratt et al., 2007)

Empowerment is an essential strategy for consumers to be more involved in the decisions of their care and treatment. Empowerment is shifting the power from the longstanding medical model to a recovery model of care allowing for more shared decision-making and building on the strengths of the person. In the past, the patient was given instructions on how they should live their life and allow others to make all the decisions for them, promoting a more dependant relationship instead of independence and autonomy (Caldwell, Sclafani, Swarbrick, & Piren, 2010).

State hospitals have been challenged to develop a new structure to promote recovery. One of these structures is the treatment mall. Treatment malls are places that offer a variety of experiences for the patients to achieve their recovery goals.

The treatment mall is a place for patients to attend psychosocial rehabilitation (PSR) programming that is away from their living environments (Whitley, Strickler, & Drake, 2011; Longo, Marsh-Williams, & Tate, 2002; McLoughlin, Webb, Myers, Skinner, & Adams, 2010; Ballard, 2008). A treatment mall can be in any location, but the ideal is a physical entity set up to offer a variety of services and resources (Whitley et al., 2011). Services that are being offered must be driven by the consumers' needs and create an environment that is conducive to learning and demonstrating skills for daily living, cognitive therapies, substance abuse counseling, building socialization skills, and peer-run groups (Whitley et al., 2011). The field of PSR is not owned by any one discipline. In fact, implementing a PSR program through a treatment mall will take an interdisciplinary approach and cooperation in order to implement a quality program (Pratt et al., 2007).

Developing a treatment mall involves every department and employee of the hospital and the willingness of the teams to work in an interdisciplinary manner. In order for the mall to be successful, the hospital staff must be vested in making the changes, because it will have an impact on the routine of care. For example, the professional staff may need to change their schedule to accommodate the patients' group schedule. Food services and housekeeping schedules may need to change to support the staff and patients' being at the mall. The success of implementing a treatment mall depends on all the disciplines' embracing the concept of the mall and believing in recovery, and the patient's ability to achieve their recovery goals (McLoughlin et al., 2010).

BUILDING A COMMUNITY WITHIN A HOSPITAL: A STATE HOSPITAL'S EXPERIENCE

A state hospital located in the western region of the United States had a survey by the Centers for Medicare and Medicaid Services (CMS). They were cited for not providing active treatment to the patients. This stimulated many changes in the hospital and required interdisciplinary work. The hospital serves adults and has three units that serve three different populations: adult civil patients, forensic criminal committed patients, and geropsychiatric, which includes both civil and criminally committed adults, older adults, and patients with a dual diagnosis of developmentally disabled and mental illness. The Adult Unit had four wards, with three wards having a capacity of 30 patients each, and one ward with 25 beds; Forensic had three wards, two of which could house 30 patients each, and one ward with 38 patients; Geropsychiatric had four wards, with the capacity of 30 beds on each ward; and the Dual Diagnosis ward had 10 beds.

The administration appointed a clinical nurse specialist (CNS) to chair the committee consisting of 11 program directors to implement active treatment throughout the hospital. This goal was to start a treatment mall that would provide centralized treatment.

The committee determined that the hospital was functioning as three separate units, and in some cases as separate wards. There was a program director for each ward, a ward management team, a unit management team, a unit programming team, a hospital programming team, and a hospital management team. Each team had some power to make independent decisions. The teams had many barriers and their decisions were frequently blocked. These decisions were blocked because the administration and key leaders had a poor understanding of recovery and did not have a vision to fully implement a recovery oriented system.

The CNS worked with the program directors, and the first step in the process of creating a treatment mall was to eliminate all the layers of decision makers by creating a Treatment Mall Steering Committee. This caused a lot of uncertainty among the ward and unit staff because the steering committee would be making decisions that would impact their work. The hospital administration was the most difficult barrier because they would have to delegate their power to the committee. Eventually the committee had complete authority and was making independent decisions. The key to the program's success was communicating to the staff and patients every step of the way and involving as many stakeholders as possible.

A recovery-based psychosocial rehabilitation treatment mall concept came to fruition in 2007. The initial program was developed specifically for the Adult Psychiatric and Forensic Services units. The units were combined into one mall. The goal was to offer programming to the patients off of their wards that resembled a college atmosphere. Similar to the college curriculum framework, the Mall offered numerous groups four hours a day, Monday through Friday.

All staff from every discipline provided the leisure, vocational, psycho-educational and process-oriented groups (Table 8.1). Each of the patients would meet with their interdisciplinary

Table 8.1 Curriculum Topics with Sample Groups Offered at the Treatment Mall

Topics	Sample Groups
Processing Groups	Managing Life's Losses; Coping with Anger; It's a Meaningful Life; Men's Issues; Women's Process Group; Finding Meaning Through Photography; Searching for Meaning
Psycho-Educational	Creating a Recovery Culture; Medication Education; Get Out, Stay Out; Symptom Management; Self Esteem; Diabetes & Metabolic Syndrome Education; FAQ; Recovery 101; WRAP; Domestic Violence Group for Men
Substance Abuse/Use	Substance Abuse; Your Brain on Drugs; Advanced Substance Abuse Studies; Alcoholics Anonymous; Narcotics Anonymous
Secondary Education	General Education Diploma Readiness
Expressive/Creativity	Arts & Crafts; Coping Through Creative Projects; Quilting; Sewing; Journaling; Learn to Play the Bass Guitar; Scrapbooking; Comedy Improv
Leisure Skills	Social Skills/Table Games; Conversation Through Sports; Art Appreciation
Physical Activity	Circuit Training; Stretch & Tone; Walking for Fitness; Gym Sports; Tai Chi
Emotional Regulation	Mindfulness; Current Events; Community Meeting: Chat Group with Staff; Reminiscing
Occupational Therapy (OT)	Horticulture Work Group; It Makes Sense; OT Sensory Task Group; Employment Resources; Meal Planning
Relaxation	Coping Through Quiet Time

treatment team to determine the individual treatment needs and select groups that would help the patient meet their treatment objectives. A personalized schedule would be generated for every patient (Table 8.2). The goal of the program was to help patients utilize their strengths and develop new skills that they would need to overcome discharge barriers and be prepared to live successfully in the community.

The programs offered at the Treatment Mall are changed on a quarterly schedule. These offering are driven by the patients' needs and focus on skill-building, healing from trauma, coping skills, wellness recovery action planning (WRAP), mental health first aid, medication and psychoeducation, illness management, and recovery. The recovery programs focus on stigma because this is key—patients must develop strategies to overcome the stigma they face in order to achieve positive health outcomes and recovery.

There were several barriers to overcome during the implementation of the Treatment Mall. One of the major barriers was the staff's perception of the patients. The staff took ownership of the patients on the ward that they worked in. Their fear was working with patients from other wards and not knowing their histories. The paradigm shift from treating "my patients" to treating "our patients" continues to be a challenge.

Table 8.2 Sample of an individualized patient schedule

	Monday	Tuesday	Wednesday	Thursday	Friday
9:00	Community Meeting	Horticulture Work Group	Creating a Recovery Culture	Horticulture Work Group	Walking for Fitness
10:00	Expressive Arts & Crafts	Get Out, Stay Out	Your Brain On Drugs	Get Out, Stay Out	Sewing
11:00	Movies and the Challenge of Change	Current Events	Movies and the Challenge of Change	Library	Men's Process Group
1:00	Circuit Training	Diabetes & Metabolic Syndrome Education	Symptom Management	Gym Sports	Community Meeting

Staff resisted mixing the patients from the different wards or units at the Mall, although the patients frequently were together during mealtimes and special events. There was an overall feeling that the forensic patients would cross boundaries or take advantage of the more vulnerable patients from the Adult Unit. After several training sessions, airing the staff's concerns and discussions, this perception dissipated. In actuality, the forensic patients, who were more stable, helped the Adult Unit patients in many ways. The stability of the forensic patients helped to give the Adult Unit patients hope that they, too, could be stabilized. Assisting the Adult Unit patients helped the forensic patients feel needed and gave them a sense of contributing to the community.

THE PARALYZING EFFECTS OF STIGMA

The Institute of Medicine report *Improving the Quality of Health Care for Mental and Substance-Use Conditions* (2006) states:

> Residual stigma, discrimination, and the multiple types of coercion that sometimes bring individuals with mental and/or substance-use illness into treatment have substantial implications for their ability to receive care that is respectful of and responsive to their individual preferences, needs, and values is what the "Quality Chasm" report refers to as patient-centered care.

The report further explains that people with mental illness are treated in dehumanizing ways due to the stigma that they are not responsible enough to make their own decisions and are more violent than the general population. If people understood the biological aspects of mental illness and understood the humanity we all share, they might be treated in a much different way.

Both inpatient and outpatient treatments must focus on helping individuals understand stigma and the consequences of this for their lives. People who are hospitalized must receive structured programming that begins to work on self-esteem and then is continued and carried out further in the community. Having a strong sense of self will lead to recovery and better medication compliance, but the person must believe in herself or himself. People suffering from chronic mental illness must understand the relationship between stigma, self-esteem, self-efficacy, and recovery. All treatment programs should have anti-stigma groups built into the curricula to help patients and consumers gain an understanding of this concept so they can develop strategies to adapt and conquer stigma.

Stigma not only influences how others perceive people with mental illness but it also influences how patients perceive themselves. Link and Phelan (2001) concluded that there is a positive correlation between suffering from a mental illness and experiencing a lower self-esteem. In addition, people with mental illness have fewer relationships and tend to isolate from others, and this leads to loneliness and the risk of relapse.

Structuring programs around self-efficacy is needed to help patients understand that they have the ability to recover. *Self-efficacy* refers to a person's belief that they are able to achieve their goals (IOM, 2006). Instilling hope in the people receiving treatment is essential so they can build the confidence that recovery is possible.

In order to assist patients in their recovery process, hospitals must develop and implement curricula that teach people about illness-management and recovery. The focus of these programs teaches people about self-management, the day-to-day task an individual must carry out to live successfully with a chronic illness. Lorig and Holman (2003) published a review of the evidence of self-management education. They identified five core skills that would meet patient needs: 1) problem-solving, 2) decision making, 3) resource utilization, 4) formation of an effective patient–provider relationship, and 5) taking action. These skills should be provided when the patient is in the hospital, which will set their foundation for community living and the continuation of building a meaningful life.

In a review of research of professional-based programs on illness management for persons with severe mental illness, Mueser and colleagues (2002) found that psychoeducation improved people's knowledge of their mental illness. They also found that relapse prevention programs successfully reduced symptom relapses and rehospitalizations. Utilizing cognitive-behavioral training, coping skills training reduced the severity of persistent symptoms. There are several illness-management programs that are used throughout the country. One of these is the Illness Management and Recovery program (IMR), which is sponsored by Substance Abuse and Mental Health Services Administration (SAMSHA). Another program that is offered throughout the country is the Wellness Recovery Action Plan (WRAP) developed by Mary Ellen Copland. Cook and her colleagues (2009) studied the WRAP program for its effectiveness in improving the psychosocial symptoms of patients. They found that the participants attending six or more group sessions had a significant improvement in the symptoms that would interfere with recovery.

This makes the argument that both the community and the hospital should be offering WRAP groups to promote progress toward recovery. Both IMR and WRAP can be implemented in the hospital and continued in the community, improving patients' ability to manage their illness and improve their quality of life.

Structuring programs around self-efficacy is also needed to help patients understand that they have the ability to recover. *Self-efficacy* refers to a person's belief that he or she is able to achieve their goals (IOM, 2006). Instilling hope in the people receiving treatment is essential so they can build the confidence that recovery is possible.

THE SUCCESS STORY OF LORI

It is not uncommon for patients to have multiple hospitalizations when suffering from chronic mental illness. The primary focus of treatment cannot solely be medication. Medications are an important part of recovery and necessary to reduce the patient's biological vulnerability and to correct any imbalance and manage symptoms. However, a person's recovery cannot be reduced to a handful of pills, and treatment teams must understand the person and identify their psychosocial needs.

The initial goal for treating Lori was to engage her and to build a trusting and empathetic relationship. She was suffering not only from a mental illness but traumatic events that numbed her to the point of expressing the pain and anguish through anger and hostility. The treatment approach was to lower the tension in the environment through establishing realistic expectations and developing a therapeutic relationship with her. It is essential to create a supportive environment by reinforcing small improvements and provide the positive reinforcement.

Lori's goals were achieved by beginning her recovery journey in the hospital. She developed new coping skills and learned the benefits of her medications. She was able to talk about the trauma of the loss of first her husband and the violence of her second husband. Processing and addressing the effects of trauma significantly reduced the symptoms of her anxiety and depression and the use of her self-destructive coping mechanisms. She was discharged with the diagnosis of "bipolar disorder with psychosis." The Axis II diagnosis of mixed personality disorder (histrionic and narcissistic with antisocial traits) was eliminated from her discharge diagnosis after the treatment team discovered the maladaptive behaviors were a response to the traumatic events and not pathological. Her treatment team helped her gain a sense of hope and self-worth. The last hospitalization engaged her to take on an active role in her own recovery and continue on this path in the community to fully recover.

CONCLUSION

The mental health system has gone through many changes since the 1800s and the days of Dorothea Dix. We are in a new era of reform, where mental health care systems are driven by the consumer of services. The consumer voice is being heard at the local, state, and national legislative levels, influencing policy changes. Consumers are now recognized as the experts in the mental health field, as they are able to describe and explain the failures of the system based on their lived experiences. Consumers are gaining the skills to be their own advocate and partner with providers to work collaboratively to meet their needs.

Future research on the recovery model framework and the psychosocial rehabilitation interventions will be instrumental in guiding further reform, national standards of care, and evidence-based practices. Further research is also needed to measure the attitudes and beliefs of providers regarding recovery so that educational strategies can be developed.

People with serious mental illness can and do recover. This simple yet profound statement is at the heart of a sea change in service delivery for people with mental disorders. Still, the concept of mental health recovery represents a seismic shift in attitudes, beliefs, and priorities.

REFERENCES

Anthony, W., Cohen, M., Farkas, M., & Gagne, C. (2002). *Psychiatric Rehabilitation* (2nd ed.). Boston, MA: Center for Psychiatric Rehabilitation.

Anthony, W. A. (1993). Recovery from mental illness: The guiding vision of the mental health service system in the 1990s. *Psychosocial Rehabilitation Journal*, 16, 521–537.

Ballard, F. A. (2008). Benefits of psychosocial rehabilitation programming in a treatment mall. *Journal of Psychosocial Nursing*, 46, 26–32.

Caldwell, B. A., Sclafani, M., Swarbrick, M., & Piren, K. (2010). Psychiatric nursing practice and the recovery model of care. *Journal of Psychosocial Nursing*, 48, 42–48.

Cook, J. A, Copeland, M. E., Hamilton, M. M., Jonikas, J. A., Razzano, L. A.,...Grey, D. D. (2009). Initial outcomes of a mental illness self-management program based on wellness recovery action planning. *Psychiatric Services*, 60, 246–249.

Davidson, L., O'Connell, M., Tondora, J., Styron, T., & Kangas, K. (2006). The top ten concerns about recovery encountered in mental health system transformation. *Psychiatric Services*, 57, 640–645.

Fardella, J. A. (2008). The recovery model: Discourse ethics and the retrieval of the self. *Journal of Medical Humanity*, 29, 111–126.

Geller, J. L. (2000).The last half-century of psychiatric services as reflected in psychiatric services. *Psychiatric Services*, 51(1), 41–67.

Improving the Quality of Health Care for Mental and Substance-Use Conditions. (2006). Washington, DC: Institute of Medicine.

Interprofessional Education Collaborative Expert Panel. (2011). *Core Competencies for Interprofessional Collaborative Practice: Report of an Expert Panel.* Washington, DC: Interprofessional Education Collaborative.

.Linhorst, D. M. (2006). *Empowering People with Severe Mental Illness.* New York: Oxford University Press.

Link, B. G., & Phelan, J. C. (2001). Conceptualizing stigma. *Annual Review of Sociology*, 27, 363–385.

Longo, D. A., Marsh-Williams, K., & Tate, F. (2002). Psychosocial rehabilitation in a public psychiatric hospital. *Psychiatric Quarterly*, 73, 205–215.

Lorig, K. R., & Holman, H. R. (2003). Self-management education: history definition, outcomes, and mechanisms. *Annals of Behavioral Medicine*, 27(1), 1–7.

McLoughlin, K. A. & Geller, J. L. (2010). Interdisciplinary treatment planning in inpatient settings: From myth to model. *Psychiatric Quarterly*, 81, 263–277.

McLoughlin, K. A., Webb, T., Myers, M., Skinner, K., & Adams, C. H. (2010). Developing a psychosocial rehabilitation treatment mall: An implementation model for mental health nurses. *Archives of Psychiatric Nursing*, 24, 330–338.

Mueser, K. T., Corrigan, P. W., Hilton, D. W., Tanzman, B., Schaub, A.,...Herz, M. I. (2002). Illness management and recovery: A review of the research. *Psychiatric Services*, 53(10), 1272–1284.

National Consensus Statement on Mental Health Recovery. (2004). Retrieved from www.samhsa.gov. Rockville, MD.

New Freedom Commission on Mental Health. (2003). *Achieving the Promise: Transforming Mental Health Care in America. Executive Summary* (DHHS Pub. No. SMA-03–3831). Rockville, MD: Substance Abuse and Mental Health Service Administration.

Olmstead vs. LC, 527 US 581, United States Supreme Court (1999).

Pratt, C. W., Gill, K. J., Barrett, N. M., & Roberts, M. M. (2007). *Psychiatric Rehabilitation* (2nd ed.). San Diego, CA:

Ralph, R. O. (2000). *Review of Recovery Literature: A Synthesis of a Sample of Recovery Literature.* Southern Maine: National Association of State Mental Health Program Directors; National Technical Assistance Center for State Mental Health.

Ranz, J. M., & Mancini, A. D. (2008). Public psychiatrists' reports of their own recovery-oriented practices. *Psychiatric Services*, 59, 100–104.

Whitley, R., Strickler, D., & Drake, R. E. (2012). Recovery centers for people with severe mental illness: A survey of programs. *Community Mental Health Journal, 48*, 547–546.

The Institute of Medicine. (2001). *Crossing the Quality Chasm: A New Health System for the Twenty-first Century.* Washington DC: National Academies Press

Young, H. M., Siegel, E. O., McCormick, W. C., Fulmer, T., Harootyan, L. K. & Dorr, D. A. (2011). Interdisciplinary collaboration in geriatrics: Advancing health for older adults. *Nursing Outlook,* 59, 243–251.

CHAPTER 9

THE IMPORTANCE OF PREPARING MEDICAL STUDENTS FOR COMMUNITY PSYCHIATRY

JULIE NIEDERMIER

There are ample statistics illustrating the devastating impact of mental illness in the United States. Statistics from the National Institute of Mental Health are grim: suicide is the fourth leading cause of death for adults aged 18 to 65. Additionally, the prevalence of mental disorders in a given year is over 25 percent of the adult population.

With such compelling data, one would anticipate that future doctors receive considerable education about and exposure to patients with mental illnesses during medical school. Yet behavioral health–related didactic and clinical experiences of medical students are highly variable nationwide. Furthermore, the academic medical community is challenged with addressing public concerns of the adequacy, professionalism, and ability of physicians, in addition to the struggle to keep pace with the growth of knowledge in medicine. Thus, prioritizing education about mental illness for students occurs amid the vast responsibilities shouldered by academic medical centers.

There is considerable literature supporting the relationship between patients having both psychiatric illnesses and comorbid medical conditions. Studies have repeatedly demonstrated excess mortality from both natural and unnatural causes among psychiatric patients (Felker et al, 1996). In addition, psychiatric patients suffer a high rate of comorbid medical illnesses, which are largely undiagnosed and untreated and which may cause or exacerbate psychiatric symptoms (Felker et al, 1996). These patients comprise the population receiving care in community settings, while the data underscore the importance of all physicians-in-training, regardless of ultimate specialty choice, receiving considerable exposure to patients with mental health issues.

The importance of medical students' obtaining competency and skill in addressing patients with mental illness is compounded by changes within the healthcare environment itself. For instance, there is mounting pressure to contain the nation's skyrocketing healthcare expenditures and to circumnavigate the implications of the Patient Protection and Affordable Care Act of March 2010. It is vitally important to have adequately trained physicians capable of managing the mental health needs of patients within the revolutionary context of contemporary health care in America.

In coming decades, for both patient welfare and economic necessity, the concept of integrated health care is paramount. Physicians will not only be expected to consolidate care with other doctors, but more importantly, the model of interdisciplinary care will take center stage. Outcomes will be driven by the patients' satisfaction and well-being, and also by measures such as mortality, rehospitalization rate, compliance, and illness course. These drivers of health care command an integrated, multidisciplinary approach—a model well-suited for and already in place at many community practices, yet inconsistently applied in the training settings for medical students.

In this chapter, we will explore the general state and challenges of training medical students about behavioral health care. Additionally, we will consider medical education in the context of an evolving modern healthcare delivery system. Challenges and opportunities amid this backdrop are explored.

THE CURRENT STATE OF MEDICAL STUDENT EDUCATION IN COMMUNITY PSYCHIATRY

The Liaison Committee on Medical Education and the American Osteopathic Association Commission on Osteopathic College Accreditation (COCA) are responsible for accrediting allopathic and osteopathic medical schools, respectively. These and other organizations, such as the Association of American Medical Colleges and the United States Medical Licensing Examination, directly and indirectly outline the components comprising the four-year medical school education.

Medical schools are challenged to provide a comprehensive and efficient curriculum to students within the rapidly changing world of medicine. Public outcry about blatantly neglectful care of patients by physicians, the recognition of the need to update archaic medical school instructional methods, and the rapid expansion of medical knowledge and technology have led academicians to rethink the medical student learning process. Now, greater emphasis is being placed on the development of critical appraisal skills, procedural skills, and the interpersonal and professional abilities of medical students.

Certainly changes in medical school curricula have the potential to ultimately improve patient care and physician accountability; yet, medical schools are at varying stages of redefining and implementing contemporary education goals. Additionally, there is a defined duration of schooling, and yet explosive amounts of material that can be covered in the four-year curriculum, medical schools are challenged to teach approaches to and methodology of critical thinking about medical problems in an efficient, organized, and testable manner. Curricula revision can, in some instances, be at the expense of, rather than optimally integrated complementarily to, clinical experiences.

Thus, the state of medical student education has affected the learning experiences of medical students with respect to psychiatry. For instance, the duration of psychiatry clerkships, the primary and core training ground for exposure of students to patients with mental health issues, are trending downward nationwide (Rosenthal et al., 2005). Additionally, there is considerable variability in the overall content, setting, and exposure of psychiatry to medical students.

Some medical schools are working to integrate exposure to psychiatry with other core specialties such as family medicine or pediatrics. With data supporting that primary care providers see the bulk of patients with mental illness, efforts to incorporate learning about psychiatry in these domains are intuitively obvious although sometimes tactically difficult to orchestrate. Nonetheless, at some medical schools, exposure of students to psychiatry may suffer due to competing priorities and time constraints within the schools.

While there is a sizable literature discussing residency and fellowship learning experiences in community settings (Faulkner et al., 1984), relatively less information describes medical student learning in community psychiatry settings, despite such sites being frequently utilized by medical schools. Much of the data that are available describe successful locally relevant training opportunities (Christensen, 2005). Overall, there is considerable variability in degree of utilization, medical student roles, and quality of experiences by students at community and other clinical psychiatry sites (von Schlageter et al., 2006). Medical schools also vary with respect to students' time spent with and exposure to faculty working with mentally ill patients. For instance, some schools have psychiatrists among the principle instructors of introductory classes about the doctor–patient relationship, basic interviewing techniques, and professionalism. In other schools, future psychiatrists may have very few required didactic or clinical encounters with medical students during the first two years of medical school. Fortunately, many schools are involved in updating their curricula with greater attention to the need for improved exposure to the behavioral health aspects of medicine.

ENVISIONING THE FUTURE

Despite limitations within and across medical schools, with evidence accumulating about the detrimental impact of mental disorders on health, there is recognition of the intrinsic value of teaching students to appreciate the patient within their biopsychosocial context. Other factors, such as the focus on overall wellness and preventative medicine, suggest greater opportunities for providing students with ample knowledge of mental health. Expanding upon this appreciation is crucial to developing a construct for psychiatric education of the contemporary medical student.

Community psychiatry can serve as a fruitful and ideal training ground for students to learn these critical concepts. To envision the utility and value of community psychiatry in the education of all future physicians, one must consider a number of converging principles. These principles include the following: 1) the medical student and social responsibility; 2) the alliances of community and university resources; and 3) the politics and economics of healthcare delivery.

MEDICAL STUDENTS AND SOCIAL AND ETHICAL RESPONSIBILITIES

Medical students, when asked about their profession choice, are quite reflexive in offering that they "want to help people." Yet, the technological age of global medicine, overt healthcare disparities, and international disasters and crises have furthered the call for medical students to assume some degree of social responsibility for the care of the sick. This rejuvenated *social responsibility* is more and more being nourished at the level of medical student training.

Faulkner and McCurdy (2000) have defined the "socially responsible" individual as a person who takes part in activities that contribute to the happiness, health, and prosperity of a community and its members; they have also raised key questions relevant to developing a medical school curriculum rooted in social responsibility. The Association of American Medical Colleges (AAMC) has declared that medical schools have some responsibility for fulfilling an implicit social contract with the community (Blumenthal and Meyer, 1996). Interpretations of this social contract for medical schools have coincided with the public call for further attention to the moral and professional development of medical students (Thompson, 1997; Wear, 1997).

Thus, it would seem that the combination of a fertile academic landscape and the personal investment of students have intersected to nourish the growth of socially responsible physicians. With this backdrop, students are primed to accept that community psychiatry settings may offer fruitful training opportunities. Indeed, studies have already shown that having students participate in psychiatry rotations can improve their attitudes about community-based treatments for mental illness (Galka et al., 2005).

Finally, if social responsibility does not appeal to today's medical student, oftentimes other situations will provide incentives to learn about mental health issues. For instance, students often have family members or even personal experiences with mental illness. Physicians also have an ethical responsibility involving their profession and are increasingly experiencing stress in the workplace. Therefore, physicians need to be well-versed in mental health issues not only because they affect their patients, but also because they affect their colleagues (Clemens et al., 2011). This unfortunate reality can serve as motivation for students unmoved by other circumstances.

ALLYING COMMUNITY AND ACADEMIC RESOURCES

The World Health Organization estimates that neuropsychiatric disorders are the leading contributor to the total burden of disability. There is a plethora of studies supporting the benefits of community-based care and answering the question of why mental health treatment matters (Druss and von Esenwein, 2006; Casalino et al., 2003). For instance, having a source (physician offices or hospital outpatient services) of care has been associated with lower prevalence of depression among community-dwelling Medicare beneficiaries (Li et al., 2011).

Combined with existing state mental hospital facilities, the infusion of funds to support the establishment of mental health centers across the United States decades ago has rendered the psychiatric profession uniquely situated to lead community-based medical education. In actuality, these facilities already serve as learning sites at many medical schools across the country. However, little emphasis has been placed on the reciprocal nature of partnerships between communities and medical schools (Hunt et al., 2011).

In examples that do exist, obvious gains have been realized. Specifically, service to military personnel and their families by partnerships of academic medical centers and the Veterans Administration have generally translated into successful patient care. Dalack et al. (2010) have described a partnership involving the University of Michigan, Michigan State University, and the Michigan Army National Guard designed to meet the needs of returning soldiers. Such examples support the claim that these partnerships are ideal, if not crucial, especially in light of the alarming suicide rate among military personnel.

Medical students most commonly interface with the community on assigned rotations or through volunteer or service activities. However, more and more academic medical centers, largely through fiscal, social, and political reconsideration, are looking to redefine their academic missions by reaching out to the local communities. These partnerships generally produce obvious benefits for both the medical school and the community.

THE POLITICS OF HEALTH CARE DELIVERY

The report of the National Advisory Mental Health Council has previously identified and called for overcoming inequities in the public and private sectors toward patients with mental as opposed to physical illnesses (NAMHC, 1993). After all, untreated mental illness is devastating for patients, not to mention its effect on the physical well-being of these patients. Not having medical insurance was predictive of lower preventive-health-service use by patients with severe mental illness (Xiong et al., 2010).

More recently, the impact of national healthcare reform on adults with severe mental disorders remains to be seen. Garfield et al. (2011) have estimated that the expansion of insurance coverage under reform will lead to more than a million new users of mental health services. Experts have already recognized that the vast population of patients seeking mental or medical care will greatly exceed the availability of healthcare providers (Leighton et al., 2011). Such statistics underscore the importance of adequately and efficiently training medical students and "physician-extenders" for the next generations. Essentially, it will be imperative for healthcare providers to not only be capable of treating and preventing illness, but to also be skillful at managing limited economic and medical resources throughout the nation.

KEY FEATURES OF THE "NEW" MEDICAL STUDENT EDUCATION: WHY COMMUNITY PSYCHIATRY TRAINING MATTERS

During medical school, students historically have had relatively little exposure to the business of health care. However, key elements of healthcare reform—including the following concepts: sustainable expense growth over time, continuum of care, accountable medical home, reimbursement rewards value, electronic information, and performance measures—will redefine contemporary medical school education. Community psychiatry, which already is faced with a scarcity of resources amid abundant demand, is poised to offer medical students education about the real world.

In many community psychiatry settings, there are already quality-indicators in place. For instance, patients with severe mental illness have been shown to show significant improvement in symptoms and functioning when enrolled in illness management and recovery programming (Fujita et al., 2010). Similarly, states have ample statistics regarding hospitalization and pharmaceutical use—two of the costliest expenditures involving the treatment of mentally ill individuals.

Community psychiatry settings have additional leverage as training grounds for other reasons as well. Most settings are well versed in the concept of multidisciplinary team based care. In recent decades, fragmented care has resulted in an erosion of the construct of interdisciplinary management. The merits of this approach are well documented and perhaps represent the greatest example of the traditional mental health center and its impact on recovery (Wells et al., 2004).

Kemp (2011) described strategies of chronic disease self-management and its application to psychiatry. This model, based on active collaboration between the patient and physician, has been widely utilized in other medical disciplines, yet its application in mental health fields is relatively new. Community psychiatric settings, with a host of healthcare team members, would seem primed to embrace and further expand its utility.

The Rand Corporation and Dartmouth have projected that at least 30 percent of healthcare dollars are wasted due to clinical decision-making, poor management, and fragmentation of care (*Health News Digest*, 2009). Newer medical school curricula are incorporating business management and looking at continuous quality improvement opportunities, such as working in teams with administrators and reviewing medical costs to address unnecessary tests and procedures. It will be helpful for mental health organizations to do their part to scrutinize internal operations and work in alliance with the resources of academic medical centers not only to add to the education of students, but also to improve their own quality of care.

REDEFINING COMMUNITY PSYCHIATRY WITH HEALTH CARE REFORM

There remain unanswered questions about what precisely will become of the traditional mental health center or other organizations serving the mental health population in the age of health care reform. Yet community psychiatry will need to further define itself by the population that it serves. In fact, the term *community* can, if it is not already, be applied to mean the discipline of medicine that addresses the mental health needs of a community. That is, community psychiatry can take on multiple functions and populations, using multiple care providers, to treat illness and encourage wellness to those with and without resources in families. While in practice this may already exist, one can argue that the general public may or may not see community psychiatry as beneficial. However, there is ample evidence to support the claim that direct and indirect benefits ultimately enhance the maintenance of healthy families and communities. Educators, students, and patients all can be instrumental in furthering this mission.

The mission and its underlying financing, as well as ties to academic medical centers, offer promise that community psychiatry sites are among those most poised and ready for a new era of health care. Thornicroft et al. (2010) described lessons learned from international data as well as identified initiatives at the national and local levels to improve the likelihood of success. Emphasizing community health also offers an approach toward aligning the priorities of academic medical centers with those of the general population (Hunt et al., 2011).

SUMMARY

Both medical student education and community psychiatry are in states of flux. The context of healthcare delivery is also evolving, with a multidisciplinary, integrated model of care becoming the norm. Multiple demands, such as increasing community accountability and refining medical school curricula, as well as national and statewide health care reform, are driving this era of change. Most importantly, academic medical centers and the breadth of agencies and personnel involved in community psychiatry will have unprecedented opportunities for redefining mental health education for the next generation of physicians.

REFERENCES

Blumenthal D, Meyer GS. Academic health centers in a changing environment. *Health Aff* 1996;15:201–215.

Casalino L, Gillies RR, Shortell SM, et al. External incentives, information technology, and organized processes to improve health care quality for patients with chronic diseases. *JAMA* 2003;289:434–441.

Christensen R. Community psychiatry and medical student education. *Psychiatr Serv* 2005;56:608–609.

Clemens NA, Horwitz M, Sharp J. Addressing impairment in a colleague. *J Psychiatr Pract* 2011;17(1):53–56.

Dalack GW, Blow AJ, Valenstein M, et al. Working together to meet the needs of Army National Guard soldiers: an academic-military partnership. *Psychiatr Serv* 2010;61:1069–1071.

Druss B, von Esenwein S. Improving primary medical care for persons with mental and addictive disorders: systematic review. *Gen Hosp Psychiatry* 2006;28:145–153.

Faulkner LR, Rankin RM, Eaton JS Jr, et al. The VA psychiatry service as a setting for residency education. *Am J Psychiatry* 1984;141:960–965.

Faulkner LR, McCurdy RL. Teaching medical students social responsibility: the right thing to do. *Acad Med* 2000;75:346–350.

Felker B, Yazel JJ, Short D. Mortality and medical comorbidity among psychiatric patients: a review. *Psychiatr Serv* 1996;47(12):1356–1363.

Fujita E, Kato D, Kuno E, et al. Implementing the illness management and recovery program in Japan. *Psychiatr Serv* 2010 ;61:1157–1161.

Galka SW, Perkins DV, Butler N, et al. Medical students' attitudes toward mental disorders before and after a psychiatric rotation. *Acad Psychiatry* 2005;29(4):357–361.

Garfield RL, Zuvekas SH, Lave JR, Donohue JM. The impact of national health care reform on adults with severe mental disorders. *Am J Psychiatry* 2011;168: 486–494.

Health Care Reform for Americans with Severe Mental Illnesses: report of the National Advisory Mental Health Council. *Am J Psychiatry* 1993;150(10):1447–1465.

Weil, Henry (2009) Health care reform medical education: the untapped aspect of health care reform. *Health News Digest*.com; http://www.healthnewsdigest.com/news/health%20care%20reform0/Medical_Education_The_Untapped_Aspect_of_Health_Care_Reform.shtml.

Hunt JB, Bonham C, Jones L. Understanding the goals of service learning and community-based medical education: a systematic review. *Acad Med* 2011;86:246–251.

Kemp V. Use of "chronic disease self-management strategies" in mental health care. *Curr Opin Psychiatry* 2011;24(2):144–148.

Leighton K, Jones K, Shin P, et al. The states' next challenge—securing primary care for expanded Medicaid populations. *N Engl J Med* 2011;364:493–495.

Li C, Dick AW, Fiscella K, et al. Effect of usual source of care on depression among Medicare beneficiaries: an application of a simultaneous-equations model. *Health Serv Res* 2011; February 9. doi: 10.1111/j. 1474-6773.2011.01240.x.

Rosenthal RH, Levine RE, Carlson DL, et al. The "shrinking" clerkship: characteristics and length of clerkships in psychiatry undergraduate education. *Acad Psychiatry* 2005;29:47–51.

Shultes von Schlageter MS, Park EM, Tucker P. Inter-site consistency at a multi-site psychiatry clerkship. *Acad Psychiatry* 2006;30:356–359.

Thompson JN. Moral imperatives for academic medicine. *Acad Med* 1997;72:1063–1070.

Thornicroft G, Alem A, Antunes Dos Santos R, et al. WPA guidance on steps, obstacles and mistakes to avoid in the implementation of community mental health care. *World Psychiatry* June 2010;9(2):67–77.

Wear D. Professional development of medical students: problems and promises. *Acad Med* 1997;72:1056–1062.

Wells K, Miranda J, Bruce M, et al. Bridging community intervention and mental health services research. *Am J Psychiatry* 2004; 161:955–963.

Xiong GL, Iosif AM, Bermudes RA, et al. Preventive medical services use among community mental health patients with severe mental illness: the influence of gender and insurance coverage. *Prim Care Companion J Clin Psychiatry* 2010:12(5). Pii:PCC.09m00927.

CHAPTER 10

THE POWER OF GROUPS IN SERIOUS MENTAL ILLNESS

Integrated Pathways to Recovery

HARRIET P. LEFLEY AND PHIL SHAPIRO

THE REVIVAL OF "HENRY"

After 20 years of unremitting schizophrenia, failures of psychotherapy and first-generation antipsychotics, and a life spent mainly at home and in bed, "Henry" joined a research study on medications. His brother had learned that the local medical school was one of the sites of the Clinical Antipsychotic Trials of Intervention Effectiveness (CATIE) and insisted that Henry apply. Henry had lost his job, wife, and infant son, and later suffered the death of his caregiver parents. He was alternately paranoid and depressed, and gave little credence to the efficacy of medications. Yet as the research progressed, he seemed to do better. When he was unblinded, he found that a particular antipsychotic seemed to be helpful in clarifying his thoughts. Nevertheless, he still avoided talking to the neighbors, taking the bus, or seeking employment, because most human interactions were frightening and evoked paranoid ideation. When the local CATIE investigators decided to offer a support group for the research subjects, Henry's brother insisted on driving him there for weekly meetings.

That was almost ten years ago. The group has continued as a no-fee psychoeducational support group open to anyone with a serious psychiatric disorder, and Henry is still coming to meetings. During this period, Henry has learned a great deal about schizophrenia. He has become a teacher and role model for new members. He has developed a list of coping skills, which he records and applies to the management of his daily chores. Henry has learned to handle his paranoia (it is not completely gone), developed some computer skills, and coped with some serious life events. At the group's urging, he fulfilled his dream of reuniting with his now-adult son by writing to explain his illness and to apologize for not being able to fulfill a parental role.

This led to a satisfying meeting and a continuing relationship. When Henry's caregiver brother died, Henry was able to arrange the funeral, deal with the loss, and ultimately move from the house they shared to a small apartment. At each step of the way, the group members encouraged him and reinforced their conviction that he had the ability to succeed. Henry religiously takes his medication, loves his new apartment, and is currently enrolled in a psychosocial research project and a professional weight-loss program. Still unable to work, but structuring both his days and his weeks with self-assigned tasks, Henry says he feels that he is now in the process of recovery.

In this chapter, we deal with recovery from serious mental illness as a growth process in which professional interventions and peer supports have an integrated role. A range of models of group support are pathways to recovery, both professional and peer-led. Groups that are exclusively peer-led perhaps represent an end-point rather than a pathway, a personification of long-sought independence and self-determination. In most practice, however, professional expertise is enmeshed with group support, which augments education with experiential understanding, role-modeling, and motivation for change.

SOCIAL NETWORKS AND PEER SELF-HELP GROUPS

Numerous studies have found that the social networks of persons with schizophrenia and other major psychiatric disorders are smaller and less functional than those of nonclinical populations, and are not necessarily supportive (Albert et al., 1998). Cutler and Tatum (1983) had earlier noted that patients had few long-term relationships except with kin, toward whom there were sometimes negative or ambivalent feelings. Their few interpersonal relationships tended to be shallow, with little complexity or reciprocity. People with serious mental illness did not acknowledge doing much for other people, and their interactions with others were typically unidimensional.

With growing deinstitutionalization, the Community Support Program (CSP) at the National Institute of Mental Health (NIMH) as well as concerned community psychiatrists turned their attention to creating adequate social support systems for community reintegration of this patient population. A comprehensive model presented by Cutler and Tatum (1983) expanded a patient's personal network of family members or group home co-residents to four other segments: psychiatric services, productive activities, recreation, and socialization. This larger network would facilitate development of social, living, leisure, and work skills. In this model, as in most others, social networks were conceptualized as a necessary aid to reintegrating and maintaining individuals in the community, with an array of concerned others providing help—family, friends, clinicians, case managers, volunteers, co-workers, and the like. It was also implied that an expanded social network might ultimately lead to improved interactive skills and more multidimensional social interactions. These developments were concurrent with a rapidly emerging emphasis on community-based psychiatric rehabilitation programs and the relearning of social and vocational skills that might facilitate recovery.

Meanwhile, the expansion of peer self-help groups has provided a different type of social network: one of mutual rather than external support. Peer self-help is an interactive model in which patients share their experiences and adaptive strategies and help others with their problems. They not only are helped by others, but learn and grow by giving to others. The glue that holds them together is common experience of personal traumas or negative life events, and their healing comes from helping each other cope.

In the mental health field, numerous self-help groups deal with an array of conditions that range from existential problems to serious psychiatric disorders. At this writing, the online American Self-Help Group Clearinghouse provides a database for over 1,100 national, international, and demonstration model self-help support groups, with many local affiliates (retrieved December 20, 2010 from http://mentalhelp.net/self-help). Peer support groups may be available to persons with any history of mental illness (or their families), such as those offered by the National Alliance on Mental Illness (NAMI) or the Mental Health Association (MHA). Others target specific diagnoses, like Schizophrenics Anonymous (SA) or Depressive and Bipolar Support Alliance (DBSA). There are also groups for various addictions, bereavement, disabilities, abuse and trauma recovery, parenting, caregiver concerns, and many other categories of stressful life situations. There are 12 Step and 10 Step programs modeled on Alcoholics Anonymous (AA) or Narcotics Anonymous (NA), and national campus-based groups for college students contemplating suicide (Active Minds). Some groups focus solely on mutual support and recovery, while larger organizations such as DBSA promote basic research, publish educational literature, conduct conferences, and engage in political advocacy. More detailed descriptions of groups focusing on serious mental illness may be found in Lefley (2008).

CONSUMER POLITICAL ADVOCACY SELF-HELP GROUPS

More than two decades ago, Emerick (1990) studied the characteristics of 104 self-help groups of present and former psychiatric patients and identified two major service models: social movement and individual therapy. The social movement groups were oriented toward social change and offered public education, legal advocacy, information and referral networking, and technical assistance to other consumers. The individual therapy groups offered more "inner-focused" individual change through mutual support meetings with a focus on coping with their illness. This distinction is still valid today, particularly with the growth of the consumer movement.

A scientific national survey in 2002 found 7,467 groups and organizations run by and for mental health consumers and/or family members in the United States. Included were 3,315 mutual support groups, 3,019 self-help organizations, and 1,133 consumer-operated services (Goldstrom et al, 2006). Most of these consumer- and family-run organizations merge mutual support with a social-change philosophy. In addition to public education and anti-stigma initiatives, they espouse a stronger role for service recipients in policy-making, design, funding, and administration of mental health services. This role has been legitimized in President Bush's New Freedom Commission on Mental Health Report (2003). The consumer and family movements have also had a profound influence in generating the new focus on recovery in mental health systems.

PEER AND PROFESSIONAL INTERVENTIONS

Regular attendance at Twelve Step groups, particularly AA and NA, is frequently a required component of professional addiction programs. Many state mental health systems, with funding and encouragement from the Substance Abuse and Mental Health Services Administration

(SAMHSA) provide funding for training and hiring consumers as peer specialists in public mental health programs. There is also a movement for states to fund special trainers for implementing illness self-management recovery plans such as the Wellness Recovery Action Plan (WRAP), developed by consumer-professional Mary Ellen Copeland, Ph.D. (Copeland, 1997). A recent quasi-experimental study comparing WRAP groups with matched standard service groups at five community mental health centers in the Midwest showed significant improvements in psychiatric symptoms and feelings of hope after the WRAP intervention (Fukui et al., 2011). Nevertheless, consumer- and professionally run programs typically operate in separate spheres. Although consumer-run enterprises have now been in existence for more than three decades, encouraged and funded by the CSP, first through NIMH and later though the Substance Abuse and Mental Health Services Administration (SAMHSA), these are usually time-limited and function as a parallel rather than integrated system of care. More recently, a joint project of the Temple University Collaborative on Community Inclusion (2010) and the National Mental Health Consumers Self-Help Clearinghouse published a compendium of consumer-run programs that have developed initiatives designed to help people with psychiatric disabilities reconnect to the everyday world around them. The emphasis increasingly is on integration of consumers into the larger community rather than diagnosis-related programs.

Although there is certainly an accelerated growth of consumer-run enterprises, it seems clear that the main body of psychiatric care will continue to be the domain of mental health professionals. Yet it is also evident that medications, psychotherapy, and other professional interventions do not provide the full array of resources needed for recovery. Although the federal CSP tried for many years to provide a comprehensive network of rehabilitative programs and residential care, such resources have diminished in many areas of the country. Homelessness and inappropriate jailing are ubiquitous problems, and numerous patients with serious and persistent mental illness still continue to lead marginal and often isolated lives. With the current focus on recovery and utilization of peer specialists as role models, how do we combine consumer and professional expertise in offering knowledge and hope to people with serious and persistent psychiatric disorders?

In this chapter, we present two models of working with this population that focus on recovery through education and group support. Both models merge professional knowledge with the experiential expertise of consumers, and both are recovery-oriented. One is a pragmatic, atheoretical model that offers psychoeducation, self-knowledge, and mutual support, utilizing group members as co-educators and co-therapists. The other is a more transformative model that focuses on recovery through skillful pain management and spiritual growth. In both models, group members inspire and participate in each other's recovery.

PSYCHOTHERAPY, PSYCHOEDUCATION, AND GROUP SUPPORT

Mental health services, particularly the vast array of psychotherapies, are based on numerous theoretical models, only a few of which have been empirically validated as evidence-based practices. In a study of 5,142 patients with schizophrenia from 44 trials conducted between 1988 and 2009, 1,400 received psychoeducation. The researchers found that psychoeducation significantly reduced relapses and readmissions, encouraged medication compliance, and reduced the length of hospital stays in hospital-based studies (Xia, Merinder, & Belgamwar, 2011). Family psychoeducation, with the attendance of the member with serious mental illness, has been empirically validated as evidence-based treatment for schizophrenia and other major psychiatric disorders. There is now a substantial body of evidence, from numerous international studies over a period of many years, of symptom improvement, relapse prevention, fewer hospitalizations, and improved quality of life (Lefley, 2009a). There is some evidence that multi-family education has more beneficial effects than single-family psychoeducation (McFarlane, 2002; Mueser et al., 2001). A meta-analysis of 199 studies found that interventions with families and patients were even more effective than psychoeducation with patients alone (Lincoln et al., 2007). Both areas of research suggest that the presence of supportive others enhances the benefits of psychoeducational interventions.

Group psychoeducation is not group psychotherapy. In a current psychiatric textbook, *group psychotherapy* is defined as a time-limited process with the therapist's role and group process derived from a specific theoretical approach (dynamic, supportive, or specialized focus). Clients must agree to attend meetings, formulate specific treatment goals, use the group for therapeutic and not social purposes, and assume responsibility for fees (Stone, 2008). Nevertheless, Stone expressly differentiates group therapy for persons with severe and persistent mental illness from other models.

Patients are prone to attend erratically, and a more flexible format that accepts this propensity may serve these individuals well. In the flexible format, core and peripheral subgroups develop, and over extended periods, groups develop a sense of continuity and cohesion. Treatment goals are generally formulated to help patients with adapting to everyday problems, improving social relations, and managing feelings. Patients may be encouraged to socialize outside of the meetings. Therapists attempt to help patients manage their isolation and sense of shame over their illness (Stone, 2008, p. 1916).

THE UNIVERSITY OF MIAMI PSYCHOEDUCATIONAL SUPPORT GROUP

Here we present a model that is clearly concordant with the type of group work recommended above. The focus is on everyday problems, and patients are indeed encouraged to socialize outside of meetings. Yet, despite their intrinsically therapeutic aspects, psychoeducational groups are not "group therapy." Their focus is on contemporary illness-management and improved quality of life rather than on resolving long-standing personal problems. The basic components of the psychoeducational model are education about major psychiatric disorders and their treatment, illness management techniques, and problem-solving strategies, together with support, understanding, and encouragement. Although there are some didactic components, this psychoeducational model has no formal lectures. Rather, it is responsive to discrete needs for knowledge as they arise. Information may be conveyed by the professional leader, by visiting psychiatric residents, or by knowledgeable members.

This model also differs from group therapy in its open, unlimited, non-fee structure. There are no attendance requirements, records, or time limits. Members are referred from the psychiatric outpatient and day treatment units, from community mental health professionals and advocacy groups, or they may come as walk-ins. The only requirement is a diagnosis of a major psychiatric disorder of more than one year and evidence of current psychiatric treatment or professional oversight. Most attendees have diagnoses of schizophrenia, bipolar disorder, or major depressive disorder. At this writing, almost all attest that they have attempted suicide at least once in the past. The group has accepted a few members with dual diagnosis (with substance abuse in remission) but not substance abuse alone.

The group meets weekly for 90 minutes with a typical attendance of 10 to 15 people. Members vary in levels of functioning and knowledge, yet all seem to work well together. Many are highly articulate and some have partial employment, including two who are peer counselors. During the past ten years, core groups have emerged and stayed for prolonged periods of time. Occasional members, with irregular attendance due to part-time jobs or other commitments, return periodically and consider themselves part of the group. There is considerable socialization outside of the meetings. Many members keep in touch by telephone and sometimes meet during the week, with encouragement from their peers and the professional leadership.

The group is led by a psychologist, with occasional attendance by psychiatric residents, who have found this a valuable learning experience. (Some have reported that hearing about the day-to-day lives of patients was one of the most important experiences of their training.) Residents answer questions about medications, the metabolic syndrome, and other medical matters. Information is based on contemporary research and tends to be general. Group members are constantly urged to discuss their medications and any adverse reactions with their individual psychiatrists.

The major goals of the group are to: (a) combat social isolation—a too-frequent problem of deinstitutionalized patients living in the community, especially those with no supportive families; (b) redeem a sense of self-esteem and hope; (c) encourage people with serious mental illness to accept challenges that will advance them beyond their present life situation without undue stress. (See Lefley, 2009b, for case examples.)

Meetings generally begin with participants' describing their past week, including specific concerns or examples of coping. The group leader prepares a discussion topic, but this is frequently discarded when a major issue arises from these recitals. Some meetings may focus, on request, on the latest research on schizophrenia or bipolar disorder, but more often we deal with topics that may arise organically from the group discussion. Examples are self-assertiveness in illness-management (being open with your psychiatrist and taking control of your own recovery); improving the mental health system; ways of maintaining good health; family relationships; dating and mating; social and gender roles; even current political issues. Some members discuss negative developmental experiences. Others express appreciation of their families and guilt about the burden of their illness. A major focus is on self-appraisal as an adult with mental illness, on recognizing and dealing with the negativity of societal stigma, self-stigmatization, and diminished hopes for the future. The group leader regularly, and legitimately, reframes their experience of mental illness as one of courage, of overcoming greater odds and climbing higher mountains than so-called normal people. The group's major focus is on the appreciation of one's personal strengths, coping capabilities, and potential for leading a satisfying life despite the constraints of a major mental illness.

The group performs tasks that are difficult to perform for the professional leader. They may urge their comrades to takes risks in order to move forward, actions that may be tacitly approved but cannot be openly recommended by a clinician. An important risk is disclosure of a psychiatric diagnosis in applying for employment. In a case vignette described elsewhere in greater detail (Lefley, 2009b), a member with bipolar disorder, highly trained in computer science, agonized for weeks about applying for a community college job for which he was well qualified. He had to answer questions on an employment questionnaire about his criminal history, and was afraid to disclose a brief stay in jail incurred during a manic episode. Group members, applauding his skills and exploring his options and risks, urged him to apply and explain his history. With great anxiety he applied, explained, and got the job. In another case, a member openly disclosed her diagnosis to an employer, stating she could only work three days a week and must avoid stressful demands. She had special skills as an interpreter and her requests were honored. The group is familiar with the Americans with Disabilities Act and its promised protections. They are aware of the field's current emphasis on recovery, and the potential for applying their consumer status as a positive rather than negative factor in finding appropriate employment or higher education.

By definition, the pragmatic model is atheoretical. Both patient and family psychoeducation, however, benefit from behavioral, cognitive, and social learning theories to the extent that they are applicable (see Lefley, 2009a). We give patients the knowledge they ask for, including skills that will benefit their survival. Typically this involves illness-management education, answers to etiological speculations, and coping techniques based on today's knowledge base. They are taught to be assertive in medication self-management; since too many express reluctance to infringe on the time or question the decisions of their doctors. Because social isolation is a major factor, members are encouraged to maintain contact and establish personal relationships outside of the clinical setting.

There are multiple therapeutic advantages to groups. In addition to mutual support and an end to isolation, they offer the type of information exchange that is typically missing in the individual encounter. They offer experiences with similar problems, their coping techniques and solutions, both successful and unsuccessful. They also offer resource information on issues important in the lives of people with major psychiatric disorders. These may include how to apply for Social Security and other federal entitlements, Medicaid/Medicare, housing, free dental care, bus coupons, disability transportation, college offices with special services for persons with disabilities, etc. The members also offer encouragement, hope, and sometimes success stories.

This section has described a psychoeducational group for individuals with major psychiatric disorders such as schizophrenia, bipolar disorder, and major depressive disorder, most of whom are highly motivated to understand their illness and improve their lives. Almost all voluntarily take medication and are interested in exploring its effects. Many have learned to enrich their group participation by joining consumer networks, resuming creative writing or painting, combating loneliness with telephoning, texting, or just hanging out with others, and gaining spiritual strength from religious worship. A very small number have found full-time employment. A few have been able to find part-time jobs, some as trained peer-counselors.

Unfortunately, the majority of our patients are not always able to attain this level of functioning and productivity. The next section deals with a treatment model that addresses the needs of more-impaired individuals. These are people who may be treatment-resistant, homeless, off their medications, reluctant to attempt change. Many must be sought out and eased into a sequence of stages leading to recovery.

THE CENTRAL CITY CONCERN OLD TOWN RECOVERY CENTER

THE EGG SALAD SANDWICH STORY

An African-American woman with paranoid schizophrenia attends community meetings at the Central City Concern Old Town Recovery Center in Portland, Oregon. They discuss recovery and healing principles, and the ten-step pathways to recovery more fully described below. The woman listens, and then takes her meager few dollars and buys egg salad sandwiches. She goes to a local nursing home and asks to see people who almost never get visitors. She visits with these people and gives them the sandwiches. She returns to the community meeting and reports what she has done. She tells the group that her father taught her to do this kind of thing when she was a child, and she wondered whether this was what we were talking about. Of course the group supported and praised her, and said this is exactly the kind of thing that reflects the power of healing, both for the recipients and for the donor.

This is an important story because the experience of mental illness is inevitably one of self-absorption. From paranoid ideation to severe depression, the focus is primarily on one's personal agonies, on external or internal threats to the self. It is extremely difficult for an individual suffering the turmoil of mental illness to understand or focus on the needs of others. Yet the egg salad sandwich story illustrates how discussions of recovery and healing, with ensuing self-awareness, can free the mind to conduct a charitable, self-sacrificing act. This is an example of how individuals focusing on self-healing can in the process achieve the capacity to abandon preoccupation with the self and concentrate on others.

The Central City Concern Old Town Recovery Center is a community mental health center with the professed goal of moving from being a clinic to being a community-healing center. In addition to the customary medication and case management services, they aim to build a community with a recovery and healing culture. Open for three hours three days a week, the Center offers a Living Room with free coffee and doughnuts for group socialization, as well as hour-long group sessions on recovery and healing principles. The patients are frequently those most difficult to treat, rotating in a recognizable "spin" phase of street-hospital-jail-street. The intervention hopes to advance to a "float" phase of medication, financial support, and housing. The ultimate aim is the "integration" phase of recovery, such as resuming school or work, or other functional indicators of community reintegration. The recovery group discussions use Shapiro's (2010) *Healing Power: Ten Steps to Pain Management and Spiritual Evolution* as a text, stimulating discussion of member-suggested topics, such as how to get along with difficult people or how to deal with painful emotions or negative thinking. Together with the standard clinical treatment, the group discussions, explorations of alternatives, and socialization experiences have the goal of advancing people from the "spin" to the "float" phases, and hopefully to "integration."

For those who want to go deeper into the topic of spirituality and healing, there is a separate group that utilizes the Shapiro text more comprehensively. There has been a resurgence of interest in spirituality in psychiatric practice as a potentially positive aspect of recovery. A randomized trial of outpatients with schizophrenia found that many patients seem interested in discussing religion and spirituality with their psychiatrists (Huguelet et al., 2011). A study of religion and spirituality in the lives of 1,824 people with serious mental illness defined *religion* as participation in institutionalized doctrine, and *spirituality* as an individual pursuit of meaning outside of the world of immediate experience. They found that nearly 90 percent of consumers identified themselves as "religious" or "spiritual," with nearly one-half at the "very" or "extremely" end of the scale. Both religion and spirituality were significantly associated with indicators of well-being and symptom reduction (Corrigan et al., 2003). Although many clinicians are ill at ease with this topic, these investigators assert that clinicians' ability to recognize this important aspect of their patient's lives falls under the rubric of cultural competence.

Patients' discussions in both Miami and Portland often focus on spirituality and appeals to a "higher power." Psychiatrists cannot deal with religious differences, but in the 12th Street model, spirituality can be part of the self-healing process, using a cognitive behavioral approach of changing negative to positive schemata. In *Healing Power*, Shapiro (2010) outlines a host of spiritually oriented cognitive behavioral methods that are proven effective tools for cultivating healing qualities. Detailed instructions explain how these methods help us cultivate love, peace, strength, and courage in response to pain of the body, mind, or soul. Continued practice of the recommended methods helps patients manage difficulties that life may bring. In the Miami program, church attendance and prayers are common coping mechanisms of group members. The group leader helps them interpret answers to prayers as the award of new capabilities for personal change. A positive response from a higher power means that supplicants are given the spiritual resources to change negative distortions, and the mandate to recognize and utilize their untapped strengths. They are given tools for improving their lives, and a moral imperative to use them.

There is great similarity in the core elements of recovery in the Miami and Portland programs. In Portland, the Living Room has formulated ten essential steps to recovery. These are:

1. *Hope* (as motivator)
2. *Power* (from helplessness to empowerment and goal-planning)
3. *Responsibility* (from dependency to choice and self-help)
4. *People* (from taking to giving, contributing to others, integration in community support network)
5. *Activities* (constructive meaningful activities including school, work, volunteering, sports, cultural pursuits, and hobbies)
6. *Belief systems* (spirituality and healing; the power of positive thoughts)
7. *Self-knowledge* (reinterpreted and appreciated identity—"I am not a disease, I am a human being with a heart, mind, and soul, equal to all others")
8. *Success* (meaningful real-life roles, accepting support in high-risk situations)
9. *Renewal* (maintaining a recovery agenda)
10. *Mastery* (power, responsibility, productivity, inner peace)

In this model, healing starts with hope. People begin to recognize their power for fulfilling hope, moving from "I can't" to "I can." When hope, power, and responsibility are activated, the psychology of recovery begins to take root. With that in place, the individual can begin building four universal recovery and healing zones: *people*, *activities*, *belief system*, and *self-knowledge*. With repetition, practice, and perseverance, there can be success, renewal, and mastery.

Although they may be formulated differently, all of these goals are incorporated in the two programs described in this chapter. Their implementation is reinforced by discussion, acceptance, and the concern of their peers. The group is also a microcosmic community in which a more salutary conception of self and its possibilities may be tested, retested, and hopefully internalized as individuals prepare to improve their lives in the outside world.

CONCLUSIONS

Almost thirty years ago, Cutler and Tatum (1983) pointed out that "much of what has developed in outpatient mental health settings seems to rely on a one-to-one model and the wishful fantasy that therapy will enable the patient to develop his own support system" (p. 15). Like many others, these authors worked to develop a model community-based social support network for persons with severe and persistent mental illness, but in the ensuing decades, too little of this has come to pass. Despite the emergence of member-run Fountain House models, drop-in centers, and consumer-run services, supportive friendships are too often missing from the lives of patients receiving standard outpatient services. Moreover, in addition to findings of smaller, less functional social networks among persons with schizophrenia when compared with the non–psychiatric patient population, some investigators have reported significant within-group differences. There were even smaller social networks among patients with negative symptoms than those with positive symptoms (Hamilton et al., 1989). This suggested that withdrawn, apathetic, self-isolating patients, those most in need of social interaction, may have the fewest resources for socialization.

In this chapter we have described adventitiously created social networks and their effect as agents of change and growth. The therapeutic effects of groups are highly interactive, and may extend well beyond those offered in the individual clinical encounter. As we have indicated, self-absorption is a prevailing feature of serious mental illness. Dealing with voices, paranoid fears, or intractable depression, or seeking relief through substance abuse, the person is engaged with himself to the exclusion of others except as sources of need-satisfaction. In a psychotic state, thoughts are intrinsically solipsistic. Participation in a group enables individuals with serious mental illness to understand the thoughts and desires of others, and to abandon obsessive ruminations on past and present insults. The "egg salad sandwich story" illustrates the resumption of an empathic ability to comprehend and serve the needs of those perceived as less fortunate than oneself.

The mental health professional provides persons with a serious mental illness education about their conditions, illness-management techniques, and a cognitive framework for reevaluating their personal strengths and potential for control of their lives. The professional may provide a structured model for recovery. The group adds socialization, experiential understanding, and encouragement. With similar diagnoses and similar concerns, members acknowledge mutual problems of isolation, shame, and low self-esteem. They exchange information and coping techniques, and encourage overcoming unwarranted fears and perceived social stigma. To help their peers advance toward recovery, they provide role-modeling, friendship, and practical and emotional support. And ideally, all members apply what they have learned to facilitate their own recovery.

REFERENCES

Albert, M., Becker, T., McCrone, P., & Thornicroft, G. (1998). Social networks and mental health service utilization—a literature review. *International Journal of Social Psychiatry, 44,* 248–266.

Copeland, M.E. (1997). *Wellness Recovery Action Plan*. Brattleboro, VT: Peach Press.

Corrigan, P., McCorkle, B., Schell, B., & Kidder, K. (2003). Religion and spirituality in the lives of people with serious mental illness. *Community Mental Health Journal*, 39, 487–499.

Cutler, D.L., & Tatum, E. (1983). Networks and the chronic patient. *New Directions for Mental Health Services*, 19, 13–22.

Emerick, R.R. (1990) Self-help groups for former patients: Relations with mental health professionals. *Hospital and Community Psychiatry*, 41, 401–407.

Fukui, S., Starnino, V.R., Susana, M., Davison, L.J., Cook, K., Rapp, C.A., et al. (2011). Effect of Wellness Recovery Action Plan (WRAP) participation on psychiatry, sense of hope, and recovery. *Psychiatric Rehabilitation Journal*, 34, 214–222.

Goldstrom, I.D., Campbell, J., Rogers, J.A., Lambert, D.B., Blacklow, B., Henderson, M.J, et al. (2006). National estimates for mental health mutual support groups, self-help organizations, and consumer-operated services. *Administration and Policy in Mental Health and Mental Health Services Research*, 33, 92–103.

Hamilton, N.G., Ponzoha, C.A., Cutler, D.L., & Weigel, R.M. (1989). Social networks and negative symptoms versus positive symptoms of schizophrenia. *Schizophrenia Bulletin*, 15, 625–633.

Huguelet, P., Mohr, S., Betrisey, C., Borras, L., Gillieron, C., Marie, A.M., et al. (2011). A randomized trial of spiritual assessment of outpatients with schizophrenia: Patients' and clinicians' experience. *Psychiatric Services*, 62, 79–86.

Lefley, H.P. (2008). Advocacy, self-help, and consumer-operated services. In A. Tasman, J. Kay, J. Lieberman, M. first, & M. Maj . (Eds.), *Psychiatry* (3rd. ed., vol. 2., pp. 2083–2096). Chichester UK: John Wiley & Sons.

Lefley, H.P. (2009a). *Family Psychoeducation for Serious Mental Illness*. New York: Oxford University Press.

Lefley, H.P. (2009b). A psychoeducational support group for serious mental illness. *Journal for Specialists in Group Work*, 34, 369–381.

Lincoln, T.M., Wilhelm, K., & Nestoriuc, Y. (2007). Effectiveness of psychoeducation for relapse, symptoms, knowledge, adherence and functioning in psychotic disorders: A meta-analysis. *Schizophrenia Research*, 96, 232–245.

McFarlane, W. R. (2002). *Multifamily Groups in the Treatment of Severe Psychiatric Disorders*. New York: Guilford.

Mueser, K.T., Bond, G.R, & Drake, R.E. (2001). Community-based treatment of schizophrenia and other severe mental disorders: Treatment outcomes. *Medscape General Medicine*, 3(1), 1–24.

New Freedom Commission on Mental Health. (2003). *Achieving the Promise: Transforming Mental Health Care in America: Final Report*. DHHS Pub. No. SMA-03–3832, Rockville, MD.

Shapiro, P. (2010). *Healing Power: Ten Steps to Pain Management and Spiritual Evolution* (Rev. ed.). Bloomington, IN: AuthorHouse.

Stone, W.N. (2008). Group psychotherapy. In A. Tasman, J. Kay, J. Lieberman, M. First, & M. Maj . (Eds.), *Psychiatry* (3rd ed., vol. 2, pp. 1904–1919). Chichester, England: Wiley.

Temple University Collaborative on Community Inclusion (2010). *Into the Thick of Things: Connecting Consumers to Community Life: A Compendium of Community Initiatives for People with Psychiatric Disabilities at Consumer-Run Programs*. Philadelphia, PA: Temple University Collaborative on Community Inclusion of Individuals with Psychiatric Disabilities. Available at www.tucollaborative.org.

Xia, J., Merinder, L.B., & Belgamwar, M.R. (2011). Psychoeducation for schizophrenia. *Schizophrenia Bulletin*, 37, 21–22.

CHAPTER 11

CULTURAL COMPETENCY

DOMINICA F. MCBRIDE AND CARL C. BELL

INTRODUCTION

A strong, yet unnoticed undercurrent exists today in the United States. This undercurrent is nearly pervasive, affecting most of behavior, variations in thinking, and guiding people in their actions and interactions. For centuries, this underlying phenomenon has influenced our society and professions without being explicitly acknowledged and addressed, until recently. Due to the ever-increasing diversity in America, culture and multiculturalism have begun to be of focus in research and healthcare. However, this focus is not yet strong enough to have the necessary impact to create a society where all are equally healthy or have equal opportunity to succeed. Culture is a multidimensional and potent construct that influences health behaviors, ways of thinking, beliefs and values, language, relationships and relating, among many other human dynamics. Because of its omnipresence, it is often forgotten or ignored. Further, due to ethnocentrism and the human propensity to favor those in-group or similar, multiculturalism is also devalued or unnoticed. This natural tendency is further complicated in helping professions and interdisciplinary teams—when there are also multiple cultural influences (values, beliefs, history) on various levels (individual, interpersonal, teams). Those who are trying to help change behavior and enhance health necessarily must meet and face these challenges. Since improving health and society is most effective through sound interdisciplinary teamwork (Langer, 1999; Purden, 2005; Bell, McBride, Redd, & Suggs, 2012), the interdisciplinary team must travel on the path toward cultural competence. This chapter explicates the need for cultural competence, the process of enhancing cultural competence, cultural competence in interdisciplinary teams or "interprofessional cultural competence" (Pecukonis, Doyle, & Bliss, 2008), and assessing cultural competence.

STEREOTYPING AND CONSEQUENT BEHAVIORS: EVERYONE DOES IT

Cultural competence is a construct that many may deem either unnecessary or irrelevant due to color-blindness (Burkard & Knox, 2004) or a denial of prejudice (Alexandar, 2010; Greenwald & Banaji, 1995). With the passing of the Civil Rights Act of 1964 and the years following, people of the United States find it difficult to admit to any prejudice, discrimination, or tendency to stereotype. However, prejudice, discrimination, and stereotyping are natural human mechanisms (Pinderhughes, 1979; Greenwald & Banaji, 1995; Pecukonis, Doyle, & Bliss, 2008; Fiske, 1992) that have protective and psychological value. Due to automaticity (i.e., the natural tendency of the brain to conserve energy and automate processes and behavior), we create associations and stereotype. Ofttimes, these associations and stereotypes are constructive (Fiske, 1992). For example, even if a chair is a different shape or color than we are used to, we know we can sit in it and not have to use mental energy figuring out if it is something upon which we can sit. Our energy is saved for something more significant, like danger and protection. This function can be used not only to preserve energy but also to cope with uncertainty, especially in social situations. According to Pecukonis, Doyle, and Bliss (2008),

> Reducing this subjective sense of uncertainty within our important social interactions promotes predictability and control. One way to reduce uncertainty is to utilize stereotypes.... These biased, but easily available templates or prototypes provide a roadmap for behavior within these social situations, and thus reduce uncertainty (p. 422).

However, like many human phenomena, these psychological protective mechanisms can become exaggerated and maladaptive. When unnecessarily transposed onto people or groups, gratuitous fear and divisions can ensue, which work against social protective factors, like collective efficacy or community. In short, certain stereotypes incite prejudice and discrimination (American Psychiatric Association, 2006). These attitudes and behaviors often work below the surface of consciousness (i.e., "implicit cognition") and are affected by experiences and exposure. Stereotyping and attitudes have "implicit modes of operation," which means that even if a person explicitly denies adopting a certain stereotype or prejudice, a feeling or belief may still very well be operating and driving behaviors but on an subconscious level (Greenwald & Banaji, 1995). Therefore, we must be aware of the presence of underlying stereotypes and prejudice despite believing we may be color-blind or see everyone neutrally. Furthermore, *any judgment placed upon implicit processes needs to be ameliorated*, especially in order to recognize, identify, and address them.

THE HARM OF CULTURAL INCOMPETENCE

Due to this implicitness and the influence of implicit cognition on behavior, myriad unintentional slights occur toward marginalized groups (e.g., people of color, low socioeconomic status (SES) communities, disabled, and women). These slights are called microinsults and *microaggressions* (Pierce, 1995; American Psychiatric Association, 2003; Sue et al., 2007), a form of cultural incompetence. An example of a microaggression is if a customer in a grocery store mistakes a black man for a store employee, when in actuality he is another customer. Another example is a woman in a healthcare setting who is presumed to be a nurse when she is a physician. Microaggressions have been identified as contributing to current racial disparities in this nation, including education (Gordon & Johnson, 2003), health (Betancourt, Green, Emmilio, Carrillo, & Park, 2005; Gilmore, 2007; Langer, 1999), and equal opportunities for employment (Alexandar, 2010; Gordon & Johnson, 2003). These offenses can take many forms, including ignoring a group's history (e.g., oppression) and/or context (e.g., structural barriers to success for people of color) and being condescending to a person or group (Sue et al., 2007). In the criminal justice system, these slights are demonstrated through a disproportionate focus of police officers on young black men. This focus has led to significant and devastating racial disparities in the criminal justice system and the creation (or perpetuation) of a "racial undercaste" (Alexandar, 2010).

In health care, these insults can manifest in the doctor–patient relationship. The doctor may ignore contextual struggles of a person from a low SES community that hinder compliance to a medical regimen and, therefore, label the person "noncompliant." Van Ryn and Burke (2000) found that race affects physicians' perceptions of patients. Despite controlling for SES and education, Black patients were perceived as more likely to abuse alcohol and substances, less likely to comply, less likely to accept or go along with recommendations or prescriptions, less intelligent and educated (despite being educated), and black patients from low SES communities were less likely to be seen as pleasant or rational. (Remember: Implicit cognition affects behavior [Greenwald & Banaji, 1995].) Subsequently, the Agency for Health Care and Research Quality (AHCRQ, 2006) conducted a study examining the variation in relationships that patients of different ethnicities had with their healthcare providers. The findings are not surprising, given the aforementioned differences in implicit cognitions of physicians. African Americans, Asian American/Pacific Islanders, and Hispanics reported they were not listened to carefully, were not given proper explanations, or were denied respect more often than their European American counterparts. Further, Asian Americans/Pacific Islanders, African Americans, Native Americans, and Hispanics reported sometimes or never having good communication with healthcare professionals more often than their white counterparts. All this exists despite research supporting the patient–doctor relationship influences the patient's health status and outcomes (AHCRQ, 2006). This type of negligence or incompetence can also affect prescriptions and effectiveness of medication (Herbeck et al., 2004). For example, because of biological variation between ethnic groups (e.g., ability to metabolize CYP 2D6 substrates: Lin, Smith, & Ortiz, 2001), different ethnic groups have different levels of tolerance for psychiatric medications (Lin & Elwyn, 2004). Therefore, the general doses doctors may prescribe to the American majority—Caucasians—may not be healthy for the American minority—people of color (Bell, 2008). We must realize and acknowledge that Western medicine is not a panacea, nor is it always "best practices" (Katz, 1985). The efficacy of any treatment, even so-called evidence-based, can depend on cultural and contextual variations (Basic Behavioral Science Task Force of the National Advisory Mental Health Council, 1996). Thus, for a clinician to disregard or ignore culture and context is irresponsible and goes against the Hippocratic Oath and healthcare ethics of non-maleficence and beneficence.

This lack of consideration has also been present in the relationships of mental health professionals and their clients (Thomas & Sillen, 1972). Burkard and Knox (2004) found that professionals who hold color-blind racial attitudes are likely to avoid attributing a person of color's plight to racist institutions or history. Instead, they attributed it solely to "laziness" or lack of effort, thus, perpetuating racism and increasing the chances of that person not completing therapy. Those indicating higher color-blindness exhibited statistically significantly less empathy and placed the responsibility of solving the problem on the black clients more often than on the white clients, which has led to premature termination, amplifying the extant distrust of psychiatric services in people of color (See Wade & Bernstein, 1991).

DEFINING CULTURAL COMPETENCE

Ostensibly, cultural incompetence has deleterious effects on health and society. Therefore, building cultural competence within health professions and society in general is vital and necessary to achieving social justice on all fronts.

The root of cultural competence is culture. Various definitions have been used for *culture*. The American Psychological Association (2003) has a comprehensive definition. Therefore, we have adopted their definition, which is:

> the belief systems and value orientations that influence customs, norms, practices, and social institutions, including psychological processes (language, caretaking practices, media, educational systems) and organizations…[and] the embodiment of a worldview through learned and transmitted beliefs, values, and practices, including religious and spiritual traditions. It also encompasses a way of living informed by the historical, economic, ecological, and political forces on a group (p. 380).

Culture can be seen as many things; however, there are constructs that culture is often confused with, like race. Although race is related to culture, they are not synonymous (U.S. Department of Health and Human Services, 2001). Their relationship is through context. Due to the shared contextual and/or historical experience of many racial groups (e.g., slavery, internment camp oppression), the people within those groups *generally* have adopted similar beliefs and values. The term *generally* is emphasized here because all groups have more variation within the group than between (Rogoff, 2003; McBride, 2011). Thus, it is important, when moving toward cultural competence, that people do not adopt new stereotypes based on the information learned in the process.

Cultural competence is knowing this fact, balancing it with culture and shared experience and values of groups, and recognizing and responding to the aforementioned implicit cognitions and microaggressions. Furthermore, cultural competence is: 1) the awareness of one's own biases and attitudes, cultural influences, behaviors, and communication style, and how they differ from others'; 2) the knowledge of one's own cultural influences and the cultures of others, how cultures have developed over time and are shaped by context, how current macro- and micro-structures can affect the individual or a group; 3) the skills in responding to differences in culture and communication and addressing macro- and micro-structures that perpetuate social injustice (Sue, 2001; Sue, Arredondo, & McDavis, 1992). Cultural competence is also seen as compassion, empathy, listening, and understanding. Since culture can be applied to various groups, including organizations, disciplines, and professions, cultural competence also applies to interdisciplinary work (Fanchet, 1995). Pecukonis, Doyle, and Bliss (2008) call this "interprofessional cultural competence." Overall, the purpose of cultural competence is to interact with and effectively respond to people of different backgrounds and belief systems, abate extant disparities, and ameliorate social injustice still present in organizations and society.

THE IMPORTANCE OF CULTURAL COMPETENCE

Cultural competence has been found effective in addressing many problems, especially around mental, behavioral, and physical health, which is the focus of this section. Wade and Bernstein (1991) found that when black female clients were randomly assigned to counselors with and without cultural competence training, the clients with the culturally competent counselors fared better in therapy. They attended more sessions, completed therapy, and were more satisfied with their treatment than those who had received therapy from a counselor without cultural competence training. A similar effect has been found in HIV prevention. Responding to and incorporating the culture of the participants has been effective in changing behavior. Kalichman et al. (1993) showed three videos discussing HIV/AIDS to African American women, with the goal of reducing risky behaviors. One video showed Caucasians talking about the epidemic and how to protect oneself; another video showed black women giving the same information in the same context; and the final video showed black women giving the information, but in a community setting with culturally relevant context (e.g., community, family). The culturally relevant video was the most effective. Significantly more women who viewed this video were tested for HIV following the viewing and came to receive condoms at follow-up; they were also more concerned about the epidemic. Using culturally relevant messages and communication has also been effective in preventing substance abuse. The Strong African American Families program (Brody et al., 2004) found inclusion of racial socialization to be effective in preventing substance abuse with black adolescents. For one of the most fatal diseases plaguing African Americans, culture was found, again, to be an integral factor in effective prevention. Paz (2002) asserted the same—culturally competent substance abuse prevention works—with Latinos. Stolley, Fitzgibbon, Wells, and Martinovich's (2004) intervention incorporated issues such as "soul food" and gave recipes and training on making healthy soul food; disseminated information on low-cost, easily accessible healthy behaviors (e.g., exercise tapes at homes, walking); addressed family and their behaviors; and integrated religion/spirituality in their teaching of healthy living. The culturally specific intervention worked well and was much appreciated by the participants. Bell et al. (2008) illustrate how adapting a U.S.-based HIV prevention intervention to a South African Zulu culture increases acceptance of the intervention. Zeller (2008) described a program integrating Aboriginal culture for Aboriginal men in prison for battering. The program infused cultural beliefs (spiritual, medicine wheel), values (peace, good relationships), rituals (corners of the earth/directions), and practices (sweat lodge) in rectifying behavior. The use of culture was effective in increasing openness to others, enhancing social skills, and improving communication.

Within medical care, the lack of cultural competence can lead to prolonged morbidity and premature mortality, for if patients do not comply with (competent) suggested medical regimens, they may die. Therefore, developing a solid working alliance is essential to positive health outcomes; cultural competence and sensitivity is integral in developing this quality relationship. Further, true understanding of a patient's predicament and ability to apply recommended behaviors depends on the level of cultural competence and openness of the doctor (Langer, 1999). Diabetes is one example of the necessity for cultural understanding. This is a lifelong disease that is greatly affected by health behaviors, and culture influences behavior that can affect health. The health professional should be knowledgeable about the culture(s) and the related behaviors in order to make accurate assessments and provide good recommendations or responses (Langer, 1999; Tang, Fantone, Bozynski, & Adams, 2002). Understanding these influences will also help the professional in understanding why adherence did not occur. Examples of some of the barriers to health behavior related to context/culture are poverty, overcrowded housing, neighborhood crime (inhibiting exercise), diet, and a lack of transportation (Langer, 1999).

As with health problems like diabetes and substance abuse, both general and interprofessional cultural competence are integral in optimal care, especially since such disorders require addressing both the mind and the body (Langer, 1999). Therefore, interdisciplinary team functioning can directly affect patient care. Purden (2005) found, in Canada with the Aboriginal people, effective health services are respectful and understanding of the culture, include the community, and use an interprofessional or interdisciplinary approach in order to bridge the gap in health services in certain areas. If the various professionals cannot effectively relate and communicate, the common mission is compromised. Cultural competence in this arena, like all others, encompasses openness, self-exploration (Richardson & Molinaro, 1996), listening, and understanding (Langer, 1999).

THE PROCESS OF CULTURAL COMPETENCE

Cultural competence is a process of becoming that can be adopted on multiple levels, from the micro to the macro (see Figure 11.1). Sue (2001) described a comprehensive model for cultural competence called the "multidimensional model for cultural competence," which includes: 1) dimensions—race/ethnicity/culture specific (e.g., Black, Native, Hispanic, Asian, and White); 2) components of cultural competence—self awareness, knowledge, skills; and

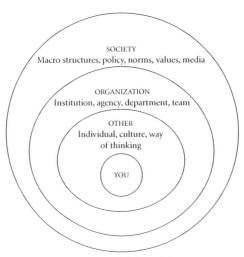

FIGURE 11.1 Levels of Cultural Competence

3) foci—individual, professional, organizational, societal. It can be manifested within the individual in thought, attitude, and action, within the organization in policy, practice, and philosophy, and within society through social equity and competent policy. In Figure 11.1, the you represents each one of us—both our internal processes and dynamics and overt behaviors. The other represents other individuals that we can influence (e.g., our colleagues, friends). Organizations represent structured entities comprised of people, policies, and institutions. Lastly, society is the larger social structure, including people, communities, norms, and greater policies.

INDIVIDUAL/OTHER/PROFESSIONAL

This process begins with the individual, starting with the three components: awareness of beliefs and attitudes, knowledge, and skills (Sue, 2001; Sue, Arredondo, & McDavis, 1992). Becoming aware of and acknowledging one's implicit and explicit beliefs and attitudes involves introspection. This aspect encompasses a growing awareness of biases and how they influence psychological processes and relationships with clients/treatment. It means being sensitive to one's own cultural influences and biases, recognizing one's limits, and being aware of cultural differences between oneself and others (clients) and emotional reactions toward clients of other cultures, races, and ethnicities (Richardson & Molinaro, 1996; Sue, Arredondo, & McDavis, 1992).

The aspect of knowledge includes knowledge of one's own cultural influences, personal and professional, and how they impact decisions, definitions, and biases of abnormality and normality (Reich & Reich, 2006; U.S. Department of Health and Human Services, 2001). What are various aspects of American culture? How do these cultural influences (e.g., individualism, capitalism, materialism) affect living for different individuals and groups in society? For instance, American culture is highly individualistic. This dynamic can create problems not only for those who grew up in and adopted the culture but also for those who are in one cultural milieu but who have a different dominant culture (e.g., Asian, African). This individualism can work against true personhood and recovery, since it is a fact that social support through family and/or community is often healing (Bell, 2008).

Knowledge should span past individual, internal boundaries into context. The helping professional should know of how professional style impacts others (e.g., communication). Professionals should be knowledgeable about sociopolitical influences and how racism, discrimination, and oppression impact themselves (e.g., white privilege, own biases) and others. For instance, since 1982, the onset of the "war on drugs," there has been a transformation of the old Jim Crow era into a New Jim Crow, which is deliberately placing black individuals into a new "racial undercaste" (Alexandar, 2010). Now, there are more black men disenfranchised and black families disrupted than in 1870 (Alexandar, 2010; Loury, 2008). Information such as this directly relates to knowledge of a target group/culture (client/patient). General knowledge about a group includes how culture influences personality, help-seeking behavior, and disorder manifestation. It also includes how culture can be destructive (as in the New Jim Crow) or curative. Culture can provide protective factors for people through shaping practices that increase and maintain constructs like optimism, resilience, satisfaction, spiritual wellbeing, wisdom, worldview, connectedness, and trust (Bell, 2011). For example, in some Eastern cultures, collectivism is valued over individualism. Collectivism or collective efficacy/social fabric, alluded to previously, is a protective factor, effective in preventing HIV/AIDS, violence, substance abuse, and strengthening families (Bell et al., 2008; Bell, Flay, & Paikoff, 2002; McBride & Bell, 2011).

Health professionals should also be knowledgeable about bias of assessments and instruments (Fraga, Atkinson, & Wampold, 2004; Langer, 1999) like the Minnesota Multiphasic Personality Inventory (MMPI).

Culturally competent skills include the ability to take the awareness and knowledge gained and apply it appropriately. Appropriate actions can include additional education, referring when necessary, and obtaining consultation. These skills include self-examination, actively growing in cultural competence, and seeking out multicultural experiences. They also include the ability to decipher whether a problem is due to or influenced by structural discrimination or preju-dice (e.g., racism, sexism, heterosexism) and enact apt interventions and actions. A culturally competent professional should also be able to conduct culturally sensitive assessment (e.g., using appropriate instruments, including family). Culture constitutes meaning and shapes the meaning of events for others. If this meaning is ignored, a great deal of pertinent and necessary information is lost in the assessment, diagnosis, and treatment plan. Assessment should not only include the individual's presenting problem and traditional assessment components (e.g., mental health history, substance abuse, past treatment) but also past experiences of societal oppression and subjugation (Bell, 2011).

Prelock et al. (2003) described a culturally competent process used in interdisciplinary assessment of children with autism. Their assessments included genograms and ecomaps (a pic-ture of the family and its context), including and focusing on the family and their environment. Information from assessments (both formal and informal) is used to feed clinical interpretation, which also requires cultural competence. Assessments should also include the strengths of a person's culture and how connected the patient is to their cultural strengths (Bell & McBride, 2011). Cultural competence also avoids the pitfall of misdiagnosis. Three decades ago, Bell and Mehta (1980; 1981) highlighted the problem of misdiagnosis of African Americans who suffered from "manic-depressive illness" as having schizophrenia—a lesson that still has to be reinforced, as misdiagnosis of this population continues to this day (Chien & Bell, 2008). Conflicts or dif-ferences in cultural values can lead to miscommunications and inaccurate interpretations. For example, European American culture is doing- and future-oriented. It values planning, schedul-ing, and a "time is money" philosophy. A clinician or physician who is influenced by these cul-tural values may interpret a therapy client who is of another culture and late to be resistant when the client actually is committed but has a different values system as it relates to time (Carter, 1991). Furthermore, a physician may interpret a patient to be noncompliant when, in actuality, the patient is restricted by the environment and, thus, cannot comply (Langer, 1999).

Metaphorically, culture is like "water to a fish"—it is pervasive and influences so much of human life but often goes unnoticed. The process of gaining cultural competence on an individ-ual level begins with noticing this water, how it affects one's own daily life, thoughts, and actions, and how it affects others. It then moves to learning about the water, the particles and structures, and how it differs in different places and for different "fish." It culminates with "swimming delib-erately", cooperating, peacefully coexisting, and effectively interacting with others.

ORGANIZATION

Individual cultural competence, especially with helping and healthcare professionals, tran-scends the intrapsychic processes and interpersonal interactions to target structures. The pur-pose of these professional services is to heal. Unfortunately, mental health services in this nation can be deleterious and unintentionally cause further harm through cultural incompetence and microaggressions. Therefore, it can actually contribute to social injustice, widening the gap of mental health service accessibility. Thus, mental health clinicians, educators, and researchers must work against this and manifest cultural competence in every sense of the meaning, including countering structural injustice. What good is it to bolster and develop a culturally competent professional if they just to go work in a monocultural, ethnocentric organization that discourages or punishes cultural competence (e.g., accepting certain gifts, doing alternative therapies, working with a shaman)? Thus, professionals must also work to propagate cultural competence in systems—educational, professional, organizations, and society (Sue, 2001).

Organizations have their own culture. For instance, some work as a "machine," with strict and immovable practices and policies, with an operator that pushes a button and all others fall into place; while others work as an "organism," flexible, molding, and growing with time, context, and people (Morgan, 1997). Organizations also exhibit or fail to manifest cultural competence, falling somewhere on a spectrum of organizational cultural competence (Sue, 2001, Jackson & Holvino, 1988; and see Figure 11.2). The monocultural or culturally incompetent organization not only disregards or devalues cultural variation but also stringently adheres to ethnocentric, monocultural policies and practices (Sue, 2001). On the other side of the spectrum, multicultural organizations parallel the multicultural competence in the individual; a truly multicultural organization not only manifests multiculturalism internally by appreciating, soliciting, and being open to diversity of many kinds, but also being proactive, such as fighting oppression and "isms" externally—in society (Jackson & Holvino, 1988).

Interdisciplinary team. Interdisciplinary teams can fall under these same categories of organizational cultural competence and develop the same process of becoming culturally competent (e.g., individual understanding and openness, increasing and respecting diversity within the team, applying culturally sensitive practices, moving toward social justice). As stated previously, a discipline is a culture too. Therefore, the interdisciplinary teams are also susceptible to interpersonal and interprofessional slights or devaluing, which can cause problems on the team and, thus, compromise treatment or the mission. "Similar to ethnocentrism, profession-centrism

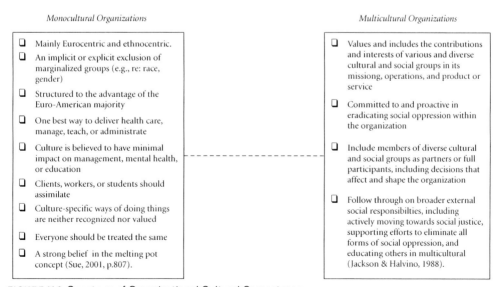

FIGURE 11.2 Spectrum of Organizational Cultural Competence

(professional centric thinking) is a constructed and preferred view of the world held by a particular professional group developed and reinforced through their training experiences" (Pecukonis, Doyle, & Bliss, 2008, p. 420). This profession-centrism, like ethnocentrism, can be abated with deliberate work and training. Perceiving the value or strengths in another profession, especially when working together, can provide an opportunity for utilizing those assets for the good of the client or patient (or achieving the goal, in general). For instance, physicians are educated in the biological bases of human life and how these mechanisms impact health, wellbeing, and sometimes even behavior. Social work has a rich tradition of studying and addressing the intersection of the individual, family, community, and ecology. There is much for each profession to learn from one another. When the two are combined, the picture of the human being becomes clearer and more accurate.

Various scholars have described experiences, findings, and conclusions in creating interprofessional cultural competence. Two core principles in good interdisciplinary functioning and cultural competence are effective communication (Lu, 2003) and true collaboration (Marcus, 2000). Reich and Reich (2006) described various pitfalls to plan for and avoid in doing culturally competent interdisciplinary work, including 1) tokenism: do not place disciplines on the team without an intent to equally include them and integrate their knowledge and skills; 2) silence and power: ensure that power is equally distributed and no person's opinion or knowledge is neglected (e.g., in data, resource allocations, and access to information); and 3) disciplinary policing: people may be averse to others or themselves' crossing disciplinary boundaries. Pecukonis, Doyle, and Bliss (2008) suggested, in enhancing intraprofessional cultural competence and addressing some of these dilemmas, the professional should have a "good IDEA":

Interaction with people from other health disciplines to gain familiarity with other disciplines;

Data (accurate) on other professions and on each individual as a person and not just a profession;

Expertise in effective communication with other disciplines—being able to both communicate one's own discipline to others, including values and principles, and openly listen to others;

Attention to one's own discipline—its culture, history, values, norms and attention to others or "professional self-reflection," should be able to discuss similarities and differences between professions with one another.

Levinson and Thornton (2003) suggested six components in successful interdisciplinary teamwork. Although their team's process was general and not related to culture, medicine, or psychology, their lessons learned are essential in interdisciplinary cultural competence. According to them, each team needs to: 1) have a strong leader, 2) check their egos at the door, 3) have a commitment to the project, 4) have rules of inclusiveness that are respected and maintained, 5) have young researchers focus on their discipline—for professional growth and clout, and 6) have a focus on developing the next generation of scientists. Strong leadership, especially in a culturally competent interdisciplinary team, is essential (Bell, McBride, Redd, & Suggs, 2012). Culturally competent leaders must be aware of "biases and assumptions" that exist in their organization or team. They must be willing to take unpopular positions on social issues to promote social justice, target oppression, and address injustices in their team, and recruit people who are underrepresented in their profession (Arredondo, 2008). Others have found easy yet efficacious tactics that can be used with those outside of leadership, supplementing some of the aforementioned core principles with individual roles, including a "jargon buster" and "equalizer," who ensures everyone has equal "air time" and is respected (Prelock et al., 2003).

CULTURAL COMPETENCE TRAINING

Regardless of the process or structure, cultural competence often begins with humility (Tervalon & Murray-Garcia, 1998), education, and/or experience. Training can provide (or elicit) each of these scaffolds. Cultural competence training has been found to be an effective tool in moving one along in the process (Beach et al., 2005; American Psychological Association, 2003; Webb & Sergison, 2003) and has been suggested for growing cultural competence in clinical interdisciplinary teams (Lu, 2003). It has caused statistically significant improvements in counselors' and doctors' behavior with clients and patients, which had improvements in clients' health (Tang, Fantone, Bozynski, & Adams, 2002; Langer, 1999). Particularly in a medical setting, training has been shown to enhance experience with sociocultural issues, understanding of the importance of and relationship among sociocultural background, health, and medicine, and improve the doctor–patient relationship (Tang, Fantone Bozynski, & Adams, 2002). Such training can come in various forms, from small-group discussion, lecture, immersion (Warner, 2002), case examples, storytelling or sharing experiences (Papadopoulos, Tilki, & Lees, 2004), personal journaling, videotaping and feedback, and professional role modeling from one's own and other cultural groups (Tervalon & Murray-Garcia, 1998). Regardless of the methodology used within the training, it should focus on cultural understanding and awareness over stereotypic information of a particular group (e.g., providing a "menu" for different groups, such as "in treating Latinos, you should . . ."; Webb & Sergison, 2003).

MEASURING CULTURAL COMPETENCE

As with any program or professional activity, knowing the value or effect of the initiative helps to affirm or disconfirm the validity or soundness of practices and guide future practice. Fortunately, there are ways that we can evaluate and measure cultural competence. There are several reliable and valid assessment instruments (Suarez-Balcazar et al., 2011; Doorenbos, Schim, Benkert, & Borse, 2005). The Cultural Competence Assessment (CCA) has been found to be the best measure for competence with healthcare providers. The CCA is a valid and reliable instrument for measuring cultural diversity experience, cultural awareness and sensitivity, and cultural competence behaviors and is especially applicable and relevant for healthcare providers. It was also made to fill the gap in available cultural competence instruments for interdisciplinary healthcare teams (Doorenbos et al., 2005).

CONCLUSION

In the previous decades, culture and diversity were unrecognized and deeply undervalued. This pervasive ethnocentrism has hindered national progress in nearly all areas, including education, economics, and national health. Fortunately, in recent years, the value of diversity and the importance of culture have started to be recognized and used. Now there is sound research that evidences the need to focus on and include cultural variation. From the harm of microaggressions, cultural ignorance, and color-blindness to the rectifying effects of cultural responsiveness, culture competence can now soundly be spotlighted and integrated throughout service development and delivery. Despite the deleterious aftermath of cultural incompetence, we can remedy our social situation with cultural competence, which can be attained through awareness, humility, and training. There is enough empirical support for widespread endeavors, such as requiring all professions to take cultural competence training and making cultural competence an ethical imperative (Niermeier, Burnett, & Whitaker, 2003). "To top it off," we are able to measure our progress with reliable tools. Recognizing the data, evidence, harm, and corrective possibilities, there is no better time to move toward making cultural competence ubiquitous.

REFERENCES

Agency for Health Care and Research Quality. (2006). *National Health Disparities Report.* Retrieved June 24, 2011, from http://www.ahrq.gov/qual/nhdr06/report/.

Alexandar, M. (2010). *The New Jim Crow: Mass Incarceration in the Age of Colorblindness.* New York: The New York Press.

American Psychiatric Association. (2003). *American Psychiatric Glossary*, 8th ed. Washington, DC: American Psychiatric Press, p. 120.

American Psychiatric Association. (2006). *Resolution Against Racism and Racial Discrimination and Their Adverse Impacts on Mental Health.* Washington, DC: American Psychiatric Association.

American Psychological Association. (2003). Guidelines on multicultural education, training, research, practice, and organizational change for psychologists. *American Psychologist, 58,* 377–402.

Arredondo, P. (2008). Using professional leadership to promote multicultural understanding and social justice. *Journal of Pacific Rim Psychology, 2,* 13–17.

Basic Behavioral Science Task Force of the National Advisory Mental Health Council. (1996). Basic behavioral science research for mental health: Sociocultural and environmental processes. *American Psychologist, 51,* 722–731.

Beach, M. C., Price, E. G., Gary, T. L., Robinson, K. A., Gozu, A., Palacio, A., et al. (2005). A Systematic Review of Health Care Provider Educational Interventions. *Medical Care, 43,* 356–373.

Bell, C. C., & Mehta H. (1980). The misdiagnosis of black patients with manic depressive illness. *Journal of the National Medical Association, 72,* 141–145.

Bell. C. C., & Mehta H. (1981). The misdiagnosis of black patients with manic depressive illness II. *Journal of the National Medical Association, 73,* 101–107.

Bell. C. C., Flay, B., Paikoff, R. (2002). Strategies for health behavior change. In: Chunn, J., (Ed.), *The Health Behavioral Change Imperative*, (pp. 17–39). New York: Kluwer Academic/Plenum Publishers.

Bell, C. C. (2008). Should culture considerations influence early interventions? In Blumenfield, M., & Ursano, R. J. (Eds.), *Intervention and Resilience after Mass Trauma,* pp. 127–148. Cambridge, NY: Cambridge University Press.

Bell, C. C, Bhana, A., Petersen, I., et al. (2008). Building protective factors to offset sexually risky behaviors among black South African youth: A randomized control trial. *Journal of the National Medical Association, 100,* 936–944.

Bell, C. C. (2011). Trauma, culture, and resiliency. In Southwick, S. W., Litz, B. T., Charney, D., & Friedman, M. J. (Eds.), *Resilience and Mental Health: Challenges Across the Lifespan.* (pp. 176–188) New York: Cambridge University Press.

Bell, C. C., & McBride, D. F. (2011). A commentary for furthering culturally sensitive research in geriatric psychiatry. *Journal of Geriatric Psychiatry, 19,* 397–402.

Bell, C. C., McBride, D. F., Redd, H., & Suggs, H. (2012). Team-Based Treatment. In McQuistion, H., Feldman, J., Ranz, J., & Sowers, W. (Eds.), *Handbook of Community Psychiatry (pp. 211–222).* New York: Springer.

Betancourt, J. R., Green, A. R., Emmilio Carrillo, J., & Park, E. R. (2005). Cultural competence and health care disparities: Key perspectives and trends. *Health Affairs, 24,* 499–505.

Brody, G. H., Murry, V. M., Gerrard, M., Gibbons, F. X., Molgaard, V., McNair, L., Brown, A. C., Wills, T. A., Spoth, R. L., Luo, Z., Chen, Y., & Neubaum-Carlan, E. (2004). The Strong African American families program: Translating research into prevention programming. *Child Development, 75,* 900–917.

Burkard, A. W., & Knox, S. (2004). Effect of therapist color-blindness on empathy and attributions in cross-cultural counseling. *Journal of Counseling Psychology,* 51, 387–397.

Carter, R. T. (1991). Cultural values: A review of empirical research and implications for counseling. *Journal of Counseling and Development, 90,* 164–173.

Chien, P. L., & Bell, C. C. (2008). Racial differences and schizophrenia. *Directions in Psychiatry, 28,* 285–292.

Doorenbos, A. Z., Schim, S. M., Benkert, R., & Borse, N. N. (2005). Psychometric evaluation of the cultural competence assessment instrument among healthcare providers. *Nursing Research, 54,* 324–331.

Fanchet, R. T. (1995). *Cultures of Healing—Correcting the Image of American Mental Health Care.* New York: W.H. Freeman and Company.

Fiske, S. (1992). Thinking is for doing: Portraits of social cognition from daguerreotype to laserphoto. *Journal of Personality and Social Psychology, 63,* 877–889.

Fraga, E. D., Atkinson, D. R., & Wampold, B. E. (2004). Ethnic group preferences for multicultural counseling competencies. *Cultural Diversity and Ethnic Minority Psychology, 10,* 53–65.

Gilmore, J. A. (2007). Reducing disparities in the access and use of Internet health information. A discussion paper. *International Journal of Nursing Studies, 44,* 1270–1278.

Gordon, J ., & Johnson, M. (2003). Race, speech, and hostile educational environment: What color is free speech? *Journal of Social Philosophy, 34,* 414–436.

Greenwald, A. G., & Banaji, M. R. (1995). Implicit social cognition: Attitudes, self-esteem, and stereotypes. *Psychological Review, 102,* 4–27.

Herbeck, D. M., West, J. C., Ruditis, I., Duffy, F. F., Fitek, D. J., Bell, C. C., et al. (2004). Variations in use of second-generation antipsychotic medication by race among adult psychiatric patients. *Psychiatric Services, 55,* 677–684.

Jackson, B. W., & Holvino, E. (1988). Developing multicultural organizations. *Journal of Religion and Applied Behavioral Sciences, 9,* 14–19.

Kalichman, C., Kelly, J., Hunter, T., Murphy, D., & Tyler, R. (1993). Culturally tailored HIV-AIDS risk-reduction messages targeted to African-American urban women: Impact on risk sensitization and risk reduction. *Journal Consulting and Clinical Psychology, 61,* 291–295.

Katz, J. H. (1985). The sociopolitical nature of counseling. *The Counseling Psychologist, 13*, 615–624.

Langer, N. (1999). Culturally competent professionals in therapeutic alliances enhance patient compliance. *Journal of Health Care for the Poor and Underserved, 10*, 19–26.

Levinson, B., & Thornton, K. W. (2003). Managing interdisciplinary research: Lessons learned from the EPA-STAR/NSF/USDA Water and Watersheds Research Program. In Renard, K., McElroy, S., Gburek, W., Canfield, H., & Scott, R. (Eds.), *First Interagency Conference on Research in the Watersheds*. (pp. 675–679). U.S. Department of Agriculture, Agricultural Research Service. Accessed online at http://www.tucson.ars.ag.gov/icrw/Proceedings/Levinson.pdf on May 11, 2011

Lin, K. M., Smith, M. W., & Ortiz, V. (2001). Culture and psychopharmacology. *Psychiatric Clinics of North America, 24*, 523–538.

Lin, K. M., & Elwyn, T. S. (2004). Culture and drug therapy. In Tseng, W. S., & Streltzer, J. (Eds.), *Cultural Competence in Clinical Psychiatry*, pp. 163–180. Washington, DC: American Psychiatric Press.

Loury, G. C. (2008). *Race, Incarceration, and American Values*. Cambridge, MA: MIT Press.

Lu, F . (2003). Culture and inpatient psychiatry. In Tseng, W ., & Stretlzer, J. (Eds.), *Cultural Competence in Clinical Psychiatry* (pp. 21–36). San Diego, CA: Academic Press.

Marcus, M.T. (2000). An interdisciplinary team model for substance abuse prevention in communities. *Journal of Professional Nursing, 16*, 158–168.

McBride, D. F. (2011). Sociocultural theory: Providing more structure to culturally responsive evaluation. . *New Directions for Evaluation, 131*, 7–13.

McBride, D. F., & Bell, C. C. (2011). Human immunodeficiency virus prevention in youth. *Psychiatric Clinics of North America, 34*, 217–229.

Michelle van Ryn, Jane Burke (2000). The effect of patient race and socio-economic status on physicians' perceptions of patients. *Social Science & Medicine, 50*, 813–828.

Morgan, G. (1997). *Images of Organization*. Thousand Oaks, CA: Sage Publications.

Niermeier, J. P., Burnett, D. M., Whitaker, D. A. (2003). Cultural competence in the multidisciplinary rehabilitation setting: Are we falling short of meeting needs? *Archives of Physical Medicine and Rehabilitation, 84*, 1240–1245.

Papadopoulos, I., Tilki, M., Lees, S. (2004). Promoting cultural competence in healthcare through a research-based intervention in the U.K. *Diversity in Health and Social Care*, 107–116.

Paz, J. (2002). Culturally competent substance abuse treatment with Latinos. *Journal of Human Behavior in the Social Environment, 5*(3–4), 123–136.

Pecukonis, E., Doyle, O., & Bliss, D. L. (2008). Reducing barriers to interprofessional training: Promoting interprofessional cultural competence. *Journal of Interprofessional Care, 22*, 417–428.

Pierce, C. (1995). Stress analogs of racism and sexism: Terrorism, torture, and disaster. In Willie, C., Rieker, P., Kramer, B., & Brown, B. (Eds.), *Mental Health, Racism, and Sexism*, pp. 277–293. Pittsburgh, PA: University of Pittsburgh Press.

Pinderhughes, C. (1979). Differential bonding: Toward a psychological theory of stereotyping. *American Journal of Psychiatry, 136*, 33–37.

Prelock, P. A., Beatson, J., Bitner, B., Broder, C., & Ducker, A. (2003). Interdisciplinary assessment of young children with autism spectrum disorder. *Language, Speech, and Hearing Services in Schools, 34*, 194–202.

Purden, M. (2005). Cultural considerations in interprofessional education and practice. *Journal of Interprofessional Care, 1*, 224–234.

Reich, S. M., & Reich, J. A. (2006). Cultural competence in interdisciplinary collaborations: A method for respecting diversity in research partnerships. *American Journal of Community Psychology, 38*, 51–62.

Richardson, T. Q., & Molinaro, K. L. (1996). White counselor self-awareness: A prerequisite for multicultural competence. *Journal of Counseling & Development, 74*, 238–242.

Rogoff, B. (2003). *The Cultural Nature of Human Development*. New York: Oxford University Press.

Stolley, M., Fitzgibbon, M., Wells, A., & Martinovich, Z. (2004). Addressing multiple breast cancer risk factors in African-American women. *Journal of the National Medical Association*, 96(1), 76–86.

Suarez-Balcazar, Y., Balcazar, F., Taylor-Ritzler, T., Portillo, N., Rodakowsk, J., Garcia-Ramirez, M., et al. . (2011). *Journal of Rehabilitation*, 77, 4–13.

Sue, D. W., Arredondo, P., & McDavis, R. J. (1992). Multicultural competencies/standards: A call to the profession. *Journal of Counseling & Development*, 70, 477–486.

Sue, D. W. (2001). Multidimensional facets of cultural competence. *Counseling Psychologist*, 29, 790–821.

Sue, D. W., Capodilupo, C. M ., Torino, G. C., Bucceri, J. M., Holder, A. M. B., Nadal, K. L., et al . (2007). Racial microaggressions in everyday life: Implications for clinical practice. *American Psychologist*, 62, 271–268.

Tang, T. S., Fantone, J. C ., Bozynski, M. E. A., & Adams, B. S. (2002). Implementation and evaluation of an undergraduate sociocultural medicine program. *Academic Medicine*, 77, 578–585.

Tervalon, M., & Murray-Garcia, J. (1998). Cultural humility versus cultural competence: A critical distinction in defining physician training outcomes in multicultural education. *Journal of Health Care for the Poor and Underserved*, 9, 117–125.

Thomas, A., & Sillen, S. (1972). *Racism and Psychiatry*. New York: Brunner/Mazel.

U.S. Department of Health and Human Services. (2001). *Mental Health: Culture, Race, and Ethnicity—A Supplement to Mental Health: A Report of the Surgeon General*. Rockville, MD: U.S. Department of Health and Human Services, Substance Abuse and Mental Health Services Administration, Center for Mental Health Services.

Wade, P., & Bernstein, B. L. (1991). Culture sensitivity training and counselor´s race: Effects on Black female clients' perceptions and attrition. Journal of Counseling Psychology, 38, 9–15.

Warner, J. R. (2002). Cultural competence immersion experiences: Public health among the Navajo. *Nurse Education*, 27, 187–190.

Webb, E., & Sergison, M. (2003). Evaluation of cultural competence and antiracism training in child health services. *Archives of Disease in Childhood*, 88, 291–294.

Zeller, E. (2008). Culturally competent programs: The first family violence program for Aboriginal men in prison. *The Prison Journal, 83,* 171–190.

CHAPTER 12

RECOVERY FACILITATING SERVICE PLANNING

An Interdisciplinary Responsibility

MARIANNE FARKAS, RICK FORBESS, AND DANIEL W. BRADFORD

INTRODUCTION—CASE STUDY

John S. is a 38-year-old individual with a diagnosis of schizophrenia. He has been hospitalized eight times in the past ten years for brief stays each time. Currently, he lives in a supported housing program, in an apartment with a roommate. His family lives about 50 miles away in another town. As a client of the Rosedale Behavioral Health Center (RBHC), John has been working with a new case manager to coordinate his various services both within and outside the Center. RBHC has recently implemented a "Recovery Facilitating Service Planning" approach to help the agency achieve its stated aim to promote recovery. The case manager begins the process of revising and updating his service by helping John establish his view of what a meaningful life would look like in three to five years, or his vision for his recovery. "My dream would be to live in a nice apartment close to the college. I would be living alone, but I would like to have some friends who lived nearby and have a girlfriend who would spend time at the apartment. Ideally, I would have a part-time job as a library assistant either at the college or at one of the city libraries. I'd like to take a course in astronomy, have a dog, and spend time at the dog park, meeting other dog owners." The challenge for the case manager is to "sell" John's dream to the rest of the team as "appropriate" for him. His psychiatric nurse is concerned that "going along" with this idea will give John "false hope" and will lead him to return to hospital from the "stress of it all." The psychiatrist is also not sure about the level of risk to John, considering that he will probably want to reduce his level of medications in order to have the energy to do all this. She worries about negative clinical outcomes, not to mention her malpractice liability. The social worker is less worried about John getting a part-time job and is more concerned about John's idea of having a girlfriend spending time at his apartment, not to mention John's mother's probable reaction to the idea of his living alone. John and the case manager are discouraged by the response of the rest of his team, with the case manager feeling that, at the "bottom" of the professional hierarchy, he has little influence on the rest of the team.

Although the overall system of behavioral health care has adopted a stronger focus on recovery, there is still wide variance in understanding of the implications for service planning in a recovery facilitating system, and changes in the actual process, including issues such as the role of the person receiving services; the identification of service plan components remains more traditionally provider-driven and medically focused. The resolution of the planning challenges for John includes a major shift in the team's view of its role in planning from that of presenting its analysis of what it considers appropriate for John for his agreement, to one of consulting with John to identify the process required to achieve his vision over a three- to five-year period.

The field of mental health care has come to agree with the *President's New Freedom Commission Report* (2003), which boldly states that mental health care in America fails a wide variety of individuals, but particularly fails those with serious mental illnesses because it is "not oriented to the single most important goal of the people it serves, that of recovery." Recovery from mental illnesses has become the overarching concern of mental health service recipients, family members, practitioners, policy makers, and researchers. Although there is still much to learn about the experience of recovery and how to support it, research has shown that recovery is possible for most people with psychiatric disabilities (e.g., reviewed by Harding & Zahniser, 1994). One of the key concepts about recovery emerging from both research and consensus in the field is that it is a highly individualized process that can occur with or without professional intervention covering a variety of dimensions. In addition to objective outcomes such as increased successful functioning in a range of life roles (worker, student, wife, softball team member, etc.), physical health, or symptom reduction, subjective outcomes are equally important: such as an increased sense of self-worth, empowerment, and well-being (Farkas, 2007; Farkas, Gagne, Anthony, & Chamberlin, 2005). Perhaps the definition of *recovery* most accepted in the field has been that proposed by William Anthony: "Recovery is a deeply personal, unique process of changing one's attitudes, values, feelings, goals, skills and/or roles. It is a way of living a satisfying, hopeful, and contributing life even with limitations caused by the illness. Recovery involves the development of new meaning and purpose in one's life as one grows beyond the catastrophic effects of mental illness" (Anthony, 1993). Within the context of recovery, facilitating service planning that enhances both the experience and the outcomes of recovery is a critical element for effective services (Adams & Grieder, 2005).

The kinds of difficulties experienced by the Rosedale Behavioral Health Care staff in promoting a recovery-facilitating process are unfortunately not unique. The traditional approach to service-planning encountered by most individuals seeking and receiving mental health services offers an experience that is far from person-centered or recovery-enhancing (Adams & Grieder,

2005; White & Davidson, 2006). In most systems, service planning is conducted during the initial period of contact, when the tone for the relationship between practitioners and the individuals receiving services is often set with an emphasis on impairment and dysfunction. While Engel's bio-psychosocial model (1977) has informed the practice of psychiatry for over 30 years, the field's focus remains on helping individuals through mitigating illness and its manifestations. A focus on deficits, rather than a focus on the person's hopes, dreams, and aspirations, undermines the possibilities for establishing a partnership of hope, empowerment, or self-worth. Putting the individual receiving services at the center of care and supporting that person's autonomy have been recognized in general medicine as a basic underlying premise for the provision of modern healthcare in general (Grol, 2001; Sensky, 2002), if not yet fully implemented in mental health or behavioral health care. Furthermore, in traditional planning services, involvement of the individual served is often limited to little more than agreeing to sign a poorly understood document, developed by others, in order to begin receiving services, despite the fact that research data suggest that involving individuals in the planning of their services, at least in rehabilitation services, improves outcome (Majumder, Walls, & Fullmer, 1998).

Recovery Facilitating Service Planning (RFSP) is designed to directly involve individuals in charting a course for building the life they would like to have. Service planning typically heavily emphasizes evaluating whether documentation of the service plan is timely and meets wording criteria, e.g., measurable, designates target dates. Although standards for documentation are adhered to, and although RFSP is adaptable to a wide range of service planning guidelines, standards, and record-keeping formats, evaluation of the effectiveness of RFSP focuses on the impact of the service-planning process. Key factors of an evaluation of an individual's RFSP include: the individual's sense of hope, confidence, and self-esteem; the service team's understanding of his or her perspective about the service plan components, progress, and assessment results; the individual's understanding of the treatment team's perspective about her or his treatment plan components, progress, and assessment results; and finally, the individual's understanding of and decisions about the components of the service plan.

Focus on these evaluation factors underscores the purpose of RFSP; that is, to facilitate the person's recovery or achievement of his or her vision of what a meaningful life would be. As such, it requires a highly interactive process among the individual and service team members in which the use of interpersonal skills that foster partnership, respect, responsibility, and self-worth is paramount.

GUIDING VALUES

The service planning process itself is guided by basic values for all recovery-oriented services (Farkas, Gagne, Anthony, & Chamberlin, 2005), (i.e., person orientation, growth potential or hope, self-determination or choice, partnership), merged with additional values more specifically associated with rehabilitation services (support, outcome orientation, role-centered, functioning) (see Table 12.1 and p. 179). Person orientation, or conceptualizing and delivering services from the perspective of the individual as a person of talents, strengths, and interests, as well as someone with deficits and limitations, has been recognized as important in the mental health field for decades.

The second value guiding RFSP is that of hope. Service planning that promotes activities focused on simple maintenance or the prevention of relapse, without opportunities and support

Table 12.1 Guiding Values of Recovery Facilitating Service Planning

Person-orientation	A focus on the individual as a person with talents, interests, and strengths beyond the diagnostic label.
Growth potential/hope	A focus on the inherent capacity of anyone to grow and to recover.
Self-determination, or choice	A focus on people having the right to make choices and decisions for themselves throughout their recovery journey.
Partnership	A focus on people being involved in all aspects of planning, conducting, and evaluating services and interventions related to their recovery—sometimes called "person-centered."
Support	A focus on providing assistance for as long as it is needed and wanted by the person served.
Outcome orientation	A focus on evaluating a person's progress in terms of the measurable results of service delivery.
Environment/Role Centered	A focus on the real world context of living, learning, working, or socializing.
Functioning	A focus on performance of day-to-day activities.
	(Adapted from Farkas & Anthony, 1989; Farkas, Gagne, Anthony & Chamberlin, 2005)

to move beyond maintenance, is not recovery-facilitating (Farkas, 2007). The third guiding value, self-determination or choice, is the cornerstone of a recovery process. The opportunities to choose one's long-term goals, the methods to be used to get to those goals, and the individuals or providers who will assist in the process are all components of a service acknowledging this value (Farkas, 2007).

Research has demonstrated the importance of including partnership or person-centered planning for people who receive services (Holburn, Jacobson, Schwartz, et al., 2004; Robertson, Emerson, Hatton, Elliott, et al., 2005, 2007; Sanderson, Thompson, & Kilbane, 2006), without leading to a significant increase in costs (Robertson, Emerson, Hatton, Elliott, et al., 2007). Finally, while rehabilitation also includes the four critical recovery values, the additional rehabilitation values of support (i.e., providing assistance for as long as it is needed and wanted by the person served); outcome orientation (i.e., evaluating a person's progress in terms of the measurable results of service delivery); environment- and role-centered (i.e., focus on the real-world context of living, learning, working, or socializing); and functioning (i.e., focus on performance of day-to-day activities) shape the nature of the elements in the RFSP process.

PROCESS

RFSP is guided by these critical recovery values in the development of a process to organize the provision of services focusing on assisting an individual to reach goals reflective of that person's recovery aspirations. RFSP is a goal-driven process, not a problem-driven process. The overriding question RFSP intends to answer is, "What are the individual's hopes for a better life, and what services are needed and wanted to help the person make progress toward that life?" While the process yields goals, objectives, interventions, and other service plan components, the individual's increased sense of hope, self-confidence, and motivation is an equally important outcome. The process is conducted more as a *recovery-facilitating process* than a staff service-planning activity. Consequently, unless the health or safety of the person receiving services or another would be in jeopardy, or the person receiving services is informed, engaged, and still unwilling to participate in the planning process, the service plan is developed with the person him- or herself.

The interdisciplinary team's composition includes the individual in recovery as well as those currently providing a service or support. Although the individual, a facilitator, and a core group of people usually remain as service team members, the composition of the service team may change over time, depending on the needs and preferences of the individual. Modifying and updating the service plan is an ongoing process responsive to the person's needs, wishes, and progress that may well be independent of service team meetings, which may occur at arbitrary time intervals based on regulatory practices. Service team meetings *may* occur at prescribed times or on an as-needed and as-possible basis, but are primarily opportunities for the service team and recipient to review decisions that have been made during the ongoing service planning process. Regularly involving the individual in a review and possible revision of her or his goals and objectives before, during, and after the delivery of services is a key characteristic of RFSP; consequently, the delivery of services and planning services are closely integrated. Providers interact with the person and each other on an "as needed" basis to discuss progress with the plan and to make additions or modifications.

PROCESS COMPONENTS

The RFSP process generates an integrated set of components intended to support the consumer's recovery from mental illness (see Table 12.2: RFSP Components). Each component is developed with full involvement of the person receiving services and can be described by its defining characteristics and purpose. In keeping with the dynamic, ongoing RFSP process, the components are developed, refined, and replaced based on the individual's preferences, progress, and insights.

The RFSP process is essentially an insight-building process designed to support the actions necessary to facilitate recovery. The process requires that an active role be played by service team members, including sharing knowledge based on their background and training, experiences, and beliefs that expand options for the individual to consider in the process of mapping out her or his road to recovery. Individual ownership of the service plan is based on the person's

Table 12.2 Recovery Facilitation Service Planning (RFSP) Components

Recovery View	Articulation of my ideal life circumstances 3–5 years in the future.
Goals	Statements of what I intend to accomplish within the next 3–12 months that would move me closer to the Recovery View.
Strengths	Skills, knowledge, attitudes, supports, and resources that I believe I can rely on to reach a goal.
Barriers	Skills, knowledge, symptom control, may impede my goal attainment unless reduced or limited.
Objectives	Targeted solutions to barriers, to accomplish in less than 3–12 months.
Actions Steps	What the service team and I agree to do in order to accomplish objectives.

understanding of the plan as well as the extent to which the plan reflects personally meaningful needs, desires, and priorities. Consequently, the person must be both able and willing to participate in the process. It is the responsibility of the service team to make coordinated efforts to engage the person in the RFSP process in those instances in which either of these barriers to participation is present. For example, while it is by no means *necessary* that a person be symptom-free in order to be able to participate, if either positive or negative symptoms prevent the person from being able to understand the process or to interact with the service team with a commonly held purpose, the service plan should begin by overcoming these barriers to engagement in order to move forward with the RFSP process.

RECOVERY VIEW

The Recovery View is a brief articulation of the individual's ideal life circumstances three to five years in the future. (As with all RFSP components, time frames are intended as general guides and should not be used as rigid standards, unresponsive to the individual's wants and needs.) It is a description of the person's hopes, dreams, and aspirations if all current problems, challenges, and so on were eliminated or lessened to the extent that they no longer posed a significant barrier to having the life the person wants to have. Since the Recovery View is not intended to be a specific goal to achieve (i.e., a desired future outcome that a person is committed to taking action to accomplish at the present time), but rather a hoped-for life situation, it does not need to conform to what either the individual, the facilitator, or the service team member perceives to be "realistic." The purpose of the Recovery View is to rekindle a hope for a better life that both inspires the individual to take on challenges and is the focal point for the development of all subsequent RFSP components. For example, one person's Recovery View was stated thus:

> My dream for a long time has been to live in an apartment, within walking distance of my parents' house. I wouldn't mind having a roommate if he was quiet and had some of the same interests I do, but living on my own would be okay too, especially if I had a case manager who could visit from time to time. I'd like to have a job working with plants, spending most of the time outside. I might want to take some classes to get a GED, but it would depend on where the class was and what the teacher was like. In my spare time, I'd just watch TV, draw, and go bowling now and then with a friend or two.

Once the Recovery View has been developed, it becomes a touchstone throughout the planning and service-delivery process. It is discussed frequently to encourage the individual and to provide a reminder for that person and each member of the service team about the focus and ultimate direction of services. Documentation in RFSP service plans ensures that the Recovery View is prominent.

GOALS

RFSP goals represent milestones toward the individual's Recovery View. Goals in traditional service planning are typically statements developed by practitioners that describe the resolution of problems assessed by the interdisciplinary team (symptoms, addictions, disability, etc.). RFSP goals, however, are statements of what the individual intends to accomplish within the next three to 12 months that would move her or him closer to the Recovery View. In most instances, one overarching goal is the focus of all subsequent team service-planning and delivery. Goals, reflective of the individual's perspective, focus on the specific types of environmental roles described in the Recovery View; that is, living, learning, working, and socializing. These goal statements use words and phrases that the individual understands and that allow goal-accomplishment to be easily recognized and measured. For example, a goal statement might be expressed as "I am willing to begin choosing a role and a setting in which I would like to be successful and satisfied," rather than "John will resolve his fears of success," a statement that is ambiguous, focused on "John" in the third person, and difficult to measure.

STRENGTHS

The specific goal statements imply the presence or absence of certain strengths of the individual, related to accomplishing them. "Strengths" include both internal characteristics of the individual, such as skills and knowledge, and external characteristics, such as resources that are available to the person. Rather than a list of generic strengths, RFSP strengths are those that relate directly to the goal, reflecting the skills, knowledge, attitudes, supports, and resources that the individual believes s/he can rely on to be as effective as possible at reaching her or his goal.

BARRIERS

The barriers to accomplishing the goal are the absence of strengths. Barriers are the lack of skill, knowledge, symptom control, and resources perceived to obstruct the individual's goal attainment. Barriers, like strengths, are written in first person, nonjudgmental "I" statements to underscore individual understanding and agreement. They also describe specific obstacles that are current and thought to be possible to resolve; for example, "I have a hard time controlling my drinking when I get stressed out," rather than a generic "history of substance abuse." John's barriers to beginning an astronomy course at college included getting nervous around people he does not know well, not being able to think clearly when he hears voices, not having enough funds to buy books, and lacking a place to study that works for him (see Table 12.3).

OBJECTIVES

RFSP objectives are targeted solutions to the barriers to accomplishing the goals, with perhaps more than one objective required in order to eliminate or lessen a particular barrier. Unlike objectives that focus on individual participation and compliance—such as "Attend all scheduled day program activities," or "Take medication as prescribed"—RFSP objectives are outcome statements. Unless there is an assessed risk to the health or safety of the individual or another person, the objectives are ones the individual agrees with and understands. John's plan (Table 12.3) provides an example of objectives related to the barrier of being nervous around people he doesn't know well. The process would also create objectives for each of the other identified barriers on his list.

Table 12.3. Example: John's Recovery Facilitating Service Plan

Recovery View	I'd like to live in an apartment in my home town close to the college. I wouldn't want to have a roommate, but I would like to have some friends who live near by and to have a girlfriend who would spend some time at the apartment. Ideally I'd have a part-time job as a library assistant at the library, either at the college or at one of the city libraries. I'd like to take a course in astronomy, either at the college or through adult education. I'd like to have a dog and to spend time at the dog park meeting other people and their dogs.
Goal	I'll begin classes in an astronomy program at Jones County Technical College by September 20__.
Strengths	I have a lot of knowledge about politics, science, and sports. I have a high school education. My brother is willing to provide transportation to classes. I know when to ask for support and how to do it.
Barriers	I get really nervous around people I don't know well. I can't think clearly when I hear voices. I don't have enough money in SSDI to buy books. I don't have a quiet place to study.
Objectives for Barrier # 1	I will feel relaxed enough to spend at least 30 minutes at the mall by June 1, 20__. I will feel relaxed enough to spend at least 30 minutes at the mall three times in one week by August 15, 20__.
Action Steps	*John*: I will attend each individual therapy session and skills teaching class scheduled for me or will call no later than three hours beforehand to let someone know if I won't be attending. I will practice using skills I'm taught in class if the leader suggests it. *Service Team*: Dr. F. will provide individual therapy to help John learn ways to recognize and reduce his anxiety. The sessions will be at the clinic, will last one hour, from 10:00 a.m.–11:00 a.m. on Monday, and will be provided for six weeks in a row beginning on October 7, 20__, and ending on November 20, 20__. Mrs. B. will provide a class to teach John how to express feelings and how to request support, once a week at the clubhouse on 6th Avenue. The class will be each Wednesday at 6:30 p.m. and will last one hour. The classes will begin on October 9, 20__, and end on December 10, 20__.

ACTION STEPS

Action steps include the actions that both the individual and the service team members will take in order to accomplish each objective. In most planning procedures, there is no practice or requirement to document individual action steps. Often, however, individual action steps, such as "Take medication as prescribed," are listed as objectives, in contrast to RFSP objectives, which clarify the intended outcome of service team and individual actions, rather than the actions themselves. Individual action steps, stated in clear first-person language and consistent with RFSP values and principles, are those that the person understands and agrees to be responsible for performing.

Most service planning documents use terms such as "intervention" or "service type" for service team action steps. RFSP team action steps identify the interventions that will be provided within the service suggested. Identifying a program to be offered, for example, "Day Treatment" or "Clinic," is not the same as identifying the intervention(s) offered within the program, intended to be the tool to accomplish the person's objective, such as "skill teaching group," "educational group," or "individual therapy." John's action steps include attending therapy sessions as well as a skill teaching class (see Table 12.3).

RFSP AND THE INTERDISCIPLINARY TEAM

RFSP is a process that enhances the functioning of a collaborative interdisciplinary team due to three factors: 1) Focus of the process on a common, overarching goal; 2)the inherent requirement for ongoing interaction among team members and the concomitant facilitator role to ensure that interaction, and 3) team composition limited to those who are actively providing services.

The standard approach to service planning typically generates multiple goals, each derived from the assessment of the professional disciplines represented on a particular team and based on the area of expertise of each discipline member. The resulting objectives and interventions often generate a set of services that are somewhat separate from each other in both structure and process. The now much-derided "service silo" system of care is an artifact of this approach. Although the more effective traditional service teams coordinate their separate services well so that the timing, frequency, and duration of their separate services are in synch, the absence of an overarching goal to provide a common context and purpose for their assessments and subsequent service planning and delivery lessens the need for a group effort of cooperation, which is a hallmark of teamwork.

The level of integration of service planning and service delivery and the emphasis on ongoing communication among the service team members is another feature of RFSP that enhances interdisciplinary teamwork. Regular and frequent assessment of progress toward the accomplishment of service objectives and goals as a component of service delivery, and the resultant modification of the plan in response, create a high need for service team members to communicate among themselves on a regular basis. The facilitator role to ensure that the perspectives of the consumer and team members are mutually understood and to inform team members of revisions of the service plan as they occur rather than making and/or learning about changes in the service plan during service team meetings that occur at prescribed times, often months apart, supports and strengthens interdisciplinary team work.

The third factor of RFSP that enhances interdisciplinary team functioning is that the members of the interdisciplinary team at any one time are those who are providing services at that time. The result is a heightened sense of investment in both the individual's progress and in collaborating with other team members. The traditional interdisciplinary team structure brings together a group representing various professional disciplines, who may or may not be providing direct services to a particular person. Those not doing so can be considered to perform their duties as team members well, even if they do not collaborate with other team members in response to a particular person's needs and wishes. RFSP team members, on the other hand, all have a direct stake in providing services in a collaborative fashion.

UNIQUE CHALLENGES AND CONCERNS FOR PSYCHIATRISTS IN AN INTERDISCIPLINARY APPROACH TO RFSP

Working with individuals who engage in RFSP presents a set of unique challenges for psychiatrists, which, when overcome, can result in corresponding benefits for individuals, psychiatrists, and service systems. Aspects of psychiatric practice relevant to RFSP include: therapeutic focus, composition of service activities as dictated by the service system, role identity relative to other mental health providers, and risk of negative outcomes. In the paragraphs below, we review the challenges, solutions (overcoming challenges), and benefits of RFSP relative to each of these aspects of psychiatric practice.

Therapeutic focus: While mental health service providers of other disciplines may also share an "illness focus" to varying degrees, psychiatry residency training experiences serving individuals in the greatest states of distress (e.g., in psychiatric emergency services or on locked inpatient psychiatric wards) may provide psychiatrists with a particular orientation toward illness-centered approaches. A therapeutic focus on illness can be particularly limiting and sometimes unrewarding for psychiatrists working with individuals with serious mental illnesses, a proportion of whom may have symptoms that only modestly or minimally respond to psychiatric treatments. Some individuals may reject psychiatric treatments offered solely in the framework of illness-focus and symptom-mitigation, thus further reinforcing feelings of futility among psychiatrists working with this population. In this context, the paradigm shift (Figure 12.1) required of providers, from the traditional treatment-planning model focused on deficit and dysfunction, to RFSP focused initially on the hopes, dreams, and aspirations of the person may be met with resistance by some psychiatrists and prove challenging even for those more open to change.

Composition of service activities: Regardless of service setting, psychiatrists uniformly provide pharmacotherapy. In many practice settings, influences of third-party payers, both public and private, have forced an emphasis on the provision of pharmacotherapy as the main, or even sole, professional activity of psychiatrists. Biomedical knowledge and approaches are thus appropriately important aspects of psychiatric training and practice. Along with the increasing emphasis on this service in modern psychiatric practice, such training can serve to reinforce the illness-centered approach, making symptom-reduction the main goal and placing psychiatrists at odds with the RFSP approach and professionals who practice it.

"Standard" Treatment Planning	Recovery Facilitating Service Planning
PROBLEM • Symptoms • Addictions • Dysfunctional Behaviors • Skill Deficits • Resource Deficits	RECOVERY VIEW • Hopes • Dreams • Ambitions •
GOAL • Lessen • Eliminate • Develop • Participate • Comply	GOAL • Achieve, accomplish • Milestones
	STRENGTHS/BARRIERS • Knowledge • Skills • Supports • Resources
OBJECTIVES • Lessen • Eliminate • Develop • Participate • Comply	OBJECTIVES • Develop • Apply • Utilize

FIGURE 12.1 Standard Planning and Recovery Facilitating Service Planning: Goals and Objectives

Role identity: With competencies and training in biological and psychological treatments, as well as the authority often granted to physicians in treating illnesses in health care settings, psychiatrists may view a more traditional, illness-focused service approach as reinforcing their identity as leaders of mental health providers. In this framework, other mental health providers are sometimes viewed as ancillary to the role of the psychiatrist, providing treatments to address manifestations of illness as the psychiatrist prescribes (e.g., a nurse administering medications prescribed; a social worker addressing resource deficits and social issues related to the identified illness; a psychologist providing therapy to help mitigate symptoms of the illness). Traditional treatment planning may be seen as largely taking place in initial psychiatrist visits focused on illness-assessment and treatment-prescription, with modification in follow-up visits based on treatment response. In the process of RFSP, the development of a Recovery View and associated goals is likely to take place over an extended time period in the more frequent and probably longer visits with other mental health providers, rather than in less frequent, shorter visits with the psychiatrist. Modification of such plans takes place in response to changes in the person's life in the community and progress toward the Recovery View. Psychiatrists may be challenged to adjust to a role of responding to and working within a service plan developed with individuals by other mental health providers, as opposed to the prior role of leading the illness-focused service plan.

Risk of negative outcomes: The threat of litigation and professional sanctions resulting from negative clinical outcomes can understandably have an impact on the way that mental health service providers practice, making them more averse to both treatment choices and the individual's goals that are perceived to be associated with a higher risk of these negative outcomes. Given the nature of clinical decisions involved in the practice of psychiatry (e.g., whether or not to initiate involuntary hospitalization in the setting of a person's increased risk of harm to self or others; medication prescription in complex situations) and the leadership role psychiatrists often play on teams of service providers, psychiatrists are exposed to higher liability-risk than other mental health providers. Psychiatrists pay higher malpractice insurance premiums than other mental health providers: almost 11 times the rates charged for psychologists, for example (see http://www.americanprofessional.com/).

In RFSP, individuals may decide to pursue goals that alter the balance of risks and benefits that are acceptable to that person. For example, a person who decides to pursue a college education may desire lower medication doses, or a trial of a new medication to which the individual is not known to respond. Should the psychiatrist view proposed changes as increasing the risk of symptomatic relapse that could lead to harmful behaviors, liability issues may make the psychiatrist uncomfortable in supporting the medication change or even the overall goal.

OVERCOMING CHALLENGES TO RECOVERY FACILITATING SERVICE PLANNING

Overcoming challenges to effective participation in RFSP for psychiatrists can be accomplished by applying the values and elements of this approach to psychiatric practice (Farkas, 2007; Anthony & Farkas, 2011), with resulting substantial benefits for individuals, psychiatrists, and service systems.

Values such as outcome-orientation and functioning in RFSP offer a broadened therapeutic focus where psychiatrists can assist and support individuals in attaining goals in a variety of domains, such as living, learning, working, and socializing, despite continuing symptoms. RFSP values of self-determination and growth potential may also provide a welcomed return to values emphasized in residency training in psychotherapy, which may have become less prominent in subsequent psychiatric practice. Participation in a setting where RFSP is practiced provides psychiatrists with information (e.g., statement of goals, strengths, and interests in an accessible format) often collected by other professionals, which facilitates these types of interactions even where patient volume is high.

The values and practice of RFSP can help both to enhance the practice of pharmacotherapy and also to broaden the role of psychiatrists beyond high-volume pharmacotherapy. Ineffective services that are not linked to what the individuals actually want and need can lead to disengagement in some individuals. For other individuals, this lack of linkage between services provided and desired outcomes can lead to an increased demand for services, including an overemphasis on pharmacotherapy as the solution to problems, as the person seeks more of the service offered to try to address problems. Effective practice of RFSP provides a method for identifying outcomes that are individually meaningful to individuals and linking these objectives to services that are most likely to facilitate achieving these desired outcomes. Linking of pharmacotherapy to these individually defined desired outcomes makes the purpose of the treatment clearer to both the psychiatrist and the consumer, and provides an individually defined balance of medication benefits and risks that are acceptable to each person. Linking of desired outcomes to other types of services that are more likely to help the person achieve them (e.g., supported employment, social skills teaching) mitigates the potential for the inappropriate use and overuse of medications that can result when a medication is used to attempt to achieve an outcome it is unlikely to produce (e.g., an antidepressant dose being increased when a person is unhappy about not having meaningful work or friends).

RFSP is best achieved in the context of interdisciplinary teams, which provide potential additional roles and activities for psychiatrists beyond the sometimes-isolating practice of high-volume pharmacotherapy. Finally, the outcome orientation of RFSP provides the possibility of psychiatrists being held accountable less for the simple volume of clinical encounters and instead for outcomes achieved. More-satisfied individuals can lead to a lower demand for pharmacotherapy visits, allowing the psychiatrist to broaden the variety of services they provide in each encounter (e.g., adding meaningful supportive therapy or rehabilitation counseling to sessions), and even justify visits of greater length. An illness-centered approach to mental health services has traditionally served to reinforce leadership roles of psychiatrists. RFSP may indeed lessen, or at least change, the leadership role of the psychiatrist on the mental health service team, as various professionals assume leadership roles for outcomes and service activities linked closely to their professional training. However, this diffusion of leadership on service teams has significant benefits for psychiatrists as it enables them to focus their leadership efforts on service activities that they are appropriately and sometimes uniquely trained for (e.g., clinical assessment and diagnosis, provision and monitoring of medications, and crisis intervention). Psychiatrists can then assume a contributing and collaborating role on the team relative to services where there is overlap in the training of various professionals or where the psychiatrist may have minimal training. As all team members begin to assume leadership for services activities linked most closely to their respective training, teams are likely to function more effectively with less potential for conflict over roles, leaving the team members more able to achieve synergy relative to skills and service activities that are common across disciplines. In this framework, selection of the individual(s) to perform overall roles of clinical and administrative leader is more appropriately linked to the skills, interests, and aptitudes of team members in leadership, such that the psychiatrist would not be assumed to fill this role, but would not be excluded from consideration either.

While psychiatrists may be much more risk-averse than other mental health professionals, driven by their exorbitant insurance premiums and the actual frequency and cost of malpractice suits, rehabilitation services provide a basis for challenging assumptions leading to concerns over increased liability risk in environments where RFSP is practiced. For example, the evidence-based practice of supported employment has been shown to be neutral with regard to psychiatric symptoms (i.e., psychiatric symptoms are not shown, in the aggregate, to increase as individuals attain competitive employment). The approach of RFSP includes an emphasis on shared decision-making, informed consent, and often, family involvement. In RFSP, the individual is more likely to have explicitly identified goals and to acknowledge, own, and accept the risks associated with pursuit of these goals. Families or other supports would be more likely to be involved and to have knowledge of the expected risks and benefits of services provided. RFSP provides a framework where the individual is viewed, not as the passive recipient of treatment decisions of the psychiatrist, but rather as a well-informed equal, actively involved in decisions. These factors, along with the enhanced therapeutic alliance resulting from RFSP, should serve to actually mitigate the risk of negative outcomes and the risk of malpractice lawsuits when negative outcomes do occur, and encourage psychiatrists to become involved in the process.

In conclusion, Recovery Facilitating Service Planning, based on critical values of recovery-oriented services and enhanced by a psychiatric rehabilitation process, provides individuals with serious mental illnesses and other team members a framework and a process with which to become effectively engaged in a collaboration to identify and achieve the individual's long-term vision for his or her own recovery.

REFERENCES

Adams, N., & Grieder, D. M. (2005). *Treatment Planning for Person-Centered Care*. Burlington, MA: Elsevier Publishers.

Anthony, W. A. (1993). Recovery from mental illness: The guiding vision of the mental health service system in the 1990s. *Psychosocial Rehabilitation Journal,* 16(4): 11–23.

Anthony, W.A., & Farkas, M. (2011) *The Essential Guide to Psychiatric Rehabilitation Practice*. Boston, MA: Center for Psychiatric Rehabilitation, Boston University. See http://www.bu.edu/cpr/products/books/titles/essentialguide.html.

Bassman, R. (Winter, 2000). Consumers/survivors/ex-patients as change facilitators. *New Directions for Mental Health Services*, 88, 93–102. Available at http://ronaldbassman.com/pdfs/ChangeFacilitators.pdf.

Blackwell, B., Eilers, K., & Robinson, D., Jr . (2000). The consumer's role in assessing quality. In: Stricker, G., & Troy, W. G. (eds.), *Handbook of Quality Management in Behavioral Health*. Dordrecht, The Netherlands: Kluwer.

Crawford, M. J., Aldridge, T., Bhui, K., Rutter, D ., Manley, C., Weaver, T., et al. (2003). User involvement in the planning and delivery of mental health services: A cross sectional survey of service users and providers. *Acta Psychiatrica Scandinavia*, 107, 410–414.

Deegan P. (1990) Spirit breaking: When the helping professions hurt. *Humanistic Psychology*, 18, 301–313.

Engel, G. (1977). The need for a new medical model: The challenge for biomedicine. *Science*, April 8, 196 (4286), 129–136.

Farkas, M., & Anthony, W. A. (1989) *Psychiatric Rehabilitation: Putting Theory into Practice*. Baltimore, MD: John Hopkins University Press.

Farkas, M., Cohen, M., McNamara, S., Nemec, P., & Cohen, B . (2000). *Psychiatric Rehabilitation Training Technology: Assessing Readiness for Rehabilitation*. Boston, MA: Boston University Center for Psychiatric Rehabilitation.

Farkas, M, Gagne, C., Anthony W. A. A., & Chamberlin, J. (2005). Implementing recovery oriented evidence based programs: Identifying the critical dimensions. *Community Mental Health Journal*, 41(2): 141–158.

Farkas, M. (2007). The vision of recovery today: What it is and what it means for services. *World Psychiatry*, 6(2): 1–7.

Grol, R. (2001). Improving the quality of medical care: Building bridges among professional pride, payer profit, and patient satisfaction. *Journal of the American Medical Association*, 286, 2578–2585.

Harding, C., & Zahniser, J. (1994). Empirical correction of seven myths about schizophrenia with implications for treatment. *Acta Psychiatrica Scandinavica Supplementum*, 90(Suppl 384), 140–146.

Holburn, S., Jacobson, J. W., Schwartz, A. A., et al. (2004). The Willowbrook futures project: A longitudinal analysis of person-centered planning. *American Journal on Mental Retardation*, 109(1): 63–76.

Majumder, R. K., Walls, R. T., & Fullmer, S. L . (1998). Rehabilitation client involvement in employment decisions. *Rehabilitation Counseling Bulletin*, 42(2): 162–173.

McQuillan, B . (1994). My life with schizophrenia. In: Spaniol, L., & Koehler, M. (eds.), *The Experience of Recovery*. Boston, MA: Center for Psychiatric Rehabilitation.

New Freedom Commission on Mental Health. (2003). *Achieving the Promise: Transforming Mental Health Care in America. Final report* Rockville, MD: U.S. Department of Health and Human Services.

Peterson, C., & Bossio, L. M. (1991). *Health and Optimism*. New York: Free Press.

Priebe, S., McCabe, R., Bullenkamp, J., Hansson, L., Lauber, C., Martinez-Leal, R., et al. (2007) Structured patient-clinician communication and 1-year outcome in community mental healthcare. Cluster randomized controlled trial. *British Journal of Psychiatry*, 191, 420–426

Robertson, J., Emerson, E., Hatton, C., Elliott, J., McIntosh, B., et al. (2005). *The Impact of Person Centred Planning*. Lancaster, UK: Institute for Health Research, Lancaster University.

Robertson, J., Emerson, E., Hatton, C., Elliott, J., McIntosh, B., et al. (2007). *The Impact of Person Centred Planning for People with Intellectual Disabilities in England: A Summary of Findings*. Lancaster, UK: Institute for Health Research, Lancaster University.

Russinova, Z. (1999). Providers' hope-inspiring competence as a factor optimizing psychiatric rehabilitation outcomes. *Journal of Rehabilitation*, October–November, 55(4): 50–57.

Sanderson, H., Thompson, J., & Kilbane, J. (2006). The emergence of person-centered planning as evidence-based practice. *Journal of Integrated Care*, 14, 2, 18–25.

Sensky, T. (2002). Withdrawal of life sustaining treatment. *British Medical Journal*, 325, 175–176.

Snyder, C. R., Irving, L. M., & Anderson, J. R. (2). Hope and health: Measuring the will and the ways. In Snyder, C. R., Donelson, R., & Forsyth, L. (eds.), *The Handbook of Social and Clinical Psychology: The Health Perspective*, pp. 285–307. Elmsford, NY: Pergamon Press.

Substance Abuse Mental Health Services Administration (SAMHSA). (2004). *National Consensus Statement on Mental Health Recovery*. Retrieved November 20, 2011. Accessed at: http://store.samhsa.gov/shin/content//SMA05–4129/SMA05–4129.pdf.

Tondora, J. (2011). *Person-Centered Care: From Theory to Practice*. Available from: http://www.ct.gov/dmhas/cwp/view.asp?a=2913&q=456036.

Weingarten R. (1994). Despair, learned helplessness and recovery. *Innovative Research*; 3.

White, W., & Davidson, L. (2006) Recovery: The Bridge to Integration? *Behavioral Healthcare*, November. Available at: http://www.behavioral.net/ME2/dirmod.asp?sid=&nm=&type=Publishing&mod=Publications%3A%3AArticle&mid=&id=275C497AD93D4F3AA4EB10C64B0D12E1&tier=4.

CONSUMER–PROFESSIONAL PARTNERSHIPS DURING THE RECOVERY ERA

SUZANNE VOGEL-SCIBILIA AND FRED FRESE

CASE EXAMPLE

Theo is a 37-year-old disabled bookkeeper who has had severe symptoms of psychosis and social isolation. After he was charged with defiant trespass by the local police who were tired of responding to his neighbors' calls when he wandered onto their property, Theo was placed on probation and referred to a recovery-focused psychiatric rehabilitation program.

Theo is very tenuously engaged in the provided services and tries to avoid both facility-based activities as well as peer support services and mobile outreach. He often claims that he is physically ill or "the weather" is hindering his participation.

Multiple agencies—including welfare, Social Security, at-risk homeless services, the federally qualified medical clinic, and probation services—all weigh in on Theo's needs, yet none look at Theo holistically. The treatment team at the psychiatric rehabilitation center attempts to provide continuity of care and recovery-based services for Theo, but the systems' shortfalls often provide huge barriers that frustrate solution-based collaboration between Theo and the clinicians.

Within the rehabilitation program, peer support specialists, traditional rehabilitation specialists, administrative support, the psychiatrist, and the rehabilitation administrator all conceptualize Theo's issues differently, while Theo is a reluctant participant in his own care. He is not interested in setting goals or advancing his recovery, but he does acknowledge that he likes meeting with the peer support specialist, who is a man of similar age and interests.

After a period of focused welcoming and social engagement, Theo begins going for coffee at the local Eastern European coffee shop with the peer support specialist and attends the Wednesday "Lunch and a Movie" outing at the rehabilitation center. Collaborative work by the treatment team over the next year assists Theo in obtaining a library card, learning how to ride a bus, and establishing a structured routine that has social contacts in a low-pressure setting. Theo develops more trust in his therapist and physician, which leads to more discussion about his goals. He decides to change his medication to one that he may be more able to adhere to. He successfully completes his probation without being incarcerated and decides to volunteer with the rehabilitation center's Buddy Budgeting Group.

Provider systems have an increased awareness that mental health treatment as well as clinical programs need to be consumer-focused and consumer-driven. This philosophy can only be accomplished by prioritizing the needs and opinions of consumers and the consumer community, then incorporating this into clinical practice. This is best accomplished by valuing, nurturing, and integrating consumer-valued concepts and services into grassroots mental health treatment.

This chapter will address this concept by describing consumer-informed approaches to mental health care, implementing recovery best practices, embracing model recovery programs, and integrating consumer clinicians into the behavioral health workforce.

CONSUMER-INFORMED APPROACHES TO MENTAL HEALTH CARE

The hallmark of consumer-informed care is the understanding and implementation of recovery principles in clinical practice. While recovery from mental illness has been discussed intensively for over three decades in psychiatric literature, the majority of programs continue to struggle with defining "recovery" and adopting recovery-oriented care (Drake, 2000).

Recovery has been defined as person-centered, individualized growth that is self-directed, empowered, peer-supported, and holistic, which focuses on strengths, respect, responsibility, and hope, while occurring in a nonlinear fashion (United States Department of Health and Human Services, 2005). While much of recovery literature focuses on the individual, deeply personal experience of recovery, there is much about recovery that involves the social environment and interactions with others (Topor, Borg, DiGirolamo, and Davidson, 2011). These factors include interpersonal relationships, adequate material conditions, and recovery supports—all of which necessitate a willing collaborator. These collaborators—professionals, peers, or friends—need the understanding of one's personal experience of living with a mental illness.

First-person accounts often function as recovery narratives that expand the research base for recovery concepts and allow non-consumer providers to understand the lived experience of

Table 13.1 Personal Narrative–Derived Concepts of Recovery

Recovery is a reawakening of hope after despair.

Recovery is breaking through denial and achieving understanding and acceptance.

Recovery is moving from withdrawal to engagement and active participation in life.

Recovery is active coping rather than passive adjustment.

Recovery means no longer viewing oneself primarily as a person with a psychiatric disorder and reclaiming a positive sense of self.

Recovery is moving from alienation to a sense of meaning and purpose.

Recovery is a complex and nonlinear journey.

Recovery is not accomplished alone—the journey involves support and partnership.

Formatted from Text: Ridgway (2001)

mental illness. Ridgway (2001) gives a clear description of eight fundamental recovery concepts from narrative research, summarized in Table 13.1.

Many clinicians have grappled with these subjective values and continue to struggle with translating them into concrete clinical strategies and system change. Davidson (2007) argued that some systems have labeled as "recovery-oriented" longstanding services and introduced as "transformative" new programs that do not change much of the prior paternalistic, provider-driven system. Davidson suggested that a minimum criterion for transformation would be fulfilling the promise made at the beginning of deinstitutionalization over 70 years ago that consumers would be able to "live in the community in a normal manner" (Davidson, 2007).

Others argue whether an evidence-based medical model is able to incorporate the recovery model of care (Frese, Stanley, Kress, and Vogel-Scibilia, 2001, 2002; Fisher and Ahern, 2002).

Subsequent establishment of best practices and delineation of theoretical constructs that implement recovery-based services in traditional treatment programs show that an evidence-based medical model can embrace recovery services. This process has been evolving for over ten years. The suggestions that follow are examples.

RECOVERY-FOCUSED ILLNESS MANAGEMENT

Recovery-focused illness management can be seen as a diverse group of interventions designed to help consumers partner with professionals in coping with symptoms and improving their quality of life. Recovery work includes focusing on consumer strengths and personal goals, determining a personalized recovery plan that decreases symptoms, and developing an identity that is not defined by the mental illness (Mueser et al., 2002). Illness management encompasses psychoeducation, behavioral tailoring, relapse prevention, and coping skills training—all of which can be undertaken in a consumer-driven, self-determined orientation that engenders recovery.

While traditional illness management programs may concentrate on adherence to medication or treatment, recovery-oriented services shift the focus away from psychopathology and address individualized self-efficacy, self-esteem, and skills training. Research interviews conducted with consumers struggling to recover suggest that formation of an enduring sense of self as an active, responsible individual is a crucial factor in improvement (Davidson and Strauss, 1992).

Illness management and recovery (IMR) is a standardized, curriculum-based recovery-oriented intervention that can be implemented in an individual or group format. Recent research has produced positive results in terms of both effectiveness and feasibility (Hasson-Ohayon, Roe, and Kravetz, 2007). One year after the illness management and recovery intervention, consumers reported 1) improvement of cognition, coping, and social support; and 2) the perception that this intervention remained unique in comparison to other rehabilitative programs (Roe, Hasson-Ohayon, Salyers, and Kravetz, 2009). Addressing ways to incorporate IMR into recovery-oriented grassroots clinical care is now the next step of investigation.

SHARED DECISION MAKING

Shared decision making involves two knowledgeable individuals, provider and consumer, who work together to review the consumer's treatment and evaluate how it is furthering the consumer's recovery (Deegan and Drake, 2006). The consumer's desires, goals, and opinions about his treatment are a major factor in the collaborative process. This is especially effective when involving aspects of care that have a high rate of non-adherence, such as medication management. Traditional psychiatric settings have a prominent focus on compliance with the provider-conceptualized treatment plan, which stifles the consumer's voice and often dooms this strategy to failure. Frustration by the provider and consumer then strain the therapeutic alliance. Shifting to a shared decision-making model requires skill in communication and collaboration with the client, providing increased educational information to increase the degree that the decisions are adequately consumer-informed, and taking the necessary time to explore these goals.

MOTIVATIONAL INTERVIEWING

Motivational interviewing is a consumer-centered, guided counseling style that encourages changes in behavior by resolving ambivalence (Rollnick and Miller, 1995; Miller and Rollnick, 2002). Motivational interviewing works because exploratory and conflict-resolution styles of interaction between consumer and clinician mirror helpful interpersonal interactions and focus the consumer's energy on productive change. This model assists consumers in learning coping strategies and provides empowerment using concepts from humanistic psychology. Motivational interviewing has many separate concepts and techniques that are often best learned using practical workbooks that have examples of model clinical dialogue that illustrates these concepts (Rosengren, 2009).

CONSUMER-RUN SUPPORT GROUPS AND RECOVERY CURRICULUM

Consumer-run self-help agencies correctly emphasize the importance of peer-driven agency-based services (Salzer, 2002), while mental health advocates such as the National Alliance on Mental Illness (NAMI) focus on community-based programs like NAMI Connections support groups (National Alliance on Mental Illness, 2011a) and NAMI Peer to Peer recovery education courses (National Alliance on Mental Illness, 2011b). Currently NAMI Peer to Peer and NAMI Connections are two of the most widely disseminated consumer recovery programs throughout the United States. Accessing the NAMI website at www.nami.org allows any practitioner to find local NAMI members who can bring these free services to consumers in their area.

Another United States peer recovery program, BRIDGES, an acronym for: Building Recovery of Individual Dreams and Goals through Education, includes both a ten-week recovery education program and ongoing peer support groups that resulted from a 1994 collaboration by Tennessee's Office of Mental Health Substance Abuse Services, Tennessee's Mental Health Consumers' Association, and NAMI Tennessee (BRIDGES, 2011). BRIDGES has pockets of intense utilization throughout the United States but is less commonly available than the NAMI signature programs listed above.

STAGES OF CHANGE MODELS OF RECOVERY/ PSYCHO-DEVELOPMENTAL MODEL OF RECOVERY

Defining a model of how recovery occurs has been elusive. This leads to a sense that "recovery" is not a scientific concept or is incompletely understood. Davidson, Roe, Andres-Hyman, and Ridgway (2010) reviewed the body of literature, including ten models that advocate stages of change involving segmented, discrete stages that a person progresses through spontaneously, from initially being overwhelmed to overcoming the impact of the psychiatric illness. The authors then summarized these models into an emerging pattern of stages of change that provided five discrete changes: pre-contemplation, contemplation, preparation, action, and living beyond the disability. They pointed out several concerns.

First, viewing recovery as a personal behavioral change runs the risk of absolving others and the mental health system from the responsibility to help. The authors feel that any model should address person-disorder-environment interactions. Another concern involved clinicians believing recovery is linear simply because a stages model is used and despite an explanation that a model involving stages could be nonlinear. The authors emphasized that understanding regulatory mechanisms and change points within a model with stages would be helpful.

One stages model published one year before, and not discussed in the Davidson et al. paper, fits the five common stages of the other models, addresses their concerns, and provides answers about the nature of regulatory mechanisms and change points. This is a psycho- developmental model (Vogel-Scibilia, McNulty, Baxter, Miller, Dine, and Frese, 2009) that frames recovery from psychiatric illness as similar to how all humans develop and deal with the inexorably difficult and often traumatic stresses of developing and aging, using stages akin to Erik Erikson's developmental schema. This model integrates diverse recovery precepts into a useable clinical strategy for providers of psychiatric care and provides an understandable strategy for conceptualizing the nonlinear and environmentally interactive nature of recovery (see Table 13.2).

CERTIFIED PEER SUPPORT SPECIALISTS (CPSP)

Georgia was the first state to reimburse Medicaid services provided by certified peer support specialists (CPSP), who are consumers living in recovery. Over the following decade more than six states instituted similar policies, which allowed peer support specialists to work in a variety

Table 13.2

Nonlinear Stages of Recovery:			Erikson's Stages of Human Development		
Trust Versus Doubt	Acceptance of psychiatric disability	Trust in the concept of recovery	**Trust Versus Mistrust**	Is the world reliable?	Will my needs be met? **Result: Hope**
Hope Versus Shame	Grapple with loss of control of mind; illness sx.	Coping skill development; hope for personal recovery	**Autonomy Versus Shame/Self Doubt**	Struggle for personal control	Understanding of separation from others. **Result: Will**
Empowerment Versus Guilt	Address frustration and anger; empower self; minimize disability.	Focus on empowerment; search for personal recovery plan. Use strengths; banish guilt	**Initiative Versus Guilt**	Concept of autonomy to pursue new tasks	Use of newfound skills to cope with disability and advance recovery. **Result: Purpose**
Action Versus Inaction	Fight static disability and isolation; create "social niche"	Seek purposeful work and leisure pursuits	**Industry Versus Inferiority**	Acquire skills and interests	Build self-esteem. **Result: Competence**
"New" Self Versus "Sick" Self	"Am I my disease?"	Separate personal identity from illness	**Identity Versus Role Confusion**	"Who am I? What are my values and self-concepts?"	Personal identity and adult role development. **Result: Fidelity**
Intimacy Versus Isolation	Establish intimate relationships; integrate recovery	Seek out intimacy with a peer to share recovery life.	**Intimacy Versus Isolation**	Engaging in intimate relationships; sharing life with a peer	Development of intimate relationships with peers. **Result: Love**
Purpose Versus Passivity	Establishing a "life niche"; altruistic giving back	Living well with a mental illness	**Generativity Versus Stagnation**	"Is this all there is?"	Accomplishing meaningful goals in life. **Result: Care**
Integrity Versus Despair	Reflecting on life lived with psychiatric recovery	Provide mentorship and wisdom	**Integrity Versus Despair**	Looking back on the life that one has lived	Life review/ addressing mortality. **Result: Wisdom**

of environments and utilize a broad range of interventions (Salzer, Schwenk, and Brusilovskiy, 2010). Certified peer support specialists most often are agency-based, and provide individual rather than group care. They frequently provide peer support in the areas of self-determination, health and wellness, hope, communication with providers, illness management, and dealing with stigma (Salzer et al., 2010). This body of research concluded that CPSP roles were different depending on the agency and setting in which they worked. Most received 80 hours or less of basic training; it was suggested that increased, individualized continuing education would be helpful, based on the type of work each CPSP was provided. This was supported by the Pennsylvania CPSP Initiative, which reported 97 percent of consumers were able to finish the training and 82 percent were working one year later. The Pennsylvania study showed that the peers described job satisfaction, felt accepted by co-workers, and reported receiving good but infrequent supervision (Salzer, Katz, Kidwell, Federici, and Ward-Colasante, 2009).

One expanding role for certified peer specialists involves the establishment and staffing of peer-run "warm lines" (as distinct from "hotlines"). Having an outlet to discuss both emergency and non-emergency issues that occur after hours when traditional care centers are closed can assist with symptom management, loneliness, and recovery skill enhancement, and can triage clients with more severe problems to a higher level of care (Dalgin, Maline, and Driscoll, 2011).

WRAP—WELLNESS, RECOVERY, ACTION PLAN

For over twenty years, Mary Ellen Copeland has advanced her recovery-oriented coping skill plan—WRAP—"Wellness Recovery Action Plan." It is a structured plan devised by the consumer that assists in coping with either illness-related or life challenges by identifying what makes them feel better and what maintains wellness, known as "wellness tools" (Copeland, 1997). The use of WRAP is well disseminated in the consumer community and has had sustained growth over the last 15 years. WRAP also stresses the importance of psychiatric advance directives for consumers. WRAP has recently been listed by the National Registry for Evidence-Based Programs and Practices (Copeland, 2011). Recent advocacy efforts by Dr. Copeland include eliminating seclusion and restraint.

PSYCHIATRIC ADVANCE DIRECTIVES

A psychiatric advance directive (PAD) is legal in twenty-five states as a document of a consumer's treatment wishes should he or she become incapacitated and unable to make informed decisions about mental health care (National Resource Center on Psychiatric Advance Directive, 2011). For clients who have an illness that creates periods of impaired decision-making, these directives can give them the sense of empowerment that desired treatment interventions made when a they do have capacity will be respected if they become incapacitated. Problems with the mental health care delivery system, lack of reimbursement for time spent enacting an advance directive, fears about consumers hamstringing providers, and lastly, unreasonable fears about adverse outcomes or litigation from advance directives limit non–recovery oriented professionals' investment in PADs and therefore prevent their dissemination.

TRAUMA INFORMED CARE

A significant aspect of consumer disengagement from the mental health system of care is the lack of sensitivity toward trauma encountered by consumers by virtue of having a mental illness, living in environments that expose the individual to violence, and from violence within the mental health care system. The National Association of State Mental Health Program Directors (NASMHPD) has a National Center for Trauma-Informed Care. This Center has reported about a consensus by knowledgeable providers that most consumers of mental health services have survived trauma and that their reactions to service provisions are shaped through the consumer's prior traumatic experiences (National Center for Trauma-Informed Care, 2011).

An emphasis on addressing trauma stems from three precepts: that violence is endemic, that trauma survivors ignore the symptoms or deny their impact, and lastly that the effects of the violence are very disabling. The Substance Abuse and Mental Health Services Administration (SAMHSA) maintains a directory of model programs and services that shows the broad array of strategies to address this problem (SAMHSA, 2011).

HOUSING FIRST PROGRAMS AND FAIRWEATHER LODGES

For some professionals, the presence of safe and affordable housing is an undervalued aspect of recovery. Much of the country utilizes intensive case managers or agency-based treatment teams to be the collaborators with a consumer on housing issues, often relying on non–recovery-based options. Two recovery-focused models will be discussed.

Housing First focuses on the premise that expecting clients to accept services and treatment or be sober before housing will be provided is contrary to the nature of mental illness and/or addictions. Often, consumers cannot accept services and care until there is a safe place for them to recover. Housing First does not tie the housing to acceptance of care, and it works to engage the client in treatment and support services after housing is provided.

Much of the research in Housing First has been with high utilizers of costly safety-net services or with the homeless. One study comparing "residential treatment first," then placement in supported housing, versus being placed into independent housing, showed that clients immediately placed into independent housing had more days living in their own place, fewer days incarcerated, and reported more choice over treatment. The study also showed no difference for "residential or transitional placement first" clients in the other clinical or community adjustment outcomes (Tsai, Mares, and Rosenheck, 2010).

Often programs blend intensive case management and healthcare services with housing for better housing outcomes compared to "local care as usual" (Mares and Rosenheck, 2011). The authors of that study also found that substance use, health status, and community adjustment outcomes are not changed with addition of case management or healthcare services in persons with chronic homelessness.

In one study that combined Housing First living and a consumer-driven Assertive Community Treatment (ACT) Team versus "treatment as usual," the majority of consumers in the Housing First/ACT group were able to maintain permanent independent housing (Stefancic and Tsemberis, 2007).

Another recovery-centered housing option that is far under-utilized is known as Fairweather Lodges. Developed in California in 1963 by George Fairweather as a result of his research into what prevents people with psychiatric disabilities from returning to a hospital, the Fairweather Lodge is founded on the notion that consumers do better living and working together as a group than individually (Coalition for Community Living, 2011). The Fairweather Lodge model allows people to live in the community more, provides employment as a component of Fairweather Lodge membership, costs less than conventional living strategies, and allows the members to govern their own community and solve problems with assistance as needed in a recovery-oriented fashion. Clients with varying levels of skills and functional abilities are divided into groups of four to eight to share a house. They elect their leaders and vote on who joins their community. They decide on a business to provide employment and develop a business plan with a variety of both house and employment leadership positions. No staff live at these lodges, but the members have access to consultants when they need help. This process supports empowerment and independence, which facilitates recovery.

Promoting Fairweather Lodges in an area means rethinking how one provides services to consumers. This model should be an element of any consumer-oriented compendium of services in the community. It provides a wonderful opportunity for professional–consumer partnerships.

ANTI-STIGMA INITIATIVES

Addressing stigma within the community and within provider agencies as well as consumer self-stigma is crucial to fostering recovery in clinical practice. All three areas of stigma are addressed by the NAMI signature program, "In Our Own Voice" (IOOV). The IOOV program sends consumers into the community, to places such as local organizations, police departments, provider agencies, and churches, where they discuss living in recovery from a mental illness and facilitate a discussion over 90 minutes (National Alliance on Mental Illness, 2011c).

Now self-stigma is understood to negatively impact a consumer's recovery, so specific interventions are being explored to address this. "Ending Self Stigma" is a recently described nine-session group intervention that shows promise to reduce internalized stigma among people with severe mental illness (Lucksted, Drapalski, Calmes, Forbes, Deforge, and Boyd, 2011). This pilot study, conducted at Department of Veterans Affairs (VA) mental health locations, addresses clients' internalized beliefs about stigma, empowerment, recovery orientation, perceived social support, and beliefs about societal stigma.

RECOVERY-ORIENTED EMPLOYMENT OPPORTUNITIES

Consumers and research literature both cite positive benefits from obtaining employment, but persons with mental illness remain significantly underemployed (Rinaldi, Perkins, Glynn, Montibeller, Clenaghan, and Rutherford, 2008). These authors cite external barriers to employment, including low expectations on the part of providers and a lack of knowledge that certain models of employment are more helpful than others. Pre-vocational training has been found to be less helpful than supported employment. Internal barriers include medication side effects, fear of losing welfare benefits, low motivation and confidence, employers' attitudes, and perceived stigma (Rinaldi et al., 2008). Employers have verbalized a high degree of concern in four areas over employing individuals with prior or existing mental health issues: trust, need for supervision, lack of initiative, and working with the public (Biggs, Hovey, Tyson, and MacDonald, 2010)

A Cochrane Systems review of vocational rehabilitation (Crowther, Marshall, Bond et al., 2001) and later studies comparing traditional vocational placement initiatives (Catty et al., 2008) shows that individual placement and support (IPS) is a more effective model than other approaches. A major emphasis of this model is targeting relational skills for potential employees and maintaining high IPS fidelity. Clients with previous work history, fewer unmet social needs, and better relationships with their vocational counselors were more likely to be offered work and work for longer durations.

Clients of the IPS model reported receiving more help in seeking and maintaining employment, but not having enough follow-up support, which is an integral part of the IPS model (Koletsi, Niersman, van Busschbach et al., 2009).

IMPLEMENTING RECOVERY BEST PRACTICES WITH PROFESSIONAL–CONSUMER PARTNERSHIPS

Utilizing the previously discussed best practices in collaboration with consumers, as colleagues, clients, and community members, is the goal of any recovery-oriented program. The first impression given by a recovery-focused environment is that it is welcoming and engaging. Feedback is solicited about the clients' further needs and ways to improve care. Assistance is provided for nontraditional needs such as rehabilitative goals, educational assistance, improved access to medical care, healthy living precepts, and social and leisure activities.

The core challenge of implementing professional–consumer partnerships involves overcoming barriers to recovery-focused best practices that exist both inside and outside provider agencies. Twelve barriers to recovery-oriented practice and recommendations for change were discussed at the Pennsylvania Consensus Conference in 2006 (Rogers, Vergare, Baron, and Salzer, 2007). These barriers included lack of knowledge about recovery, discouragement due to clients who are perceived as failing to improve, limited time to pursue recovery goals, lack of leadership by psychiatrists in promoting recovery, paucity of community psychiatrists, low mental health reimbursement rates, too few recovery-oriented programs, lack of coordination among systems and services, lack of a systematic way to assess the effectiveness of mental health treatment, community prejudices toward persons with psychiatric disabilities, limited financial reimbursement for community supports, and low socioeconomic status leading to victimization of consumers.

Other barriers can be grouped as either external or internal to the system. External barriers, including psychiatric infrastructure deficits, inadequate reimbursement to fund new recovery initiatives, lack of affordable housing, inadequate recovery and rehabilitation service access, limited availability of collaborative medical and psychiatric care, funding cutbacks for entitlements and transportation, and a lack of safe recovery communities which leads to criminalization, all create a perfect storm of frustrations for clients and providers.

Internal barriers include providers' resistance to relinquishing paternalistic or coercive practices that inhibit recovery, lack of access to best practices involving recovery practices, and provider burnout involving learning new skills or innovation. Several other internal barriers shall be addressed in more detail in the bullet points that follow.

- Power dynamics between consumer and provider goals

It is important to surrender the illusion of control when providing care to individuals who are competent to decide the nature of their care. The medical community has grappled and reckoned with this concept in relation to clients with cognitive impairment who reject medical care. Yet many psychiatric providers still struggle. Consumers, by non-adherence to or departure from care, will reject treatment plans that they are not invested in. Theo in this chapter's initial case study only accepted care that helped his recovery when he had been welcomed, engaged, and involved in his own recovery.

- Fear by providers that consumer-driven care will increase their liability exposure

Recovery precepts and consumer-focused programs increase engagement and improve outcomes for clients at high risk for adverse outcomes. Adequate charting of the rationale and recovery-focused discussion that leads to collaborative decisions, along with improved engagement with clients, will decrease, not increase a provider's risk of liability.

- Pessimistic view of consumers' ability to recover

An internalized belief that consumers cannot in fact recover is more pervasive in the psychiatric community than is acknowledged (Hocking, 2003). Part of this belief stems from long-outmoded teachings about severe psychiatric illness and prior more limited options for recovery. Clinicians in crisis centers, inpatient wards, extended acute treatment centers, and state hospitals provide repetitive care to a sub-segment of the consumer community who have symptoms at the peak of their severity, and who may chronically reject care or lack insight into and investment in treatment. This leads to a warped perspective on the potential for all consumers to recover. Recovery precepts dictate that all consumers have the ability to recover, no matter how severe their symptoms may be at any given time. Additionally, consumers in outpatient centers who have established recovery in the community require less care—so the proportion of time rendering care to recovered individuals is decreased compared to the smaller proportion of consumers who struggle. Suggestions exist to encourage stigma-reduction strategies for mental health professionals (Horsfall, Cleary, and Hunt, 2010).

- Fear of being marginalized in a recovery framework of care

The reality is that within a consumer-driven recovery system of care the provider becomes the mentor and learned consultant in the consumer's recovery program. This role is not one that can be assumed by another discipline. One study of consumer-run self-help agencies produced an unexpected factor in goal advancement—faith in one's psychiatrist as a source of responsibility for treatment decisions (Hodges and Segal, 2002).

EMBRACING MODEL RECOVERY PROGRAMS

Two model psychiatric rehabilitation programs are highlighted in this section to express both the potential and diversity of successful recovery programs in the United States.

Fountain House, founded in New York City in 1948, "is dedicated to the recovery of men and women with mental illness by providing opportunities for our members to live, work, and learn, while contributing their talents through a community of mutual support" (Fountain House website, 2011). Fountain House is a membership organization, with the creed "We are not alone." Members and staff work side by side. Fountain House is not a clinical program. It has no therapists or psychiatrists. It has an intense focus on employment programming.

Fountain House has become the template for the Clubhouse model of rehabilitation. With Fountain House as a model, in 1994 the International Center for Clubhouse Development (ICCD) was established. This organization now claims to have over 325 clubhouses in 28 countries worldwide.

The Village is an integrated service agency in Long Beach, California, that practices recovery-oriented, holistic care through a collaborative, multifaceted compendium of services within a psychosocial rehabilitative model (Village website, 2011). The Village, which began in 1990, serves adults and young adults with mental illness. In doing so, the Village incorporates many types of mental health care, including treatment, rehabilitation, self-help, and family and community involvement, while following a "no fail" approach. The Village employs psychiatrists and other professionals as well as paraprofessionals, including individuals who have recovered from mental illnesses. In 2002, President Bush's New Freedom Commission on Mental Health selected the Village as a model of "programs that work."

INTEGRATING CONSUMER CLINICIANS INTO THE BEHAVIORAL HEALTH WORKFORCE

For a care system to be consumer-driven, consumers need to be involved in all aspects of the evidence-based system. The areas in which consumers are now engaged in transforming the mental health care system include consumer-operated and/or consumer-advised services, research and development, mental health policy planning, anti-stigma initiatives, community and government relations, and membership on various forms of treatment teams and as functioning clinicians and administrators.

One of the most ingrained areas of stigma toward persons with mental illness involves both external and self-stigma toward consumer-providers (Solovitch, 2007; Baxter, 1998). Over the last two decades, a small number of providers have acknowledged their severe mental illness as a form of recovery advocacy, coining the term *prosumer* to describe open provider-consumers working to transform the system (Frese, 1993; Frese, Knight, and Saks, 2009; Vogel-Scibilia, 2001). Despite this cohort of practitioners possessing special insight into the lived experience of mental illness, there are few formalized avenues of input within mental health care systems to utilize their suggestions. Working on strategies to tap into this knowledge would help advance consumer–professional partnerships.

True integration and collaboration will only occur when the system transforms itself into one that encourages and engages its consumer members and shifts the philosophy of care away from paternalistic, provider-centered control toward a more strength-based client-driven recovery plan.

REFERENCES

Baxter, E.A. (1998). Personal accounts: Turn of the tide. *Psychiatric Services*, *49*, 1297–1298.

Biggs, D., Hovey, N., Tyson, P.J., & MacDonald, S. (2010). Employer and employment agency attitudes towards employing individuals with mental health needs. *Journal of Mental Health*, *19*(6): 505–516. Epub September 2010.

BRIDGES (2011). Available at http://www.recoverywithinreach.org/education/bridges. Retrieved 9/23/11.

Catty, J., Lissouba, P., White, S., Becker, T., Drake, R.E.... & EQOLISE Group (2008). Predictors of employment for people with severe mental illness: results of an international six-centre randomized controlled trial. *British Journal of Psychiatry*, 192(3): 224–231.

Copeland, M.E. (Sep 1997). *Wellness Recovery Action Plan, 1ˢᵗ edition,* pp. 9–18. Peach Press, 1st edition, September, 1997. pages 9–18. ISBN-10: 0963136615.

Copeland, M.E. (2011). Wellness Recovery Action Plan—Mary Ellen Copeland, available at http://www.mentalhealthrecovery.com/. Retrieved 9/29/11.

Crowther, R., Marshall, M., Bond, G.R., & Huxley, P. (2001). Vocational rehabilitation for people with severe mental illness. *Cochrane Database of Systemic Reviews*, Issue 2, Epub online—April 23, 2001. Retrieved 9/23/11.

Dalgin, R.S., Maline, S., & Driscoll, P. (Summer 2011). Sustaining recovery through the night: Impact of a peer-run warm line. *Psychiatric Rehabilitation Journal*, 35(1): 65–68.

Davidson, L., & Strauss, J.S. (Jun 1992). Sense of self in recovery from severe mental illness. *British Journal of Medical Psychology*, 65(pt 2): 131–145.

Davidson, L. (Aug 2007). A basic criterion for transformation. *Psychiatric Services*, 58, 1029.

Davidson, L., Roe, D., Andres-Hyman, R., & Ridgway, P. (2010). Applying stages of change models to recovery from serious mental illness: Contributions and limitations. *Israel Journal of Psychiatry and Related Sciences*, 47(3): 213–221.

Deegan, P.E., & Drake, R.E. (Nov 2006). Shared decision making and medication management in the recovery process. *Psychiatric Services*, 57, 1636–1639.

Drake, R.E. (2000). Introduction to a special series on recovery. *Community Mental Health Journal*, 36(2): 207–208.

Fisher, D.B., & Ahern, L. (2002). Evidence-based practices and recovery. *Psychiatric Services*, 53, 632–633.

Fountain House website (2011). Available at http://www.fountainhouse.org/content/mission. Retrieved 9/23/11.

Frese, F.J. (1993). Cruising the cosmos, part three: Psychosis and hospitalization. A consumer's personal recollection. In A.B. Hatfield and H.P. Lefley (Eds.), *Surviving Mental Illness*. New York: Guilford Press.

Frese, F.J., Stanley, J.D., Kress, K., & Vogel-Scibilia, S. (Nov 2001). Integrating evidence-based practices and the recovery model. *Psychiatric Services*, 52, 1462–1468.

Frese, F.J., Stanley, J.D., Kress, K., & Vogel-Scibilia, S. (May 2002). Evidence-based practices and recovery. *Psychiatric Services*, 53, 633–634.

Frese, F.J., Knight, E.L., & Saks, E. (2009). Recovery from schizophrenia: With views of psychiatrists, psychologists, and others diagnosed with this disorder. *Schizophrenia Bulletin*, 35(2): 370–380.

Hasson-Ohayon, I., Roe, D., & Kravetz, S. (Nov 2007). A randomized controlled trial of the effectiveness of the Illness Management and Recovery program. *Psychiatric Services*, 58(11): 1461–1466.

Hocking, B. (May 2003). Reducing mental illness stigma and discrimination—everybody's business. *Medical Journal of Australia*, 178(Suppl:S): 47–48.

Hodges, J.Q., & Segal, S.P. (2002). Goal advancement among mental health self-help agency members. *Psychiatric Rehabilitation Journal*, 26(1): 78–85.

Horsfall, J., Cleary, M., & Hunt, G.E. (Jul 2010). Stigma in mental health: Clients and professionals. *Issues in Mental Health Nursing*, 31(7): 450–455.

Koletsi, M., Niersman, A., van Busschbach, J.T., Catty, J., Becker, T.... & EQOLISE Group. (Nov 2009). Working with mental health problems: Clients' experiences of IPS, vocational rehabilitation and employment. *Social Psychiatry and Psychiatric Epidemiology*, 44(11): 961–970. Epub March 12, 2009.

Lucksted, A., Drapalski, A., Calmes, C., Forbes, C., Deforge B., & Boyd, J. (2011). Ending self-stigma: Pilot evaluation of a new intervention to reduce internalized stigma among people with mental illnesses. *Psychiatric Rehabilitation Journal, 35*(1): 51–54.

Mares, A.S., & Rosenheck, R.A. (2011). A comparison of treatment outcomes among chronically homeless adults receiving comprehensive housing and health care services versus usual local care. *Administrative Policy in Mental Health, 38*(6): 459–475.

Miller, W.R., & Rollnick, S. (2002). *Motivational Interviewing, 2ⁿᵈ edition*. New York: Guilford Press.

Mueser, K.T., Corrigan, P.W., Hilton, D.W., Tanzman, B., Schaub A., Gingerich, S., et al. (2002). Illness management and recovery: A review of research. *Psychiatric Services, 53*, 1272–1284.

National Alliance On Mental Illness (2011a). NAMI Connection Support Group. Available at http://www.nami.org/template.cfm?section=nami_connection; retrieved 9/20/11.

National Alliance on Mental Illness (2011b). NAMI Peer to Peer—consumer recovery education program. Available at http://www.nami.org/template.cfm?section=Peer_to_Peer. Retrieved 9/20/11.

National Alliance on Mental Illness (2011c). In Our Own Voice. Available at http://www.nami.org/template.cfm?section=In_Our_Own_Voice. Retrieved 9/20/11.

National Center for Trauma-Informed Care (2011). Welcome to the National Center for Trauma-Informed Care. Available at http://www.samhsa.gov/nctic/default.asp. Retrieved 9/25/11.

National Resource Center on Psychiatric Advance Directives (2011): Review of State Legislation. Available at http://www.nrc-pad.org. Retrieved 9/24/11.

Ridgway, P. (2001). Restorying psychiatric disability: Learning from first-person recovery narratives. *Psychiatric Rehabilitation Journal, 24*(4): 335–343.

Rinaldi, M., Perkins, R., Glynn, E., Montibeller, T., Clenaghan, M., & Rutherford, J. (2008). Individual placement and support: From research to practice. *Advances in Psychiatric Treatment, 14*, 50–60.

Roe, D., Hasson-Ohayon, I., Salyers, M.P., & Kravetz, S. (2009). A one year follow-up of illness management and recovery: Participants' accounts of its impact and uniqueness. *Psychiatric Rehabilitation Journal, 32*(4): 285–291.

Rogers, J.A., Vergare, M.J., Baron, M.A., & Salzer, M.S. (2007). Barriers to recovery and recommendations for change: The Pennsylvania Consensus Conference on Psychiatry's Role. *Psychiatric Services, 58*, 1119–1123, August, 2007.

Rollnick, S., & Miller, W.R. (1995). What is motivational interviewing? *Behavioral and Cognitive Psychotherapy, 23*, 325–334.

Rosengren, D.B. (2009). *Building Motivational Interviewing Skills—A Practitioner Workbook*. New York: Guilford Press.

Salzer, M.S. (2002). Mental Health Association of Southeastern Pennsylvania Best Practices Team: Consumer-delivered services as a best practice in mental health care delivery and the development of best practices guidelines. *Psychiatric Rehabilitation Skills, 6*, 355–382.

Salzer, M.S., Schwenk, E., & Brusilovskiy, E. (2010). Certified peer specialist roles and activities: Results from a national survey. *Psychiatric Services, 61*, 520–523.

Salzer, M.S., Katz, J., Kidwell, B., Federici, M., & Ward-Colasante, C. (2009). Pennsylvania Certified Peer Support Specialist Initiative: Training, employment and work satisfaction outcomes. *Psychiatric Rehabilitation Journal, 32*(4): 301–305.

SAMHSA (2011). Healing from Trauma—Trauma-Specific Interventions. Available at http://www.samhsa.gov/nctic/healing.asp. Retrieved 9/21/11.

Solovitch, S. (2007). Conspiracy of silence. *BP Magazine, 3*(1): 28–34.

Stefancic, A., & Tsemberis, S. (2007). Housing First for long-term shelter dwellers with psychiatric disabilities in a suburban county: A four-year study of housing access and retention. *The Journal of Primary Prevention, 28* (3–4): 265–279.

The Coalition for Community Living (2011). Available at http://theccl.org/Fairweather.htm. Retrieved 9/28/11. "Frequently Asked Questions," pp. 1–3.

Topor, A., Borg, M., DiGirolamo, S., & Davidson, L. (2011). Not just an individual journey: Social aspects of recovery. *International Journal of Social Psychiatry, 57*(1): 90–99.

Tsai, J., Mares, A.S., & Rosenheck, R.A. (2010). A multi-site comparison of supported housing for chronically homeless adults: "Housing First" versus "residential treatment first." *Psychological Services, 7*(4): 219–232.

United States Department of Health and Human Services (2005). National Consensus Statement on Mental Health Recovery. Retrieved 9/18/11 from http://store.samhsa.gov/product/National-Conse nsus-Statement-on-Mental-Health-Recovery/SMA05-4129, pp. 1–3.

Village website (2011). Available at http://www.village-isa.org, retrieved 9/23/11.

Vogel-Scibilia, S.E. (Winter 2001). Reflections on recovery. *NAMI Advocate*, pp. 5–6.

Vogel-Scibilia, S.E., McNulty, K.C., Baxter, B., Miller, S., Dine, M., & Frese, F.J. (Dec 2009). The recovery process utilizing Erikson's stages of human development. *Community Mental Health Journal, 45*(6): 405–414. Epub June, 2009.

CHAPTER 14

INTERDISCIPLINARY MENTAL HEALTH CONSULTATION

A Key Skill for Mental Health Professionals

DAVID L. CUTLER AND ANITA EVERETT

We also reach out to assist non-professional care giving individuals and organizations, especially those who provide mutual help to fellow sufferers.

—Gerald Caplan

INTRODUCTION

There are many barriers to achieving success in mental health work. As things change (and things are always changing), the challenges increase. We are contributing this chapter in the hope that future readers will think seriously about the importance of working thoughtfully and collaboratively to build on the knowledge and skills of one another to assure positive outcomes for the people we serve. Although this seems simple, it isn't, really. Sharing skills and knowledge does occur by teaching and mentoring, but when relationships do not exist, nothing is transferred.

We both have had extensive, although different, experiences on opposite sides of the country working as mental health consultants either formally or informally in various mental health and other community agencies. As we think about those experiences working at various levels in very complex systems, in a very complex society, in these very complex times, we wonder at how often it has been difficult, even for those of us with much experience, to be able to "see the forest through the trees" and provide effective help to other professionals. These days, it often seems as if there is a pervasive assumption that communication is electronic and automatic. It would seem that in an age of instant computerized linking, communication should be as simple as e-mail, Facebook, or Twitter. But, actually this wired sort of connectedness only creates an illusion of connectivity and perhaps a false sense of confidence that effective communication or even consensus has been reached, when nothing of the sort has happened. Both of us have worked in ordinary and sometimes extraordinary situations and at times have been faced with dilemmas that were in and of themselves difficult, but taken within the high-tech culture we currently are bathed in, they were well nigh impossible. For us, thinking and acting within a face-to-face consultation framework has yielded a way for us to maintain our balance, in order to be more helpful and effective with other professionals and non-professionals providing support.

In this chapter, we will try, as often as possible, to demonstrate the importance and utility of consultation by providing case discussions. In particular, we will try to emphasize examples of cases managed by healthcare professionals such as nurses and primary care physicians, although lots of other sorts of providers require similar consultation support. We are taking this opportunity because we suspect that, as we move forward to build integrated health/mental health treatment systems, healthcare providers will need lots of consultation if they are to be effective in serving all sorts of difficult mental health problems in primary care clinics.

Here is an example of a case that could have turned out better had some form of consultation been available: a case one of us recently heard about in the course of a clinical meeting concerning a periodically psychotic young woman who had been stabilized with intensive case-management and involuntary outpatient treatment requiring medications. She responded well to all of this support until the day before her involuntary outpatient commitment term was to expire. On that day, she had a medical appointment with a new primary care doctor, who examined her without explaining what he was going to do or warning her what parts of her he would touch before doing the physical. She quickly relapsed, became psychotic, and wound up in the hospital the next day. So this was a case of a failure to communicate properly, or perhaps a failure to appreciate the meaning of touching to a person who may have had a traumatic history, which may have triggered a bad outcome. Such events occur every day and perhaps are increasing because we actually think we are communicating or understanding one another when we really are not. It may also be viewed as a cautionary tale, illustrative of the perils ahead as we work to integrate health and mental health into a seamlessly functioning healthcare system.

How can we learn to understand what our colleagues may be thinking, and how can we help each other get it more right? In this chapter, we will try to outline for the reader how we have used the principles and methods of mental health consultation to encourage, support, and educate our colleagues so that we can all succeed in helping those who come within our sphere of influence, whether we are therapists, social workers, teachers, doctors, nurses, administrators, or police. Why is this important now? Berlin (1969) in an important article on consultation in schools pointed out; "The traditional role of school social worker is doomed by sociological pressures. Although trained in casework skills they cannot make a dent in meeting the needs of the school population." That was true then, and it remains true now. Although community mental health work implies, first and foremost, a population-oriented approach, on a face-to-face level, success is still very much contingent upon a relationship or multiple relationships. Professionals cannot hope to meet the needs, one at a time, of all those school children and all the adults who may have or may be on the verge of having mental health problems in a given population. Consequently, although what we have learned in the past hundred years about the nature of relationships continues to be relevant, including the ideas of early twentieth-century psychoanalysts such as Freud, Jung, Adler, and Erikson, we need to have a way to generalize the effect of good, positive relationships in a manner that takes advantage of naturally occurring supports.

NATURAL HELPING NETWORKS

Unfortunately, the wisdom of the psychoanalysts is limited to one-to-one relationships, which are not the standard social construct within which we live. Indeed, we are all, to some degree, a part of our own personal support networks, made up of multiple individuals connected to us through relationships and sometimes also to one another as well. Such networks can be measured and visualized diagrammatically and can be likened to little solar systems of 20 to 30 people. The inner "planets," so to speak, are those who are very close to us, like family. The outer concentric rings contain friends, work associates, teachers, and church members (Boissevain, 1974). These "natural" support people are crucial to our daily existence. They allow us to interact around daily events and thoughts and help us feel in balance with the culture and society around us. We gain self-esteem by receiving positive feedback daily, even minute-to-minute, from such people, who are quietly quite important to us. Not surprisingly, these folks can be very effective helpers when crises occur in our lives (Collins and Pancoast, 1976).

Sokolovsky et al. (1978) describe the case of "A.P.," a 27-year-old gentleman from New York who suffered from schizophrenia and had been going in and out of the hospital every three to five months with catatonia. After he moved into an single-room-occupancy (SRO) hotel in Manhattan, which contained mixed-tenant groups for social and food preparing activities, he began joining groups and stopped becoming acutely psychotic for a period of over 12 months. Access to these groups and individuals via consultation can translate into an important influence on individuals in need of help and sustenance in order to cope with major stresses such as chronic illness, divorce, job loss, war trauma, or death of a family member (Lindemann, 1944; Cutler and Madore, 1980). Natural helpers can be all sorts of folks from all walks of life, including schoolteachers, public health nurses, police, barbers, and even retired social workers living in SRO hotels (Levin and Straun, 2011), although it is not always possible to access such people in the midst of a crisis. Consultation relationships do need to exist prior to the crisis if the natural helper is likely to be able to act effectively. With help from a mental health consultant, they can become good screeners, problem-solvers, connectors, and providers of instrumental and emotional support. Gerald Caplan's views of the value of consultation (1964) are based on these ideas. Griffith and Libo (1968) demonstrated how in the remote, rural Four Corners of New Mexico, where essentially no mental health services existed in the early 1960s, mental health consultants were able to piece together a cadre of effective services by first establishing rapport with, and then making themselves useful by providing support to the staff of universities, local ministers, welfare departments, law enforcement agencies, physicians, and public media. Their volunteer work stimulated a reciprocal return of support from the various organizations and ultimately resulted in community mental health programs developing out of these collaborations.

Helping the helpers to help: All of us develop negative beliefs about various others because of what we might have experienced throughout our lives with certain similar people. We carry these beliefs with us unless someone has helped us see them differently over time. We need to recognize that our skills and knowledge will actually be effective in establishing rapport and providing meaningful help to people who may seem to fit into a category of futility. For example, in this day and age, we are coming to believe that it is possible for people to essentially recover from the effects of schizophrenia. But for centuries, that has not been the case. Now we have a variety of treatments—biological, psychological, and social—which are evidence-based and effective.

Yet many people, even trained professionals, harbor negative old beliefs deep in their collective unconsciousness about the hopelessness of schizophrenia.

An example of this occurred at a training for group home operators who provided structured housing for persons discharged from state hospital living in the community but still somewhat disabled. After hearing a lecture on cognitive behavioral approaches to developing recovery plans for the residents, a housing program manager approached the speaker and asked the following question; " I understand you are well-meaning in the schemes you have presented, but how can people like this who are by devils ever recover?" This case is not unusual. The individual was unusually open about this belief because it was shared openly by many others in that rural community. But more often, these beliefs can only be sensed or inferred, because they are not overtly stated. Either way, the consultation problem is, how does one go about helping this person see the future of treatment for the folks they are taking care of from a more positive, recovery-oriented point of view?

TWENTY-FIRST—CENTURY ORGANIZATIONS AS COMMUNITIES

Before one can help a group of professionals or natural helpers, one must first make contact with the organization that group is a part of (Karno & Schwartz, 1974). This could be anything from a family support group to a hospital-based primary care practice. All organizations have formal and informal power and authority structures: when considering a consultation with an agency, it is important for us to recognize that there are subtleties in the power structure that may be less than obvious, as well as formal administrative lines of authority. All agencies develop somewhat different cultures. Often the original values associated with the beginnings are still an underlying influence decades later, even after the mission may have been altered, funding streams have changed, and the original staff and founders are now gone. These atmospheric differences can be sensed but often are not articulated clearly by verbal or written documentation. For example, some originally faith-based programs that are no longer connected to a religious order continue to carry a certain missionary quality that can seem quite different from the flavor which emanates from a hospital-based system or a government-operated county, state, or former federal Community Mental Health Center (CMHC) or Federally Qualified Health Center (FQHC) program. There are also differences in theoretical models. For example, mental health programs may be formulated around certain treatment approaches such as cognitive therapy, dialectical behavior therapy (DBT), or psychodynamic therapy. Insurance companies operate under strict business models, and schools are highly politicized public facilities embedded in their communities and influenced by their parent groups.

There are also often informal power structures that differ markedly from what is on the organizational chart. If the King is weak then the barons are probably strong (Jay, 1967). In mental health organizations, highly skilled and charismatic therapists may possess more influence than administrative managers ("bean counters"). Just as there is no guarantee that a king is born competent and becomes powerful, there is also no guarantee that a manager will be more powerful than a smart therapist. So what appears to be an organized hierarchy may on some operational level be an illusion. The effective power to make things happen may lie in an informal network of relationships that is not spoken about directly but can be observed as one gets to know the organization. Good managers know how to parlay these informal power bases into effective team functioning. Good consultants also need to figure out who has influence, what sort of influence it is, and if possible, form a working relationship or alliance with these people. So, when encountering a new organization or program, it is useful to have, not just an understanding of the written formal organizational chart, but also a sense of the informal leadership structure or hidden barriers or unanticipated obstacles that are likely to arise.

A recent example of this was a consultation by one of the authors that involved the supervision of a physician new to an assertive community treatment team. This particular team had a team leader who either was not particularly experienced in leadership roles or had difficulty with the responsibility of supervising a psychiatrist. The team case-management staff often functioned as a substitute for the team leader, and this was the case especially for one unusually strong, assertive staff member who was very verbal but not very knowledgeable clinically. This awkward situation resulted in frequent conflict with the physician and a flood of management problems within the team on a daily basis, as well as several split opinions on the team regarding the best way to manage particular aspects of individual persons' treatment. The difference between "designated team supervisor" and "informal team leader" was critical for the new physician to understand and cope with until roles and relationships could be clarified. Such situations are very typical and may require careful relationship-building by the physician with all staff before they can actually become effective as clinical leaders On the other hand, when these subtleties are missed, effectiveness is delayed or never happens, and the team functions at the lowest-common-denominator level rather than achieving quality care above and beyond the norm.

For the purposes of our discussion, let's note some fundamentals about the current state of social disintegration versus how organizations work (Leighton et al., 1963). Leighton (1963) described the concept of social disintegration as a combination of factors, including unemployment, crime, divorce, etc., leading to higher incidence of mental illness in communities. Although most mental health systems start out with the best of intentions, it takes good structure, function, and leadership to produce success. Social service agencies have grown in recent years, in some cases to rather extraordinary proportions compared to what was available after the mid–twentieth century, yet multitudes of needy individuals continue to lack tailored, appropriate services. Over the ensuing half century, mental health programs have evolved to serve a very wide range of problems, yet people continue to slip through some very wide cracks, even though there are a lot of recovery-oriented and somatic treatments available. Homelessness continues to be quite prevalent in American cities, which makes it ever more difficult to get services to those in need. In the mid 1950s, state hospital clinics and psychoanalysis were most of what was available in follow-up, or outpatient mental health aftercare, with nothing in between. But what about all those in-between folks who needed something else? This included children, adults, and elderly, each of whom can be predicted to experience failure to achieve their life goals at a rate that may seem unbelievable, given the range of services now available. Generally, natural networks were what filled in the gaps for people before formal supportive services were available. This sort of thing has always more or less worked in less-complicated societies. But our society is anything but uncomplicated. There are rules for everything we do, and getting through and around them takes energy. Much of what staff in mental health agencies actually do turns out to be coping with barriers as opposed to working face-to-face with clients. In addition, the support network functions that organizations exist to carry out develop their own power structures and traditions, which often come into conflict with the original mission of the organization, forcing professionals to make choices that deprive people of the appropriate tailored services that could meet their needs. Keeping one's "eyes on the prize" is becoming harder to do and requires good leadership. Caricatured adages or folk-wisdom concepts like "Murphy's law" and "the Peter Principle" often appear to be more in play in the absence of strong leaders and supervisors. Add to that the ubiquitous funding problems, and one can see how morale in large human services agencies can often hit rock bottom. The result is, despite what we know and have the ability to do, appropriate help does not get to those in need. Consultation is not a cure-all for all this, but it can help staff get goals and function back in line with one another in an agency.

THE ROLE OF SUPERVISION IN AN ORGANIZATION

For most mental health professionals, it in important to be able to give and receive supervision and consultation just as a means of overcoming these negative forces. Yet these functions frequently do not get filled. The results may include a lack of access and bad outcomes for clients. For example: most people complain about how difficult it is to get adequate time with their doctor nowadays. Many wind up switching providers and even insurance plans. Meanwhile, physicians are given little time to see patients. In a fee-for-service model, there is little incentive to stop and take the time to build rapport and develop a relationship. If one does take the time to get to know the client, then one is likely to be late for the next patient, and appointments get backed up so that it begins to seem like the old county hospital waiting room (first come, first served) or worse yet an emergency department where the triaging system means that, unless you are close to death and can be saved, you are going to wait until the doctor is exhausted but can see you.

Many mental health agencies, instead of supplying formal supervision, have a tendency to function as if they were democracies when in reality they are not. To some extent, this is derived from the fact that therapists and other professionals need to be able to stimulate hopeful, empowering feelings in their clients but have trouble doing this if they themselves feel undervalued in their jobs. But functional organizations to some extent have to combine an empowering atmosphere for their staff with fiscal accountability and a solid organizational authority structure. This is a difficult balancing act for many administrators. Often the much-ignored, basic functional areas of ongoing staff training and career development get forgotten, and staff are neglected. This sort of vacuum causes stress for the staff, which leads to what we often refer to as burnout. Consultation in such a situation may not alleviate the problem, and a high turnover may well ensue. Nevertheless, a consultant who finds him/herself working with such circumstances can often help by simply being there and providing encouragement.

One of us was recently consulting with a group of psychiatric nurse practitioners who had lost their supervisor but did not lose their heavy caseloads. In fact, caseloads of difficult dual-diagnosis patients needing medicine, and a lot more, continued to pile up, without a manager there to set limits. The consultant who had been discussing tough cases on a consultee-centered basis had to switch to comments praising the heroic nature of these nurses (absolutely true) who against all odds continued to do exceptional work (also true). A detailed look at problem areas would have been counterproductive under these circumstances.

WHAT IS MENTAL HEALTH CONSULTATION?

Sadly, the term *consultation* has become ubiquitous in that it has evolved into multiple connotations. For this reason, it might be useful to start by pointing out some of what it is not. For our purposes, we do not want to imply here "expensive men in fancy suits," nor do we mean "mental health consultants who are a category of workers with mental health skills." What we are talking about when we say "mental health consultation" is a special skill that involves one professional helping another to be more effective and successful in providing service to persons who may be on the verge of, or are already in the midst of, a definable mental health problem. Furthermore, a consultant usually does not have a supervisory relationship with a consultee but rather is available on a voluntary basis for others to take advantage of. The voluntary nature of the relationship implies a discourse between equals or peers that is non-hierarchical. The advantage of this is that there is no loss of self-esteem in the relationship, since it is an exchange between peers (who may or may not be of the same professional discipline). Another aspect of consultation that is related to this egalitarian feature is that the consultee has the choice whether or not to use and take responsibility for implementing the suggestions of the consultant, as opposed to a supervisory relationship where there is always shared responsibility for a case and joint liability for mistakes. This allows for a more relaxed approach to problem-solving with fewer psychological and legal risks interfering with trust-building. Unfortunately, although the early days of community mental health development in the United States had a strong emphasis on consultation as a strategy (Cutler et al., 2012), in the current climate it is not a billable service and is difficult to fund with service dollars. For that reason it has been slowly disappearing, like an endangered species, from mental health training programs and from the skill sets of modern interdisciplinary mental health workers, much to the overall detriment for the mental health field. The decline of this methodology essentially means that building community support in non-medical settings is much more difficult.

There is quite a bit of literature on mental health consultation as a methodology for primary prevention in mental health. But most of it dates to the third quarter of the twentieth century, and it has received little attention in recent years. The effects of it have not been measured, so it hardly seems likely to emerge as an evidence-based practice. On the other hand, primary preventive strategies have been gaining traction, and there is reason to suspect that it will be possible to revisit these ideas, not only for the purpose of prevention but also for understanding and providing effective service delivery skills in interdisciplinary mental health and integrated health and mental health settings (McGorry, 1998). Brown et al. (1993) recommended that psychiatry residency programs provide training in negotiating and carrying out mental health consultation in a community agency. Such training has had little effect, however, because standards for training in psychiatry and other disciplines do not require mental health consultation as part of the curriculum and are no longer funded by federal grants. Such training was present in many places and in particular it was core for several decades within the Community Psychiatry Training Program at the Oregon Health and Sciences University (Goetz et al., 1998; Krishnan and Cutler, 2005). This training model was closely tied to Gerald Caplan's model (Cutler and Huffine, 2004) and provided supervised training to psychiatry residents, social work students, and nursing students in an interdisciplinary seminar on consultation skills, as well as other important knowledge and practical material needed for mental health work. Faculty from all the disciplines collaborated on the content of the interdisciplinary seminar, which was updated every six months in order to remain ahead of the changes in the field. Only consultation remained unchanged throughout the 30 years from 1975 until 2005. These skills based on relationship formation continue to be important even though everything changes as if we were constantly in a mental health revolution of sorts. High-tech communication methods and novel schemes to control costs are what grab the most attention these days, but core competencies remain vital.

Gerald Caplan's last book (Caplan, 2001) was a sort of tragic commentary on the consequences of the failure to prevent bad outcomes, which may actually be directly related to a lack of the availability of consultation. It focused on how agencies and their staffs, for a variety of reasons, can fail to understand and support their clients, and how that failure can actually cause psychological damage to those who rely on their services. Caplan refers to this as "iatrogenic harm," and blames the damage induced in patients on well-meaning caregivers such as social workers, clergy, teachers, physicians, or judges in the course of professional interventions where the goal was actually to prevent mental disorders but the result was to worsen them. The book, written toward the end of his career, contains case studies and first-hand accounts of caregivers he worked with to diminish this iatrogenic effect. His earlier work, on the other hand, lays out a more optimistic exposition of his "crisis theory," where he suggests that timely interventions can result in growth and health.

Caplan outlines his theory in his classic text *Principles of Preventive Psychiatry* (1964). In it, he draws from the earlier work by his mentor Eric Lindemann (1944) and colleague George Saslow following their observations of the survivors of the Coconut Grove nightclub fire in Boston in 1942. Saslow interviewed the survivors of that fire and reported his finding to Eric Lindemann, who published his classic article on the stages of grief in 1944. Caplan (1961) may have derived his theory on crisis intervention from these early observations. His idea was that people in crisis have an opportunity to get stronger as they cope with the crisis and gain competence and self esteem from mastering a stressful situation, or they may descend into anxiety and perhaps dysfunction due to their inability to resolve the crisis. When surrounded by family, friends, and natural helpers, they can use these supports to solve problems, but alone or in hostile, unsupportive situations, they resort to dysfunctional stress disorders, which, as we know, seem to have multiplied exponentially over the years (Linehan, 1986).

A key aspect of Caplan's approach to mental health consultation and collaboration involves mental health professionals consulting with teachers, clergy, nurses, doctors, police, and other service providers to address mental health issues within the contexts in which they occur instead of having to intervene directly. These natural-environment settings offer the advantage of not being official mental health agencies and therefore not requiring an individual to accept the role of "patient." Caplan in his many books includes a recipe for conducting consultations along with case discussions illustrating how this methodology can be applied in a variety of natural settings where mental health professionals such as social workers, psychologists, psychiatrists, nurses, and other mental health workers can be effective by using the skills and insight they have acquired as consultants to influence and improve the skills of community agencies and institutions to support the people receiving services. By improving the support within these organizations, the population they serve will be more likely to get the help they need when they need it in order to master crisis situations, and thereby become more resilient rather than more anxious or despairing, leading to failure or perhaps mental illness or even criminal behavior (Masuda et al., 1978).

MAKING CONTACT AND GETTING ACQUAINTED

In *The Theory and Practice of Mental Health Consultation* (1970), Caplan outlines the steps involved in developing a consultation program, including selecting and approaching the right agencies, determining where in the organization an intervention will be useful, negotiating a formal consultation contract, assessing the underlying reasons for the difficulties the organization is currently experiencing, and offering the consultees assistance. Target groups or agencies can be schools, nursing homes, or groups of natural helpers who are in contact with a population at risk such as children or the elderly. A key to establishing rapport and developing relationships is recognizing how exquisitely sensitive people are to issues of power, authority, and self esteem in the workplace. Griffith and Libo (1968) point out that success in community consultation depends to a large extent on establishing rapport with community providers and natural helpers and breaking through the fear people have of appearing ignorant or disorganized. There is a tendency in particular for folks to assume psychiatrists and psychologists can read minds, detect lies, and make judgments about people's character structure (a sort of counter-transference, one might say) which of course is not true, but creates considerable resistance. As a result, the folks who need the most help may be the hardest to get close to. Usually consultants are very successful in working with highly self-confident staff who do not have these fears, but they are usually the ones who need help the least. This is not a problem in an agency with a strong supervisory system, since staff are accustomed to sharing problems with supervisors, and consultants, under these circumstances, are seen as desirable extra help for unusual problems. But, although most agencies may look good on paper, they often are not actually performing effective supervision. In this more common situation, starting with high-functioning, more confident staff can eventually lead others to join in to get some extra help with tough cases.

Also in his 1970 book, Caplan outlines various types of consultation. The first he calls "client-centered case consultation," which is similar to typical inpatient hospital consultations. In these cases a consultant is called in to see a patient and offer a written opinion of what is gong on and what to do about it. In Caplan's model this can be done with or without the consultant's actually seeing the patient. The main feature is that the discussion and report center on the patient and provide suggestions for this patient alone. The goal is to help the consultee take care of the one case. Certainly, most consultation relationships begin this way. Over time, however, it is usually more effective to focus on the patterns of consultee's particular blind spots that may interfere with a successful outcome with certain patients or clients.

CASE EXAMPLE

A psychiatrist was asked by a civil commitment monitor to see and give an opinion about a hospitalized psychotic woman who had pushed a nurse down some stairs. The hospital staff were extremely distressed by this, and most of them wanted the patient charged with assault and discharged from the hospital because "the behavior was sociopathic and deliberate." The psychiatrist saw the patient and reported to the commitment monitor that the patient was quite psychotic and delusional and that voices had told her to push the nurse. The psychiatrist's opinion was conveyed by the commitment monitor, but the patient was released from the hospital and returned there within 24 hours, still quite psychotic. This case is an interesting example where a consultant gave an opinion but it was completely ignored, and in essence, nothing was learned. Fortunately, nothing really bad occurred as a result of this, but there was certainly a risk of a very bad outcome here. In fact, the patient returned to the same hospital and treatment team, who were obligated to treat the psychosis and did so successfully. The patient left finally after a couple of weeks, thinking clearly and not a danger to anyone.

Consultee-centered case consultation is quite different. It focuses attention on the consultee, not the patient/client. It can only happen as a part of a trust relationship developed with the consultee, and the issue becomes, not diagnosis, but improving the consultee's performance in certain areas. Some staff may lack specific knowledge, skills, or experience that may be necessary to be successful with certain client problems. The consultant must respond with knowledge- or skill-building suggestions that the consultee can then use in their work with a client. At times the problem is not lack of knowledge or skill, but a lack of self confidence or a lack of objectivity. If the former is the case, simple support and encouragement are helpful in the short run, but in the long run a good supervisory system is usually what is needed. Caplan, in his three books that discuss consultation (1964, 1970, and 1993) mentions these sorts of difficulties, which are universal among staff. No one has all the knowledge, skill, and objectivity to be successful with every case. It is just not possible, given what we do not know about the human condition. It is important to note that training programs in social work, nursing, psychology, and psychiatry do not produce perfect people. Graduates need experience in the real world under supervision to develop good judgment in clinical situations. Consequently, improvement in these areas is a constant training and supervisory need in a mental health organization. All human services agencies need to provide supervision, mentoring, and continuing education for their staff in order for a staff to thrive. If they do not, the ultimate result is burnout, or as Caplan (1970) called it, "lack of self confidence." When this happens among a large portion of staff, one sees high turnover, which is never good for the vulnerable populations we deal with who are sensitive to loss.

LACK OF OBJECTIVITY

Beyond burnout, in particular, what we understand about the constructs of transference and counter-transference gives us clues to the generic objectivity problems that affect our thinking and the assumptions that each of us makes relatively automatically when we are faced with a new or difficult client. These assumptions are also not necessarily always conscious, but they are available to substitute for missing experience, skill, or knowledge. It is human nature for us to seek some sort of objective "hook" or theoretical framework to hang our understanding of the person upon, which will enable us to systematically evaluate and plan for what we can do to help. With training and experience we refine these into habits as we grow as professionals. But this growth takes time and in most cases good supervision along the way, and while we are learning, we are likely to insert subconsciously our own early personal and culture-based beliefs and reactions into the knowledge gaps we have. These beliefs are injected into the treatment process, temporarily replacing specific science-based knowledge and judgment that we acquire later as we mature as professionals. If the work problem stems from a lack of objectivity, then what group of individuals does this person have difficulty with and what sort of negative belief does this consultee have about such groups of people? Often these negative beliefs at best do no harm, but what if they include negative or hopeless expectations regarding treatment?

Some of these problems are fairly prosaic, such as boundary problems, over-identification with the client, transference distortions, and distortions of perception regarding certain clients based on the consultee's personal issues. Nowadays, many workers in mental health and adjacent fields are actually suffering from themselves or recovering from a serious mental illness. Finally, Caplan (1964) describes a typical objectivity problem that can stymie an otherwise effective consultee. This can be thought of as a ubiquitous form of minor misunderstanding akin to stigma. Caplan coined the term "theme interference" and suggested that staff fail with certain people because they unconsciously fit them into "initial categories" that they also believe lead to "inevitable bad outcomes." Because they expect the worst, that is usually what they get.

Theme interference is basically a negative belief system about a certain class of individuals. In a pluralistic, ever-shrinking world, people of various shapes, cultures, genders, and religions are constantly coming into contact with service agencies staffed by dominant cultures (Marris, 1974, McBride & Bell, chapter 11, this volume). Any professional or nonprofessional may grow up with certain beliefs or expectations about people who are different in some way. Theme interference occurs when someone is expected to fail because they appear to belong to a certain category. Caplan (1964) divides these concepts into initial categories and inevitable bad outcomes. In other words, if you are in such a category you inevitably can't be helped. What's the use? The consultant, once she figures out what is happening, helps the consultee to reduce the theme interference over time by showing how the consultee can in fact help such an individual. It is mostly a matter of encouragement and persistence on the part of the consultant that helps the consultee feel they can be successful. As mentioned earlier, for centuries it was commonly thought that schizophrenia was a hopeless condition. As recent as the mid–twentieth century, it was commonly taught that people with this condition were incapable of forming attachments; therefore, psychotherapy was a waste of time. We now recognize that the opposite is true, that such individuals are exquisitely sensitive to rejection, and that relationships are in fact very important to them just like anyone else (Strauss et al., 1985).

According to Caplan (1970), theme interference can be reduced and perhaps eliminated by using a technique he called "theme interference reduction," either through supervising or by consulting with staff and demonstrating over time they can be successful even with people they always thought were hopeless. It has worked for patients with schizophrenia ("hopeless cases" not so many years ago), borderline personality ("hopeless cases" not so long ago) and various cultural froups ("hopeless cases" not long ago). Case by case, clinician by clinician, self-esteem is built, along with confidence that they can be helpful and perhaps even successful with people they were convinced they would fail with. Of course along the way they also begin to admire rather than fear people whom they previously considered hopeless.

CASE EXAMPLE

Consultation interventions occur at some unusual levels. A psychiatrist consultant working with a team of Medicaid-utilization review staff listened to a case about a 12-year-old male with an eating disorder. The child quit eating and drinking for no apparent reason. When asked why, she said "I don't know." The child was from an Asian culture and the parents didn't speak English. The child was hospitalized for several weeks but would not start eating on her own. She had to be fed with a tube. Eventually a plan was developed to send her to a day-treatment program where she began to eat and drink without the feeding tube but refused to eat or drink at home on the weekends. The day-treatment program began to wonder whether they should continue with the case, even though they had succeeded in getting the child to eat.

The utilization social worker became reluctant after several weeks of no progress to discuss this case. She was frustrated that little progress was being made but understood that having the child in day treatment was more effective than the hospital and offered the chance of helping the family cope. The psychiatrist supported the social worker in continuing to encourage the day-treatment program to stay on the case, and they both agreed that a culturally competent consultant was needed to evaluate the family. Such a psychologist was found and made a visit to evaluate the child in the home environment. There she spoke to the father, who described the problem in their native tongue as "an extended family disagreement." But when she met with the child, an unusual rapport developed between them that hadn't happened with any of the previous providers. They sat and ate a meal together, and the girl described a situation that had terrified her involving her mother, who had become wildly psychotic. No one could speak about it, and the child couldn't speak or eat. Once that was possible to discuss, the child improved rapidly.

Where was the consultation focus in this case? Was it with the child? Was it with the provider? Or was it with the utilization worker?

There are multiple levels of answers to this question. One of them, for our purposes, is the utilization social worker. We offer this as an illustration of how far removed from direct clinical action a consultation intervention may be. Had the utilization worker supported the day-treatment staff's desire to give up, the progress the child had made would be lost, she would have been re-hospitalized, the parents would have failed, and there would be a new team starting over with a demoralized family.

What were the consultee's issues with this case? Was it knowledge, skill, or objectivity? In this case, it would be difficult to answer that question, since we know little about the consultee. Clearly, the cultural gap prevented the providers from understanding the problem, and they reacted with a misunderstanding of the issues—perhaps a theme interference that could have led to a bad outcome. Over time, however, patterns emerge in a long-term consultation relationship that should eventually give a consultant a theory as to which issue is affecting the consultee. This example illustrates a skilled but overworked social worker who knew what to do but was responding to a pressured situation in the day-treatment staff. The day-treatment staff was demoralized perhaps by "theme interference," which would mean that they believed that this sort of situation would inevitably lead to a bad outcome. In this case, there was not enough evidence to make that assumption, but even if that were true, the intervention supporting the placement helped the consultee experience a positive outcome for this case. The day treatment staff may have had a lack of skill regarding dealing with the cultural issues but the problem was solved by finding a culturally competent consultant and everyone involved came out winners especially the patient who improved dramatically.

ADMINISTRATIVE CONSULTATION

As we have noted, organizations are managed by people, and people at the highest level may also have objectivity issues, blind spots, or skill and knowledge deficits. These problems can easily become, in a way, habit-forming in large, stable organizations. A rule of thumb we have noticed is that when staff are hired at any level, they will do whatever they know how to do from their training. If that is what is needed, there is no problem; but if it isn't, if they are not supervised and trained in models and service methods relevant to the needs of the populations they are supposed to be serving, they will simply apply whatever they know how to do to whomever they serve until a crisis comes along that forces them to change. In the early days of community mental health, most of what people knew how to do was insight-oriented psychotherapy, something relevant to only a small portion of the population. But, outside forces like Justice Department lawsuits, The Joint Commission on Hospital Accreditation, or other official sorts of interventions by government agencies threatening a loss of funding will get people's attention. These circumstances are often the basis for administrative consultations.

Each of us has had experience with these sorts of situations. One of us served as the state Inspector General in a large Eastern state. That role included surprise visits to hospitals and Community Mental Health Centers (CMHCs) to deal with evidence of some sort of dysfunction or lack of accessible appropriate services to the public. A visit from that person would be immediately noticed, but the Inspector behaved more like a consultant than a detective, and program staff were grateful for the advice they received. One of us also worked for the Joint Commission on Hospital Accreditation (1979) in the late 1970s and early 1980s when they were using the "Balanced Service System" model for community mental health center standards. Centers who wanted accreditation had to design their programs as systems and undergo a three-day site visit to determine if they conformed to key principles in each of five defined functional areas (services, administration, research and evaluation, staff development, and citizen participation). These site visits included workshops and consultations in the areas of medical records and administration given by experienced mental health experts trained in the model. In those early days of community mental health, these system consultations were a powerful force that moved simple one-to-one private-patient-model outpatient clinics into true community mental health/community support system agencies that were planning and delivering accessible services for a range of target populations. Both of these examples relied heavily on both program-centered and consultee-centered administrative consultation to achieve their goals.

PROGRAM-CENTERED ADMINISTRATIVE CONSULTATION

In program-centered administrative consultation, a consultant studies an organization or program and then writes a report and makes written recommendations on how to perform certain functions or operate certain programs. This is similar to client-centered case consultation, except the program is the focus, not the client. Such consultations are very typical and generally involve an expert and a detailed report outlining steps one should take to solve a problem or improve productivity.

A recent example of this involved the National Council on Community Behavioral Health, which was concerned that many of its member mental health programs were having trouble maintaining a medical workforce. They contacted the American Association of Community Psychiatrists and worked with a consultant from that group to start an executive leadership course for psychiatrist medical directors. A critical component of this program was the development of a performance improvement project that individual medical directors could take from a structured seminar back into their home community mental health center. In addition, expert faculty were recruited to help with the design and planning for the project, and throughout the implementation, course participants had access to both an individual coach-mentor as well as a group webinar experience, which offered the opportunity to troubleshoot problems and barriers in implementation with a group of peers as well as experienced executive coaches. The program enabled local programs to secure expert training and mentoring for their medical/psychiatric staff, thereby making the jobs more attractive for young physicians and more effective for the local programs. (See http://www.comunitypsychiatry.org/.)

CONSULTEE-CENTERED ADMINISTRATIVE CONSULTATION

Consultee-centered administrative consultation is where the consultant develops a relationship with an administrative or supervisory consultee and the focus is on improving the consultee's performance as an administrator. Here again, all the issues associated with consultee-centered case consultation come into play. A real and common example of a sort of agency-wide theme interference or "prognostic pessimism," if you will, can be seen with smoking-cessation policies. It is very common for healthcare providers and physicians, including psychiatrists and primary care physicians, to exclude smoking-cessation counseling from their interactions with patients. Attitudes such as "this individual with schizophrenia will never quit," or "persons of this group always smoke, so it is hopeless to encourage them to quit," or "persons of this group have a lower value on their health and it will be annoying to the patient to bring up smoking cessation" are quite common.

The following example is based on the smoking cessation issue and possible preconceived pessimistic ideas leadership in an organization might harbor.

CASE EXAMPLE

A local city government with a particularly compassionate city health commissioner passed a no-smoking ordinance so that individuals could not smoke in public settings anywhere within the city limits. This ordinance included the campus grounds of the community mental health center. Leadership at the center, while tacitly supportive of the big idea that smoking is unhealthy, considered an appeal for a waiver based on the idea that their consumers and patients would not be able to refrain from smoking and that it would deter attendance, and that their staff were not expert in smoking cessation. Consultation resulted in the staff's learning about smoking cessation. Focus groups with the patients determined that many patients were in fact very interested in smoking cessation and that many would welcome a program offering assistance with smoking cessation.

In this example the leadership had a strongly held belief that this effort would fail. The majority would agree that smoking is not good for people, but in fact, most of the resistance to change came from the assumptions of the leadership, not the reluctance of the patients. Consultation was important in this situation in order to reduce a "theme interference" in the leaders so that progress could be made with this difficult health problem, which is associated with increased morbidity for an already stressed population.

Consultee-centered administrative consultation is very interesting and also very creative. Changes on a large scale may ensue that can move programs to higher levels of functioning. Strong leaders are usually the case in these situations, unless the consultation is something required by higher authority. Having a consultant to help with these difficult administrative pressures is seen by good leaders as something of a luxury. The need for such "consultants" was understood as far back as the Romans. Scipio Aemilianus had a Greek consultant who accompanied him during the third Punic War and was at his side to the very end, giving advice. The Greeks themselves consulted the Oracle at Delphi when they needed important advice. It is still a good idea.

CONCLUSIONS

Mental health consultation as conceived by Caplan and Caplan (1993) and Berlin (1969) and many others continues to be a crucial component of mental health work. It requires experienced clinicians who possess a certain cadre of skills and competencies to be successful. But it can be key in helping programs and staff to be successful in solving difficult and confusing mental health problems. This may be even truer now than it was in the early days of community mental health, particularly because of the trend toward integrating health and mental health programs into single funding streams and "one-stop" integrated programs. The so-called Cartesian body/mind split that has existed for centuries will not be easy to reunify just because it sounds like a good idea. There continue to be many reasons why it is more convenient to keep the two apart, not least of which is a wide cultural gap between medical model and mental health model programs. They will need to learn to understand each other in an age characterized by too much information. Complex consultation schemes such as the National Council/ American Association of Community Psychiatrists AACP collaboration will need to be developed for community mental health centers and primary care clinics if this great idea is to actually come to fruition.

But health and mental health integration is not the only challenge. All sorts of social service agencies exist to help people struggling with all sorts of problems—school problems, old age problems, homelessness, unemployment, or veterans returning home to families from war zones, to name but a few environments in which stress, crisis, and the potential for serious mental health problems persist in our society. Even with modern access to the Internet, where enormous amounts of information is easily available, none of us can know everything or solve everything, let alone develop interpersonal skills, from looking at a computer. Good consultation, mostly on a face-to-face basis, is still fundamental in our field.

REFERENCES

Berlin IN (1969). Mental health consultation for school social workers: A conceptual model. *Community Mental Health Journal, 5*(4): 280–288.

Boissevain J (1974). *Friends of Friends; Networks, Manipulators, and Coalitions.* New York: St. Martin's Press.

Brown DB, Goldman CR, Thompson KS, Cutler DL (1993). Training residents for community psychiatric practice: Guidelines for curriculum development. *Community Mental Health Journal, 29*(3):271–283.

Caplan G (1961). *An Approach to Community Mental Health.* New York: Grune and Stratton.

Caplan G (1964). *Principals of Preventive Psychiatry.* New York: Basic Books.

Caplan G (1970). *The Theory and Practice of Mental Health Consultation.* New York: Basic Books.

Caplan G and Caplan R (1993). *Mental Health Consultation and Collaboration.* San Francisco: Jossey-Bass.

Caplan G (2001). Helping *the Helpers Not to Harm: Iatrogenic Damage and Community Mental* Health. New York: Brunner Routledge. Collins AH and Pancoast DL (1976). *Natural Helping Networks: A Strategy for Prevention.* Washington, DC: NASW Publications.

Cutler DL and Madore E (1980). Community-family network therapy in a rural setting. *Community Mental Health Journal, 16*(2): 144–155.

Cutler DL and Huffine C. (2004). Heroes in community psychiatry: Gerald Caplan. *Community Mental Health Journal, 40*(3): 193–197.

Cutler DL Sills G, Svendsen D, and Yeager K (2012). *Public Mental Health in America: "Enlightenment" to Accountable Care. Textbook of Modern Community Mental Health Work: An Interdisciplinary Approach.* New York: Oxford University Press.

Goetz RR, Cutler DL, Pollack D, Falk N, Birecree E, McFarland B, et al. (1998). Community and public psychiatry training in Oregon: Evolution and adaptation. *Psychiatric Services, 49*(9): 1208–1211.

Griffith CR and Libo LM (1968). *Mental Health Consultants: Agents of Community Change.* San Francisco: Jossey-Bass. Publishers.

Jay A (1967). *Management and Machiavelli; an Inquiry into the Politics of Corporate Life..* New York: Holt, Rinehart and Winston.

Joint Commission on Accreditation of Hospitals (1979). *Principals for Accreditation of Community Mental Health Service Programs.* Chicago: JCAH.

Karno M and Schwartz D (1974). *Community Mental Health Reflections and Explorations.* Flushing, New York: Spectrum Publications.

Krishnan B and Cutler D (2005). A resident's view of training in public psychiatry. *Community Mental Health Journal, 41*(5): 505–508.

Leighton DA, Harding JS, Macklin DB, Macmillan AM, and Leighton AH (1963). *The Character of Danger; Psychiatric Symptoms in Selected Communities.* New York, London: Basic Books.

Levin A and Straun TC (Jul 2011). Some barbershops aren't just for haircuts anymore. *Psychiatric News, 46*(14): 9.

Lindemann E (1944). Symptomatology and management of acute grief. *American Journal of Psychiatry, 101*, 141–148.

Linehan MM. (1986). Suicidal people: One population or two? *Annals of the New York Academy of Sciences, 487*, 16–33.

Marris P (1974). *Loss and Change.* New York: Pantheon Books.

Masuda M, Cutler D, Hein L, and Holmes T: (1978). Life events and prisoners: A study of the relationship of life events to prison incarceration. *Archives of General Psychiatry, 35*(2): 197–203.

McGorry PD (1998). "A stitch in time"…the scope for preventive strategies in early psychosis. *European Archives of Psychiatry and Clinical Neuroscience, 248*(1): 22–31.

Sokolovsky J, Cohen C, Berger D, and Geiger J (Spring 1978). Personal networks of ex-mental patients in a Manhattan SRO hotel. *Journal of Human Organization, 37*(1): 5-15.

Strauss JS, Hafez H, Lieberman P, and Harding CM (1985). The course of psychiatric disorder, III: Longitudinal principles. *American Journal of Psychiatry, 142*, 289–296.

Website: http://www.communitypsychiatry.org/aacp/cppms.aspx American Association of Community Psychiatrists. Accessed: September 28, 2012.

CHAPTER 15

PHYSICAL HEALTH AND MENTAL HEALTH CARE

ELIZABETH REISINGER WALKER, SHERRY JENKINS TUCKER, JAYME LYNCH, AND BENJAMIN G. DRUSS

INTRODUCTION

An increasing number of individuals in the United States experience both mental disorders and physical health conditions. The co-occurrence of two conditions, in this case mental and physical disorders, within the same person is called *comorbidity* (Valderas, Starfield, Sibbald, Salisbury, & Roland, 2009). Challenges to effectively treating medical and physical conditions include the high prevalence of comorbidities, the complex links among comorbid conditions, and the long-standing fragmentation between the mental and medical healthcare systems. Evidence-based treatments exist for improving care in this population; however, these treatments are not routinely integrated into primary care and community-based settings. Given the increasing number of individuals with comorbidities and recent changes in healthcare policy, it is a high priority to improve the quality and efficiency of care for this population. Additionally, a multilevel and holistic approach is warranted in order to promote overall wellness and quality of life. This chapter discusses the connections between mental and physical disorders, evidence-based approaches for treating comorbid mental and physical conditions, and future directions for mental health and physical health care.

COMORBID MENTAL AND PHYSICAL CONDITIONS

Comorbidity between mental and physical conditions is the rule rather than the exception. According to a large nationally representative survey, 68 percent of adults with a mental disorder reported having at least one general medical disorder, and 29 percent of individuals with a medical disorder had a comorbid mental health condition (Druss & Walker, 2011). High rates of comorbidity are also found between specific medical and mental disorders. For example, the risk of depression is two times higher for people with diabetes (Egede, Zheng, & Simpson, 2002) and 2.3 times higher for people with asthma (Strine et al., 2008) compared to individuals without the medical conditions. Additionally, individuals with cardiovascular disease (CVD) have 1.43 times the risk of having a lifetime anxiety disorder compared to those without CVD (Goodwin, Davidson, & Keyes, 2008).

The *Faces of Medicaid III* report shows similar patterns among disabled Medicaid recipients (Kronick, Bella, & Gilmer, 2009). Over half of the recipients with psychiatric conditions also had diabetes, CVD, or pulmonary disease, while those without psychiatric conditions had lower rates of these physical conditions. Based on the high prevalence of psychiatric diagnoses among people with physical conditions, the authors recommend prioritizing improved integration of mental and physical health care.

The pathways connecting mental and physical disorders are complex, bidirectional, and involve a variety of exposures and behaviors (Katon, 2003). Physical conditions can increase the likelihood of developing mental disorders, mental disorders can increase the risk of physical conditions, and physical and mental disorders share common risk factors. For example, medical conditions with a high symptom burden, like back pain or migraine headaches, can lead to depression (Patten, 2001). Conversely, major depression is a risk factor for physical conditions that involve pain and inflammation, such as CVD (Patten et al., 2008).

Common risk factors for mental and physical disorders include childhood adversity (Felitti et al., 1998), stress and trauma (Honkalampi et al., 2005), and low socioeconomic status (Harper & Lynch, 2007; Lantz et al., 1998; Lorant et al., 2003). Social factors, low income, unemployment, low educational attainment, and lack of support are major contributors to poor health outcomes (Murphy & Athanasou, 1999; Phelan, Link, Diez-Roux, Kawachi, & Levin, 2004; Turner, 1999). Comorbid conditions are also linked by adverse health behaviors, which results in elevated symptom burden and poor quality of life. Adverse health behaviors, notably tobacco use (Glassman et al., 1990; Lasser et al., 2000), alcohol and illicit drug consumption (Carney, Jones, & Woolson, 2006; Carney & Jones, 2006; Grant et al., 2004), lack of physical activity, and poor nutrition (Compton, Daumit, & Druss, 2006; Daumit et al., 2005), are common among people with mental disorders, which increases their risk for physical conditions and poor outcomes. Finally, comorbid conditions require paying strict attention to self-care regimens, including medication adherence and lifestyle changes, in order to manage symptoms and prevent disease progression. However, people with mental disorders are less likely to adhere to self-care procedures than are those without psychiatric conditions (DiMatteo, Lepper, & Croghan, 2000; Piette, Heisler, Ganoczy, McCarthy, & Valenstein, 2007). Ultimately, based on these pathways, people with mental and physical disorders experience elevated symptoms-burden, functional impairment, decreased quality of life, and increased mortality (Dickerson et al., 2008; Eaton et al., 2008; Egede, 2007; Stein, Cox, Afifi, Belik, & Sareen, 2006).

PROBLEMS IN QUALITY OF CARE FOR COMORBID CONDITIONS

People with comorbid mental and physical conditions experience barriers to receiving adequate care. A major barrier is the fragmentation between the mental health and medical healthcare systems. In primary care, common mental disorders, such as depression and anxiety, are often under-recognized and under-treated (Higgins, 1994). Many individuals with these disorders present with somatic, or bodily, symptoms, such as headache, fatigue, or gastrointestinal problems, that mimic those of other medical conditions (Seelig & Katon, 2008). Another challenge to diagnosing mental disorders is the lack of systematic screening for these conditions in primary care. Conversely, in specialty mental health settings, medical conditions often go untreated (Druss & von Esenwein, 2006). People with severe mental illness are also less likely than individuals in the general population to receive preventive services such as immunizations, cancer screenings, and smoking-cessation counseling (Druss, Rosenheck, Desai, & Perlin, 2002).

Once patients are diagnosed, providers face time constraints in managing multiple conditions. Limited time with patients and competing demands may prevent primary care providers from being able to adequately address psychological issues, which contributes to poor quality of care (Collins, Westra, Dozois, & Burns, 2004). Similar problems exist in specialty mental health settings, where having comorbid medical conditions predicts worse quality of care for more serious mental disorders (Chwastiak, Rosenheck, & Leslie, 2006). The challenges of managing and accessing care for comorbid conditions, as well as coping strategies, are illustrated in the case example presented in Box 15.1.

BOX 15.1 PERSONAL STORY

Clint Taylor is a certified peer specialist and assistant director at the Peer Support and Wellness Center in Decatur, Georgia. He has had physical and mental health challenges for as long as he can remember. Some of his physical challenges include Type 2 diabetes, asthma, hyperthyroidism, high blood pressure, endocrine issues, joint issues, back problems, irritable bowel syndrome (IBS), and other unresolved gastrointestinal problems.

"When I was 12 years old I had ulcers," Clint says, "and they took me to the hospital for some very intrusive, painful, embarrassing tests. I remember after all the tests had been done, I was sitting in the hospital room with the doctor and my parents, and they just said, 'Well here's his problem. Change his diet for the next six months and it should clear up.' I remember standing, looking out the window of my room, watching my parents walk to the car in the parking lot, and I was just *furious* that no one had asked me what is going on that a 12-year-old boy would have ulcers! They never gave me the chance to say what was bothering me."

As an adult, Clint sought medical services intermittently, but often he couldn't afford the care. "Even on Medicare, you still pay 20% co-pay," he said. "For example: I went to a cardiologist, and my portion of the bill for an examination was $400! And they wanted it right then and there! After that, I became very selective and I wouldn't see a doctor unless I was in great pain or something. I just wouldn't even bother.

"My physical health improved remarkably between the ages of 17 and 25," he continued. "I could do anything I wanted without suffering physical consequences. But during that period I had a lot of significant depressions going on."

After several psychiatric hospitalizations, Clint remembers, "I would be sitting in my mother's home staring at the wall for hours just drooling all over myself and being enormously hungry all the time. Between Lithium, Depakote, and Zyprexa, I gained 120 pounds. I now have Type 2 diabetes." He notes, "I was never told that if I took these medications, it could shorten my life span by 25 years. I'm still on a neuroleptic and an anti-convulsant, and these supposedly can damage the way your organs work. My liver has been damaged seriously.

I haven't been medication-free for 16 years," he said, "and I don't know what I'm really like without medication."

In 2008, Clint attended the certified peer specialist training, where he learned about the value of peer support, the possibility of recovery, and moving toward wellness. The following year he began working at the Peer Support and Wellness Center and believed for the first time that his life had meaning and purpose.

"Essentially, the Peer Support and Wellness Center has given me a reason to want to bother," he says. "And when I went to the Peer Support Whole Health training, I liked how they emphasized that really small changes made consistently over time were the key to changing the quality of your overall health. That was helpful because I used to think I'd have to radically alter what I do.

"Like today, I brought a salad to work. I'm also signed up on a spiritual literacy program that offers different courses in spirituality on different topics, and the one I selected was on Transformation. Before working here, I never would have done something like that.

"I'm crossing over from contemplation to behavioral change, and this is new for me. I am finally in a period of my life where I want to be alive now. I'm looking forward to how things are going to happen in the future. I've been doing pretty well for a while now, and I don't know what it would take for me to go back again. I am able to trust more in my recovery."

Comorbid conditions are also associated with substantial health care costs (Druss, Marcus, Olfson, & Pincus, 2002). The presence of comorbid mental disorders significantly increases medical and mental healthcare expenditures, with the majority of the increase occurring in medical expenditures (Melek & Norris, 2008). Mental disorders exact a high cost from individuals and employers. Individuals with severe mental illnesses experience reduced earnings compared to those without mental disorders (Kessler et al., 2008). Persons with comorbid mental and medical conditions cost employers approximately twice as much as those with either condition alone (Druss, Rosenheck, & Sledge, 2000), due to increases in presenteeism, absenteeism, and sick days (Glassman et al., 1990; Goetzel, Hawkins, Ozminkowski, & Wang, 2003). Finally, people with mental disorders have high rates of uninsurance and underinsurance, which further limits access to care (Druss & Rosenheck, 1998).

EVIDENCE-BASED APPROACHES FOR TREATING COMORBID MENTAL AND PHYSICAL CONDITIONS

Evidence-based approaches can minimize the barriers patients face in receiving quality care for comorbid conditions. Strong evidence supports the effectiveness of collaborative care approaches

(Gilbody, Bower, Fletcher, Richards, & Sutton, 2006). Under the collaborative care framework, multidisciplinary teams work together to screen, treat, and track mental conditions in primary care settings. These approaches are based on the "chronic care model," which outlines the clinical and community characteristics necessary for fostering collaboration between patients and healthcare teams in order to improve illness management (Wagner, Austin, & VonKorff, 1996). The core elements of the chronic care model include:

- Self-management support—treatment plans, self-management education, goal setting, modeling and support from peer consumers
- Decision support—guidelines and flowcharts for referring patients to specialty care
- Delivery system design—multidisciplinary team with clear roles
- Clinical information systems—electronic records and registries, reminder and feedback systems
- Health care organization—support from leadership, prioritization of chronic care, reimbursement policies
- Community resources—collaborations with community groups (Bodenheimer, Wagner, & Grumbach, 2002; Wagner et al., 2001; Wagner et al., 1996)

Effectively treating comorbid conditions requires integration of all of these core elements in order to be successful; simply implementing screening or provider education is not sufficient to improve outcomes (Gilbody, Whitty, Grimshaw, & Thomas, 2003). Two key active ingredients of collaborative care models are care managers and stepped-care approaches to managing multiple conditions (Bower, Gilbody, Richards, Fletcher, & Sutton, 2006). Care managers educate patients, provide support in patient decision-making, monitor symptoms, follow up with patients, and communicate with the care delivery team (Christensen et al., 2008). Stepped care involves monitoring physical and mental symptoms in order to inform adjustments to services to either a higher or lower intensity, as needed (Mauer & Druss, 2007).

Collaborative care models have traditionally been implemented in primary care settings, particularly for improving outcomes for common mental disorders such as depression and anxiety. In programs for depression, such as Improving Mood-Promoting Access to Collaborative Treatment (IMPACT; Unutzer et al., 2002) and Depression Improvement Across Minnesota, Offering a New Direction (DIAMOND; Jaeckels, 2009), the patient, care manager, and provider work together to develop a treatment plan that may include antidepressant medication or brief psychotherapy. The team meets weekly with a psychiatrist to discuss the treatment plan and make adjustments as necessary. Care managers monitor the patient's symptoms and coordinate follow-up. Patients enrolled in these programs experience significant improvement in depressive symptoms, as well as higher levels of satisfaction with care and quality of life compared to individuals in the control groups (Jaeckels, 2009; Unutzer et al., 2002). Additionally, new financing models, such as case-rate payment for depression care, are being introduced. These financing models aid in facilitating integration of mental healthcare into primary care. In the DIAMOND project, a monthly rate is paid under a single billing code to participating clinics for a bundle of services, including care management and psychiatry consults. In addition to streamlining the process, there is an opportunity for health plans paying for the program to accrue cost savings because payments are being made from the health care side of the system.

Katon and colleagues (2010) demonstrated how collaborative care can be used to target both depression and chronic illnesses. Patients with depression and poorly controlled diabetes, coronary heart disease, or both were randomized to either a treatment-as-usual control group or the collaborative care intervention group. Individuals in the intervention group interacted with a nurse care-manager, who collaborated with the patient's physician. These individuals showed significant improvement for depressive symptoms and several risk factors for the chronic conditions compared to the control group (Katon et al., 2010).

In contrast to the robust literature supporting collaborative care in primary care, fewer researchers have examined how these models can be used to treat physical conditions in specialty mental health settings. Initial evidence, however, indicates that multidisciplinary teams can improve the quality of medical care for people with severe mental illness by decreasing barriers to access and increasing coordination of care (Druss, Rohrbaugh, Levinson, & Rosenheck, 2001; Druss & von Esenwein, 2006). Druss and colleagues (2001) conducted a randomized controlled trial in which individuals who were enrolled at the Veterans' Affairs (VA) mental health clinic were randomly assigned to an integrated clinic or the VA general medical clinic. The integrated clinic was located in the VA mental health clinic and consisted of a nurse practitioner who provided primary medical services, a family practitioner who oversaw the nurse practitioner, a nurse case-manager, and an administrative assistant. The medical staff kept in close communication with the mental health providers and coordinated appointments to follow mental health visits. In the year following randomization, veterans in the integrated clinic had more primary care visits, more preventive services, higher satisfaction with care, and greater improvements in their physical health compared to the veterans referred to the general medical clinic. Additionally, the integrated clinic appeared to be cost-neutral when taking total health care expenditures for both groups into account (Druss et al., 2001). Multidisciplinary teams could also be instrumental in integrating healthy lifestyle programs targeting weight loss and physical activity among people with serious mental illness in order to reduce the burden of chronic diseases such as diabetes and cardiovascular disease (Bartels, Desilets, & Dartmouth Health Promotion Research Team, 2012; Dixon et al., 2010).

Innovative approaches to improving access to and quality of mental and physical health care include community-based care, in which partnerships are fostered between mental and general health practitioners, academics, and community organizations. Examples of community-based mental health care in the research literature are currently limited, but this number is growing. Community-based work is challenging because it requires significant commitment from a variety of stakeholders and substantial time to build relationships, identify common goals, and implement programs. Dobransky-Fasiska and colleagues (2010) describe a process in which community members, community organizations, healthcare providers, and researchers collaborated to improve depression care. In particular, they focused on disadvantaged and hard-to-reach individuals, such as elders and minority groups. The researchers partnered with Meals-on-Wheels to reach elders, developed a peer-education program to reduce stigma around mental health issues, implemented mental health outreach and depression screenings, and trained staff of community organizations to identify and handle common mental disorders. Initial feedback indicates that community members feel they have already benefited from being involved in the collaboration (Dobransky-Fasiska et al., 2010).

Another community-based approach involves integrating mental health consumers as part of the multidisciplinary team. The role of these consumers is to support and empower their peers to take a more active role in their treatment and recovery, promote self-management and overall wellness, and improve social networks (Sterling, von Esenwein, Tucker, Fricks, & Druss, 2010). In Georgia, consumers can become certified peer specialists (CPS) whose responsibilities include providing direct services to help consumers in the recovery process, being models for the possibility of recovery, and acting as change agents in the mental health system (Sabin & Daniels, 2003). One example of CPS involvement is through the consumer-run Peer Support and Wellness Center, located in Atlanta, Georgia (see Box 15.2). Another example is the Health and Recovery Peer (HARP) Program, in which CPS lead six group sessions about chronic disease and mental health self-management (Druss et al., 2010). Results of a randomized controlled trial indicate that participants assigned to the HARP program demonstrated greater improvement in patient activation and rates of primary care visits compared to individuals in the usual care condition. Additional, though non-significant, intervention improvements were found for physical health–related quality of life, physical activity, and medication adherence. This program demonstrates the benefits of streamlining mental health recovery and medical disease management in order to improve patients' overall health (Druss et al., 2010).

BOX 15.2 PEER SUPPORT AND WELLNESS CENTER

A project of the Georgia Mental Health Consumer Network, the Peer Support, Wellness, and Respite Centers (PSWRC; see Figure 15.1) are a peer-run alternative to traditional mental health services. The PSWRCs follow the motto "We are about wellness, not illness." Staff at the three PSWRC locations are certified peer specialists (CPS) and are also trained in Intentional Peer Support, a program created by Shery Mead. The PSWRCs offer daily "Wellness Activities," a 24/7 "Warm Line," and "Respite."

Daily *Wellness Activities* focus on whole health, wellness, and recovery. These activities include the Wellness Recovery Action Plan (WRAP), Double Trouble in Recovery (DTR), Art Explorations, Aroma Therapy, Creative Writing, and Job Readiness. Consumers are free to attend sessions based on their interest and availability.

FIGURE 15.1 Peer Support, Wellness, and Recovery Center

The **Warm Line** provides peer support over the phone, 24 hours a day, across the state of Georgia. The warm line is staffed by CPS, who listen to callers, share their own experiences, and connect callers to community resources.

Respite offers a trauma-informed alternative to psychiatric hospitalization. The PSWRCs have private rooms, where an individual can stay for up to seven nights. Before a respite stay is needed, consumers complete a **Proactive Interview**, which is an interactive dialogue with peer staff. The vast majority of individuals who stay in Respite report that it has helped them avoid a psychiatric hospitalization.

FUTURE DIRECTIONS

Comorbid mental and physical conditions can be challenging to manage effectively due to the high prevalence of and complex connections between diseases. However, evidence-based approaches, particularly those based on collaborative care, can improve quality of care and health outcomes. Despite the progress that has been made, however, additional development is needed to continue integrating physical and mental health care—from staffing to financing—as well as testing programs that address multiple conditions. Innovative approaches, such as community-based partnerships and peer support programs, that can influence social determinants of health outside of the clinic, deserve particular attention. Holistic and multilevel approaches facilitate the ultimate goal of better health and quality of life.

REFERENCES

Bartels, S., Desilets, R., & Dartmouth Health Promotion Research Team. (2012). *Health Promotion Programs for People with Serious Mental Illness*. Washington, D.C.: SAMHSA-HRSA Center for Integrated Health Solutions.

Bodenheimer, T., Wagner, E. H., & Grumbach, K. (2002). Improving primary care for patients with chronic illness. *Journal of the American Medical Association, 288*(14), 1775–1779.

Bower, P., Gilbody, S., Richards, D., Fletcher, J., & Sutton, A. (2006). Collaborative care for depression in primary care—making sense of a complex intervention: Systematic review and meta-regression. *British Journal of Psychiatry, 189*, 484–493.

Carney, C. P., & Jones, L. E. (2006). Medical comorbidity in women and men with bipolar disorders: A population-based controlled study. *Psychosomatic Medicine, 68*(5), 684–691.

Carney, C. P., Jones, L., & Woolson, R. F. (2006). Medical comorbidity in women and men with schizophrenia: A population-based controlled study. *Journal of General Internal Medicine, 21*(11), 1133–1137.

Christensen, H., Griffiths, K. M., Gulliver, A., Clack, D., Kljakovic, M., & Wells, L. (2008). Models in the delivery of depression care: A systematic review of randomised and controlled intervention trials. *BMC Family Practice, 9*, 25.

Chwastiak, L., Rosenheck, R., & Leslie, D. (2006). Impact of medical comorbidity on the quality of schizophrenia pharmacotherapy in a national VA sample. *Medical Care, 44*(1), 55–61.

Collins, K. A., Westra, H. A., Dozois, D. J., & Burns, D. D. (2004). Gaps in accessing treatment for anxiety and depression: Challenges for the delivery of care. *Clinical Psychology Review, 24*(5), 583–616.

Compton, M. T., Daumit, G. L., & Druss, B. G. (2006). Cigarette smoking and overweight/obesity among individuals with serious mental illnesses: A preventive perspective. *Harvard Review of Psychiatry, 14*(4), 212–222.

Daumit, G. L., Goldberg, R. W., Anthony, C., Dickerson, F., Brown, C. H., Kreyenbuhl, J., et al. (2005). Physical activity patterns in adults with severe mental illness. *Journal of Nervous and Mental Disease, 193*(10), 641–646.

Dickerson, F., Brown, C. H., Fang, L., Goldberg, R. W., Kreyenbuhl, J., Wohlheiter, K., et al. (2008). Quality of life in individuals with serious mental illness and type 2 diabetes. *Psychosomatics, 49*(2), 109–114.

DiMatteo, M. R., Lepper, H. S., & Croghan, T. W. (2000). Depression is a risk factor for noncompliance with medical treatment: Meta-analysis of the effects of anxiety and depression on patient adherence. *Archives of Internal Medicine, 160*(14), 2101–2107.

Dixon, L. B., Dickerson, F., Bellack, A. S., Bennett, M., Dickinson, D., Goldberg, R. W., et al. (2010). The 2009 schizophrenia PORT psychosocial treatment recommendations and summary statements. [Consensus Development Conference Practice Guideline Research Support, N.I.H., Extramural Research Support, U.S. Gov't, Non-P.H.S. Review]. *Schizophrenia Bulletin, 36*(1), 48–70.

Dobransky-Fasiska, D., Nowalk, M. P., Pincus, H. A., Castillo, E., Lee, B. E., Walnoha, A. L., et al. (2010). Public-academic partnerships: improving depression care for disadvantaged adults by partnering with non-mental health agencies. *Psychiatric Services, 61*(2), 110–112.

Druss, B. G., & Rosenheck, R. A. (1998). Mental disorders and access to medical care in the United States. *American Journal of Psychiatry, 155*(12), 1775–1777.

Druss, B. G., Rosenheck, R. A., & Sledge, W. H. (2000). Health and disability costs of depressive illness in a major US corporation. *American Journal of Psychiatry, 157*(8), 1274–1278.

Druss, B. G., Rohrbaugh, R. M., Levinson, C. M., & Rosenheck, R. A. (2001). Integrated medical care for patients with serious psychiatric illness: a randomized trial. *Archives of General Psychiatry, 58*(9), 861–868.

Druss, B. G., Marcus, S. C., Olfson, M., & Pincus, H. A. (2002). The most expensive medical conditions in America. *Health Affairs, 21*(4), 105–111.

Druss, B. G., Rosenheck, R. A., Desai, M. M., & Perlin, J. B. (2002). Quality of preventive medical care for patients with mental disorders. *Medical Care, 40*(2), 129–136.

Druss, B. G., & von Esenwein, S. A. (2006). Improving general medical care for persons with mental and addictive disorders: Systematic review. *General Hospital Psychiatry, 28*(2), 145–153.

Druss, B. G., Zhao, L., von Esenwein, S. A., Bona, J. R., Fricks, L., Jenkins-Tucker, S., et al. (2010). The Health and Recovery Peer (HARP) Program: a peer-led intervention to improve medical self-management for persons with serious mental illness. *Schizophrenia Research, 118*(1–3), 264–270.

Druss, B. G., & Walker, E. R. (2011). *Mental Disorders and Medical Comorbidity.* Princeton: Robert Wood Johnson Foundation.

Eaton, W. W., Martins, S. S., Nestadt, G., Bienvenu, O. J., Clarke, D., & Alexandre, P. (2008). The burden of mental disorders. *Epidemiologic Reviews, 30*(1), 1–14.

Egede, L. E., Zheng, D., & Simpson, K. (2002). Comorbid depression is associated with increased health care use and expenditures in individuals with diabetes. *Diabetes Care, 25*(3), 464–470.

Egede, L. E. (2007). Major depression in individuals with chronic medical disorders: prevalence, correlates and association with health resource utilization, lost productivity and functional disability. *General Hospital Psychiatry, 29*(5), 409–416.

Felitti, V. J., Anda, R. F., Nordenberg, D., Williamson, D. F., Spitz, A. M., Edwards, V., et al. (1998). Relationship of childhood abuse and household dysfunction to many of the leading causes of death in adults—The adverse childhood experiences (ACE) study. *American Journal of Preventive Medicine, 14*(4), 245–258.

Gilbody, S., Whitty, P., Grimshaw, J., & Thomas, R. (2003). Educational and organizational interventions to improve the management of depression in primary care—A systematic review. *Journal of the American Medical Association, 289*(23), 3145–3151.

Gilbody, S., Bower, P., Fletcher, J., Richards, D., & Sutton, A. J. (2006). Collaborative care for depression: A cumulative meta-analysis and review of longer-term outcomes. *Archives of Internal Medicine, 166*(21), 2314–2321.

Glassman, A. H., Helzer, J. E., Covey, L. S., Cottler, L. B., Stetner, F., Tipp, J. E., et al. (1990). Smoking, smoking cessation, and major depression. *Journal of the American Medical Association, 264*(12), 1546–1549.

Goetzel, R. Z., Hawkins, K., Ozminkowski, R. J., & Wang, S. (2003). The health and productivity cost burden of the "top 10" physical and mental health conditions affecting six large U.S. employers in 1999. *Journal of Occupational and Environmental Medicine, 45*(1), 5–14.

Goodwin, R. D., Davidson, K. W., & Keyes, K. (2008). Mental disorders and cardiovascular disease among adults in the United States. *Journal of Psychiatric Research, 43*(3), 239–246.

Grant, B. F., Stinson, F. S., Dawson, D. A., Chou, S. P., Dufour, M. C., Compton, W., et al. (2004). Prevalence and co-occurrence of substance use disorders and independent mood and anxiety disorders—Results from the national epidemiologic survey on alcohol and related conditions. *Archives of General Psychiatry, 61*(8), 807–816.

Harper, S., & Lynch, J. (2007). Trends in socioeconomic inequalities in adult health behaviors among U.S. states, 1990–2004. *Public Health Reports, 122*(2), 177–189.

Higgins, E. S. (1994). A review of unrecognized mental illness in primary care. Prevalence, natural history, and efforts to change the course. *Archives of Family Medicine, 3*(10), 908–917.

Honkalampi, K., Hintikka, J., Haatainen, K., Koivumaa-Honkanen, H., Tanskanen, A., & Viinamaki, H. (2005). Adverse childhood experiences, stressful life events or demographic factors: which are important in women's depression? A two-year follow-up population study. *Australian and New Zealand Journal of Psychiatry, 39*(7), 627–632.

Jaeckels, N. (2009). Early DIAMOND adopters offer insights. *Minnesota Physician, 23*(1), 1–2.

Katon, W. J. (2003). Clinical and health services relationships between major depression, depressive symptoms, and general medical illness. *Biological Psychiatry, 54*(3), 216–226.

Katon, W. J., Lin, E. H., Von Korff, M., Ciechanowski, P., Ludman, E. J., Young, B., et al. (2010). Collaborative care for patients with depression and chronic illnesses. *New England Journal of Medicine, 363*(27), 2611–2620.

Kessler, R. C., Heeringa, S., Lakoma, M. D., Petukhova, M., Rupp, A. E., Schoenbaum, M., et al. (2008). Individual and societal effects of mental disorders on earnings in the United States: Results from the National Comorbidity Survey replication. *American Journal of Psychiatry, 165*(6), 703–711.

Kronick, R. G., Bella, M., & Gilmer, T. P. (2009). *The Faces of Medicaid III: Refining the Portrait of People with Multiple Chronic Conditions.* Hamilton, NJ: Center for Health Care Strategies, Inc.

Lantz, P. M., House, J. S., Lepkowski, J. M., Williams, D. R., Mero, R. P., & Chen, J. M. (1998). Socioeconomic factors, health behaviors, and mortality—Results from a nationally representative prospective study of U.S. adults. *Journal of the American Medical Association, 279*(21), 1703–1708.

Lasser, K., Boyd, J. W., Woolhandler, S., Himmelstein, D. U., McCormick, D., & Bor, D. H. (2000). Smoking and mental illness: A population-based prevalence study. *Journal of the American Medical Association, 284*(20), 2606–2610.

Lorant, V., Deliege, D., Eaton, W., Robert, A., Philippot, P., & Ansseau, M. (2003). Socioeconomic inequalities in depression: A meta-analysis. *American Journal of Epidemiology, 157*(2), 98–112.

Mauer, B. J., & Druss, B. G. (2007). *Mind and Body Reunited: Improving Care at the Behavioral and Primary Healthcare Interface*. Albuquerque, NM: American College of Mental Health Administration.

Melek, S., & Norris, D. (2008). *Chronic Conditions and Comorbid Psychological Disorders*. Seattle, WA: Milliman.

Murphy, G. C., & Athanasou, J. A. (1999). The effect of unemployment on mental health. *Journal of Occupational and Organizational Psychology, 72*, 83–99.

Patten, S. B. (2001). Long-term medical conditions and major depression in a Canadian population study at waves 1 and 2. *Journal of Affective Disorders, 63*(1–3), 35–41.

Patten, S. B., Williams, J. V. A., Lavorato, D. H., Modgill, G., Jette, N., & Eliasziw, M. (2008). Major depression as a risk factor for chronic disease incidence: Longitudinal analyses in a general population cohort. *General Hospital Psychiatry, 30*(5), 407–413.

Phelan, J. C., Link, B. G., Diez-Roux, A., Kawachi, I., & Levin, B. (2004). "Fundamental causes" of social inequalities in mortality: A test of the theory. *Journal of Health and Social Behavior, 45*(3), 265–285.

Piette, J. D., Heisler, M., Ganoczy, D., McCarthy, J. F., & Valenstein, M. (2007). Differential medication adherence among patients with schizophrenia and comorbid diabetes and hypertension. *Psychiatric Services, 58*(2), 207–212.

Sabin, J. E., & Daniels, N. (2003). Managed care: Strengthening the consumer voice in managed care: VII. The Georgia peer specialist program. *Psychiatric Services, 54*(4), 497–498.

Seelig, M. D., & Katon, W. (2008). Gaps in depression care: why primary care physicians should hone their depression screening, diagnosis, and management skills. *Journal of Occupational & Environmental Medicine, 50*(4), 451–458.

Stein, M. B., Cox, B. J., Afifi, T. O., Belik, S. L., & Sareen, J. (2006). Does co-morbid depressive illness magnify the impact of chronic physical illness? A population-based perspective. *Psychological Medicine, 36*(5), 587–596.

Sterling, E. W., von Esenwein, S. A., Tucker, S., Fricks, L., & Druss, B. G. (2010). Integrating wellness, recovery, and self-management for mental health consumers. *Community Mental Health Journal, 46*(2), 130–138.

Strine, T. W., Mokdad, A. H., Balluz, L. S., Gonzalez, O., Crider, R., Berry, J. T., et al. (2008). Depression and anxiety in the United States: Findings from the 2006 Behavioral Risk Factor Surveillance System. *Psychiatric Services, 59*(12), 1383–1390.

Turner, R. J. (1999). Social support and coping. In A. V. Horowitz & T. L. Scheid (Eds.), *A Handbook for the Study of Mental Health: Social Contexts, Theories, and Systems* (pp. 198–210). Cambridge, UK: Cambridge University Press.

Unutzer, J., Katon, W., Callahan, C. M., Williams, J. W., Jr., Hunkeler, E., Harpole, L., et al. (2002). Collaborative care management of late-life depression in the primary care setting: A randomized controlled trial. *Journal of the American Medical Association, 288*(22), 2836–2845.

Valderas, J. M., Starfield, B., Sibbald, B., Salisbury, C., & Roland, M. (2009). Defining comorbidity: implications for understanding health and health services. *Annals of Family Medicine, 7*(4), 357–363.

Wagner, E. H., Austin, B. T., & VonKorff, M. (1996). Organizing care for patients with chronic illness. *Milbank Quarterly, 74*(4), 511–544.

Wagner, E. H., Austin, B. T., Davis, C., Hindmarsh, M., Schaefer, J., & Bonomi, A. (2001). Improving chronic illness care: Translating evidence into action. *Health Affairs, 20*(6), 64–78.

BEST PRACTICES AND CURRENT EVIDENCE FOR CLINICAL PRACTICE

CHAPTER 16

EVIDENCE-BASED PRACTICE IN COMMUNITY MENTAL HEALTH

An Overview

LENORE A. KOLA, DAVID E. BIEGEL, AND ROBERT J. RONIS

Over the past two decades, there has been an enormous growth in the number of evidence-based practices for adults with severe and persistent mental illnesses and/or co-occurring mental health and substance use disorders as well as for children and adolescents with severe emotional disorders. However, in the behavioral health field as in health care in general, for a number of reasons discussed below, these practices have not been routinely utilized. This chapter begins with a definition of *evidence-based practice*, followed by a discussion of frameworks for adoption of new models of evidence-based practice. We then discuss the emerging field of *implementation science*, followed by a discussion of the implementation of core components of evidence-based practice and presentation of strategies to overcome barriers to implementation. Our concluding remarks discuss recommendations for future implementation research that over time may help achieve a wider dissemination and adoption of evidence-based practice in community mental health settings.

WHAT IS EVIDENCE-BASED PRACTICE?

The concept of evidence-based practice began in the field of medicine and is now being utilized in health, behavioral health, and social welfare fields. Some erroneously believe that evidence-based practice can be defined solely on the basis of whether a practice is using interventions and treatments that are supported by the best or most rigorous evidence. This is a necessary but not sufficient condition for defining evidence-based practice. "Evidence-based practice" (EBP), as defined in medicine, requires "the integration of the best research evidence with our clinical expertise and our patients' unique values and circumstances" (Straus, Richardson, Glasziou, & Haynes, 2005, p. 1). Similarly, the American Psychological Association's Council of Representatives in 2005 defined evidence-based practice in psychology as "the integration of the best available research with clinical expertise in the context of patient characteristics, culture, and preferences" (APA Task Force on Evidence-Based Practice with Children and Adolescents, 2008). Thus, evidence-based practice requires a melding of research evidence of effectiveness with clinical expertise and patient characteristics, culture, and preferences. While there is no total consensus as to the level of evidence required to designate a practice as "evidence-based," consistent with this volume, "evidence-based practices" will be defined as interventions that have strong empirical support, usually including at least several randomized controlled trials conducted by different research groups.

As we discuss below, decisions made in the design of research studies to obtain evidence of treatment effectiveness often offer only a limited view of patient attributes. Too often, in the desire to minimize threats to internal validity, research studies of interventions limit external validity by selecting very homogenous populations to study that are often quite different from the heterogeneous populations found in community-based mental health settings.

ADOPTING NEW MODELS OF EVIDENCE-BASED PRACTICE

The gap between research and the translation of research findings into practice in community-based health settings has been extensively documented in all fields of medicine and behavioral health (Institute of Medicine, 2000). In the mental health field over a decade ago, findings from the Schizophrenia Patient Outcomes Research Team (PORT) study indicated that even those interventions with demonstrated effectiveness were utilized in less than half of all treatment settings (Lehman et al., 1998). In addition, many of the ancillary services needed by clients, such as housing, job training, or social skills training, were available in an even more limited fashion. Although there are many reasons for the lack of using evidence-based research findings in practice, such as the characteristics of the intervention or the situation of the intended target settings (Glasgow & Emmons, 2007), a repeated theme is that the practical adaptation of the evidence gathered is often ineffective because the research that has been conducted sacrifices external validity for internal validity by studying very select and homogeneous groups that may not be analogous to the heterogeneous populations that need the practice. Glasgow (2007), in writing about improving evidence for family medicine, quoted Larry Green: "If we want more evidence-based practice, then we need more practice-based evidence." The field of behavioral health has grown more complex and requires models of practice that are more consistent with the complexity of the client population. "Technology transfer" refers to the process whereby innovation in practice or an evidence-based practice (EBP) that has been rigorously evaluated and found to be effective through research (usually randomized controlled trials) is translated and strategically disseminated and implemented (Roman et al., 2010).

"Translational research" refers to the knowledge gained from research that ultimately influences practice and policy (Drolet & Lorenzi, 2011; Kerner & Hall, 2009; Manuel et al., 2009).

Kerner and Hall (2009) make a distinction between two different types of translational research: "Translation 1" relates more to the early process of research whereby basic science developments are translated into new clinical interventions and tested in carefully controlled clinical trials, and "Translation 2" primarily focuses on the dissemination and implementation of evidence-based interventions; in other words, the translation of results from clinical studies into routine clinical practice and health decision-making (Woolf, 2008). Many models place this entire process on a continuum rather than defining two distinct processes. Drolet and Lorenzi (2011) speak to the fact that although innumerable basic science discoveries represent the beginning of the translation (i.e., Translation 1), few actually result in applied clinical practice and health gains (Translation 2). As Woolf (2008) discusses, there is a much greater focus by the National Institutes of Health (NIH) on Translational 1 research than on Translational 2 research. In fact, T2 research only receives about 1% of the funding that T1 research receives (Eccles et al., 2009).

There are many different frameworks that are useful in translating and adopting an evidence-based-practice. One model put forward by Glasgow (2006, 2009) that does appear to have considerable practical application and would be applicable to Kerner & Hall's model "Translation 1" (i.e., evaluating the usefulness of scientific evidence), takes into consideration the social context in which the behaviors occur. The RE-AIM model is designed to provide a translational framework that can be used in intervention planning, implementation, analysis, reporting, and refining of the intervention model (Glasgow, 2006). RE-AIM is an acronym that stands for *reach* (participation rate as well as representativeness of the sample), *effectiveness* (both positive and negative consequences), *adoption* (representativeness of settings), and *maintenance* or *sustainability* (at both the individual level as well as the setting level). This model asserts that in evaluating the efficacy of a new innovation (intervention), the individual level as well as the setting adopted must be considered using each of the above dimensions in order to enhance the external validity of the intervention, thereby addressing criticisms that much research on evidence-based practice has, in the past, sacrificed external for internal validity (Glasgow & Emmons, 2007).

IMPLEMENTATION SCIENCE

Within the behavioral sciences, translating lessons learned from research into service settings as well as public policy is a complex and complicated process (Fixsen et al., 2009; Kerner & Hall, 2009). Fixsen and colleagues (2005) make a clear distinction between "paper implementation" where policies or procedures related to EBPs are put into place, and "performance implementation" where the actual implementation of these policies or procedures occurs. Performance implementation within the mental health field involves the incorporation of the procedures and processes of the EBPs into clinical practice with, hopefully, positive outcomes for consumers of that practice, with the engagement of a variety of stakeholders including consumers. This process requires considerable financial as well philosophical investment by the mental health system (Bond et al., 2009; Fixsen et al., 2005; Kruszynski & Boyle, 2006; Simpson et al, 2007).

This interest in successfully moving scientific findings to service has led to literature dealing with both evaluating the models of EBPs as well as what is described as "implementation science" (Fixsen et al., 2009; Soydan, 2009). Fixsen et al. (2005) address the challenges and complexities of implementation efforts and focus on "methods that are grounded in research and elaborated through accumulated experience." This includes efforts at the clinical, organizational, and systemic levels that begin with the readiness of programs to implement innovations, but continue through subsequent stages of adoption, implementation, and sustainability using a stage-based conceptual framework (Fixsen et al., 2009; Kruszynski & Boyle, 2007; Prochaska, Prochaska, & Levesque, 2001; Simpson & Flynn, 2007). A number of the implementation models have been structured around this "Transtheoretical Model of Change," a conceptual model that has been applied to matching treatment approaches to patient readiness in a variety of EBPs (Prochaska et al., 1992; Simpson et al., 2007; Simpson, 2009). The adaptation of this model to the implementation of EBPs reflects this parallel to client recovery. Indeed, Prochaska and colleagues (2001) originally adopted this model in an effort to integrate various frameworks for organizational change (Prochaska et al., 1992; Prochaska, Prochaska, & Levesque, 2001).

The adoption of EBPs is a process that begins with cultivating the political and social environment to allow for encouraging changes in organizational, programmatic, and clinical practices. Fixsen et al. (2005, 2009) describes this process as a very active one in which "outside experts (purveyors)…work with organizations, systems, and practitioners to achieve high fidelity use of the products of science to assure benefits to consumers," as opposed to the more passive approach of managers and practitioners utilizing research literature in a less systematic fashion, even though the described innovation may be relevant to improving the quality of care (Simpson, 2009). Successful implementation requires active and planned implementation efforts, as opposed to what historically was an assumption that published research would bring about effective and successful treatment innovations through passive diffusion (Drake & Bond, 2007).

A number of models have been proposed to describe this evolving science of implementation and dissemination in mental health programs. The National Institute of Mental Health (NIMH) (Department of Health and Human Services [DHHS], 2003) provided support for mental health providers and researchers through the Interventions and Practice Research Infrastructure Program (IPRISP) as a means of bridging the gap between science and service (Brekke et al., 2009). Brekke et al. (2009) presented two models of implementation practices for behavioral health agencies: "the external specialist purveyor model" and the "embedded generalist purveyor model." A *purveyor* is defined as "…an individual, or group of individuals who actively work to implement that practice or program with fidelity and good effect" and is typically an expert in the particular EBP (Fixsen et al., 2009). The work of Brekke and his colleagues (2009) moves away from the external specialist model (Biegel et al., 2003) and proposes the embedded generalist purveyor model, which differs in that the purveyor is one who is schooled in the science of implementation research and practice and is an employee of the agency. The actual implementation activities would appear to be similar in the two models (Fixsen et al., 2005; Kruszynski et al., 2006), but what differs is the integration of the external specialist purveyor activities into the responsibilities of an actual employee of the agency; that is, the embedded generalist purveyor who may be responsible for implementing more than one EBP.

Thus, implementing clinical and programmatic innovations can be seen as a stage-based process that must consider and address the variety of elements mentioned, including the assessment of organizational readiness for the change. The preparatory phase of assessing the need for implementation and gaining consensus of the organization plays a significant role and ultimately assists in bringing about better outcomes through the adoption of the innovation, its implementation, and efforts to ensure fidelity to it over time (Kruszynski et al., 2006; Simpson, 2009).

A number of authors have discussed organizational functioning and readiness for this technology transfer to occur (Fixsen et al., 2005; Prochaska, Prochaska, & Levesque, 2001; Simpson et al., 2007; Simpson, 2009), spelling out the actual steps that need to be taken to implement an evidence-based or best practice innovation (Fixsen et al., 2005; Kruszynski et al., 2006; Kruszynski & Boyle, 2006).

IMPLEMENTATION OF CORE COMPONENTS OF EVIDENCE-BASED PRACTICE

In the mental health field, there has been a very strong movement encouraging the implementation of evidence-based practice (New Freedom Commission on Mental Health, 2003). The federal government through SAMHSA has identified and funded a number of EBPs that have been successfully implemented across this country. Examples include: ACT (Assertive Community Treatment); Supported Employment, Illness Management and Recovery; Family Psychoeducation; and Integrated Dual Disorders Treatment (Drake et al., 2001). This movement toward integrating research and practice toward the promotion of implementation of evidence-based practice builds upon the earlier literature of technology transfer.

In addition to the many models of implementation that are extant, the terminology used to describe the these models is often confusing, with different terms being used to mean the same thing or something totally different (Kerner & Hall, 2009). In the implementation literature, a clear distinction is made between the many conceptual models of the development of building knowledge for implementation and the actual efforts, or "core components," of implementation (Fixsen et al., 2009; Manuel et al., 2009). In special issues of the *Journal of Substance Abuse Treatment* (2007) and *Research on Social Work Practice* (2009), studies are included that focus on the factors involved in innovation adoption that precede the complex and crucial implementation challenges. Within the core components of evidence-based practice are several guiding principles: Critical to the process and similarly to client recovery, implementation must be viewed as a long-term, incremental endeavor that may take two to four years (Simpson, 2009; Simpson & Flynn, 2007). The lack of successful outcomes may represent a failed implementation process at any stage (Bond et al., 2009).

There are a number of models in the literature that deal with this implementation process that share similar experiences and characteristics, but they all begin with the notion of organizational readiness and end with practice improvement, with issues of fidelity and sustainability in between. Many use a stage-based conceptual framework. Kruszynski et al. (2006) using the Prochaska et al. (1992) and Prochaska, Prochaska, and Levesque' (2001) transtheoretical model of change relate the various tasks of the stages of implementation to the appropriate organizational-change strategies employed, ranging from consideration of the success of their current treatment program (contemplation) to adoption of an innovation (action) to sustaining a high-fidelity treatment program (maintenance). These steps vary in language, but would appear to be similar in operations and are related to this stage-based process. As with many stage-based models, the process is not seen as linear, but rather each stage "impacts the others in complex ways," and every element is seen as crucial (Fixsen et al., 2009). These models include: "Exploration and Adoption," a conceptual model initially proposed by Rogers in 1995, but the reference I used is Rogers (2004), that describes "diffusion" of information beginning with assessing the organization's needs and the availability of community resources, progressing through leadership and staff "buy-in" of the innovation, and ending with the decision to move ahead to the implementation—the crucial step that connects the decision to adopt with the actual practice of the organization.

The inclination toward adopting an innovation will most often require a cultural shift in organizational vision and philosophy, consensus among the key stakeholders, changes in staff attitudes and in clinical staff's programmatic skills. Recruitment and selection of the individuals to carry out the implementation process may represent a threat for the staff to their current way of doing business and may require not only in-service training, but ongoing coaching (preparation stage) (Fixsen et al., 2009; Wieder et al., 2007; Kruszynski & Boyle, 2006). Deloitte & Touche (1996), in a survey of 400 organizations, found that the number one reason why organizations fail in their efforts to bring about change is resistance as a result of attempts to impose change on employees who are not yet prepared. Prochaska et al. (2001) take the position that an approach to this problem is one of social influence, insuring that planned interventions such as training and program consultation are matched to the employees' stage of readiness, so as to insure greater participation.

Once this organizational and individual readiness process has been determined, training then may occur. Simpson et al. (2007) assert that manuals have become a preferred tool for delivering training of an intervention as well as guiding its fidelity (Kruszynski et al., 2006). Following training, the adoption stage or actual implementation of the practice or program innovation is the next crucial step (action stage) (Simpson & Flynn, 2007). By this time, the questions about adequate resources (both sufficient staffing and financial support) as well as acceptance of the principles of the EBP should have occurred.

Ongoing training and consultation are necessary elements for maintaining high fidelity to the EBP model as well as managing sustainability (maintenance stage)—these are elements that are costly and require ongoing staff resources. These must often occur despite significant turnover in practitioners and loss of billable hours for training, and so forth, within the mental health system. This stage requires considerable financial resources for trainers and consultants (Simpson, 2007). As stated by Fixsen et al. (2005), "the goal during this stage is the long-term survival and continued effectiveness of the implementation in the context of a changing world."

STRATEGIES TO OVERCOME BARRIERS TO IMPLEMENTATION OF EVIDENCE-BASED PRACTICE

ORGANIZATIONAL BARRIERS

Policy, leadership and infrastructure. Significant challenges must be met to successfully accept, adopt, implement, and maintain a practice innovation. Barriers can occur along a continuum from the individual practitioner level to the state mental health authority. Leadership at the state mental health authority must not only be philosophically supportive, but also fiscally supportive as well, which, given the current fortunes of most mental health state authorities, may be difficult to achieve. However, barriers at one level, such as funding issues for programs within a mental health center, can sometimes be dealt with by changes in policy at another level, such as changes in reimbursement rates by the state mental health authority (Salyers et al., 2007). Most recently, concerns about Medicaid programs, which are the funding basis for a significant portion of persons with serious mental illness, also present a potential barrier to implementation of innovative practices and programs. Barriers also may include the cultural beliefs and value systems of all the stakeholders about the relevance and importance of the EBP, as well as the lack of necessary infrastructure at the state, agency, and board levels.

Brown & Flynn (2002) stated the belief that it is the role and responsibility of the federal government to take the lead in supporting and facilitating this technology transfer. However, while the government may lead the provision of resources for implementation of an evidence-based practice, without the commitment of the various stakeholders and mental health leadership, and a mechanism to achieve this transfer—for example, creating technical assistance centers within the states or individuals trained in the implementation sciences, as suggested by Brekke and his colleagues (Biegel et al., 2003; Brekke et al., 2009)—this technology transfer will not occur (Kola & Kruszynski, 2010).

PROGRAM BARRIERS

Program planning. At the mental health program level, administrators, team leaders, supervisors, et cetera, often do not have clear guidelines as how to proceed to implement evidence-based practice. Program planning must occur before intensive training, as establishing the organization's readiness, including the structural and functional program environment as well as consumer and staff needs, is required (Simpson, 2007). It is necessary to insure that there is no conflict between the leadership of the organization who are prepared to take action, and the staff in the organization who may be poorly prepared or do not see the benefits of the innovation adoption (Prochaska et al., 2001). The lack of an implementation plan, inadequate leadership (no necessary champions), no buy-in from staff, or model specification not made clear for the staff who may not understand the relevance or importance of the planned innovation, all contribute to what may be perceived as resistance (Drake, Goldman, et al., 2001; Fixsen et al., 2005).

Practitioner and supervisor characteristics that have been found to promote successful implementation include enthusiasm for the new innovation and "positive energy" toward the consumers of the model, optimism about outcomes, and a willingness to learn all aspects of the model. In addition, the implementation supervisor should have strong supervisory skills and the necessary substantive clinical skills to work with the particular population, and be trained in evidence-based practice (Wieder & Kruszynski, 2007). Given the current state of most mental health agencies, just keeping up with existing clinical demands makes it difficult to devote time and effort to developing new clinical skills, so there must be both psychological as well as fiscal incentives to motivate the staff.

Program planners may underestimate the infrastructure needs, practitioner skills, and leadership required for successful implementation, including adequate training that is easily understood and can be implemented such as using toolkits, manuals, etc., and done by competent trainers and consultants. The National EBP Project researchers have developed a comprehensive training-consultation model that includes a number of elements, such as: consultation to the state mental health authority and mental health administrators; a comprehensive needs assessment; baseline fidelity evaluations; a public "kickoff" event including all the major stakeholders from within the mental health system as well as consumers; skills trainings; ongoing consultation to the sites implementing the EBP; and, systematic monitoring of fidelity through a variety of methods of periodic fidelity reviews (Bond et al., 2009; Kruszynski et al., 2006; Torrey et al., 2001a).

Program fidelity. In addition to the lack of planning and program readiness assessment, many mental health agencies simply do not have the quality assurance and outcome procedures in place to adequately evaluate the process of EBP implementation or the consumer, family, or programmatic outcomes. Research consistently supports that programs that demonstrate high fidelity; i.e., those faithful to the model as it was empirically developed, produce better outcomes, so the need to adhere to the evidence-based models is critical (Ho et al., 1999; Jerrell & Ridgely, 1999; McHugo et al., 1999). Bond et al. (2007) in the National EBP project found a number of barriers to effective use of the fidelity reviews. These included problems coming not only from the sites, but also from the trainer/consultants, in that reports may not be valued by the agency; or the reviews may not have provided timely feedback or incorporated concrete action steps.

The maintenance of high fidelity increases the probability that an EBP will be successful over time. Basic to the implementation process is a clear set of shared objectives that measure achievement and success, as well as a quality improvement system that allows for collection of data not only on the outcomes, but also on the organizational process of implementation (i.e., fidelity reviews using standardized fidelity instruments, preferably done by outside reviewers who then provide feedback including action steps to improve or sustain fidelity).[1]

Unfortunately, not all mental health agencies have the capacity to engage in effective fidelity monitoring, outcome tracking, or ongoing organizational process evaluations related to the implementation of EBPs. There may be a lack of data systems to inform and sustain these practices, or the organizational culture from the leadership to the staff may simply not regard fidelity reviews as critical to ongoing quality improvement (Bond et al., 2009). The development of such systems requires ongoing consultation and technical assistance dedicated to a quality improvement process and an administrative investment in an outcomes process.

CLINICAL BARRIERS

Staff selection and training. In addition to both structural and functional organizational change, adequate implementation of practice innovation requires careful selection of staff who have the capacity and willingness to learn new skills, adequate training provided by competent trainers, adequate ongoing consultation by consultants who have clinical and programmatic experience and are skilled trainers, and retention of the workforce that has been trained (Wieder, Boyle, & Hrouda, 2007). Mental health clinicians typically lack systematic training in EBPs; and they rely on self-initiated opportunities for learning current interventions (Drake et al., 2001), continuing to do what they have historically been trained to do. Training must be made available if practitioners are to gain the clinical expertise required to adhere to models of EBP. Training needs to be provided to staff on an ongoing basis to assure that the frequent turnover in staffing experienced by many mental health agencies does not impede agencies' abilities to sustain fidelity in implementation (Woltmann & Whitley, 2007). However, it is now recognized that barriers to implementation of EBPs in mental health cannot be overcome solely by traditional methods of training and provision of written materials. Torrey et al. (2001b) state that these strategies may be a necessary component of program change, but are insufficient in themselves to bring about the required changes in behavior.

Research has demonstrated that there must be a good match between the treatment model selected for implementation and the staff implementing it (Wieder et al., 2007). Staff selection may be one of the key ingredients to successful implementation. Central to the staffs' ability to deliver successful quality interventions was their knowledge, skills, and talents. In addition, openness to learning was also a critical aspect; i.e., staff must be motivated to learn about the EBP and be receptive to the possibility of more successful outcomes following implementation.

Also, there must be financial incentives to keep caseloads small as required by most EBP models in order to retain the trained workforce, and time-unlimited technical assistance to address both turnover of trained staff as well as organizational changes.

CONCLUSION AND RECOMMENDATIONS FOR FUTURE IMPLEMENTATION RESEARCH

In an attempt to develop a comprehensive approach to innovation implementation and to overcome some of the barriers, the Implementing Evidence-Based Practices for Severe Mental Illness Project, funded by the MacArthur Foundation, Johnson & Johnson, and the Robert Wood Johnson foundation, the Substance Abuse and Mental Health Services Administration (SAMSHA), the National Alliance for the Mentally Ill (NAMI), and state and local mental health organizations promoted three program elements: Predisposing/disseminating strategies (educational materials and training), enabling methods (practice guidelines and decision support), and reinforcing strategies (practice feedback mechanisms) via an array of technical supports (Torrey et al., 2001a; McHugo et al., 2007; Rapp et al., 2008).

The adoption of EBPs is a process that begins with cultivating the political and social environment to allow for encouraging clinical and programmatic practices, and a commitment to bridging this gap between science and service in order to overcome some potential barriers. Challenges to implementation can be successfully met if there is widespread advocacy for the development of EBPs, such as financial and leadership resources to support innovation, training and supervision for practitioners at both the clinical and programmatic levels, as well as developing dissemination mechanisms that include consumers so that they may also advocate for the implementation of these programs (Drake et al., 2001; Mueser et al., 2003).

In conclusion, despite what we have learned about implementation from the emerging field of implementation science over the last few years, there remain many unanswered questions. Researchers have identified a variety of recommendations for future research pertaining to conceptualization, measurement, and capacity to undertake future implementation research (Bhattacharyya, Reeves, & Zwarenstein, 2009: Eccles et al., 2009; Proctor et al., 2011); to whit:

- There is a need for consistency and a common understanding of key terms and concepts used in intervention research.
- Testing of theory in implementation research is essential.
- Further development of valid and efficient measures for implementation outcomes is needed.
- Studies of the impact of context on implementation and the attributes of that context (role and modifiability) are key.
- Research is needed to better understand the level or unit of analysis that is most appropriate for particular implementation outcomes.
- Research is required to model the interrelationships among implementation outcomes.

- Research is needed to understand the attributes of implementation sustainability, such as the maintenance of behavioral changes in individuals and organizations, as well as to understand effective strategies to engage practitioners and managers in implementation.
- Strategies are needed to build capacity to do implementation research.

These recommendations can help us further understand the implementation process and thus improve both the extensiveness and the effectiveness of evidence-based practice in the mental health system over time.

NOTE

1. Personal communication by trainer/consultants of the Center for Evidence-based Practices at Case Western Reserve University.

REFERENCES

American Psychological Association Task Force on Evidence-Based Practice for Children and Adolescents. (2008). *Disseminating Evidence-Based Practice for Children and Adolescents: A Systems Approach to Enhancing Care.* Washington, DC: American Psychological Association.

Bhattacharyya, O., Reeves, S., & Zwarenstein, M. (2009). What is implementation research? Rationale, concepts and practices. *Research on Social Work Practice, 19* (5), 491–502.

Biegel, D.E., Kola, L.A., Ronis, R.J., Boyle, P.E., Delos Reyes, C.M., Wieder, B., et al . (2003).The Ohio Substance Abuse and Mental Illness Coordinating Center of Excellence: Implementation support for evidence-based practice. *Research in Social Work Practice, 13* (4), 531–554.

Bond, G.R., Drake, R.E., McHugo, G.J., Rapp, C.A., & Whitley, R. (2009). Strategies for improving fidelity in the National Evidence-Based Practices Model. *Research on Social Work Practice, 19* (5), 569–581.

Brekke, J.S., Philips, E., Pancake, L., Anne, O., Lewis, J., & Duke, J. (2009). Implementation practice and implementation research. *Research on Social Work Practice 19* (5), 592–601.

Brown, B. S., & Flynn, P. M. (2002). The federal role in drug abuse technology transfer: A history and perspective. *Journal of Substance Abuse Treatment, 22,* 245–257.

Deloitte & Touche (1996). Executive survey of manufacturers (on-line). Available at http://www.dtcg.com/research.

Drake, R.E., Essock, S.M., Shaner, A., Carey, K.B., Minkoff, K., Kola, L., et al. (2001). Implementing dual diagnosis services for clients with severe mental illness. *Psychiatric Services, 52,* 469–476.

Drake, R.E., Goldman, H.H., Leff, H.S., Lehman, A.F., Dixon, L, Mueser, K.T., et al. (2001). Implementing dual diagnosis services for clients with severe mental illness. *Psychiatric Services, 52,* 469–476.

Drake, R.E., & Bond, G.R. (2007). Case studies of evidence-based practice implementation. *American Journal of Psychiatric Rehabilitation, 10,* 81–83.

Drolet, B.C., & Lorenzi, N.M. (2011). Translational research: understanding the continuum from bench to bedside. *Translational Research, 157*(1), 1–5.

Eccles, M.P., Armstrong, D., Baker, R., Cleary, K., Davies, H., Glasziou, P., . . . Sibbald, B. (2009). Editorial: An implementation research agenda. *Implementation Science, 4* (18). doi: 10.1186/1748-5908-4-18.

Fixsen, D.L. Naoom, S.F., Blasé, K.A., Friedman, R.M., & Wallace, F. (2005). *Implementation Research: A Synthesis of the Literature*. Tampa, FL: University of South Florida, Louis de la Parte Florida Mental Health Institute, The National Implementation Research Network (FMHI Publication #231).

Fixsen, D.L., Blasé, K.A., Naoom, S.F., & Wallace, F. (2009). Core implementation components. *Research in Social Work Practice, 19* (5), 531–540.

Glasgow, R.E. (2006). RE-AIMing research for application: Ways to improve evidence for family medicine. *Journal of the American Board of Family Medicine, 19* (1), 11–20.

Glasgow, R.E. (2009). Critical measurement issues in translational research. *Research on Social Work Practice, 19* (5), 560–568.

Glasgow, R.E., & Emmons, K.M. (2007). How can we increase translation of research into practice? Types of evidence needed. *Annual Review of Public Health, 28*, 413–433.

Ho, A.P., Tsuang, J.W. Liberman, R.P., Wang, R., Wilins, J.N., Eckman, T.A., et al . (1999). Achieving effective treatment of patients with chronic psychotic illness and comorbid substance dependence. *American Journal of Psychiatry, 156*, 1765–1770.

Institute of Medicine (2000). Crossing the quality chasm: A new health system for the 21st century. Washington, DC: National Academy Press.

Jerrell, J.M., & Ridgely, M.S. (1999). Impact of robustness of program implementation on outcomes of clients in dual diagnosis programs. *Psychiatric Services, 50*, 109–112.

Kerner, J.F., & Hall, K.L. (2009). Research dissemination and diffusion: Translation within science and society. *Research on Social Work Practice, 19* (5), 519–530.

Kola, L.A., & Kruszysnki, R. (2010). Adapting the integrated dual disorder treatment model for addiction services. *Alcoholism Treatment Quarterly, 28*, 437–450.

Kruszynski, R., & Boyle, P.E. (2006). Implementation of the Integrated Dual Disorders Treatment Model: Stage-wise strategies for service providers. *Journal of Dual Diagnosis, 2* (3), 147–155.

Kruszynski, R., Kubek, P., Boyle, P.E., & Kola, L.A. (2006). *Implementing IDDT: A Step-by-Step Guide to Stages of Organizational Change*. Ohio Substance Abuse and Mental Illness Coordinating Center of Excellence, Center for Evidence-Based Practices. Cleveland, OH: Case Western Reserve University.

Lehman, A.F., Steinwachs, D.M., Dixon, L.B., Goldman, H.H., Osher, F. Postrado, L., et al. (1998). Translating research into practice: The Schizophrenia Patient Outcomes Research Team (PORT) treatment recommendations. *Schizophrenia Bulletin, 24* (1), 1–10.

Manuel, J.I., Mullen, E.J., Fang, L., Bellamy, J.L., & Bledsoe, S.E. (2009). Preparing social work practitioners to use evidence-based practice: A comparison of experiences from an implementation project. *Research on Social Work Practice, 19* (5), 613–627.

McHugo, G.J., Drake, R.E., Teague, G.B., Xie, H. (1999). Fidelity to assertive community treatment and client outcomes. *Psychiatric Services, 50*, 818–824.

McHugo, G.J., Drake, R.E., Whitley, R., Bond, G.R., Campbell, K., Rapp, C.A., et al. (2007). Fidelity outcomes in the National Implementing Evidence-Based Practices project. *Psychiatric Services, 58* (10), 1279–1284.

Mueser, K.T., Noordsy, D.L., Drake, R.E., & Fox, L. (2003). *Integrated Treatment for Dual Disorders: A Guide to Effective Practice*. New York: Guilford Publications.

New Freedom Commission on Mental Health (2003). *Achieving the Promise: Transforming Mental Health Care in America. Final Report* (DHHS Pub. No. SMA-03-3832). Rockville, MD: Dept. of Health and Human Services.

Prochaska, J.M., Prochaska, J.O., & Levesque, D.A. (2001). A transtheoretical approach to changing organizations. *Administration and Policy in Mental Health, 28* (4), 247–261.

Prochaska, J.O., DiClemente, C.C., & Norcross, J.C. (1992). In search of how people change: Applications to addictive behaviors. *American Psychologist, 9*, 1102–1114.

Proctor, E., Silmere, H., Raghavan, R., Hovmand, P., Aarons, G.,...Hensley, M. (2011). *Administration and Policy in Mental Health and Mental Health Services Research, 38* (2), 65–76.

Rapp, C.A. Etzel-Wise, D., Marty, D., Coffman, M., Carlson, L., Asher, D., et al. (2008). Evidence-based practice implementation strategies: Results of a qualitative study. *Community Mental Health Journal, 44,* 213–224.

Rogers, E.M. (2004). A prospective and retrospective look at the diffusion model. *Journal of Health Communication, 9,* 13–19

Roman, P.M., Abraham, A.J., Rothrauff, T.C., & Knudsen, H.K. (2010). A longitudinal study of organization formation, innovation adoption, and dissemination activities with the National Drug Abuse Treatment Clinical Trials Network. *Journal of Substance Abuse Treatment, 38* (Supp. 1), 544–552.

Salyers, M.P., McKasson, M., Bond, G.R., McGrew, J.H., Rollins, A.L., & Boyle, C. (2007). The role of technical assistance centers in implementing evidence-based practices: Lessons learned. *American Journal of Psychiatric Rehabilitation, 10,* 85–101.

Simpson, D. D. (2002). A conceptual framework for transferring research to practice. *Journal of Substance Abuse Treatment, 22,* 171–182.

Simpson, D. (2009). Organizational readiness for staged-based dynamics of innovation implementation. *Research on Social Work Practice, 19* (5), 541–551.

Simpson, D.D., & Flynn (2007). Moving innovations into treatment: A stage-based approach to program change. *Journal of Substance Abuse Treatment, 33,* 111–120.

Soydan, H. (2009). Guest editorial: Implementation and translation research: theory and practice. *Research on Social Work Practice, 19* (5), 489–490.

Straus, S.E, Richardson, W.S., Glasziou, P., & Haynes, R.B. (2005). *Evidence-Based Medicine: How to Practice and Teach EBM.* Edinburgh, UK: Elsevier Churchill Livingstone.

Torrey, W.C., Drake, R.E., Dixon, L., Burns, B.J., Rush, A.J., Clark, R.E., et al. (2001a). Implementing evidence-based practices for persons with severe mental illness. *Psychiatric Services, 52,* 45–50.

Torrey, W.C., Drake, R.E., Cohen, M.C., Fox., L.B, Lynde, D., Gorman, P., et al. (2001b). The challenge of implementing and sustaining integrated dual disorder treatment programs. *Community Mental Health Journal, 38* (6), 507–521.

Wieder, B.L., Boyle, P.E., & Hrouda, D.R. (2007). Able, willing, and ready: Staff selection as a core component of IDDT implementation. *Journal of Social Work Practice in the Addictions, 7* (1/2), 139–165.

Wieder, B.L., & Kruszynski, R. (2007). The salience of staffing in IDDT implementation: One agency's experience. *American Journal of Rehabilitation, 10,* 103–112.

Woltmann, E., Whitley, R. (2007). The role of staffing stability on the implementation of integrated dual disorders treatment: An exploratory study. *Journal of Mental Health, 16* (6), 757–769.

Woolf, S.H. (2008). The meaning of translational research and why it matters. *Journal of the American Medical Association, 299* (2), 211–213.

CRISIS INTERVENTION AND SUPPORT

DAVID L. CUTLER, KENNETH R. YEAGER, AND WILLIAM NUNLEY

The early twentieth century was a period characterized by the collapse of social institutions, authority structures, governments, and political and economic alliances throughout Europe prompting the famous lines; "things fall apart, the centre cannot hold" (W. B. Yeats, 1921). One might imagine there was a need to formulate something to address the overwhelming uncertainty in the world in the wake of the fall of the great ruling houses of Europe, the Russian Revolution, and World War I. This was the context within which the idea of stress reduction was developed as a principle in the emerging "mental hygiene" movement. Adolph Meyer, a Swiss psychiatrist/alienist who settled in America in the early 1900s, was the first to advocate a realistic, commonsense approach to understanding the effects of stress on the human condition. Meyer (1922), perhaps reacting to the chaotically changing world of his times, rejected the so-called Cartesian dualism of mind and body and postulated a "psycho-biological whole" and "a broader social understanding." As a professor at Johns Hopkins University he taught physicians about the "Life Chart," which he would illustrate on a chalkboard. He marked the points in a person's life cycle when stressful events were occurring and noted the ensuing onset of illness following particularly stressful periods.

Ultimately, he devoted his career to the study of the course of schizophrenia, which he believed was caused by an accumulation of psychological stress throughout one's life. His wife, Mary Potter Brooks, is considered the first American social worker (Meyer, 1922). Meyer along with Clifford Beers also fathered the mental hygiene movement, which in turn marked the beginning of the idea that mental illness could be prevented, and ultimately evolved into the roots of community mental health in America as we know it today.

In the midst of World War II, on November 28, 1942, a fire broke out at the Coconut Grove, a nightclub in Boston, where 492 people were killed and hundreds more injured. Eric Lindemann, along with his colleague George Saslow (Cutler, 2006), interviewed the survivors, and they later reported their findings in the classic paper on grief reactions: "Symptomatology and Management of Acute Grief" (Lindemann 1944). That paper gave impetus to Meyer's prevention ideas and created a paradigm within which to understand normal versus pathological grief reactions. Gerald Caplan, also working with Lindemann after the war, further developed this framework by postulating a "crisis theory," which became the basis for his book *Principles of Preventive Psychiatry* (1964). This view of grief as a sort of prelude to depression led to the idea that prevention methodologies could actually intervene to avoid frank mental illness, particularly if natural supports were developed or reinforced and made more powerful though existing cultural and family networks. (The question of what is grief, what is pathological grief, and what crosses the line into mental illness is still being debated as the American Psychiatric Association DSM V is being developed [Frances, 2010]).

At mid-century, Erik Erikson's (1950) eight stages of the life cycle provided a theoretical underpinning for understanding the stressful effects of internal developmental transitional phases also leading to personal crisis. For example, a teenager may fail to resolve the crisis of identity by making career choices or love choices prematurely and may struggle in adulthood with an uncertain sense of self if earlier conflicts go unresolved.

When crisis intervention does not occur, professional crisis support becomes necessary. Leighton et al. (1963) linked "sociocultural disintegration" with an increased incidence and prevalence of psychiatric disorders in communities experiencing a malfunction of sociocultural ecology such as poverty, high unemployment, and heavy use of mood-altering substances (all currently serious problems throughout the world). Evidence of the validity of Meyer's, Erikson's, and Caplan's theories was soon scientifically documented by a number of researchers. Tyhurst (1958) theorized that certain stressful situations, such as major life transitions or turmoil in disasters and migration, usually have to get worse before an individual fully mobilizes and tries to make things better. Holmes and Rahe (1967) were able to quantify the effects of external life changes into stress measurements and then show the temporal relationships of accumulations of stress to the onset of various forms of illnesses, including physical, mental, and also social ones (Masuda et al., 1978).

Shneidman and Farberow's work at the Veterans Administration Hospital in California in the late 1950s led to the establishment of the Los Angeles Suicide Prevention and Crisis Service in 1958. This was followed closely by the Erie County (Buffalo, N.Y.) 24-hour Suicide Prevention and Crisis Service. Indeed, the early days of community mental health witnessed a rapid growth of crisis hotlines and walk-in clinics established to allow people to come in while in crisis and speak with a therapist who could help them through the crisis with support, encouragement, and sometimes social interventions. People needing referrals to social welfare agencies were helped with paperwork, and benefits were acquired. The idea was to stop the crisis before it turned into some sort of formal mental illness diagnosis. This notion of providing crisis services as far out into the natural environment as possible to prevent folks from having to become patients was systematized in the 1970s with the creation of the "balanced service system" model (Gerhard et al., 1981). That model began in Georgia when James Earl "Jimmy" Carter was governor and eventually became the basis of the Joint Commission on Accreditation of Hospitals (JCAH) standards for community mental health centers in the 1970s and 1980s.

Looking at crisis from the frame of culture-clash, Maris (1974) in his small book *Loss and Change* studied the effects of mid-century slum clearance projects in developed and developing countries. He noticed that all these examples contained the opposite poles of "innovation" or change versus what he called "the conservative impulse," which is resistance to change. Since the people who lived in neighborhoods targeted for demolition seldom had any say in the matter, the relocation projects were carried out against their will and resulted in massive increases of stress and crisis and disruption of natural support systems, leading to an increased incidence of diagnosable mental illness in what had previously been stable, homogeneous populations living supportively and adjacent to one another. Roberts (2005) recently described *crisis* as: "an acute disruption of psychological homeostasis in which one's usual coping mechanisms fail and there exists evidence of distress and functional impairment. It is the subjective reaction to a stressful life experience that compromises the individual's stability and ability to cope or function." According to crisis theory, a *crisis event* is a subjective response to external stimuli involving stress or a traumatic life event, or a series of events that are perceived by the person as hazardous, threatening, or extremely upsetting, which does not resolve using inherent coping mechanisms.

A crisis can be viewed either as an opportunity or as a dangerous and life-threatening situation. Stressful or traumatic events can combine with life-stage issues and lead to a crisis reaction representing a turning point in the individual's life. When the individual can be helped to mobilize hidden strengths, protective factors, or capabilities, the crisis can result in personal growth. When these factors are not present, the opposite occurs, and the individual proceeds on a course toward personal or psychosocial disaster. The impact of a crisis on an individual is also based on (a) the individual's perception of the events as the cause of considerable upset and/or disruption, and (b) the individual's inability to resolve the disruption through her or his usual coping mechanisms. The following factors should be considered when addressing a crisis:

- Each person will at some point in her/his life experience an acute or traumatic stress that is not necessarily harmful of emotionally toxic. It is the overall context of the event in the person's life that determines whether or not the stressor becomes an acute crisis.
- Homeostasis is a natural state of equilibrium that all people seek. An individual is more amenable to intervention when in a state of disequilibrium caused by an acute event.
- Untapped resources or new coping mechanisms are needed to deal with a traumatic event, and the traumatic event can serve as the catalyst for the development of new coping mechanisms.
- The dearth of prior experience with the crisis event creates increased anxiety, and strategic efforts by the individual can result in the discovery and implementation of hitherto hidden coping strategies.
- The duration of any crisis is limited, depending on the precipitating event, response of the individual, and availability of resources.
- Certain affective, cognitive, and behavioral tasks must be mastered through a series of identifiable and predictable stages of crisis stabilization. (Roberts & Yeager, 2009)

It is important that crisis workers understand processes and evidence associated with crisis intervention. However, crisis intervention, like a lot of other pure concepts in mental health, has evolved. Silently, every day, countless crises are occurring but never coming to the attention of professionals. On the other hand, due to the proliferation of hotlines, walk-in clinics, and crisis respite facilities, more and more crises are dealt with by trained mental health workers and peer support specialists. We will try to illustrate in this chapter how these things currently work through a number of case examples interwoven with response systems ranging from the natural to the more formal.

CASE EXAMPLE 1

Mrs. X. was a 48-year-old woman experiencing sadness, sleeplessness, and loss of appetite following the death of her husband, who was a prominent scholar at a local college. She attended several memorial events in honor of her dead spouse, but reported to her family that she was surprised by the outpouring of sadness from so many people she did not know. She had lots of invitations from friends and neighbors following his death and accepted many of them. Within two weeks she returned to work. Her sleep and appetite did not improve for several weeks, so she spoke to a colleague about sleep remedies. That person suggested she try light therapy and daily morning walks with friends. She agreed, took that advice seriously, and over the course of the next year her mood improved, her appetite improved, and her sleep normalized. An occasional visit to her pastor was also helpful. She continued periodically to complain to friends about the loss and sometimes, when home alone, to cry to herself when something reminded her of her husband.

What occurred here? This is an example of a crisis that occurred in the natural environment. This person was able to receive support from her friends and neighbors following the death and took some advice from a supportive colleague. Although she was deeply grief-stricken, to the point where her mood, appetite, and sleep were affected, she was still able to maintain her balance and at no time made contact with any public or private mental health professionals. Work was also a big factor here. Because she had a job, she kept busy with meaningful activities, which maintained her self esteem and also generated money, which she could use to help pay for the expenses of ceremonies, her husband's burial, and extra help around the house to do things that used to be done by him. All of this support was informal, so she never had to face the stigma of "failure" that is often associated with seeking mental health care. From the point of view of Caplan's crisis theory, a mental illness may have been prevented before it ever happened (primary prevention).

PREVENTING A CRISIS FROM BECOMING AN ILLNESS

The formal mental health system was never a part of this case. This person, though, would be considered to be in a group at high risk for depression because of the magnitude of her loss. A community mental health program that had funding for primary prevention might want to supply consultation and support to local widow-support groups or church groups so that supportive, attentive friends and colleagues are encouraged to be helpful to those who have lost loved ones. One of us asked to do a consultation to a church in an Arizona suburb many years ago. The minister was concerned about parishioners who had moved to a planned senior community there from the Northeast and Midwest to retire and play golf. They left their friends and families for the dream of a warmer climate, but when they arrived, the husbands grabbed their golf clubs and went directly from their garage to the golf course for 18 holes, leaving their wives behind.

The men quickly made friends with other golfers and also became activists in the church. But the wives were home alone, with no friends, nothing to do, and did not connect with other women (a situation that makes little sense, because women are usually much more sociable than men). Golf was the common denominator for the men, but for the women there was a suicide epidemic, and the question was; What can the church do to reach out to and form support for these women? As a result of the consultation, activity groups for women were organized in the church and an outreach to newcomers was implemented.

CASE EXAMPLE 2 (CRISIS INTERVENTION IN THE NATURAL ENVIRONMENT)

Mr. K. was a 55-year-old single man who had lived alone most of his life. He had graduated from an important college in the West and tended to work outdoors in the woods along the Northwest coast as a ranger, fisherman, tour guide, etc. He never married, but had a number of relationships; but all dissolved, including one that had been particularly important to him. Although his parents had died long ago, he still had two brothers and two sisters, but the brother he was closest to died recently, and Mr. K. had lost his job. After a year of unemployment, he began to run out of resources.

Although very self-reliant throughout his life, he suddenly became overwhelmed with remorse and despair and tried to asphyxiate himself with exhaust from his car. When that didn't work he considered borrowing a gun, but instead sought out a brother and sister-in-law in a city. They took him in "as a roommate," asked him to perform household chores collaboratively with them to help out around the house, and became very attentive for fear he would make a repeat suicide attempt. Their unconditional support had an immediate effect on his mood, and thoughts of suicide quickly dissipated. He also agreed to see a counselor twice a week to help him understand what caused his mood to suddenly drop.

What occurred here? This example is that of a crisis that occurred and was stabilized; mostly in the natural environment, but there was also a private counselor involved. It would qualify as an example of secondary prevention because it was a very quick response to a rapidly developing dangerous situation and perhaps diagnosable depression. This person was able to receive effective support, mostly from family, despite coming close to suicide. Men are very endangered when they become suicidal, and this man had plans and means, but at the last moment he sought out support from relatives. Without the family to rely on, he might have easily found a successful method to kill himself. He was also not using drugs, and was willing to get help: two factors that gave him a much greater chance to survive.

But he was also without funds, which made him unlikely to receive services in the private sector, and without Medicaid or Medicare there were few public programs able to accept him in services. Nevertheless, in this case he was able to find enough support because of his family to remain alive and begin to rebuild his life. Many like him, however, fall through the gaps in what is often an inadequate safety net.

CRISIS SYSTEMS, RURAL AND URBAN: HOW DO THEY WORK?

For people who require more attention, public mental health systems have evolved into increasingly sophisticated models. In small communities, the natural supports are very important and can usually be activated quickly and effectively in dangerous crisis situations. Police and other officials tend to personally be acquainted with folks who are likely to have crises. People in small towns help each other out.

Local mental health clinics usually have on-call systems, and people are available to answer calls and often know the person who calls after hours. Generalist staff who spend most of their time doing case-management psychotherapy also must do involuntary holds and civil commitments (Nunley et al., 2013).

In larger communities, there is much less informal knowledge of the people in crisis and generalization of skills in responding. Figuring out how to solve a crisis means starting from scratch with each person, many of whom don't mention or are estranged from their families. Most of these communities have multiple entry points to their systems for people in crisis. All are arranged a little differently.

For example, Columbus, Ohio, has one behavioral health program that provides most of the crisis services in the county out of multiple locations, including twenty-four-hour mental health and substance abuse crisis intervention, stabilization, and assessment. Two of these sites allow police drop-off of suicidal or psychotically dangerous people. One site has a walk-in clinic, a hotline, and a large respite facility where relatively stable people needing temporary respite can stay while their crisis situation is evaluated and stabilized. People are either seen in counseling or in some cases are referred to local acute psychiatric units in general hospitals or the Columbus state hospital if they are medically stable but require longer stay mental health treatment.

In Portland, Oregon, the crisis system consists of a crisis hotline based in the Multnomah County Mental Health and Addictions Division office, which connects directly to a large crisis contractor, Cascadia Behavioral Health, Inc., which operates "Project Respond" (an outreach team of mental health staff who join with Crisis Intervention Team (CIT) -trained police to intervene in homes and neighborhoods). Cascadia also operates a crisis walk-in clinic and a respite facility. There is an additional 16-bed sub-acute unit operated by a different contractor, Telecare, Incorporated, which is linked to hospital emergency departments, where people with severe mental health problems and also with potential additional medical problems are screened and either admitted or diverted to the sub-acute Crisis Assessment and Treatment Center (CATC). Although the CATC added a missing element to the system, it was not funded well enough to be able to take direct admits from police-officer holds. Police still needed to transport people to hospital emergency departments for medical screening before they could be admitted there.

This use of police to transport results in severely ill folks having to ride in a squad car in handcuffs, exacerbating the existing crisis for many of them by having so much contact with police even though they have committed no crimes. A Bazelon Center–funded grant project (Safer PDX) (Bernstien, R. (2112) managed by Cascadia Behavioral Health strongly recommended that this contact be reduced for most people with mental health crises, since every contact with police also carries with it the danger that the police might take them to jail, or worse, cause them physical harm if a confrontation occurs (Cutler et al., 2002).

The Police Department, working with "Safer PDX" and the county, agreed to funnel mental health crisis calls from their 911 line directly to the crisis call center at the county instead of automatically dispatching officers. The crisis line could then determine the extent of risk and either give advice over the phone to the caller, contact Project Respond to make a home visit, or re-contact police if there was imminent danger and it was absolutely necessary.

This one small procedural change had a huge effect by reducing police calls and increasing hotline calls screened by mental health professionals, and it saved all involved considerable stress (see Fig. 17.1).

CASE EXAMPLE 3

Ms. S. was a 21-year-old college student who had recently been experiencing increasing levels of stress, anxiety, and depression. She had been in a relationship, but this was not going well. She feared her boyfriend was interested in another young woman in one of his classes. For several months, Ms. S. had been experiencing increasing episodes of sadness, where she felt unable to keep going with her life. She reported that this fluctuated between moments of hope and then intense anxiety in which she was unable to catch her breath. She complained of "feeling down" most of the day for the past three months. When asked to explain this further, she described pervasive feelings of "emptiness, and a paralyzing fear of being alone." She also experienced difficulty getting out of bed in the morning and more often than not felt excessive fatigue throughout the day, reporting having difficulty staying awake to complete coursework even while in class. When asked to describe her day-to-day activity, she described a diminished ability to think, leading to feelings of worthlessness. She reported her grades had dropped, and she was having fewer and fewer interactions with her friends, giving up most social activities.

Her friends also began noticing changes: one reporting that she seemed "scattered"; another that she was "moving so slow"; and yet another reported that she was "just not her usual self."

On the other hand, she tried devoting much energy to fixing her relationship. But this led to decreased attention to schoolwork and missed days at her job at a coffee shop on campus. She had been placed on probation at work, had received two failing grades on final exams, received late notices on her electric and cable bill, and was eventually told by her boyfriend that he wanted out of this relationship. She arrived at the crisis center in tears with suicidal ideation, stating she "just can't take it anymore."

Ms. S. was observed for 48 hours in a crisis emergency center and was given anti-anxiety medications and crisis-supportive therapy. She discussed with the crisis therapist methods of understanding of her situation and also reducing her reactions to the stress she was experiencing. She was quite capable of verbalizing

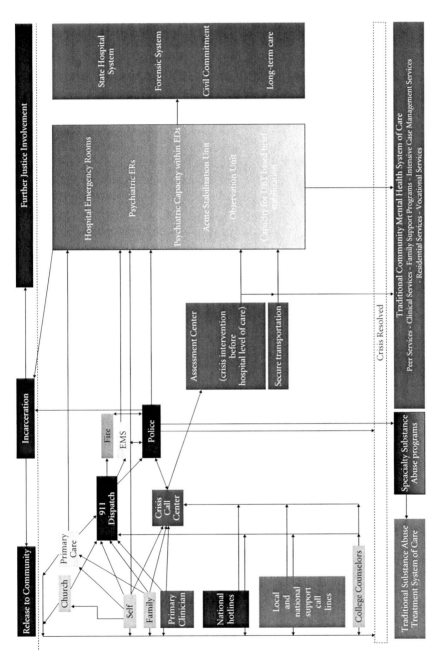

FIGURE 17.1 An Example of an Urban Crisis System.

that she had been caught in a situation of control and perfection that spiraled out of control. But she was not able to manage the emotions that went with it. But within a short period she demonstrated sufficient stabilization and was discharged to weekly individual counseling sessions at the local crisis walk-in clinic. At the walk-in clinic she was treated with cognitive behavioral therapy, and her medications were slowly reduced because of the risk for abuse (Power et al., 1990). She continued in counseling for six months, initially meeting with her counselor on a weekly basis, then bi-monthly for two months, and then monthly for the remainder.

What occurred here? This example is that of a crisis that led to a diagnosable condition, but one that could be and was stabilized in a supportive clinical environment. This young woman was a student, away from home in a competitive academic environment that contains a lot of people, but all of whom are under the various stresses associated with that transitional stage of life and being faced with the demands of school and the seduction of intimate relationships. The stress was overwhelming for her.

On the other hand, she was cooperative and insightful and able to follow through with treatment. Resources were available to her, and she used them effectively to get back on her feet and quickly resume her life as a student, despite the painful loss she had experienced. Since the treatment was sufficient to get her back on track, her case could be seen as successful secondary prevention. In other words, she briefly crossed the invisible line of mental illness, but the treatment helped her cross back into a shaky but stable state of mental health. She avoided being in the hospital, so this episode will carry less stigma in her mind and that of her friends. Medications were used but withdrawn, giving her the opportunity cope with her issues without risking an addiction. She also knows she can return if she needs to for more supportive therapy. Hopefully, success with her work and studies will help to keep her on course with her life and also give her the self esteem she will need to maintain her balance in a future intimate relationship.

CASE EXAMPLE 4 (EARLY PSYCHOSIS INTERVENTION CRISIS CASE VIGNETTE)

Mr. M. was a 21-year-old first-generation naturalized son of an East European family living with both parents and many siblings. He was recently discharged from a three-week stay on an acute-care psychiatric ward for his first hospitalization due to symptoms of escalating impulsive, erratic, aggressive, defiant and disorganized behavior, insomnia, and possible hallucinations. He had a marked change in his presentation about six months prior to being hospitalized, during which time he had an auto accident and seriously disrupted his family's home.

After his discharge from the hospital, he entered an Early Intervention for Psychosis (EIP) program in Portland, Oregon. He and his family began attending family education and support groups held in the evenings where families were given matter-of-fact information about psychosis and how they can be of help. But, two months later, he abruptly stopped his antipsychotic medication due to side effects. This soon became apparent when his family noted his prior symptoms reemerging. As a result of increasing insomnia and nighttime activity, he began having serious conflicts with the brother with whom he shared his bedroom. Mr. M. became increasingly irritable and agitated with his brother as well as with other family members who tried to intervene, including younger siblings also living in the home. Family members called Mr. M.'s mental health consultant, who made a home visit later that day once it was determined that Mr. M. was not imminently dangerous.

During the meeting with the family, Mr. M. expressed his frustration with recent headaches, a rash, and excess salivation, which he attributed to the medications. He uncharacteristically became provocative, accusing other family members of lying about his behavior and insomnia. He was clear that the tension with the family had become critical, but despite his frustrations, he did agree to meet with his psychiatrist to discuss an alternative medication.

Despite his obvious agitation and dysphoria, he agreed to a short stay with a local crisis Respite facility to escape the stress of being around his family. He also agreed to see his psychiatrist that day and consented to a trial of a different medication on the way to the Respite home. After a one-night stay, he returned home without his medication. He continued to have family conflict severe enough that the police were called at one point due to his aggressive behavior with a younger sibling.

His mental health consultant again met with him and the family. The roommate brother continued to express considerable frustration, focusing on his own inability to sleep and study for his newly started college courses. Mr. M. was vague about why he left Respite but did admit feeling more comfortable with his new medication. He was able to describe his ambivalence about being around his family and ultimately agreed to a return to crisis Respite, where he stayed for four more nights. Upon his return home he had become stable. Symptoms and family conflict had both vanished. He identifies Respite services as an important part of his relapse prevention plan, has returned to his job that he left before being hospitalized, and is now working on a long-term goal of attaining independent housing and independent management of his illness. In the meantime, his relationships with his family have remained positive and constructive.

What occurred here? This example demonstrates a crisis that occurred in the midst of treatment; in this case, within an elaborate program to prevent the onset of disability associated with a diagnosable mental illness (Melton et al., 2013). Both the client and the family had already received considerable support and education before the crisis occurred, which began when he stopped his medication because of side effects. This sort of event is the rule, not the exception (Falk et al., Chapter 24, this volume). No one likes side effects, and when they occur with psychotropic medications, they can be very disturbing. Taking medications for the purpose of controlling symptoms of mental illness is also stigmatizing and in young people likely to be resisted, until it becomes clear to them that it can be directly useful to them. Ironically, street drugs tend to be viewed in a much more positive light by young people, since they often symbolize membership in a sort of "cool" youth subculture and also provide a brief conscious respite from the sometimes brutal reality of everyday life.

This case illustrates the power of the family to help a person heal, provided they are given the necessary tools. In this structured program, families are taken in as allies and are always included so that they feel supported and empowered. The opportunity to utilize the formal mental health system briefly via the crisis Respite facility enabled the young person to save face and maintain self esteem by not having to go back to the hospital in the midst of the crisis. Since he was not dangerous, the secure facilities of a hospital psychiatric ward were not needed.

DISCUSSION

As we have said, not all crisis intervention occurs in traditional crisis centers, nor is all crisis intervention conducted by mental health professionals in settings in which they are trained to practice. The truth is there are thousands of persons from all walks of life enacting crisis intervention and stabilization scenes on a daily basis. The degree to which individuals interact with family members, peer support systems, local churches and civic organizations, self-help and support groups will mitigate the risk for progression of a crisis situation into a diagnosable condition. Crisis intervention is based on the individual response to the situation at hand. The individual's response is based on a complex interaction of inherent coping skills combined with the ability to ask for and to access community-based support systems. Some support systems are not linked in any form to mental health centers. The cumulative awareness of any support system and response to individual need may in fact be the strongest support in the fight against the progression of a crisis into more serious, diagnosable mental or physical illness. Regardless of the basis of the support—be it family, community, or professional—support and understanding are the most potent sources for building resilience.

Just as stigma is still very much alive and well, there is a growing force of persons with a unique, deep, and personal understanding of mental health crises: these people are working to take part in situations where people with little to no understanding of mental illness interface with those who have or are on the verge of mental illness. We face a crisis of funding for traditional mental health settings. But at the same time there is growing diversity among professionals, non-professional people, and organizations dedicated to improving the lives of those vulnerable to mental illness.

CONCLUSIONS

We have provided some examples of people in crisis in a variety of social settings and stressful situations. These examples are by no means comprehensive and do not illustrate even a fraction of the possible informal and formal systems wherein people get help. All of us are potentially vulnerable. We live and survive as conservative, structure-loving organisms in an ever-changing, sometimes incoherent-seeming world. Grief and loss are always lurking around the corner of the next accident, illness, or death of a loved one. All it takes is circumstance to activate a spiral of agonizing disequilibrium in most of us. We cope with minor losses every day without too much pain, but when losses pile up or involve the disintegration of stable attachments and predictable environments, we are far more susceptible to breakdown. This "breakdown" may take a variety of forms, but in vulnerable individuals, depending upon the magnitude of the loss, it often leads to grief, crisis, and depression along with its biological sequelae.

How, then, can we counter such a destructive force? Is this not the inevitable outcome of social Darwinian theory? Should we as a society intervene or should we let the chips fall where they may? These sorts of questions are not so easy to answer, because they are rooted in a shared pan-human ethos but with variable symbols and interpretations infinitely too diverse to simplify. But since the "center cannot hold," we are destined to struggle with these dilemmas from generation to generation, despite the incredible technological revolutions we have witnessed, are witnessing, and will continue to witness in the decades to come. Crises cannot always be predicted, and stressful events do not mean the same things to different people. But stress adds up and crises will always lurk at some unexpected point in our future. Crisis intervention and management is a skill we must continue to cultivate if we are to have any effect on the global burden of mental illness (Murray & Lopez, 1996).

REFERENCES

Bernstien, R. (2112). Bazelon Center in Brief and Annual Report Summer 2012 Newsletter & 2011 Annual Report Page 9. Washington DC: Bazelon Center.

Caplan, G. (1964). *Principals of Preventive Psychiatry*. New York: Basic Books.

Cutler, D.L., Bigelow, D., Collins, V., Jackson, C., & Field, G. (2002). Why are severely mentally ill persons in jails and prisons. In P. Backlar & D. Cutler (Eds.), *Ethics in Community Mental Health Care: Commonplace Concerns*. Kluwer Academic.

Cutler D.L. (2006). Heroes in community psychiatry: George Saslow, M.D. Ph.D. *Community Mental Health Journal, 42*(3): 259–262.

Erikson, E. (1950). *Childhood and Society*. New York: Norton.

Frances, A. It's not too late to save "normal." *Los Angeles Times,* March 1, 2010.

Gerhard, R.J., Miles, D.G., and Dorgan, R.E. (1981). *The Balanced Service System: A Model of Personal and Social Integration*. Clinton, OK: Responsive Systems Associates.

Holmes, T.H., & Rahe, R.H. (1967). The social readjustment rating scale. *Journal of Psychosomatic Research, 11*(2): 213–218.

Leighton, D. C., Harding, J.S., Macklin, D.B., Macmillan, A.M., & Leighton, A.H. (1963). *The Character of Danger: Psychiatric Symptoms in Selected Communities. Volume III: The Stirling County Study of Psychiatric Disorder & Sociocultural Environment*. New York: Basic Books.

Lindemann, E. (1944). Symptomatology and management of acute grief. *American Journal of Psychiatry. 101*, 141–148.

Marris, P. (1974). *Loss and Change*. New York: Pantheon Books.

Masuda, M., Cutler, D., Hein, L., Holmes, T. (1978). Life events and prisoners: A study of the relationship of life events to prison incarceration. *Archives of General Psychiatry*, 35(2): 197–203.

Melton, R.P., Roush, S.N., Sale, T.G., Wolf, R.M., Usher, C.T., & Rodriguez, C. L. (2012). *Early Intervention and Prevention of Long-Term Disability in Youth and Adults: The E.A.S.A. Model. Modern Community Mental Health Work: An Interdisciplinary Approach*. New York: Oxford University Press.

Murray, C.J., & Lopez, A.D., (1996). *The Global Burden of Disease*. Cambridge, MA: Harvard University Press, p. 21.

Meyer, A. (1922). A historical sketch in outlook of psychiatric and social work. *Hospital Social Service Quarterly, 5,* 22.

Nunley, W., Nunley, B., Dentinger, J., McFarland, B.H., & Cutler, D.L. (2013). Involuntary civil commitment: Applying evolving policy and legal determination in community mental health. In: *Modern Community Mental Health: An Interdisciplinary Approach* (Ch 4). New York: Oxford University Press.

Roberts, A.R., (2005). Bridging the past and present to the future of crisis intervention and crisis management. In A. R. Roberts (Ed.), *Crisis Intervention Handbook: Assessment, Treatment and Research* (3rd ed., pp. 3–34). New York: Oxford University Press.

Roberts, A.R., and Yeager, K.R. (2009). *Pocket Guide to Crisis Intervention.* New York: Oxford University Press.

Tyhurst, J.S. (1958) The Role of transitional states-including disaster -in mental illness. In *Walter Reed Army Institute of research, Symposium on Preventive and Social Psychiatry.* Washington DC U.S. Gov. Printing Office

Yeats, W.B. (1921). The Second Coming. *Michael Robartes and the Dancer.* Churchtown, Dundrum, Ireland: The Chuala Press.

CHAPTER 18

EARLY INTERVENTION AND PREVENTION OF LONG-TERM DISABILITY IN YOUTH AND ADULTS

The EASA Model

RYAN P. MELTON, SEAN N. ROUSH, TAMARA G. SALE, ROBERT M. WOLF, CRAIGAN T. USHER, CHRISTINA L. RODRIGUEZ, AND PATRICK D. MCGORRY

EARLY PSYCHOSIS INTERVENTION: OVERVIEW

In a typical high school of 2,000 students, one percent, or twenty, of its students will develop schizophrenia. Symptoms most commonly begin during teen and young adult years (Hafner et al., 1993; Kaplan, Sadock, Grebb, 1994; McGorry, 2005; Yung et al., 2007). Without appropriate supports, schizophrenia can result in interrupted individuation, school drop-out, long-term unemployment and reliance on disability funding, loss of social network, involuntary care, legal involvement, homelessness, suicide, or premature death from other causes. These consequences are often avoidable, yet few communities have access to the most effective services (Drake & Essock, 2009). Schizophrenia costs the United States over $60 billion annually, much of which is spent without positive outcomes (Rupp & Keith, 1993; Ho, Andreasen & Flaum, 1997; Woodside, Krupa, & Pocock, 2008; Nelson et al., 2009; McGorry, 2005; McGorry & Yung, 2003; Mueser & McGurk, 2004).

Without early intervention, psychosis commonly persists for a year or more before treatment (Ho & Andreasen, 2001; Jackson & McGorry, 2009; Keshavan et al., 2003). The functional decline of schizophrenia is most significant during a "critical period" of the first two to five years, and the level of functional disability established during this time tends to persist long-term. Intervention during this early "critical period" may help establish a higher level of functioning early on in the illness (Birchwood, Todd, & Jackson, 1998; Carpenter & Strauss, 1991; Crumlish et al., 2009; Drake et al., 2000; Dube et al., 1984; McGlashan, 2006; Jackson & McGorry, 2009). With proactive community education, early identification, and evidence-based care, young people get treatment sooner and have better short-term to medium-term outcomes (Harris et al., 2005; Johannessen et al., 2001, 2007; Norman & Malla, 2009; Addington et al., 2004; Yung et al., 2007; Simonsen et al., 2010).

Research into the onset of psychosis and effective interventions has multiplied rapidly in the last two decades, with thousands of relevant studies. A thriving international network of researchers, clinical programs, and individuals with lived experience has led to systems reform. A growing number of countries have adopted national early-psychosis strategies, including Australia, New Zealand, United Kingdom, Canada, Switzerland, Germany, Norway, and Denmark (Jackson & McGorry, 2009; McGorry et al., 2006, 2010). Although the United States has been slower to adopt early-psychosis intervention, interest and momentum is building. In 2004, the International Early Psychosis Association and the World Health Organization issued a joint consensus statement articulating a vision and specific goals for international development of early-psychosis intervention (Bertolote & McGorry, 2005).

Research findings suggest that early intervention programs produce better outcomes (de Hann et al., 2002), and there is emerging consensus on the essential intervention components, including a focus on community connections, engagement, initial assessment, and non-pharmaceutical and pharmaceutical interventions in a team approach (Marshall, Lockwood, & Fiander, 2005). An analysis of participants' experiences in specialized first-episode programs indicated an adherence to best practice guidelines contributed to participant satisfaction (O'Toole, Ohlsen, Taylor, Walter, & Pilowsky, 2004). EASA follows guidelines addressing all of these components, which are updated periodically from the most recent literature.

EARLY INTERVENTION IN MANAGED CARE AND HEALTH CARE REFORM: EASA

Fragmented, inadequate service delivery causes many young people with psychosis to go without care, and the services that do exist often ignore their needs (President's New Freedom Commission, 2003). Managed healthcare organizations (MHOs) are able to reorient funding toward accessible, effective care. However, MHOs manage specific insurance plans, and since young adults often transition between insurers and frequently have no insurance, a systemic solution cannot rely on a single insurer. Even with insurance, barriers to access include the symptoms of the illness itself, unfamiliarity with or negative preconceptions of mental health services, requirements such as showing up on time and having insight into illness, and service limitations such as large caseloads and separate programs for youth and adults. In order to address these challenges, it is necessary to blend multiple funding streams, create new funding where none currently exists, and provide policy and regulatory leadership. Thus, successful implementation requires the cooperation and flexibility of numerous partners.

Mid-Valley Behavioral Care Network (MVBCN) is a managed mental health care organization focused on bringing evidence-based and preventive strategies to the Medicaid recipients (Oregon Health Plan) in five Oregon counties (Linn, Marion, Polk, Tillamook, and Yamhill). MVBCN's board of directors consists of county commissioners, and its operational direction combines advocates and providers. In 2001, MVBCN created the Early Assessment and Support Team (EAST), modeled on the Early Psychosis Prevention and Intervention Center (EPPIC) in Melbourne, Australia (McGorry et al., 1996). EAST evolved to include additional evidence-based practices over time (Sale, 2008; Sale & Melton, 2009). Initially the program blended the Oregon Health Plan (OHP), private insurance, and private foundation funds. Beginning in 2008, Oregon's legislature funded a statewide dissemination of EAST called the Early Assessment and Support Alliance (EASA). Written practice guidelines, as well as training, supervision, and fidelity review processes, have helped guide consistent, successful implementation of EASA (MVBCN, 2008). By the end of 2011, EAST/EASA had served over 800 families.

CASE STUDY

The EASA team met seventeen-year-old John as a high school senior, a talented guitarist and basketball player. For several months, however, his family and friends had noticed his growing social withdrawal, plummeting grades, and uncharacteristic suspicion and odd statements. He would stand up and abruptly leave the classroom, and by the beginning of his senior year, he refused to attend school. He had started to believe that cameras were tracking him in the classroom and at home. John confided to his mother that he "might be going crazy."

John's school counselor had learned the early signs of psychosis from a community education presentation and contacted EASA, which provided a brief screening of the presenting symptoms and consultation on how to best respond. John's mother, JoAnne, recognized a problem and was eager to get EASA involved, while his father, Peter, felt his son was being defiant and undisciplined. Furthermore, Peter was a first-generation immigrant from the former Soviet Union, and was wary of abuse by government officials. Sensitive to the family's concerns, the EASA clinician came to the family's house and shared food with them. She spent time introducing herself, getting to know the parents, explaining how EASA operates, and responding to their concerns. She discovered that John's maternal grandmother had spent decades in a state hospital. Thus, it was necessary to allow plenty of time to hear the parents' fears, build trust, and help them set aside negative preconceptions.

The counselor gently introduced information about teenage brain development and psychiatric illness using a stress-vulnerability framework that views psychiatric symptoms as resulting from a variety of factors, many of which can be modified (Substance Abuse and Mental Health Services Administration, 2009a; Jackson & McGorry, 2009; Nuechterlein et al., 1992; Nuechterlein & Dawson, 1984; Zubin & Spring, 1977). She helped them regain hope as they realized that they could play an active role in their son's success. Recognizing their state of crisis and marital conflict, she explained that these are normal reactions that most families experience. The counselor helped create a good short-term crisis plan, while she began to engage with their son.

John was initially wary of and resistant to the counselor. He became willing to talk as the counselor showed genuine interest in his music and basketball, and his goal of finishing school. The counselor introduced the family to the rest of the EASA team: the psychiatrist and nurse, vocational specialist, and occupational therapist. The team members coordinated closely, reinforcing the strengths of John and his family. They provided opportunities for the family to meet and learn from others in successful recovery, offered expertise to support well-informed decisions, helped the family re-envision a positive long-term future, and explored options for meeting their short-term and long-term goals. The family participated in educational workshops and groups, learning about symptoms, coping skills, and communication techniques. The support from the EASA team and other families helped John's family calm down and take things one step at a time.

The EASA staff shared the strengths and occupational therapy assessments with John's high school counselors and administrators, helping identify and implement accommodations. John's symptoms gradually improved. He learned ways to cope with his persistent symptoms and was able to successfully complete high school with his peers. The employment specialist helped him find a summer job. John lived at home and went to community college for a year after high school. In the fall when he started college, he had a significant relapse, but he was able to return with a temporarily reduced class load and accommodations. Eighteen months after first joining EASA, John and his family gradually, over a six-month stretch, transitioned into ongoing services through his school and a local community health center. EASA remained a resource as the family ran into new challenges. John and his father spoke several times to families who were new to EASA, and talked to a legislative committee. John went on to receive his associate degree at the community college and then transferred to a four-year university.

STAGING MODEL

Schizophrenia rolls in like a slow fog, becoming imperceptibly thicker as time goes on. At first, the day is bright enough, the sky is clear; the sunlight warms your shoulders. But soon, you notice a haze beginning to gather around you and the air feels not quite so warm. After a while the sun is a dim light bulb behind a heavy cloth. The horizon has vanished into a gray mist, and you feel a thick dampness in your lungs as you stand, cold and wet, in the afternoon dark.

(Elyn Saks, *The Center Cannot Hold: My Journey Through Madness*, 2007)

As Elyn Saks, a law and psychiatry professor with schizophrenia eloquently describes, like many illnesses, schizophrenia often begins insidiously and later picks up momentum. Early changes may seem non-specific, commonly including neurocognitive changes like reduced processing speed and difficulty with working memory, as well as affective changes, and mild sensory distortions. Progression into hallucinations and delusions is often gradual, with weeks, months, or even years before the person loses insight and begins to modify his or her behavior based on a newly emerging explanatory model (Cornblatt et al., 2003; Jackson & McGorry, 2009). The person's needs and appropriate response vary depending on whether they are showing signs that they may be at high risk (i.e., early symptoms with insight), acutely ill (loss of insight, impaired ability to communicate, and changed behavior directly resulting from symptoms), in early recovery (no longer acute, and able to engage in reciprocal conversation), or in a later stage of recovery. Increasingly, practice guidelines acknowledge these different stages of illness and recovery and provide recommendations for each stage (Jackson & McGorry, 2009; McGorry et al., 2007; Johannessen, Martindale, & Cullberg, 2006).

Individuals in the "high risk" category are assessed through careful differential diagnosis and use of a specialized assessment tool such as the Structured Interview for Prodromal Syndromes (SIPS) or its predecessor, the Comprehensive Assessment of At-Risk Mental States (CAARMS), which interview for common psychotic symptoms using a gradation scale (McGlashan et al., 2010; Miller et al., 2003; Yung et al., 2005). There is not yet a way to accurately predict who will develop schizophrenia. The only universal prevention strategies currently available include wide-scale education about brain functioning and early signs of illness, preventable risk factors such as drug use, and healthy lifestyle practices that promote resiliency. Early intervention focuses on individuals with early clinical presentations that are consistent with a possible onset (Jackson & McGorry, 2009; Yung et al., 2007).

The earlier illness is identified, the more diagnostic ambiguity clinicians face (Baldwin et al., 2005; Rahm & Cullberg, 2007; Salvatore et al., 2009; Whitty et al., 2005). The need for care typically precedes the utility and ability of assigning a traditional diagnosis of schizophrenia. This uncertainty leads to ethical concerns about potentially iatrogenic interventions, particularly related to premature diagnostic labeling and use of medications. Thus, EASA emphasizes functioning and targeted symptoms, and approaches diagnosis and medications with care (Jackson & McGorry, 2010; Jackson & McGorry, 2009; Petersen et al., 2005; Thorup et al., 2005).

OVERVIEW OF EASA

At the time EASA was created, early psychosis intervention was widespread internationally but still very rare within the United States. EASA profoundly changed the experiences of young people with early psychosis. Before EASA, local stories of people with schizophrenia often began with a long series of unsuccessful attempts to get help, escalating traumatic crises, entry into services through involuntary crisis services, and requirements that the person enter the disability system to access care. Today, those stories are giving way to stories of rapid and effective response and young people continuing on their developmental tracks. Beginning with the local Managed Healthcare Organization (MHO), state and local policy makers came together to commit to providing accessible, evidence-based support and treatment for teenagers and young adults with early signs of psychosis, regardless of insurance issues or other barriers.

Local transdisciplinary teams (Bruder, 1994) were created in each EASA county, including a psychiatrist or prescribing nurse practitioner, registered nurse, counselor/case manager, vocational specialist, and occupational therapist. The teams engage in ongoing, proactive community education and outreach to engage individuals and families. Services are based on the most current evidence-based care, and continue to evolve as new research and participant feedback become available. All services emphasize individualized strengths and adaptation, with a planned transition over a two-year period moving individuals and their families from EASA services and into community services and supports.

TEAM STRUCTURE

EASA teams are based on the Assertive Community Treatment (ACT) model, a well-researched intervention for individuals at risk for repeated hospitalizations or who have been homeless. ACT incorporates multiple disciplines, shared caseload and direct service delivery among team members, frequent contact, low staff ratios, and outreach (Kreyenbuhl, Nossel, & Dixon, 2009; SAMHSA, 2008; Teague, Bond, & Drake, 1998). Individuals with a first episode of psychosis are at high risk of hospitalization (ACCESS Economics, 2009), and there is growing research demonstrating the benefits of ACT with early psychotic illness (Dixon et al., 2009; McFarlane et al., 2010; Nordentoft et al., 2006; Petersen et al., 2005; Rosen, Mueser, & Teeson, 2007; Verhaegh, 2009). Individuals need and receive different levels of service intensity, and the optimal service mix is still an issue of active scientific debate and study.

EASA also built on McFarlane's Family-Assisted Community Treatment (FACT) model, integrating multi-family psychoeducation with a specialized ACT team. This approach aligns efforts and reduces conflict in the person's environment (McFarlane et al., 1992). EASA teams operate in a "transdisciplinary" manner. On a multidisciplinary team, each professional provides services based on their own discipline, with periodic meetings to coordinate and discuss the case. Transdisciplinary teams work to optimize the benefits of each professional's skill set, with one common plan. Bruder (1994) describes this approach in more detail:

> A transdisciplinary approach requires the team members to share roles and systematically cross discipline boundaries. The primary purpose of this approach is to pool and integrate the expertise of team members so that more efficient and comprehensive assessment and intervention services may be provided. The communication style in this type of team involves continuous give-and-take between all members on a regular, planned basis. Professionals from different disciplines teach, learn, and work together to accomplish a common set of intervention goals for a individual and her family. The role differentiation between disciplines is defined by the needs of the situation rather than by discipline-specific characteristics. Assessment, intervention and evaluation are carried out jointly by designated members of the team. This teamwork usually results in a decrease in the number of professionals who interact with the child on a daily basis (p. 61).

The EASA team provides community education, outreach, multi-family groups and other family support, psychoeducation and counseling, vocational support using the Individual Placement and Support model (Swanson & Becker, 2011; SAMHSA, 2009c), supported education, occupational therapy, psychiatry, nursing, and opportunities to meet and learn from peers. The team provides most of the outpatient mental health services needed by the individual, including substance-abuse treatment using a harm-reduction model. The team meets twice per week to coordinate care, collaborate, and provide feedback on clinical decisions. Team members routinely meet with the individual and family.

COMMUNITY EDUCATION, RECRUITMENT, AND SCREENING

Community education and consultation is essential, since a primary goal is early identification and referral. Community education targets people most likely to come in contact with teenagers and young adults, including school professionals, parent groups, primary care physicians, emergency and mental health services, law enforcement, and clergy and youth groups. Messages target the individual group, with goals of "normalizing" psychotic illness as a common and treatable condition, increasing their familiarity with the common process of its onset and observable early signs, and encouraging rapid referral for help where psychosis is suspected. Examples of changes that might warrant a referral include the person having new trouble reading, understanding complex sentences, or speaking; fearfulness that is not grounded in reality; uncharacteristic and bizarre statements or behavior; strange new beliefs such as a concern that others are putting thoughts in the person's head or the person's thoughts are being broadcast; social withdrawal; and statements such as "I think I'm going crazy." Referents are also coached to look for perceptual anomalies such as hearing voices or colors appearing psychedelic, faces looking distorted, or straight lines looking wavy (Birchwood et al., 2000; Jackson & McGorry, 2009; EASA website www.easacommunity.org). Once a person is referred, the EASA intake clinician follows up to learn more and do an initial diagnostic screening, including connection to primary care to address any potential medical conditions. The majority of people referred to EASA do not have psychosis, but EASA plays an important role in clarifying their needs and connecting them to appropriate care.

ENGAGEMENT

The patient's level of engagement in treatment is critical to outcomes (Kreyenbuhl et al., 2009). Many mental health programs expect that individuals with mental illness will request help, find their way to a clinic, and follow through consistently. This expectation ignores barriers such as unfamiliarity with the system; negative preconceptions about mental health services; symptoms such as paranoia, disorganization, and cognitive problems; lack of insight; resource gaps; and cultural differences (U.S. Department of Health and Human Services, 2001). EASA attempts to overcome these barriers through flexible and proactive outreach, and aligning services to the needs and interests of the person and family. Initial engagement happens in an environment where the individual is comfortable. The EASA team works with the family to understand the family's culture, how they explain what they are experiencing, and their preferred strategies for responding. EASA staff members focus on the individual's strengths and interests, as well as his or her perceived needs. A process of collaborative empiricism helps bridge the person's experience and explanations to other potential explanations such as the medical model. The goal is not to convince the individual and family of an explanation, but to construct a shared understanding that strengthens their autonomy and self-efficacy, and respects their perceptions, culture, and values.

All EASA team members who do outreach programs pay attention to the physical setting of their programs in order to make them positive and youth-friendly. A lead clinician coordinates care within and outside of the team. Different team members may participate or play the primary role in engagement. For example, the employment specialist may play a primary role in engaging the person whose chief interest is finding a job. All team members become familiar with the unique strengths and perspective of the family and engage in a similar fashion. For example, the psychiatrist may have the first visit in the home and spend most of the time talking about the person's interests, such as sports, video games, or music. The psychiatrist might then meet with the family and provide some psychoeducation within the context of the family's culture. From the earliest stage, the clinicians also work with the family to build a common understanding and to help them interact more effectively with their loved one. EASA clinicians model and coach the family in empathetic listening, problem solving, and limit setting, introducing methods such as the four steps of Xavier Amador's LEAP model (Amador, 2007):

- Listen to what the person says and how they feel.
- Empathize with them rather than immediately contradicting what may not make sense.
- Agree on common ground; this may include agreeing to disagree.
- Partner around a mutually acceptable plan (p. 56).

ASSESSMENT

The assessment is ongoing from the first contact. Assessment is viewed as an engagement strategy, so it is done largely in a narrative, observational, and story-telling format. Assessment is comprehensive with a bio-psycho-socio-cultural framework. It incorporates a comprehensive history, mental health/medical assessments, strengths assessment, cognitive screening, and substance abuse screening. A baseline physical and medical exam are strongly encouraged, with the registered nurse playing an important role in monitoring baseline risk factors for metabolic disorder or other complicating diagnoses, nutritional and wellness practices including physical exercise and sexuality (Jackson & McGorry, 2009). An explicit and detailed strengths assessment is core to both engagement and treatment planning (Rapp & Goscha, 2008). The assessment attempts to understand the person's and family's cultural context and explanations of the phenomena they are experiencing, as well as their preferences for communication and care. Clinicians actively incorporate the individual's and family's language and preferences into the assessment and plan.

Psychosis can rapidly result in significant consequences, and EASA tries to prevent traumatizing involuntary measures, which may themselves create their own iatrogenic effects. Thus, early risk assessment and crisis planning are central elements of EASA's practice. Risk assessments include the content of the individual's psychotic symptoms (i.e., command hallucinations, delusional content) that may result in elopement and unintended harm; impulsivity and drug or alcohol use; family support and conflict; access to weapons and potentially lethal substances (including Tylenol and other over-the-counter medications), and potential for victimization by others (Jackson & McGorry, 2009).

TREATMENT

Many individuals are at a high level of acuity and risk when they are first introduced to EASA and require more intensive treatment in the beginning. Team members may arrange daily check-ins or extra outreach, with all clinicians on the team covering for each other in order to ensure availability for the family. Families must have access to a 24-hour crisis response, although this is often provided through the local crisis team. A risk assessment/crisis plan is completed early on by team members and may be shared with local crisis providers as well.

All treatment goals are written from the perspective of the individual and attempt to bridge the person's functional strengths and clinical needs. All team members contribute to and build on one shared treatment plan. John's initial "recovery plan" had three goals, which helped guide all interventions. The goals used John's specific words:

- "I want to get back into playing basketball with my friends."
- "I want to pass my classes."
- "I want to go to college."

The individual's goals provide a common framework to analyze the impact of symptoms and frame interventions. For example, the lead counselor helped John access tutoring resources and helped break down his academic goal into concrete steps, such as completing this week's math homework and visiting a college campus. The doctor prescribed medicine in order to help reduce the intensity of John's belief that he was being monitored by cameras, and his auditory hallucinations and anxiety, which were getting in the way of social interaction and completing homework. The occupational therapist addressed how cognitive and sensory changes and needs (Brown, Cromwell, Filion, Dunn, & Tollefson, 2002; Brown & Dunn, 2002; Champagne, 2011; Champagne, Koomar, & Olson, 2010) were impacting functioning (i.e., the ability to tolerate different levels of light and sound, retention of information, organizing and sequencing a daily schedule, etc.) (American Occupational Therapy Association [AOTA], 2008). The employment specialist helped John with resume writing, finding and keeping a summer job, and signing up for college. The nurse addressed issues related to meals, sleep, and medication side effects. An EASA graduate who was in college provided mentoring. Practical challenges such as how to explain his long absence to his basketball teammates were addressed in multi-family group.

COUNSELING AND CASE MANAGEMENT

EASA uses a clinical case management model that integrates practical day-to-day support for life activities, cognitive behavioral therapy (CBT) (Dobson & Dobson, 2009), motivational interviewing (Miller & Rollnick, 2002; Rollnick, Miller, & Butler, 2008), and psychoeducation (Jackson & McGorry, 2009; McFarlane, 2002; SAMHSA, 2009b; Walsh, 2010). All clinicians may be involved in this process at some point. The goals of these interventions are to:

- Reduce or prevent internalized stigma, while maintaining a positive view of the future
- Help the person progress developmentally and toward personal goals, and
- Enable them to master symptoms and improve functioning (National Early Psychosis Project, 1998)

Many mental health providers emphasize the importance of "accepting" that one has an illness in order to recover. Yet, if a person thinks that having schizophrenia means being unreliable and dangerous, accepting the diagnosis is tantamount to giving up. The EASA team works with young people like John to help build a self-concept based on their strengths (someone who loves basketball, is musical, has great friends and family, and also has a manageable condition). Cognitive behavioral therapy (CBT) techniques, meeting others with the illness, and focusing on positive goals can help identify and challenge negative assumptions (Jackson & McGorry, 2009).

There is substantial international research into CBT, with results showing modest efficacy in reducing symptoms, helping individuals adjust to their condition, and improving their subjective quality of life. However, CBT has demonstrated only minimal efficacy in reducing relapse (Orygen, 2010; Penn et al., 2005). Two CBT models were embedded in early intervention programs: the Graduated Recovery Intervention Program for First Episode Psychosis (GRIP) at the University of North Carolina–Chapel Hill (Waldheter et al., 2008) and the Cognitively Oriented Psychotherapy for Early Psychosis (COPE) model at the Early Psychosis Prevention and Intervention Centre (EPPIC) in Melbourne, Australia (Orygen, 2010; Jackson et al., 2005).

EASA provides integrated substance-abuse treatment, using a harm-reduction approach. In John's situation, he disclosed to the counselor that he had been drinking and using marijuana occasionally. The counselor shared research with him about the impact of marijuana on the brain, and explored John's use with him using a motivational interviewing harm-reduction approach. The issue was also addressed in a multi-family group. Although abstinence is ideal, these behaviors are common in the young adult population. Motivational interviewing (MI) is a core part of the skill set for all EASA team members. MI provides a construct for a transtheoretical "stage of change model." Stages of change and relevant interventions include the pre-contemplation phase in which there is no intention to change behavior in the foreseeable future, followed by the contemplation, action, maintenance, and termination phases. EASA clients are often in a pre-contemplative stage, and MI is effective across a spectrum of behaviors such as substance use and returning to work (Miller & Rollnick, 2002; Rollnick, Miller, & Butler, 2008). The Illness Management and Recovery (IMR) framework (SAMHSA, 2009a; Mueser et al., 2006) combines three key elements of the EASA program: psychoeducation, CBT, and MI approaches, along with consumer recovery perspectives. Although IMR was not developed for early psychosis, it is a useful tool when adapted to the clinical and developmental differences of this population.

EASA clinicians choose from a range of clinical methods and resources, based on the person's needs (Prochaska et al., 2010). Research suggests that the relationship may be more important to outcomes than the choice of therapeutic methods. Staff continuity and participant feedback are important to prevent premature drop-out and relapse in a population at high risk for both. Risk of drop-out and poor outcomes can often be detected within the first few sessions, and changing the provider significantly increases these risks. To address these concerns, EASA guidelines emphasize staff continuity, and EASA clinicians routinely use feedback tools such as the Outcome Rating Scale and Session Rating Scale, simple instruments that measure levels of stress in several life domains and give feedback to the clinician about the person's perspective on how therapy is going. Research suggests that use of these instruments as much as doubles the likelihood of clinically significant change (Miller et al., 2006; Duncan et al., 2004; Duncan & Miller, 2000; Wampold, 2001; Bringhurst et al., 2006; Lambert et al., 2003; Whipple et al., 2003).

MEDICAL SERVICES

Like all EASA team members, psychiatrists and nurses practice flexible, strength-based engagement and use person-centered language. Whether medications are prescribed, and which medications are used, is a collaborative decision based on full informed consent. If the person chooses against medicine and is symptomatic, the medical team remains engaged, and the entire team continues to work with both the person and the family to maximize their functioning, using a strengths orientation, problem solving, and addressing safety concerns. The team has a "start low, go slow" philosophy of prescribing, which is facilitated if the individual is identified prior to developing acute symptoms and offered a range of additional recovery strategies. The emphasis in prescribing is to establish a positive experience with the physician where the individual feels a sense of control and in which prescribing is sensitive to targeted symptoms, potential alternative ways of managing symptoms, and potential side effects. One way EASA psychiatrists or psychiatric nurse practitioners promote a climate of collaboration is by regularly posing these questions to the individuals they are working with:

1) How do you feel?
2) Are there ways you would like to think, feel, or live differently?
3) Can we consider ways that medications help you achieve these goals?
4) Do you know about the benefits of the medications you are taking or considering taking?
5) Are you familiar with the side-effects of the medications you are taking or considering taking?

A conservative approach is warranted for those who are at an early stage in the illness. Individuals with first-episode psychosis, especially adolescents, tend to experience more side effects more intensely than older individuals, and improvement in the early stages usually occurs more quickly (Kahn et al., 2008; Jackson & McGorry, 2009; Correll 2008; Correll & Carlson, 2006). Sometimes the person will already be on medicines from previous crisis involvement or hospitalizations, often in excessive dosage. In these situations, the EASA psychiatrist or psychiatric nurse practitioner may taper the person down to a level with fewer side effects. While a higher dose of medicine or polypharmacy may be warranted in a short-term acute situation, side effects may outweigh benefits. Benzodiazepines are often used in the beginning as an alternative to neuroleptics to address agitation and anxiety. Careful attention to both symptoms and side effects is critical for treatment effectiveness in-the-moment and also because these early experiences of working with a psychiatrist or nurse practitioner can have a lasting impact on the person's willingness to participate in treatment. In some situations, medication use may not be necessary or desired, in which case the physician continues to meet with the individual and family and support them by providing ongoing assessment and recommendations, problem solving, coordination with the team, and psychoeducation with the person and family. Other team members routinely join medical visits.

The EASA nurse, along with others on the team, pays close attention to risks associated with neuroleptic treatment, including individual's waist circumference, fasting blood sugar, triglycerides, and cholesterol levels, as well as monitoring for movement disorders. EASA nurses are encouraged to chart their findings using the Automatic Involuntary Movement Scale (AIMS) and the Barnes Akathisia Scale. EASA medical staff discuss and encourage sleep hygiene, abstinence from or reduced use of alcohol and other drugs, good nutrition and exercise, and safe sex practices.

Initially, the psychiatrist met weekly with John and his parents, and recommended laboratory tests and Omega-3 polyunsaturated fatty acid capsules. The psychiatrist did not prescribe medicine at first, because John's symptoms were less severe and John was able to participate in other forms of treatment. John continued to meet with the psychiatrist and nurse, who talked with him about what was going on in his life, and encouraged him to exercise and participate in occupational therapy, counseling, and vocational support. The psychiatrist played guitar with him and encouraged his interest in song writing, while also talking about the lyrics he was writing and how things were going at school. When John's paranoia and delusions became severe, the doctor prescribed a low dose of antipsychotic medicine. After several months, John collaborated with the psychiatrist and EASA team to taper off of the medicine with careful monitoring.

OCCUPATIONAL THERAPY

Occupational therapists (OTs) provide interventions focused on the integrated functioning of the person. OTs may assess for functional cognition (executive functioning, problem solving, methods for new learning, orientation); sensory functioning, preferences, and needs (Brown & Dunn, 2002; Champagne, 2011; Champagne, Koomar, & Olson, 2010); visual and auditory memory and ability to maintain dual attention; and visual perception. Interventions may include task modification (e.g., changes to class schedules, changes in task complexity, etc.), compensatory strategies (e.g., visual supports to compensate for auditory processing limitations), environmental modifications, sensory strategies, strategies for managing symptoms, daily routine, and education of the team and support system (AOTA, 2008; Brown & Dunn, 2002; Champagne, 2011; Champagne, Koomar, & Olson, 2010). These interventions are important to help the individual overcome common underlying cognitive problems such as impaired working memory, inability to maintain attention, and problems with registering and responding appropriately to stimulation in the environment.

The OT initially engaged with John by playing basketball. The OT developed an occupational profile describing John in relation to the things he enjoyed doing, needed to do, and was expected to do. The OT evaluated and clarified John's cognitive and sensory challenges as well as his information processing style. For example, she learned John felt overwhelmed by the incessant buzz of fluorescent lights in his classrooms, noting that this is why he felt compelled to stand up and leave class, and this noise also contributed to the delusion that cameras were watching him. Using the OT assessment and recommendations, the EASA team members worked with John's family and school staff to create accommodations to support John.

FAMILY PSYCHOEDUCATION

Families are core partners in treatment, and team members focus on understanding and supporting the needs of all family members. Most families in EASA participate in multi-family psychoeducation groups (MFGs) (McFarlane 2002). Group facilitators meet with the family for several "joining" sessions, which explore family experiences, strengths, and coping, and introduce them to simple family guidelines. The sessions provide illness education, help families cope with and recognize early relapse symptoms and protective factors, orient the family to the multi-family group process, and encourage MFG participation. Families attend a one-day family workshop provided by all EASA team members: reviewing common symptoms, diagnoses, causes, communication and problem solving skills, the recovery process, and family guidelines. Finally, families join ongoing groups with families in a similar situation. The first two groups are "get-to-know-each-other" groups focused on strengths and the impact of illness. All of the remaining groups follow the same process of problem solving.

Multi-family problem-solving groups follow the same sequence, starting with socialization, a check-in, problem identification and clarification, brainstorming solutions, brainstorming pros and cons, and completing an action plan. The predictability, simplicity, and practicality of the structure responds to the high level of sensitivity of individuals with psychosis to emotional expression, family conflict, and disagreement, executive processing issues that impact problem solving capacities, and the "overload" that comes with managing the complexity of dealing with psychotic illness. The groups expand the social support network, provide a supportive opportunity to for socialization, and help family members and clinicians think of solutions they would not have considered (McFarlane, 2002).

For example, during one check-in, John's mother, JoAnne, expressed anxiety about John drinking alcohol with friends on the weekends. She was concerned about his safety and the impact on symptoms. The group problem-solved the question, "What can JoAnne do to help reduce her anxiety about John's drinking on the weekends?" John was one of the people brainstorming solutions, which ranged from "Insist that John stop drinking" to "Go to a movie and forget about it." All group members, including John and his parents, were involved in identifying pros and cons for each possibility, and the final action plan was agreed upon by everyone in the family. The whole family agreed to sit down with a counselor and come up with some ground rules; using a harm reduction approach, the counselor was able to get John to agree to reduce his alcohol use and established periodic check-ins on the issue within the team.

SUPPORTED EMPLOYMENT AND EDUCATION

School and work are core developmental tasks, and so are core to EASA. The Individual Placement and Support (IPS) model has demonstrated success in facilitating competitive employment by individuals with chronic mental illness, and research suggests it may be even more effective for individuals with early psychosis (Swanson & Becker, 2011; SAMHSA, 2009c). Early studies have concluded that implementation of an IPS model significantly increased the rate of returning to work or school of first-episode schizophrenia patients, with lower attrition rates than traditional vocational rehabilitation (Killackey et al., 2008; Nuechterlein et al., 2005). Core features of IPS include:

- Full integration of the supported employment specialist on the clinical team
- No additional "hoops" or assessments required to enter competitive job search
- Rapid competitive job search and ongoing on-the-job support (SAMHSA, 2009c)

In John's situation, the employment specialist met with him and helped him develop a career plan. The employment specialist supported John in completing a resume and finding a summer job clearing invasive plants. John called the employment specialist several times for problem solving when he was dealing with workplace conflict and other stressors.

EASA's approach to supported education is similar to supported employment, with an emphasis on helping individuals pursue competitive education. EASA works with the student on campus or wherever is most helpful, identifying and supporting their educational goals, assessing the need for accommodations and on-site support, advocating for accommodations as needed, and providing hands-on practical support for career planning, completing applications, financial aid, campus orientation, registration, scheduling, homework, test taking, etc. (Downing, 2006; Sin & Wellman, 2005; Mowbray, 2004; Mowbray et al., 2002; Unger, 1999). The EASA team promotes understanding among school counselors and teachers, so that they may take an empathic, flexible approach to students with psychotic illness. The following interventions were helpful to John in returning to school: sitting in the back of the room and being allowed to take breaks as needed; getting extended test-taking time (time and a half) and a quiet, separate space for testing; copies of class notes; use of an audio recorder; tutoring, and regular check-ins with instructors.

TRANSITION

EASA is a two-year transitional program, and its transitional nature is emphasized in the beginning, with all interventions targeted toward building lasting understanding, skills, resources, and connections that will facilitate long-term success. Six months prior to discharge, the patient's transition plan is finalized. Prior to discharge, the individual and family meet with longer-term providers and ensure that the plan works well. The transition plan addresses insurance coverage, medical care, and access to ongoing care as needed, as well as informal supports, housing and community living needs, and vocational or school functioning needs. The process of entering recovery requires a level of effort and new knowledge equal to an academic degree program, and EASA intentionally recognizes that accomplishment through a voluntary graduation celebration. After leaving EASA, graduates sometimes look to EASA for advice when they face new challenges such as changes in insurance or resource issues, and EASA graduates are a resource to clinicians as they begin to work with people new to EASA. As EASA evolves, one of the most important areas of its focus is continuing a level of support by the programs for as long as five years in order to maintain gains (Norman et al., 2011).

EMERGING RESEARCH

Early intervention for psychosis is a rapidly evolving field internationally, with programs in sixty countries, particularly Australia, Western Europe, the United Kingdom, Canada, Asia, and the United States. As less intrusive and more effective methods become available, it is important that services continue to evolve. One example of emerging research that may have significant value for early intervention programs is cognitive remediation, which attempts to directly address neurocognitive deficits (Vinogradov et al., 2008). Olfaction testing also holds promise, as olfaction has been shown to be one of the earliest and most pronounced areas of sensory system deficits (Keshavan et al., 2009). Other hopeful areas of research and development include nutritional interventions such as the use of Omega-3 fatty acids (Amminger et al., 2007); structured supported education approaches (Unger, et al., 2000); and expanded integration of peer support and participation (Tonin, 2007). A thoughtful and structured method for integrating new knowledge and participant perspectives is critical to early psychosis intervention.

SUMMARY

EASA reflects a significant change in a field historically dominated by entrenched pessimism about schizophrenia. Starting with the assumption that young people with schizophrenia and related conditions can be expected to do well, the challenge to professionals, families, and communities is how to optimize the support, knowledge, and skill sets available to give young people the best chance of lasting recovery. Not only can individuals do well, but systems can be transformed. EASA and the other early psychosis programs throughout the world offer the hope that policy, funding, and service delivery can evolve rapidly and profoundly based on a shared vision and commitment, the strengths of the professional disciplines, the experiences of service participants and advocates, and new research.

REFERENCES

ACCESS Economics (2009). The Economic Impact of Youth Mental Illness. Retrieved from http://www.headspace.org.au/_uploads/documents/2009%20media%20releases/CostYM_H_Dec2009FINAL.pdf.

Addington, J., Van Mastigt, S., & Addington, D. (2004). Duration of untreated psychosis: impact on 2-year outcome. *Psychological Medicine, 34*, 277–284.

Amador, X. (2007). *I Am Not Sick, I Don't Need Help.* New York: Vida Press.

American Occupational Therapy Association [AOTA]. (2008). Occupational therapy practice framework: Domain and process (2nd ed.). *American Journal of Occupational Therapy, 62*, 625–683.

Amminger, G., Schaefer, M., & Papageorigiou, K. (2007). Omega-3 fatty acids reduce the risk of early transition to psychosis in ultra-high-risk individuals: A double-blind randomized placebo-controlled treatment study. *Schizophrenia Bulletin, 33*, 418–419.

Baldwin, P., Browne, D., Scully, P. J., Quinn, J. F., Morgan, M. G.,…Waddington, J. L. (2005). Epidemiology of first-episode psychosis: Illustrating the challenges across diagnostic boundaries through the Cavan-Monaghan study at 8 years. *Schizophrenia Bulletin, 31*(3), 624–638.

Bertolote, J., & McGorry, P. (2005). Early intervention and recovery for young people with early psychosis: consensus statement. *British Journal of Psychiatry, 187*, s116–s119.

Birchwood, M., Todd, P., & Jackson, C. (1998). Early intervention in psychosis: The critical period hypothesis. *British Journal of Psychiatry Supplement, 172*(33), 53–59.

Birchwood, M., Spencer, E., & McGovern, D. (2000). Schizophrenia: Early warning signs. *Advances in Psychiatric Treatment, 6*, 93–101.

Bringhurst, D. L., Watson, C. W., Miller, S. D., & Duncan, B. L. (2006). The reliability and validity of the Outcome Rating Scale: A replication study of a brief clinical measure. *Journal of Brief Therapy, 5*(1), 23–30.

Brown, C., Cromwell, R., Filion, D., Dunn, W., & Tollefson, N. (2002). Sensory processing in schizophrenia: Missing and avoiding information. *Schizophrenia Research, 55*, 187–195.

Brown, C. E., &Dunn, W. (2002). *Adolescent/Adult Sensory Profile: User's Manual.* San Antonio, TX: Pearson.

Bruder, M. (1994). *Working with members of other disciplines: Collaboration for success.* In M. Woolery and J. Wilbers (Eds.), *Including Children with Special Needs in Early Childhood Programs* (pp. 45–70). Washington, DC: National Association for the Education of Young Children.

Carpenter, W. T., &Strauss Jr., J. S. (1991). The prediction of outcome in schizophrenia. IV: Eleven year follow-up of the Washington IPSS cohort. *Journal of Nervous and Mental Disorders, 179*(9), 517–525.

Champagne, T., Koomar, J., & Olson, L. (March 2010). Sensory processing evaluation and intervention in mental health. *OT Practice, 15*(5), CE1-CE8.

Champagne, T. (2011). *Sensory Modulation and Environment: Essential Elements of Occupation (3rd ed., rev.)*. Sydney, Australia: Pearson.

Cornblatt, B. A., Lencz, T., Smith, C., Correll, C., Auther, A., & Nakayama, E. (2003). The schizophrenia prodrome revisited: A neurodevelopmental perspective. *Schizophrenia Bulletin, 29*(4), 633–651.

Correll, C. (2008). Assessing and maximizing safety and tolerability of antipsychotics used in the treatment of children and adolescents. *Journal of Clinical Psychiatry.* 69(suppl 4), 26–36.

Correll, C., & Carlson, H. (2006). Endocrine and metabolic effects of psychotropic medications in children and adolescents. *Journal of American Academy of Child Adolescent Psychiatry*; 45, 7.

Crumlish, N., Whitty, P., Clarke, M., Browne, S., Kamali, M., . . . O'Callaghan, E. (2009). Beyond the critical period: Longitudinal study of 8-year outcome in first-episode non-affective psychosis. *British Journal of Psychiatry, 194*(1), 18–24.

de Hann, L., Peters, B., Dingemans, P., Wouters, L., & Linszen, D. (2002). Attitudes of patients toward the first psychotic episode and the start of treatment. *Schizophrenia Bulletin, 28*, 431–442.

Dixon, L., Dickerson, F., Bellack, A., Bennett, M., Dickinson, D., . . . Kreyenbuhl, J. (2009). The 2009 Schizophrenia PORT psychosocial treatment recommendations and summary statements. *Schizophrenia Bulletin, 36*(1): 48–70.

Dobson, D., & Dobson, K. S. (2009). *Evidence-Based Practice of Cognitive-Behavioral Therapy.* New York: Guilford Press.

Downing, D. (2006). The impact of early psychosis on learning: Supported education for teens and young adults. *OT Practice, 11*, 7–10.

Drake, R., & Essock, S. (2009). The science-to-service gap in real-world schizophrenia treatment: The 95% problem. *Schizophrenia Bulletin, 35*(4), 677–678.

Drake, R. J., Haley, C. J., Akhtar, S., & Lewis, S. W. (2000). Causes and consequences of duration of untreated psychosis in schizophrenia. *British Journal of Psychiatry, 177*, 511–515.

Dube, K. C., Kumar, N., & Dube, S. (1984). Long term course and outcome of the Agra cases in the international pilot study of schizophrenia. *Acta Psychiatrica Scandinavica, 70*(2), 170–179.

Duncan, B., & Miller S. (2000). *The Heroic Client: Principles of Client-Directed, Outcome-Informed Therapy.* San Francisco: Jossey-Bass.

Duncan, B., Miller, S., Reynolds, L., Sparks, J., Claud, D., . . . Johnson, L. (2004). The session rating scale: Psychometric properties of a "working" alliance scale. *Journal of Brief Therapy, 3*(1), 3–12.

Hafner, H., Riecher-Rossler, A., An Der Heiden, W., Maurer, K., Fatkenheuer, B., & Loffler, W. (1993). Generating and testing a causal explanation of the gender difference in age at first onset of schizophrenia. *Psychological Medicine, 23*(4), 925–940.

Harris, M. G., Henry, L. P., Harrigan, S. M., Purcell, R., Schwartz, O. S., . . . McGorry, P. D. (2005). The relationship between duration of untreated psychosis and outcome: an eight-year prospective study. *Schizophrenia Research, 79*(10), 85–93.

Ho, B., Andreasen, N. C., & Flaum, M. (1997). Dependence on financial support early in the course of schizophrenia. *Psychiatric Services, 48*(7), 948–950.

Ho, B., & Andreasen, N. C. (2001). Long delays in seeking treatment for schizophrenia. *Lancet, 357*, 898–899.

Jackson, H., McGorry, P., Edwards, J., Hulbert, C., Henry, L., . . . Power, P. (2005). A controlled trial of cognitively oriented psychotherapy for early psychosis (COPE) with four-year follow-up readmission data. *Psychological Medicine, 35*, 1295–1306.

Jackson, H., & McGorry, P. D. (2009). *The Recognition and Management of Early Psychosis: A Preventive Approach* (2nd ed.). New York: Cambridge University Press.

Johannessen, J. O., McGlashan, T. H., Larsen, T. K., Horneland, M., Joa, I., . . . Vaglum, P. (2001). Early detection strategies for untreated first episode psychosis. *Schizophrenia Research, 51*(1), 39–46.

Johannessen, J.O., Martindale, B. V., & Cullberg, J. (Ed.). (2006). *Evolving Psychosis: Different Stages, Different Treatments.* New York: Routledge.

Johannessen, J. O., Friis, S., Joa, I., Haahr, U., Larsen, T. K.,…McGlashan T. (2007). First-episode psychosis patients recruited into treatment via early detection teams versus ordinary pathways: Course, outcome and health service use during first 2 years. *Early Intervention in Psychiatry, 1*(1), 40–48.

Kahn, R.S., et al. (2008). Effectiveness of antipsychotic drugs in first-episode schizophrenia and schizophreniform disorder: An open randomized clinical trial. *Lancet, 371*(9618):1085–1097.

Kaplan, H. I., Sadock, B. J., & Grebb, J. A. (1994). *Kaplan and Sadock's Synopsis of Psychiatry.* Baltimore, MD: Williams & Wilkins.

Keshavan, M. S., Haas, G., Miewald, J., Montrose, D. M., Reddy, R.,…Sweeney, J. A. (2003). Prolonged untreated illness duration from prodromal onset predicts outcome in first episode psychoses. *Schizophrenia Bulletin, 29,* 757–769.

Keshavan, M. S., Vora, A., Montrose, D., Vaibhav, D. A., & Sweeney, J. (2009). Olfactory identification in young relatives at risk for schizophrenia. *Acta Neuropsychiatrica, 21*(3): 121–124.

Killackey, E., Jackson, H., & McGorry, P. (2008). Vocational intervention in first episode psychosis: individual placement and support v. treatment as usual. *British Journal of Psychiatry, 193*(2): 114–120.

Kreyenbuhl, J., Nossel, I., & Dixon, L. (2009). Disengagement from mental health treatment among individuals with schizophrenia and strategies for facilitating connections to care: A review of the literature. *Schizophrenia Bulletin, 35*(4): 696–703.

Lambert, M., Whipple, J., Hawkins, E., Vermeersch, D., Nielsen, S., & Smart, D. (2003). Is it time for clinicians routinely to track patient outcome? A meta-analysis. *Clinical Psychology, 10,* 288–301.

Marshall, M., Lockwood, A., & Fiander, M. (2005). Essential elements of an early intervention service for psychosis: The opinions of expert clinicians. *BMC Psychiatry, 4,* 17. Retrieved from http://www.ncbi.nlm.nih.gov/pmc/articles/PMC455683/.

McFarlane, W. R., Stastny, P., & Deakins, S. (1992). Family-aided assertive community treatment: A comprehensive rehabilitation and intensive case management approach for persons with schizophrenic disorders. *New Directions in Mental Health Services, 53,* 43–54.

McFarlane, W. R. (2002). *Multifamily Groups in the Treatment of Severe Psychiatric Disorders.* New York: Guilford.

McFarlane, W. R., Cook, W. L., Downing, D., Verdi, M. B., Woodberry, K. A., & Ruff, A. (2010). Portland identification and early referral: A community-based system for identifying and treating youths at high risk of psychosis. *Psychiatric Services, 61*(5), 512–515.

McGlashan, T., Walsh, B., & Woods, S. (2010). *The Psychosis-Risk Syndrome: Handbook for Diagnosis and Follow-up.* New York: Oxford University Press.

McGlashan, T. H. (2006). Is active psychosis neurotoxic? *Schizophrenia Bulletin, 32*(4), 609–613.

McGorry, P. D., Edwards, J., Mihalopoulos, C., Harrigan, S. M., et al. (1996). EIPIC: An evolving system of early detection and optimal management. *Schizophrenia Bulletin, 22*(2), 305–326.

McGorry, P. D., &Yung, A. R. (2003). Early intervention in psychosis: An overdue reform. *Australian and New Zealand Journal of Psychiatry, 37*(4), 393–398.

McGorry, P. D. (2005). Royal Australian and New Zealand College of Psychiatrists clinical practice guidelines for the treatment of schizophrenia and related disorders. *Australian and New Zealand Journal of Psychiatry, 39*(1), 1–30.

McGorry, P. D., Hickie, I. B., Yung, A. R., Pantelis, C., & Jackson, H. J. (2006). Clinical staging of psychiatric disorders: A heuristic framework for choosing earlier, safer and more effective interventions. *Australia and New Zealand Journal of Psychiatry, 40*(8), 616–622.

McGorry, P. D., Purcell, R., Hickie, I. B., Yung, A. R., Pantelis, C., & Jackson, H. J. (2007). Clinical staging: A heuristic model for psychiatry and youth mental health. *Medical Journal of Australia, 187*(7 Suppl), S40–S42.

McGorry, P., Dodd, S., Purcell, R., Yung, A., Thompson, A.,…Killackey, E. (Eds.). (2010). *Australian Clinical Guidelines for Early Psychosis* (2nd ed.). Melbourne: Orygen Youth Health Research Centre.

Mid-Valley Behavioral Care Network (2008). *Guidelines for Oregon Early Psychosis Dissemination.* www.easacommunity.org

Miller, S., Duncan, D., Brown, J., Sorrell, R., & Chalk, MB. (2006). Using formal client feedback to improve retention and outcome: Making ongoing, real-time assessment feasible. *Journal of Brief Therapy, 5*(2), 5–22.

Miller, T., McGlashan, T., Rosen, J., Cadenhead, K., Ventura, J.,…Woods, S. (2003). Prodromal assessment with the structured interview for prodromal syndromes and the scale of prodromal symptoms: Predictive validity, interrater reliability, and training to reliability. *Schizophrenia Bulletin, 29*(4), 703–715.

Miller, W. R., & Rollnick, S. (2002). *Motivational Interviewing: Preparing People for Change* (2nd ed.). New York: Guilford Press.

Mowbray, C. T., Brown, K. S., Furling-Norman, K., & Sullivan-Soydan, A., (Eds.). (2002). *Supported Education and Psychiatric Rehabilitation: Models and Methods.* Linthicum, MD: International Association of Psychosocial Rehabilitation Services.

Mowbray, C. T. (Ed.). (2004). Special issue on supported education. *American Journal of Psychiatric Rehabilitation, 7*(3), 215–365.

Mueser, K., Meyer, P., Penn, D., Clancy, R., Clancy, D., & Salyers, M. (2006). The illness management and recovery program: rationale, development and preliminary findings. *Schizophrenia Bulletin, 32*(suppl 1), S32–S43.

Mueser, K. T., &McGurk, S. R. (2004). Schizophrenia. *The Lancet, 363*, 2063–2072.

National Early Psychosis Project (Australia) (Ed.). (1998). *The Australian Clinical Guidelines for Early Psychosis* (1st ed.). Melbourne: National Early Psychosis Project, University of Melbourne.

Nelson, B., Sass, L. A., Thompson, A., Yung, A. R., Francey, S. M.,…McGorry, P. D. (2009). Does disturbance of self underlie social cognition deficits in schizophrenia and other psychotic disorders? *Early Intervention in Psychiatry, 3*, 83–93. doi: 10.1111/j.1751-7893.2009.00112.x.

Nordentoft, M., Thorup, A., Petersen, L., Ohlenschlaeger, J., Melau, M.,…Jeppesen, P. (2006, June). Transition rates from schizotypal disorder to psychotic disorder for first-contact patients included in the OPUS trial. A randomized clinical trial of integrated treatment and standard treatment. *Schizophrenia Research, 83*(1), 29–40.

Norman, R. M. G., &Malla, A. K. (2009). Pathways to care and reducing treatment delay in early psychosis. In H. J. Jackson & P. D. McGorry (Eds.), *The Recognition and Management of Early Psychosis: A Preventive Approach* (pp. 161–174). Cambridge, UK: Cambridge University Press.

Norman, R. M., Manchande, R., Mallai, A. K., Windell, D., Harricharan, R., & Northcott, S. (2011). Symptom and functional outcomes for a 5-year early intervention program for psychosis. *Schizophrenia Research, 129*(2), 111–115.

Nuechterlein, K., Subotnik, V., Gitlin, J., Green, M., Wallace, C.,…Mintz, J. (2005). Advances in improving and predicting work outcome in recent-onset schizophrenia. *Schizophrenia Bulletin, 31*(2), 530.

Nuechterlein, K. H., & Dawson, M. E. (1984). A heuristic vulnerability/stress model of schizophrenic episodes. *Schizophrenia Bulletin, 10*(2), 300–312.

Nuechterlein, K. H., Dawson, M. E., Gitlin, M., Ventura, J., Goldstein, M. J.,…Mintz, J. (1992). Developmental processes in schizophrenic disorders: Longitudinal studies of vulnerability and stress. *Schizophrenia Bulletin, 18*(3), 387–425.

Orygen Youth Health Research Center (1998, update 2010). *The Australian Clinical Guidelines for Early Psychosis.* Australia: University of Melbourne.

O'Toole, M., Ohlsen, R., Taylor, T., Walter, J., & Pilowsky, L. (2004). Treating first episode psychosis—the service users' perspective: A focus group evaluation. *Journal of Psychiatric and Mental Health Nursing, 11*, 319–326.

Penn, D., Waldheter, E., Perkins, D., Mueser, K., & Lieberman, J. (2005). Psychosocial treatment for first-episode psychosis: A research update. *American Journal of Psychiatry, 162*(12), 2220–2232.

Petersen, L., Jeppesen, P., Thorup, A., Abel, M. B., Ohlenschlaeger, J., ... Nordentoft, M. (2005). A randomized multicenter trial of integrated versus standard treatment for patients with a first episode of psychotic illness. *British Medical Journal, 331*, online publication. doi:10.1136/bmj.38565.415000. E01.

President's New Freedom Commission on Mental Health (2003). *Achieving the Promise: Transforming Mental Health Care in America.* http://store.samhsa.gov/product/Achieving-the-Promise-Transfor ming-Mental-Health-Care-in-America-Executive-Summary/SMA03-3831

Prochaska, J. O., &Norcross, J. C. (2010). *Systems of Psychotherapy: A Transtheoretical Analysis.* Belmont, CA: Brooks/Cole.

Rahm, C., &Cullberg, J. (2007). Diagnostic stability over 3 years in a total group of first-episode psychosis patients. *Nordic Journal of Psychiatry, 61*(3), 189–193.

Rapp, C., & Goscha, R. (2008). *Strengths-Based Case Management.* Guilford Publications.

Rollnick, S., Miller, W. R., & Butler, C. (2008). *Motivational Interviewing in Health Care: Helping Patients Change Behavior.* New York: Guilford Press.

Rosen, A., Mueser, K. T., & Teeson, M. (2007). Assertive community treatment—issues from scientific and clinical literature with implications for practice. *Journal of Rehabilitation Research and Development, 44*(6), 813–826.

Rupp, A., &Keith, S.J. (1993). The costs of schizophrenia: Assessing the burden. *Psychiatric Clinics of North America, 16*, 413–423.

Saks, Elyn (2007). *The Center Cannot Hold: My Journey Through Madness.* New York: Hyperion.

Sale, T. (2008). EAST helps people with schizophrenia out west. *Behavioral Healthcare, 28*(6), 28–31.

Sale, T., & Melton, R. (2009). A long-term approach to early psychosis intervention. *National Council Magazine, 2*, 28–30.

Salvatore, P., Baldessarini, R. J., Tohen, M., Khalsa, H. M., Sanchez-Toledo, J. P.,...Maggini, C. (2009). McLean-Harvard international first-episode project: Two-year stability of DSM-IV diagnoses in 500 first-episode psychotic disorder patients. *Journal of Clinical Psychiatry, 70*(4), 458–466.

Simonsen, E., Friis, S., Opjordsmoen, S., Mortensen, E. L., Haahr, U., ... McGlashan, T. H. (2010). Early identification of non-remission in first-episode psychosis in a two-year outcome study. *Acta Psychiatrica Scandinavica, 122*, 375–383.

Sin, J., Moone, N., & Wellman, N. (2005). Developing services for the careers of young adults with early-onset psychosis-listening to their experiences and needs. *Journal of Psychiatric and Mental Health Nursing, 12*, 589–597.

Substance Abuse and Mental Health Services Administration. (2008). Assertive Community Treatment. Retrieved from http://store.samhsa.gov/product/Assertive-Community-Treatment-ACT-Evidence -Based-Practices-EBP-KIT/SMA08-4345.

Substance Abuse and Mental Health Services Administration. (2009a). Illness Management and Recovery. Retrieved from Evidence-based practice KIT website: http://store.samhsa.gov/product/Il lness-Management-and-Recovery-Evidence-Based-Practices-EBP-KIT/SMA09-4463.

Substance Abuse and Mental Health Services Administration. (2009b). Family Psychoeducation. Retrieved from http://store.samhsa.gov/product/Family-Psychoeducation-Evidence-Based- Practices-EBP-KIT/SMA09-4423.

Substance Abuse and Mental Health Services Administration. (2009c). Supported Employment. Retrieved from http://store.samhsa.gov/product/Supported-Employment-Evidence-Based- Practices-EBP-KIT/SMA08-4365.

Swanson, S. J., & Becker, D. R. (2011). *Updated and Expanded Supported Employment: Applying the Individual Placement and Support (IPS) Model to Help Clients Compete in the Workforce.* Center City, MN: Dartmouth PRC-Hazelden.

Teague, G., Bond, G., & Drake, R. (1998). Program fidelity in assertive community treatment: Development and use of a measure. *American Journal of Orthopsychiatry, 68,* 216–232.

Thorup, A., Peterson, L., & Jeppsen, P. (2005). Integrated treatment ameliorates negative symptoms in first episode psychosis—results from the Danish OPUS trial. *Schizophrenia Research, 79,* 95–105.

Tonin, V. (2007). Young people seeking mental-health care. *Lancet. 369* (9569), 1239–1240.

Unger, K. V. (1999). *Handbook on Supported Education.* Baltimore MD: Brooks Publishing Co.

Unger, K. V., Pardee, R., & Shafer, M. S. (2000). Outcomes of post-secondary supported education programs for people with psychiatric disabilities. *Journal of Vocational Rehabilitation, 14*(3), 195–199.

U.S. Department of Health and Human Services (2001). Mental Health: culture, Race and Ethnicity. A Supplement to *Mental Health: a Report of the Surgeon General.* Substance Abuse and Mental Health Services Administration.

Verhaegh, M. J. M. (2009). *Effectiveness of Assertive Community Treatment in Early Psychosis.* Eindhoven, The Netherlands: Tilburgh University.

Vinogradov, S., Luks, T. L., Schulman, B. J., & Simpson, G. V. (2008). Deficit in a neural correlate of reality monitoring in schizophrenia patients. *Cerebral Cortex, 18*(11), 2532–2539. doi:10.1093/cercor/bhn028.

Waldheter, E., Penn, D., Perkins, D., Mueser, K., Owens, L., & Cook, E. (2008). The graduated recovery intervention program for first episode psychosis: Treatment development and preliminary data. *Journal of Community Mental Health, 44*(6), 443–455.

Walsh, J. (2010). *Psychoeducation in Mental Health.* Chicago: Lyceum Books.

Wampold, B. E. (2001). *The Great Psychotherapy Debate: Models, Methods, and Findings.* Mahwah, NJ: L. Erlbaum Associates.

Whipple, J., Lambert, M., Vermeersch, D., Smart, D., Nielsen, S., & Hawkins, E. (2003). Improving the effects of psychotherapy: The use of early identification of treatment and problem-solving strategies in routine practice. *Journal of Counseling Psychology, 50,* 59–68.

Whitty, P., Clarke, M., McTigue, O., Browne, S., Kamali, M., . . . O'Callaghan, E. (2005). Diagnostic stability four years after a first episode of psychosis. *Psychiatric Services, 56*(9), 1084–1088.

Woodside, H., Krupa, T., & Pocock, K. (2008). How people negotiate for success as psychosis emerges. *Early Intervention in Psychiatry, 2,* 50–54.

Yung, A. R., Yuen H. P., McGorry, P. D., Phillips, L. J., Kelly, D., . . . Buckby, J. (2005). Mapping the onset of psychosis: the comprehensive assessment of at-risk mental states. *Australia and New Zealand Psychiatry 39,* 964–971.

Yung, A. R., Killackey, E., Hetrick, S. E., Parker, A. G., Schultze-Lutter, F., . . . McGorry, P. D. (2007). The prevention of schizophrenia. *International Review of Psychiatry, 19*(6), 633–646.

Zubin, J., & Spring, B. (1977). Vulnerability—A new view of schizophrenia. *Journal of Abnormal Psychology, 86*(2), 103–126.

CHAPTER 19

FAMILY PSYCHOEDUCATION

KEN DUCKWORTH, JOYCE BURLAND, LISA HALPERN, AND HARRIET P. LEFLEY

FEAR, FRUSTRATION, AND TRIUMPH: MY FAMILY AND MY JOURNEY

When my father flew from Los Angeles to Boston to see me, I wouldn't let him in my door. I remember thinking: I can't handle the stimulation and stress of his visit—but I couldn't put my thoughts into logical order and explain this to him—I just knew that I wouldn't see him. He was persistent; after making the trip, he came to my neighborhood and called my mother (who was staying with me) on his cell phone. "Is there any way Lisa would be willing to see me, even for a few minutes; maybe if I wait outside, she'll change her mind?" So my father waited— walking around my neighborhood while talking to my Mom on his cell phone. But I did not budge. I was inexplicably terrified of my father, even though he was incredibly supportive of me with my schizophrenia. I had become scared of people, even my father. So my father flew back to California without seeing me.

Before entering graduate school at Harvard and before my diagnosis, I was living in Washington, D.C., and driving a car my brother had loaned me. We had always been very close growing up (he's two years my senior), and he was quite protective of me. When I was ready to leave Washington and he wanted to retrieve the car, I refused to let him visit me. He mistakenly thought I did not want to give him his car back—when, in truth, I was isolating to a new degree and could not logically explain why to him. This became a pattern; I was unable to speak my feelings or explain the (lack of) logic behind them. My brother thought I was "just being difficult," and we ceased communication for about a year. It was a very painful time.

A few months later, when I was speaking to my mother on the phone, I told her, "I can't understand what you're saying to me." "Stop joking," she responded. "You're always a quick study and comprehend everything I say very well." "No, you're not hearing me," I shot back and collapsed in tears. "I literally can't understand the words you're saying to me." My mom panicked but then went online and found a phone number for McLean Hospital, near Boston. She called and managed to get me an appointment with a prominent psychiatrist who then referred me to the doctor I still see. My mother also started making frequent trips to Boston while I went on medical leave from school. When I couldn't even read or write, she started reading very simple books to me and helped guide me toward retraining my brain.

I was hospitalized twice that year. The first time, I faked behavior when my mother rapidly arrived from California so I could be released quickly. How did my family relationships change so that, by the time I was hospitalized for the second time, my mother and brother came from California to be with me on the inpatient unit and I welcomed their visit? They were waiting when visiting hours began at 10:00 a.m. and stayed until 10:00 p.m. every day. They walked with me around the bucolic McLean campus, talked about happy times, and met with my doctors. They were there so much they were mistaken for either patients or staff. My brother took leave from graduate school to be with me; my father participated by phone because he couldn't be away from work. During this hospitalization I finally received an accurate diagnosis: schizophrenia and depression.

Several things contributed to the change in interactions with my family. First, I was conscious of stress and tried to explain to my family that I needed low stimulation. My mind was playing tricks on me and we decided that I would simplify communication with my family by talking only to my mother. Something as simple as the change of cadence in voices set me off—so my mother spoke for my father and brother when I was experiencing intense symptoms. Second, out of self-preservation, I began to educate my family on what I needed by telling them specifically what they should ask me about, trying to find the words to explain what I was feeling, and suggesting they read books and articles to better understand my illness. They would ask me pertinent questions: what does akathesia actually feel like, and, what is the difference between being insecure versus paranoia—and I tried to answer as best I could. My parents took the Family-to-Family course of the National Alliance on Mental Illness (NAMI) and found it very helpful. With greater understanding of what I was going through, my family rallied around me and tried to help me accept realistic limitations while maintaining an attitude that one can thrive and not just survive with schizophrenia. They had high expectations for me—they held out hope when I couldn't see a way out, and they believed I was going back to graduate school even when I couldn't read or write. And that has made all the difference. Today I check in daily with my parents—they remind me to reduce stress when possible, ask if I've taken my medications and about my sleep. Their support, along with that of my brother, is an important constant in my life.

—Lisa Halpern

The role of the family in promoting the well-being and recovery of its members is now well established in a large number of studies. This chapter focuses on two empirically tested models of psychoeducational work with families (Family-to-Family) or for families and the people they love who are coping with an illness (the multi-family group model). Family-to-Family is a relatively brief 12-week course that focuses on educating families about specific psychiatric disorders, relieving their distress, and teaching them how to interact more effectively with their ill family members. These are manual-based courses that are typically taught by well-trained family members; sometimes but not always in conjunction with mental health professionals, and usually with the patient absent. Outcome measures target benefits to family participants, although often there is anecdotal evidence of benefits to patients as well. This model is usually called "family education" (Solomon, 1996).

Evidence-based family psychoeducation (FPE), on the other hand, is an empirically validated treatment for schizophrenia, bipolar disorder, and increasingly, other disorders as well. FPE is administered by mental health professionals in 6- to 12-month courses. In most models both family members and patients participate. FPE may be tailored to individual families, but is currently more available in McFarlane's (2002) multi-family group (PMFG) model. There is some evidence that PMFG may be superior in outcome to single-family treatment (McFarlane, 2002; Mueser, Bond, & Drake, 2001). Interventions are tested in randomized controlled studies. Results are measured in terms of patient variables such as reduction in symptoms, relapse, and rehospitalizations, sometimes with the addition of caregiver variables such as reduced depression or improved quality of life.

A BRIEF HISTORY OF FAMILY PSYCHOEDUCATION

When family therapy emerged as a separate discipline, it was based on the premise that the symptoms of schizophrenia and other major psychiatric disorders were functional in maintaining a pathological homeostasis in disturbed family systems. Research found that this approach failed to benefit families or alleviate symptoms (Howells & Guirguis, 1985) and anecdotally did a great deal of harm (McElroy, 1990). A number of events put an end to this model and ushered in the era of family psychoeducation—an intervention finally responsive to families' expressed desires for education about mental illness and training for illness management. The international expressed emotion (EE) research, which preceded this new intervention, demonstrated the enormous variability of families of people with schizophrenia. Some families were hostile and critical or emotionally over-involved (high EE), while others were patient, calm, and respectful (low EE), despite similar levels of family burden. Studies indicated that patients from high EE families were significantly more likely to relapse (Leff & Vaughn, 1985). However, when high EE family members were educated about the adverse effects of their attitudes toward the patient, FPE readily produced changes in their behaviors that led to more salutary patient outcomes (Barrowclough, 2005; Leff, 2005).

The development and study of FPE at research institutes at the Institute of Psychiatry in London (Leff, 2005); the University of Manchester, United Kingdom (Barrowclough, 2005); the University of Birmingham, United Kingdom (Fadden & Birchwood, 2002); the University of Pittsburgh's Western Psychiatric Institute in Pennsylvania (Anderson, Reiss, & Hogarty, 1986); the University of California at Los Angeles (Falloon, Boyd, & McGill, 1984) and others produced data on FPE's efficacy in promoting patients' progress. Today we have data from hundreds of well-designed research studies from countries throughout the world—including numerous rigorously controlled studies from China—attesting to the efficacy of FPE in symptom improvement, reduction of relapse and rehospitalizations, fewer hospital days, enhanced quality of life, and improvement of family understanding and well-being (see Magliano & Fiorillo, 2007; Lefley, 2009; and Luckstead, McFarlane, Downing, & Dixon, 2011, for comprehensive overviews). Among these, McFarlane's (2002) multi-family group model is attaining world-wide prominence, particularly for early interventions among young people showing prodromal signs of schizophrenia (McFarlane, 2011; Schmidt, 2007).

FAMILY EDUCATION MODELS

According to Corrigan et al. (2008), there have been at least five randomized trials and one quasi-experimental design of family education, all showing positive effects on families. NAMI's Family-to-Family, cited in the opening vignette, is undoubtedly the most prominent model of educating family members. In this program, well-trained family members teach a manualized course to other families about the etiological theories, treatment, and management of major psychiatric disorders, together with problem-solving skills. Families learn how to validate and deal with their own emotional reactions and the most beneficial ways of dealing with disturbed behaviors. The research on Family-to-Family, now administered to over 300,000 families, is described in greater detail below. An earlier model, the eight-week Journey of Hope (JOH) program, has been largely administered in one state by NAMI of Louisiana. Several controlled studies of JOH have shown participants reported fewer depressive symptoms; greater gains in knowledge about mental illness, problem-management, and community resources; and fewer negative relationships with their ill family members than controls (Pickett-Schenk et al., 2008).

The Training and Education Network (TEC), administered by the Mental Health Association of Southeastern Pennsylvania, is a collaborative of families and mental health professionals experienced in providing a 10-week psychoeducational course. Controlled research indicated a significant increase in self efficacy; i.e., "confidence in one's ability to understand mental illness in a relative and to cope with its consequences" (Solomon, Draine, Mannion, & Meisel, 1996, p. 46). The Pacific Clinics Institute, which developed *Schizophrenia: A Family Education Curriculum,* has been administering 12 hours of lectures for over 25 years to over 50,000 families in eight languages, sometime as an adjunct to Family-to-Family in California. Further descriptions are found in Amenson and Liberman (2001). Descriptions of many other family education programs may be found in Lefley (2009).

FPE has grown in scope and interest and is now being applied in novel settings, often in conjunction with other patient-centered interventions. It is an integral component of Ian Falloon's Optimal Treatment Project, which promotes the routine use of evidence-based strategies for schizophrenic disorders in clinics in numerous European countries, as well as Turkey and New Zealand (Magliano & Fiorillo, 2007). McFarlane's multi-family model is critical to early intervention efforts for psychosis, such as the Portland Identification and Early Referral (PIER) program (McFarlane, 2011; Schmidt, 2007), and has also been applied in conjunction with Assertive Community Treatment (McFarlane, 1997).

Nevertheless, despite its strong and growing research base, psychoeducation for families and consumers remains an underutilized and at times under-funded resource in the service of recovery. Barriers to implementation are discussed in greater detail in Lefley (2009).

This chapter describes two creative and effective models that have been well studied and are still the most highly utilized in the field: 1) NAMI's Family-to-Family course, led by family members to provide information, stress relief, and a sense of agency to family members who are supporting loved ones who are living with serious psychiatric illnesses; and 2) multi-family psychoeducational support groups led by professionals for multiple individuals living with psychotic processes, and their families (McFarlane, 2002).

BACKGROUND: HISTORICAL TENSIONS

Before discussing these primary models, it is essential to address the often difficult and complex relationship that psychiatry and families historically have had. The concept of the "schizophrenogenic mother" (Fromm-Reichmann, 1948), active in the 1950s, 1960s and even 1970s, may be viewed by professionals as simple misapplication of psychoanalytic theory, but it scarred many mothers of people living with mental illness who simply were searching for better care for their ill children. This dynamic—of blaming mothers and families for complex illnesses—generated mistrust and was a key theme that led to the formation of NAMI in 1979. NAMI now has over 1,100 affiliates nationally and is the largest family and consumer organization in the nation.

Today, while many of these historical tensions based on family blame have now eased and the overall connection between the mental health field and families is improving, families continue to report that they at times feel excluded from information about their loved one's care, and that the Health Insurance Portability and Accountability Act (HIPAA) regulations (U.S. Department of Health & Human Services, 1996) or other confidentiality concerns are overemphasized by health care providers. They often find that psychiatry's primary emphasis on the individual can be a problem when the family is helping to provide love and practical support in many forms, such as money management, housing support, and daily structure. Although family members often feel major responsibility for the person's outcome, they often report the experience of doing their best without good or complete information from the care team. Practitioners who involve families are greatly appreciated by them. Many practitioners who engage families find that their professional efforts are helpfully reinforced and complemented in the family setting. This is particularly the case when families are educated about their loved one's illness.

THE NAMI FAMILY-TO-FAMILY EDUCATION PROGRAM

Family-to-Family is conducted under the auspices of national NAMI, and administered at local levels. In the 20 years that this program has been operating, 7,500 NAMI volunteers have been trained to teach this free, peer-directed, 12-week program in their home communities. Since 1991, it has graduated over 300,000 people in 49 states, Canada, Mexico, and Italy, and has been translated into Spanish, Italian, Vietnamese, Mandarin, and Arabic. The program now is offered to family members of veterans in Veterans Administration hospitals across the country. In addition, more than two-thirds of the NAMI organizations managing the program at the state and affiliate level have been successful in securing ongoing funding to sustain the course from state and county departments of mental health; thus, it is recognized by state and federal funders as a valuable family education tool.

The course is open to any family member, partner, or consumer who has a first-degree relative suffering from a serious mental illness (schizophrenia, bipolar disorder, major depression, co-occurring brain and addictive disorders, borderline personality disorder, post-traumatic stress disorder, panic disorder, and obsessive-compulsive disorder). Over the life of the course, Family-to-Family has maintained a participant dropout rate of less than 10 percent.

THE DEVELOPMENT OF FAMILY-TO-FAMILY

When NAMI was founded in 1979, many of its early advocates were mental health professionals who helped originate the literature on the problems inherent in having a family member living with a serious mental illness (Hatfield & Lefley, 1987; Lefley & Johnson, 1990; Lefley, 1996; Vine, 1982; Wasow, 1992). Among the first academic accounts to investigate the objective and subjective stresses on family caregivers as well as their important role in the rehabilitation of their loved ones, these books urged the mental health system to initiate family education as an essential component of clinical care.

Calculating that decades of theoretical family-blaming and system overloading made it highly unlikely that education would be widely undertaken by providers on behalf of families, the founder of the Family-to-Family Education program[1] introduced an alternative approach as a way to bring vital information and support to family caregivers (Burland, 1991; Burland, 1995). Expanding on the established understanding of family caregiver experience as stress, adaptation, and coping, the Family-to-Family program added a new dimension: focus on the trauma visited on families who must suddenly cope with the profound loss, grief, fear, and uncertainty brought on by a loved one's descent into mental illness (Burland, 1998).

Through Dr. Burland's own experience over 30 years as a caregiver of a sister and a daughter with paranoid schizophrenia, she noted a substantial gap in the education and support of the families who were so crucial in helping their loved ones. Her vision was to develop a program that helped families maintain their dignity as loving caregivers, celebrated their strengths, and addressed the traumatic upheaval in their lives. The Family-to-Family course was designed to give them the tools needed to understand, support, and voice their rights in a decisive, effective advocacy role. Given this perspective, the primary themes in Family-to-Family revolve around trauma healing, consciousness-raising, and empowerment. After 20 years and many thousands of evaluations from family member participants, it is apparent that the course has sparked a response that is profoundly psychological, intensely personal, and transforming for many.

UTILIZING A TRAUMA MODEL OF RECOVERY: ENCOURAGING FAMILY HEALING

In the language of family pain, the constant repetition of words like "shattering," "devastating," "horrendous," "agony," and "desperation" reflects the degree of personal anguish families experience in the crucible of mental illness. Families are surely loaded down with difficult burdens in mental illness, but they are also traumatized, meaning that the shockwaves of this event go to the deepest personal moorings that hold one's life together. To neglect this aspect of emotional experience in educational work with families is to miss the crucial element that, when given attention, can transform family anguish into action and power. To this end, in the opening class of Family-to-Family, participants are introduced to the stages of normative emotional reactions to trauma applied to mental illness. They are taught that their various responses to severe life-dislocation caused by their loved one's mental illness are not wrong or bad—that people in this situation travel a predictable emotional path from shock and disbelief, to anger and grief, to understanding and acceptance. They are also introduced to the ultimate learning goal of the course—how to place living with trauma into a life perspective that fosters self-care and self-realization.

The theoretical base of the course draws on understanding trauma theory (Herman, 1992) and developing adaptive responses to it. In Family-to-Family, the architecture of the course allows family members, over a period of three months, to attain a bonding and comfort level in the group where they can safely "speak pain," reveal their feelings of loss and grief, and break the silence of their negative feelings of entrapment, guilt, and self-blame—the essential healing steps in mitigating the personal trauma of mental illness. Classes in the course contain all the requisite educational elements about brain disorders, and skill-training workshops also are included. Moreover, they actually model the final step in trauma recovery, demonstrating that the wisdom they have gained can be used to assist others. They are carefully trained to refrain from any sort of therapeutic intervention with participants, allowing family members to find and claim their own level of emotional resolution.

MODELING EMPATHY AND LEARNING TO ADVOCATE

To ease the anxieties associated with attending a course on loving someone with a serious mental illness, Family-to-Family is led by two caregivers like them who have survived their own fears. They hear that, although the curriculum offers a lot of information, they are the experts about their own circumstances and are trusted to take from the course whatever is personally relevant to them. Released from any expectation of performance or retention, while at the same time exposed to a torrent of new ideas and approaches to consider, family members can seek their own learning level, permitting them in many cases to reach further than they had expected. Aware that everyone in the class is responding to different emotional triggers in the lectures, discussions, and group exercises, teachers are trained to attend to the feelings that are aroused, alert to the fact that each person is working on a highly charged personal mosaic of understanding. In a program that hopes to lead family caregivers into lifelong learning, empowerment is gained by having the courage to stay the course.

Later, as family members develop learning confidence, they are introduced to the goal of advocating for their loved one—asking for explanations of treatment decisions and persisting in getting services essential to their relative's recovery, even though providers might not always welcome or respond to their efforts. By this time, families perceive very quickly that their experience would be altogether different if their stricken relative were struggling with any other medical illness—that no one could possibly imagine people with heart disease or cancer, and their families, putting up with the endless frustrations involved in navigating America's mental health system. By including advocacy training in the course, Family-to-Family makes the claim that preparing caregivers to challenge the conditions that limit them is a more effective means of alleviating families' burdens than any form of previous family "treatment."

A FAMILY-TO-FAMILY CASE STUDY: A TRUE STORY

Fran and Joe Holden have two sons who joined the Army in 2008. The older son, Harry, experienced a year of combat in Iraq and was discharged with severe PTSD. His brother, Tom, stationed to desk duty, became ill with bipolar psychosis and was hospitalized stateside soon after. Harry returned to his parent's home feeling angry and despondent. Tom also came home, soon went off his medications, and began to abuse alcohol and drugs. Fran and Joe had never coped with mental illness before and had great difficulty understanding their sons' difficult behaviors and odd reactions. Nothing they did to try to help their sons had any effect. "I couldn't reach them at all, they were so different," Fran said. "Suddenly, Joe and I had to function 24/7 as doctor, therapist, warden, case-manager—we felt totally isolated, really afraid for our boys and utterly lost, for months and months. We were completely overwhelmed." They found themselves in constant conflict over their sons' inactivity, sullenness, and erratic behaviors, with Joe protesting that the boys should just straighten up and go out and get a job, while Fran insisted they just needed a little more time to get back to normal after their army experience.

It was only after Harry's sudden suicide attempt that his parents realized this might be a long-term situation. Hearing about Family-to-Family from a social worker where Harry was hospitalized, Fran finally persuaded Joe to go with her to take the course. Here they joined 20 other family members under the tutelage of two NAMI volunteers with personal experience as caregivers. "That first class was a real eye-opener," Fran recalled. "They focused on the trauma of our experience, they normalized our reactions to it, they spoke to us with kindness and respect, they said a lot of information in the course had been denied to families and that we could use it any way we saw fit. They told us to trust our instincts and honor our expertise as the ones who knew our loved one best. I immediately felt validated and absolutely safe."

Over the early weeks of the class, the Holdens learned to identify the core symptoms of their sons' illnesses and understand how those symptoms affect behavior. Their unrealistic expectations for their sons to "pull themselves up by their own bootstraps and get on with it" faded in the face of repeated scientific evidence that brain disorders are serious medical illnesses. Week by week, they gained a growing realization of the painful isolation these illnesses bring to young people stricken in this manner. They began to talk openly of their problems, eventually joining the others in disclosing feelings of wanting to escape all the responsibilities that caused them to neglect their own relationship and well-being. They learned how to set reasonable boundaries, and how to see themselves through the inevitable ups and downs of their sons' adjustment to radically changed life circumstances. Through the communication class and the empathy class, they learned better and more compassionate ways to approach both young men, and saw their relationships improving so they could effectively assist their sons. Joe explained: "The understanding of their inner experience that I gained enabled me to see how much guts it took to get through each day with a mental illness. Boy, did I ease up. I turned all that frustration into advocating for my boys so they would get what they need—particularly their service benefits. I couldn't have done that without taking the course." Fran claimed the course enabled them to approach problems from the same level of understanding and acceptance. "It saved our marriage and it saved me—I was so desperate early on that I sought counseling," she said. "The course was really more valuable because it answered so many of my personal and practical questions. Far from being the distraught and depressed mom I was, I now see myself as a strong ally for my boys."

Harry has joined a PTSD program offered at the VA where he receives treatment; Tom has been hospitalized again after another bout of psychosis. "I know it will be a while before he's ready to accept his illness and learn what he has to do to manage it," Joe says, "but we're ready to see him through it. I can't thank NAMI enough for making this class available to our family. It was absolutely life-changing."

DEFINING THE EVIDENCE BASE: RESEARCH ON FAMILY-TO-FAMILY

Three studies have been conducted by Dr. Lisa Dixon, M.P.H., when she was the director of the Division of Health Services Research at the University of Maryland, along with her colleagues.

PILOT STUDY 1

In the first study, a prospective, longitudinal evaluation, a total of 37 consenting family members were drawn from five classes in Baltimore, Maryland. When compared with baseline assessments, completion assessments indicated that the program participants felt significantly more empowerment in the community, in their family, and with the service system. They also experienced less displeasure and worry about their ill family member. No significant improvements or deteriorations were noted for any measure between program completion and the six-month follow-up. Though limited by its small size and scope and the lack of a control group, the study results were encouraging with respect to the efficacy of Family-to-Family. (Dixon et al., 2001)

PILOT STUDY 2

This study conducted a controlled evaluation of the effectiveness of the program. Ninety-five participants were recruited from 15 classes in six different Maryland counties and Baltimore City. While the majority of participants were Caucasian, a substantial minority (27%) were African-American. A fidelity protocol was conducted to ensure that classes were delivered according to the manualized format; all classes met the fidelity standard. Results showed that participants' self-reported subjective burden and worry were significantly reduced after attending the course. Empowerment in all three domains (community, family, and service) was greatly enhanced. Depression symptoms of attendees significantly improved from waitlist and pre-test to the six-month follow-up, and all other reported improvements were also sustained at six-month follow-up. This study replicated the results of Pilot 1, and within the constraints of this study's non-randomized design, provides the strongest evidence available that Family-to-Family has important salutary effects on the family-member experiences of serious mental illness. Overall, the study indicated that its peer/family teachers provided effective information and support to family members and helped them resolve barriers to their participating in clinical care. As such, it has provided a solid first step in the evaluation of Family-to-Family as evidence-based practice for assisting family members (Dixon et al., 2004).

PILOT STUDY 3

This study, conducted over four years, was constructed to test the effectiveness of Family-to-Family with a randomized controlled design. A total of 318 consenting participants in five Maryland counties were randomly assigned to take Family-to-Family immediately (160) or to wait at least three months for the next available class, with free use in the meantime of any other NAMI or other community support (158). As in earlier studies, the majorities of participants were women and were middle-aged parents. Consistent with previous studies, Family-to-Family increased the participants' empowerment within the family, service system, and community, and significantly reduced the depression, anxiety, and overall distress in family member attendees. Knowledge about mental illness increased, extending the previous finding that evaluated only self-reported knowledge. Emotion-focused coping improved with respect to acceptance of mental illness, the dimension of emotion-focused coping most relevant to Family-to-Family's curriculum. The study also evaluated family functioning and found significant improvements in the Personal Skill subscale of the Family Assessment Device, suggesting that Family-to-Family may influence how family members solve internal problems and navigate emotional difficulties. Such a finding is noteworthy, given Family-to-Family's brevity and its reliance on the participation of the family member without the individual with the illness. These findings suggest the possibility that distal benefits such as enhanced family relationships may accrue as the family member uses these skills and insights gained via Family-to-Family within the family system.

Overall, these study results highlight the value of such community-based, free programs as a complement to services within the professional mental health system, and suggest that Family-to-Family merits consideration as evidence-based practice, which we should encourage practitioners to recommend to their patients and family members affected by serious mental illness (Dixon et al., 2011).

PSYCHOEDUCATIONAL MULTI-FAMILY GROUPS

THE DEVELOPMENT OF PSYCHOEDUCATIONAL MULTI-FAMILY GROUPS

Psychoeducational multi-family groups (PMFG) aim to improve the recovery and experience of individuals with psychiatric illnesses in groups with families by creating a positive and problem-solving community. The model's emphasis on the individual with their family in a group setting is a different approach than NAMI's Family-to-Family program, which serves family members. The use of professional staff is another key distinction from the all-volunteer

Family-to-Family model. PMFGs began for individuals with schizophrenia, but have evolved to serve many different populations with psychiatric illnesses.

PMFGs are based on Dr. William McFarlane's hypothesis that the state of the individual with schizophrenia is determined by a continuing interaction of specific biological dysfunctions of the brain with regard to social processes. The corollary to the hypothesis is that an optimal outcome can occur if *and only if* the biological and social determinants are addressed together (McFarlane, 2002). Significantly, the illness—not the person—is the focus of the groups, because the person is not the problem, the illness is.

A BRIEF HISTORY OF THE PSYCHOEDUCATIONAL MULTI-FAMILY GROUPS MODEL

Dr. H. Peter Laqueur is generally regarded as the pioneer of multi-family groups. The early groups were intended to promote the social functioning of inpatients who participated in them and improve the morale of the family as well. The basic idea behind multi-family groups is that families can learn or be taught what they do not know, increasing their coping skills in managing symptoms, vulnerability, and disability. Dr. William R. McFarlane worked with Laqueur at the Vermont State Hospital from 1973 through 1975, and then McFarlane built upon Laqueur's concept by adding a formal emphasis on psychoeducation and problem solving. The multi-family group offers the opportunity to create "visible villages"—prosthetic social networks—in contrast with invisible villages (McFarlane, 2002). McFarlane refined the PMFG concept as a hybrid of psychoeducational single-family treatment groups (PSFT), such as cognitive behavioral therapy, and multiple-family groups, where the goal is social networking without psychoeducation (McFarlane et al., 2003).

PSYCHOEDUCATIONAL MULTI-FAMILY GROUPS STRUCTURE

In the PMFG model, two professional clinicians, referred to as "family clinicians," lead a group of families. The model proposes that the main "goal in working with families is to help them develop the knowledge and skills instrumental in promoting the recovery of their family member while eschewing family dysfunctional etiological theories of the past" (Jewell et al., 2009). Importantly, the person living with mental illness is intricately involved in the groups. Based on the guiding principle that "almost all types of severe illnesses have a better course if the afflicted person has a large and knowledgeable social support system" (McFarlane, 2002), and because families can have a significant effect on their loved one's recovery (McFarlane et al., 2003), PMFG "is a treatment modality designed to help individuals with mental illness attain as rich and full participation in the usual life of the community as possible" (National Registry of Evidence-based Programs and Practices [NREPP], 2006). A group of five to nine families participates in each PMFG and becomes a microcosm of society for the person with mental illness to try out relationships in a real social setting. "Family" is defined as anyone committed to the care and support of the person with mental illness, and consumers often ask a close friend or neighbor to be their support person in the group (NREPP, 2006). Thus a PMFG is a three-sided partnership, involving the clinicians, family members, and people living with the illness.

ORGANIZATION OF PSYCHOEDUCATIONAL MULTI-FAMILY GROUPS

There are three stages to a PMFG: the joining phase, the educational workshop, and a series of biweekly meetings with the families and patients. In the joining phase, treatment begins as a bond forms between the family clinicians and the family members. The family clinician meets separately with the individuals living with mental illness and with the families at this stage because, after an acute episode of psychosis (for example), it may prove difficult for the individual to sustain the attention necessary to focus for an entire session. There are at least three joining meetings with each family and individual in the joining phase before they move on to the educational workshop. Session 1 helps everyone get acquainted with one another, separate from the illness. Session 2 centers on the impact of the illness—the emotional burdens exacted by the illness on the family and the individual. During Session 3, the family clinician "finishes gathering information, paying special attention to work, school, and other institutional connections, as well as areas of personal strengths and resources" (McFarlane, 2002).

After the three joining sessions, families attend a full-day educational workshop, usually held on a weekend, to underscore PMFG's core values and to ensure that the "families and patients know in no uncertain terms that they did not cause this disorder and that the professionals who are asking for their help do not hold any such beliefs" (McFarlane, 2002). The rationale behind the educational workshop portion of the PMFG model is that there is a fallacy of cause and care. Historically, families were responsible for the care of their sick loved ones, but, especially in the case of schizophrenia, families were also believed to be the perpetrators and cause of the illness. The educational component covers the seriousness of the illness; the role of stress in precipitating episodes; early signs of relapse; the more mysterious aspects of symptoms, especially the negative variety (see Dyck et. al., 2000); the ways in which psychiatric medications affect brain function and cause side effects; the ways that families are affected by severe mental illness in one of their members; effective coping strategies and illness-management techniques; the causes and general prognosis of the illness; and the psychoeducational treatment process itself.

The third stage of PMFG is made up of biweekly support group meetings, which are held for a minimum of six months and can continue for up to four years. At the first group meeting, usually held two weeks after the educational workshop, families are reminded that patients are invited to all subsequent multi-family group meetings. The goal of the first meeting is to get to know each other. The second meeting focuses on how the illness has affected everyone's lives. "It is helpful to emphasize that there is increasing hope with each passing year for treating and preventing this illness [schizophrenia], and that the members of the group will benefit from one of those developments, just by attending and participating in the group" (McFarlane, 2002). For the individual with mental illness, benefits include reduction in symptoms and reduced proclivity to relapse (Pollio et al., 2002).

After the first two multi-family group meetings, all subsequent group meetings focus on problem solving, with the same format for each 90-minute meeting. Problem solving in multi-family groups mitigates negative attitudes, stimulates brainstorming, and increases participants' hope that progress is possible through experiencing success in small steps (McFarlane, 2002). Group members also gain resilience at the social level because, even though the burden does not change in the aggregate amount, the relative burden on each person decreases as it is divided among more people. The problem-solving aspect of PMFG has been shown to be particularly effective in dealing with first-episode psychosis (McWilliams et al., 2010; McFarlane, 2011).

The problem-solving stage has six distinct steps (McFarlane, 2002):

Step 1: Define the problem or goal (family and clinicians)
Step 2: List all possible solutions (all group members)
Step 3: Discuss first advantages and then disadvantages of each possible solution in turn (family and clinicians; group members)
Step 4: Choose the solution that best fits the situation (family)
Step 5: Plan how to carry out this solution in detail (family and clinicians)
Step 6: Review implementation (clinicians)

Significantly, the problem-solving meetings begin and end with time spent socializing. It is critically important for the family members to get to know each other as people first, which simple socializing allows. The relationships that form are part of the fabric of recovery.

THE EVIDENCE BASE FOR PSYCHOEDUCATIONAL MULTI-FAMILY GROUPS

The Bergen County trial reported that among three types of family therapy—PMFG, PFST (psychoeducational single family therapy), and dynamic multi-family groups (DMG)—PMFG yielded the lowest relapse rate after four years (50% for patients in PMFG, vs. 78% for those in PSFT). Multi-family group therapy alone (without psychoeducation) yielded a 57% relapse rate. (McFarlane et al. 1995) Another study, the New York State Family Psychoeducation Study (trial at six sites), showed that the PMFG relapse rate was one-third less than the PSFT rate (28% compared to 42%) (McFarlane, et al. 1993).

Another benefit of PMFG is its cost-effectiveness. The PMFG approach is designed to require one-half of the staff time per patient compared to the PSFT format: one hour per month per patient for PMFG, compared to two hours for PSFT. Every dollar spent on PMFG or PSFT treatment ($34 or $17, respectively) was saved in hospitalization costs during that period (McFarlane, 2002). Scheduling multi-family groups is at times an obstacle to participation by multiple families, and individual family psychoeducation has a place in the service continuum.

Recovery typically requires a long time trajectory, and the benefits of PMFG appear to increase over time. "It has become clear from a clinical perspective that social support, recently observed to be a significant predictor of outcome, requires much longer developing than is possible in an 8- to 12-week course…the implication is that longer-term work, extending for at least one year, appears to be necessary to achieve these effects" (McFarlane, 2002). As shown by Courtney Harding's seminal "Maine vs. Vermont" study, examining data from a time period of 30 years, recovery is possible but happens gradually (DeSisto et al., 1995). A PMFG needs to challenge the individual to achieve goals but to moderate that vision with awareness of the stress that higher demands can create.

PMFGs have been shown to be effective in helping relatives deal with mental illness, thereby helping the individual with the illness. Reviews by Murray-Swank and Dixon (2004), Jewell et al. (2009), and Rummel-Kluge and Kissling (2008) have all come to similar conclusions: PMFGs offer a solid, evidence-based, effective practice for reducing relapse rates and hospitalizations. In keeping with these conclusions, the Substance Abuse and Mental Health Services Administration (SAMHSA) of the U.S. Department of Health and Human Services includes McFarlane's PMFG as evidence-based practice and has released a toolkit to promote its widespread implementation (SAMSHA, 2009). Additionally, recently updated Patient Outcome Research Team (PORT) treatment recommendations suggest that family interventions should last from six to nine months and include illness education, crisis intervention, emotional support, and training for coping skills (Dixon et al., 2009).

PMFGs have been implemented in twelve states, ranging from California to New York. Internationally, the method has been used in thirteen countries. It is estimated that several thousand sites are presently using PMFG, not including applications to other psychiatric or psychosocial disorders. Tens of thousands of consumers have participated in multi-family groups (NREPP, 2006).

Multi-family groups offer a coherent, clear and supportive milieu for an individual who experiences a psychotic process and his or her family to find support, education, and strategic aids for fostering recovery. Organizing a PMFG can be a logistical challenge for clinicians and families alike, but the results are worth the effort. The American Psychiatric Association (2004) "lists family psycho-education among their psychosocial interventions with substantial evidence bases, and cites reduced family burden and reductions in relapse rates" (cited in McWilliams et al., 2011). PMFGs represent a creative, cost-effective, and replicable opportunity for individuals and their families to move forward in their lives.

CONCLUSION

In a field that has historically been driven by attention to the individual's mental illness and or health, the emergence of well-studied and applied models of family psychoeducation add to the spectrum of recovery options and resources. This connection with families results in improved family experience and in individual outcomes. Evidence now clearly meets the experience of those who have used both NAMI's Family-to-Family and psychoeducational multi-family groups in the promotion of well-being for families and individuals impacted by serious psychiatric illness. These programs offer the powerful perspective that can only be gained from combining firsthand experience with support, education, problem-solving, and collaboration. These free or cost-effective and practical capacity-building resources are an important and growing part of the fabric of mental health services to promote individual recovery and improve the family experience of coping with mental illness.

NOTE

1. Family-to-Family was initially called "The Journey of Hope."

REFERENCES

Amenson, C. S., & Liberman, R. P. (2001). Dissemination of family psychoeducation: the importance of consensus building. *Psychiatric Services*, 52, 589–592.

American Psychiatric Association Work Group on Schizophrenia. (2004). *Practice Guideline for the Treatment of Patients with Schizophrenia*. 2nd edition. Washington, DC: American Psychiatric Association.

Anderson, C. M., Reiss, D. J., & Hogarty, G. E. (1986). *Schizophrenia and the Family: A Practitioner's Guide to Psychoeducation and Management*, New York: Guilford.

Barrowclough, C . (2005). Families of people with schizophrenia. In N. Sartorius, J. Leff, J. Lopez-Ibor, M. Maj, & A. Okasha . *Families and Mental Disorders: From Burden to Empowerment.* (pp. 1–24). Chichester, UK: Wiley.

Burland, J . (1991). *NAMI Family-to-Family Education Program.* Arlington, VA: National Alliance on Mental Illness.

Burland, J . (1995). Journey of hope: A family-to-family self help education program. *The Journal of Self Help,* 6 (3), 20–22.

Burland, J . (1998). Family-to-family: A trauma-and-recovery model of family education. *New Directions in Mental Health Services,* 77, 33–41.

Corrigan, P. W., Mueser, K. T., Bond, G. R., Drake, R. E., & Solomon, P . (2008). *Principles and Practice of Psychiatric Rehabilitation.* New York: Guilford.

DeSisto, M., Harding, C., McCormick, R., Ashikaga, T., & Brooks, G. (1995). The Maine and Vermont three-decade studies of serious mental illness: Matched comparisons of cross-sectional outcome. *British Journal of Psychiatry,* 167, 331–338.

Dixon, L., Stewart, B., Burland, J, Delahanty J, Lucksted A., & Hoffman M. (2001). Pilot study of the effectiveness of the family-to-family education program. *Psychiatric Services,* 52, 965–967.

Dixon, L., Lucksted, A., Stewart, B., Burland, J., Brown, C. H., Postrado, L.,…Hoffman, M. (2004). Outcomes of the peer-taught 12-week family-to-family education program for severe mental illness. *Acta Psychiatrica Scandinavia.* 109, 207–215

Dixon, L., Luckstead, A., Medoff, D., Burland, J., Stewart, B.,…Murray-Swank, A. (2011). Outcomes of a randomized study of a peer-taught family-to-family education program for mental illness. *Psychiatric Services,* 62, 591–597.

Dixon, L. B., Dickerson, F., Bellack, A. S., Bennett, M., Dickinson, D.,…Kreyenbuhl, J . (2009). Schizophrenia PORT psychosocial treatment recommendations and summary statements. *Schizophrenia Bulletin,* 36, 48–70.

Dyck, D. G., Short, R. A., Hendryx, M. S., Norell, D., Myers, M., & Patterson, T. (2000). Management of negative symptoms among patients with schizophrenia attending multiple-family groups. *Psychiatric Services,* 51, 4, 513–519.

Fadden, G., & Birchwood, M. (2002). British models for expanding family psychoeducation in routine practice. In H. P. Lefley & D. L. Johnson (Eds.), *Family Interventions in Mental Illness: International Perspectives* (pp. 25–41). Westport, CT: Praeger.

Falloon, I. R. H., Boyd, J. L., & McGill, C. W. (1984). *Family Care of Schizophrenia.* New York: Guilford.

Falloon, I. R. H. (1999). Optimal treatment for psychosis in an international multisite demonstration project. *Psychiatric Services,* 50, 615–618.

Fromm- Reichmann, F. (1948). Notes on the development of the treatment of schizophrenia by psycho-analytic psychotherapy. *Psychiatry, 11,* 263–273.

Hatfield, A., & Lefley, H. P. (Eds.). (1987) *Families of the Mentally Ill: Coping and Adaptation.* New York: Guilford.

Herman, J. L. (1992). *Trauma and Recovery.* New York: Basic Books.

Howells, J. G., & Guirguis, W. R. (1985). *The Family and Schizophrenia.* New York: International Universities Press.

Jewell, T. C., Downing, D., & McFarlane, W. R. (2009). Partnering with families: Multiple family group psychoeducation for schizophrenia. *Journal of Clinical Psychology,* 65, 868–878.

Leff, J., & Vaughn, C. (1985). *Expressed Emotion in Families.* New York: Guilford.

Leff, J. (2005). *Advanced Family Work for Schizophrenia: An Evidence-Based Approach*. London, Gaskell.

Lefley, H. P ., & Johnson, D. L . (Eds.), (1990). *Families as Allies in Treatment of the Mentally Ill: new Directions for Mental Health Professionals*. Washington, DC: American Psychiatric Press.

Lefley, H. P. (1996). *Family Caregiving in Mental Illness.* Thousand Oaks, CA: Sage.

Lefley, H. P. (2009). *Family Psychoeducation for Serious Mental Illness.* New York: Oxford University Press.

Luckstead, A., McFarlane, W., Downing, D., & Dixon, L. (2011). Recent developments in family psychoeducation as an evidence-based practice. *Journal of Marital and Family Therapy*. doi: 10.1111/j.1752–0606.2011.00256x.

Magliano, L., & Fiorillo, A. (2007). Psychoeducational family interventions for schizophrenia in the last decade: from explanatory to pragmatic trials. *Epidemiologia e Psichiatria Sociale*, 16(1), 22–34.

McElroy, E. M. (1990). Ethical and legal considerations for interviewing families of the seriously mentally ill. In H.P. Lefley & D.L. Johnson (Eds.), *Families as Allies in Treatment of the Mentally Ill: New Directions for Mental Health Professionals* (pp. 173–193). Washington, DC: American Psychiatric Press.

McFarlane, W. R., Dunne, E., Lukens, E., Newmark, M., McLaughlin-Toran, J., & Horen, B. (1993). From research to clinical practice: Dissemination of New York State's family psychoeducation project. *Hospital Community Psychiatry*, 44, 265–270.

McFarlane, W. R., Link, B., Dushay, R., et al. (1995). Psychoeducational multiple family groups: Four-year relapse outcome with schizophrenia *Family Process*, 34, 127–144.

McFarlane, W. R. (1997). FACT: Integrating family psychoeducation and assertive community treatment. *Administration and Policy in Mental Health and Mental Health Services Research,* 25, 191–198.

McFarlane, W. R . (2002). *Multi-Family Groups in the Treatment of Severe Psychiatric Disorders*. New York: Guilford.

McFarlane, W. R., Dixon, L., Lukens, E., & Luckstead, A. (2003). Family psychoeducation and schizophrenia: A review of the literature. *Journal of Marital and Family Therapy*, 29, 223–227.

McFarlane, W. R. (2011). Prevention of the first episode of psychosis. *The Psychiatric Clinics of North America*, 34, 95–107.

McWilliams, S., Egan, P., Jackson, D., Renwick, L., Foley, S., Behan, C., et al. (2010). Caregiver psychoeducation for first-episode psychosis. *European Psychiatry*, 25, 33.

McWilliams, S., Hill, S., Mannion, N., Fetherston, A., Kinsella, A., & O'Callaghan, E. (2011). Schizophrenia: A five-year follow-up of patient outcome following psycho-education for caregivers. *European Psychiatry*, doi: 10.1016/j.eurpsy.2010.08.012.

Mueser, K. T., Bond, G. R., & Drake, R. E. (2001). Community based treatment of schizophrenia and other severe mental disorders: Treatment outcomes. *Medscape General Medicine*, 3(1), 1–24.

Mullen, A ., Murray, L., & Happell, B. (2002). Multiple family group interventions in first episode psychosis: Enhancing knowledge and understanding. *International Journal of Mental Health Nursing*, 11, 4, 228.

Murray-Swank, A. B., &, Dixon, L. (2004). Family psychoeducation as an evidence based practice. *International Journal of Neuropsychiatric Medicine*, 9, 12, 905–912.

Pickett-Schenk, S., Lippincott, R. C., Bennett, C., & Steigman, P. J. (2008). Improving knowledge about mental illness through family-led education.: The Journey of Hope. *Psychiatric Services*, 59, 49–56.

Pollio, D., North, C., & Osborne, V. (2002). Brief report—Family-responsive psychoeducation groups for families with an adult member with mental illness: Pilot results. *Community Mental Health Journal*, 38, 414.

Rummel-Kluge, C., & Kissling, W. (2008). Psychoeducation in schizophrenia: New developments and approaches in the field. *Current Opinion in Psychiatry*, 21, 168–172.

Schmidt, C. (2007). Putting the brakes on psychosis. *Science*, 316 (May 18), 976–977.

Solomon, P. (1996). Moving from psychoeducation to family education for adults with serious mental illness. *Psychiatric Services*, 47, 1364–1370.

Solomon, P., Draine, J., Mannion, E., & Meisel, M. (1996). The impact of individualized consultation and group workshop family education and interventions on ill relative outcomes. *Journal of Nervous and Mental Disease*, 184, 252–254.

Substance Abuse & Mental Health Services Administration (SAMHSA). (2006). National Registry of Evidence-Based Programs and Practices. (NREPP). Psychoeducational Multi-family Groups. Date of Review: December 2006.

Substance Abuse & Mental Health Services Administration (SAMSHA). (2009). *Family Psychoeduction: How to Use the Evidence-Based Practice Kits.* HHS Pub. No. SMA-09–4422. Rockville, MD: Center for Mental Health Services, Substance Abuse and Mental Health Services Administration, U.S. Department of Health and Human Services (available at http://mentalhealth.samhsa.gov/cmhs/CommunitySupport/toolkits/family/).

U.S. Department of Health & Human Services (1996). The summary of the Health Insurance Portability and Accountability Act (HIPPA) privacy rule. Available at http://www.hhs.gov/ocr/privacy/hipaa/understanding/summary/privacysummary.pdf. Retrieved November 12, 2011.

Vine, P . (1982). *Families in Pain.* New York: Pantheon Press.

Wasow, M. (1992). *Coping with Schizophrenia: A Survival Manual for Parents, Relatives and Friends.* Palo Alto, CA; Science and Behavior Books.

CHAPTER 20

ASSERTIVE COMMUNITY TREATMENT TEAMS

LISA T. SCHMIDT, NARSIMHA R. PINNINTI, BUDDY GARFINKLE, AND PHYLLIS SOLOMON

People living with serious mental illnesses have varying needs for treatment and support. While most can manage their illness using conventionally delivered medication, therapy, and rehabilitation, the formal system of care fails to connect with some. An alternative treatment approach is needed to engage these individuals. Assertive Community Treatment (ACT) is one such alternative.

OVERVIEW OF THE ASSERTIVE COMMUNITY TREATMENT MODEL

Assertive Community Treatment was developed in the early 1970s at the height of deinstitutionalization in the United States, by Marx, Test, and Stein (1973). "Training in Community Living," as it was originally named, was to take the interdisciplinary treatment team of the hospital into the community and function as a community-based alternative to inpatient psychiatric service. These innovators had observed that training patients in the hospital setting about living in the community and then having them transfer these skills to a community setting was not successful, as these patients tended to be "concrete learners" with limited ability to generalize knowledge and skills to new environments (Bellack, Mueser, Gingerich, & Agresta, 1997).

Like the hospital, ACT was designed to be a comprehensive, self-contained program that was to meet the medical and psychosocial needs of the patients by providing all psychiatric treatment, rehabilitation, and social services (Stein & Santos, 1998). ACT is delivered by a multidisciplinary team that includes at minimum a psychiatrist, nurse, therapist/clinician, and a case manager who serves the coordinating function for the team. In addition, contingent on the target population of consumers served by the team, each program has a number of specialists such as employment and substance-abuse counselors (Allness & Knoedler, 2003). It is becoming increasingly common for teams to also have peer recovery specialists as well as family members who function as advocates, educators, and support people. Peer and family involvement is transforming the orientation of mental health services toward recovery, as was called for by President Bush's New Freedom Commission on Mental Health (2003).

Similar to the hospital, ACT teams are available 24 hours a day, seven days a week. This availability includes mobile crisis services and affords continuity of care. Thus, ACT enhances integrated and well-coordinated services on a long-term, continuous basis. A no-discharge policy has been a hallmark of the program, although research has found that consumers can be transferred with no negative consequences, if it is done in a planned manner (Phillips, Burns, Edgar, Mueser, et al., 2001; Salyers, Masterton, Fekete, Picone, & Bond, 1998). Each team offers a staff–consumer ratio of one to 10–12, with a maximum of 120 consumers served by a given team. Teams offer continuous care that is flexible and personalized to each individual served. Teams meet on a daily basis so all staff members are aware of the current clinical status of each consumer. This structure assures that there is no break in service should a provider be unavailable. Also, teamwork and a low staff-to-consumer ratio reduce work-related stress and staff burnout (Rosen, Mueser, & Teesson, 2007).

Services are delivered *in vivo* wherever a person lives, works, learns, and recreates. Consumers can be visited more than once every day if needed. Given its intensity of service and assertive outreach, the ACT team is generally reserved for people who do not engage with services, have numerous hospitalizations, are homeless, and have a great number of crises. Based on these criteria, this service is intended for about 20 percent of persons with severe psychiatric disorders. The goals of ACT from its inception were to reduce a person's need for psychiatric hospitalizations, increase their independence from the formal mental health service system, and increase social inclusion in community settings of their choosing.

ACT is currently considered an evidence-based practice and is widely implemented internationally. Extensive research has consistently found that, with fewer drop-outs from service, ACT decreases hospitalizations or lengths of stays when consumers are hospitalized, and decreases homelessness and emergency-service use. It has also been shown to increase housing stability and is associated with greater consumer and family satisfaction when compared to broker or intensive case management services (Dixon, Dickerson, Bellack, Bennett, Dickinson, et al., 2010). Findings regarding reduction in symptoms, fewer arrests, improved functional status (including employment and social skills), higher quality of life, and medication compliance are less consistently demonstrated (Corrigan, Mueser, Bond, Drake, & Solomon, 2008; Rosen et al., 2007). It has, however, been found to be cost effective due to reductions in hospitalization expenses. When ACT is assessed as having high fidelity to identified standards, consumers experience better outcomes (Bond, Drake, Mueser & Latimer, 2001; Rosen et al., 2007). However, as conventional service systems evolve, fewer hospitalizations and far shorter lengths of hospital stay are now typical. In addition, "usual services" such as intensive case management now employ features of ACT, including an integrated team approach, *in vivo* services, and assertive outreach. Thus, recent research reviews have concluded that ACT's advantage over usual care in reducing hospitalization is not sustained. In areas where standard services effectively use elements of ACT, it may be time to be more judicious in the use of ACT, but where there are persons with severe mental illnesses cycling between homelessness, jail, and the community and scarce high-quality services, it is not a time to abandon ACT (Burns, 2009, 2010; Dieterich, Irving, Park, & Marshall, 2010).

TEAM DYNAMICS

As described above, the ACT model requires a clinically skilled, multidisciplinary team of practitioners working in close collaboration with each other and with a shared caseload of consumers. Diverse clinical training, competing philosophies of care (e.g., medical model vs. rehabilitation model) and a well-established hierarchy among health professionals present challenges to ACT team collaboration. In conventional treatment settings, those with the highest medical degrees typically control clinical decision making, yet they often spend limited time in direct contact with consumers. Those with less formal training provide adjunct support and carry out many of the day-to-day tasks of care management. The ACT model, however, requires all team members to share responsibility for tasks and deemphasizes hierarchical decision-making in favor of a client-centered approach and shared decision-making. Teams must find ways to break down professional "silos" and view the consumer as an active member of the team so that a collaborative effort ensues. Additionally, ACT teams include member roles and perspectives that are often unfamiliar to those with more conventional training. For instance, a family advocate or a certified peer specialist does not have the formal training of the other professionals on the team but does bring the voice of "lived experience" (Deegan, 1988). This voice often challenges traditional notions of what is helpful and what is possible. When everyone is open to this alternate perspective, new ways of solving intractable problems often come to light. This opportunity is important, considering that most ACT consumers have not responded to more conventional approaches to treatment.

Consumers are perhaps the most important members of the team, not only because they are the focus of assessment and treatment, but also because, without their active collaboration, ACT services will be ineffective. ACT consumers typically have long histories of rejecting conventional services. In part this is due to their belief that treatment has not helped them in personally meaningful ways. The quality of consumers' participation is improved when special efforts are made to engage and empower them.

An ACT team must preserve the expertise of its individual members while fostering a common trans-disciplinary philosophy. Specifically, the team must believe that recovery from serious mental illness is possible and that all team members can contribute equally to facilitating recovery. High-performing teams value the unique perspectives of its members and use this diversity to creatively address the needs of consumers.

Effective leadership and supervision is essential to insuring that this collaboration takes place. The effective leader helps team members to value interdependence through mutual assistance, cooperation, and support. The leader continually insures that everyone understands the mission of the program, their individual roles, and the goals of each consumer. In ACT practice, the master's-level clinician typically doubles as service provider and team leader, and shares clinical oversight with the psychiatrist. The team leader is the primary person in charge of team process and function. The team leader is responsible for (a) insuring fidelity to the ACT model, (b) enhancing the clinical skills of each team member, (c) monitoring how time is spent, and (d) offering feedback regarding team interaction. This last element is particularly important.

The interactional behavior of an ACT team can be assessed and managed within the framework of group dynamics principles (Stewart, Manz, & Sims, 1999). The team leader must effectively manage the contributions of the members, making sure that everyone is heard and that members feel comfortable expressing differences of opinion. The team leader ensures that issues are explored in enough depth so that all potentially useful data are gathered and then used to inform decision making. The leader must also skillfully facilitate the team's integration and application of their diverse disciplines and skills.

Group dynamics also are affected by how long the team has been working together. Groups are thought to go through various phases described by Tuckman (1965) as the *forming, storming, norming,* and *performing* stages. Given high staff turnover, the team may cycle through these phases several times during the course of an individual's treatment. Effective team leadership recognizes the rewards and perils of storming and aims to establish a culture of sharing, discovery, and growth. New team members are hired as much for their clinical skills as their practical life experience, their enthusiasm for working in groups, and their commitment to involving consumers in making decisions about their treatment. Norms are established through careful fidelity to the ACT model (Teague, Bond, & Drake, 1998). A fully empowered team embraces an assertive philosophy and does not need constant direction from the leader. Team members develop protocols for discussing their improvement strategies and conducting team-building sessions.

CASE EXAMPLE

The person described below illustrates some of the compelling problems experienced by ACT consumers. The example demonstrates how members of an ACT team work in an integrated manner over a long period of time to address problems and promote recovery. The person in this example has been involved in ACT for seven years, and thus offers a longitudinal examination of team development and client progress.

At the point of referral to ACT in 2004, Mr. H. was a 39-year-old single African American male, diagnosed with schizoaffective disorder. He exhibited symptoms including persecutory and self-referential delusions, agitation, depressed mood, and an inability to control his anger. He was on probation for assault. His illness had taken a chronic course starting at age 18 with numerous periods of symptom exacerbation, crisis visits, and involuntary psychiatric hospitalizations. He had been bounced from one mental health program to another due to his angry outbursts. He was estranged from his family of origin. His two brothers were incarcerated, and his mother, who had severely abused him as a child, had moved from New Jersey to Florida.

Mr. H. dropped out of school in the ninth grade and did not learn to read or write. He used cannabis, alcohol, and inhalants regularly from age 10 to 13, which contributed to his lack of achievement, but then he stopped using completely. He had brief periods of employment doing physical labor, but could not sustain a job due to interpersonal conflicts and problems with authority figures. He had brief romantic encounters with women and fathered a child who was given up for adoption.

TEAM PROCESS: THE ENGAGEMENT PHASE

When someone is referred for ACT services, the team leader and possibly a second team member reach out to the person to start the engagement process. Enrollment in ACT is voluntary, yet people who could most benefit from ACT services are often skeptical about receiving help. Initial contacts occur wherever the person prefers, and may take place in the hospital or at an agreed-upon community setting. The engagement process may continue for quite a while before the person officially decides to join the program. On first encounter, Mr. H. expressed hopelessness, defeat, and suspicion. Thus, it was very important for the team leader to be open, nonjudgmental, and flexible in order to gain his trust and build his motivation for participation in the service. Once he was enrolled, it took a number of additional months and a variety of strategies for Mr. H. to engage with other members of his ACT team. All team members employed a common set of transdisciplinary strategies, including (a) offering unconditional positive regard, (b) focusing on his life goals, (c) empowering him to set his own priorities and direct his treatment, and (d) addressing his immediate needs for housing, food shopping, and transportation. At any time, any available team member worked on whatever issue he presented. This included promptly responding with help to situations he perceived as emergencies. After three months of regular contact by multiple members, Mr. H. was able to verbalize his appreciation of the ACT team and what they were doing for him.

TEAM PROCESS: COMPREHENSIVE ASSESSMENT AND RECOVERY PLANNING

As positive and respectful relationships grow, the team is able to develop a clear picture of the consumer's perspective on his/her strengths, problems, concerns, preferences, and life goals. Initially, Mr. H. was focused on successfully staying out of the hospital and completing probation for physical assault. He also expressed interest in getting a job and in finding a new girlfriend. All team members became aware of these personally relevant goals through direct contact with Mr. H. and through team discussions.

Once a consumer is enrolled in ACT services, team specialists conduct discipline-specific assessments including psychiatric, nursing, substance use, and vocational evaluations. These assessments highlight the strengths and problems related to achieving personal goals. After Mr. H. participated in each of these assessments, he met with one member of the team to review all the data. This person then helped Mr. H. develop a recovery plan documenting his goals and aspirations. The plan also identified intervention strategies, which the full team then implemented.

Over the course of seven years of treatment, many assessments and plans were developed and evaluated. As his initial goals were accomplished, Mr. H. identified longer-term priorities for his recovery, such as achieving successful employment and a satisfying romantic relationship. Over time, he developed new skills, experienced success in work and love, and gained insights into his thoughts and feelings. Mr. H. worked on overcoming his traumatic memories of abuse by his mother, was able to forgive her, and reestablished contact with her before she died. Given a history of similar family problems, the peer specialist was instrumental in helping him talk about his family, develop new insights, and work through his grief.

TEAM PROCESS: ACTIVE TREATMENT
AND REHABILITATION PHASE

The ACT team meets daily to briefly review every person on the caseload. Consumers who are new or who are having difficulty are discussed in more depth. The last person to see a consumer usually presents the update. Together, the team then develops plans for the rest of the day, assigning visits and tasks. Whenever a new assessment or plan is developed, the team discusses who will do what to meet the goals and objectives as outlined. When specific credentials are required to complete a task or intervention, such as medication administration or psychotherapy, the person with the appropriate background is designated. If a more generalized intervention is required, such as psychoeducation, skills teaching, or emotional support, team members take turns assisting. This offers the consumer a variety of interpersonal experiences and facilitates a multidisciplinary evaluation of the person's progress and interventions. This process also reinforces teamwork and reduces the emotional burden on any one member when crises or setbacks occur. It also enables the consumer to establish a relationship with the team rather than one individual member. This approach reduces problems when a team member terminates her or his employment from an ACT position.

Meeting on a daily basis also helps the team respond to incidents in a timely fashion. On one occasion, Mr. H. lost his housing. The team discussed options for temporary placement. The task of making a housing connection was assigned to the mental health advocate, and Mr. H. was housed promptly, reducing the risk for relapse. When he stopped medication, the nurses would visit Mr. H. more frequently and identify early signs of symptom recurrence, which they brought to his attention. These interventions always led him to restart medication. Over time he learned to talk about side effects and thoughts about discontinuing medication before doing so, which allowed for collaboration on changes in his medication regimen without significant gaps in adherence.

Through ongoing discussions, the team and Mr. H. could clearly see that his aggressive behavior interfered with his personal goals of living in the community, working a job, and engaging in satisfying interpersonal relationships. Using their specific areas of expertise, the team formulated various interventions to help Mr. H. manage his anger. All team members were actively involved in implementing these intervention strategies. The clinician taught Mr. H. a variety of anger management skills, including self-monitoring of emotions, and self-soothing techniques such as distraction, avoidance of triggering situations, and positive self-talk. The psychiatrist prescribed medications and helped Mr. H. identify beliefs about himself and others that led to medication non-adherence and aggression. The nurses engaged in collaborative medication management of his distressing symptoms and dysfunction. When angry outbursts resulted in crises, other team members stepped in to offer support, guidance, and skills teaching, all the while driving home the idea that this behavior kept Mr. H. from achieving his most important goals of work and love.

Mr. H. had frequent outbursts with team members, which led to team discussions about how to respond to this behavior. Although each team member understood that they served as his support system, and needed to help him address his frustrations so they would not build up, there was disagreement regarding how to construct consequences. Some team members felt that firm limit-setting should be applied, so that whenever an angry outburst occurred, he would receive unpleasant consequences or even be excluded from contact until he calmed down. Other members of the team however, felt that they should be more accepting of his outbursts by playing the role of "emotional punching bag," so that later they could review the situation with him and help him understand how this behavior impeded his success. The team leader helped build consensus by suggesting both strategies be tried and evaluated in the spirit of testing hypotheses about what worked. One thing that everyone agreed on was that over time, he developed alternative modes of handling his frustrations.

A priority for Mr. H. was having a girlfriend. During the early course of treatment he dated a few women but had several verbal fights and a physical altercation with one of them that ended the relationship. Then, five years ago, Mr. H. met a woman who was also an ACT consumer, and this relationship has survived many threats: chiefly his anger management problems and her family's disapproval of him. Although Mr. H. did not expressly ask for help in coping with this conflict, several team members wanted to help him improve his interpersonal communication skills. Others on the team were less willing to intervene in a matter that they perceived as private. However, as each member of the couple was seriously emotionally impacted by their conflicts, putting them at risk for relapse, the team resolved to work with both consumers individually and together, teaching them skills to build and maintain a healthy relationship.

Another thing Mr. H. wanted to do was work. He obtained some jobs but none of them lasted more than a few weeks. His illiteracy contributed to some of these failures. The team worked with him weekly for several months using a commercially available literacy program called "Hooked on Phonics." He was eventually able to read and write well enough to take public transportation for the very first time in his life. Mr. H. also received supported employment services, initially working with the vocational specialist to find a job he liked, and then with the whole team to support him through times of frustration. His employer was also included in discussions about how to help accommodate his needs to calm down and sometimes take time off to regain his emotional balance.

CHALLENGES TO TEAMWORK

PHILOSOPHICAL CONFLICTS

Given the interdisciplinary nature of ACT teams and the complex problems experienced by consumers of this service, there are numerous opportunities for team conflict that must be managed. Themes, many of which have been illustrated in the case example, include consumer independence and self-determination, natural consequences, harm reduction, and professional boundaries. Team discussions often center on these themes and are guided by some overarching principles and goals, including informed choice, recovery, community integration, and normalization.

When consumers make poor choices, teams often struggle with the extent to which they should allow natural consequences to occur. Effective teams value calculated risk-taking because it often leads to growth and change. But it can also lead to negative consequences that can harm the person and their relationships. For instance, Mr. H. wanted to take medication in smaller doses or to try medication holidays. Some team members rejected this idea and recommended eyes-on medication monitoring to avoid noncompliance. Others preferred letting him try these changes and watching for an increase in symptoms before intervening. Since the psychiatrist is clinically responsible for prescribing medication, he worked directly on this issue with Mr. H., using cognitive-behavioral strategies. Together they evaluated the risk–benefit of reducing the dose and came to a collaborative agreement that Mr. H.'s preferences would be honored as long as he was willing to participate in more frequent doctor visits, self-monitor his symptoms, and inform the team of any increase in symptoms.

Tension between fostering recovery by building self-reliance and fostering safety by offering intensive support is always present. Even though client self-determination is valued, sometimes team members take this to an extreme, insisting that if the client does not ask for help, then none should be given. As was described earlier, Mr. H. was having trouble with his relationship with his girlfriend. It was clear to some on the team that helping him develop interpersonal skills would promote better communication between the couple. Some members wanted to discuss this with Mr. H., while others felt this was not an area in which they should get involved because it was not "clinically significant." In the balance, the team members agreed that helping in this way served to promote Mr. H.'s stated goal.

Although it was not an issue for Mr. H., consumers with substance-use disorders present potential conflict over how to respond to lapses in use. A progressive substance-use disorders specialist will help the team understand that lapses and even relapse are part of the process of recovery from addiction, and should be anticipated rather than punished. Also, there may be disagreement over when and how to use harm reduction strategies rather than insist on abstinence. Since ACT is deemed for people who have not succeeded with conventional help, it is critical that team members remain open to trying new strategies and embrace emerging as well as evidence-based best practices.

Openness and empathy are required for effective teamwork in this program setting. Some people may be less empathetic to the consumer's struggles and become hardened to the consumer's needs. Others become overly concerned and offer support indiscriminately, even when the consumer might be able to do things for themselves. There needs to be an understanding of the balance between self-determination and protection; between dependence and independence. Teams that work well together engage in open, dialectical discussion of these positions. Over time, all tend to become more empathetic and also more accepting of consumer behavior. Perhaps this is due in part to a growing shared experience among consumers and co-workers, affording a stronger, more personal connection among them. As the team works through conflicts and embraces the principles and practices of the ACT model, members begin to operate in a trans-disciplinary manner, transcending their individual disciplinary roles, and taking on tasks and perspectives that promote effective team discussion and function. This fosters an "eyes on the prize" mentality that serves to invigorate motivation to work together to resolve differences and reach consensus on solutions that are both effective and creative.

DIFFERING VIEWS ON RECOVERY

ACT has been criticized for being coercive by focusing on treatment adherence and avoiding hospitalizations (Gomory, 2001). From a medical perspective, these outcomes are the primary indicators of recovery. However, consumers often define recovery very differently, focusing more on quality of life issues and successful participation in normal adult roles such as employee, student, spouse, and citizen. This calls into question the extent to which ACT can assume a recovery orientation that empowers consumers. A recent qualitative study by Salyers and colleagues (2011) found that ACT teams do indeed differ in their use of recovery-oriented practices and behaviors. ACT teams must work diligently to insure that organizational and community environments are conducive to recovery. Teams must learn how to preserve and incorporate the unique perceptive of peer specialists rather than co-opt their input. Staff attitudes toward consumers (coaching vs. parenting), expectations of consumer self-determination, the degree to which recovery language is employed, and the processes associated with working with consumers, all affect the team's ability to overcome medical model traditions and promote recovery.

TURNOVER

For many consumers, the ACT team constitutes their primary support system. Inevitable staff turnover can be upsetting, even when special care is taken to ease the process of termination. Over the course of seven years, Mr. H.'s entire ACT team, except for the psychiatrist, turned over at least once. The team leader position turned over twice. Changes in staff require adjustment and accommodation of new personalities, differing work experiences, and varying treatment philosophies. Teams with high turnover also experience frequent storming and norming phases. Regular team meetings develop common ground by offering opportunities for sharing and discussing different treatment strategies. An effective team leader also fosters accommodation and adaptation of team members to new circumstances and new staff. Cross-training of staff can ease the burden of a staff vacancy in the short term, and a strong new-employee orientation helps new members fit into the ACT culture and workflow expeditiously and efficiently.

The team has diligently helped Mr. H. understand and expect staff turnover while helping him develop his own natural support system. Yet, despite his own support network, Mr. H. has strong reservations about his transition out of ACT, because he believes it is the family he never had. The team also feels like Mr. H. is family. Some of this sentiment is a reflection of the strong therapeutic relationships that have developed between individual team members and Mr. H. These sentiments are also fostered by the flexible boundaries between consumer and provider that come from caring for the whole person, not just the illness. Team members truly care about Mr. H. and will undoubtedly experience his program exit as a personal loss. This situation makes it difficult to transition Mr. H. to conventional services and natural supports, yet all understand the importance of promoting this transition.

CONCLUSION

Mr. H.'s team has experienced significant changes since its inception seven years ago, but its current stability can be attributed to strong leadership, hiring the right people, and improved systems support for implementing evidence-based best practices. The latter includes a comprehensive state-wide monitoring program insuring program fidelity to the ACT model, as well as training in such practices as motivational interviewing, cognitive behavioral therapy (CBT), illness management and recovery, integrated co-occurring disorders treatment, and wellness recovery action planning. Of course, the diligence with which training is applied in practice at the local level is pivotal to achieving successful outcomes. Mr. H.'s team has taken particular interest in learning, practicing, and disseminating information about CBT (Pinninti, Fisher, Thompson, & Steer, 2010). Team members, including the psychiatrist, a nurse, and two peer advocates, have presented at a national ACT conference on the use of CBT with ACT consumers.

Over the past decade, the changing focus of behavioral health systems toward recovery-oriented services has provided a hopeful framework for all providers and particularly for ACT members. Seeing and believing that people with long-term mental illnesses can improve their functioning and live successfully in integrated settings in the community presents an unwavering goal for the team's efforts. The use of effective interventions undoubtedly increases job satisfaction as ACT consumers experience improved outcomes with these practices. Thus, additional evidence-based practices and wellness strategies are now included in ACT services to help people improve their integration into the community, expand their social connections, and regain their physical, emotional, and spiritual health. While the training and supervision of new practices challenge ACT teams to learn while providing services, the implementation of additional evidence-based practices has become integral to enhancing team development and program outcomes. Effective teams nurture a culture of continuous learning and self-improvement. This promotes their ability to view interventions as hypotheses to be tested in practice, which in turn develops the team's capacity for evaluating and modifying approaches until proven effective.

As the ACT team in this example has grown and changed, so, too, has Mr. H. He has avoided psychiatric hospitalization and criminal arrest. He is in a long-term committed relationship and has been working steadily for several years. He has come to terms with his abusive past and reconciled with his mother. His reading has improved, and he uses public transportation independently. He appreciates his vulnerability to stress and negative thinking and has developed coping skills to manage his emotions. Even though he is not totally free of symptoms and problems, he is hopeful that his recovery will continue, whether he stays with the ACT team or moves on to less intensive services.

REFERENCES

Allness, D. J., & Knoedler, W. H. (2003). *A Manual for ACT start-up: Based on the PACT Model of Community Treatment for Persons with Severe and Persistent Mental Illnesses.* Arlington, VA: NAMI.

Bellack, A. S., Mueser, K. T., Gingerich, S., & Agresta, J. (1997). *Social Skills Training for Schizophrenia. A Step-by-Step Guide.* New York: The Guilford Press.

Bond, G., Drake, R., Mueser, K., & Latimer, E. (2001). Assertive community treatment for people with severe mental illness: Critical ingredients and impact on patients. *Disease Management and Health Outcomes, 9,* 141–159.

Burns, T. (2009). End of the road for treatment-as-usual studies? *The British Journal of* Psychiatry, *195,* 5–6.

Burns, T. (2010). The rise and fall of assertive community treatment? *International Review of Psychiatry, 22,* 130–137.

Corrigan, P., Mueser, K., Bond, G., Drake, R., & Solomon, P. (2008). *Principles and Practice of Psychiatric Rehabilitation: An Empirical Approach.* The Guilford Press, New York.

Deegan, P. E., (1988) Recovery: The lived experience of rehabilitation. *Psychosocial Rehabilitation Journal, 9*(4), 11–19.

Dieterich, M., Irving, C., Park, B., & Marshall, M. (2010). *Intensive Case Management for Severe Mental Illness. The Cochrane Collaboration.* John Wiley & Sons, Ltd. Retrieved June 1, 2011 at http://www. thecochranelibrary.com.

Dixon, L., Dickerson, F., Bellack, A., Bennett, M., Dickinson, D., Goldberg, R., et al. (2010). The 2009 Schizophrenia PORT psychosocial treatment recommendations and summary statements. *Schizophrenia Bulletin, 36,* 48–70.

Gomory, T. (2001). A critique of the effectiveness of assertive community treatment. *Psychiatric Services, 52,* 1394–1395.

Marx, A., Test, M., & Stein, L. (1973). Extra-hospital management of severe mental illness. *Archives of General Psychiatry, 29,* 505–511.

New Freedom Commission on Mental Health (2003). *Achieving the Promise: Transforming Mental Health Care in America: Final Report* (DHHS Publication No. SMA-033832). Rockville, MD: DHHS.

Phillips, S., Burns, B., Edgar, E., Mueser, K., Linkins, K., Rosenheck, R., et al. (2001). Moving assertive treatment into standard practice. *Psychiatric Services, 52,* 771–779.

Pinninti, N. R., Fisher, J., Thompson, K., & Steer, R. (2010). Feasibility and usefulness of training assertive community treatment team in cognitive behavioral therapy. *Community Mental Health Journal, 46*(4), 337–341.

Rosen, A., Mueser, K., & Teesson, M. (2007). Assertive community treatment—Issues from scientific and clinical literature with implications for practice. *Journal of Rehabilitation Research & Development, 44,* 813–826.

Salyers, M., Masterton, T., Fekete, D., Picone, J., & Bond, G. (1998). Transferring clients from intensive case management: Impact on client functioning. *American Journal of Orthopsychiatry, 68,* 233–245.

Salyers, M., Stull, L., Rollins, A., & Hopper, K. (2011). The work of recovery on two assertive community treatment teams. *Administration Policy and Mental Health Services Research, 38,* 169–180.

Stein, L., & Santos, A. (1998) *Assertive Community Treatment of Persons with Severe Mental Illness.* New York: W. W. Norton.

Stewart, G. L., Manz, C. C., & Sims, H. P. (1999). *Team Work and Group Dynamics.* New York: John Wiley & Sons.

Teague, G. B., Bond, G. R., & Drake, R. E. (1998). Program fidelity in assertive community treatment. Development and use of a measure. *American Journal of Orthopsychiatry, 68,* 216–232.

Tuckman, B. W. (1965). Developmental sequence in small groups. *Psychological Bulletin, 63*(6), 384–399.

CHAPTER 21

CRISIS INTERVENTION TEAMS

A Boundary-Spanning Collaboration Between the Law Enforcement and Mental Health Communities

DAVID P. KASICK AND CHRISTOPHER D. BOWLING

CASE EXAMPLE

At 2:43 a.m. on a warm summer Saturday night, the distraught mother of a 23-year-old man called 911 due to his aggressive and belligerent behavior. The mother explained to the police dispatcher that she had not seen her son in four days, and that he had abruptly returned home several minutes before in a highly agitated state. He was unkempt, sweating profusely, wearing only his underpants, ranting loudly and incoherently about "demons" and "being chased by spies," and appeared to not have been sleeping for several days. She reported further that her son had not seen his psychiatrist in over a month, and she was concerned that he had recently stopped taking his prescribed medications. While on the phone with the dispatcher, his mother watched him cut the power cord to the television with a pair of scissors, saying something about "not being watched anymore."

Several police officers were dispatched to the scene, including two officers who were members of the department's Crisis Intervention Team (CIT). Officers proceeded to encounter the man lying down in the back yard of the home, praying loudly and wildly flailing his arms in the air. Although he was initially suspicious and hostile toward the officers, the CIT officers were able to engage and verbally de-escalate him over the next several minutes. One of the CIT officers had encountered the man at his apartment a year before when he had overdosed in a suicide attempt. The man seemed to vaguely remember this officer and the rapport they had established during this previous encounter.

Recognizing the signs and symptoms of a decompensated mental illness, the officers discussed going to the local mental health crisis facility with the man. He was agreeable to being transported there by police, saying that he would "feel safe with their protection." Upon arrival at the crisis facility, officers conveyed the incident details as well as their observations of the man's behavior to the crisis workers. Following further triage care at the crisis facility, he was admitted to a psychiatric hospital for inpatient care later that morning.

INTRODUCTION

Over the past 20 years, the exponential growth of the Crisis Intervention Team (CIT) model reflects an increasing awareness for the need to develop collaborative approaches to mental health work at the first opportunity that many acutely mentally ill individuals have to receive help: through contact with law enforcement officers. CIT programs generally comprise front-line patrol officers within a law enforcement agency who have received additional training in identifying, assessing, de-escalating, and resolving situations in which law enforcement has encountered an individual in a mental health crisis. Through improving integration of roles and relationships between the criminal justice and mental health communities, CIT aims to simultaneously improve attention to the needs of the mentally ill, without compromising the goals of public safety (Morrissey et al. 2009). These first responders become both generalists and specialists in that they continue to perform general police duties, but are also sent as police specialists to service calls involving persons in a mental health crisis.

When calls to police dispatchers are thought to involve a person experiencing a mental health crisis, CIT trained officers are selected to respond. Linking officers who have the most training and expertise in working with at-risk consumers was designed to have a positive impact on the safety and outcomes of such encounters. After initial conceptualization and success of CIT in Memphis, Tennessee, the subsequent evolution of the "Memphis Model" has since been repeatedly adapted and replicated by individual communities, leading to a national and international network of CIT programs. Developing, training, and maintaining CIT programs at the local level has led to partnerships between law enforcement and several key community stakeholders, including mental health consumers and families, mental health advocacy groups, and local mental health treatment providers. Joining forces to span the traditional boundaries between the criminal justice and mental health communities has led to numerous perceived benefits, as well as an emerging evidence base that suggests that CIT is contributing to achieving mutually safe and effective outcomes for individuals in crisis and the police officers encountering them.

HISTORY OF CIT

The birth of the modern crisis intervention team model has been widely attributed to the program developed by the Memphis (TN), Police Department in 1988. In September 1987, Memphis police officers were involved in the fatal shooting of a mentally ill individual who, after cutting himself with a knife while possibly suicidal, was threatening officers and unable to comply with their instructions. Although review of the incident did not find the officers guilty of any criminal wrongdoing, an analysis of the factors surrounding the incident elicited the need to develop further training for officers to better understand the behavioral manifestations of mental illness and their potential impact on police encounters.

Law enforcement agencies have long recognized the likelihood that police officers will find themselves in situations involving individuals displaying aberrant behaviors driven by active, severe mental illnesses (Bittner, 1967). In 1996, a survey of larger urban police departments suggested that the number of police contacts and investigations thought to involve an individual with a mental illness was approximately seven percent (Deane et al. 1999). At that time, fewer than half of the survey respondents indicated that their department had any type of specialized mental health response for such situations. These situations commonly afford the officer to exercise significant discretion in deciding how to resolve the encounter, balancing the need to protect the welfare of the larger community as well as protecting citizens with mental illness who cannot care for themselves (Lamb et al. 2002).

Prior to the late 1980s and the development of the CIT model, standard police academy training for law enforcement officers in working with individuals with mental illness was highly variable and oftentimes sparse. Academy classroom hours were generally devoted to core topics such as response to and management of criminal activity and disorder, police professionalism, understanding and application of criminal and traffic laws, legal issues, use of weapons, driving skills, and defensive tactics. These core elements often overshadowed more in-depth exploration of understanding individuals with characteristics that could lead to a wide range of behaviors potentially warranting the assistance or attention of law enforcement officers in the community. For example, in 2006, the minimum standard in the State of Ohio for training peace officers was a minimum total of 16 hours of training (out of 582 total hours) for dealing with "special populations," which included individuals with mental illness, developmental and physical disabilities, and physical handicaps. Beyond these minimum requirements for training at the basic academy level, the growth of the CIT model has thus provided a continuing educational framework for additional officer training and skill development.

The timing of the development of the CIT movement coincided, perhaps not surprisingly, with the growing, unintended consequences of the deinstitutionalization movement. As the population of individuals with serious mentally illness in the United States both grew and shifted from hospital to community settings over the past 40 years, funding and service shortfalls, including the closure of inpatient psychiatric treatment beds, led to many mentally ill individuals' receiving significantly less support than in previous decades (Lamb and Weinberger 2005). As opposed to being treated in asylums or hospitals a generation before, the closure of these inpatient beds was offset by growing numbers of seriously mentally ill individuals being housed and treated in jails and other correctional settings. When coupled with the added vulnerabilities of homelessness and addictive disorders, the opportunity for mentally ill individuals to have street-level contact with law enforcement increased, leading to police officers becoming a primary referral source for psychiatric emergency facilities (Borum et al. 1998). Other outcomes of such encounters could include criminal arrest, many of which may have been misdemeanor charges stemming from behaviors driven by undertreated mental illness. With this transfer of serious behavioral pathology from behind the doors of the traditional mental health treatment system to the street and the criminal justice system, police agencies and communities recognized the need for more sophisticated training and community partnerships to reflect the diverse and changing needs of the population served by police officers. Interest in CIT as a mechanism for facilitating jail diversion has also grown (see Munetz, Chapter 30, this textbook, Jail Diversion: Using the Sequential Intercept Model").

CIT PROGRAM STRUCTURE AND CURRICULUM DESIGN

Following the success of the initial Crisis Intervention Team in Memphis, other communities and law enforcement agencies across the country began developing their own versions of crisis intervention training. Many of these programs were founded on grassroots efforts at the local level to capture the unique needs of the local law enforcement agency, the local mental health system, and the specific population of the community being served. Conversely, other agencies participated as members of statewide programs (in the State of Georgia, for example) driven by a centralized, top-down approach with a common curriculum and administrative structure, (Oliva and Compton 2008).

As the various curricula were adapted to meet the goals of the stakeholders, many agencies continue to refer to the elements and structure first conceptualized in Memphis, leading to the concept of the "Memphis Model" (Dupont et al. 2007). The goals of this model emphasize CIT programs as being "more than just training," with an focus on improving officer and consumer safety and redirecting mentally ill individuals from the criminal justice system to the healthcare system (Dupont et al. 2007). Individual programs continue to pragmatically weave the core ongoing, operational, and sustaining elements suggested by the Memphis Model into their programs to meet the unique and dynamic needs of their communities.

Ongoing program elements emphasized in the Memphis Model include active partnerships between leadership of law enforcement agencies—for example, police departments and sheriff's offices, members of the judiciary, and corrections agencies—with members of the advocacy community and mental health professionals. Coordinators from each group are identified and act as liaisons to each of the other key stakeholder groups. Joining the individuals who interact on the front lines through encountering, de-escalating, transport and disposition, risk assessment, and care provision, with advocates who are able to humanize and promote the interests of consumers, is felt to be critical in the planning and implementation of policies guiding the development of local CIT programs. The mutual benefits of education, training, and shared community ownership in crisis situations are difficult to capitalize upon without the existence of such partnerships (Dupont et al. 2007).

Operational elements set forth in the Memphis Model center around policies and procedures within law enforcement and mental health agencies felt necessary to effectively handle each crisis situation (Dupont et al. 2007). Adequate numbers of patrol officers should be trained to have around-the-clock availability. Accordingly, all police dispatchers should also be trained to properly identify a mental health crisis and route the nearest CIT officer to the scene. Ideally, a range of inpatient and outpatient referral options should be available to officers, with specific policies in place to facilitate easily accessible, immediate mental health care when necessary. Turnaround time for CIT officers transporting an individual to mental health care settings should be minimal and not exceed the time needed to process a criminal arrest, so as to remove the potential for jail booking to be preferred as less time-intensive option.

Patrol officer CIT training under the Memphis Model focuses on building crisis de-escalation skills through experience, ideas, and information from a variety of individuals from the mental health, law enforcement, and advocacy communities (Dupont et al. 2007). Volunteer officers apply for training and are selected for a 40-hour course.

Based on a review of training schedules for programs around the United States, CIT core curricula typically consist of the following major categories: mental illnesses and their treatments, co-occurring disorders such as substance use disorders and personality disorders, interaction with family members and consumers, legal issues, the local community mental health system, and de-escalation skills.

Program curricula vary in the organization of content; for example, mental illness diagnostic terminology or psychotropic medications and their effects may be presented in an aggregate fashion or be broken into blocks corresponding to major diagnostic categories. Some programs include specific blocks on suicide risk assessment and child/adolescent mental health issues. Substance use disorders are the most commonly presented co-occurring disorder. Programs may also provide training and education on those who have either independent or co-occurring mental illnesses and developmental disabilities, helping law enforcement officers understand the differences between these conditions and the entities that that provide services to these persons.

CIT core training curricula provides methods for law enforcement officers to interact with family members of those who have a mental illness and with consumers of mental health services. These methods include panel discussions, facility visits, and riding in the field with mental health case managers. Panel discussions are held in the classroom, and consumers and family members have distinct times to present their information to the law enforcement officers in the class. When resources permit, law enforcement officers ride in the community with case managers from mental health service–providing agencies. The goal for riding with case managers is to let law enforcement officers observe case-manager interaction with clients to provide a context for the de-escalation skills to be taught and to allow law enforcement officers to observe persons with mental illnesses when they are not in crisis. Interacting with persons with a mental illness who are not in crisis provides an additional perspective to law enforcement officers, as officers are typically called when a crisis state exists. Officers learn about effective communication skills by listening to consumer perspectives and by observing the communication and interaction methods used by case managers with clients.

The legal aspects of local civil commitment laws are part of the core training curricula. Topical matter includes a review of the state's statutes and methods for taking a person into emergency custody to have the person evaluated by a medical professional, any procedures that have been codified by the state to take a person into emergency custody, and client rights. Law enforcement officers learn how to write effective probable cause statements and how to take a person into custody and deliver that person to a place of care and safety.

The final large block of training consists of training officers in the use of de-escalation skills and then having the officers demonstrate those skills in a practicum. Verbal de-escalation patterns and communication methodologies are provided during core training sessions and are taught either as part of an action-response framework or independently. Additional framing can be used to help law enforcement officers tailor their responses based on their observations of the subject's mood, thoughts, anxiety, and personality at the scene of a call for service. Once law enforcement officers receive the designed de-escalation training, a practicum is often utilized to allow the officers to apply the newly learned skills in a practical setting. The practicum method most often used is role-play. Role-play scenarios are built with guidelines and rule sets for role players so that law enforcement officers experience success when they us the taught de-escalation skills. CIT programs use a variety of role players, to include mental health professionals, medical actors, experienced Crisis Intervention Team officers, family members, or consumers. The role-plays differ from program to program and in design. Some scenarios are designed to allow a specified team of law enforcement officers to complete a single role-play scenario, and others allow multiple teams of officers to complete a single scenario, switching when the allotted time has expired. When the role-play is completed, debriefing of the scenario takes place and permits direct learning for participants and vicarious learning for those who were observing the role play.

Reciprocal training for the course faculty is also recommended under the Memphis Model, including a patrol ride-along "in order to fully understand the complexities and differences that exist between mental health care and law enforcement" (Dupont et al. 2007). Graduating officers from many programs receive a special CIT uniform pin, which elevates awareness of the CIT program and signifies their CIT training status to fellow officers, consumers, and the general public.

CURRENT STATE OF CIT PROGRAMS

By 2006, there were an estimated 400 law enforcement agencies with active CIT programs across the United States (Watson et al. 2008). Although the common goals of improving safety, outcomes, and jail diversion may exist across agencies, the specific policies, needs, and challenges surrounding sustaining individual CIT programs may vary widely. CIT programs exist in small rural sheriff's offices, large urban metropolitan police departments, suburban police departments, and university and airport police departments. Each setting brings significant variations in the diversity of population, resources available in the community, and number and density of officers working in a given area at any given time. Accordingly, providing adequate training to the number of officers and dispatchers requiring to provide 24/7 CIT availability can present hardships in small departments needing to provide coverage for staff attending 40 hours of training (Compton et al. 2010). Implementation in areas without access to a psychiatric emergency receiving facility with a "no refusal" policy, or in rural areas with limited proximal mental health resources, can lead to challenges in sustaining functional CIT programs (Compton et al. 2010).

Other examples of collaborative response to mental health crises exist outside of the CIT police-based, police officer response model. Non-sworn police-based mental health employees have been used in some locales to provide on-scene and telephone consultations to sworn police officers, as have mobile mental health crisis teams deployed independently through the local community health system (Borum et al. 1998). Despite the growing popularity of the CIT model, more study is needed to clarify the precise advantages or disadvantages it may confer in comparison to other modes of crisis response.

GENERAL IMPACT OF CIT ON STAKEHOLDER CULTURE CHANGE

Given the potential for CIT programs to impact community mental health work, and the inherent boundary spanning partnerships behind each program, the academic community has begun to accumulate an evidence base to study and support the growth of the CIT phenomenon. The parallel evolution of research partnerships between local police departments in Memphis, Tennessee; Akron, Ohio; Chicago, Illinois; as well as at the state level in Georgia and Florida, with corresponding local university faculty, has led them to begin to collect data and examine the factors thought to contribute to the anecdotal success, as the deployment of CIT transitions from a common-sense response to a community need to an evidence-driven, sustainable model worthy of financial support.

Programs and their stakeholders have organized at the national and international level, with yearly conferences since 2005 that disseminate innovations in teaching techniques and tactical practices. As a vehicle for collaborative research between community and university based mental health professionals, further study of CIT program outcomes related to training differences, community differences, disposition of interactions, costs, and benefits of law enforcement and community safety all appear to be viable avenues of outcomes-oriented research (Morrissey et al. 2009).

Compton and colleagues (2008) conducted a systematic review of the available research conducted on CIT, noting that compared to the enthusiasm surrounding the opportunity for collaboration between stakeholders, as well as the resources being devoted to CIT training, there remain relatively limited outcomes research available. Much of the current research has been done by authors from mental health backgrounds, rather than criminologists or social scientists. Of the available studies, Compton suggests that CIT may have positive effects ranging from officers' attitudes and training, to jail diversion and improved consumer outcomes. Among the current studies, officer-level and system-level outcomes such as dispositions of police calls eliciting a CIT response and pre-booking jail diversion are better represented than patient-level outcomes. Critics of the rapid spread of the CIT concept across the United States cite a lack of rigorous outcomes data beyond descriptive evidence, as well as the lack of universal access to adequate receiving facilities serving as a transport destination for officers considering jail alternatives, which is thought to be a key to the initial success in Memphis (Geller 2008).

More research is also needed into how CIT may affect the operation of local mental health systems. For example, officers may be aware that they are interacting with a mentally ill individual, but may perceive barriers which lead to the belief that criminal arrest is a more reliable disposition. Such barriers could include long waits to access mental health emergency services, more rigid mental health criteria for holding individuals, and problems with information exchange between officers and mental health crisis workers that could lead to quick release (Lamb et al. 2002). Though uniting and facilitating regular communication among stakeholders, CIT could plausibly impact the coordination of solutions for these and other common problems officers report when accessing local emergency mental health resources.

CIT IMPACT ON POLICE OFFICERS AND LAW ENFORCEMENT CULTURE

CIT training has attempted to mitigate the historical challenges perceived by police officers in managing situations with individuals in mental health crisis. Having exposure to CIT training led Memphis officers to perceive that they were more effective at meeting the needs of mentally ill individuals in crisis, at keeping the mentally ill out of jail, minimizing the amount of officer down-time while dealing with mental health crisis calls, all while maintaining community safety (Borum et al. 1998).

Police officers have several options for how to resolve dispatched calls or encounters with individuals possibly experiencing the effects of a mental illness, including leaving the individual at the scene, transporting them to a hospital or treatment facility, or transporting them to jail. At times, legal obligations do not preclude officer discretion (e.g., "must arrest" situations). Ritter et al. examined the role that both dispatcher call coding and CIT training appeared to have in Akron, Ohio, on the disposition of each encounter, finding that both dispatch codes and officers' on-scene assessments had an impact on transport decisions (Ritter et al. 2011). Specifically, calls dispatched as a "suspected suicide" or "mental disturbance" were more likely to result in transport to treatment than calls dispatched as "needing assistance," "disturbance," "suspicious person," "assault," "suspicion of a crime," and "meet a citizen." Ritter and colleagues also found that CIT officer-recognition of specific signs and symptoms of mental or physical illness emphasized in CIT training, or other issues such as substance abuse and nonadherence to medication, led to increased rates of transport to treatment, regardless of how the call was dispatched. Their study underscored the importance of dispatcher training as a component of CIT training, as well as support for the concept that CIT officers are more likely to consider treatment options over other potential outcomes.

Other studies have similarly concluded that CIT has led to improvement in officers' understanding and beliefs about specific mental illnesses, and has led to increased referrals to psychiatric services (Broussard et al. 2010, Compton et al. 2006, Demir et al. 2009, Dupont and Cochran 2000). CIT training is also thought to have increased the safety of both officers and individuals through a reduction of officer injuries, and may lead to a reduction in the use of force between officers and individuals with mental illness (Compton et al. 2011, Dupont and Cochran 2000).

Georgia CIT-trained officers have suggested that their training curriculum enhances the self-efficacy of police officers in interacting, interviewing, de-escalating, and referring individuals with depression, schizophrenia, and alcohol and cocaine dependence to treatment (Bahora et al. 2008). Similarly, this study also revealed a correlation between CIT training and a reduction of need for social distance; for example, living near, working with, or being friends with an individual with mental illness. The extent to which these changes in perceived confidence or stigma would affect interactions or officer decision-making was not evaluated.

CIT appears to have benefits that can be replicated in large, urban police departments. CIT training in the Chicago Police Department has been successfully implemented, as evidenced by application of skills from training to actual cases, police collaboration with community service providers, diversion to mental health services, voluntary officer response to mental health calls, and community requests for CIT-trained officers (Canada et al. 2010). Watson and colleagues also found that CIT training in Chicago appeared to have a more substantial impact on the decision making of officers who had a personal familiarity with mental illness or who had positive perceptions of mental health services in their area (Watson et al. 2010). However, in Chicago, CIT training has shown less clear benefit in reducing injury during encounters (Kerr et al. 2010).

CIT IMPACT ON MENTAL HEALTH PROFESSIONALS AND THE MENTAL HEALTH SYSTEM

As a mechanism for fostering stakeholder interaction, CIT has provided an opportunity for mental health care providers to interact and strengthen alliances with the law enforcement community. While these two professional cultures have presumably had past interactions, views, and curiosities about each other through the common ground of assisting consumers in crisis, misperceptions and unrealistic expectations may have more readily persisted prior to such a partnership. Interestingly, little has been written to date examining the impact of CIT training on the attitudes and perceptions of mental health professionals, although their beliefs and attitudes toward the role of police officers is important to consider. The accessibility, responsiveness, and perceived helpfulness of mental health emergency services appeared to have an impact on the perceptions of officers, and could have an impact on the disposition of police interventions (Borum et al. 1998). Accordingly, the attitudes, beliefs, and understanding of police culture by mental health workers are likely to play a substantive role in shaping these relationships and spanning previous boundaries.

Further study could investigate how the collaboration necessary to develop and implement CIT programs may lead to improved communication, reduction of systemic friction, and more appropriate understanding of the limitations of each side of the intervention continuum. Aside from the opportunity to develop academic research, clinicians may find involvement in the implementation and teaching of CIT programs to be an important conduit for community involvement, helpful in reducing burnout, and perhaps could even improve a sense of workplace safety though officer presence at crisis facilities. The opportunity to collaborate with other professional agencies through involvement with CIT programs could also appeal to students considering a career as a mental health professional. Exposure and involvement with CIT training programs may also be an important tool for elevating the awareness of trainees (physicians, nurses, social workers, counselors) to the network of community resources as well as challenges facing consumers and providers outside of traditional treatment settings.

CIT IMPACT ON CONSUMERS, FAMILIES, AND ADVOCATES

From the consumer-advocacy perspective, CIT programs provide an opportunity to achieve positive outcomes for individuals with mental illness following contact with law enforcement officers. Among these advocacy-oriented goals, the ability to facilitate treatment for consumers in crisis, when indicated, in lieu of incarceration or no intervention, is perhaps the most important. Although the research currently available about the impact of CIT is frequently focused on officer-level outcomes, data supporting the outcomes of CIT from the consumer perspective is beginning to emerge.

The appropriateness of CIT referrals to psychiatric emergency services has been examined by two studies that reviewed patient-focused outcomes. Broussard et al. (2010) examined whether CIT training leads to excessive or inappropriate referrals by examining the characteristics of patients brought to treatment settings by CIT-trained officers, in comparison to non-CIT-trained officers and family members. Their findings suggested that CIT-trained officer referrals, based on patient characteristics, are similar to the characteristics of patients referred by non-trained officers. This suggests that CIT training does not lead to a narrower (referring only severely ill individuals) or broader (referring individuals not needing emergency services) view of patients needing emergency services based on severity of illness.

An earlier study by Strauss et al. (2005) in Louisville, Kentucky, revealed similar findings and concluded that CIT officers were able to adequately identify patients requiring emergency care, although a higher proportion patients with schizophrenia were referred by CIT-trained officers. Strauss and colleagues suggest that CIT programs may reduce psychiatric morbidity by referring severely ill individuals the appropriate level of treatment earlier than might occur otherwise.

Consumers in crisis appear to have been positively impacted by the development of the CIT model through increased linkage to treatment. In data collected and analyzed from the Akron, Ohio, Police Department, CIT-trained officers appear to transport individuals experiencing mental health crises to treatment at a higher rate than non-CIT officers (Teller et al. 2006). Additionally, a greater proportion of individuals were transported to treatment voluntarily for both CIT-trained and non-trained officers, possibly due to a diffusion of training techniques or the referral of more challenging situations to CIT officers. Since the inception of the Akron program, the number and proportion of calls to police dispatch involving persons who possibly had a mental illness increased. Teller and colleagues theorized that this could be related both to increased dispatcher assessment and awareness of mental health emergencies, and possibly increased consumer comfort in calling police to identify mental health crises due to awareness of the program. This study did not find a reduction in the arrest rate between trained and non-trained officers, perhaps attributable to a referral bias of more difficult cases or CIT officer awareness of the Akron Mental Health Court post-arrest diversion program (Teller et al. 2006).

Similarly, a more recent study capturing data from the Chicago Police Department also suggests that their CIT officers have a higher likelihood of directing persons with mental illness to the mental health system (Watson et al. 2010). In examining the effects of CIT training, this study revealed that direction of individuals to the mental health system and reduction in "contact only" encounters was most robust among officers who had a positive view of mental health resource availability, and among officers with prior familiarity with mental illness. Like in Akron, the Chicago study did not demonstrate a reduction in arrests, although the Memphis program has reported low rates of arrests (Teller et al. 2006, Watson et al. 2010, Dupont and Cochran 2000, Steadman et al. 2000). Among the limitations noted in studying the effects of CIT were a lack of pre-training controls, non-randomization of officers to CIT, lack of independent verification of mental illness in subjects encountered by trained and non-trained officers, and a possible lack of recognition or documentation of mental illness in subjects encountered by non-CIT officers (Watson et al., 2010).

SUMMARY

As community mental health work continues to evolve in the post–deinstitutionalization era, the role of police officers acting as initial points of contact during mental health emergencies will undoubtedly persist. The opportunity for these first responders to work as members of crisis intervention teams, while bridging the gap between the street and the front door of the crisis care system, will continue to be a crucial safety net for consumers, especially as more recent economic uncertainty has taken a toll on mental health care budgets. The collective goals of CIT as a boundary-spanning partnership, underscored by the opportunity to strengthen communities, represents the potential for high-quality, informed, collaborative community mental health work to be at its best.

REFERENCES

Bahora M., Hanafi S., Chien V.H., & Compton M.T. (2008). Preliminary evidence of effects of crisis intervention team training on self-efficacy and social distance. *Administration and Policy in Mental Health and Mental Health Services Research*, *35*(3), 159–167.

Bittner, E. (1967). Police discretion in emergency apprehension of mentally ill persons. *Social Problems, 14*(3), 278–292.

Borum R., Deane M., Steadman H., & Morrisey J. (1998). Police perspectives on responding to mentally ill people in crisis: Perceptions of program effectiveness. *Behavioral Sciences and the Law, 16*(4), 393–405.

Broussard B., McGriff J.A., DemirNeubert B.N., D'Orio B., & Compton M.T. (2010). Characteristics of patients referred to psychiatric emergency services by crisis intervention team police officers. *Community Mental Health Journal, 46*(6), 579–584.

Canada K.E., Angell B., & Watson A.C. (2010). Crisis intervention teams in Chicago: Successes on the ground. *Journal of Police Crisis Negotiations, 10*(1–2): 86–100.

Compton M., DemirNeubert B., Broussard B., McGriff J., Morgan R., & Oliva J. (2011) Use of force preferences and perceived effectiveness of actions among crisis intervention team (CIT) police officers and non-CIT officers in an escalating psychiatric crisis involving a subject with schizophrenia. *Schizophrenia Bulletin, 37*(4), 737–745.

ComptonM.T., Esterberg M.L., McGee R., Kotwicki R.J., & Oliva J.R. (2006). Crisis intervention team training: Changes in knowledge, attitudes, and stigma related to schizophrenia. *Psychiatric Services 57*(8), 1199–1202.

Compton M.T., Bahora M., Watson A.C., & Oliva J.R. (2008). A comprehensive review of extant research on crisis intervention team programs. *The Journal of the American Academy of Psychiatry and the Law, 36*(1), 47–55.

Compton M.T., Broussard B., Hankerson-Dyson D., Krishan S., Stewart T., Oliva J.R., & Watson A.C. (2010). System- and policy-level challenges to full implementation of the crisis intervention team (CIT) model. *Journal of Police Crisis Negotiations, 10*(1–2), 72–85.

Deane M.W., Steadman H.J., Borum R., Veysey B., & Morrissey J. (1999). Emerging partnerships between mental health and law enforcement. *Psychiatric Services, 50*(1), 99–101.

Demir B., Broussard B., Goulding S., & Compton M. (2009). Beliefs about causes of schizophrenia among police officers before and after crisis intervention team training. *Community Mental Health Journal, 45*(5), 385–392.

Dupont R. & Cochran S. (2000). Police response to mental health emergencies—barriers to change. *The Journal of the American Academy of Psychiatry and the Law, 28*(3), 338–344.

DupontR., Cochran S., & Pillsbury S. (2007). *Crisis Intervention Team Core Elements*. Retrieved from The University of Memphis School of Urban Affairs and Public Policy, Department of Criminology and Criminal Justice, CIT Center website: http://cit.memphis.edu/pdf/CoreElements.pdf. Last accessed October 5, 2012.

Geller J.L. (2008). Commentary: Is CIT today's lobotomy? *The Journal of the American Academy of Psychiatry and the Law, 36*(1), 56–58.

Kerr A.N., Morabito M., & Watson A.C. (2010). Police encounters, mental illness and injury: An exploratory investigation. *Journal of Police Crisis Negotiations, 1*(10), 116–132.

Lamb H.R., Weinberger L.E., & DeCuir W.J. (2002). The police and mental health. *Psychiatric Services, 53*(10), 1266–1271.

Lamb H.R., & Weinberger L.E. (2005). The shift of psychiatric inpatient care from hospitals to jails and prisons. *The Journal of the American Academy of Psychiatry and the Law, 33*(4), 529–534.

Morrissey J.P., Fagan J.A., & Cocozza J.J. (2009). New models of collaboration between criminal justice and mental health systems. *The American Journal of Psychiatry, 166*(11), 1211–1214.

Oliva J.R., & Compton M.T. (2008). A statewide crisis intervention team (CIT) initiative: Evolution of the Georgia CIT program. *The Journal of the American Academy of Psychiatry and the Law, 36*(1), 38–46.

Ritter C., Teller J.L., Marcussen K., Munetz M., & Teasdale B. (2011). Crisis intervention team officer dispatch, assessment, and disposition: Interactions with individuals with severe mental illness. *International Journal of Law and Psychiatry 34*(1), 30–38.

Steadman H., Deane M., Borum R., & Morrisey J. (2000). Comparing outcomes of major models of police responses to mental health emergencies. *Psychiatric Services, 51*(5), 645–649.

Strauss G., Glenn M., Reddi P., Afaq I., Podolskaya A., Rybakova T., . . . El-Mallakh R.S. (2005). Psychiatric disposition of patients brought in by crisis intervention team police officers. *Community Mental Health Journal, 41*(2), 223–228.

Teller J.L., Munetz M.R., Gil K., & Ritter C. (2006). Crisis intervention team training for police officers responding to mental disturbance calls. *Psychiatric Services, 57*(2), 232–237.

Watson A., Morabito M., Draine J., & Ottati V. (2008). Improving police response to persons with mental illness: A multi-level conceptualization of CIT. *International Journal of Law and Psychiatry, 31*(4), 359–368.

Watson A.C., Ottati V.C., Morabito M., Draine J., Kerr A., & Angell B. (2010). Outcomes of police contacts with persons with mental illness: The impact of CIT. *Administration and Policy in Mental Health, 37*(4), 302–317.

CHAPTER 22

CASE MANAGEMENT CONTRIBUTIONS TO CARE

CHRISTY DARON AND KENNETH R. YEAGER

IN THE BEGINNING

To some, case management may be a relatively new service; however, its roots date back to 1863 in the United States when it was developed to coordinate public human services. Mary Richmond, often recognized as a pioneer for the social work profession of the 1800s in the United States, is linked to the early model of case management as she mobilized communities to help others who struggled—using activities that were a bridge for the individual to their social environment. Through investigation and assessment of available resources to meet the challenges of a population, Mary Richmond developed practices that charity organizations and settlement houses began using in the 1880s. The Henry Street Nurses' Settlement was founded by Lillian Wald in 1895. As the earliest recognized public-health nurse, she developed a role as a link between a family's social, economic, and health needs, in addition to contributing to service cost-containment while doing so; and, her contributions were precursors to what insurance companies use today as principles for payment structure in case management (Gursansky, Harvey, & Kennedy, 2003). Until the early 1980s, case management was largely recognized as "mission work" and not professionally based. It was later, into the 1990s, that case management took a role in guarding against fraud and ensuring efficient use of resources (2003).

The deinstitutionalization of the mentally ill, aged, and disabled in the 1960s, followed by the Adoption Assistance and Child Welfare Act of 1980 created new opportunities to deliver services that were community-based and away from the self-contained service provisions of the large institutions and long-term care facilities. Concurrently, advancements in medical technology in the postwar years gave new opportunities to those living with a chronic health condition to live in the community in lieu of spending their days in an acute care facility (Gursansky et al., 2003). Additionally, the Community Support System that was created by the National Institute of Health in 1977 "envisioned case management as a mechanism for helping clients navigate this

fragmented social service system" (Center for Substance Abuse Treatment, 2011). These historical changes in society gave rise to the traditional role that case managers have today.

CASE MANAGEMENT AND THE SOCIAL SECURITY ACT

While there are many levels of variation in those providing case-management activities within
a variety of roles and settings, it is important to remember that case-management activities are
strictly defined under Medicaid regulations. Furthermore, it is important to note that Medicare
regulations regarding coverage and funding, provider qualifications, and payment have significantly affected the development of case-management programming.

Prior to the 1980s, Medicaid founded only two categories of case-management services:
Administrative services were designed to determine the eligibility for Medicaid services,
help beneficiaries locating Medicaid services and, to a limited extent, monitor the provision
of services. *Case-management activities* were provided in conjunction with the delivery of a
Medicaid-funded service.

Three separate legislative reforms of the Social Security Act authorized the coverage of case
management as a "stand-alone" Medicaid service. The sections are: section 1915(b) of the Social
Security Act, section 1915(c), and section 1915(g).

- Section 1915(b) of the Social Security Act permits states to obtain waivers to operate
  case-management services within "primary care" settings.
- Section 1915(c) of the Social Security Act permits states to deliver home and
  community-based services (HCBS) as an alternative to Medicaid-reimbursable institutional services; e.g., hospital or extended care facilities. Yet there are limitations, including
  providing services to only one target group or any subgroup that the state may define—age
  or persons with disabilities (or both), persons with mental retardation of developmentally
  disabilities (or both) and persons with mental illness. States have flexibility in establishing target criteria consistent with this regulation, but are required to provide all people
  enrolled in the waiver with the opportunity for access to all needed services covered by
  the waiver and the Medicaid state plan.
- Section 1915(c) identifies "case management" as part of the services to be offered through
  the HCBS waiver program, but does not provide a definition for the term. Thus, states are
  required to propose their own definition, which must then be give federal approval. The
  Center for Medicare Services (CMS) provided a template for states submitting waivers for
  HCBS. In 2006, a definition of core case-management services was defined as: "Services
  that assist participants in gaining access to needed waiver and other state plan services,
  regardless of the funding sources for the services to which the access is granted." (CMS,
  2006, p. 132) Therefore, under an HCBS waiver, activities may include the following for
  any approved population:
  - Evaluation and/or reassessment of the need for waiver services
  - Evaluation/reevaluation of level of care
  - Development and review of service plan
  - Coordination of multiple services and/or multiple providers of services
  - Monitoring and implementation of the service plan

- To address problems within the service plan
- Response to participant crisis
- Determination of cost neutrality of waiver services for any given individual

Section 1915(g) of the Social Security Act authorizes states to provide "target case-management services" on a free-standing basis as a regular benefit under specific state Medicaid plans. This section was modified by the Omnibus Reconciliation Act of 1987 and the Deficit Reduction Act (DRA) in 2005 to clarify the circumstances under which payments may be authorized. This provision, while approving target case-management services, is optional for states, thus contributing further to variations from state to state. States that choose to cover case-management services under their Medicaid plan must define the target population, the scope of activities, and the providers and provider qualifications. As in other sections of this legislation, the Medicaid program requires that any services included within a state program must be available to all Medicaid recipients. However, within section 1915(g), states are allowed to limit the delivery of targeted case management to specific groups of Medicaid recipients (Mollica & Gillespie, 2004). States must indicate any limitations of disease or condition, age, institutional or non-institutional status, or other characteristic(s) of any given target group receiving limited services. Furthermore, the state must also define case-management services as they apply to the target population and specify any limitations (Mollica & Gillespie, 2004). For this discussion it is important to note that CMS does not attempt to define "targeted case-management services," indicating that these services may include a wide range of activities designed to help individuals obtain and retain the services they need. These services may include monitoring and follow-up activities, including activities and contacts that are necessary to ensure the care plan is effectively implemented and adequately addressing the needs of the individual (CMS, 2000). According to CMS recommendations, states can use targeted case management as an avenue to implement the *Olmsted* decision. This in reference to the Supreme Court Decision in *Olmstead v. LC* (21999), which is an interpretation of Title II of the Americans with Disabilities Act (ADA), which affirms the right of people with disabilities to receive services in the most integrated setting.

What we have outlined above begins with a description of a function within community mental health that has evolved and changed across time as understanding of the populations' needs has evolved and changed across time. We have seen how different systems define the role of case management differently. We have documented different roles within case management, and we have discussed the legislation that has in part provided the foundation for variation in the definition and application of case-management services to meet the ever-changing population needs. In general, payer groups follow the lead of CMS, which is the foundation for state definition of many case-management services.

Next arises the question of how we know that the services being provided are the right or most effective services. Within the transformational aspects of community case management, the question of how we know that what we are doing is effective is daunting to answer. To do so, we will next examine currently recognized best practices within case management.

CONCEPTUALIZING THE PRACTICE

Definitions of *case management* are as broad as the professions that apply the practice, and there is no universally accepted definition for it. In fact, some see case management as a function within other professions such as social work and nursing, while others see it as a separate profession that stands alone. For example, the function of case management within the treatment of substance abuse is recognized as one of eight counseling skills utilized by the National Association of Alcoholism and Drug Abuse Counselors (1986). However, widely accepted across fields are the set of functions that comprise case management, including: assessment, planning, linkage, monitoring, and advocacy.

Traditionally, case management has been practiced in the human service and nursing fields, though it is currently used in criminal justice, rehabilitation, school-based professions, and more recently, managed-care companies. The diversity of case-management services and the definition of the role of a case manager are defined by the program arrangement within which the position works. Examples of this would be a direct services case manager who holds a caseload of clients and orchestrates the management of many aspects in the person's life (e.g., adult psychiatric services), versus another case manager who is viewed as a resource for referrals to services (e.g., homeless services, inpatient medical facilities). Nurse case managers often have population-specific caseloads (e.g., chronic health conditions, psychiatric needs, etc.), while others may be limited within a managed-care facility to contacting patients who are identified as "high utilizers of services" to assess the needs of the patient who may require referrals or medication assessment to reduce the cost of care for that patient. Institutional case managers operate differently than those who are based in the community. Case management as a framework offers person-centered care through a process of collaborative assessment, planning, facilitation of services, and evaluation to address the problems a person or a family is identified to have. Most commonly, case managers work intensely with the complex needs of higher risk populations. No matter their focus, case managers provide the same dimension of services.

Most will agree case-management activities generally function as a connection assisting individuals with accessing services and supports to assure their needs are met through available services provided within the community. The overarching goal is to meet reasonable standards of quality of care delivery that will in turn lead to improved outcomes for individuals served within the community. In most case-management settings, activities may vary, depending on population's service, but they generally include the following:

- Screening and intake: Determination of the client's eligibility for services and need for case management.
- Comprehensive assessment: In-depth evaluation of the client's current situation, including strengths and limitations and need for services and support.
- Development and monitoring of the planning of care: Development of a care plan to include the most appropriate services and supports addressing all the needs identified during the assessment process.
- Service arrangement: Provision of information, referrals, or actively arranging client's access to services and supports.
- Monitoring: Evaluation of the quality of services and supports, and determination if the goals established within the care plan are being executed in a manner that supports the desired outcome.
- Reassessment: Reevaluation of the goals and care plan developed during the comprehensive assessment, in an effort to adjust the care plan to meet individualized needs and to lead to the best possible outcome.

As indicated above, within this framework, case-management systems differ greatly, depending on the overall and individual needs of the population served, the range of services provided by case managers and each agency, reimbursement structures within payor groups, and across various cities, counties, states, and regions. Additional roles within case management have been redefined by service need and have shifted for persons performing the work, depending on system variance. For example:

- A "broker" traditionally has been a person who identifies, arranges, and coordinates services. Within a variety of systems this role can be completed by a variety of persons in a variety of roles. An Employee Assistance Professional may serve this function, linking persons with benefits provided by a company or corporation. A social worker may be completing this function within a community mental health center; a nurse functioning in the role of discharge coordinator may be filling this role in a primary health care setting. A counselor in vocational or occupational rehabilitation may serve a similar function linking individuals to work or occupation-related services.
- A "gatekeeper" traditionally has been a person who contains costs and monitors resource allocation. Within community settings, a range of persons may be responsible for this role, including the chief financial officer, who may have a keen interest in managing practice accounts of "shared risk" in which practice groups are participating in "pay for performance" programming. "Pay for performance" means groups that hit specified quality indicators receive higher reimbursement rates for the practice plan. For example, if specific targets such as readmissions within 30 days are kept at or below an industry-established benchmark or target (e.g., below 10% of total admissions), then reimbursement will be higher and dollars saved can be reallocated to other areas of programming. Within a managed-care setting the gatekeepers may have varying levels of mental health training, but still be charged with monitoring resource allocation by following specific criteria for admission. Yet a different face may be a gatekeeper within a clinic setting where schedules are tight and appointments are carefully guarded to permit enhanced patient/client access and flow throughout the system of care.
- An "evaluator" who assures that case-management goals are attained is yet another role that may vary from system to system. For example individuals may fulfill this role as a quality director, conducting audits on records to determine compliance with goal attainment. Efforts may be focused toward attaining a quality goal to lead to improved outcomes within an organization. Within the same institution there may be a compliance officer (a person with an accounting or legal background) who is working to assure case-management goals are billed within accordance within payor standards such as Centers for Medicare and Medicaid Services to avoid missed billing or fraudulent billing. Still another person with risk management (a legal or nursing or social work background) may be auditing records to assure case-management goals were attained to reduce medical legal risk, such as circumstances that may have resulted in unintended outcomes when clients deviate from their care plan, placing them at greater risk of harming themselves or others.

While the definition of persons completing the work may change, the overall goals remain the same—that is, to focus on processes that help clients maximize their ability to use available resources to improve their quality of life. Therefore, those functioning as case managers may be providing education or transportation, assisting with scheduling appointments, helping to develop special diets, or facilitating a link with and integration into housing, employment services, or medical care, to mention a few. Additionally, the case manager also acts as a mediator between the system and the client, acting as an advocate on behalf of the client.

It should be noted that, while certain constructs differ greatly between areas of case management, other areas seem to transcend approaches to case management. The following are examples of these skill and practices:

Continuity of care: sadly, this term has become somewhat of a bureaucratic buzzword and in the process has lost clinical relevance. The term initially reflected the need to establish and maintain rapport with populations who require time to establish trusting relationships that over the long term function as the foundation for ongoing care communication processes. In this role, case managers became the historians of the case, providing valuable information relating to the variety of symptoms that had presented across time. This information functioned as the foundation for understanding the manifestation of illness across time, and how past presentation of illness related to current treatment needs, social functioning, and utilization of social networks to stabilize patient populations across time. Studies have shown that progress in illness management is made through extended relationships and experimentation with care approaches including client, case manager, and psychiatric caregivers. Essentially, the clinical team, with the input of the client, develops an individualized understanding of the best approach to treatment through trying a variety of treatment approaches across time. Case managers monitor and schedule care based on assessment of manifestation of symptoms, combined with social stressors and response to supportive efforts. If a client's condition worsens and hospitalization is required, the case manger can work with the client and care team to negotiate a voluntary admission or work with other care providers as necessary to inform the level of care needed, up to and including the need to obtain a commitment order.

Use of case-management relationship: Individualized care requires more than complex discharge planning. The key is interactive and collaborative relationships with clients, families and other caregivers. Collaborative relationships enable case managers to avert crises when external resources and stressors lead to client destabilization. Thus case-management intervention is a function of the ongoing relationship, which provides the opportunity to assess patient capabilities and limitations in interacting with a complex social and healthcare system.

Flexibility: One of the challenges of mental health management is the challenge of responding to the ever-changing internal and external world of the client population. This constant state of flux requires case managers to be flexible in approach, strategy, and intervention processes to accommodate the diverse population and needs within the population served. In short, this flexibility insists that achieving goals within the treatment plan is not a sufficient measure of success. The measure of success is actually the means that permits the accomplishment of client goals, the strategies designed that reflect an appreciation of each individual patient's need. This is demonstrated through actions such as varying frequency and duration of meetings, revision of goals based on emerging situations, inclusion of family and community supports in treatment plan revisions, and inclusion of clients in decision making processes, which lead to greater acceptance of the treatment plan, transparency in implementation of the treatment plan, and an overall increased value in and adherence to the care plan of all working to support the client. This is not to say that flexibility is to replace firmness; in many situations, firmness is a necessary tool for supporting the next step of the care plan (e.g., transition to injectable medication as a necessary precursor to transition into a supervised apartment living situation). Yet flexibility is, within the framework of case management, the key to individualized care.

Care coordination: Within traditional case-management models care coordination was for the most part tied to and directly identified members of the care team assuring that key elements of the care plan were implemented. For the most part, this included day-to-day activities, making appointments, building support networks, and establishing relationships between a variety of care providers. This last element holds particular importance to the multidisciplinary team aspect of modern community mental health practice. As many others have mentioned throughout this text, the diversity of multidisciplinary team members in the care plan is continuing to grow. To indicate the complexity of mental health management has grown would be an understatement.

Today, thanks to changing models of care, combined with patient advocacy concerns, increasing knowledge of comorbid illness, and changing definitions of comorbid illness, the treatment process is exponentially more complex than even 10 years ago. In the future, the role of the case manager will include aspects such as data gathering, examining correlations between improvement in illness and interventions provided, and working with diverse team members to tweak and sharpen already complex plans of care and to manage costs of care within new and emerging reimbursement models. Within these new reimbursement models both insurers and providers enter into agreements of "shared risk" in which dollars for care are allocated to agencies and the agencies provide care with this set amount. The next section will examine what a traditional case-management model may look like as time progresses, as well as examine some traditional approaches to case management.

PRINCIPLES OF CLINICAL CASE MANAGEMENT

Within the framework of case management, it is important to understand certain constructs of care management models; we will next examine a clinical case-management approach. The review in this section will examine traditional clinical case-management components combined with potential factors associated with future intervention processes and will discuss how the framework for future case-management models may be affected. Figure 22.1 depicts this framework.

ENGAGEMENT

Describes the basic components in a step model of clinical case management. It is important to note that the cycle of care is a continually reviewed process always liking to Engagement, Assessment, and Planning.

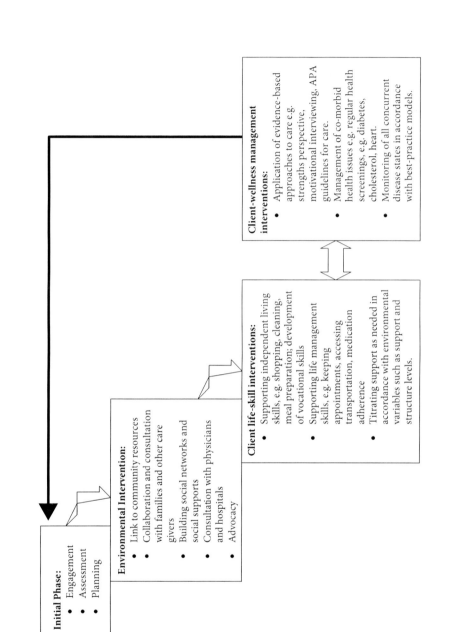

FIGURE 22.1 Components of Clinical Case Management

Establishing rapport with clients is the foundation of case management. It is a process that requires skill, sensitivity, and above all, patience. While the patient may have severe mental illness that is clear to the observer, this is not always clear to the client, who frequently denies the extent and severity of their illness, leading the individual to being reluctant to collaborate in any helping relationship. Frequently, clients are concerned that engaging in case management will require relinquishing their autonomy and becoming a part of a system, frequently a system they do not trust. While the literature may suggest this can be accomplished within weeks or even months, the reality of establishing true collaborative relationships with severely mentally ill populations may take years.

ASSESSMENT

Case-management assessment of severely mentally ill populations requires more than evaluation of the patient's history, symptom constellation and medication response, stated wishes, daily living skills, and available resources. It requires establishing a comprehensive understanding and appreciation for the client's clinical status, overt and covert responses to case management, ability to comprehend and to function within a variety of settings, responses to external and internal stimuli, and social networks. This requires repeated contacts across time, including observations of previous caregivers, family members, and others with knowledge of the functioning of the individual. Once gaining a true understanding of the presenting concerns of the case, the care manager in concert with the team can begin the process of developing care plans and care networks in which the plans can be implemented. It is important to understand both the clients and family and their informal support network's response to prior care plans and that this be considered in the assessment process. The best care plan on paper is not worthy of implementation if it is not realistic within the functional world of the individual.

PLANNING

More than ever, the future of mental health care will be based on the ability of case management to serve as a reflection of each client's conflicting desires and needs. While some clients will be able to verbalize their desires in a clear and straightforward manner, each individual's needs are usually much more complex, and frequently in conflict with what is needed. For example, the desire for autonomy can be in conflict with the need for support provided within the parental home. Working with clients and their support systems to address the inherent conflicts that arise within case management is both an art and a science. It is extremely important that the reality of the client's situation and needs be considered within the framework of safety and growth. In doing so, the case worker will frequently find they are trapped between the proverbial rock and a hard place.

The natural response is to attempt to develop a treatment plan that takes into account the aims of all constituents. However, this is not always possible; even the most carefully constructed care plans can result in less than desirable outcomes. In many situations the best case-management plan is designed to help clients address their internal struggles, while when possible helping them avoid crisis situations. It is important to openly acknowledge when situations arise when a clear estrangement exists between what the client desires and what the client needs. In situations it is extremely for case managers to clarify with the client the reason for this choice and the actions taken. Of course, case managers, like other mental health professionals, may feel uncomfortable with the explicit and implicit authority of their role. The best approach in such cases is the team approach, frequently a team approach based on evidence-based practices that support the decision-making process. This approach lessens the burden of decision and builds on the consensus of the team in an approach to care that sets the foundation for the best patient outcome. It is important to openly acknowledge that, in situations where the there is a clear estrangement between desire and need, choosing to act in the client's best interests often covers both. While the client may resent such actions, it is important that case managers understand and act in accordance with the authoritative elements of their professional role.

Within planning, the role of the team is to address all aspects of care, from medication management, to social interaction, to management of potential complications of any type within care. The case-management aspect of care provides the eyes and ears of the treatment team. The case manager will provide data on patient functioning within the community environment and responses to planned interventions. Treatment plans will evolve initially out of the processes of engagement and assessment, but ultimately will be revised based upon the client's response to care provided within the complex environment of the community. Case management will in the future work to provide data in the form of observation, completion of standardized measures, and client self-report to inform care revisions. Figure 22.2 provides a visual of the interaction between treatment engagement, assessment, and planning with interventions throughout the treatment process.

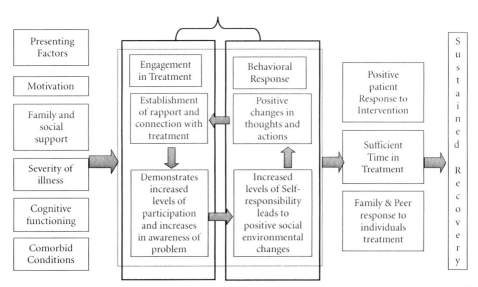

FIGURE 22.2 Clinical case management interventions designed to enhance and strengthen aspects of recovery should occur in engagement and behavioral response areas of treatment.

ENVIRONMENTAL INTERVENTION

LINKING TO COMMUNITY RESOURCES

Most of us know and agree that case management has a long history of linking clients to community resources. When linking clients with the needed community resources, case managers will continue to work to determine how much assistance is the right amount of assistance needed; however, in the future the case manager will be working with the team to determine access to community resources based upon current evidence-supported decision making processes. Working with a multidisciplinary teams, case mangers will establish personalized working relationships with staff not only from their agencies but from others within the community. They, with team input, will negotiate service linkage, integrating the needs of the client and developing a true appreciation of the concerns of other agencies as they prepare both clients and staff for what can be expected from one another. Case management in the future of community mental health care will bear the responsibility of solidifying, through team interaction and interaction with external partner agencies, the integrative rationale for proactive interventions to establish, nurture, and measure the effectiveness of the treatment plan. These negotiations and evaluations will provide clients with a "model of care" for operating within the community as capable and secure individuals able to function at increasingly higher levels.

COLLABORATION WITH FAMILIES AND OTHER CAREGIVERS

The importance of interacting with families and other caregivers cannot be underestimated. The relationship of the care team with important caregivers does not end once the plan of care is developed. Nor should they be limited to interactions with the case manager. The role of the case manager is to spearhead interactions with family and caregivers, either formal or informal. Care managers should initiate consultations on an ongoing or intermittent basis, depending upon individual client needs. In most cases the quality of the patient's care within the community depends on the competence, dedication, and support of caregivers. Care managers must function as the communication mechanism providing information, education, and support on how best to interact with the team to support the client. Common issues include medication management, changes in mood and behavior, availability of community resources, and availability of crisis services if needed (Angell, 2003).

Most families are more concerned than other care providers regarding future prospects for the individual's recovery and adaptation to living within the community. Many may feel the burden of the obligation to care for their loved one; they may become resentful as the burdens increase. When burdens become excessive, the case manager and team can help families make suitable modifications to the plan of care to support the recovery process. While some questions can be addressed via education, most will require an ongoing consultative relationship that will be managed by the case manager on behalf of the entire care team.

BUILDING SOCIAL NETWORKS AND SOCIAL SUPPORTS

When families and caregivers become overly burdened, the case manager has the unique ability to provide additional support systems for both clients and family members. The importance of building social networks for the client is that the support provided extends beyond the individual to the family. Conversely, building support systems for family members will extend the network of options available to family members and the client as family members and caregivers begin to have a greater understanding of the trial-and-error aspects of care management. When support networks grow and expand, they address both social and physical needs, allowing families and team members to focus their energies on specific care needs. A word of caution regarding establishments of support networks: because supportive relationships are difficult to assess, families, case managers, and team members should work together to maintain an ongoing interest in such contacts to assure that a truly safe and supportive relationship is maintained (DiMatteo, 2004).

CONSULTATION WITH PHYSICIANS AND HOSPITALS

The most notable of the collaborations between case managers and physicians is the observation of and reporting on the effectiveness of medication regimes. This is important, as medication response is often more apparent to caregivers and family members than to the client; therefore, psychiatrists, general practitioners, advanced practice nurses, and others on the care team frequently will depend on case managers to monitor patient functioning between interviews. One growing role of the case manager in the future will be to assist in identifying the emergence of medication side effects and monitoring long-term medication side effects such as weight gain, and implementing counter-measures like a healthy diet combined with moderate exercise activities. Case managers will also provide data related to the home environment that can assist psychiatrist and other care providers in establishing dosage schedules and to facilitate client compliance with medications, monitoring of blood sugar and blood pressure, and other aspects of behavior and physical health need.

The relationship with hospitals is equally important, as the case manager is able to promote effective interventions when patients are hospitalized and to provide hospitals with information about premorbid functioning, precipitators of relapse, and effective past treatment modalities. The case manager's knowledge of the community resources will play an important role in facilitating a seamless transition back to the community by providing access to increasingly difficult-to-access community resources.

ADVOCACY

In recent years, the role of the advocate has evolved to include a variety of disciplines, fulfilling different roles to attain different goals. For example, the consumer movement has functioned to improve advocacy for those with mental health issues; legal services are frequently provided through agencies; and increasingly, social workers, nurses, and patient advocates are filling the role of patient advocate by emphasizing client empowerment. New roles have emerged that did not formally exist years ago, such as the role of "support broker" or "personal agent" or "patient advocate"; all of these positions function to facilitate client self-determination and have added new dimensions to the role of advocacy by providing person-centered care strategies that work to shift the decision-making balance in favor of the client and his or her family. The person-centered approach is rapidly becoming a best practice, focusing on individual needs and preferences for care, provided in a way that increases the person's capacity to manage their individual care needs.

CLIENT LIFE-SKILL INTERVENTIONS

SUPPORTING INDEPENDENT LIVING SKILLS

Within the future of community mental health, treatment teams will come together around client management with increasing focus on maintaining clients within community settings in which collaborative initiatives will serve as a network for meeting the needs of the populations served. Some larger agencies will house multiple programs under a single roof, while others, in rural areas, may build collaborative relationships designed to pool resources to meet diverse client needs. Case managers and others will function an a manner similar to wrap-around service teams or ACT teams; they may look more like life coaches facilitating the resolution of a variety of concerns, including social relationships, impulse control, affect modulation, and the like. They may teach activities of daily living, like grocery shopping, meal preparation, cleaning, and the development of vocational or (increasingly) social network skills using technology. While it is not clear what will emerge as key aspects of care, it is safe to say that technology will play a larger role in case management. Greater access to smartphones, and associated programs such as Skype and face-to-face technology, facilitate access to support, and checks can be immediate and mobile. Thus the age-old issue of whether the patient has both a case manager and a therapist will probably take on a different face.

SUPPORTING LIFE-MANAGEMENT SKILLS

Although case managers may not label resolving conflicts with co-workers, life mates, or family members as "therapy," the skills involved are largely based on coaching and skill development—this may require cognitive restructuring as in CBT, or building plans to deal with future conflicts as in solution-focused approaches. The goal of the team will probably shift to developing life-management skills, as payment structures move from payment for service to payment for performance. When incentives move from fee for service to overall care management, the structures supporting individual counseling, therapy, and medication management as traditional reimbursed services fade, permitting the development of new and innovative approaches to overall care (Gingerich & Mueser, 2005).

TITRATING SUPPORT AS NEEDED

The transition from fee for service to overall care management will also permit the ability to apply a variety of interventions: from providing electronic devices to assist with access and communication, to coaching, to internet-based services—the options are limitless. The key is that services will be based upon the degree of support needed to manage overall care rather than traditional structures where the focus has been on justifying the need for sessions that are reimbursed by type or time structures. The care team may also change as the interventions change. Individuals who are in crisis may require more intense medication management and stabilization services, while others may require more family focused, or peer support services. The key will be using the multidisciplinary team to manage individual needs rather than building services based on reimbursement structures.

CLIENT—DISEASE MANAGEMENT INTERVENTIONS

APPLICATION OF EVIDENCE-BASED APPROACHES TO CARE

Within the past decade, there has been a remarkable emergence of evidence-based practice approaches (Roberts & Yeager, 2004). With the emergence of evidence-based and
evidence-informed approaches, agencies, care providers and researchers work together to
determine new and potentially effective models. Sources for evidence are now easily accessible. The *Cochrane Database of Systematic Reviews* provides a remarkable resource for the
examination of new evidence-based approaches. For example, Dieterich, Irving, Park, and
Marshall (2010) examined the effectiveness of intensive case management (ICM) for severe
mental illness. ICM is a community-based package of care that seeks to provide long-term care
for severely mentally ill people who do not require immediate hospitalization for the preserva-
tion of safety. ICM evolved from two original community models of care: assertive community
treatment (ACT) and case management (CM). In a matter of ten minutes, practitioners can
enter the *Cochrane Database*, enter a search for approaches to care, and have a three-page
summary outlining the background, objectives, search strategy, selection criteria, data collection and analysis, results of randomized control trials, meta analysis, and other key factors to
inform their decision-making.

Having said this, not all is as simple as this will sound. There are points where evidence
does not yet exist to answer all care questions; not all evidence has been effectively applied
in community settings; and what works in a study may not work with your client or meet
the desires of your client. However, these commonly made arguments cannot outweigh the
importance of evidence-based or evidence-informed approaches to care. While it is not possible to review all approaches to case management in this chapter, it is important to note
that linking evidence-based approaches and theoretical constructs will be important factors in driving outcomes. Interventions may include applications of best practices, practice
guidelines and theoretical constructs such as stages of change, strengths perspective, and
solution-focused approaches. The decision of what evidence or theoretical construct to apply
will require team development of a treatment plan informed by the best evidence available,
considered within the structure of the clients' desires for approaches to care (Schneider,
Hussey, & Schnyer, 2011).

MANAGEMENT OF COMORBID HEALTH ISSUES

Just as evidence-based or evidence-informed approaches are important to behavioral and
mental health approaches, the application of these strategies to manage comorbid health
issues will be a key factor in improving outcomes in community mental health populations.
Within healthcare, there are already best-practice approaches associated with health screenings that are currently driving clinical outcomes. The merging of physical and mental health
may in fact lead to the greatest improvement of outcomes for this population. The role of
the case manager remains essentially the same, but applies methods traditionally reserved
for mental health management to the healthcare of the mentally ill population (Hunter &
Goodie, 2010).

RECOGNIZED BEST PRACTICES

In spite of critics, evidenced-based practice (EBP) continues to transform service delivery, particularly in the psychiatric and substance abuse fields. These practices are backed by scientific and systematic clinical testing that is linked with consumer outcomes that show an increase in levels of functioning, insight, self efficacy, and living to their maximum potential.

THE STAGES OF CHANGE (TRANSTHEORETICAL MODEL)

A person's readiness to change is often defined by clinicians in the fields of social work and chemical dependency as their "stage of change" and is recognized as being in one of five categories: pre-contemplation, contemplation, preparation, action, and maintenance. The basic premise of this model is that human behavior change is a circular process (Porche, 2004). Use of the theory by clinicians is a way to match the interventions with the behaviors and views of the client about the problem, thus improving outcomes.

Each stage has characteristics that are easily identified. An individual who is unaware of the health risks of smoking, for example, and has no intention to change is identified as being in the *pre-contemplation* stage of change. A person who is aware of the risks but is also considering the self-defined benefits to smoking and may be willing to consider reducing the use of smoking, is identified as in *contemplation* stage. In the preparation stage, a person is taking steps toward change. For example, they may be researching the alternatives to smoking to reduce anxiety, or talking with their doctor about treatment options to help them stop. The *action* stage is characterized when overt behavior modifications have taken place. The *maintenance* stage is not achieved until the person's behaviors have been modified for a minimum of six months and no repeat of the unhealthy behavior has been seen (Porche, 2004).

During the fluid movement through the stages, a person performs a constant reevaluation of pros and cons of the change. Porche (2004) stated that people evaluate "instrumental gains to self, instrumental gains for others, approval of self, and approval from others" as evaluators for continuing to change the behavior. Interventions are then used to assist the person in progressing to achieve the behavior modification. It is important to remember that the stages of change are not static, rather, they are in movement and negotiation as the person continues to evaluate the pros and cons and reap the rewards of their success thus far. This theory works in tandem with other best practices and is often used as a framework for interventions, while the ways the person is engaged in the process of change using other intention tools.

MOTIVATIONAL INTERVIEWING

Engaging the client is paramount to moving a person through the recovery journey. To do this, it is important that practitioners know how to utilize motivational interviewing (MI) as a tool in this process. MI bases its practice on "rolling with resistance" and has been shown to engage even the hardest-to-reach people in moving through change. Used widely in the field of social work, motivational interviewing is equally applicable for physicians, dental hygienists, diabetes educators, peer counselors, and a variety of other professionals in the helping or corrections fields (Rosengren, 2009). The philosophy of MI involves helping the person recognize the need for change (identifying there is a problem), getting the person to resolve their ambivalence and move in the direction of change, and practicing persuasion and support rather than argumentative intervention to move the person through the stages of change. Building motivation for change is the key to helping a person acknowledge that there is a problem and then be willing to take steps to solve it.

Five principles that practitioners follow in MI include: expression of empathy, developing discrepancies, avoiding argumentation, rolling with resistance, and supporting self-efficacy. Utilizing MI takes training and practice, though the knowledge of basic strategies in MI can be an easy place to start. Referred to as "OARS"—asking *open-ended* questions, using *affirmations*, using *reflective* listening, and making *summaries* (Rosengren, 2009), these strategies are used to move the client through the process. These skills are seen most in counseling to keep sessions moving in the direction of progress, but are invaluable in any profession that is helping a person change. It is important to note that OARS are not locked in order during use; rather, they are to be practiced with fluidity and to move the conversation toward change talk.

Gathering information through use of open-ended questions is useful and reduces the client's defensiveness while exploring their view of the issue at hand. For example, asking "When you drink alcohol, tell me about the circumstances," is better than asking "How often and how much to do you drink?" Or, when expressing concerns of a loved one, it may be phrased "Your wife expressed concerns over your smoking. What's your sense on why she finds this concerning?" This is an example of using open-ended questions with placing the problem outside of the person and thereby depersonalizing it, making it easier for the person to discuss. Another form of open-ended question is that of an open-ended statement. These are used to preface the change in topic with a client. For example, when a client is showing ambivalence about stopping smoking, you can say, "I wonder what it would be like if you decided to stop smoking." This gives the client permission to explore without committing, and it gets them to provide more information on their fears, concerns, and ambivalence about changing their behavior. Once the undercurrent of reasoning has been established, interventions to support those can be put in place.

Affirmations are used to build a person's feelings of empowerment and self-efficacy and dispel their beliefs that past efforts to change have failed, and therefore the "problem" becomes that of others around them, or a reflection of deficits of their own (Rosengren, 2009). Affirmations are more than reflective listening, they are statements that describe a person's behaviors or feelings and can be a powerful tool of self-reflection. Additionally, the use of affirmations involves the use of "you" statements. For example, to address a client's anxiety over coming to appointments, it could be said, "You must have felt a lot of pressure coming in to your appointment today, but it took a lot of determination on your part to do it anyway." After an affirmation is given, it is helpful to then use follow-up questions as a way to get the person to elaborate on their success. For example, "How did you keep this commitment to yourself?" or "What did you do differently to prepare for coming here today than in other times where you chose to miss?" Affirmations are used to bridge the recognition of strengths in a client to the next step: using those strengths to address other problems, which may in fact be completely unrelated.

Reflective listening and summaries are akin to one another. Reflective listening involves paraphrasing a person's thoughts in a way that clarifies and amplifies their points. This involves having the clinician stay focused on the points of the client and avoid inserting the clinician's agenda. A good use of reflective listening is done so in short statements such as "So the decision to stop smoking really has anxiety attached to it for you." A "summary" of the same subject involves a more elaborate narrative of the subject, still reflecting the client's views. Summaries help the client organize their experiences (Rosengren, 2009). Miller and Rollnick (2002) describe summaries as a special application of reflective listening, but they are also used to select the elements that will aid the client in moving forward (staying true to MI). As the primary goal of MI is to elicit change talk, summaries give weight to the statements the client has made that reflect change talk. An illustration of these ideas, used when talking with "Bob" about his smoking habit, may help:

> You are here today because you reported to the nurse having shortness of breath, a deep cough. Your wife has shared concerns that smoking two packs of cigarettes per day may be contributing to your health concerns. You worry that if you stop smoking you will gain weight and become more anxious when you are around big crowds. At the same time, you recognize that smoking would be a hard thing to stop doing but you care about how your wife feels and you don't want to worry her. The next task at hand is to find ways to help you reduce anxiety and manage weight to help you be successful.

This type of summary is described by Miller and Rollnick (2002) as a "collecting summary": to gather information together, present it back to the client, and keep the conversation moving in the direction of change. Summaries can be placed throughout the session with the client and not exclusively at the end. They can be particularly helpful as a technique for clarifying the client's position on a matter while amplifying the change talk that has occurred.

STRENGTHS MODEL

The strengths model steps away from the psychoanalytical theory that may stigmatize and label people with mental illness. The model highlights the need for cooperation of practices between the medical science and strengths-approach, focusing on helping people as individuals rather than as victims, clients, or patients. The principles of the model involve engagement, strengths assessment, personal planning, and resource acquisition (Rapp & Goscha, 2006). People with severe and persistent mental illnesses (SPMI), for example, are often encountered by clinicians who see them as people plagued with problems and barriers. In response, and based on bias fostered by a deficit model the interventions employed often reinforce the oppression experienced by the client. hough it is rarely done with intention or malevolence, professionals dress up the interventions with compassion and caring (Rapp & Goscha, 2006, p. 3). Empirical testing of the strengths model finds that it is "superior to traditional approaches" (2006), particularly with those with SPMI. The model was developed as a framework for giving notice to clinicians that adults with SPMI are human: thereby, the theory operates on these beliefs:

- Treatment must include a major focus on each client's strengths rather than just symptoms.
- Clients and families have not only rights but insights into their problems.
- The mentally ill are not labels, such as "schizophrenics," but humans who have value, worth, and personal strengths.

- Individuals and families deserve a voice and appropriate power within America's mental health systems (Saleebey, 1997).

Meant to be used jointly with other interventions, the strengths model focuses on helping the client develop empowerment and self-determination as the change agents in managing their own difficulties. This model helps clinicians realize the importance of not blaming clients and their families for their problems; rather, they are people with feelings, insights, hopes, and civil rights (1997). The model does not, however, replace the need for diagnosis and biologically based medication interventions. It simply challenges workers to view the clients, patients, or consumers as *people* with a diagnosis. Hence, treating the person, not the diagnosis, is the mantra.

CHALLENGES AND FUTURE IMPLICATIONS TO CASE MANAGEMENT

"Two of the most oppressed groups in mental health are clients and their case managers" (Rapp, 2006, p. 66). Recognized by most in the social services field, case managers are the lowest paid, the least credentialed, and the lowest in the organizational hierarchy, and yet they have the most responsibility in working with the most intensely high-risk populations. They are also the ones with the least influence and decisional voice in their organizations. Morale in the profession of social service case management can be particularly low, with high turnover of staffing, perpetuating yet more stress in the job and subsequently lower morale.

Establishing the value of case management as a service has been accomplished, though doing the same for the profession continues to be a challenge. The first challenge is one involving policy vs. practice. In fact, according to the Case Management Society of America (CMSA), founded in 1990 for the support and professionalization of case managers, case management is not a "service"; rather, it is a "profession." In similar form, the National Association of Social Workers (NASW) established standards for social work case management in 1992 to help provide a structure and expectations for social workers who provide case management, as well as to clarify the role of a social work case manager, which is to be respected as valuable and has techniques and trained practices. The social work case manager is expected to follow the basic NASW social work code of ethics. The challenge that faces these supportive organizations in making case management a profession is seen in the variety of expectations that employers have in their selection of case managers. The CMSA, for example, declares that "case managers are licensed professionals with experience to support individuals and their families" (CMSA, 2011). The practice of case management transcends health and human service professions and adapts to the multiple needs of many populations that the social work profession serves. With this dominant presence comes the concern for fidelity to the model of case management, which cannot be defined solely by its functions. Serving as gatekeepers of resources, case managers are expected to maintain a monitoring, collaborative, and efficiency role regarding the care of a person's individual needs, or *case*. Like the professions that utilize it, case management has evolved throughout the years to satisfy the changing face of populations that need it, policies that manage the fiscal payment of it as a service, and the politics that demand a model for cost reduction and collaborative service delivery.

The U.S. Affordable Care Act of 2010 catapulted case management as the leading factor in meeting the efforts in collaborative care. Promoting quality care through a more transparent and accountable health care system, while asking the public to be held accountable for their health, services such as preventive and wellness services are coupled with chronic disease case-management services all around the country. Policy makers are being influenced by grassroots advocates from organizations that promote case management as essential to health care reform.

As called for under the Act of the Department of Health and Human Services, a National Strategy for Quality Improvement in Health Care was released that, in part, calls for evidence-based practices in service delivery. To meet this expectation at the micro level, employers must make adjustments in their selection of candidates for case-management positions and utilize the professional direction that the NASW and CMSA have proposed to standardize case management. Training and support of case managers must improve if systems of care are to meet the expectations of government in reducing costs and improving services. As health care reform takes shape in the United States "case management" will undoubtedly become viewed more as "care management" to reflect the emphasis on the individual nature of the services being offered; thereby establishing "case managers" as care coordinators. The relatively recent addition of managed care to the field of human services management is beginning to transform the way services are delivered. The slow dismantling of established service arrangements is being replaced by provisions of care that address the duplication of services across providers of the same person. True collaboration through communication and service planning is the future of care; therefore, case managers will become the central coordinators of a person's treatment.

Now, with an understanding of the history, roles, some of the evidence-based practices used, and the implications for the future of case management, let us take a look at a case example of case management on a daily basis. Though case management is expanding into different fields, our case example involves working with adults with disabilities who require a moderately high amount of intervention and support—a modern use of case management today.

DAY-TO-DAY CASE MANAGEMENT PROCESSES

To define the case manager's day as "typical" would not only be insulting to the profession but inaccurate. No two days are alike, and each day is an orchestration of a symphony of tasks, demands, crises, and documentation requirements. The calendar is a case manager's best friend and worst enemy alike. Tasks must routinely be reviewed and prioritized on a monthly, weekly, and daily basis. Sometimes, hourly adjustments must be made to accommodate clients in crisis and the occasional traffic jam. Based in the community, the day consists of making home and vocational visits, developing and modifying plans of care, coordinating client referrals, scheduling collaborative treatment meetings, and documenting all the above events. Returning voicemails, responding to emails, and staying accessible to others throughout the day makes the job complex. Scheduling is dictated by the needs of the clients, the restriction of hours of other service providers (doctors' offices, Social Security offices, entitlement offices, etc.), family members, courts, and the clients themselves. Saddled as they are with too many tasks and not enough time in the day, flexibility and organization are survival tools of the case manager.

A good case manager is capable of prioritizing, adapting to change, meeting deadlines, understanding their role in fiscal responsibilities, and utilizing community resources to meet the needs of the population they serve, and is efficient in their work. Goal setting is not foreign to the case manager and must be done with purpose and timeliness. Filing reports to the Social Security Administration on their agency's management of client funds, for example, is fitted snugly between returning calls, answering emails, and advocating for the client. Staying calm in volatile situations, and practicing self awareness, compassion, and good use of rapport with the client are requirements. Case managers must be able to dance in the light of the successes with their clients and hold a hand out to those who are struggling. Skills used on a daily basis include time management, self motivation, multitasking, knowledge of community resources, and patience. As they are the "point guard" of their case load, knowledge of community resources and how to navigate them is paramount to a successful case manager. And having the ability to work as a team player goes without saying, as the case manager would contribute to their own demise operating alone. Planning, prioritization, and scheduling are at the center of the case manager's success.

The decision of in what order a case manager will do things is largely dependent upon rating of the direct impact to the client and the self efficacy of said client on that given day, as well as balancing the expectations of the agency. For example, the plan for completing paperwork related to a client's monthly budget is notably important but pales in comparison to the sudden emotional needs of a second client trying to overcome the loss of a friend weeks before. Likewise, to assist a client with transportation to a doctor's appointment for a diabetes check is without argument very important. Though, with use of the strengths model and community resources, that client can use the bus system or perhaps a family member to get them to this appointment. Assessing a person's ability to meet their own needs, via their immediate resources or the use of other community resources, is crucial to prioritizing and managing the daily grind. Attending regularly scheduled meetings, supervision sessions, and mandatory profession trainings are non-negotiables in the schedule; however, placing an office visit with a client to complete a service plan or review their progress toward goals helps manage the time constraints. With all of this, we ask: "Lunch? Well, that wasn't on the agenda for today—maybe tomorrow."

REFERENCES

Angell, B. (2003). Contexts of social relationship development among assertive community treatment clients. *Mental Health Services Research*, 5(1):13–25.

Case Management Society of America. (2012). Website: www.cmsa.org.

Center for Substance Abuse Treatment. *SAMHSA/CSAT Treatment Improvement Protocols*. Rockville (MD): Substance Abuse and Mental Health Services Administration (US). Accessed 11/29/11

Center for Medicare Services. (2000). *Olmstead* Updates No.3, HCFA Update (CMS, July 25, 2000.) Available online: http://www.cms.hhs.gov/smdl/downloads/smd072500b.pdf. Accessed 11/29/11

Center for Medicare Services. (November, 2006). "Application for a §1915 (c) HCBS Waiver—Version 3.4: Instruction, Technical Guide and Review Criteria," p. 132. Available online: http://www.hcbs. org/files/100/4982/Final_Version_3_4_Instructions_Technical_Guide_and_Review_Criteria_ Nov_2006.pdf.

Dieterich, M., Irving, C. B., Park, B., Marshall, M. (2010). Intensive case management for severe mental illness. *Cochrane Database System Review*. October 6(10):CD007906.

DiMatteo, M. R. (2004). Social support and patient adherence to medical treatment: A meta-analysis. Health Psychology, 23(2):207–218.

Gingerich, S., & Mueser, K. T. (2005). Illness management and recovery. In R. E. Drake, M. R. Merrens, & D. W. Lynde (Eds.), *Evidence-Based Mental Health Practice: A Textbook* (pp. 395–424). New York: Norton.

Gursansky, D. ; Harvey, J. & Kennedy, R. (2003). *Case Management: Policy, Practice, and Professional Business*. New York: Columbia University Press.

Hunter C. L., & Goodie J. L. (2010). Operational and clinical components for integrated-collaborative behavioral healthcare in the patient-centered medical home. *Families, Systems, & Health*, 28(4):308–321.

Miller, W. R., & Rollnick, S. (2002). *Preparing People for Change* (2nd ed.). New York: Guilford Press.

Mollica, R. and Gillespie, J. (2004). *Targeted Case Management Discussion*. Rutgers Center for State Health Policy/National Academy for State Health Policy, 2004. Available online: http://www.cshp.rutgers.edu/TACCMSconfPapers/MollicaGillespieTargetedCaseMgt.Pdf. Accessed 12/2/11

National Association of Alcoholism and Drug Abuse Counselors Certification Commission Oral Exam Guidelines. National Association of Alcoholism and Drug Abuse Counselors; Arlington, Va: 1986.

National Association of Social Workers. (June 1992). *Standards for Social Work Case Management*. Available at http://www.socialworkers.org/practice/standards/sw_case_mgmt.asp#def.

Porche, D. J. (2004). *Public and Community Health Nursing Practice: A Population-Based Approach*. Thousand Oaks, CA: Sage Publications.

Rapp, C., & Goscha, R. (2006). *The Strengths Model: Case Management with People with Psychiatric Disabilities*. New York: Oxford University Press.

Roberts, A. R., & Yeager, K. R., (2004). *Evidence-Based Practice Manual: Research and Outcome Measures in Health and Human Services*. New York: Oxford University Press.

Rosengren, D. (2009). *Building Motivational Interviewing Skills: A Practitioner Workbook*. New York: Guilford Press.

Saleebey, D. (Ed.). (1997). *The Strengths Perspective in Social Work Practice* (2nd ed.). New York: Longman.

Schneider, E. C., Hussey, P. S., & Schnyer, C. (2011). Payment Reform: Analysis of Models and Performance Measurement Implications. Study conducted by RAND Health and sponsored by the National Quality Forum, February 22, 2011.

CHAPTER 23

PRINCIPLES AND PRACTICES OF MEDICATION MANAGEMENT FOR PEOPLE WITH SCHIZOPHRENIA

Evolution within a Recovery-Based Framework of Care

PETER F. BUCKLEY AND ANTHONY O. AHMED

INTRODUCTION

Treating patients with schizophrenia can be highly rewarding, especially as there is the opportunity to reduce illness burden for the patient and family. There is the possibility of return to a good level of functioning, even to prior employment in a minority of patients. That said, treatment is challenging for many—even the majority of patients—and requires a taking a long-range perspective. Although certainly not the only aspect of care, medications play a central role. Medication treatments are complex and dynamically evolving over time—both because of the availability of new information as well as the new drugs coming "on line." This chapter does not cover the finer details of psychopharmacology. Nor does it provide an exhaustive account of the relative merits of each available antipsychotic. These important aspects are very well covered elsewhere (Van Os & Kapur, 2009; Jones & Buckley, 2006).

In this chapter, we provide a succinct overview of the principles and clinical practice of modern-day drug treatments for schizophrenia, specifically incorporating a recovery-based framework of care. Rather than address the complexities of medication management for all severe mental illnesses—an overly ambitious undertaking for a single chapter—we discuss medication practices for schizophrenia as a prototype for other severe mental illnesses. We hope that this approach will enable clinicians (some of whom may not be medication prescribers) to appreciate the broader context of care, discover how medication practices can be inculcated into a recovery-based framework, and realize the invaluable role that non-prescribers can and should play to support recovery-based medication management.

WHAT MEDICATIONS WILL—AND WILL NOT—DO

TWO CASES

Marilyn, aged 26, had schizophrenia since her early teens. Her parents were shocked to learn about her condition and, after seeking herbalist and other nontraditional cures, they eventually brought her to see a psychiatrist. A medication was tried, though Marilyn's parents were most concerned because the psychiatrist had warned them about the risk of her developing diabetes and Marilyn's brother had actually died five years earlier from complications of diabetes. Marilyn was less concerned about diabetes, and she actually thought that the medication was poison. She stopped the medication after three weeks and ended up in a hospital. Trials of other drugs invariably had the same outcome. Reluctantly, she and her parents agreed to her going on a long-acting injection form of medication. She often stops that, too, though now the clinic nurse calls her parents any time that she misses a clinic appointment for her injection.

Anne, aged 33, was diagnosed with schizophrenia five years ago. She has been able to return to college, though she has relapsed on two occasions. The first was three weeks after she stopped her medication following a painful muscle spasm of her neck. The second time was coming up to her exams, when she felt overwhelmed and "all stressed out." Anne has found the opportunity to talk with a peer support specialist to be really helpful to her, especially as both of them share similar experiences with medications that have only partially worked and have caused them both to gain weight. Twice a week they go to the gym together. Recently, Anne was about to quit her medications altogether, and her peer counselor persuaded her to go back to her psychiatrist, talk it over, and see if there was a better, newer drug now available for her.

These two brief stories illustrate the complexities of decisions as well as the various influences that keep a person engaged in their treatment. These themes will resonate as we now delve into the practical aspects of treating people with antipsychotic medications.

TARGET SYMPTOMS

Despite over fifty years of increasingly sophisticated neuroscience research, it is still unclear how antipsychotic drugs alter brain chemistry and functioning to achieve their therapeutic benefit (Van Os & Kapur, 2009) (Table 23.1). Antipsychotic medications work most effectively on positive symptoms of psychosis; that is, delusions (fixed, false beliefs), thought disorder (disorganized thinking and incoherent speech), and hallucinations (experiences of hearing or seeing things when there is nothing there). It was originally thought that they take about two weeks (of build-up) to work on these symptoms, though more recent research suggests an onset of action

Table 23.1 Putative Mechanisms of Action of Antipsychotic Medications

- Stimulate brain repair and generation of new cells
- Correct brain receptor dysfunctions:
  - Too much dopamine
  - Too much serotonin
  - Too little glutamate
- A combination of effects on many brain receptors
- Stabilize and repair lipids that make up nerve cells
- Improve blood flow and brain chemistry (e.g., glucose utilization) in key areas of the brain
- Correct signaling deficits in the "electrical wiring" of brain cells
- Many other theories

within days. Moreover, the earlier they "kick in," the more likely the person is to respond well to the drug.

DEFINING RESPONSE

"Response" is a complicated term to define because it depends on whether you consider the definition of response as the eradication of illness and return to prior level of functioning ("recovery," as the term is used in cancer therapy), or as keeping the person symptom-free ("remission"), or as reduction in distressing and debilitating symptoms of an acute relapse. The drugs are not curative in the sense of eradicating illness ("recovery" has a different connotation—see below) and at best, patients can achieve remission of symptoms, which usually comes along with improved functioning (Andreasen et al., 2005; Kane, 2006; Kane et al., 2007). For people who have experienced their first episode of psychosis, approximately 83 percent can anticipate achieving full remission within the first year. Most respond early to treatment, within days or weeks, although the time to remission is reported to average 35.7 weeks (Lieberman et al., 1993). When people relapse, regaining remission can be both harder to achieve and take longer. It appears that this pattern occurs with subsequent relapses, probably reflecting a gradual deterioration rather than accruing tolerance, or drug immunity.

For a small percentage of people, however, the medications appear to be relatively ineffective from early on, and these people appear to have a more severe, treatment-refractory illness (Kane et al., 1988). The earlier the onset of illness and the more insidious its presentation and course, the more likely it is that this will be a treatment-refractory illness. Additionally, some patients whose response to medications declines over successive treatments can end up with treatment-refractory illness. Recognizing these patterns early as opposed to following a continued "trial-and-error" process is important because these patients are de facto candidates for clozapine therapy (Kane et al., 1988; Jones et al., 2006), instead of repeated trials of each successive new antipsychotic (see below).

EFFECTIVENESS AGAINST OTHER SYMPTOMS

Antipsychotics work best against positive symptoms (Buchanan et al., 2009). They are effective in reducing manic symptoms and behaviors. They are effective for anxiety symptoms. They also reduce agitation, and they are often used as first-line treatments to reduce aggressive behaviors (even though they are not FDA-approved as "anti-aggressive agents"). These effects are powerful and are observed within minutes to hours, leading to the widespread use of these drugs in acute inpatient units and emergency rooms. This is also why they are used for dementia and for a host of other conditions, none of which are FDA-approved indications (Maher et al., 2011). These drugs are considerably less effective in treating "negative" symptoms of schizophrenia—that is, apathy, lack of motivation, self-neglect, impoverished speech, and social isolation. Unfortunately, these features, when present, are more disabling than positive symptoms (Van Os & Kapur, 2009). It has also increasingly become—at least in research circles—a focus to consider whether medications might be given early, even to "manage" prodromal symptoms of schizophrenia (Crossley et al., 2010).

Similarly, these drugs have, at best, marginal benefit in improving cognitive performance in schizophrenia (Keefe et al., 2007). These features, especially when prominent, add substantially to the disability of schizophrenia. While many people gain insight into their illness when medications relieve their delusions and hallucinations, it is not evident that the drugs themselves directly improve insight as a core domain of treatment. This distinction is important because, parenthetically, patients with poor insight are those who are least likely to accept treatment and who default on treatment over time.

Also, given that lack of insight is the commonest feature of psychosis and is more on a continuum than an "all-or-nothing" phenomenon, the extent to which a patient sees benefit from medication powerfully determines whether they will remain on medication (Buckley et al., 2007; Buckley, 2008; Byerly, 2007). Medications do not address many of the common concerns and consequences of psychosis: lack of friendships, impaired relationships, lack of work skills or job availability, general lack of well-being, insecurity, or lack of self-confidence. Accordingly, if a patient does not appreciate the impact of medications upon their positive symptoms and the ability to remain stable and avert relapses, patients can perceive little or no tangible benefit to them from continuing on treatment (Buckley et al., 2007).

SELECTING THE RIGHT MEDICATION

TRIAL-AND-ERROR CLINICIAN CHOICE

Although other areas of medicine are fast laying claim to "personalized medicine"—that is, the ability to tailor treatment for any given individual—unfortunately, the selection and choice of antipsychotic medication is still more of a trial-and-error process than anything else. A list of commonly used antipsychotic medications and their profile is given in Table 23.2. In the largest treatment study ever conducted on schizophrenia—the Comparative Antipsychotic Treatments Inventions Effectiveness (CATIE) trial—all of the tested antipsychotics proved generally similar in efficacy for people with chronic schizophrenia (Lewis & Lieberman, 2008; Lieberman et al., 2005; Lieberman & Stroup, 2011). The same was found in a comparative study of antipsychotics in first-episode schizophrenia (Kahn et al., 2008). The great paradox here is that, while each drug appears to be equal in effect from studies involving many patients, it is true that there is wide variability in response between patients: that is, one person might respond well to Drug A while another person might do poorly on Drug A and respond well to Drug B, while yet another

Table 23.2 Profile of Commonly Prescribed Antipsychotic Medications

Drug Name	Recommended Dose (mg/day)[a]	Available in Formulations Other Than Tablet (Yes/No)	Chief Side Effects
Haloperidol	6–20	Yes—IM PRN for acute use and depot, liquid	EPS, anticholinergic effects, weight gain, sedation, hypotension
Fluphenazine	6–20	Yes—IM PRN for acute use and depot	EPS, anticholinergic effects, hypertension, hypotension, NMS
Risperidone	2–8	Yes—IM depot, ODT, liquid	Prolactin elevation, weight gain, glucose and lipid abnormalities, EPS, QTc elongation
Paliperidone	3–15	Yes—IM depot	EPS, NMS, QTc elongation, glucose and lipid abnormalities, akathisia
Olanzapine	10–20	Yes—IM for acute use and depot, ODT	Weight gain, glucose and lipid abnormalities, sedation, hypotension, EPS, anticholinergic effects, akathisia
Quetiapine	300–750	No	Sedation, EPS, anticholinergic effects, weight gain, glucose and lipid abnormalities, hypotension
Ziprasidone	80–160	Yes—IM PRN for acute use	EPS, prolactin elevation, QTc elongation
Aripiprazole	10–30	Yes—Oral solution, ODT, IM for acute use	Nausea, headache, sedation, EPS
Asenapine	10–20	Wafer (ODT)- no tablet	EPS, sedation, somnolence, dizziness, weight gain, oral hypoesthesia
Iloperidone	12–24	No	Hypotension, sedation, dizziness, somnolence
Lurasidone	40–80	No	Akathisia, weigh gain, somnolence, Parkinsonism
Clozapine	150–600	No	Weight gain, glucose and lipid abnormalities, agranulocytosis, seizures, myocarditis

[a] Dosages are maintenance phase doses partly based on the Schizophrenia Patient Outcome Research Team (PORT) guidelines (Buchanan et al., 2009).

Key: IM = Intramuscular, usually in the form of long-acting injectables. ODT = Orodispersable tablet. EPS = Extrapyramidal symptoms. NMS = Neuroleptic malignant syndrome. Asenapine is currently available in only ODT form.

patient finds benefit only in Drug C or Drug D. This variability underscores the need to have availability, access, and choice to many medications rather than limited use of just a few drugs (Lieberman & Stroup, 2011). Moreover, at present, we have no way of determining in advance which drug might work best for a given patient. There is some research suggesting that variation in the genetics of key brain chemistry receptors (dopamine, serotonin receptors) might help us predict treatment response (Van Os & Kapur, 2009). This work is still in its infancy and not clinically relevant yet. There is also renewed evaluation of the comparative efficacy between old and new antipsychotic medications. On balance, new antipsychotics are (marginally) more effective than older drugs, although this point remains hotly debated and is still a point of inquiry in ongoing studies (Lewis & Lieberman, 2008; Lieberman & Stroup, 2011).

AVOIDING SIDE EFFECTS AS A STRATEGY FOR DRUG SELECTION

While as a general assessment it can be stated that antipsychotics are largely similar in efficacy, they do differ substantially in side-effect profiles (McEvoy et al., 2006; Stroup et al., 2011). These are important distinctions. Some drugs are more likely to cause weight gain, others to cause muscle stiffness, others to influence blood pressure, others to be more sedating, others to affect prolactin hormones. While no patient wants to "trade off" one side effect for another, it is often possible to evaluate the relative risk and impact of these side effects for a given patient. This can inform treatment choices. As an example, a patient who is already overweight might be better advised to select a drug with a lower liability for weight gain. As another example, a patient who has chronic sleeping difficulty may prefer a more sedating antipsychotic that can be given at night. Just as was the case in describing the efficacy profile of these drugs, these attributes are not absolute. Accordingly, it is important to bear in mind that a given patient may gain a lot of weight on a drug that appears—at least at face value and from available studies—to have a low propensity for promoting weight gain. Drug selection based on side-effect profile is like playing the odds and represents the other half of the equation in the trial-and-error decision-making process.

SHARED DECISION-MAKING

Recognizing the complexity of this decision to choose a medication, as well as how individual this choice will be, clinicians are increasingly engaging patients in a joint evaluation process. While this may seem intuitive, many patients heretofore left decisions about which medications to take in the hands of their doctor, recognizing his or her expertise and benevolence to act in their best interest. Consumerism, widespread availability of lay information about medications, and more active involvement of patients and their families in care all favor the shift toward shared decision-making. Studies suggest that most patients desire to participate in decision-making related to the course of their treatment and medication choices (Adams, Drake, & Wolford, 2007; Hamann et al., 2010; Levinson et al., 2005). Furthermore, most patients including people with schizophrenia are able to participate in shared decision-making (Bunn et al., 1997; Carpenter et al., 2000; Hamann et al., 2006). Educational interventions and decision aids have also been shown to help patients with impaired decisional capacity to work with providers in decision-making contexts (Carpenter et al., 2000; Deegan et al., 2008). Shared deci-sion-making has been shown to be feasible even within relatively short psychopharmacological visits (Hamann et al., 2006). With regard to clinical outcomes, shared decision-making has been shown to improve the quality of treatment decisions, treatment adherence, patient knowledge, and overall satisfaction with treatment (Hamann et al., 2006; Hamann et al., 2007; Loh et al., 2007; Malm et al., 2003).

STAYING ON MEDICATIONS—OR SWITCHING OFTEN?

ACHIEVING STABILITY AND RECOVERY OVER TIME

For people who have experienced more than one psychotic episode, medications offer the best hope of stability over time, as they have been shown unequivocally to reduce the risk of relapse (Kreyenbuhl et al., 2010). Treatment over time aims to use the lowest-dose effective drug to avert relapse while also minimizing the risk of side effects (Van Os & Kapur, 2009) (see Table 23.3). In principle, this seems straightforward. In practice, however, this is very complicated (Buckley, 2008). The amount of drug needed to achieve a sustained effect differs from patient to patient. Also, it is not clear that more of a given drug will result in a better outcome over time. On the other hand, it is clear that higher doses of a medication increase the risk of side effects. Thus, the patient and her or his clinician engage in a continual process of evaluation: Is the drug work-ing well enough? Should we try more? Should we just wait longer at the present dose? Should we switch to another drug instead that might work better? Added to these considerations is the equally important evaluation of side effects: Are the side effects tolerable or not? Would they get

Table 23.3 Key Considerations in the Use of Medications for Treating Schizophrenia

- Drug Choice
- Dose:
  - Amount
  - Frequency
- Mode of ingestion:
  - Tablet
  - Liquid
  - Dissolvable
  - Injection—
    - Acute
    - Long-Lasting
- Known efficacy:
  - Target symptoms
  - Other symptoms
- Known tolerability and side effects
- Use in combination with other drugs

worse and/or new ones appear if we tried a higher dose of drug? Should the dose of medication be reduced to relieve the present side effects? Should we switch to another drug that is less likely to have these side effects? These are vexing questions that clinicians are making decisions about with their patients on a daily basis—and unfortunately, we have not yet provided sufficient information from research to help with these complicated decisions.

With more medications come more choices, so that you could imagine how a patient might want to switch drugs repeatedly, trying each of the available medications in an effort to chase down the elusive "best fit" drug (Buckley, 2008). There is, of course, some merit to this strategy, which is in essence the trial-and-error approach extended over time. On the other hand, this strategy is risky because each time is essentially a roll of the dice all over again. The patient does not truly know how well the drug will work or what side effects will occur until he or she has tried the drug for an adequate trial. The term *adequate trial* is also important: it is estimated that it might take up to eight weeks to determine whether a medication is beneficial or not. That "adequate trial" also assumes that the drug is given at a reasonable dose that is likely to be beneficial. Again, there is variability in how people metabolize drugs, and some patients will require higher doses of a drug. Plasma levels of drugs are not available—apart from clozapine—to help guide treatment decisions.

THE RISKS AND GAINS OF SWITCHING MEDICATIONS

Switching medications is, in itself, a tricky proposition (Weiden & Buckley, 2007). It is best to avoid going "cold turkey"—that is, stopping one drug abruptly to start a new drug. This runs the risk of withdrawal side effects and increases the risk of relapse. However, being on two medications over time runs the heightened risk of side effects. It is best to adopt a gradual cross-taper of medications: gradually reduce the dose of the first medication while the new medication is being slowly titrated up in dose over time. This is, at present, more art than science (see Table 23.4).

Reviews suggest that whereas clozapine and olanzapine are associated with the highest risk of weight gain and metabolic disturbances, ziprasidone and aripiprazole may be associated with the lowest risk. Other second-generation antipsychotics such as risperidone and quetiapine pose low to moderate risks (Newcomer, 2005; Rummel-Kluge et al., 2010). It is possible that weight gain due to antipsychotics with high weight-gain risk might be reversible by switching to low weight-gain-risk antipsychotics. A recent study compared switching medications or staying on medications for patients who had weight gain or metabolic side effects of their treatment. Patients were randomized either to stay on risperidone, olanzapine, or quetiapine or to switch

---

Table 23.4 Key Principles in Switching Antipsychotic Medications

- Give an adequate trial first of the original medication
- Jointly review all options with patient and family
- Explain risks and potential benefits in basic terms and pertinent to this patient
- Gradual cross-titration
- Observe closely for withdrawal effects
- Observe closely for early relapse
- Complete the switch to avoid leaving patient unnecessarily on two medications
- Monitor to determine the benefit of the medication switch over time

to aripiprazole (Stroup et al., 2011). Both groups showed similar symptom outcomes over time, while weight loss was much better in patients who switched to aripiprazole. However, 44 percent of these patients discontinued treatment early on during one switch. This study illustrates the complexities of treatment choices.

MONITORING MEDICATIONS OVER TIME

MEDICATION NON-ADHERENCE

Taking any medication long-term is a challenge, whether it is an antihypertensive, antipsychotic, or any other medication that is prescribed for a chronic condition. This ubiquitous problem is all the more difficult in the long-term care of people with schizophrenia, in whom the very nature of the illness diminishes their insight, capacity, and judgment concerning the perceived benefits of medications. And it gets worse...the patient may even be paranoid about the clinician and the medication, believing that he or she is being poisoned. In such circumstances, it is highly unlikely that the patient will adhere to medication treatment over time. There are many other valid reasons (see Table 23.5) why a patient stops medication (Byerly, 2007). One or several reasons may prevail in any given circumstance. It is important to inquire both about the extent of medication adherence (most patients have partial adherence) as well as risk factors for non-adherence with medication. There are various techniques used to assess medication adherence, varying from simple "pill counts" to electronic monitors. Obtaining a detailed history about the pattern of medication use—from the patient and their friends and relatives—can be effective, but it does require a comprehensive and time-consuming evaluation. Brief, simple questions such as "Are you taking your medication?" are less likely to be reliable at assessing adherence in most patients.

Efforts to enhance medication adherence should of course depend upon the cause(s) of non-adherence. For example, if a patient quits his/her medication due to weight gain, it does not make sense to reinstate that medication, and the patient is more likely to be adherent to a drug with a lower likelihood of inducing weight gain. Medications can also be given in different formulations that can help detection of non-adherence. Instead of tablets, some antipsychotics (haloperidol, fluphenazine, risperidone, paliperidone, olanzapine) can be given as a long-acting

Table 23.5 Factors Contributing to Medication Non-Adherence in Schizophrenia

- Lack of insight about being ill
- Delusional about treatments and/or clinician
- Impaired access to medication
- Medication costs
- Ineffectiveness of medication
- Side effects
- Stigma about medications
- "Forgetfulness" and other cognitive deficits
- Substance abuse
- Poor continuity of care
- Lack of social, family support
- Taking too many medications already

injection. Although these seem pharmacologically no better than their oral counterparts, they can reduce the risk of relapse because clinicians are immediately aware of medication non-adherence when the patients do not show up for their scheduled appointments to receive their injections (Leucht et al., 2011).

MONITORING MEDICATION SIDE EFFECTS

Patients, relatives, and clinicians collectively need to remain vigilant for side effects of antipsychotic medications. Some (e.g., dry mouth) are troublesome but do not pose a serious medical risk. Others are serious and life-threatening, either acutely (as in one now-uncommon neuroleptic malignant syndrome) or over time (weight gain, elevated cholesterol, elevated triglycerides, glucose dysregulation: Weiden, 2007; Weiden & Buckley, 2007). In either circumstance, they may contribute to medication non-adherence and thereupon to a relapse of illness. It is essential to evaluate for side effects regularly. Since weight gain and metabolic disturbances now dominate the care of people with schizophrenia, it is important that these serious adverse effects be carefully monitored during treatment. Available evidence suggests that weight gain in the first three weeks of treatment will predict continued weight gain. Therefore, switching medications once weight gain occurs is a reasonable consideration (bearing in mind the caveats above). Equally, dietary management, exercise, and reducing sedentary behaviors are key to minimizing the risk of weight gain (Hassapidou et al., 2011; Loh, Meyer, & Leckband, 2006; Maayan & Correll, 2010). The preemptive use of statins or other anti-obesity agents (e.g., atorvastatin) has been studied, but this is not routine practice. Recently, metformin has gained attention as an intervention for antipsychotic-induced metabolic dysfunction. Studies suggest that alone or in combination with lifestyle modification, metformin might reverse weight gain induced by antipsychotics, including olanzapine, by the eighth week of treatment (Chen et al., 2008; Praharaj et al., 2011; Wu et al., 2008).

RESPONSE AND RECOVERY

It is also essential to continually evaluate the benefit of medications over time and to adjust the dosage of medications up or down accordingly. It is also important to consider whether it is time to try another medication or to add in a medication in an effort to boost the effect of the present medication. Knowing what to expect from the medication and how the patient is, or is not, improving over time is key to taking stock of the medication's risk–benefit profile for this patient. Enlisting the opinion of friends and family here is very helpful.

THE NEXT MEDICATION CHOICE?

POLYPHARMACY

It is estimated that about one-third of patients are receiving two antipsychotics simultaneously. Traditionally, this practice has been frowned upon and has been considered to be without scientific merit. However, a recent meta-analysis statistical compilation of studies stretching back 20 years showed a modest benefit for antipsychotic polypharmacy (Correll et al., 2009). Additionally, a recent randomized clinical trial of antipsychotic monotherapy versus polypharmacy showed better outcome in the multiple medications group—though these patients also experienced more weight gain (Essock et al., 2011). If this strategy is chosen, the reason for the selection of the second drug should be explicit, and both response and side effects should be carefully evaluated overtime. The decision to stop polypharmacy is often as important as the decision to start again; caution is warranted here. A summary of some polypharmacy combinations is given in Table 23.6.

WHEN TO TRY CLOZAPINE

When all else fails, clozapine should be tried. The problem is that clinicians should not wait to exhaust all options before going to clozapine. It is still recommended that clinicians consider clozapine after a failed trial of two antipsychotic medications (Moore et al., 2007). A history of suicidality or aggressive behavior might prompt earlier consideration. Clozapine is a complex and highly effective drug of proven superiority to other antipsychotics. It has, however, many serious side effects, including the requirement for regular (initially weekly) blood monitoring for agranulocytosis, neutropenia, and other hematological abnormalities. For these reasons, it is not used as a first-line treatment for schizophrenia.

"IT'S NOT ABOUT THE MEDICATIONS . . . STUPID"

BROADER CONTEXT

While medications are the bedrock of the treatment of schizophrenia, they are not "cure-alls" nor are they alone of benefit. Hogan (2010) and others have espoused a broader treatment con-

---

Table 23.6 Combinations of Medications for Treating Schizophrenia

- Antipsychotic + antipsychotic:
  - Second generation + second generation
  - Second generation + first generation
  - First generation + first generation
  - Clozapine + second generation
  - Clozapine + first generation
  - Injectable formulation + tablet formulation
- Antipsychotic + antidepressants
- Antipsychotic + anti-anxiety drug
- Antipsychotic + mood stabilizer
- Antipsychotic + cognitive enhancing drugs
- Antipsychotic + drugs used to treat side effects:
  - Benztropine for muscle side effects
  - Cholesterol-lowering drugs
  - Anti-obesity drugs
  - Stimulants

text in which medications play a role but without being "the last word." Hogan emphasizes the following objectives in managing psychosis:

- Early identification and intervention
- Continuity of care and trust
- Hope
- Housing "first"
- Maximizing normal development

It is therefore important that our care be considered in a broader framework. Specifically, there are national efforts to enhance the quality of care in medicine. Such expectations should also pertain to mental health care. Proposed measures of quality for schizophrenia are given in Table 23.7.

RECOVERY-BASED CARE

While most of this chapter has focused on medications and the practicalities of their use, it is salient that people's own resilience may be the most powerful determinant of outcome over the long haul (Peebles et al., 2007). Much has been written about recovery—viewed more as a journey or process than an outcome. Of course, recovery-based care that emphasizes the patient as the driver of care is not antithetical to good medication practices. Dr. Robert Liberman, a psychiatrist who has combined good medication practices with psychosocial rehabilitation practices, gives a wise account of how to "practice what you preach" (see Table 23.8). Similarly, Noordsy and colleagues (2000) use the term *recovery-oriented psychopharmacology* to envision a role for psychiatrists that places recovery as an overarching principle that guides medication management and a goal to be accomplished in concert with rehabilitative interventions for schizophrenia.

The recovery model has implications for the practice of medication management in a number of notable ways:

1. *Psychopharmacology goals*: One implication of a recovery focus in psychopharmacology is that it encourages practitioners to adopt a new strategy for managing symptoms. The goal of psychopharmacology has evolved within recovery-based systems, from a focus on symptom remission, to maximizing overall wellness and community living. Treatment objectives include careful management of symptoms and side-effect profiles—activities that now involve a collaborative effort between the practitioner and

---

Table 23.7 Proposed Quality-of-Care Measures in the Treatment of Schizophrenia

- Use and continuity of antipsychotic medications
- Cardiovascular health and diabetes screening
- Cardiovascular health and diabetes monitoring
- Follow-up after hospitalization for schizophrenia
- Emergency department utilization
- Cervical cancer screening for women with schizophrenia

Source: National Committee for Quality Assurance (NCQA), September 2011 http://www.ncqa.org.

Table 23.8 Lieberman's (2010) Principles of Recovery-Based Care

- *Individualized*: Treatment is tailored to the individual patient, attending to personal goals, cultural and individual values, and phase of illness.
- *Skill building*: Treatment focuses not merely on reducing symptoms, but on building the individual's own capacity to manage his or her overall wellness.
- "*Remediate cognitive deficits*": Patients often report that cognitive deficits impact their lives more than other symptoms and reduce their sense of efficacy. Attending to cognitive deficits is consistent with recovery principles.
- *Patient voices*: Providers must give patients voices and be willing to listen. Incorporating the services of peer-support specialists would be invaluable in this respect.
- *Family involvement*: Families should be incorporated into treatment teams and treatment decision-making.
- *Strength-focus*: Underscore the individual's own strengths, supports, and personal resources in treatment planning.
- *Progress*: Small improvements are not to be taken lightly but built on. Encourage the patient's own improvements and continue to instill hope.
- *Quality*: Providers should provide with fidelity and evidence-based practices, offering choices of treatment options whenever these choices are available.

Source: Liberman, R. P. (2010).

the patient to reclaim a life once derailed by mental illness. Efforts to manage symptoms may involve taking medication but should also include learning about mental illness, treatment, and other means besides medications to cope with symptoms. For example, many patients report that employment provides a focus for their attention on tasks outside of their internal experience, which may assist them in reducing the attention that they give to their symptoms (Mueser et al., 1997). This typically results in symptoms' being experienced as more remote or less powerful, and over time, in an experience of greater control or mastery over symptoms.

2. *Self-management*: A number of illness self-management programs, including Wellness Recovery Action Planning (WRAP; Copeland, 1997) and Illness Management and Recovery (IMR; Mueser et al., 2006), teach people with psychiatric illnesses strategies for managing their own symptoms. IMR includes a module focused on strategies for medication self-management—such as adaptation strategies for people who may suffer memory impairments that impact taking medications. It also incorporates social skills training that can be used to help patients learn how to ask questions related to medication use, side effects, and emerging symptoms. Whereas IMR incorporates evidence-based psychosocial interventions, WRAP derives more from consumer experiences and includes various coping strategies for maintaining wellness. IMR and WRAP training have been shown to improve outcomes in people with schizophrenia, including their self-management, recovery attitudes, and overall functioning.

3. *Rethinking medication adherence*: Most practitioners consider treatment adherence paramount for experiencing immediate and long-term improvements from psychiatric symptoms. The traditional adherence/compliance model has been criticized on the grounds that it is a paternalistic approach to treatment that requires the patient to comply with the practitioner's treatment recommendations (Deegan & Drake, 2006). Furthermore, the practitioner intervenes in ways to increase conformity rather than

encourage the patient's own self-direction and independence. Paradoxically, the adherence/compliance model has been associated with high rates of non-adherence and treatment disengagement (O'Brien, Fahmy, & Singh, 2009). Deegan and Drake have recently brought to light the role of complex decision-making processes and decisional conflicts in the medication-use behavior of people with long-term illnesses (Table 23.9). They encourage practitioners to embrace shared decision-making (described earlier) as a means of resolving such decisional conflicts and evaluating the impact of medications on the patient's valued social roles and quality of life. In this context, the patient's own involvement and investment in the decision-making process improve the quality of the treatment strategy and drive improvements in their symptoms and quality of life.

4. *Motivational interviewing*: Miller and Rollnick (2002) developed motivational interviewing as a directive, yet person-centered style of communication to resolve ambivalence by harnessing the individual's own motivations to change. In motivational interviewing, the practitioner seeks to understand the "whole person's" interests, goals, and aspirations. Given that the goal of recovery-focused medication management is to assist the individual in reclaiming such interests and life goals, the focus on goals provides them an intrinsic motivation to engage actively in psychopharmacological treatment. The practitioner empathizes with the patient's apparent resistance to taking medications by helping the individual resolve contradictory motivations to improve or at least stay the same. This involves instilling a state of cognitive dissonance by underscoring the discrepancy between the patient's own life goals and current behavior. Studies suggest that this approach may improve insight and treatment adherence of people with schizophrenia (Martino et al., 2000; Rusch & Corrigan, 2002).

5. *Continuity with other treatment models*: It is quite common for the activities of physicians within some treatment teams to be discordant with the objectives of rehabilitation and recovery-based interventions. This often leads to poorly coordinated care in the service of the patient. Consider a situation in which a patient's rehabilitation objectives include participating in psychoeducation, social skills training, and computerized cognitive remediation geared toward vocational life goals. In disjunctive care, psychopharmacologists prescribe without significant input from other treatment team members about the role of alternative and adjunctive interventions in the patient's care and how medications may enhance or detract from the effects of such interventions. In such a situation, medications with a more benign side-effect profile— fewer anticholinergic, EPS, cognitive, and sedative effects—may allow the patient to better participate in such interventions. The recovery model provides a context for coordinating services and fostering communication and collaboration across treatment disciplines. We discuss this issue in more detail in the next section.

Table 23.9 Deegan and Drake's (2006) Medication-Related Decisional Conflicts

- Is the effect of this medication regimen more tolerable than the actual illness?
- Am I better of taking medications all the time or when symptoms are most distressing?
- Is taking medications worth the associated stigma, discrimination, and social rejection?
- Is this regimen an unwanted reminder of my illness?
- Is this medication regimen actually beneficial?
- Is this regimen interfering with activities and roles that I value?

RECOVERY-FOCUSED MEDICATION MANAGEMENT: OPERATING WITHIN INTERDISCIPLINARY TEAMS

Interdisciplinary treatment teams are a characteristic of modern community mental health settings, often comprising a treatment team coordinator, psychiatrists, psychologists, behavioral specialists, social workers, case managers, physician assistants, nurses, peer specialists, and other therapists and support staff. An interdisciplinary approach to the care of people with severe mental illnesses is consistent with a biopsychosocial approach that recognizes that patients have needs that span several life domains, including interpersonal, vocational, recreational, and psychological domains. Interdisciplinary teams offer the benefit of representing expertise from various disciplines, which may contribute to overall treatment quality, continuity, and effectiveness, and provide truly holistic care (Jefferies & Chan, 2004). Despite their potential benefits, interdisciplinary teams are fraught with interdisciplinary tension resulting from conflicting treatment goals and objectives, overlapping professional roles, overlapping boundaries of practice, and strong professional identification unmatched by team identification (Byrne, 2005; Donnison, Thompson, & Turpin, 2009). The role of providers from various disciplines in the larger context of the treatment team and the quality of their interaction with other providers is one that impacts the quality of patient care, organizational efficiency, and the professional satisfaction of providers.

The practice of medication management on interdisciplinary teams is one that presents a unique challenge but a great opportunity for psychiatrists and other mental health professionals in community mental health settings. While most mental health professionals defer to psychiatrists about medication-related decisions, the contributions of non-medical practitioners to medication decisions and their benefits can be invaluable. Yet some psychiatrists may view the opinions of other team members as an impingement on their professional territory. The bone of the contention is whether non-medical interdisciplinary team members should obtain, contribute to, or provide information that informs psychopharmacological practice and decision-making. The spectrum of opinion among mental health professionals regarding this issue ranges from those who believe that confluence and continuity in mental health practice is best served when other professionals are involved, to those who believe that all medication-related discussions and practice should be circumscribed to psychiatrists and other medical doctors.

In the context of an overarching vision of recovery, it would appear that when all practitioners focus on fostering a patient's experience of recovery, the shared vision would encourage an interest in sharing, collaborating, and consulting across disciplines, rather than turf wars (Noordsy et al., 2000). In contrast, Harrison and colleagues' (2011) recent proposal that psychiatry increase its focus on psychopharmacology in order to distinguish itself from other mental health professions and secure its future as a medical discipline does little to promote such confluence between psychiatry and other mental health professions. What, then, are practices that non-medical team members can and should engage in to inform and support psychopharmacological treatment? In a similar vein, what role should psychiatrists play in informing and supporting the rehabilitative efforts of other mental health professionals?

In most community mental health settings, non-medical providers have longer and more frequent contact with patients and are thus in position to evaluate the patient's adherence to and response to medications, any side effects, emerging symptoms, and functioning in their community in between psychiatric visits. By regularly communicating their impressions to psychiatrists, non-medical providers would be in position to inform the course of psychophar-macological treatment. A collaborative discussion of the patient's aspirations, strengths, inter-ests, abilities, history, and other information emerging from psychotherapy visits may inform the relatively shorter psychopharmacological visits, allowing them to be spent efficiently. Such discussions also allow the psychopharmacologists to practice within the context of the rehabili-tation goals, such as tailoring a medication regimen to allow the patient to address vocational goals (e.g., adjusting medication schedule around their work schedule) or sex and intimacy goals (providing medications less likely to elevate prolactin levels). Psychologists complete com-prehensive evaluations that inform diagnosis and medication management. Such evaluations typically include a comprehensive history of psychiatric treatment, medication use history, and treatment response that may inform subsequent treatment. It is our experience that psychop-harmacologists welcome discussions as well as formal and informal assessments of patients' ongoing functioning by non-medical providers in order to inform their psychopharmacological practice.

The activities of non-medical providers can go a long way toward accentuating the benefits of medication management. Certain psychosocial interventions such as social skills training (SST; Bellack, 2004), functional adaptive skills training (FAST; Patterson et al., 2006), and IMR include modules that help patients collaborate better with prescribers during psychopharma-cological visits, and take their medications correctly. For example, SST includes modules that teach patients to ask their psychiatrist questions about health problems and medications, report problematic side effects, and negotiate adjustments. The FAST intervention teaches patients the benefits of medications and uses modeling and skill-building exercises to show them how to read medication labels and correctly follow physician recommendations. Other interventions such as cognitive adaptation training and cognitive remediation may be beneficial to patients for whom cognitive deficits such as memory and attention impact their medication adherence (Velligan et al., 2008). Patients whose lack of financial resources may undermine medication adherence may benefit from an efficient collaboration between a psychiatrist and a case manager to match medication needs with community programs that support medication needs. The col-laborative effort of the psychiatrist and the rehabilitation specialist would be required to deter-mine which psychosocial interventions may be indicated to support medication management and implement such intervention. The aforementioned examples illustrate not only the potential of non-medical providers to contribute to psychopharmacological efforts, but the confluence of psychopharmacology and psychosocial rehabilitation in promoting recovery.

Psychiatrists should similarly support the rehabilitative work of other disciplines by encour-aging the patient's participation and inquiring about the patient's progress at accomplishing rehabilitative goals. As treatment team leaders, psychiatrists should assume the responsibility of integrating the perspectives of multiple disciplines into a comprehensive picture of the patient's challenges and encourage the coordination of services across disciplines to promote the patient's recovery. This includes monitoring and partnering with other disciplines to ensure that other treatment objectives beyond medication management—including psychotherapy, case manage-ment, and advocacy needs—are met. All disciplines should assume the role of educating other disciplines about skills and knowledge they possess that are germane to the patient's care, with-out sacrificing their own unique contributions. For example, interdisciplinary teams provide an opportunity for non-prescribing practitioners to learn about medications, and for all disciplines to learn about psychological treatments, behavioral support, advocacy, peer-led interventions, and case management. This not only provides an opportunity for professional development but advances the integration and continuity of all treatment modalities.

CONCLUSIONS

Medication management is central to the care of people with schizophrenia. The complexity of the illness and the myriad of available medication choices require complex decision-making that includes evaluating symptoms, patient-by-drug responses, side effects, and overall wellness. Recent advances in the practice of medication management include the implementation of a recovery-based approach to psychopharmacological practice. The recovery model challenges practitioners to adopt new goals, strategies, and definition of outcomes in the treatment of schizophrenia and other severe mental illnesses. Rather than operate within a strict compliance/adherence model, recovery-oriented practitioners engage in collaborative, shared decision-making to establish treatment goals and design medication strategies. Medication management can be practiced in a way that is consistent with recovery by incorporating shared decision-making, self-management programs, and motivational interviewing into psychopharmacological practice. Interdisciplinary teams offer a unique opportunity for providers from non-medical disciplines to contribute to and accentuate the benefits of medications.

REFERENCES

Adams, J. R., Drake, R. E., & Wolford, G. L. (2007). Shared decision-making preferences of people with severe mental illness. *Psychiatric Services, 58,* 1219–1221.

Andreasen, N. C., Carpenter Jr., W. T., Kane, J. M., Lasser, R. A., Marder, S. A., & Weinberger, D. R. (2005). Remission in schizophrenia: Proposed criteria and rationale for consensus. *American Journal of Psychiatry, 162,* 441–449.

Bellack, A. S. (2004). Skills training for people with severe mental illness. *Psychiatric Rehabilitation Journal, 27,* 375–391.

Buchanan, R. W., Kreyenbuhl, J., Kelly, D. A., Noel, J. M., Boggs, D. L., Fischer, B. A., et al. (2009). The 2009 Schizophrenia PORT psychopharmacological treatment recommendations and summary statements. *Schizophrenia Bulletin, 36*(1), 71–93.

Buckley, P. F., Wirshing, D. A., Bhushan, P., Pierri, J. M., Resnick, S. A., & Wirshing, W. C. (2007). Lack of insight in schizophrenia: Impact on treatment adherence. *Central Nervous System Drugs, 21* (2), 129–141.

Buckley, P. F. (2008). Factors that influence treatment success in schizophrenia. *Journal of Clinical Psychiatry,* 69(suppl 3), 4–10.

Bunn, M. H., O ' Connor, A. M., Tansey, M. S., Jones, B. D., & Stinson, L. E. (1997). Characteristics of clients with schizophrenia who express certainty or uncertainty about continuing treatment with depot neuroleptic medication. *Archives of Psychiatric Nursing, 11,* 238–248.

Byerly, M. J. (2007). Antipsychotic medication adherence in schizophrenia. *Psychiatric Clinics of North America,* 30(3), 437–452.

Byrne, M. (2005) Community mental health team functioning: A review of the literature. *The Irish Psychologist,* 21(12), 347–350.

Carpenter, W. T., Gold, J. M., Lahti, A. C., Queern, C. A., Conley R. R., Bartko, J. J., et al. (2000). Decisional capacity for informed consent in schizophrenia research. *Archives of General Psychiatry, 57,* 533–538.

Chen, C., Chiu, C., Huang, M., Wu, T. H., Liu, H. C., & Lu, M. L. (2008). Metformin for metabolic dysregulation in schizophrenic patients treated with olanzapine. *Progress in Neuro-Psychopharmacology and Biological Psychiatry, 32*(4), 925–931.

Copeland, M. E. (1997). *Wellness Recovery Action Plan.* Dummerston, VT: Peach Press.

Correll, C. U., Rumell-Kluge, C., Corves, C., Kane, J. M., & Leucht, S. (2009). Antipsychotic combinations vs. monotherapy in schizophrenia: A meta-analysis of randomized controlled trials. *Schizophrenia Bulletin, 35*(2), 443–457.

Crossley, N. A., Constante, M., McGuire, P., & Power, P. (2010). Efficacy of atypical v. typical antipsychotics in the treatment of early psychosis: Meta-analysis. *British Journal of Psychiatry, 196,* 434–439.

Deegan, P. E., & Drake, R. E. (2006). Shared decision-making and medication management in the recovery process. *Psychiatric Services, 57*(11), 1636–1639.

Deegan, P. E., Rapp, C., Holter, M., & Riefer, M. (2008). Best practices: A program to support shared decision making in an outpatient psychiatric medication clinic. *Psychiatric Services, 59*(6), 603–605.

Donnison, J., Thompson A.R., & Turpin, G. (2009). A qualitative exploration of communication within the community mental health team. *International Journal of Mental Health Nursing, 18*(5), 310–317.

Essock, S. M., Schooler, N. R., Stroup, S., McEvoy, J. P., Rojas, I., Jackson, C., et al. (2011). Effectiveness of switching from antipsychotic polypharmacy to monotherapy. *American Journal of Psychiatry, 168,* 702–708.

Hamann, J., Langer, B., Winkler, V., Busch, R., Cohen, R., Leucht, S., et al. (2006). Shared decision making for inpatients with schizophrenia. *Acta Psychiatrica Scandinavica, 114,* 265–273.

Hamann, J., Cohen, R., Leucht, S., Busch, R., & Kissling, W. (2007). Shared decision making and long-term outcome in schizophrenia treatment. *Journal of Clinical Psychiatry, 68,* 992–997.

Hamann, J., Kruse, J., Schmitz, F. S., Kissling, W., & Pajonk, F. G. (2010). Patient participation in antipsychotic drug choice decisions. *Psychiatry Research, 178,* 63–67.

Harrison, P. J., Baldwin, B. S., Barnes, T. R. E., Burns, T., Ferrier, I. N., & Nutt, D. J. (2011). No psychiatry without psychopharmacology. *British Journal of Psychiatry, 199,* 263–265.

Hassapidou, M., Papadimitriou, K., Athanasiodou, N., Tokmakidou, V., Pagkalos, I., Vlahavas, G., et al . (2011). Changes in body weight, body composition and cardiovascular risk factors after long-term nutritional intervention in patients with severe mental illness: An observational study. *BMC Psychiatry, 11* (31), Retrieved October 26, 2011, from http://www.biomedcentral.com/1471-244X/11/31.

Hogan, M. (2010). Updated schizophrenia PORT treatment recommendations: A commentary. *Schizophrenia Bulletin, 36*(1), 104–106.

Jefferies, N., & Chan, K. K. (2004). Multidisciplinary team working: Is it both hostile and effective? *International Journal of Gynecological Cancer, 14*(2), 210–211.

Jones, P. B., Barnes, T. R., Davies, L., Dunn, G., Lloyd, H., Hayhurst, K. P., et al. (2006). Randomized controlled trial of the effect on quality of life of second- vs. first-generation antipsychotic drugs in schizophrenia: Cost Utility of the Latest Antipsychotic Drugs in Schizophrenia Study (CUtLASS 1). *Archives of General Psychiatry, 63*(10), 1079–1087.

Jones, P. B., & Buckley, P. F. (2006). *Schizophrenia.* London: Elsevier.

Kahn, R. S., Fleischacker, W. W., Boter, H., Davidson, M., Vergouwe, Y., Keet, I. P. M., et al. (2008). Effectiveness of antipsychotic drugs in first episode schizophrenia and schizophreniform disorder: An open randomized clinical trial. *The Lancet, 371*(9618), 1085–1097.

Kane, J. M., Honigfeld, G., Singer, J., Meltzer, H. Y., and the Clozaril Collaborative Study Group. (1988). Clozapine for the treatment-resistant schizophrenic. *Archives of General Psychiatry, 45*(9), 789–796.

Kane, J. M. (2006). Commentary on the Clinical Antipsychotic Trials of Intervention Effectiveness (CATIE). *Journal of Clinical Psychiatry, 67,* 831–832.

Kane, J. M., Crandall, D. T., Marcus, R. N., Eudicone, J., Pikalov, A., Carson, W. H., et al. (2007). Symptomatic remission in schizophrenia patients treated with aripiprazole or haloperidol for up to 52 weeks. *Schizophrenia Research, 95,* 143–150.

Keefe, R. S., Bilder, R. M., Davis, S. M., Harvey, P. D., Palmer, B. W., Gold, J. M., et al. (2007). Neurocognitive effects of antipsychotic medications in patients with chronic schizophrenia in the CATIE trial. *Archives of General Psychiatry 64*(6), 633–647.

Kreyenbuhl, J., Buchanan, R. W., Dickerson, F. B., & Dixon, L. (2010). The Schizophrenia Patient Outcome Research Team (PORT): Updated treatment recommendations, 2009. *Schizophrenia Bulletin, 36*(1), 99–103.

Leucht, C., Heres, S., Kane, J. M., Kissling, W., Davis, J. M., Leucht, S. (2011). Oral versus depot antipsychotic drugs for schizophrenia—A critical systematic review and meta-analysis of randomised long-term trials. *Schizophrenia Research, 127*(1), 83–92.

Levinson, W., Kao, A., Kuby, A., & Thisted, R. A. (2005). Not all patients want to participate in decision making. *Journal of General Internal Medicine, 20,* 531–535.

Lewis, S., & Lieberman, J. A. (2008). CATIE and CUtLASS: Can we handle the truth? *British Journal of Psychiatry, 192,* 161–163.

Liberman, R. P. (2010). The Ten Commandments of Psychiatric Rehabilitation (online). Retrieved November 1, 2011 from http://www.nami.org/Content/Microsites125/NAMI_Ventura_County/Home116/Committee_Meetings_and_Announcements/TenCommandments.pdf.

Lieberman, J., Jody, D., Geisler, S., Alvir, J., Loebel, A., Szymanski, S., et al. (1993). Time course and biological correlates of treatment response in first-episode schizophrenia. *Archives of General Psychiatry, 50,* 369–376.

Lieberman, J. A., Stroup, T. S., McEvoy, J. P., Swartz, M. S., Rosenheck, R. A., Perkins, D. O., et al. (2005). Effectiveness of antipsychotic drugs in patients with chronic schizophrenia. *New England Journal of Medicine, 353,* 1209–1223.

Lieberman, J. A. & Stroup, T. S. (2011). The NIMH-CATIE Schizophrenia Study: What did we learn? *American Journal of Psychiatry, 168*(8), 770–775.

Loh, H., Meyer, J. M., & Leckband, S. G. (2006). A comprehensive review of behavioral interventions for weight management in schizophrenia. *Annals of Clinical Psychiatry, 18*(1), 23–31.

Loh, A., Simon, D., Wills, C. E., Kriston, L., Niebling, W., & Härter, M. (2007). The effects of a shared decision making intervention in primary care of depression: A cluster-randomized controlled trial. *Patient Education and Counseling, 67,* 324–333.

Maayan, L., & Correll, C. U. (2010). Management of antipsychotic-related weight-gain. *Expert Review of Neurotherapeutics, 10*(7), 1175–1200.

Maher, A. R., Maglione, M., Bagley, S., Suttorp, M., Hu, J., Ewing, B., et al. (2011). Efficacy and comparative effectiveness of atypical antipsychotic medications for off-label uses in adults: A systematic review and meta-analysis. *Journal of the American Medical Association, 306,* 1359–1369.

Malm, U., Ivarsson B., Allebeck P., & Falloon I. (2003). Integrated care in schizophrenia: A two-year randomized controlled study of two community-based treatment programs. *Acta Psychiatrica Scandinavica, 107,* 415–423.

Martino, S., Carroll, K. M., O' Malley, S. S., & Rounsaville, B. J. (2000). Motivational interviewing with psychiatrically ill substance abusing patients. *American Journal on Addictions, 9,* 88–91.

McEvoy, J. P., Lieberman, J. A., Stroup, T. S., Davis, S. M., Meltzer, H. Y., Rosenheck, R. A., et al. (2006). Effectiveness of clozapine versus olanzapine, quetiapine, and risperidone in patients with chronic schizophrenia who did not respond to prior atypical antipsychotic treatment. *American Journal of Psychiatry, 163,* 600–610.

Miller, W. R., & Rollnick, S. (2002). *Motivational Interviewing: Preparing People for Change* (2nd edition). New York: Guildford Press.

Moore, T. A., Buchanan, R. W., Buckley, P. F., Chiles, J. A., Conley, R. R., Crismon, M. L., et al. (2007). The Texas Medication Algorithm Project antipsychotic algorithm for schizophrenia: 2006 update. *Journal of Clinical Psychiatry, 68*(11), 1751–1762.

Mueser, K. T., Becker, D. R., Torrey, W. C., Xie, H., Bond, G. R., Drake, R. E., et al. (1997). Work and nonvocational domains of functioning in persons with severe mental illness: A longitudinal analysis. *Journal of Nervous and Mental Disease, 185,* 419–426.

Mueser, K. T., Meyer, P. S., Penn, D. L., Clancy, R., Clancy, D. M., & Salyers, M. P. (2006). The illness management and recovery program: Rationale, development, and preliminary findings. *Schizophrenia Bulletin, 32,* 32–43.

Newcomer, J. W. (2005). Second-generation (atypical) antipsychotics and metabolic effects: A comprehensive literature review. *CNS Drugs, 19* (Suppl 1), 1–93.

Noordsy, D. L., Torrey, W. C., Mead, S., Brunette, M., Potenza, D., & Copeland, M. E. (2000). Recovery-oriented psychopharmacology: Redefining the goals of antipsychotic treatment. *Journal of Clinical Psychiatry, 61,* 22–29.

O'Brien, A., Fahmy, I. R., & Singh, S. P. (2009). Disengagement from mental health services: A literature review. *Social Psychiatry and Psychiatric Epidemiology, 44*(7), 558–568.

Patterson, T. L., Mausbach, B. T., McKibbin, C., Goldman, S., Bucardo, J., & Jeste, D. V. (2006). Functional adaptation skills training (FAST): a randomized trial of a psychosocial intervention for middle-aged and older patients with chronic psychotic disorders. *Schizophrenia Research, 86,* 291–299.

Peebles, S. A., Mabe, P. A., Davidson, L., Frick, L., Buckley, P. F., & Fenley, G. (2007). Recovery and systems transformation for schizophrenia. *Psychiatric Clinics of North America, 30,* 567–583.

Praharaj, S. K., Jana, A. K., Goyal, N., & Sinha, V. K. (2011). Metformin for olanzapin-induced weight gain: a systematic review and meta-analysis. *British Journal of Clinical Pharmacology, 71*(3), 377–382.

Rummel-Kluge, C., Komossa, K., Schwarz, S., Hunger, H., Schmid, F., Lobos, C. A., et al. (2010). Head-to-head comparisons of metabolic side effects of second generation antipsychotics in the treatment of schizophrenia: A systematic review and meta-analysis. *Schizophrenia Research, 123* (2–3), 225–233.

Rusch, N., & Corrigan, P. W. (2002). Motivational interviewing to improve insight and treatment adherence in schizophrenia. *Psychiatric Rehabilitation Journal, 26* (1), 23–32.

Stroup, T. C., McEvoy, J. P., Ring, K. D., Hamer, R. H., LaVange, L. M., Swartz, M. S., et al. (2011). A randomized trial examining the effectiveness of switching from olanzapine, quetiapine, or risperidone to aripiprazole to reduce metabolic risk: comparison of Antipsychotics for Metabolic Problems (CAMP). *American Journal of Psychiatry, 168,* 947–956.

Van Os, J., & Kapur, S. (2009). Schizophrenia. *Lancet, 22,* 635–645.

Velligan, D. I., Diamond, P. M., Mintz, J., Maples, N., Li, X., Zeber, J., et al. (2008). The use of individually tailored environmental supports to improve medication adherence and outcomes in schizophrenia. *Schizophrenia Bulletin, 34*(3), 483–493.

Weiden, P. J. (2007). EPS profiles: the atypical antipsychotics are not all the same. *Journal of Psychiatric Practice, 13*(1), 13–24.

Weiden, P. J., & Buckley, P. F. (2007). Reducing the burden of side effects during long-term antipsychotic therapy: the role of switching medications. *Journal of Clinical Psychiatry*,*68* (suppl 6), 14–23.

Wu, R., Zhao, J., Jin, H., Shao, P., Fang, M. S., Guo, X. F., et al. (2008). Lifestyle intervention and metformin for treatment of antipsychotic-induced weight gain: a randomized control trial. *Journal of the American Medical Association*, *299*(2), 185–193.

CHAPTER 24

OPTIMIZING MEDICATION IN THE SERVICE OF RECOVERY

Is There a Path for Reducing Over-Utilization of Psychiatric Medications?

NEIL FALK, DANIEL B. FISHER, AND WILL HALL

INTRODUCTION

There was a time when mines in the United States produced ores to go into blast furnaces to produce steel to go to factories that produced cars, radios, toasters, televisions, or other things we could buy at the hardware store or corner store. Now, instead of huge factories rising to the sky and puffing smoke from their furnaces making steel, we have huge medical centers rising above the hills, producing steam for their heating systems to warm their clinics where medical care is provided. There is a lot of momentum to this. There are treatments for all illnesses, and diagnoses to go with all treatments that can be billed to someone, and even though 50 million people in this country currently have no "official" access to health care, most of them—and the rest of us who have some sort of health insurance—still find a way to get pills from somewhere. Sometimes it seems like in America today the gross national product has become medical care: it is as if the purpose of our existence is to be patients so that perhaps we can help the economy recover. Truthfully, we are all consumers of healthcare products cradle to grave.

But what if we don't want to be patients (and most of us really don't want to be patients)? What if we are worried about the long-term effect of taking various chemical substances into our bodies (most research drug trials only last six months)? For each of us to be smart patients, we need to know the risks and benefits of receiving treatment and the risks and benefits of refusing treatment. Sadly, for some of us, remaining alive is a matter of accepting some kind of medical care. If we have a heart attack we usually want something done to fix the problem (a stent or a triple bypass, for example) so that we may live a while longer. If we become depressed and suicidal there is still often a part of us that says, "I want some treatment that will help me feel better" (like a good therapist, or an antidepressant medicine, or both). But an even more subtle question is, At what point is treatment enough or no longer necessary? At what point may the treatment be worse for me than the illness? How do we know when? What happens if we get it wrong?

Wouldn't it be great if we could answer these questions? In this chapter we will raise these issues as food for thought, so to speak, although we doubt if anyone has the definitive answers as yet. Perhaps if we can shed light on this question, a new balance will be struck between the medical establishment and the community of patients, a balance that will give us a sense of equality and mindfulness as we decide what treatment we might need for whatever mental health problem we may have.

Our motivation for putting these thoughts into words comes from the fact that, of the three authors of this chapter, two of us have experienced extensive mental health treatment with medications. The other author provides treatment to a variety of people, including young persons experiencing symptoms of psychosis. All of us are mental health professionals involved in recovery or prevention services for people who suffer from severe forms of psychosis.

Each of us who suffers has a unique story to tell, with ups and downs. Although perhaps not typical of anyone else here, is a brief vignette of one of us:

> *Our family rarely talked about feelings. My sister and I underwent traumas our family did not discuss. So the chemical causation idea fit with our need for denial. From a sense of duty and guilt, I decided I should become a neurochemist and discover the pill to make my sister behave as she should. In the course of my post-doctoral research at the NIMH and in my own life, I felt betrayed by the chemical explanation of psychological issues. In the lab, the more deeply I examined the regulation of neurotransmitters dopamine and serotonin, the more I realized the futility of reducing our lives to a test tube. There were far too many factors involved in regulating the amounts of neurotransmitters. So I concluded that each of us was more than a machine and it was far more important to understand ourselves and our relationships than the behavior of our individual chemicals. This realization dissolved my sense of purpose in life.*
>
> *I was diagnosed with schizophrenia and hospitalized on three occasions. I was given antipsychotic medications at each hospitalization. I tried to come off the Thorazine after my first hospitalization. However, I still thought mental illness was due to faulty chemistry, so I was fearful I might relapse. Indeed, one year later, after a failure in love, I did relapse and was re-hospitalized. After the second hospitalization I was convinced I had to make a major life change in my way of relating to people and in my profession. I realized that medication alone would not solve these problems. I fortunately had a psychiatrist who believed in my potential to recover. He saw a positive side to my psychoses. He described them as "regression in service of the ego." This term was used by Dr. Ernst Kris, during his work in ego psychology, indicating the creative benefits of regression. He felt that the aims of the ego were sometimes enhanced by the ability of people to regress and use the irrational processes of the unconscious and the id to develop alternative ways of thinking, feeling, and behaving. While this is of obvious advantage to artists, he was thinking to of the wider benefits of such flexibility (Kris, 2000).*

That time I was able to successfully come off all medication for a four-year period. During that period I worked as a peer counselor for people who came in distress to a free clinic. I entered a variety of group therapies and rap sessions. These experiences gave me the courage to share feelings, become more involved romantically and with friends, and enter a new career as a psychiatrist. (Fisher, 2008)

—D. F.

THE LITERATURE

While increased attention has been paid in recent years to non-medical models of approaching mental distress (Amminger, 2010; Brosse, 2002; Strohle, 2008; Gorczynski, 2010; Karon and VandenBos, 1980; Miklowitz, 2007; Dickerson, 2000; Dixon et al., 2000; Dilk and Bond, 1996; Becker, 2004), the use of prescription mental health medications has risen. While an exploration of the factors behind this paradox is beyond the scope of this paper, it is striking that very little attention has been given to the issues involved in *discontinuing* medications. Specifically, the past 20 years have seen only sporadic publications in the medical literature of data reflecting how long we should continue treatment, when to attempt discontinuation of medications, or how to safely discontinue them. What has been published looks primarily at relapse rates of people who stop medications versus those who continue them, with an underlying assumption that relapse after stopping is at best common, and at worst inevitable. In addition, these studies assume that a recurrence of symptoms indicates the relapse of a chronic condition, and they do not address the question of whether the recurrent symptoms might actually represent long-term results of medication use (most of us, whether we take thyroid or Thorazine, notice side effects). These studies do not include data on what (if any) non-pharmacological treatments were used as adjuncts to, or replacements for, medication.

The studies do suggest a common theme, however: that slower discontinuation of medications (tapering off) carries a lower risk for relapse than a rapid or abrupt discontinuation. For example, a literature review from the mid-1990s (Baldessarini, 1996) concluded that people with a diagnosis of bipolar disorder who discontinued Lithium rapidly (within 1–13 days) relapsed five times sooner than those who discontinued their Lithium slowly (over 14 or more days). What was not overtly reported, however, was that 12% of people remained stable for 3½ years after discontinuing Lithium, with approximately 2% of the rapid discontinuers and 37% of the slow discontinuers remaining stable (with 30% remaining stable out to five years after discontinuing Lithium). One of the studies (Faedda, 1993) included in this meta-analysis pessimistically concluded that gradual discontinuation of Lithium delays but does not reduce risk of mania recurrence in bipolar affective disorder (BAD) 1, but delays and reduces risk of depressive recurrence in both BAD 1 and BAD 2.

Similarly, a mid-1990s literature review on discontinuing antipsychotics (Viguera, 1997) examined rapid (20 or less days, many within one day) versus slow (21 or more days) tapering of antipsychotics among people with a diagnosis of schizophrenia. While they reported that the relapse rate at six months among the rapid discontinuers was double that of the gradual discontinuers, the data reveal that approximately 50% of those who abruptly stopped antipsychotics actually remained stable after six months, and 40% remained stable for a full 24 months. The best results were among those being treated in an outpatient setting who discontinued medications slowly, with over 50% of this group remaining stable four years after stopping medications. More recently, a longitudinal study revealed that 19% of people diagnosed with schizophrenia were in recovery 15 years after diagnosis, 67% of whom were off medication (Harrow & Jobe, 2007). Most of these people stopped medication one to two years after diagnosis, and remained in recovery for many years afterward.

More recently, a moderate-sized study looked at rapid (1–7 days) versus slow (14 or more days) discontinuation of antidepressants in people with various mood and anxiety diagnoses (Baldessarini, 2010). The primary conclusion was that people who stopped antidepressants quickly relapsed 2.3 times more rapidly than those who stopped gradually, and the study identified numerous issues correlated with more rapid relapse. However, the data reveal that 22.3% of the rapid discontinuers, and 40.9% of the gradual discontinuers, remained symptom-free after 12 months. These results are similar to a prior meta-analysis, which found that 59% of those who stopped antidepressants remained relapse-free after a modal study length of 12 months (Geddes, 2003).

It would appear that there are people taking psychiatric medications who could successfully discontinue them (Rappaport, 1977). Even Pepper et al. (1981) predicted in the "rule of thirds" that one third of those with a psychotic break would need medication but two thirds either did not need meds or would only require treatment if they experienced a relapse. This is consistent with naturalistic data from the pre-medication era. Multiple studies prior to 1955 revealed that roughly 50% to 70% of people diagnosed with schizophrenia were successfully living in the community between three and six years after release from state hospitals or similar institutions (Cole, 1959; Lehrman, 1961; Warner, 1985). Data from the early years of the medication era suggest that those who stop antipsychotic medication may in fact have better long-term outcomes than those who continue to take them long-term (Harrow, M 2007). Harrow found that the members of the cohort who were able to come off antipsychotic medication (39%) showed a greater degree of recovery than those who stayed on medication. He also showed that those who did not take antipsychotic medication during the 15-year period had a greater internal locus of control than those who stayed on medication (Harrow and Jobe, 2007). (However, it is unclear if this represents a negative effect of medication use, or a selection bias such that those with worse symptoms remain on medications longer.) Similar naturalistic studies in those diagnosed with depression suggest better long-term outcomes for those who did not use antidepressant medications than for those who did. Data reveal that those who did not take medication to treat their depression were 50% more likely to remain relapse-free (Weel-Baumgarten, 2000), had 42% less time feeling depressed (Patten, 2004), had better overall one-year outcomes (Goldberg, 1998), returned to work after short-term disability 27% faster, and were 50% less likely to develop long-term disability (Dewa, 2001). (Again, it is unclear whether these data describe a negative effect of antidepressants or a phenomenon that people with more severe pathology take medications more often.)

Unfortunately, there is scant scientific data on identifying those who are best treated without medications and those who would do better with only short-term use of medication. Likewise, there is a lack of scientific literature on how to support those who opt to go off medications. As poor pre-morbid functioning is the most common trait associated with higher risk for relapse after stopping medication, it stands to reason that improving an individual's functioning and coping skills would help in his/her effort to stop or decrease medications (or not use them at all). This practice also supports the concept of not solely deferring or stopping medications, but finding alternate non-pharmacological methods to address symptoms (actual or potential). Many such methods are used concomitantly with medications when treating mental illness, and many can be used on their own without medications.

The most commonly used non-pharmacological treatment to address mental health symptoms is psychotherapy. Many studies support the use of several types of psychotherapy, including cognitive therapy, behavioral therapy, cognitive behavioral therapy, dialectical behavioral therapy, interpersonal therapy, and dynamic therapies (Dickerson, 2000). Most studies agree that medication and therapy offer similar success rates in treating depression, with therapy having more long-lasting benefits than medications after therapy is stopped, and with placebos playing an important role in antidepressant medication efficacy (Moncrieff et al., 2005). Similar data exist to support the use of psychotherapy as adjunctive treatment in bipolar disorder (Miklowitz, 2007) as well as schizophrenia (Miklowitz, 2007). Similarly, family therapy and psychoeducation are proven effective in supporting people diagnosed with bipolar disorder (Miklowitz, DJ 2007) and schizophrenia (Dixon, 1995; Dixon, 2000)

Addressing issues outside of a disease treatment model has also been proven helpful for those concerned about mental health symptoms. For example, supported employment has proven effective for people with a variety of psychiatric diagnoses (Becker, 2004) as has social skills training (Dilk & Bond, 1996). Courtney Harding's (Harding et al., 1987, 1994) well-documented Vermont State Hospital study of 269 persons diagnosed with long-term schizophrenia who were given hope and a recovery-oriented approach showed highly positive results. Forty percent of the group were able to get off meds completely, and another 28% showed marked recovery. In contrast, a comparison of Vermont's outcomes with those in Maine, where the state subscribed to a disease model and maintenance, showed there was a lower recovery rate in Maine (DeSisto et al., 1995). In addition, research into so-called holistic health approaches is suggesting the usefulness of some of these approaches. For example, an article in *Psychiatric News* (October 2011) features a psychiatrist in Washington, D.C., organizing free bikes and docking stations for his patients to ride around the city. Exercise has a demonstrated positive effect in affective disorders (Brosse, 2002; Strohle, 2008) and has shown promise in addressing symptoms in schizophrenia (Gorczynski, 2010). And many small studies address the role of food allergies and support the use of diet or specific herbal remedies, such as the use of hypericum for affective disorders (Linde, 2008) and Omega-3 oils for a variety of symptoms, including potentially emerging psychosis (Amminger, 2010).

Recovery philosophies regarding the cause and treatment of mental health symptoms, such as the Soteria House (Mosher, 1999) and Open Dialogue models (Seikkula et al., 2003), have also been helpful to those diagnosed with severe mental illness, with no or reduced medications. The Open Dialogue approach in Finland views extreme distress as social, rather than medical, in nature. Open Dialogue de-emphasizes American-style pharmaceutical intervention and instead establishes a dialogue with the patient, provides immediate help, and organizes a treatment meeting within twenty-four hours of the initial contact. The results consistently show that this way of working reduces hospitalization, lowers use of medication, and leads to less recurrence of crises when compared with psychosis treatment as usual. For example, in a five-year follow-up (Seikkula,, 2006), 83% of patients had returned to their jobs or studies or were job-seeking, thus not receiving government disability. In the same study, 77% did not have residual psychotic symptoms, and fewer than 20% were taking antipsychotic medication.

Soteria House, a residential hospital alternative, also demonstrated promising results. Director Loren Mosher wrote:

> Results from 6-week outcome data for all Soteria House Ss and 2-year outcome data for the Ss admitted between 1971 and 1976 are discussed. The interpersonally based therapeutic milieu of Soteria House was as effective as neuroleptic drugs in reducing acute symptoms of psychosis in the short term (6 weeks) in newly diagnosed psychotics. Longer-term outcomes (2 years) were as good as or better than those of hospital treated control Ss in terms of independence, autonomy, and peer-based social networks. (Mosher, 1991)

The model of describing the problem and the approach to help was likewise interpersonal and recovery based, and the use of medication was lower and the relapse rate was much lower than hospitalization (Mosher, 1999).

Peer-run respites similar to Soteria House have also shown promising results. These alternatives to hospitalization are based on peer-support values, which rank the interpersonal as the most important element of assistance, and on recovery values of self-determination and holistic health. They show higher satisfaction rates than hospitals and a greater increase in self-esteem (see www.power2u.org/peer-run-crisis-alternatives.html).

Both the Soteria model and peer-run respites share a set of values very similar to SAMHSA's 10 components of recovery:

I.   The mental health conditions are approached holistically, and the psychosocial and spiritual factors of distress and recovery are given at least the same weight as the biological factors.

II. There is always hope that the person will recover a full role in society.

III. The person suffering's humanity is respected as being as important as that of the practitioner and other members of society.

IV. Persons with mental health issues have the right to choose the form of therapy and support they are provided; i.e., self-determination is endorsed.

V.   Peer support is a vital component of recovery.

VI. Having a greater internal locus of control is associated with recovery; i.e., empowerment is a component of recovery.

CASE VIGNETTE 1

Lisa was a 19-year-old college student who experienced the onset of paranoia, disorganization, and odd behavior during a campus festival weekend. She was presumed to have developed psychosis from substance use; however, her urine drug screen was negative for all substances, and she denied any substance use besides alcohol. She remained hospitalized for two weeks due to symptoms that were slow to improve. She was discharged home with a diagnosis of schizophrenia, given her intense psychosis and development of prominent negative symptoms. Despite continued medication use and the eventual ending of her psychosis, she continued to have a flat affect and to isolate. She denied having depression, but clearly had little motivation for any social interactions or activity. She worked with an intensive treatment team, with a primary therapist who frequently visited her in the community and slowly worked to increase her activity level. Eight months after her discharge, she began to reintegrate with friends, and re-enrolled part-time in school. Twelve months after discharge, she expressed a desire to stop her medications, feeling she no longer needed them.

After a summer term class, during which she was stationed in a remote wilderness location, she returned to school full-time, and her medication was tapered off over three months. She did well at school, obtaining good grades similar to those she had in the past, working part-time in a restaurant, and volunteering at a community garden. While she intermittently had alternative and/or unusual ideas about her health and about environmental issues, she never had overt delusions, and remained highly active with friends and in the community. Her affect returned to full range, and she began dating again. As of this writing, she has been off medications for eighteen months without any recurrent symptoms or loss of social or academic functioning.

This example demonstrates a central tenet of the recovery model: that people can indeed recover from illnesses once considered chronic and debilitating (McGuire, 2000). In the past, individuals such as Lisa were told they would need to take medication for the rest of their lives, lest they have recurrent psychotic episodes. This can be devastating information, especially for individuals who have experienced their first and only episode of psychosis. In addition to consigning them to a medical model of illness and treatment to explain their experiences, it can discourage individuals from holding hope, and encourage them to not push themselves to excel. However, with early intensive treatment and adequate education, people can continue to have productive lives and experience minimal symptoms while off medications. While medications can certainly be helpful in acute psychosis, their use long term is not a given, presuming other methods of addressing symptoms are helpful.

In short, it is clear a subgroup of people taking psychiatric medications could do well without them, although there is no method to accurately distinguish this group from those who would benefit from long-term medication use. However, given the long-term risks associated with medication, and reasonable odds of any given individual doing well without medications, people should be given an opportunity to stop medications if they so desire. To do so safely, it is recommended that this titration off medication occur slowly (to minimize both the risk of future symptoms and the untoward effects of discontinuation syndromes), and that the person utilize one or more of any of the other treatment modalities proven effective in treating mental illnesses.

CASE VIGNETTE 2

Karla was a 24-year-old woman working in environmental sciences who became manic and psychotic while working in a remote forest. She experienced rapid onset of sleeplessness, expansive moods, delusions of space aliens trying to control her behavior, visual hallucinations of these aliens, and impulsivity. She responded well to the start of a mood stabilizer and an antipsychotic when hospitalized, but disliked the side effects of sedation, cognitive dulling, and weight gain. She agreed to stay on medications for six months, during which time she worked closely with a therapist to examine the general risk factors for relapse, explore her unique symptoms, and create a list of "early warning signs" indicating another psychotic episode might be developing. When such warning signs emerged, she increased her contact with her therapist and psychiatrist, and adopted appropriate behavioral responses, such as increasing her exercise, increasing her sleep, and taking one to two hours out of the day to play music or otherwise relax. She kept a small supply of an antipsychotic drugs on hand as a "safety net" should her behavioral interventions not be as helpful as she hoped.

Over the ensuing two years off medications, she had numerous episodes of "early warning" symptoms, all but two of which responded within three to five days to behavioral interventions. On these other two occasions, she used her medication in low doses for five to seven days, each time reducing her symptoms to manageable levels. She maintained part-time employment throughout these two years, needing to take time away from work only once for a few days. As of this writing, she continues to work successfully and play music in small clubs, and has established a long-term romantic relationship.

This vignette demonstrates that long-term use of medications is not always a necessity, especially when alternative methods of addressing symptoms are successful. However, many individuals opt to use medications intermittently when symptoms re-arise, in cases when these alternative methods of treatment prove ineffective for a specific episode. Unfortunately, it is impossible to know after a first episode of illness if the individual will be able to stop medications, require intermittent use of medications, or have need of medications over the long term.

However, in the interest of limiting the exposure of individuals to their long-term adverse effects, psychiatric medications should be used only after proven necessary for that individual's recovery.

APPROACHING DISCONTINUATION:
TOWARD BEST PRACTICES

What should our response be when a client questions continuing psychotropic medications, or when a prescriber is concerned about short- or long-term risks associated with continuing medications? When do medications no longer become useful, and when is their usefulness out-weighed by their risks? In addition to the limited research on the topic, developing any specific protocols for reduction and discontinuation faces an additional challenge: the subjective nature of medication therapeutic response. Assessment of and preparation for the discontinuation process will therefore begin with attention to the *therapeutic relationship* and to broader social support for the client. Once this attention is in place, clinicians can begin a careful consideration of the client's medication history and the current nature of medications' adverse effects, as well as an assessment of the subjective usefulness of the medications to the client; and from there we can consider a reduction process, at each step working with the client on their response. The most important attitude for both client and providers is that this is a mutual learning process. (Hall, 2007)

Assessing therapeutic usefulness of a client's medication profile is difficult to do from a purely pharmacological standpoint because, other than obvious psychotic symptoms or disorganized thinking, psychiatric medication response and side effects are mostly subjective, particularly once the person no longer exhibits positive symptoms. As Cohen writes, "No single theory in psychopharmacology addresses how drugs produce 'therapeutic' effects. There is no theory of 'drug response.' This is because the perception of a drug effect as therapeutic depends on human motives within particular social contexts." (Cohen, 2001) The reduction and discontinuation process will depend therefore on the attention to the therapeutic relationship, the education of the client about the nature of their diagnosis and condition, and the creation of new life possibilities around reduction and discontinuation.

With limited time and resources, prescribers may not themselves be able to give the required attention to the relationship; a team or an individual such as a case manager, peer specialist, therapist, or nurse practitioner will be important. For our purposes, let us call this person a "wellness coach": someone who unconditionally supports and advocates for the client. The role of the wellness coach would be to ensure communication between prescriber, client, and others involved with providing care such as families; create a pattern of continuity and regularity in the process; support client education and the client's decision-making process at each step of the way; discover and utilize support resources for the client; and provide the emotional support and recognition needed to foster greater autonomy and engagement with the recovery process. The U.K. Charity MIND study found that doctor–patient relations *re:* coming off meds are frequently very poor. Of patients interviewed, 40 percent saw their prescribers as "not helpful" in the process, making them the least helpful source of advice and support. (Read, 2005) Without a good relationship and the role of wellness coach who is "on the side" of the client in place, it will be difficult to effectively monitor the client's progress, address problems early, cultivate non-medication wellness tools, and avoid problems.

Rather than focus primarily on medications, at each step we should address the entirety of the client's life experience, to best understand the place of medications and discontinuation or reduction decisions within it. Priority should be put where it is needed, rather than following a preprogrammed schedule for medication changes, with flexibility to pause or resume the process as the client's overall life situation indicates. Emphasis should be not on medication reduction/withdrawal as an end in itself, but rather on the life goal the individual has and how the medication reduction can serve that. This reinforces the recovery-based understanding of medications as a tool in life, rather than a necessary treatment for disease.

The wellness coach will also coordinate an education process that sets the context and tone for reduction and discontinuation. Education is directed at the client as well as the client's larger immediate social network, such as family members, friends, and healthcare providers, and is a mutual education process, with the wellness coach seeking to learn and understand the clients' experience and needs and to help educate any providers and professionals involved. The cornerstone of this education is the values and perspectives of the peer recovery movement and its emphasis on self-determination, to foster the emergence of autonomy and responsibility in the client.

While at each step of the way prescription and medication reduction are client-centered, the prescriber also maintains a clinical and ethical responsibility to monitor the process from the standpoint of their skills and experience, with the aim to "Do No Harm." Following a prescription is the purview of the client; writing a prescription is the purview of the clinician, and the process is collaborative. Each brings their unique perspective and has the freedom to question the other, and if needed disengage from the relationship if they feel their perspective is not adequately addressed in the collaboration. For example, clients may be willing to take risks clinicians advise against, such as the risk of hospitalization or tolerance of experiences defined as symptoms, because from their experience adverse effects have become intolerable; while clinicians may be unwilling to go along with a medication requested by the client because of their assessment of medication toxicity risks. Each has a responsibility to voice their concerns and to reach compromise where possible, and prescribers are ethically and professionally bound by their role as prescribers and have the added responsibility to be aware of the power differences with their client. Where medication optimization and reduction are new to the prescribers, they will need to approach the process as a learning experience and have an attitude of humility and tolerance for the unknown.

To begin preparation, clients should be supported in examining their history with medications, any previous attempts at reduction or discontinuation, their relationships with providers, the client's desire to begin the reduction/discontinuation process, and their motivations, goals, and challenges. Comprehensive laboratory tests and tests for medication toxicity, as indicated by each medication, should be up-to-date to suggest discontinuation priorities and to consider any medical need for abrupt withdrawal. Once an initial assessment of medication adverse effects is done, an overall physical health assessment should be conducted, including from a holistic standpoint, to clarify what factors are influencing the client's quality-of-life concerns. Many clients experience quality-of-life limitations that arise from unaddressed physical issues, which have been overlooked by previous providers or mistakenly attributed to a diagnosed mental disorder. Many emotional and psychological complaints can have hidden physical origins. While there is a great range of possible considerations, some things to consider are thyroid functioning; adverse effects of other medications such as steroids; encephalopathy; vitamin deficiency; or gluten intolerance, any of which could be playing a role. Physical health assessment encourages the client to take a more active stance in their wellness and to overcome past relationships of passivity and dependence toward their treatment. To catch the earliest signs of adverse effects, clinicians should consider using the most comprehensive testing available.

A discontinuation plan then usually begins with a slow incremental taper, such as a 10 percent reduction from baseline dosage in two- to three-week increments. This can be adjusted based on the length of time the client has been on the drug and on the client's level of preparedness, motivation, and support. As reduction begins, prescriber and client check to ensure the process is tolerable, and the prescriber supports the client in waiting out withdrawal symptoms using non-medication approaches, with the option of increasing back to the previous dosage at any time that the process feels overwhelming or too fast. Clients who have been taking medications long term may need to consider an even slower rate, such as continuing the reduction every few months or longer, unless side effects are too severe. Often clients have good ideas as to where to begin, such as medications with the most troubling side effects or with those felt as not useful or necessary; the prescriber may also recommend a starting point based on the toxicity indicated by laboratory tests and observed adverse effects. In the case of polypharmacy and redundant medications, a faster taper may be successful since the client has other medications to rely on. Some medications such as for anxiety and sleep can be transitioned to an as-needed basis. Meds with shorter half-lives may be switched to those with longer half lives, especially in the case of antidepressants. Liquid formulations may make precise control of the dosage easier.

While this slow and tapering approach to reduction and discontinuation is generally advisable and has a growing body of research evidence in support of it, in practical settings this is only a guideline. For example, clinicians and clients sometimes face circumstances where abrupt withdrawal is indicated. Medication toxicity such as liver and kidney problems, signs of tardive dyskinesia, rash associated with lamotrigene, neuroleptic malignancy syndrome, serotonin syndrome, or acute reactions such as heart arrhythmia, suicidality, self-injury, or mania call for either immediate withdrawal or transfer to another medication with a different adverse effect profile. In such instances the risks associated with withdrawal are outweighed by the physical danger posed by medication continuation. Abrupt withdrawal should be cautiously considered, however, as some medications, such as benzodiazepines, can be life-threatening during abrupt discontinuation (Ashton, 2005). Clients may also choose abrupt withdrawal when adverse effects are subjectively experienced as intolerable. In these cases, clinicians should ensure that clients are informed about the possible consequences of abrupt withdrawal, while also acknowledging the motivation and concerns behind it, and any difficulties encountered are treated as a learning process.

As the process is underway, the client will explore and discuss their experience. Key areas of client education include the effectiveness of non-medication symptom management, the way medications work as psychoactive substances, the considerable research uncertainty about the nature of mental illness, the success of others who are able to reduce and go off medications, and the importance of being open to the outcome (Jacobs et al., 1999; Moncrieff, 2005; Vastag, 2001). Not everyone becomes completely medication free; therefore, the goal is improved well-being and the optimal use of medications, not necessarily *no* medications. Expectation of recovery and hope for success are the most crucial ingredients, and should be conveyed by the wellness coach and all providers involved, while emphasizing the need for patience and flexibility.

As the client will be learning to rely on non-medication tools for managing their distressing experiences, the coach makes an inventory of their existing capacities and resources. Understanding early warning signs, using person-directed planning, the Wellness Recovery and Action Plan, and psychiatric advance directives can all be helpful, and the client should be directed to opportunities to discover new wellness resources, understanding that their unique interests determine what role a specific tool may or may not play in their life, rather than imposing one method over another.

Symptom management will have two aspects in the process: the capacity to respond to withdrawal-related symptoms and emotional distress previously suppressed by medications; and the client's attitude toward those symptoms and distress. Physical symptoms such as headaches and flu-like discomfort should be met with reassurances they will usually pass as the withdrawal and detoxification process continues, while if these symptoms persist or become intolerable, presenting the option of returning to previous levels of medication until the symptoms abate and the reduction process can be resumed, perhaps at a slower pace. Wellness tools will be useful at the earliest signs of increased emotional symptoms, especially sleeplessness and anxiety. Lack of sleep is the single most important symptom to be watchful of, with quick intervention to prevent escalation. Anxiety leading to social and emotional withdrawal is the second most important symptom. The close relationship with the wellness coach is central to addressing these issues successfully.

At the same time, the client facing renewed symptoms of distress may need to learn that these are not indicators of the return of a disease process that must be medicated, but may be met on their own terms as human experiences like any other. Clients whose emotions have been limited by medications may not be familiar with the ups and downs of life from a non-pathologizing standpoint, and therefore be too quick to judge renewed fear, sadness, anger, or elation as signs of returning illness. The unique sensitivities and expression of the individual's personality should be supported, rather than assuming that what is "normal" is to be "asymptomatic" at all times.

Recurrence of emotional distress and physical withdrawal symptoms should be weighed carefully, to strike a balance between challenging and overwhelming the client. Where the process goes too fast or risks becoming unmanageable by the clients' personal resources, options such as resuming previous dosages should be considered, but only with the opportunity presented to learn and discover new ways of coping. This gradual transition to non-medication approaches requires patience and openness to meeting the client where they are at each step of the way.

If hospitalization is an option in the face of distress, a liaison with hospital staff should be created so that medication protocols while the client is an inpatient complement the continued overall reduction process, rather than just returning to or raising the levels of medication prior to the start. Any crisis should be considered transitory and part of a long-term learning process, rather than a failure and indication that the process cannot continue. Hospitalization is not a surrender of autonomy but presents opportunities for the client and their coach to be engaged with decisions and options on how to best serve the client's needs.

WHEN DISCONTINUATION IS NOT INDICATED

Unfortunately, some individuals prove to need medication long term, and quickly experience recurrences and relapses when off medications, even after a long-term and gradual reduction. It is indeed unfortunate that often there is a sort of Hobson's choice between mental health and side effects for some folks. All of our treatments, despite our best intentions, do not always work. Many individuals cannot tolerate the side effects of effective medications, or may get only limited benefits from tolerable medications. A good client–provider relationship can help you to continually assess whether medications are effective and tolerable, or if adjustments are required. These continuous assessments and adjustments are best and most safely done when alternative supports are present as well. In such cases, the road to recovery may be long and difficult. The following vignettes demonstrate examples of when medications should be continued if possible, even when clients are ambivalent at best about their usefulness.

CASE VIGNETTE 3

Lee was a 19-year-old male who was mandated to mental health treatment after assaulting his 14-year-old brother in the middle of the night while the boy was sleeping. Prior to this incident, Lee had other episodes of violence at home, including yelling at other family members, causing property damage to the home and vehicles, and attempting to hit his parents. He also often threw away food from the refrigerator, claiming it was poisoned. His violence was often associated with alcohol or marijuana use, but not always.

He began working with an intensive outreach and support team, who helped him obtain partial sobriety. While his violent behavior stopped during his two- to six-week periods of sobriety, he continued to display paranoia, throwing away food and bathroom products and accusing neighbors of persecuting his family due to their non-citizen status. He also remained isolated from his family and friends. He reluctantly began taking fish oil on the recommendation of his psychiatrist, as he refused medications, and continued to be partially adherent with this treatment for four months. When his paranoia and isolation did not improve, he agreed to try a low dose of antipsychotic. His partial adherence improved, mostly due to the efforts of his mother, resulting in decreased symptoms. He recognized the medication was somewhat helpful, and accepted a higher dose. This higher dose resulted in his paranoia's ending. He became more social with his family, and began attending substance-abuse treatment groups (while he started these due to a court requirement, he eventually came to look forward to these groups). As of this writing, he remains mostly adherent with medication, sometimes not refilling his supply for two to seven days. He recognizes that he has more difficulties thinking and interacting with others when off medication, and hopes to stay on it.

Many people, especially younger folks experiencing a first episode of psychosis, have little awareness about how their thoughts and behaviors are flawed or unreliable. As such, it may be difficult for them to view themselves as having a condition that needs treatment. In addition, confounding factors, especially substance use, may make it difficult to clarify if a mental disorder diagnosis is indeed warranted (and if medication use would thus be appropriate). In such cases, if no acute danger is present, it is best to take time to tease out these other factors, to ensure any suggested medication use is appropriate. If so, a slow introduction of medication in an environment of multiple supports helps improve long-term adherence and long-term life success for the individual.

CASE VIGNETTE 4

John was a 20-year-old male training to be a mixed martial arts fighter who came to the clinic at his parents' request. He was barely able to tolerate an interview, frequently getting up to show martial arts moves or quote from his Eastern philosophy texts. He initially refused medications, seeing no need for them. However, at his parents' urging, he agreed to take them, explaining that his body and will were so strong no medications could contain them. He intermittently took medications over the next month, and was hospitalized after he was removed from his college campus by security staff for agitation. He stabilized after 10 days of medication use, but quickly became significantly depressed. He responded well to the addition of an antidepressant, and gained insight into his recent manic behavior. He viewed this mania (and subsequent depression) as a factor of his martial arts training's raising his energy level too high, and stopped medications three months later, agreeing to restart them if asked. However, when he had recurrent mania six months later, he deferred on medications when they were encouraged by his psychiatrist. He was hospitalized two weeks later, stabilizing quickly again and becoming depressed shortly thereafter. His depression responded again to the addition of an antidepressant; however, he became hypomanic when he started taking an herbal weight loss supplement as part of his training. His supplement was stopped, and his mood stabilizer changed due to side effects of weight gain and sedation. He did well for eight months, eventually having recurrent mania despite medication adherence. A change in mood stabilizers and addition of low-dose antidepressants resulted in a stable mood, which has been stable for seven months as of this writing. He currently is working part-time, slowly reintegrating with friends, and contemplating a return to school. However, his confidence is shaken by the events of the past few years, and he remains unsure of how to proceed in his life.

Except when the individual is legally mandated to treatment, each person must decide if medications are an option they wish to use in their recovery, and if their use is a primary element of their recovery plan or a secondary adjunct to other options. However, as mental illnesses can sometimes affect one's judgment, some individuals may not recognize the benefits they gain from the use of medication. Similarly, sometimes medication can itself limit the capacity of the individual to recognize adverse effects. In such cases, a good client–provider relationship is helpful in helping the person gain understanding and better consider these benefits and risks.

APPENDIX: MEDICATIONS AND RECOVERY

RECOVERY-ORIENTED PSYCHIATRIC PRACTICE GUIDELINES

In 2010, a group of psychiatrists met to propose a recovery-oriented approach to provision of psychiatric medication:

1a. The development of a therapeutic alliance is essential for both informed choice and for more successful reduction of medication. This relationship between prescriber and consumer is enhanced by a "wellness coach" (Swarbrick et al., 2011) and is based on all parties' subscribing to four basic ground rules of engaging in dialogue (as have b een tested in business: Isaacs, 1999):

    a.   Listening together: giving equal consideration to all sides of the conversation (these principles are vital to effective networking meetings)

    b.   Respecting differences: building a positive, respectful relationship between the psychiatrist and the consumer is essential

    c.   Suspension of belief: it is particularly important that both parties be able to suspend any dogmatic beliefs of either extreme—that medications are always required for recovery, or that medications always interfere with recovery

    d.   Authentic voicing: the consumer should be encouraged to voice their true opinion about their medication

1b.   Mental health consumers have the right of informed choice and shared decision making with regard to their medication

2a.   Their psychiatrist and wellness coach should inform them and their immediate significant supports of the benefits and risks of medications, as well as non-medication alternatives that have been helpful for other persons with their mental health issues.

2b.   Part of the education should involve informing the consumer of person-directed recovery planning, WRAP, and advance directives.

2c.   The person should also learn that many of the symptoms such as insomnia and anxiety are often the expression of the withdrawal process or due to the normal ups and downs of life.

3.   Based on this information and consumers' own reactions to the medications, they have the right to choose which medication(s) to take, how much to take, when to take it, whether to stop taking it, and how to stop taking medication.

4.   Informed choice is renegotiated at each meeting between consumer and their psychiatrist and wellness coach on each visit.

5.   If a consumer chooses to discontinue their medication, we recommend that the decision be collaborative, enabling the consumer to remain in treatment during the period of withdrawal.

6.   Maintaining a relationship between the psychiatrist and the consumer is an important element in responsible tapering-off of medication.

7.   Power shared in ways that encourage the autonomy of the consumer; the concept of collaboration be reinforced by the psychiatrist having power together in the relationship, and this relationship be mirrored in relationship between the person and their pills. A psychiatrist using this collaborative approach might prescribe a pill and say, "This pill will not cure you, but you can collaborate with it so that you can take increasing control of your life."

We recommend that consumer choice to stop a medication be respected that they and their prescriber and team of mental health caregivers follow these guidelines:

    a.   Taper medications carefully and very gradually.

    b.   Be aware that every psychotropic medication may be associated with withdrawal reactions, which should be necessarily discussed but not be mistaken for relapse.

    c.   Agree that mental distress is best approached holistically, such that attention is paid to the bio-psycho-socio-spiritual dimensions of living and recovery.

d. Support social well-being by helping develop a personal network of supportive people who are understanding of recovery plans and supportive of the individual consumer.

e. Attend to psychological well-being by encouraging, learning, and practicing self-soothing and stress-reduction skills such as meditation and affirmations.

f. Attend to physical well-being by having a healthy diet, engaging in regular exercise, and getting sufficient sleep.

g. Spiritual dimensions, involving finding meaning and purpose in life, are supported and encouraged.

h. Be trauma-informed by maximizing connections and empowerment while minimizing unnecessary life stresses and trauma. Develop a positive working relationship with a nearby hospital, clinic, and/or respite center so they can continue the appropriate medication regime and plan for medication optimization when a consumer is using their services.

REFERENCES

Aldridge, M. A. Addressing non-adherence to antipsychotic medication: a harm-reduction approach. *Journal of Psychiatric and Mental Health Nursing*, 85–96, 2011.

Amminger, G. Long-chain omega-3 fatty acids for indicated prevention of psychotic disorders: a randomized, placebo-controlled trial, *Archives of General Psychiatry*, 67(2), 146–154, 2010.

Ashton, H. The diagnosis and management of benzodiazepine dependence.—*Current Opinion in Psychiatry*, 18(3), 249–255, May 2005.

Baldessarini, R. J. Effects of the rate of discontinuing lithium maintenance treatment in bipolar disorders. *Journal of Clinical Psychiatry*, 57, 441–448, 1996.

Baldessarini, R. J. Illness risk following rapid versus gradual discontinuation of antidepressants. *American Journal of Psychiatry*, 167, 934–941, 2010.

Becker, D. R. *Supported Employment for People with Severe Mental Illness*. Behavioral Health Recovery Management Project, 2004. New Hampshire-Dartmouth Psychiatric Research Center Dartmouth Medical School.

Blumenthal, J. Effects of exercise training on older patients with major depression. *Archives of Internal Medicine*, 159, 2349–2356, 1999.

Bola, J, Compi, L., Culberg, J., & Lehtinen K, "Psychosocial treatment, antipsychotic postponement, and low-dose medication strategies in first-episode psychosis: A review of the literature." *Psychosis*, 1(1), 4–18, 2009.

Brosse, A. L. Exercise and the treatment of clinical depression in adults: Recent findings and future directions. *Sports Medicine*, 32(12), 741-60, 2002.

Cohen, D. How to detoxify from common illusions about psychiatric medications. *Ethical Human Sciences and Services*, 3, 207–211, 2001.

Cohen, D. The psychiatric medication history: Context, purpose, and method. *Journal of Social Work in Mental Health*, 4, 5–28, 2003.

Cole, J. (ed.). *Psychopharmacology*. Washington, DC: National Academy of Sciences, 386–387, 1959.

DeSisto, et al. (1995). The Maine and Vermont three decade studies of serious mental illness. *British Medical Journal of Psychiatry*, 167, 338–342.

Dickerson, F. B. Cognitive behavioral psychotherapy for schizophrenia: A review of recent empirical studies. *Schizophrenia Research*, 43, 71–90, 2000.

Dilk, M. N., & Bond, G. R.. Meta-analytic evaluation of skills training research for individuals with severe mental illness. *Journal of Consulting Clinical Psychology,* 64, 1337–1346, 1996.

Dixon, L., & Lehman, A. Family interventions for schizophrenia. *Schizophrenia Bulletin,* 21, 631–643, 1995.

Dixon, L., Adams, C., & Lucksted., A. Update on family psychoeducation for schizophrenia. *Schizophrenia Bulletin,* 26, 5–20, 2000.

Donoghue, K., Lomax K., & Hall, J. Using group work to prevent relapse in bipolar disorder. *Nursing Times, 103*(19), 30–31, 2007.

Faedda, G. L. Outcome after rapid vs. gradual discontinuation of lithium treatment in bipolar disorders. *Archives of General Psychiatry,* 50, 448–455, 1993.

Fisher, D. B. Promoting recovery. In: T. Stickley and T. Basset (eds.), *Learning About Mental Health Practice.* Chichester, UK: John Wiley & Sons, 119–139, 2008.

Freedman, R. Abrupt withdrawal of antidepressant treatment. *American Journal of Psychiatry, 167,* 886–888, 2010.

Geddes, J. Relapse prevention with antidepressant drug treatment in depressive disorders. *Lancet,* 361, 653–61, 2003.

Goldberg, D. The effect of detection and treatment on the outcome of major depression in primary care. *British Journal of General Practice,* 48, 1840–1844, 1998.

Gorczynski, P. Exercise therapy for schizophrenia. *Cochrane Database of Systematic Reviews.* 2010 May 12;(5):CD004412.

Hall, W. *Harm Reduction Guide to Coming Off Psychiatric Drugs.* New York: Freedom Center & The Icarus Project, 2007. Available online at www.willhall.net/comingoffmeds

Harding, C. The Vermont longitudinal study of persons with severe mental illness, I. *American Journal of Psychiatry,* 144, 718–726, 1987.

Harding, C.. Empirical correction of seven myths about schizophrenia with implications for treatment. *Acta Psychiatrica Scandinavica,* 384, suppl. 14–16, 1994.

Harding, C. M., et al. The Vermont longitudinal study of persons with severe mental illness, I. Methodology, study sample, and overall status 32 years later. *American Journal of Psychiatry,* 144, 718–728, 1987.

Harrow, M., & Jobe, T. H. Factors involved in outcome and recovery in schizophrenia patients not on antipsychotic medications: A 15-year multi-follow-up study. *The Journal of Nervous and Mental Disease,* 195, 406–414, 2007.

Isaacs, W. *Dialogue the Art of Thinking Together.* Crown Business, 1999.

Jacobs, D., & Cohen, D. What is really known about alterations produced by psychiatric drugs? *International Journal of Risk and Safety in Medicine,* 12, 37–47, 1999.

Jin, S.Z., Wu, N., Xu, Q., Zhang, X., Ju, G.Z., Law, M.H., & Wei, J. A study of circulating gliadin antibodies in schizophrenia among a Chinese population. *Schizophr Bull,* 38(3), 514–518, 2012.

Karon, B., & VandenBos, G. *Psychotherapy of Schizophrenia.* Aronson, 1980.

Kris, E. *Psychoanalytic Explorations in Art.* Madison, CT: International Universities Press, 2000.

Lehrman, N. Follow-up of brief and prolonged psychiatric hospitalization. *Comparative Psychiatry,* 2, 227–240, 1961.

Linde, K., Berner, M., Egger, M., Mulrow, C. St John's wort for depression: Meta-analysis of randomised controlled trials. *British Journal of Psychiatry,* 186, 99–107, 2005.

Lundquist, G. Prognosis and course in manic-depressive psychoses. *Acta Psychiatrica Scandinavica,* suppl. 35, 7–93, 1945.

McGuire, P. New hope for people with schizophrenia. A growing number of psychologists say recovery is possible with psychosocial rehabilitation. *31*(2), 24, 2000.

Miklowitz, D. J. A randomized study of family-focused psychoeducation and pharmacotherapy in the outpatient management of bipolar disorder. *Archives of General Psychiatry, 64*, 419–427, 2007.

Moncrieff, J., & Cohen, D. Rethinking models of psychotropic drug action. *Psychotherapy and Psychosomatics, 74*, 145–153, 2005.

Moncrieff, J., & Kirsch, I. Efficacy of anti-depressants in adults. *British Medical Journal, 331*, 155–157, 2005.

Mosher, L. Soteria: A therapeutic community for psychotic persons. *International Journal of Therapeutic Communities,* 12(1), 53–67, 1991.

Mosher, L. Soteria and other alternatives to acute psychiatric hospitalization: A personal and professional review. *Journal of Nervous and Mental Disease,* 187, 142–149, 1999.

Patten, S. The impact of antidepressant treatment on population health: synthesis of data from two national data sources in Canada. *Population Health Metrics,* 2, 9, 2004.

Pepper, B, Kirshner, M. & Ryglewicz, H : The young adult chronic patient: Overview of a population. (originally published in 1981). *Psychiatric Services,* 51, 989–995, 2000.

Rappaport, M. Are there schizophrenics for whom drugs may be unnecessary or contraindicated? *International Pharmacopsychiatry,* 13, 100–111, 1978.

Read, J. *Coping with Coming Off.* Mind Publications, 2005.

Seikkula, J., Alakare, B., Aal-tonen, J., Holma, J., Rasinkangas, A. & Lehtinen, V. Open dialogue approach: Treatment principles and preliminary results of a two-year follow-up on first-episode schizophrenia. *Ethical Human Sciences and Services,* 5(3), 163–182, 2003.

Seikkula, J. Five-year experience of first-episode nonaffective psychosis in open-dialogue approach: Treatment principles, follow-up outcomes, and two case studies. *Psychotherapy Research,* 16(2), 214–228, 2006.

Strohle, A. Physical activity, exercise, depression and anxiety disorders. *Journal of Neural Transmission,* 116, 777–784, 2008.

Swarbrick, M., Murphy, A., Zechner, M., Spagnolo, A., & Gill, K. (2011).Wellness coaching: A new role for peers. *Psychiatric Rehabilitation Journal,* 34(4), 328–331.

Vastag, B. Pay attention: Ritalin acts much like cocaine. *Journal of the American Medical Association,* 286, 905–906, 2001.

Viguera, A. C. Clinical risk following abrupt and gradual withdrawal of maintenance neuroleptic treatment. *Archives of General Psychiatry,* 54, 49–55, 1997.

Warner, R. *Recovery from Schizophrenia.* Boston: Routledge & Kegan Paul, 74, 1985.

Weel-Baumgarten, E. Treatment of depression related to recurrence. *Journal of Clinical Pharmacy and Therapeutics,* 25, 61–66, 2000.

CHAPTER 25

SUPPORTED HOUSING, SOCIALIZATION, EDUCATION, AND EMPLOYMENT

MARGARET A. SWARBRICK AND ROBERT E. DRAKE

As the President's New Freedom Commission (2003) emphasized, recovery entails living, learning, working, and participating fully in one's community. This chapter addresses four approaches to helping people achieve these important outcomes: supported housing, supported socialization, supported education, and supported employment. These interventions share common theoretical and practical orientations. Each assumes that people know themselves and their personal recovery goals, have personal strengths, and can make use of professional as well as natural supports to live be successful in community environments of their choice. Each starts with the person's phenomenology: How do they see themselves, their situations, their needs, and their goals? Each approach assumes that people have strengths that can be identified, reinforced, and enhanced rather than deficits that must be corrected, or problems to be solved. Each assumes that people can take control of their own lives and recoveries more easily if they have access to relevant information and choices, and opportunities to learn, practice, and take risks. Each entails direct access to valued adult roles rather than stepwise training approaches. Each assumes that integrated, natural settings are preferable to segregated settings (i.e., only other people living with disabilities). Each empowers the consumer or client as *the central* member of a multi-disciplinary team. Finally, each relies on natural supports of the person's choice as well as professional supports.

We begin with a vignette to illustrate how these interventions can be combined and individually tailored. We then describe each intervention, including principles, details, research, and training. Finally, we discuss the commonalities of these approaches.

A YOUNG MAN WITH PSYCHOSIS AND DRUG ADDICTION

Manuel R. was a 23-year-old man when he came to the mental health center. He began struggling with drug use and intermittent psychotic episodes during his freshman year of college and flunked out of school the following year. Afterward, he had numerous admissions to psychiatric hospitals and addiction treatment centers, was unable to hold a job, and experienced increasing acrimony with his parents and siblings. A public altercation eventually led to his arrest and conviction on assault charges.

When he joined a multidisciplinary dual diagnosis team, Manuel was experiencing paranoia, cravings, and severe regrets regarding his school and work failures and the problems he had caused his family. His goals were to live independently, to repair relationships with his family, and to return to school and work. He initially entered a residential dual-diagnosis facility for three months, in which he became stabilized on lithium plus an antipsychotic medication, learned to manage his paranoia and cravings in cognitive-behavioral sessions, received education about his dual disorders, bonded with other young men in the residence, and began to attend Alcoholics Anonymous meetings each evening in the community with mentors (experienced AA members who were hired to help others learn about and join AA). He also applied to take one course at a local community college.

As Manuel transitioned to an apartment in the community, the dual diagnosis team helped him set up his apartment, learn to use public transportation, and enroll at the community college. They also continued to support him and his peers in attending AA meetings. When Manuel completed his first college course in accounting, with help planning his homework schedule from the team, he enrolled in another course and also began looking for a job. The team helped him find a part-time job as a bookkeeping assistant. Weekly telephone meetings with Manuel's family resulted in respectful communications and clear agreements about responsibilities. He feels that they understand his illnesses better, and they feel that they are taking care of their own needs as well as helping Manuel.

Manuel believes that his quality of life is immensely improved. He has an apartment, a job, several friends in AA, a better relationship with his family, and confidence about completing his college education. The team checks with Manuel bi-weekly and provides supports, but his needs are less each month as he begins to rely more on his friends and his own capacity to manage his life.

Manuel's story illustrates how supported housing, employment, education, and socialization are woven together and highly individualized by the same team. We next describe each intervention separately.

SUPPORTED HOUSING

Supported housing combines supports for independent housing with flexible mental health interventions and other services (Rog, 2004; Tabol, Drebing, & Rosenheck, 2010; see http://www.socwel.ku.edu/mentalhealth/projects/promising/supporthousing.shtml). It can be located in different living settings, including self-contained accommodations with professional services on site (at least during office hours) and scattered-site arrangements with regular visits by a support team.

Supported housing emphasizes several principles:

- client-centeredness—the consumer's values, goals, and preferences
- housing choice—type, housemates, supports
- tenancy—lease held by the consumer
- integrated community-living settings—not segregated enclaves
- affordable decent housing—professionals may help to locate
- permanence—do not have to move on once completing a program
- education regarding rights—tenant role rather than consumer/patient role
- separate housing supports—not linked with other services
- personal preferences—use of mental health treatment and other services
- agency oversight—many tasks related to housing
- services in the community—not in mental health settings

Teams of all kinds (assertive community treatment, intensive case management, community support, housing teams, and so on) can deliver supported housing. Members typically have expertise, not only on housing issues, but also in regard to benefits, mental health, addictions, employment, and other resources and services that may be useful or relevant. Services are usually available 24 hours a day, seven days a week. Much of the team's work entails basic support: acquiring furniture, shopping for groceries, making and keeping healthcare appointments, obtaining public benefits, paying bills, preparing meals, keeping a clean and safe home, and so forth.

People with limited education can deliver basic housing supports. Social workers are usually involved in coordination, counseling, and supervisory roles. People with specialized training may be needed to provide skills teaching, addiction counseling, peer advocacy, supported employment, or other interventions. A person with a graduate degree in some area of mental health usually leads the team. These teams may serve one or more specific populations, requiring specialized team training or skills. Examples include teams serving people with co-occurring mental health and intellectual disabilities, people with significant physical health issues, or people who are raising children.

Many supported housing programs deviate from the basic model (Tabol, Drebing, & Rosenheck, 2010). Alterations may involve required treatment, required financial management, multiple units in the same building, or shared living of some kind. Some programs diverge so far from the model that they are called "support*ive* housing" rather than "support*ed* housing." The Substance Abuse and Mental Health Services Administration (SAMHSA) emphasizes permanent supportive housing: see http://store.samhsa.gov/product/SMA10-4510?WT. ac=AD20100918HP_SMA10-4510.

Research on Housing First and other models of supported housing has shown positive out-comes in terms of maintaining residence, especially for people who have experienced homeless-ness (Tsemberis, Gulcur, & Nakae, 2004; McHugo et al., 2004). In addition to housing supports and mental health services, successful models usually emphasize harm reduction rather than immediate sobriety, also client choice, personal recovery goals, and financial services to ensure rental payments.

Dependence is a central challenge with supported housing. People easily become accus-tomed to having extensive assistance, and staff may also find it easier to do tasks for people than to teach them the skills they need to take care of themselves.

SUPPORTED EMPLOYMENT

Supported employment is an approach to vocational rehabilitation that helps people with psychi-atric disabilities attain and succeed in competitive jobs (Becker & Drake, 2003). The Individual Placement and Support (IPS) model of supported employment (see www.dartmouth.edu/~ips) is the only nationally and internationally recognized evidence-based approach to vocational rehabilitation for this population.

Several principles define IPS:

- zero exclusion—all clients who want employment are eligible
- competitive employment—client's goal
- client choice—all aspects of selecting, finding, and maintaining employment
- job development—professional approach
- rapid job search—training on the job rather than prior to employment
- service integration—vocational plus housing, mental health, addiction, physical health
- follow-along supports—as long as needed

In IPS, employment specialists help with all phases of vocational services: assessing, plan-ning, developing, acquiring, mastering, retaining, and changing jobs. An employment specialist typically works with 18 to 20 clients at a time. The client makes all decisions; e.g., choosing a type of job, how to find the job, how many hours to work, disclosure of their status, types of support, and so on, through a process of shared decision-making, in which the employment specialist provides information and options.

IPS supported employment is a team-based model. The employment specialist joins one or more multidisciplinary teams: case management, assertive community treatment, intensive case management, supported housing, or other types of teams. Rather than providing the vocational services alone, the employment specialist galvanizes the team to consider work as an essential part of recovery, one needing everyone's attention. The doctor may need to reassure the client that he or she can work and may need to adjust medications to reduce side effects. The social worker may need to educate the family about Social Security rules regarding insurance and income support when people are working. The therapist may need to help the client learn cop-ing skills to manage anxiety on the job. The case manager may need to help the client learn to use public transportation to and from work. The addiction counselor may need to make sure the workplace supports abstinence (e.g., does not serve alcohol).

The entire team is involved in helping the client select a good job match and sometimes in finding a job also. As an example, consider a young man, Albert, who had never worked and was anxious and fearful around people. The team helped Albert identify his interests and strengths in taking care of animals. All members of the team thought of their own contacts with pet stores, farms, veterinary clinics, pet owners, and so on, to identify potential employers. Each team member made contacts to help develop a part-time job. Within a month, Albert had three job offers. He chose a job on weekends taking care of recovering animals at a veterinary clinic. The employment specialist visited him regularly at work. Albert gradually expanded his time to weekday evenings, gained confidence in his ability to do a good job, and made friends with other employees at the veterinary clinic.

People with a variety of backgrounds—business, vocational services, mental health, lived experience—can become employment specialists. They can learn basic IPS skills via an online course (at www.dartmouth.edu/~ips/page26/page26.html) and can develop their skills through the mentoring of an IPS supervisor. Books, training courses, videos, training, and fidelity tools are available: see www.dartmouth.edu/~ips.

IPS has been developed and refined for over 20 years, based on continuous research. The model has a clear procedural manual, a fidelity scale, and defined training procedures (Swanson & Becker, 2010). In some states, reimbursement, licensing, or accreditation is tied to fidelity. IPS is widely used in several American states, several European countries, Canada, and Australia.

Extensive research on IPS includes 16 randomized controlled trials and numerous other studies around the world. Recent summaries of the research (Drake & Bond, 2011; Bond, Drake, & Becker, in press) show that about two-thirds of clients who enroll in IPS achieve competitive employment within 12 to 18 months. The rate is slightly higher in North American countries than in other countries, possibly due to different workforce, economic, and regulatory factors. Long-term follow-ups show that clients tend to remain employed and be steady workers for at least 10 years. When working, clients tend to improve in terms of self-esteem, quality of life, and symptom control. Current research aims at improving outcomes for the one-third of clients who are not benefiting from standard IPS; for example, by providing compensatory cognitive strategies or cognitive training.

Federal disability benefits from Social Security can be discontinued proportionately or stopped suddenly when people return to work. Health insurance can also be tied to disability status. In addition, many states tie public benefits and rents to earned income. Despite some of the challenges people may face returning to work being employed is a key to helping people to realize their full potential and helping them to be contributing members of their community and society.

SUPPORTED EDUCATION

Supported education assists people with psychiatric disabilities in pursuing academic goals in integrated post-secondary schools (Anthony & Unger, 1991). Services are individualized and flexible with an emphasis on student choice, self-determination, and career development. People are helped to manage post-secondary education, to achieve their academic goals, and to gain meaningful employment. Supports are highly variable but might encompass applying to school, gaining financial support, planning classes, negotiating with teachers, completing assignments, managing test anxiety, controlling symptoms, compensating for cognitive problems, and learning how to cope socially in an academic environment. Though most colleges offer disability services, students with psychiatric disabilities are often reluctant to access traditional disability services due to fears regarding disclosure (Collins & Mowbray, 2005).

Principles of supported education include:

- client choice—educational goals and services
- educational assessment—informs individually tailored educational plan
- career counseling—education linked with employment
- coping skills—for managing stress and symptoms
- access school resources—enrollment, financial aid, and campus resources
- time management skills—homework, papers, preparing for tests

Supported education has not been standardized by research in the same way as supported employment. Thus, models vary widely in terms of where students attend classes, where they receive supports, what types of supports are available, who provides the supports, the amount of supports, and the linkage with mental health services. For example, supports may be delivered in the classroom, at the school, at a clinic, or in one's residence. Several manuals on different approaches to supported education are available, and different groups are also working on fidelity measures. Until the basic approach is standardized and empirically validated, however, these efforts may be premature.

Supported education is sometimes offered by individual practitioners but at other times as part of a team-based approach. Many newly developed supported education services are operating in a team environment to ensure students have seamless services. The mobile team works with students in different educational settings or modes (local community college, local full-scale college or university, vocational-technical school, and home learners studying via distance learning). The current worldwide emphasis on early intervention involves working with younger people, many of whom have had their education threatened or interrupted by the early phases of mental health problems. Early-episode teams are typically multidisciplinary and include a specialist in supported education and employment (Nuechterlein et al., 2008; Rudnick & Gover, 2009). The team works together to prevent further episodes of illness and disability. Clients often pursue a mixture of education and employment, and usually the same person provides both services.

The skills and training needed to provide supported education are unclear. Experience suggests that supported education practitioners should complete some sort of formal educational or vocational training program, but in reality practitioners come from many backgrounds. Understanding psychiatric rehabilitation principles might also assist practitioners in the areas of situational assessments, direct skills teaching, resource planning, supportive counseling, and using natural supports. An important role of a supported education practitioner is to establish and maintain ongoing relationships between the supported education program and educational institutions in the community (e.g., the school's offices of disability services, admissions, and financial aid).

Supported education so far lacks rigorous research, but non-experimental studies show reasonable rates of enrollment, completion of classes, and obtaining degrees (Unger et al., 2000; Goulding, Chien, & Compton, 2010; Best, Still, & Cameron, 2008). A large, randomized controlled study is underway now, conducted by investigators at Temple University and the University of Medicine and Dentistry of New Jersey, School of Health Related Professions Department of Psychiatric Rehabilitation and Counseling Professions.

Supported education may be even more vulnerable than supported employment to funding difficulties. The current financial climate emphasizes "medical necessity" rather than people's desires to be functional citizens.

SUPPORTED SOCIALIZATION

Supported socialization, though seemingly a natural analogue of supported housing, employment, and education, has neither a consistent definition nor a consistent methodology. People with mental health problems often report loneliness, isolation, and a desire for friendships. Traditional approaches to improving social connections involve social skills training, group activities within mental health programs, clubhouses, and peer support programs. But these efforts may not transfer to new relationships outside of the mental health system.

Supported socialization aims to help people develop and sustain relationships in the community, apart from the mental health system. It emphasizes the concept of community integration rather than mental health segregation. Supported socialization involves a direct effort to help people participate in natural social, organizational, and recreational activities in the community (Davidson et al., 2004). Thus, social experiences and training groups within a day treatment center would not qualify as supported socialization; helping a participant to join a church, a softball team, or a stamp collecting group in the community would be considered supported socialization.

Other aims are often added to the concept of supported socialization; for example, to enhance the depth and quality of relationships (Davidson et al., 2004) or to facilitate exchanges of tangible goods and problem-solving opportunities (Wong, Matejkowski, & Lee, 2011). But these extensions of the concept often revert to traditional mental health efforts to change people rather than to help them find satisfying friendships and social niches in the community.

Emerging principles of supported socialization might include the following:

- highly individualized—based on personal interests, preferences, and goals
- building on strengths—rather than changing personality or skills
- relationships in the community—not in the mental health system
- community opportunities—consider many potential activities
- supports as needed—types, amounts, and durations

No consensus exists on how supported socialization should be delivered. In theory, laypeople, peers, or professionals could deliver supported socialization. Several programs partner community volunteers with mental health consumers to develop permanent supportive friendships. A small team might include a community volunteer and a mental health or rehabilitation professional to oversee the process (McCorkle, et al 2008). Alternatively, teams involved in other interventions, such as assertive community treatment teams, supported employment teams, or supported housing teams, could also provide supported socialization.

The process and skills for delivering supported socialization are also unclear. Discussions and guides on topics as varied as leisure, parenting, dating, and intimacy are widely available (see, e.g., www.tucollaborative.org). The following vignette illustrates a possible process and suggests relevant skills.

John lives alone and complains of loneliness. He currently stays mostly in his apartment but wants to socialize more. He has revealed that he used to bowl and enjoyed the social aspects of bowling. A supported socialization intervention for John might be a stepwise process like the following:

- John and a staff member go bowling together.
- The staff member helps John examine the bulletin boards at the bowling alley for a bowling team or league that he might join.
- The staff member meets with John to address practical issues (e.g., transportation and buying or renting bowling shoes) and to discuss strategies for managing his anxiety about bowling on a team with unfamiliar people.
- The staff member accompanies John during his first league night, observing from a distance and available to help if needed.
- John goes bowling on a next league night without the staff member, who is available by cell phone.
- The staff member meets with John monthly to solve problems until John feels comfortable that he is making friends on the team.

Little research exists on supported socialization. Because many clients reject or fail to benefit from other approaches to finding desired social relationships, supported socialization models need to be constructed, piloted, refined, measured, and tested. To be consistent with other supported approaches, supported socialization should emphasize natural social settings in the community rather than relationships that are paid for by the mental health system.

DISCUSSION AND CONCLUSIONS

People with mental health difficulties identify functional goals such as independent housing, education, employment, and friends as essential to the recovery process. Supported approaches to helping them to achieve these goals share several features. They begin with the consumer's perception of needs, goals, and preferences. They offer consumers choices in terms of pathways, timing, steps, and types of supports. They aim directly and rapidly at integrating in one's community and using natural supports. They encourage independence from the mental health system.

People from many different backgrounds, including people in recovery, can deliver supported services. To ensure that different types of supports are combined, individually tailored, and linked with other services, team-based approaches are usually optimal. The consumer is always the central member of the team as the director of services. The variety of supported service models usefully informs the recovery vision and outcomes.

REFERENCES

Anthony, W.A., & Unger, K.V. (1991). Supported education: An additional program resource for young adults with long term mental illness. *Community Mental Health Journal, 27,* 145–156.

Becker, D.R., & Drake, R.E. (2003). *A Working Life for People with Severe Mental Illness.* New York: Oxford University Press.

Best, L.J., Still, M., & Cameron, G. (2008). Supported education: Enabling course completion for people experiencing mental illness. *Australian Occupational Therapy Journal, 55,* 65–68.

Bond, G.R., Drake, R.E., & Becker, D.R. (in press). Generalizability of the individual placement and support model of supported employment outside the U.S. *World Psychiatry.*

Collins, M.E., & Mowbray, C.T. (2005). Higher education and psychiatric disabilities: National survey of campus disability services. *American Journal of Orthopsychiatry, 75,* 304–315.

Davidson, L., Shahar, G., Stayner, D.A., Chinman, M.J., Rakfeldt, J., & Tebes, J.K. (2004). Supported socialization for people with psychiatric disabilities: Lessons from a randomized controlled trial. *Journal of Community Psychology, 32,* 453–477.

Drake, R. E., & Bond, G. R. (in press). IPS support employment: A 20-year update. *American Journal of Psychiatric Rehabilitation.*

Goulding, S.M., Chien, V.H., & Compton, M.T. (2010). Prevalence and correlates of school drop-out prior to initial treatment of nonaffective psychosis: Further evidence suggesting a need for supported education. *Schizophrenia Research, 116,* 228–233.

McCorkle, B.H., Rogers, E.S., Dunn, E.C., Lyass, A., & Wan, Y.M. (2008). Increasing social support for individuals with serious mental illness: Evaluating the compeer model of intentional friendship. *Community Mental Health Journal, 44,* 359–366.

McHugo, G.M., Bebout, R.R., Harris, M., Cleghorn, S., Herring, G., Xie, H., et al. (2004). A randomized controlled trial of supported housing versus continuum housing for homeless adults with severe mental illness. *Schizophrenia Bulletin, 30,* 969–982.

Nuechterlein, K.H., Subotnik, K.L., Turner, L.R., Ventura, J., Becker, D.R., & Drake, R.E. (2008). Individual placement and support for individuals with recent-onset schizophrenia: Integrating supported education and supported employment. *Psychiatric Rehabilitation Journal, Spring; 31,* 340–349.

Rog, D.J. (2004). The evidence on supportive housing. *Psychiatric Rehabilitation Journal, 27,* 334–344.

Rudnick, A., & Gover, M. (2009). Combining supported education with supported employment. *Psychiatric Services, 60,* 1690.

Swanson, S.J., & Becker, D.R. (2011). *Supported Employment: Applying the Individual Placement and Support (IPS) Model to Help Clients Compete in the Workforce.* Center City, MN: Hazelden.

Tabol, C., Drebing, C., & Rosenheck, R. (2010). Studies of "supported" and "supportive" housing: A comprehensive review of model descriptions and measurement. *Evaluation and Program Planning, 33,* 446–456.

Tsemberis, S., Gulcur, L., & Nakae, M. (2004). Housing first, consumer choice, and harm reduction for homeless individuals with a dual diagnosis. *Research and Practice, 94,* 651–656.

Unger, K.V., Pardee, R., & Shafer, M.S. (2000). Outcomes of post-secondary supported education programs for people with psychiatric disabilities. *Journal of Vocational Rehabilitation, 14,* 195.

Wong, Y.L., Matejkowski, J., & Lee, S. (2011). Social integration of people with serious mental illness: Network transactions and satisfaction. *Journal of Behavioral Health Service Research, 38,* 51–67.

CHAPTER 26

RECOVERY AND COMMUNITY MENTAL HEALTH

MARK RAGINS AND DAVID A. POLLACK

T his chapter is intended to introduce and clarify the concept of recovery, the revolutionary qualities of the recovery movement, the what and how of recovery-oriented services, and how mental health organizations can and should transform to become compatible with recovery principles. The recovery movement has emerged with much energy and enthusiasm in community-based mental health programs throughout the United States and around the world. Recovery brings hopeful, value-based transformational concepts and practical skills to effectively serve people who have been difficult to serve and whose experience with the treatment system has left them frustrated, demoralized, and alienated.

The following case description, which is interspersed throughout the chapter, will be used to demonstrate key points about these challenges and the various responses to them.

CASE EXAMPLE

Robert served in the army in Korea, but long after the fighting was done. He mainly remembered using drugs sold to him by his sergeant. When he left the military, he was lost, confused, isolated, using drugs, and increasingly wrapped up in a religious guilt feeling that God was punishing him. He wandered the country and became suicidal. He went to a Midwestern Veterans Administration hospital for help, but was locked in a barren ward, deprived of any means to hurt himself. After two weeks, he promised not to kill himself, so they let him out. He hated the experience and never returned to the VA for any services or benefits.

He spent the next decade traveling around, doing odd jobs and learning some construction skills. Occasionally homeless, he often lived in hotels or shelters as he moved about. He never held a steady job or an apartment of his own, and had no long-term relationships or connections with his family.

Then a terrifying thing happened. He fell asleep on a bus and two undercover military agents sat behind him and implanted a receptor in his head so they could transmit satellite messages to him. These messages were very disturbing and crazy-making, telling him to kill himself or hurt other people, especially black people. When he saw a newspaper report that his old sergeant had been made a general, it all made sense to him. He was being discredited so he could never testify against his old sergeant.

He went to hospitals to get X-rays to find the implant and remove it, but instead was told he was crazy. He was given medications that confused him. He felt unable to "fight the machine." He struggled mightily against these messages, but sometimes did attack people. He developed headaches, severe anxiety, and insomnia. He learned that alcohol calmed him and helped him sleep, but also dulled his mind and reduced his vigilance. Speed seemed to work better, because it helped him think fast enough to outsmart the machine, but then the headaches, insomnia, and anxiety returned. He isolated himself to avoid hurting anyone, and ended up living under a bridge.

Our discussion begins by comparing and contrasting the two most common mental health treatment models—the medical model and the rehabilitation model—with the recovery model.

The *medical model* is predicated on the notion of diagnosing psychiatric illnesses, treating their symptoms, and helping persons with these conditions return to health and more productive and meaningful lives. However, it is a paradigm that fails to address some concerns for persons with mental illnesses. Many people with mental illnesses do not agree that they have an illness, at least not in the way it is defined by the medical model, and they are often difficult to engage in treatment. Even with excellent treatment, many do not experience sufficient symptom relief from treatment alone to feel healthy enough to return to life. After most symptoms are relieved, many continue to have substantial disabilities from other factors (e.g., trauma and loss, personality issues, low intelligence, poor relationship skills, poverty, lack of education, social ostracism), not to mention the immediate and longer-term impacts of involuntary and coerced treatment interventions. This leads many to seek additional, often equally insufficient, medical treatments and/or to give up on the mental health system entirely.

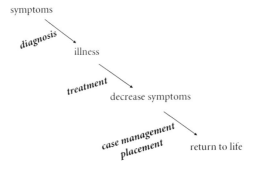

Figure 26.1 Medical Model

ROBERT'S MEDICAL MODEL SCENARIO

Robert was hospitalized and was diagnosed with a co-occurring mental illness and addiction disorder. The hospital staff explained to him in a compassionate, psychoeducational manner that there wasn't any machine. They explained that he had a chemical imbalance in his brain, probably exacerbated by substance use. The brain disorder was causing his mind to misperceive reality, and the "machine" was a delusion. The good news was that medications could restore his brain's chemical imbalance so he wouldn't be delusional anymore.

Unfortunately, Robert refused to believe this explanatory model, even though the staff were kind and compassionate. He refused the medications and never went to the outpatient clinic they referred him to. Since Robert lacked insight and was struggling to meet his basic needs, he was repeatedly hospitalized on an involuntarily basis and forcibly medicated. When not hospitalized and removed from society for his protection and public safety, he would often return to a life of alienation, homelessness, loneliness, and little hope of returning to a productive life.

The *rehabilitation model* focuses more on functioning than on symptoms. A functional assessment leads to training to reduce deficits and build strengths. When persons are sufficiently supported and perceived as likely to succeed, they are assisted in using their new and restored skills to return to life. However, this model also fails for a significant number of people. It is almost always used sequentially with the medical model, based on the presumption that symptoms must be treated and stabilized before skills training and support efforts would be effective. If symptoms cannot be controlled, such people are often deemed not ready for rehabilitation. This vulnerability is being actively addressed with various supportive rehabilitation techniques (e.g., supported employment, housing, education). The need for symptom control is not necessarily a prerequisite for effective functioning, but our system often reflects social stigma and rejection by not giving people with overt symptoms a chance to build functioning. The rehabilitation model depends on sufficient opportunity: that if someone has job skills, there is a job available, or if someone is able

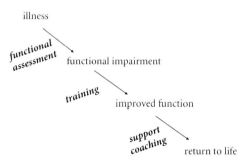

Figure 26.2 Rehabilitation Model

to live independently, there is an affordable apartment available. To be effective, rehabilitation has to be supplemented by community development to build such opportunities.

ROBERT'S REHABILITATION SCENARIO

After he was discharged from the hospital, the outpatient rehabilitation program staff told Robert that they would help him with supportive housing and employment after he was stabilized. When he became compliant with medications (by taking medications) and maintained sobriety (by completing a drug treatment program), he would be ready for rehabilitation. Alternatively, if he felt that such an approach was too difficult, they would help him get on Social Security disability. They would then offer him housing and services in a residential program where he would receive the treatment, structure, and supervision that he needed until he could again function safely and independently. When offered these choices, he refused all services and eventually wandered off and out of contact with the treatment program.

The recovery model emphasizes changes that persons make in and for themselves. When people first come for services, they often feel their illness has swallowed them up. They have struggled to overcome it on their own for quite a while, but with little success. They have experienced substantial loss, destruction, and rejection, as well as self-doubt. They often feel crippled by the illness and their life is a constant all-consuming struggle. Recovery engages the part of the person that is struggling, that may still have hopes and dreams, and aligns with that part. The recovery approach helps by decreasing the impact of the illness and by restoring or expanding the rest of the person's life. Recovery requires building meaningful roles in life.

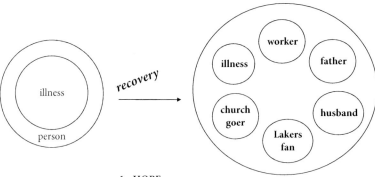

1. HOPE
2. EMPOWERMENT
3. SELF-RESPONSIBILITY
4. MEANINGFUL ROLES

Figure 26.3 Recovery Model

ROBERT'S RECOVERY SCENARIO

The staff guided Robert toward recovery step by step. They helped him rebuild hope by having him work with an outreach worker who used to be homeless and hopeless himself. "If I could make it, so can you." They helped him create an image of a better future dealing with the "implant" and other frightening thoughts and to get back to work. They helped to empower him and build up his belief in himself. They gave him self-help coping tools, including medications he could manage and administer himself. They insisted on his taking responsibility for not hurting anyone, no matter what the "satellite" or other entities would tell him. They invited him to contribute to their program in meaningful ways, making lunches for homeless people and earning money to pay rent. As he struggled to rebuild, they stuck with him to find ways to overcome the barriers that emerged.

Recovery is both a destination and a journey. Meaningful goals mark progress along the way:

1. Functions may be recovered—the ability to read, to sleep restfully, to work, to have coherent conversations, to make love, to raise children, to drive a car, etc.
2. External things may be recovered—an apartment, a job, friends, playing in a band, a spouse, a car, family relationships, a TV, educational programs, etc.
3. Internal states can be recovered—feeling good about oneself, satisfaction, self-confidence, spiritual peace, self-responsibility, a sense of identity other than as a mentally ill person, etc.

The journey of recovery is a very personal process. In the same way that Elizabeth Kübler-Ross described a set of stages that people go through as they struggle with impending death, Mark Ragins described a set of stages (hope, empowerment, self responsibility, and achieving meaningful roles) that people go through as they struggle to overcome serious mental illnesses (Ragins, 2002). Even as hospice has been developed to assist people in their journey to die with dignity, mental health is developing recovery-based programs to assist people in their journeys to live with dignity.

We will return to Robert and more details of what happened to him, later in the chapter.

THE RECOVERY REVOLUTION

In his book *The Structure of Scientific Revolutions*, Thomas Kuhn describes the process of revolutionary change in science as resulting from the failure of a dominant paradigm to explain or address the issues for which it was originally intended. A scientific revolution is a "non-cumulative developmental episode in which an older paradigm is replaced in whole or in part by an incompatible new one." Such a change is analogous to a political revolution.

The conditions that have led to the current "revolution" to transform the mental health system to accommodate the notion of recovery clearly match those described by Kuhn. Persons who had been recipients of mental health services came to feel that they were not getting better, would complain that their needs were frustrated or unmet, and often felt harmed by the system that was allegedly there to help them. They also went in and out of the system (or avoided it because of the negative experiences they had grown accustomed to) into other niches of society that were neither prepared for nor able to deal with them, reflecting the failure of the mental health system; for example, jails and prisons, safety-net health clinics, or the streets. As more persons with lived experiences in the mental health system shared their stories with peers and members of their social and support networks, a growing sense emerged that things had to change and that alternative approaches must be developed (Davidson et al., 2010; Spaniol & Koehler, 1994; Warner, 1985; Becker & Drake 2003).

Over the past 20 to 30 years, the recovery movement has progressed from being an outsider revolutionary movement to being an insider reform movement. This has been a difficult personal and tactical progression for many people in the movement. Angry advocacy is easier and more immediately satisfying than collaborative compromise. Criticizing is easier than constructive collaboration. Nonetheless, the shift is occurring, supported by a growing army of consumers, advocates, clinicians, policy makers, and influential community members. As the recovery movement has progressed, new challenges and applications have emerged. The full implications and impact of recovery are ahead of us.

Malcolm Gladwell, in *The Tipping Point* (2000), has hypothesized that a number of factors are essential for revolutionary ideas to become fully realized. These include:

1. The Power of Context: This is the realization that maintaining the status quo or incremental change is unsustainable and will fail, leading to system collapse and much worse outcomes. The evidence is mounting that the current paradigm is failing:
   - Many persons do not get better with traditional medical or rehab treatment approaches.
   - Many have become alienated from the mental health system and its coercive and sometimes harmful interventions.
   - For many who remain in the mental health system, the illness has become their identity and their lives are filled with hopelessness and passivity.
   - Unrecognized trauma has emerged as a major issue, but the system often fails to help without triggering old traumatic feelings or creating new ones.
   - The mental health system fails to recognize that many persons have significant strengths, want to take on more self-responsibility, and want to go on with their lives in the "real world."
   - Budgets for mental health services have been slashed and often disproportionately allocated to more intense forms of treatment.
   - The lack of meaningful community support contributes to more trans-institutionalization of persons with mental illnesses into the criminal justice system.
   - The lack of a welcoming and caring system results in horror stories about persons with mental illness behaving in violent ways in the popular press (even though they are much more often the victims of various forms of brutal behavior), leading to more stigma and demands that we "lock up the mentally ill."

When these failures of the usual care become more widely observed, the system is undeniably destabilized, and a new paradigm must emerge.

2. The Power of the Few: This entails developing and supporting connectors, mavens, and salesmen. Passionate and assertive champions who advocate for change make such changes happen. The primary instigators of the recovery movement have come from the consumer/survivor movement. These are people who describe themselves as having survived not only their mental illnesses, but also the traditional treatment for those illnesses. They angrily and painfully describe traumatic experiences associated with coerced treatment, institutionalization, restraints, and excessive medications, as well as social ostracism, stigma, and isolation. They actively promote system transformation through real consumer inclusion—"nothing about us without us," including choice, empowerment, increased opportunities, decreased stigma, and direct participation in all aspects of the mental health system. Over time, the recovery movement has found champions scattered throughout the field, including the 12-Step recovery movement, rehabilitation professionals, civil rights advocates, staff "doing whatever it takes" with challenging populations like homeless people, transitional-age youth, and minority cultures, and spiritually based treatment providers. Many mental health professionals have found recovery practice a return to their core personal and professional values. Many have been doing recovery-oriented practice already, although sometimes "in the closet."

3. The "Stickiness" Factor: This means compelling ideas presented in unconventional and unexpected ways and contrary to conventional wisdom. Approaches that attract attention and interest, that are "sticky," involve imagining a dramatically new vision of what we do and how we do it. Our system has incorporated a pervasive view that serious mental illnesses are chronic and deteriorating. The default position is that most people with serious mental illnesses have impaired insight, poor judgment, lack of self-responsibility, and overall inability to function effectively in society. This view stresses stabilization of symptoms, which leads to controlling and coercive interventions, lifelong social isolation, and dependency.

Two sets of data sharply challenge this "default" position: First, longitudinal outcome studies of persons with schizophrenia have shown that many have been able to substantially recover. (7,8,9). Second, there is an overwhelming number and variety of first-person accounts of persons who have achieved recovery from major mental illness. More and more people are "coming out of the closet," including celebrities, mental health professionals, leading citizens, and ordinary people everywhere, and they are sharing their stories of successful struggle and hope (Balter & Katz, 1987; Chamberlin, 1988; Saks, 2008; Jamison, 1997).

Unfortunately, both the longitudinal data and the personal stories of recovery have failed to gain much attention within the professional clinical consciousness. Actively counteracting these hopeful views has been the "clinician's illusion" that the worst outcomes are typical and to be expected, often based on the skewed experience that many clinicians have had in their training or in the failing systems in which they work; in other words, a self-reinforcing conclusion, or what Gerald Caplan would call "theme interference." (Caplan & Caplan, 1993). In recent years, this negative expectation has been increasingly replaced by the more hopeful and positively reinforcing vision that the outcome studies and personal accounts imply. The emerging descriptions of recovery have a compelling power that has attracted and inspired many people.

WHAT IS RECOVERY AND HOW DO WE MAKE IT PRACTICAL?

Recovery has been variably defined, which can be very confusing. However, some consensus was achieved in two recent initiatives.

The President's New Freedom Commission on Mental Health created a plan in 2003 to transform the entire mental health system refocusing it on recovery, and declared that

> "*recovery* refers to the process in which people are able to live, work, learn, and participate fully in their communities. For some individuals, recovery is the ability to live a fulfilling and productive life despite a disability. For others, recovery implies the reduction or complete remission of symptoms. Science has shown that having hope plays an integral role in an individual's recovery."

In 2004, SAMHSA convened a panel of professionals, consumers, and families who agreed that "*recovery* is a journey of healing and transformation enabling a person with a mental health problem to live a meaningful life in a community of his or her choice while striving to achieve his or her full potential." They described 10 fundamental components of recovery: "Self direction, individualized and person-centered, empowerment, holistic, non-linear, strengths-based, peer support, respect, responsibility, and hope" (National Consensus Statement on Mental Health Recovery, 2004).

In 2011, SAMHSA went a step further, bringing together mental health and substance abuse representatives to create a unifying Working Definition of Recovery: "A process of change through which individuals improve their health and wellness, live a self-directed life, and strive to reach their full potential" with four major dimensions—health, home, purpose, and community (SAMHSA, 2012).

Recovery is not the same as cure. For acute illnesses, recovery often results from symptom elimination and cure, but for persistent illnesses, recovery more often results from:

- Achieving self-management of the illness
- Maintaining hope and self-image
- Carrying on with life through rehabilitation and adaptation
- Replacing professional supports with natural supports
- Building strengths and resilience to handle future illness

Many people, including consumers, families, staff, and our communities, will be reluctant to give up the path of pursuing a medical cure for mental illnesses, but if taken together, those objectives offer us a realistic, practical route to recovery for almost everyone.

Successful recovery does not conclude with the person thanking the treatment providers for all their great understanding and help, but also remaining dependent upon them: "I'm so glad I met you. You really understand me. You gave me the right medications. You took care of everything. I know I can always rely on you to solve any problem for me. I'm going to stay in treatment with you and count on you forever because I'll never be well enough to handle things on my own." Instead, successful recovery leads to more self-knowledge and self-reliance: "I wouldn't have wished this illness on my worst enemy. The pain and suffering have been enormous, but in a strange way it has been a blessing in disguise. I've found and developed strengths I never knew

I had. I've learned what's really important in life. There have been deep gifts from my deepest wounds. It's made me into the person I am today." To get to that endpoint, we must change our initial response from, "You did the right thing coming to see me. I'm a good doctor. I'm going to be able to help you," to "I can already see strengths you are going to use to overcome this terrible illness." The hope in recovery is that they will develop, not that we will "cure" them.

HOW DO RECOVERY-BASED SERVICES WORK?

1. Recovery-based services are "person-centered" instead of "illness-centered."

> A homeless outreach worker, himself a veteran with a history of mental illness and alcoholism, began stopping by Robert's encampment, bringing him sack lunches, sharing stories, and listening quietly. After several months, Robert agreed to come into a drop-in center to shower and get some clean clothes.
>
> After another week, Robert was introduced to the team psychiatrist, to "see if our doctor can help you." As he listened to Robert's story, the doctor didn't ask many diagnostic questions. He asked Robert about the story of his life instead of the history of his illness. He learned that Robert was a very moral man, that he missed working, and that he was getting sick and tired of living on the streets. When the psychiatrist shared pictures of his own family, Robert said that he still hoped he could marry and have a family some day. Rather than providing corrective insights that "the machine" wasn't real and that he had a psychotic disorder that would probably respond to medication, the doctor met Robert where he was. He said he knew nothing about military satellite technology, but a lot about strengthening brains and dealing with overwhelming stressors. He was interested in Robert's efforts to strengthen his brain with alcohol and amphetamines and thought he could offer a better alternative. He offered him a prescription for a pill that "combines the effects of alcohol and speed that might calm you and focus your thinking. Would you be willing to try it instead of alcohol and speed to see if that helped you fight the machine better?" He agreed.

Put simply, the goal of recovery is not to treat mental illnesses, but to help people with mental illnesses to have better lives. However, this transformative approach ultimately affects the entire clinical process.

2. Recovery-based services are built on consumer strengths, leading to resilience, rather than on the clinical mastery of the professional treating the consumer's deficits.

> The psychiatrist told Robert that he was more vulnerable to the "machine" by staying alone under the bridge than in a hotel room, and that he'd probably cope better if he was doing something positive instead of sitting worrying about this

all day long. To take advantage of his work ethic, Robert was offered "work for a day—house for a day." He could work two hours a day in the program's café lunchroom making hamburgers and sandwiches to earn a nightly hotel voucher. He was assured there would be people there who could help if he felt overwhelmed or violent and who wouldn't lock him up. They began working together on his goal of fighting off the machine and rejoining society. They invited him to become a member of the community program (The Village).

Over the next few months, he improved. The machine quieted down enough so he could relax and sleep; the headaches went away. When he worked, the machine didn't affect him at all. He began driving the van on catering jobs. The program staff were encouraged and offered him a permanent job and help getting a subsidized apartment.

Strengths are not people's skills or talents or things we like about them. They are the resources they will use to overcome their illnesses. Strengths can be internal qualities like determination, hopefulness, self-awareness, self-responsibility, pride, a strong work ethic, family values, and spiritual faith. Strengths can be external resources like money, family, community, stable and safe housing, mentors and friends. Strengths can be discovered (or

Table 26.1 A comparison of person-centered and illness-centered approaches to care

Person-Centered	Illness-Centered
The relationship is the foundation	The diagnosis is the foundation
Begin with welcoming—outreach and engagement	Begin with illness-assessment and diagnosis
Services are based on personal suffering and help needed	Services are based on diagnosis and treatment needed
Services work toward quality-of-life goals	Services work toward illness-reduction goals
Treatment and rehabilitation are goal-driven	Treatment is symptom-driven and rehabilitation is disability-driven
Personal recovery is central from beginning to end	Recovery from the illness sometimes results after the illness and then the disability are taken care of
Track personal progress toward recovery	Track illness progress toward symptom reduction and cure
Use techniques that promote personal growth and self-responsibility	Use techniques that promote illness control and reduction of risk of damage from the illness
Services end when persons can manage their own lives and attain meaningful roles	Services end when the illness is cured
The relationship may change and grow throughout and continue even after services end	The relationship only exists to treat the illness and must be carefully restricted to maintain professional boundaries

rediscovered) or newly developed. When someone has enough strength to overcome the next symptom increase, drug relapse, relationship breakup, job loss, family disappointment, or even tragic loss without falling apart, without becoming homeless or jailed or hospitalized, without losing everything they have worked so hard for, then they have resilience. Our goal is not to protect them from tragedies but to help them build enough resilience to handle the inevitable crises when they come.

As people grow, they move along a continuum from "unengaged" to "engaged but poorly self-coordinating" to "self-responsible." People who are "unengaged" generally do not collaborate in their recovery. They might refuse all treatment, come in irregularly during crises, only want charity and entitlements but not treatment, or be brought into treatment repeatedly or involuntarily for being dangerous or disruptive. People who are "engaged, but poorly self-directed" might want to collaborate in their recovery, but have trouble coordinating the services they need. They may miss appointments, take medications poorly, abuse substances, or have poor skills or support. They need someone to help coordinate their services. People who are "self-responsible" can collaborate in their recovery and usually can coordinate it by increasing their resilience, self-sufficiency, and community integration.

These three levels of engagement are not exclusively related to consumer traits. System traits, primarily "ease of engagement" and "ease of coordination," also affect the level of engagement. Programs that are more welcoming and accessible, with few barriers to treatment and that integrate multiple coordinated services at one site instead of scattered in several separate systems, are more likely to attract or retain consumers whose level of engagement had previously been marginal.

Table 26.2 Differences in approaches between Caretaking Services and Growth Oriented Services across four stages of recovery

Stage of Recovery	Caretaking Services	Growth Oriented Services
Extreme risk	External controls—locked environment, seclusion, restraints, 1:1 monitoring. Forced sedation. Reduce external interactions and stress.	Support to increase internal controls and self-responsible problem solving. Help to reduce internal sources of distress and loss of control. Trauma sensitive interactions.
Unengaged	Forced treatment Protection Benefits establishment Acute stabilization	Outreach and engagement Peer bridging Concrete quality-of-life goals Relationship building
Engaged, but poorly self-coordinating	Structure Making decisions for people Case management Chronic stabilization Board and care	Supportive services Skill building Personal service coordination Collaboration building Halfway house
Self-responsible	Benefits retention Maintenance therapy and medication Support groups	Community integration Self-help Peer support Wellness activities Growth promoting therapy

Most consumers need both caretaking and growth-promoting services at different times in their lives and in different combinations. However, the more a program emphasizes or relies upon caretaking services, the less likely it is to promote growth, personal strength, and resilience.

Readiness is a key concept in standard mental health services and is generally understood to mean "prepared and likely to succeed." Traditional programs spend a lot of time assessing readiness and trying to create it so that people will be "ready" to leave the hospital, get a job, go to school, become their own payee, get off conservatorship or court-ordered treatment, get their own apartment, or effectively use or even get off medications. From a recovery perspective, "ready" means "motivated and excited," and the focus is on exposure and building motivation. "Prepared and likely to succeed" comes from learning by doing, sometimes with guidance, but often as a result of trial and error. The job of staff is not to prepare ahead of time, but to actively support while the client learns by doing. Instead of trying to prevent or avoid suffering, the recovery goal should be to help consumers learn as they go, building strengths and resiliency for when they will be on their own.

3.   Recovery-based services are "client-driven" instead of "professional-driven."

Robert disappeared back under the bridge. The treatment team suspected that he'd either relapsed on speed or stopped taking his medication and was more psychotic. The peer outreach worker looked for him and found that neither of those things had happened. Robert was just scared and thought they were pushing him too fast. He agreed to return to "work for a day—house for a day."

Six months later, he chose to move on to permanent work and an apartment. By the time the team celebrated his achievement with a housewarming party, he'd gained so much confidence dealing with the machine that he stopped his medications. The psychiatrist continued to see him and, although his old religious guilt returned, the machine remained very quiet. He worked on his shame and guilt without meds. He began volunteering by providing homeless outreach with his old peer counselor as a way to give back to others.

Robert felt proud of himself and the emotional closeness he had developed with the community of staff and program members, who reminded him of his lost family. The program helped him find his sister on the Internet and to visit her in a distant city. She welcomed her long-lost brother. Six months later, he decided to move to be with his sister, realizing that he was strong enough to make it without the treatment program.

Client-driven approaches were developed primarily to increase engagement and motivation in treatment. Traditional approaches incorporate a big differential in the relative power of the treatment transaction: a strong professional helping a weak person by doing something to or for them, which conveys a subtle, sometimes overt, message that the client/patient needs the professional in order to get better. A truly amazing array of client-driven approaches has been developed, primarily by non-clinicians, especially consumers in recovery. Here are some notable examples:

1. Personal Assistance in Community Existence (PACE)—A comprehensive approach to recovery built on self-directed, empowered usage of proven recovery beliefs, relationships, skills, identity, and community, especially useful for people who are not motivated by a medical approach for their "so-called mental illness." (Ahern & Fisher, 1999)

2. Shared Decision Making—People are more likely to be motivated to work on plans they have had a part in creating and that reflect their contributions. (Davidson et al., 2010)

3. Motivational Interviewing—We can "meet people where they are" in the normal process of making difficult life changes (pre-contemplation, contemplation, planning, action, and sustaining), supporting them in their inevitable ambivalence with its "ups and backs." This is likely to be more effective than always prescribing action and then getting frustrated, even coercive, and blaming them when they don't follow through. (Miller & Rollnik, 2002)

4. Wellness Recovery Action Plans (WRAP)—People can create their own plans in a notebook for maintaining mental health, dealing with moderate stressors, and serious crises. WRAP can be done individually or in groups and can be facilitated by trained peer counselors. (Copeland, 2002a,b)

5. Advance Directives—Serious mental illness can lead to times of losing control and the ability to make competent decisions, even for people who are generally doing well in recovery. Just like people prepare for medical deteriorations by creating advance directives to make their choices known ahead of time and to appoint a surrogate, people can create advance directives for future psychiatric crises. Many states have legal supports for advance directives (Backlar, 1997; Fisher, 2000).

True collaboration requires understanding how other people view themselves and their lives, rather than just teaching them our point of view. It requires understanding their goals instead of ours, looking for shared goals that both parties can value and enthusiastically pursue. It requires clinicians to be compliant with consumers' plans as much as expecting consumers to be compliant with professionals' plans. It requires sharing power and actively empowering people. In particular, it requires mutual trust.

WHAT ARE "RECOVERY-BASED" SERVICES?

A typical set of services that promote engagement, self-responsibility, and community integration, while incorporating self-help activities that facilitate recovery, would include the following:

1. *Engagement and welcoming*—Focus on relationship- and trust-building services, not on requiring diagnosis or insight or medication; "meeting people where they're at"; harm reduction; "housing first"; peer engagement; outreach; and charity.

2. *Person-centered planning and goal-driven services*—Develop a shared story of the person's life instead of a history of illness, identify strengths to be used in recovery, assist in formulating goals to pursue collaboratively, identify potential barriers and develop

shared plans to overcome barriers, develop goal-setting skills, and use a menu of services supplied by an integrated team and community.

3. *Sharing decision-making and building self-responsibility*—Develop collaborative relationships, describe service choices in understandable language and as it impacts the consumer's goals; "client-driven services," advance directives, assist clients in learning from consequences of decisions to learn to make new choices—learn from mistakes; define respective roles in achieving goals; increasing self-responsibility and self-reliance.

4. *Rehabilitation-building skills and supports*—Do things with people instead of for them; use "teachable moments," *in vivo* skill building; assist with entitlements, supports, and opportunities; psychiatric rehabilitation and psychosocial rehabilitation; clubhouses and learning roles; peer support.

5. *Recovery-based medication services*—Consider treatment optimization approaches that balance judicious use of medications with other treatment, rehab, and recovery interventions, with particular emphasis on patient/client/consumer preference. Align use of medications with the consumer's goals, instead of symptom control. Getting patients to take their medication to improve their symptoms needn't precede rebuilding lives. Medications can initially be for "short-term" effects until a "customer relationship" is built. Getting off medications happens when they're no longer needed to attain and maintain goals, not when symptoms are relieved. Medications enable self-help coping techniques, rather than competing with them. (Muesser et al., 2002)

6. *Peer support and self help*—Cultivate opportunities for outreach and engagement, peer counseling, shared stories and humanity, peer advocacy, peer bridging, acceptance, "giving back," peer support groups, 12-Step groups, coping skills, self care, WRAP. (Georgia Mental health Consumer Network, 2003; Jonikas & Cook, 2004)

7. *Adapting and integrating therapy and healing*—Provide therapeutic relationships without excessive structure or rules. Emphasize engagement, relationship building, "corrective emotional experiences." Create a healing environment—sanctuary, counterculture of acceptance, "therapeutic milieu," group therapy without walls, Carl Rogers' client centered approach that emphasizes providing empathy, authenticity, and caring to help people grow without needing a formal therapy structure.

8. *Trauma-informed care*—Increase trauma awareness, empathetic relationships, trauma healing and recovery, personal safety and boundaries. Avoid retraumatization cycles and traumatization by staff, including reducing coercion, seclusion, and restraints.

9. *Spirituality and alternative approaches*—For some persons, healing and recovery requires attention to their spiritual life. Faith and communing with others who share similar spiritual beliefs, without proselytizing or requiring participation in formal religious activities, can be a very powerful and supportive adjunct to feeling whole; inclusion of spiritual strengthening practices and healing.

10. *Community integration and quality of life support services*—Identify needs and gaps in social supports, and provide benefits assistance, re-documentation, "supported services"—housing, education, employment, medical care, community development; finding "welcoming hearts" in the community; finding a niche; meaningful roles; community inclusion; rights and responsibilities; avoiding "failures of community integration"—hospitalization, homelessness, imprisonment.

11. *Graduation and self-reliance*—Build strengths and resilience, protective factors, gifts from their suffering, overcoming fear of losing benefits and illness roles, replacing

professional supports with self-help and personal supports, developing community treatment resources, "coming out" to fight stigma and discrimination.

RECOVERY CHANGES EVERYTHING: RELATIONSHIPS, TEAMS, CULTURE, AND SYSTEM

To implement recovery-based services, there must be substantial transformation of treatment relationships. These changes are often threatening to staff who feel effective and safe within the bounds of traditional professional standards and ethics. Items like sharing bathrooms, giving choices to psychotic people, treating people without relying on medications, taking people in staff cars, eating lunch together, and encouraging relevant and ethical staff self-disclosure are lightning rods for staff resistance to recovery.

Recovery-oriented programs usually provide volunteer and staff positions for peers and family advocates. Persons with lived experiences of mental illness can provide specialized peer-based services, such as positions that involve outreach, peer-to-peer engagement, case management, life-rebuilding skills, and community development, and they can be hired in any position that they are qualified to do. The inclusion of such persons in the staff of a program can be disruptive to the traditional professional staff, who may worry or complain about risks associated with boundaries, ethics, or safety.

Recovery is not an "anything goes" model. One must be attentive to safety and ethics. Traditional ethics and safety rules evolved in a very risky and dangerous treatment arena: the isolated, secretive, individual private practice settings. It may be surprising and paradoxical, but activities that may not be safe, ethical, or appropriate within a private practice context can be provided and may be preferred in the context of a cohesive recovery-based team and program culture. Clinical rules regarding safety and ethics, and their rationale, must be reexamined and aligned with the goals of treatment and recovery: lowering boundaries and barriers, sharing power and responsibility, and engaging the community. Patricia Deegan has provided detailed guidance for the creation of new rules for new teams (Deegan, 2003). The Los Angeles County Department of Mental Health created a set of bureaucratic "Parameters for Service Relationships in a Recovery-Based Mental Health System" reconciling recovery values with existing policies and parameters (2006).

Team-based care is becoming the norm throughout all areas of health care. The relatively recent emphasis on patient-centered primary care homes and the integration of mental health and primary care are obvious examples of this rapidly growing trend. A recent report has identified the key core competencies for persons involved in collaborative care (Interprofessional Education Collaborative Expert Panel, 2011). In addition to the specific competencies associated with the person's specific clinical discipline, this report specifies collaborative care abilities in four domains: values/ethics for interprofessional practice, roles/responsibilities, interprofessional communication, and teams and teamwork. Although most community-based mental health programs have provided some form of team-based care for decades, many have failed to truly develop teams to meet the aims of a quality health system; that is, to be patient-centered, effective, efficient, equitable, timely, and safe. These collaborative care competencies are relevant and underscore the shortcomings of traditional practices, whether individual or team-based.

Recovery programs need to be team-based and to cultivate these competencies because:

- We need to integrate a range of quality-of-life services beyond any one person's competence.
- People at different stages of recovery require different staff skills—engagement, building skills and support, moving on.
- None of us is Mother Theresa, but between us we can create "one Mother Theresa": a broad "counterculture of acceptance" welcoming and engaging everyone in need.
- To safely and ethically lower boundaries and adopt multiple roles, we need to support and keep each other honest.
- To maintain staff morale and avoid our own trauma and burnout, we need to stick together and take care of each other.

Recovery-based programs are more readily differentiated from traditional programs by the values embedded in their culture than by the services they provide. Mental Health America of Los Angeles has created a recovery-culture progress report that rates programs from the perspective of consumers, families, line staff, and supervisors/administrators on seven key dimensions: Welcoming and accessibility, growth orientation, consumer inclusion, emotional healing relationships and environments, quality-of-life focus, community integration, and staff recovery and morale (Ragins, 2010). That final dimension is crucial and often overlooked: Staff should be treated in a recovery-based way, if only to increase their ability to treat their clients the same way. In many programs, staff morale is too low to allow a recovery-based culture. On the other hand, when a recovery-based culture is promoted, staff burnout diminishes and morale improves.

Recovery-based programs need to align all of their processes with recovery-based values and principles. Boston University's Center for Psychiatric Rehabilitation states that "A ROMHP [*recovery-oriented mental health program*] is characterized by program structures such as mission, policies, procedures, record keeping and quality assurance that are consistent with fundamental recovery values. Similarly, staffing concerns such as selection, training and supervision are guided by the fundamental values of recovery." The BU document identifies four fundamental values: person orientation, person involvement, self-determination/choice, and growth potential (32). As the recovery movement matures, additional refinements are emerging, such as recovery-based supervision and mentoring, recovery-based administration, recovery-based funding, and recovery-based accountability.

IMPLEMENTING RECOVERY-BASED TRANSFORMATION

It is easier to create a new recovery-based program with selected staff than to transform an existing program. Resistance to change is common (Farkas et al., 2005). Keys to transformation include: Sustained coordinated leadership, creating "learning cultures" in the programs, improving connections between programs and administration, including and hiring consumers, and moving from a predominantly crisis-response mode to a proactive, team-based, planned mode.

The American Association of Community Psychiatrists created a policy document that is: intended to facilitate the transformation to recovery-oriented services and to provide direction to organizations or systems that are engaged in this process. They should be useful to systems that have already made significant progress in creating services that promote recovery by providing a systematic way of thinking about quality improvement and management for these services.

The guidelines are organized divided into three domains of service systems: administration, treatment and supports. Each domain is composed of several elements and recovery-enhancing characteristics for each of these elements are described. Some suggestions for measurement of achievement/progress in each of these areas are included. (2003)

The revolution is still in progress:

> Successful revolutions are rare in social systems and not all revolutions succeed, even if they should. True revolutions often take a generation or more to fully unfold and actualize. Progress can be tracked through stages of development; moving from innovators and early adaptors to growing acceptance to broad-based implementation.

Looking back at the history of the recovery movement thus far, there is clear evidence of progress.

1980s: Recovery Is Possible
- Longitudinal studies of recovery
- Individual stories of recovery
- Recovery doesn't have to mean cure—Recovery can occur with chronic illnesses
- Recovery is something the person does, not the illness—recovery is "person-centered"

1990s: Recovery Services Are Better
- Quality-of-life outcomes from model programs
- Inclusion of challenging populations who were dropping out, frustrating, and without recovery services, who "needed" coercion
- Improved staff morale and satisfaction
- Enhanced employment outcomes

2000s: Recovery Is Coming
- Widespread recovery transformation proclamations—President's New Freedom Commission, Veteran's Administration, California's Mental Health Services Act, SAMHSA's transformation states, other state initiatives
- Widespread persistent transformation efforts. "It's not just a fashion—you can't wait this out"

2010s: Recovery Is Practical
- Widespread development of recovery-based practices, programs, tools, and systems of care
- Recovery requires an integrated team—including psychiatrists and consumer staff
- Recovery is reasonably cost-effective compared with standard services—and probably even compared to neglect and cost-shifting
- Moving from recovery as an add-on for "outliers" to the core of the entire system

FUTURE CHALLENGES

In this chapter, we have:

- Outlined the roots of the recovery movement in mental health,
- Compared recovery to the prior two dominant models of care, the medical and rehabilitation models, and

- Described what recovery services are and how to implement them.

As recovery-based programs continue to emerge, develop, grow, and learn from their own and others' experiences, it is essential that the providers and consumers who endorse these approaches continue to improve the quality of the programs they create. We must also keep the "tipping point" process active by spreading the news that this is the effective and preferred way to meet the needs of the populations we serve, especially persons with severe and persistent mental illnesses and addiction disorders.

In order to sustain this revolution, we must apply recovery to the administration of programs; for example, through recovery-oriented leadership, mentoring, supervision, and accountability. Programs must manage their workload and avoid excessive caseloads, by creating efficient methods for allowing clients to flow through and graduate from programs. We must expand the effort to create and provide "strengths-based" services to build resilience and a sense of community into all of our lives, whether we are providers, recipients of services, or both. As the health system changes to one that is more primary care–based, we need to make sure that recovery principles and practices are a central part of the overall integration of mental health and addiction services with primary care. History suggests this will not be easy, because health integration means "medical model." But whether our revolution succeeds is up to all of us. There will be much more work yet to be done, some of which will involve educating our colleagues.

REFERENCES

Ahern, L., and Fisher, D. (1999). *Personal Assistance in Community Existence: The Alternative to PACT.* National Empowerment Center (NEC). Available at http://www.power2u.org/pace_manual.pdf.

American Association of Community Psychiatrists (AACP). (2003). *AACP Guidelines for Recovery Oriented Services,* available at http://www.communitypsychiatry.org/publications/clinical_and_administrative_tools_guidelines/ROSGuidelines.aspx

Backlar, P. (1997). Anticipatory planning for psychiatric treatment is not quite the same as planning for end-of-life care. *Community Mental Health Journal,* 33, 4, 261–268

Balter, M., and Katz, R. *Nobody's Child.* Cambridge, MA: Perseus Books, 1987.

Becker, D.R., and Drake, R.E. *A Working Life for People with Severe Mental Illness.* New York: Oxford University Press, 2003.

Caplan, G.L., and Caplan, R.B. *Mental Health Consultation and Collaboration;* San Francisco, Jossey-Bass, 1993

Chamberlin, J. *On Our Own.* Mind Publications, United Kingdom, 1988.

Copeland, M.E. (2002a). *Developing a Wellness Toolbox.* Available at http://mentalhealthrecovery.com/art_toolbox.html.

Copeland, M.E. (2002b). *Guide to Developing a WRAP—Wellness Recovery Action Plan.* Available at http://mentalhealthrecovery.com/art_devwrap.html.

Davidson, L., et al. (2006). The top ten concerns about recovery encountered in mental health system transformation. *Psychiatric Services,* 57, 5 640–645 (May).

Davidson, L., Harding, C., and Spaniol, L. (eds.). *Recovery from Serious Mental Illnesses: Research Evidence and Implications for Practice—Volume 1.* Boston: Boston University Center for Psychiatric Rehabilitation, 2005.

Davidson, L, Rakfeldt, J, and Strauss, J. *The Roots of the Recovery Movement in Psychiatry: Lessons Learned* (West Sussex, UK: Wiley-Blackwell; 2010).

Davidson, L., Rakfeldt, J., Strauss, J., and Deegan, P. (2010). *Common Ground.* Available at http://www.patdeegan.com/commonground/about.

Deegan, P., and Advocates, Inc. (2003). *Intentional Care Employee Performance Standards That Support Recovery and Empowerment.* Available at http://www.advocatesinc.org/Resources-IntentionalCare.

DeSisto, M., Harding, C.M., McCormick, R.V., Ashikaga, T., and Brooks, G.W. (1995). The Maine and Vermont three-decade studies of serious mental illness: I. Matched comparison of cross-sectional outcome. *British Journal of Psychiatry*, 167, 331–337.

Farkas, et al. (2005). Implementing recovery oriented evidence based programs: Identifying the critical dimensions community. *Mental Health Journal*, 41, 2 145–153 (April).

Fisher, D. (2000). *Making Advance Directives Work For You.* Available at *http*://www.power2u.org/self-hep/directives_work.html.

Georgia Mental Health Consumer Network. (2003). *Georgia's Consumer-Driven Road to Recovery: A Mental Health Consumer's Guide for Participation In and Development Of Medicaid Reimbursable Peer Support Services.* Georgia Division of Mental Health, Developmental Disabilities, and Addictive Diseases; Office of Consumer Relations. Decatur, Georgia

Gladwell, M. *The Tipping Point: How Little Things Can Make a Big Difference.* Little, Brown, and Company, 2000.

Harding, C., et al. (1987). The Vermont longitudinal study of persons with severe mental illness. *American Journal of Psychiatry*, 144 727–735 (June 6).

Interprofessional Education Collaborative Expert Panel (2011). *Core Competencies for Interprofessional Collaborative Practice: Report of an Expert Panel.* Washington, DC: Interprofessional Education Collaborative.

Jamison, K. R. (1995). *An Unquiet Mind: A Memoir of Moods and Madness.* New York: Alfred A Knopf, Inc. 1995

Jonikas, J., and Cook, J. (2004). *This is Your Life: Creating Your Self-Directed Life Plan (Workbook).* Chicago: University of Illinois.

Los Angeles County Department of Mental Health Office of the Medical Director (2006). *Parameters for Service Relationships in a Recovery-Based Mental Health System.* Available at http://file.lacounty.gov/dmh/cms1_159957.pdf

Miller, W., and Rollnick, S. *Motivational Interviewing: Preparing People for Change.* New York: Guilford Press; 2002.

Muesser, K.T., Corrigan, P.W., Hilton, D.W., Tanzman, B., Schaub, A., Gingerich, S., et al. (2002). Illness management and recovery: A review of the research. *Psychiatric Services*, 53(10), 1272–1284.

Pilon, D., and Ragins, M. *Milestones of Recovery Scale (MORS) Manual.* Los Angeles: Mental Health America, 2008.

President's New Freedom Commission on Mental Health. (2003). *Achieving the Promise: Transforming Mental Health Care in America.* Available at http://www.mentalhealthcommission.gov/reports/FinalReport/downloads/FinalReport.pdf.

Ragins, M. *A Recovery Culture Progress Report.* Los Angeles: Mental Health America, 2010.

Ragins, M. *A Road to Recovery.* Los Angeles: Mental Health America, 2002.

Saks, E. *The Center Cannot Hold: My Journey Through Madness.* New York: Hyperion; 2008.

SAMHSA. (2004). *National Consensus Statement on Mental Health Recovery.* Available at http://store.
samhsa.gov/product/National-Consensus-Statement-on-Mental-Health-Recovery/SMA05–4129

SAMHSA. (2012). *SAMHSA's Working Definition of Recovery* Available at http://store.samhsa.gov/prod-
uct/SAMHSA-s-Working-Definition-of-Recovery/PEP12-RECDEF; .

Spaniol, L., and Keohler, M. (eds.). *The Experience of Recovery.* Boston: Center for Psychiatric
Rehabilitation, Boston University, 1994.

Warner, R. *Recovery from Schizophrenia.* Boston: Routledge & Kegan Paul, 1985.

CHAPTER 27

MILITARY VETERANS AND FAMILIES

JAMES SIZEMORE AND SHANÉ MARSHALL

Since September 11, 2001, many military personnel have been deployed to various regions around the world to engage in combat. This has brought the effects of these deployments on service members and their families to the attention of people within the larger society. The primary mental health issue most people focus on with military veterans is post-traumatic stress disorder (PTSD) (Department of Veterans Affairs, 2011b; Department of Defense, 2011; National Association of State Alcohol and Drug Abuse Directors and Abt Associates, Inc. 2009). While this focus is valid, it is not the sole concern of mental health care needs among veterans. Other issues affecting military veterans are:

- Readjustment to civilian life (from military life or combat situations)
- Marriage and family: Changes in family dynamics, broken bonds, etc.
- Divorce
- Parenting skills
- Family issues involving PTSD
- Depression
- Anxiety
- Sleep disturbances
- Suicide
- Military sexual trauma (MST)
- Impulsive behaviors
- Grief/bereavement
- Post-traumatic stress disorder (PTSD)
- Traumatic brain injury (TBI)
- Alcohol and other drug (AOD) issues
- Legal issues

- Housing/homelessness
- Employment/unemployment
- Service linkage and availability
- Financial troubles
- Crisis management

CASE EXAMPLE

Daniel W. is a 28-year-old married Caucasian male who has two children. He was admitted to the emergency room after a traumatic car accident and was soon taken to the intensive care unit and then the medical step-down unit. In the assessment he indicated he possibly had thoughts of self-harm prior to the accident. We also learned that Daniel is a military veteran who served two tours of duty in Southwest Asia in support of Operation Iraqi Freedom and Operation Enduring Freedom. Daniel was discharged from the military a year ago.

He attended college for a year prior to enlisting into the Army; which was soon after the 9/11 attacks. Daniel felt he should do his part in defending the United States, so he had a desire to serve in the military. Upon completion of his initial training, he was assigned to a military unit stationed in Germany that deployed to Iraq shortly after his arrival. He spent 15 months in Iraq on his first deployment. When his unit redeployed to Germany, he married a woman he met on line while taking online college courses. He deployed again two years later, to Afghanistan, for 12 months, during which his first child was born. He redeployed back to Germany after 12 months. Daniel's next tour of duty was an unaccompanied tour to Korea. During this time his wife returned to the States to live near her family, and his second child was born. Because he wished to spend more time with his family, Daniel reluctantly got out of the military upon completing his enlistment. Since getting out of the Army, Daniel doesn't feel he fits in with his family or the civilian community. He and his wife are fighting more often, and because of his absence for over half of their lives, he doesn't feel he knows his kids (ages six and three years old). Overall, he doesn't feel he fits anywhere anymore.

In the midst of this readjustment, Daniel does not have personal health insurance. While he qualifies to receive health care through the Department of Veteran Affairs (VA) Health Administration, he is reluctant to seek assistance. Therefore, he has not enrolled in the VA healthcare system, and is not certain of how to get assistance.

THE VETERANS' PERSPECTIVE

MILITARY CULTURE

When a person wears a military uniform, they and others within the military community know their role and position. The style of the uniform is different for each branch of service: Army,

Navy, Air Force, Marines, or Coast Guard. But on each uniform a service member wears their rank, combat patches, awards, and badges. When they walk into a room in uniform with other people in uniform, they know where they fit and can size up the other personnel with a quick look. Personnel have clearly defined positions within the military, and become identified by that role. For example, a person who is in a combat military occupation skill (MOS) trains to seek out and engage the enemy. While a person who is in a combat support or service support MOS is also trained to engage the enemy, if they are engaged, they typically don't try to find them.

The military has a clearly defined process for personnel to advance in their career or gain rank. There are clearly defined test scores to achieve and schools to attend in order to move up through the rank structure, and the community is designed to help them achieve these goals. If the service member does not advance in rank over a period of time, they will be discharged from military service (see afterdeployment.org). When military veterans are separated from the service, they are not afforded the necessary time or training to make an easy transition or readjustment to civilian life. Therefore, some of the most immediate feelings experienced may be becoming:

- Overwhelmed by the need to make choices
- Anxious due to a lack of structure
- Unsure where they fit in society
- Uncertain about the future
- Frustrated about starting over

SPIRITUALITY

Within the military, often the first person someone in need of mental health care will interact with is the chaplain. Whether the person is a Protestant, Catholic, Wiccan, Buddhist, or atheist is not a qualifier or disqualifier for seeing a chaplain. Chaplains are more than spiritual counselors; they also serve in the role of advisors regarding interpersonal matters and personal issues affecting people. Spiritual concerns should not be overlooked. The veteran's experience in other cultures, environments, and war zones may cause them to have personal spiritual conflicts. Veterans are often exposed to human suffering that most others do not experience. This is not all due to being in combat. Military personnel will often provide humanitarian assistance in regions of the world that are very poor or politically unstable, and will often assist during or immediately following natural disasters. Some draw upon their faith or spiritual beliefs as a source of strength, but others have their belief structures challenged or shattered by what they have seen or done. Some experiences that may bring about spiritual discord are:

- Seeing human suffering in combat zones or Third World nations
- Killing other human beings
- Survival after those nearby were violently killed
- Lacking relief from combat-related trauma
- Asking why would God do this? (Hurricane, volcano, tidal wave, tornado, etc.)
- Questioning if there is a God
- A desire to be forgiven
- A desire to be at peace within

READJUSTMENT TO THE CIVILIAN WORLD

Upon leaving the military, a veteran and his/her family are in a world of many decisions and limited community support. While they were on military posts or bases, the social service supports were easily accessible, and the loss of military structure can be difficult to handle. In addition to this, all of the friends who were their support are no longer nearby, nor are they easily accessible (Afterdeployment, 2011). They are now living in a community of people who don't understand them. When returning to the civilian community, the military veteran and their family must adapt to a whole new system of life (Duckworth, 2009):

- From a military community to one with very few veterans
- From having major responsibilities for the lives of others to very little responsibility
- From specialized training to the very beginning of a new career
- From secure employment to seeking employment in a questionable job market
- From being highly skilled and qualified to having military skills that may not be useful in the civilian job market

SEEKING HELP

One of the reasons military veterans are reluctant to seek help is because it is viewed as an admittance of weakness. This reluctance is not just involving mental health concerns, but is also for physical health issues as well (Lanham, 2007). Military members may hide or downplay physical injuries when they think it will separate them from their unit or keep them from deploying with the unit. They are even more likely to hide mental health issues, due to issues of stigmatization. The fear of seeking mental health care is compounded by the belief they will lose their security clearance and possibly be discharged from the military, or not be able to pursue a civilian career. Additionally, veterans are reluctant to seek mental health care because they hold some of the following beliefs:

- It means they are weak or "crazy"
- They should be in charge of the situation
- It implies they are unable to "get it together"
- They are not dependable in tough situations
- They can tough it out till it is over
- There is no reason to bother…it takes too much time and paperwork to get help
- They don't want everyone to know their business

MILITARY FAMILIES

Often the family will identify themselves as being "in the military" along with the service member. A spouse's status in the community is tied to the military members' rank (e.g., an officer's wife rises in status as her husband rises in rank). As a result, the spouses will see themselves as having to maintain a role as a military spouse. Military families form support networks to assist one another while their service-members are deployed, and it is typical for the spouses of the highest-ranking members to be the leaders of the family support system. The families will develop strong bonds among themselves, just as the military members will during a deployment (Duckworth, 2009). The spouses are expected to maintain the household so the service members can maintain focus on the mission and not be distracted by household concerns. Military families may experience the following:

- Long periods of separations
- Infidelity
- Parenting difficulties
- Fear of death or severe injury to the service member
- Strong reliance on extended family and friends
- Guilt for feelings of detachment
- Questioned loyalty
- Fear of changes upon the service-member's return
- Single parenthood
- Lack of social support
- Feelings of loneliness
- Development of a strong connection within the military community
- Stress of maintaining a household alone
- Neglect
- Financial strain

A service member will often make more money when they are deployed, but this is not always the case. Some Reservists and National Guard members take a pay decrease when they are activated for military service. An additional financial burden is that a military spouse will often have to pay to have things done around the household that the service member would have done when at home (e.g., lawn care, home repairs, etc.), and if there are children in the household, they need additional childcare support.

RECOMMENDED STEPS OF CARE

In the case example noted, Daniel's injuries resulting from the car accident were identified as the immediate concern, but these injuries were the result of underlying mental health issues. The car accident appeared to be a veiled attempt to commit suicide. With the compounding effects of Daniel's troubled family life and reintegration into the civilian community, he began to view suicide as a solution to his problems. In the healthcare community, adding the question, "Are you a military veteran?" to the assessment process provides a way to identify veterans and opens a process to begin identifying underlying issues and linking and/or referral to needed resources.

STEP ONE—ASK "ARE YOU A MILITARY VETERAN? DID YOU SERVE IN A COMBAT ZONE?"

Adding this question to the assessment process opens up possible sources of the issues affecting the patient, and identification of resources available to them. There are some considerations when interacting with a veteran (especially a combat veteran). As a result of military and combat experiences, veterans can seem aggressive to those who are not familiar with military personnel. A loud voice or use of harsh or vulgar language does not mean they are posturing or escalating to violent behavior. Showing respect, remaining calm, and using an appropriate tone of voice is often the best way to defuse tension that may arise in the moment. Some consideration and tips for interacting with military veterans are as follows:

- Be professional
- Be respectful
- Relax
- A priority is building rapport and trust for the life of the therapeutic relationship
- Allow the veteran time to share their experience; try to avoid rushing the process
- Avoid aggressive and authoritarian attitudes, as they can trigger an aggressive response
- Avoid use of demeaning or condescending tones or language
- Avoid minimization of their experiences and significant events
- Keep in mind the veteran does not know you, how much they can trust you, or your intentions as a mental health professional
- Obtain information related to pre-military/military/post-military experiences/homecoming
- Assess for religious and cultural factors that may impact their views of orders they carried out while on active duty

STEP TWO—IDENTIFY THE ISSUES OR PRESENTING PROBLEM

Some of the possible cultural and family concerns to consider during the assessment are identified above. For Daniel's case, there are multiple issues that are interconnected, which is likely to be true in many other cases. Nevertheless, taking the time to listen to Daniel is necessary for the exploration within the complexity of his situation. Upon review and as noted before, Daniel gave up a career he enjoyed to be with his family. But once he was with his family, he began to feel he did not fit in with them and was letting them down. He no doubt began to feel this way regarding his fellow service members because he was not able to be there for them, either. Issues that military members often experience related to their families are:

- Disconnectedness
- Infidelity
- Anger
- Feelings of abandonment and/or betrayal
- Change of family roles and loss of responsibilities
- Communication difficulty
- Concern about how much of their experiences they reveal to their family
- Don't want to burden their family with their problems

Daniel's family issues are also compounded by events experienced during his two combat tours. During these tours, one of the soldiers in his charge was killed and another was severely injured when his leg was amputated during an attack. Daniel had several other soldiers injured in enemy attacks and vehicle accidents as well. Symptoms that may be associated with exposure to combat environments such as these are:

- Stress/anxiety: for safety, experiencing full range of emotion, reactions to surroundings
- Hypervigilance: being on alert may mean the difference between life or death
- Guilt: for being alive or not being able to protect those who were injured or killed
- Dissociation: to patrol for increased arousal or triggers
- Intrusive thoughts: regarding events that occurred
- Nightmares: regarding events that occurred or are associated with fear of actual behaviors while awake
- Hallucinations: seeing, hearing, or smelling things that were present during combat
- Physical pain: both from actual injury or of a somatic nature as associated with experience(s)

STEP THREE—IDENTIFY THE RESOURCES AVAILABLE

The Veterans' Administration has many sources of healthcare and other benefits that may alleviate underlying concerns and are available to veterans. However, the complexity of qualifications for them can be overwhelming. It is then necessary to understand that the primary means for a veteran to gain access to these benefits is by having a "DD214" (pronounced *dee-dee-two-fourteen*). A DD214 is a Department of Defense Form #214 which indicates the veteran's military service and identifies where and when they served. It also indicates the type of discharge the veteran obtained from the military (e.g., honorable, general, dishonorable, etc.). All of these items will identify various resources available to the veteran. Also, there are additional state and local government agencies and nonprofit organizations that provide assistance to veterans. These organizations will require the DD214 as proof of military service as well. Accessing these agencies will be discussed below.

Some states have developed systems to connect veterans and their families to behavioral healthcare. This network can be accessed through the Department of Mental Health or the Department of Alcohol and Drug Addiction Services and the Army National Guard. These networks also provide training to the providers on the issues affecting veterans and their families, and on treatment options.

STEP FOUR—STRUCTURING THE TREATMENT ENVIRONMENT

Military veterans are used to having task lists to complete, and they are seeking answers or solutions to solve their problem. Yet, as they may want to vent regarding these problems, they remain in need of guidance on how to overcome these issues. Ways that assist in fostering an appropriate environment for care are as follows:

- Provide adequate space within the treatment environment to minimize discomfort and prevent triggers

- Explain the difference between "psychiatrist," "psychologist," "social worker," "counselor," and all the other mental health professionals they may encounter so veterans know what treatment to expect from each provider
- Educate the veteran on your scope of practice and/or influence
- Explain the treatment process, expectations, rights, confidentiality, and responsibilities
- Have clear and concise instructions and/or steps throughout the treatment process
- Ask them to repeat back what you have instructed them, for clarity and understanding
- Learn something about the culture/military/history of the war
- Foster a sense of trust, at their pace
- Provide structure throughout the life of treatment
- Assist in medication management to reduce excessive and/or debilitating side effects
- Empower the veteran for ongoing mental and medical health care maintenance
- Advocate for the veteran as needed and/or requested

STEP FIVE—FOLLOW-UP (CASE MANAGEMENT)

Veterans with PTSD or TBI often have difficulty maintaining schedules or meeting appointment schedules. They often become overwhelmed with anxiety and frustrated with multiple schedules and appointments. As a result, they will drop out of treatment or not consistently attend scheduled appointments. Therefore, it is important to assist veterans with meeting appointments. A case manager is helpful in maintaining appointments with counselors and psychiatrists. It is sometimes helpful to have a social worker accompany a veteran to appointments to ensure they communicate effectively the symptoms they are experiencing. There are times when it is helpful to involve the spouse or family in the treatment process. Family members will often reveal symptoms the veteran does not notice or is not willing to reveal. A family member will also help a veteran remember appointments and will encourage a veteran to follow through with the treatment (Department of Veteran Affairs, 2011a). Some means to help veterans make appointments or commit to the treatment process are:

- Assign a case manager
- Involve a family member
- Call to remind them of appointments
- Encourage the usage of a smartphone to maintain appointments

ACCESSING HEALTHCARE IN THE DEPARTMENT OF VETERAN AFFAIRS

The Department of Veteran Affairs (VA) Healthcare System is available to veterans who meet certain criteria. One of which is that within five years of being discharged from the military, a veteran can receive healthcare at a VA facilities for little or no cost to them. To access this system, the veteran will need a copy of their DD214, as mentioned before. If the veteran does not have a copy, one can be requested from the military, though it often takes six weeks or more for the document to arrive. There are several ways for a veteran to get a copy of the DD214 if they do not have one already. These include:

- Requesting a copy of the DD214 on the Web or by phone from the military
- Requesting the assistance of a Veteran Service Officer
- Requesting the assistance of VA Benefits Advisor
- Visiting a veteran service organizations where assistance is provided to gain access to benefits
- Calling or visiting a Vet Center

Once the veteran has a copy of his DD214, he can go to a VA hospital or clinic to enroll into the healthcare system and determine his eligibility through the Enrollment Department. The veteran can also speak with a benefits advisor to determine his eligibility for other veteran assistance programs. While many people assume a veteran has free healthcare at any VA healthcare facility, this is not always the case. Due to the complexities of eligibility, it is best to connect the veteran with a Benefits Advisor. Vet Centers are an agency within the VA that provides counseling and assistance on navigating the VA and various agencies and programs. A veteran can be directed to one of the Vet Centers to get assistance. This can be done in person or over the phone.

ADDITIONAL VETERAN SERVICE ORGANIZATIONS

The VA is the federal agency that provides assistance to veterans. There are state agencies, county agencies, city agencies, and civilian nonprofit organizations that provide assistance to veterans and their families as well. Some of these are listed below.

- State agencies
  - Governor's Office of Veteran Affairs
  - Veterans Service Commission
  - Veterans Benefits Office
- County agencies
  - Veteran Service Officers are trained to assist veterans accessing benefits
  - Areas with larger populations will offer more services
  - These agencies can provide emergency funds for rent or medications
- Civilian nonprofits
  - Veterans of Foreign Wars (VFW)
  - American Legion
  - Disabled American Veterans (DAV)
  - Marine Corps League
  - Vietnam Veterans of America
  - Iraq Afghanistan Veterans of America (IAVA)

Some veteran service organizations provide assistance for specific needs, such as:

- Amputees
- Traumatic brain injury (TBI) survivors
- Widows and orphans of service members killed in action
- Bereavement support for families (TAPS)
- Military kids

REFERENCES

After Deployment (2011). *Wellness Resources for the Military Community: Resources.* Retrieved 16 September 2011, from www.afterdeployment.org.

Department of Defense. (2011). *Demographics 2010: Profile of the Military Community.* Washington, DC.

Department of Veteran Affairs: National Center for PTSD. (2011a). *Information on Trauma and PTSD: Working with Families.* Retrieved 16 September 2011, from http://www.ptsd.va.gov/professional/pages/fslist-tx-family.asp.

Department of Veteran Affairs: National Center for PTSD. (2011b). *Mental Health Effects of Serving in Afghanistan and Iraq.* Retrieved 16 September 2011, from http://www.ptsd.va.gov/public/pages/overview-mental-health-effects.asp.

Duckworth, Darrell, LTC. (2009). *Effects of Multiple Deployments on Families; Strategy Research Project* (November 9). Retrieved 24 February 2010, from http://www.dtic.mil/cgi-bin/GetTRDoc?AD=AD A498029&Location=U2&doc=GetTRDoc.pdf.

Lanham, Stephanie . (2007). *Veterans' and Families' Guide to Recovering from PTSD: 4th Edition.* Annandale, VA: Purple Heart Service Foundation.

National Association of State Alcohol and Drug Abuse Directors and Abt Associates, Inc. (September 2009). *Addressing the Substance Use Disorder Service Needs of Returning Veterans and Their Families: The Training Needs of State Alcohol and Other Drug Agencies and Providers.* Retrieved from www.pfr.samhsa.gov.

CHAPTER 28

MENTAL ILLNESS AND INTELLECTUAL DISABILITY

JULIE P. GENTILE, CHRISTOPHER T. MANETTA, AND CARROLL S. JACKSON

There is universal agreement that all individuals with intellectual disabilities might present with behavior and interaction skills of a chronologically younger child and might maintain these characteristics throughout the lifespan. Thus, any judgment about symptom presentation must be evaluated within the context of developmental delay. (Szymanski and King, 1999)

CASE EXAMPLE

Anne is a 21-year-old female with a history of mild intellectual disability, borderline personality disorder, and obsessive compulsive disorder who is hospitalized for self-injurious behavior and elopement from her sheltered workshop setting. She also has a medical history significant for seizure disorder, esophageal ulcers, and gastro-esophageal reflux disease. During the mental health hospitalization, she is restarted on her medication regimen, which includes valproate (Depakote), quetiapine (Seroquel), fluoxetine (Prozac) and temazepam (Restoril). The precipitant of the hospitalization was the patient's feeling of abandonment when her biological mother was to pick her up for her birthday and did not show up. This has happened on numerous occasions, and Anne's fractured relationship with her mother consistently causes significant disruption in her life. At the time of the disappointment, the patient began to refuse her medications and eloped from her sheltered workshop the following day. Local law enforcement was notified of the elopement, and within several hours, the patient was located and taken to the emergency department of a local hospital for admission to the behavioral health unit.

INTRODUCTION

Mental illness and intellectual disabilities (ID) have been intimately interlaced for centuries. Individuals with either of these conditions have been marginalized, institutionalized, or left to their own devices, particularly if their families were unable or unwilling to provide appropriate care for them. In more recent years, deinstitutionalization has become more widely accepted; placement in the least restrictive environment is the norm, but the success of individuals in community settings is dependent on multiple factors, including collaboration of mental health and intellectual disability systems, as well as appropriate transition and community supports.

Many mental health professionals lack specialized training in ID, and yet persons with ID frequently present to mental health professionals with behavior problems that may or may not be related to mental health issues. The current prevalence rate of ID in the general population is approximately two to three percent, and it has also been found to be 1.5 times more common in males than in females. The prevalence is slightly higher if intelligence quotient (IQ <70) is used as the only criterion (Larson et al. 2001).

In this chapter, the unique challenges encountered by providers treating the ID patient population will be reviewed, and relevant nuances for prescribers that distinguish individuals with ID from others will be described. No evidence-based practices exist specific to individuals with ID; therefore, the clinician is left to utilize expert consensus guidelines in combination with evidence-based practices for the general population.

MENTAL HEALTH ASSESSMENT

Individuals with ID experience and suffer from the same entire range of psychiatric disorders as do those with typical cognitive functioning; in fact, behavior and psychiatric issues occur in individuals with ID at three to six times the rate of the general population (Aman et al. 2003). It is therefore vital that community organizations collaborate and work in partnership to effectively serve the ID population to avoid duplicating services, but more importantly to keep individuals from falling through the cracks.

According to the Centers for Disease Control and Prevention (CDCP), ID is characterized by both a significantly below-average score on a test of mental intelligence and by limitations in the person's ability to function in areas of daily life such as communication, meeting basic needs, and navigating social settings. Communication is the foundation of every relationship; most individuals with ID have limited expressive language skills, and this complicates obtaining subjective reports of mental health symptoms and physical discomfort. Communicative ability is affected by the severity of ID, ranging from mild to profound, and the clinician should assume that the individual's receptive language skills are better developed than are their expressive language skills. Each individual should be afforded the opportunity to communicate their thoughts in their own way and within their own developmental framework.

The relationship between a mental health provider and their patient is vital to accurate diagnosis, treatment planning, and ultimately, patient compliance (Finlay and Lyons 2002). The therapeutic dyad, which is the focus of most educational programs, typically becomes a triad due to collateral data source(s) being present during interface with the individual; the clinician must "manage the triangle" to utilize the time effectively. The clinician should address the patient with ID during the appointment, regardless of the patient's communication ability. If patients are non-verbal or have significantly limited communication abilities, the clinician should observe them for relatedness to others; impulse control; activity level, including both voluntary and involuntary motor movements; expression of affect; attention span; and any unusual, ritualistic, or repetitive behavior; among other observations related to their psychological and/or medical status. If individuals with ID use assistive or communicative devices, the devices should be treated as part of the patient's personal space. According to the American Psychiatric Association's Guidelines for the Treatment of Psychiatric Disorders (2006), providers should:

> use professionally trained interpreters with mental health experience … for those who are deaf, who have severely limited hearing and who know a sign language. Evaluation of persons with [*intellectual disability*] may emphasize behavioral observations and functional measures, depending on the patient's ability to understand questions and report on his or her own mental experiences. Co-occurring general medical conditions are often undetected in adults with [*intellectual disability*].

More detail on the mental status examination is beyond the scope of this chapter; however, Levitas et al. (2001) discuss the interview for individuals with ID in detail and the nuances specific to the ID population. As with every patient, the clinician should be aware of and respect the cultural, socio-economic, educational, and environmental background of the individual.

Historically, clinicians working in the mental health field have found that the applicability of the *Diagnostic and Statistical Manual of Mental Disorders Fourth Edition, Text Revision* (2000) and the *International Classification of Diseases, Tenth Revision, Criteria for Mental Retardation* (1996) are relatively limited in their utility for patients with ID. Many of the diagnostic criteria in these manuals are based on subjective reports from the individual on their inner mood and perceptual experiences. Patients with ID often have limited expressive language skills, and hence the *Diagnostic Criteria—Learning Disability* (DC-LD 2001; see Table 28.1) and the *Diagnostic Manual—Intellectual Disability* (DM-ID 2007; see Table 28.2) were introduced to better accommodate the increased use of observational and collateral data sources often necessary for an accurate diagnosis. These specialized classification systems are founded in evidence-based practices and expert-consensus principles; descriptions of mental disorders that differentiate patients with cognitive deficits from individuals in the general population are included, in addition to proposed alterations of criteria that take into account the developmental framework of the individual. Table 28.3 shows the proposed diagnostic criteria for the upcoming *Diagnostic and Statistical Manual (Fifth Edition)* to be published in 2013 (subject to change).

Patients with ID experience the full range of mental disorders at higher prevalence rates, and in addition, common habit-forming disorders indicative of poor self-regulatory control, including behaviors such as biting, trichotillomania, bruxism, motor and vocal tics, and Tourette's disorder (Long and Miltenberger 1998). A thorough and recent physical examination is essential. Coordination of care with the person's primary care physician is a major task of assessment and management, as both medical *and* mental health conditions may present with behavioral changes or problem behaviors. (See Table 28.4 for Sovner's [1986] four concepts to assist clinicians in the psychiatric assessment of individuals with ID.)

Table 28.1: Diagnostic Criteria for Learning Disabilities (DC-LD) for Use with Adults

- Diagnostic criteria: Criteria are used synonymously with the ICD-10 term *mental retardation.* The diagnosis of mental retardation is dependent upon the person's having an intelligence quotient below 70, together with continued impairment in adaptive behavior/social functioning, and with onset during the developmental phase (i.e., before the age of 18 years). The term *borderline learning disabilities* is not included in the ICD-10, nor is it included in DC-LD. Within most European and North American cultures, ICD-10 recommends the use of the Vineland Adaptive Behavior Scales as an assessment tool.
  Severity of learning disabilities:
  - Mild learning disabilities: IQ Range = 50–69; mental age 9 to under 12 years
  - Moderate learning disabilities: IQ Range = 35–49; mental age 6 to under 9 years
  - Severe learning disabilities: IQ Range = 20–34; mental age 3 to under 6 years
  - Profound learning disabilities: IQ Range = 20; mental age less than 3 years
  - Other learning disabilities
  - Unspecified learning disabilities
- Clinical summary sheet (this relates the DC-LD descriptive classification to its etiology, using the four dimensions of *biological, psychological, social,* and *development,* and provides an example of other summary information relevant to clinical practice)
- Diagrammatic presentation of the hierarchical approach to diagnosis that is adopted throughout DC-LD (identify severity and cause of learning disability; identify developmental disorders, psychiatric illnesses, personality disorders, problem behaviors, and other ICD-10 disorders)

The text of DC-LD provides additional information on psychiatric assessment of adults with learning [*intellectual*] disabilities.

Adapted from The Royal College of Psychiatrists, *DC-LD (Diagnostic Criteria for Psychiatric Disorders for Use with Adults with Learning Disabilities/Mental Retardation).* London: Gaskell, 2001; p. 18 and Figure 5.

CASE VIGNETTE, CONTINUED

Anne remained stable following her discharge from the hospital, for a period of three weeks, at which time her work supervisor was transferred to another location without warning. The following morning, staff noticed that Anne was talking to herself and required extra time to get ready for work. Anne stated that she would not get on the bus because "I won't be safe," and she responded to staff only after long pauses, appearing confused by some of their statements. Staff noticed that she spent 45 minutes in the bathroom (much longer than was typical for her) and insisted on carrying her family photo album with her all day long. "Someone will steal my pictures if I leave them here." Following breakfast, she wrapped up extra food in a napkin and placed it in her purse. She closed all of the curtains in the kitchen, stating she did not want the police to "come pick me up again."

This vignette illustrates some of the nuances that Sovner (1986) outlined (see Table 28.4), including subtle changes in behavior that may initially be overlooked by direct care staff (baseline exaggeration), and how the structure of a supported residential setting combined with the individual's limited socialization in the community may complicate detection of symptoms (psychological masking). Furthermore, Anne had difficulty identifying and articulating her emotions, thus adding further layers of complication (intellectual distortion).

Table 28.2: Diagnostic Manual – Intellectual Disability Criteria for Intellectual Disabilities

American Association of Intellectual and Developmental Disabilities, from Diagnostic Manual – Intellectual Disability (DM-ID, 2007)

AAIDD definition: "a disability characterized by significant limitations both in intellectual functioning and in adaptive behavior as expressed in conceptual, social, and practical adaptive skills. The disability originates before age 18" (American Association of Mental Retardation, 2005). To this they add "Five Assumptions Essential to the Application of the Definition:"

1. Limitations in present functioning must be considered within the context of community environments typical of the individual's age peers and culture.
2. Valid assessment considers cultural and linguistic diversity as well as differences in communication, sensory, motor, and behavioral factors.
3. Within an individual, limitations often coexist with strengths.
4. An important purpose of describing limitations is to develop a profile of needed supports.
5. With appropriate personalized supports over a sustained period, the life functioning of the person with mental retardation generally will improve.

(American Association on Mental Retardation, 2005)

Degrees of Severity
Mild 50–55 to 70
Moderate 35–40 to 50–55
Severe 20–25 to 34–40
Profound below 20–25

AAIDD categories
Intermittent Support
Limited Support
Extensive Support
Pervasive Support

Fletcher, R., Loschen, E., Stavrakaki, C., & First, M. (Eds.). (2007). *Diagnostic Manual – Intellectual Disability (DM-ID): A Textbook of Diagnosis of Mental Disorders in Persons with Intellectual Disability.* Kingston, NY: NADD Press. Pages 64–66.

Table 28.3: DSM V Proposed Criteria for Intellectual Disability

Proposed Criteria for Intellectual Developmental Disorder in DSM 5 (to be published in May, 2013)

Intellectual Developmental Disorder (IDD) is a disorder that includes both a current intellectual deficit and a deficit in adaptive functioning with onset during the developmental period. The following 3 criteria must be met:

A. Intellectual Developmental Disorder is characterized by deficits in general mental abilities such as reasoning, problem-solving, planning, abstract thinking, judgment, academic learning and learning from experience.

B. Impairment in adaptive functioning for the individual's age and sociocultural background. Adaptive functioning refers to how well a person meets the standards of personal independence and social responsibility in one or more aspects of daily life activities, such as communication, social participation, functioning at school or at work, or personal independence at home or in community settings. The limitations result in the need for ongoing support at school, work, or independent life.

C. All symptoms must have an onset during the developmental period.

http://www.dsm5.org/ProposedRevision/Pages/proposedrevision.aspx?rid=384

Table 28.4: Challenges in the Diagnostic Assessment of
Psychiatric Disorders in People with Intellectual Disability

Cognitive disintegration: vulnerability to decompensation under stress and subsequent overload of
  cognitive functioning may lead to bizarre, atypical, and even psychotic-like presentations
Psychosocial masking: limited life experiences and intellectual capacity can influence the content of
  psychiatric symptoms
Intellectual distortion: diminished abstract thinking and communication skills limit the ability of the
  person to accurately and fully describe their emotional and behavioral symptoms
Baseline exaggeration: pre-existing maladaptive behavior not attributed to a mental illness may increase
  in frequency or intensity with the onset of a psychiatric disorder

Sovner R. Limiting factors in the use of DSM-III criteria with mentally ill/mentally retarded persons. *Psychopharmacol
Bull* 1986; 22(4): 1055–1059.

BIOPSYCHOSOCIAL MODEL

The utility of the biopsychosocial model is vital when determining the etiology of behavior
and/or mental health symptoms in patients with communication difficulties. Many patients will
present with undiagnosed or under-treated medical conditions, and the knowledgeable clinician is often faced with the difficult task of screening for these critical aspects of care and subsequently arranging the appropriate interdisciplinary referral.

In addition to the shift in disposition management of individuals with ID from institutionalization to deinstitutionalization, there has also come a shift in the paradigm of treatment
approach with the ID population. Much like the treatment of patients with typical cognitive
ability, new literature highlights the importance of a holistic approach for individuals in need
of care. During the history-gathering and assessment phases performed by the clinician, better outcomes and more specific diagnoses are delineated when the patient is approached in a
multidimensional format. Similar to the management of delirium in determining the underlying cause of an encephalopathic presentation, approaching the patient with ID warrants a
systems-based approach, in which multiple facets of the patient are explored and analyzed. This
was originally described and outlined as the biopsychosocial model, first developed by the physician George Engel in 1977 (Engel 1977, Engel 1980).

Essentially, recognizing that an entity in one system may be influencing or affecting an entity
in another system is core to the model. For example, one's primary attachment figures throughout one's formative years most definitely impact one's characterological makeup and personality
throughout one's life. This is illustrated in the vignette, where Anne's mother, an unpredictable
and chaotic presence during Anne's childhood, significantly influences Anne's current fears of
abandonment and lack of security. This subsequently leads to Anne's acting-out behaviors and
poor coping mechanisms. All spheres, to include biological, psychological, and sociological
components, must be acknowledged and addressed by the primary mental health provider and
all collaborating treatment team members. (See Table 28.5 for Comprehensive Assessment of
Persons with Intellectual Disabilities.)

Table 28.5: Comprehensive Assessment of People with Intellectual Disabilities and Aggressive Behavior (Charlot and Shedlack)

Identify genetic syndromes with known behavioral or psychiatric phenotypes

Establish any psychiatric diagnoses, based on most recent standardized evidence based diagnostic manual for individuals with intellectual disability

Determine if there are undetected or untreated medical problems

Determine if there is a correlation between drug changes and changes in behavior

Consider possible role of drug effects, including toxicity/delirium, side effects (akathisia, disinhibition), withdrawal effects, interaction effects

Identify objective measures of symptoms or behaviors: use screening tools as appropriate, measurement of behaviors, assessment of vegetative functions, mood, memory, and other mental status information

Look for any correlation with stressful life events and changes

Assess all environments, including structure/supports to meet cognitive developmental needs

Collect detailed data on baseline functioning of the individual

Consider likely developmental effects on the problems described

Assess the individual's abilities to describe internal states and other communicative abilities

Determine behavioral repertoire, including areas of strength and weaknesses

Assess probable functions of the aggressive behavior, including escape, attention, communication, expression of pain or frustration, modulation of stimulation levels, secure tangibles. Triggers? Factors that maintain behavior? Quantify frequency and severity. Identify variables contributing to a lowering of the threshold for aggression

Identify changes in behavioral or other psychosocial treatments correlated with increased problems

Clarify past treatment trials: What helped? What did not help? Was trial adequate? Were there possible confounding variables? Were successful interventions prematurely terminated?

Charlot L, Shedlack K. Masquerade: Uncovering and treating the many causes of aggression in individuals with developmental disabilities. *NADD Bulletin*. 2002; 5: 59–64.

VIGNETTE, CONTINUED

Several months later, Anne's caregivers report episodic physical aggression to the psychiatrist at a follow-up appointment. They request an increase in her psychotropic medication, specifically her antipsychotic medicine. The psychiatrist inquires about the circumstances of the aggression: "What is the nature of the aggression (physical? verbal? property destruction?) What are the precipitating factors or antecedents? Is there a pattern such as time of day and environment (home or work)? What interventions have been tried to de-escalate the patient? What tends to increase or decrease the frequency and severity of the aggression? Has the patient had a recent physical exam and laboratory workup? What are the acute or chronic psychosocial stressors (e.g., losses, changes in staff or routine, family conflicts, among others)?"

After collecting data on the biological, psychological, and social factors of the presentation, the psychiatrist concludes that Anne's physical aggression is almost exclusively directed toward staff that encourages her to eat her meals. The aggression is worse in the evening, and her sleep has become disrupted in the previous four weeks. The psychiatrist recommends that Anne be evaluated by her primary care physician to rule out gastrointestinal conditions. Anne was found to have exacerbation of her gastro-esophageal reflux disease, a very painful condition that is common in individuals with ID, and if untreated for long periods of time puts the individual at increased risk for esophageal cancer.

Table 28.6: Clinical Pearls Based on Expert Consensus for Treating the Patient with ID Who Has Aggression or SIB

Treatment should be based upon the most specific psychiatric diagnosis possible. When only a tentative non-specific diagnosis can be made, such as in individuals with more severe ID, clinicians should focus on one or more behavioral symptoms as targets of treatment.

- Utilize neuroreceptor correlates of aggression to guide pharmacological interventions
- Utilize the biopsychosocial formulation to determine etiology
- Identify "predisposing," "perpetuating," and "protective" factors
- Rule out undiagnosed and/or under-treated medical conditions
- Depression and anxiety tend to be under-diagnosed
- Rule out physical pain (acute and chronic)
- Rule out medication side effects
- Shore up supports during transitions
- Ensure thorough physical examination and laboratory workup are conducted
- Identify grief and loss issues and address appropriately
- Manage the triangle during the data collection process
- Perform a functional analysis
- Enlist a behavioral psychologist or behavior support specialist
- Be familiar with the individual's baseline functioning

Medication Practices to Avoid:

Long-term use of benzodiazepine anti-anxiety agents (e.g., diazepam) or shorter-acting sedative hypnotics (e.g., zolpidem)

Use of long-acting sedative hypnotics (e.g., chloral hydrate)

Use of anticholinergics without extrapyramidal symptoms

Higher than usual doses of psychotropic medications

Use of phenytoin, phenobarbital, primidone as psychotropics

Long-term use of "PRN" or "as needed" medication orders

Failure to integrate medication with psychosocial interventions

Aman MG, Gharabawi GM., for the Special Topic Advisory Panel on Transitioning to Risperidone Therapy in Patients with Mental Retardation and Developmental Disabilities. *Treatment of behavior disorders in mental retardation: Report on transitioning to atypical antipsychotics, with an emphasis on risperidone. J Clin Psychiatry* 2004; 65: 1197–1210.

(See Table 28.6 for Clinical Pearls from Expert Consensus Guidelines for Treatment of Patients with Intellectual Disabilities.)

According to the American Diabetic Association (2010), life expectancy for individuals with ID has increased to the extent that young adults with ID should experience the same "expected life" as their age-matched peers without ID (American Diabetic Association [ADA] Guidelines 2010). Prevalence rates are higher for seizure disorders, heart disease, obesity, hearing and vision problems, and low bone-mineral density. They are at higher risk for medical conditions involving every organ system, further complicated by genetic conditions and the prevalence of polypharmacy. (For a review of the alterations to medical prevention and monitoring protocol for adults with ID, see Wilkinson et al. 2007.) Patients with ID are significantly less likely to participate in or be exposed to traditional preventative treatment methods for most if not all medical conditions (Havercamp et al. 2004). The obstacles to treatment must be eliminated at all costs.

NON-PHARMACOLOGICAL THERAPEUTIC INTERVENTIONS

The clinician must view behavior as a form of communication, as this will inevitably serve the patient well (Bongiorno 1996). Ultimately, understanding and identifying the underlying problem will reveal whether or not an underlying diagnosis of a comorbid psychiatric disorder or habit disorder exists. Because polypharmacy practices are so prevalent in the ID population, it is vital that the prescriber consider non-pharmacological intervention prior to any initiation of psychotropic medications. Often psychotherapy and socio-environmental interventions can be effective in and of themselves without the use of psychotropic medications. Investigation must continue to delineate the etiology of the presenting behavior (i.e., collection of behavior support data, collateral data across environments, performing a physical examination, obtaining laboratory values, and ensuring examination by a primary care physician).

Long and Miltenberger (1998) reviewed available literature on behavioral treatment modalities for individuals with ID. Those with efficacy included self-monitoring, covert sensitization, relaxation techniques, cognitive-behavioral therapy, over-correction, and positive and negative practice. In *Clinical Pearl: From the Use of Medication for the Management of Behavior Problems Among Adults With Intellectual Disabilities: A Clinician's Consensus Survey*, Unwin and Deb (2008) reported that one important finding is the very strong preference to use non-medication-based management options as one primary intervention for aggression and self-injurious behavior.

VIGNETTE, CONTINUED

Anne graduated from high school, having successfully completed an individualized educational plan. Many of Anne's peers who had been together throughout all of their school years lived with their families, and most transitioned to sheltered workshops at the same time as they were moving from family homes to supported residential group homes. Anne began compulsively checking and counting as her anxiety increased in anticipation of the two major transitions. She moved in to the group home with Jess, one of her female girlfriends with whom she had graduated. Shortly after they had moved into the group home, Anne became upset that Jess's family picked her up every weekend and visited the group home frequently. Jess's family regularly included Anne in their outings, but despite their best efforts, Anne experienced emotional upheaval every Friday evening as the young women discussed their weekend plans and Anne's mother would not return her phone calls.

The mental health team recommended consultation from a behavior support specialist who created a plan that identified the antecedents, behaviors, and consequences of the weekly emotional upheaval. Anne was given extra activities on weekends and incentives to spend more one-on-one time with her favorite direct-care staff if she was able to utilize coping strategies she learned in her individual psychotherapy. The staff was also asked to attend the last few minutes of each appointment (with Anne's consent) so that they were aware of the coping skills to be reinforced between appointments.

This part of the vignette illustrates the inherent difficulties during the transition years (from roughly 17–24 years of age) as many individuals with ID transition from family homes to supported residential systems in the community as well as from the educational to the occupational systems. Utilization of the entire multidisciplinary team is essential so that all of Anne's psychosocial needs are met and to increase her quality of life.

PSYCHOTHERAPY IN INDIVIDUALS WITH ID

Historically many mental health clinicians thought that individuals with ID could not suffer from mental illness; others believed that they did not possess the cognitive ability to benefit from psychotherapy. Over the past decade, mental health professionals have come to understand that individuals with ID can and do benefit from psychotherapy. However, the literature also suggests that several modifications to traditional treatment methods must be made in order to improve the efficacy of the treatment provided. Clinicians must adjust the mode of psychotherapy provided to fit the cognitive abilities of the patient, as insistence upon the use of traditional models of treatment will result in poor treatment outcomes and will prevent patients with ID from receiving appropriate care (Whitehouse et al. 2006). (See Table 28.7 for adaptations that should be considered regardless of the type of therapeutic intervention provided.)

There are also adjustments that can be made to specific treatment models that can help strengthen the impact of the therapeutic intervention being utilized. What follows is a brief review of several modalities that show promise with this population, along with suggestions regarding modifications that clinicians can consider when treating patients with ID.

MOTIVATIONAL INTERVIEWING

Motivational interviewing (MI) was developed by Miller and Rollnick (2002) in order to address the conflicting feelings that individuals frequently experience when thinking about making changes in problematic behaviors (Miller and Rollnick 2002). The psychotherapist targets this ambivalence and works with the patient to resolve it. MI was initially intended as a tool in the treatment of substance-use disorders; however, it has now been shown to be an effective intervention to increase motivation for treatment when dealing with a variety of mental health disorders. When using this method, psychotherapists take a nonjudgmental approach and do not confront the patient about their continued engagement in problematic behaviors. Instead, they focus on

Table 28.7: Psychotherapy Adaptations for Patients with
Intellectual Disability

Flexible sessions	Length of therapy sessions should match the individual's attention span. For some patients, this may be no longer than 30 minutes.
Simplification of interventions	Break down intervention into smaller chunks and reduce the complexity of the techniques being utilized.
Adjust language	Reduce level of vocabulary, sentence structure and length of thought to match the cognitive abilities of the patient.
Augment interventions with activities	Use of activities can help deepen change and learning and may include the use of drawing, therapeutic games, role play, and homework assignments.
Involve caregivers	Important source of collateral information necessary to ascertain progress between sessions.
Increased length of care	Most research indicates that a longer length of treatment (1–2 years) is a best practice with this population. This allows the psychotherapy to move at a slower pace so that the clinician can spend additional time on each intervention utilized, ensuring that the skills being taught are internalized. It also allows for the inclusion of additional treatment stages that may be necessary.

helping the patient develop insight regarding the nature of their problems, the potential consequences of their maladaptive behaviors, and the potential benefits of making positive changes.

MI may be a helpful treatment method when working with individuals with ID, as they are often not self-referred for care. Instead, they are typically referred by involved care providers who are concerned about some type of maladaptive behavior—which may or may not be a source of concern for the patient. This can result in patient ambivalence about participation in psychotherapy, as the referral may be seen as a punishment rather than as an opportunity for self-exploration and growth. Addressing issues related to motivation may help increase the patient's readiness and acceptance of treatment, which is necessary before problematic behaviors are addressed. When working with this population, clinicians may need to take a more directive stance than is typically utilized with this approach, as the patient may benefit from feedback regarding appropriate or socially acceptable behavior and may require assistance with identifying and expressing their feelings regarding the possibility of change.

COGNITIVE BEHAVIORAL THERAPY

Cognitive behavioral therapy (CBT) is a treatment modality that focuses on helping individuals understand how their thoughts, feelings, and behaviors are interconnected. Patients learn how their conscious thoughts, automatic thoughts, and cognitive schemas impact their sense of self-worth as well as their views of the world around them. They are taught to identify and change thinking patterns that negatively impact their feelings and behaviors, as well as learning to replace maladaptive behaviors with more appropriate responses (Romana 2003). This approach has been shown to be highly effective; however, it is also understood that the ID population may find it difficult to understand the abstract concepts that are the central focus of treatment. Therefore, the psychotherapist will need to include a preparatory phase in the treatment process, in which the patient receives the education and training needed to ensure comprehension of all components. It is helpful to involve care providers, with the patient's consent, as they can be a valuable resource. In addition to providing much-needed collateral information, they can function as a part of the multidisciplinary team and help support the patient's engagement in psychotherapy. For example, they can facilitate the learning process by helping the patient practice the skills learned between sessions, such as the identification of thought distortions. Care providers can also assist with the completion of homework, reinforcing the work between appointments assigned to the patient to solidify concepts.

DIALECTICAL BEHAVIORAL THERAPY

Dialectical behavioral therapy (DBT) was developed as a treatment for chronically suicidal patients who were not benefiting from traditional treatment methods. It is proven to be an effective technique for patients diagnosed with borderline personality disorder. The psychotherapist focuses on teaching the patient to cope with life stressors, regulate their emotions, and improve their interpersonal relationships (Lew 2011). The provision of DBT includes both weekly individual therapy sessions and weekly group skills training. There are four main skills that are taught in the skills training: mindfulness, interpersonal effectiveness, distress tolerance, and emotional-regulation skills (Linehan 1993). This approach is a good fit for individuals with ID, who can benefit from the structure and the focus on skill building that it provides. Slight modifications can be made to the traditional treatment model to ensure that the cognitive needs of the patient are adequately addressed (Charlton and Dykstra 2011). Individuals with ID may have limited concentration ability, making it difficult for them to sustain attention for the two-and-a-half-hour group sessions, further decreasing their opportunity to benefit from the material presented. Recent literature suggests that this can be addressed by decreasing the length of group sessions to 30 minutes, and either adding a second session during the week or increasing the overall length of care to ensure that there is sufficient time to cover all pertinent material. Patients with ID may also benefit from increasing the amount of time that is spent on each of the four skills, as repetition of information and additional opportunities to practice the principles taught will help to make certain that the material is internalized. DBT typically utilizes handouts, homework, and diary cards as supplements to the information presented. For patients with ID, it is important to ensure these are simplified so that they are easily understood by the patient. The use of concrete language and the addition of pictures to illustrate the concepts and will increase the patient's ability to implement the skill modules between treatment sessions.

SUPPORTIVE PSYCHOTHERAPY

Supportive psychotherapy (SP) is an eclectic approach that combines several different treatment modalities, including CBT, psychodynamic therapy, and interpersonal psychotherapy. It is based on the theory that the positive and affirming relationship between the patient and psychotherapist can serve to repair maladaptive core schemas that developed as a result of inadequate parenting (Douglas 2008). The goal of SP is to change self-destructive behavior and to improve the patient's ability to cope with stress as well as to improve their interpersonal skills and relationships. A more directive stance is taken with this modality, in which clinicians frequently provide suggestions, opinions, and feedback. The clinician also involves family members or care providers and may do some case management, such as assisting the patient in accessing community resources or engaging with an employer when necessary. SP is a sound treatment option for this population, as many individuals with ID can benefit from the validation, direction, and advocacy that is inherent in this approach. As with the other modalities, it is important for the clinician to simplify the interventions being utilized and to plan for a longer duration of care to allow for necessary practice and review of learned skills.

Overall, psychotherapy is a best practice when working with the ID population. However, it is also inherently more challenging due to their varying levels of cognitive ability. Clinicians will need to recognize and address language barriers, memory deficits, and learning variations in order to provide an intervention that will be meaningful and effective for the patient. Small modifications, such as increasing length of treatment and repetition of therapeutic interventions, significantly increase efficacy.

PSYCHOTROPIC MEDICATIONS

Primum non nocere ("first, do no harm"). Review of the literature and history indicates that the ID patient population has often been subject to polypharmacy and is known to be more vulnerable to medication side effects. The use of older or first-generation antipsychotics can cause extrapyramidal side effects, and the use of newer or second-generation neuroleptics increases the risk of cardiac and metabolic problems, including diabetes, obesity, and hyperlipidemia. In an effort to incorporate a universal and standardized level of care, The Clinical Bulletin of the Developmental Disabilities Division published a guide for prescribing psychotropic medication for the management of psychiatric disorders and problem behaviors in adults with ID (2010). The Bulletin reported that more than 30 percent of individuals with ID have a comorbid psychiatric disorder, which often has its onset in childhood and persists throughout the lifespan (Cooper et al. 2007, Einfeld et al. 2006). Of this 30 percent with ID and a co-occurring psychiatric diagnosis, 20 to 45 percent receive some form of psychotropic medication to target the identified problem, such as aggression, self-injurious behavior, or the diagnosed psychiatric disorder. More specifically, of those receiving psychotropic medication, 14 to 30 percent are receiving medication to manage their problem behavior (PB) (Clark et al. 1990, Deb and Fraser 1994).

"Problem behaviors" (PB) in the world of ID have been defined as a "socially unacceptable behavior that causes distress, harm or disadvantage to the persons, themselves or to other people, and usually requires some intervention" (Deb et al. 2006). PB is the most common justification for use of pharmacotherapy. The most effective way to navigate an investigation of the etiology of the PB is use of the biopsychosocial model; i.e., psychiatric and medical disorders, grief and loss issues, environmental factors, characterological pathology, among other etiologies. If a cause cannot be identified, the treatment goal should be to minimize the disruption to the patient's quality of life (Fletcher et al. 2007, Royal College of Psychiatrists Diagnostic Criteria for Learning Disorders (DC-LD), 2001).

Abbreviated care is unacceptable in patients with ID; therefore, serial in-person appointments, laboratory analyses with physical examinations, and diagnostic studies when deemed appropriate should be pursued according to universally accepted standards (Unwin and Deb 2008). Also, it is crucial to increase the use of standardized, measurable instruments when monitoring for extrapyramidal side effects, in particular in patients with muscular disorders such as cerebral palsy (Unwin and Deb 2008). It is recommended to begin with the lowest starting dose, to titrate slowly, and to remain within the dose range outlined by the *Physician's Desk Reference*, the Food and Drug Administration, and/or alternate prescribing authorities. Nonetheless, the following general recommendations are to be emphasized:

1. Try to stabilize the person's PB on a minimum number of medications prescribed at the lowest possible dose;
2. Withdraw one medication at a time;
3. Withdraw medication slowly;
4. If necessary, allow time after withdrawing one medication and before starting to withdraw another (Unwin and Deb, 2008).

It is a fact that patients with ID are more vulnerable to side effects of psychotropic medications, and there is often a lack of subjective complaints due to their deficits in expressive language skills. An empirical and standardized measure of target symptoms and behaviors must be instituted, including a format to quantify the benefits and adverse effects of psychotropic medication (Clinical Bulletin of the Developmental Disabilities Division, 2010).

PB remains a primary cause for clinicians' anxiety and can segue into unnecessary over-prescribing of medications and ancillary treatment strategies such as hospitalization. Nonetheless, PBs are the reason more than 90 percent of patients with ID present for mental health evaluation (even when they have undiagnosed and under-treated medical conditions). PBs are the most frequent reason for psychiatric hospitalization, the biggest cause for morbidity and mortality, and the reason many prescribers feel the only intervention available is to prescribe antipsychotic medications (Emerson et al. 2001, Lowe et al. 2007). Polypharmacy is especially common in mental health delivery systems where there is a lack of behavioral interventions, highly restrictive managed-care guidelines, and/or a lack of intersystem collaboration. Other types of disruptive behaviors have been found and included in the differential when addressing changes in patterns of behavior in the patient with ID. Aggressive, antisocial, and self-injurious behavior have been described by Aman and Gharabawi (2004) as analogous to disruptive behavior disorders as defined by the *DSM-IV TR* (2000).

Patients with ID are more susceptible to mood and anxiety disorders than others in the general population, and these tend to be under-diagnosed. They are more vulnerable to developing these disorders, in part due to their limited internal resources for dealing with stress and their circumscribed problem-solving skills. Treatment of anxiety is complicated by the paradoxical stimulation that some patients with ID experience with benzodiazepines. Other considerations with this medication class relevant to this specialized population include its potential to cause retrograde and anterograde amnesia (when memory problems already exist with cognitive deficits), impaired sensorium, sedation, and potential for respiratory depression (in patients already vulnerable to pulmonary pathology). When paradoxical stimulation occurs, it is thought to be due to disinhibition or disorientation, and this state can increase impulse control problems, agitation, or PBs. With regard to prescription of all psychotropics, it is important to be aware of medications which alter seizure thresholds (e.g., bupropion) due to the high seizure prevalence in the ID population. Psychotic disorders tend to be over-diagnosed in the ID population, and antipsychotic medications are over-prescribed.

EXPERT CONSENSUS GUIDELINES

While no evidence-based practices exist in the field of ID, consensus-based practices will suffice; every acknowledged expert in the field of ID agrees that there is a need for evidence-based research. The following is a list of citations of documents written by acknowledged prescribing authorities in the field of intellectual disabilities.

- Kalachnik JE, Leventhal BL, James DH, Sovner R, Kastner TA, Walsh K, Weisblatt SA, Klitzke MG. (1998). Guidelines for the use of psychotropic medication. In S. Reiss and M. G. Aman (Eds.), *Psychotropic Medications and Developmental Disabilities: The International Consensus Handbook* (pp. 45–72). Columbus: Ohio State University, Nisonger Center.
- *Psychotropic Medications and Developmental Disabilities: The International Consensus Handbook* (Reiss, S. and Aman, M. G., eds.); American Association of Mental Retardation, 2000.
- Aman MG, Crismon ML, Frances A, King BH & Rojahn J (eds.) (2004) *Treatment of Psychiatric and Behavioral Problems in Individuals with Mental Retardation. An Update of the Expert Consensus Guidelines for mental retardation and developmental disability populations.* Postgraduate Institute for Medicine, Englewood, CO.
- Deb S, Clarke D, and Unwin G (2006). *Using Medication to Manage Behavior Problems Among Adults with a Learning Disability: Quick Reference Guide* (QRG). University of Birmingham, MENCAP, The Royal College of Psychiatrists, London. (See www.Id-medication.bham.ac.uk.)
- Fletcher R, Loschen E, Stavrakaki C, and First M. (Eds.). (2007). *Diagnostic Manual—Intellectual Disability (DM-ID): A Textbook of Diagnosis of Mental Disorders in Persons with Intellectual Disability.* Kingston, NY: NADD Press.
- *Problem Behavior in Adults with Intellectual Disabilities: International Guide for Using Medication. Section on Psychiatry of Intellectual Disability (SPID).* The World Psychiatric Association (WPA): Working group. September 2008.
- Unwin G and Deb S. (2008) Use of medication for the management of behavior problems among adults with intellectual disabilities: A clinicians' consensus survey. *American Journal on Mental Retardation*, 113(1), 19–31.
- *Clinical Bulletin of the Developmental Disabilities Division. International Guide to Prescribing Psychotropic Medication for the Management of Problem Behaviors in Adults with Intellectual Disabilities.* World Psychiatry Association, 2010.

Expert consensus recommends utilizing the same medications for patients with ID that are used to treat disorders in the general population. No evidence exists to support inter-class or intra-class polypharmacy or to prescribe regimens that are qualitatively different from those used in the general population. Use of general evidence-based practices is appropriate and logical until more specific empirical research is available.

FINAL THOUGHTS

The parameters outlined in this chapter provide a framework for mental health clinicians to use in adhering to the guidelines of evidence-based practices in the care of the patient with ID and mental illness. There are currently no best practices or evidence-based medicine principles specific to this specialized population, but consensus-based guidelines from acknowledged experts, combined with application of evidence-based medicine principles for the general population, will suffice. Individuals with ID are vulnerable to the side effects of psychotropic medications, and in particular the extrapyramidal and metabolic side effects of antipsychotics. Depressive and anxiety disorders tend to be under-diagnosed, and psychotic disorders tend to be over-diagnosed. It must be a priority to eliminate polypharmacy and offer the full range of mental health treatments to all individuals with ID. Behavior must be viewed as a form of communication; physical and mental health must be addressed in a collaborative effort to eliminate undiagnosed and under-treated medical conditions in this medically fragile population. Utilization of the biopsychosocial formulation and the institution of multidisciplinary treatment plans are core to effective mental health treatment. Collaboration of systems works well and is a necessity.

As is the case in all medical and mental health treatment modalities for any type of pathology, long-established assumptions about treating the patient require ongoing modification and review. Treating the patient with ID is no exception. The well-known physician Hunter Campbell Adams once said, "We can never get a re-creation of community and heal our society without giving our citizens a sense of belonging." Previously marginalized individuals with ID and mental illness are important members of our society and deserve the highest-quality mental health services. Psychotropic medications should improve cognitive function, not worsen it; psychotropic medications should fully treat mental health issues. We expect no less when treating an individual in the general population. Treating the patient with ID the same as any other, with virtue and professionalism, is sure to lead to their stability and increased quality of life.

REFERENCES

American Diabetic Association. Position of the American Diabetic Association: Providing nutrition services for people with developmental disabilities and special health care needs. *J Am Diet Assoc* 2010; 110: 296–307.

Aman MG, Gharabawi GM, for the Special Topic Advisory Panel on Transitioning to Risperidone Therapy in Patients with Mental Retardation and Developmental Disabilities. Treatment of behavior disorders in mental retardation: Report on transitioning to atypical antipsychotics, with an emphasis on risperidone. *J Clin Psychiatry* 2004; 65: 1197–1210.

Aman MG, Crismon ML, Frances A, King BH, Rojahn J. *Treatment of Psychiatric and Behavioral Problems in Individuals with Mental Retardation. Expert Consensus Guidelines Update (2004) For Mental Retardation/Developmental Disability Populations.* Englewood, CO: Postgraduate Institute for Medicine, 2004.

Aman MG, Lindsay RL, Nash PL, et al. Individuals with mental retardation. In: Martin A, Scahill L, Charney DS, et al. *Psycho-pharmacology: Principles and Practice.* New York: Oxford University Press; 2003: 617–630.

APA. *American Psychiatric Association Practice Guidelines for the Treatment of Psychiatric Disorders. Compendium 2006.* Arlington VA: American Psychiatric Association.

APA. *Diagnostic and Statistical Manual of Mental Disorders, Fifth Edition* (*Proposed*). Available at http://www.dsm5.org/ProposedRevision/Pages/proposedrevision.aspx?rid=384 Access date 05/17/2011.

APA. *Diagnostic and Statistical Manual of Mental Disorders, Fourth Edition, Text Revision* (DSM-IV TR). Arlington, VA: American Psychiatric Association, 2000.

Bongiorno FP. Dual diagnosis: Developmental disability complicated by mental illness. *South Med J* 1996 December; 89(12): 1142–1146.

Charlton M, Dykstra EJ. *Dialectical Behavior Therapy for Special Populations: Treatment with Adolescents and Their Caregivers. Psychotherapy for Individuals with Intellectual Disabilities.* Kingston, NY: NADD Press; 2011: 13–36.

Clark DJ, Kelley S, Thinn K, et al.: Psychotropic drugs and mental retardation: I. Disabilities and the prescription of drugs for behavior and for epilepsy in three residential settings. *J Ment Deficiency Res* 1990; 28: 229–233.

Cooper S-A, Smiley E, Morrison J, et al. Prevalence of and associations with mental ill-health in adults with intellectual disabilities. *Br J Psychiatry* 2007; 190: 27–35.

Deb S, Clarke D, Unwin G. *Using Medication to Manage Behavior Problems Among Adults with a Learning Disability: Quick Reference Guide (QRG).* Birmingham, UK: University of Birmingham; London: Royal College of Psychiatrists, 2006; www.ld-medication.bham.ac.uk. Access date 04/04/11.

Deb S, Fraser W . The use of psychotropic medication in people with learning disability: Towards rational prescribing. *Hum Psychopharmacol* 1994; 9: 259–272.

Douglas C. Teaching supportive psychotherapy to psychiatric residents. *Am J Psychiatry*, 2008; 165: 445–452.

Einfeld SL, Piccinin AM, Mackinnon A, et al. Psychopathology in young people with intellectual disability. *JAMA* 2006; 296: 1981–1989.

Emerson E, Kiernan C, Alborz A et al. The prevalence of challenging behaviors: A total population study. *Res Dev Disabil* 2001; 22: 77–93.

Engel GL. The clinical application of the biopsychosocial model. *Am J Psychiatry* 1980; 137, 535–544.

Engel GL. The need for a new medical model: A challenge for biomedicine. *Science* 1977; 196, 129–136.

Finlay WML, Lyons E. Acquiescence in interviews with people who have mental retardation. *Ment Retard* 2002; 40(1): 14–29.

Fletcher R, Loschen E, Stavrakaki C, et al. (eds.). *Diagnostic Manual—Intellectual Disability (DM-ID): A Textbook of Diagnosis of Mental Disorders in Persons with Intellectual Disability.* Washington, DC: National Association for the Dually Diagnosed Press and the American Psychiatric Association; 2007.

Havercamp SM, Scandlin D, Roth, M. Health disparities among adults with developmental disabilities, adults with other disabilities, and adults not reporting disability, in North Carolina. *Public Health Rep* July–August 2004; 119, 418–426.

Kalachnik JE, Leventhal BL, James DH, et al. Guidelines for the use of psychotropic medication. In Reiss S and Aman MG (eds.), *Psychotropic Medications and Developmental Disabilities: The International Consensus Handbook.* Columbus: Ohio State University, Nisonger Center; 1998: 45–72.

Larson SA, Lakin KC, Anderson L, et al. Prevalence of mental retardation and developmental disabilities: Estimates from the 1994/1995 National Health Interview Survey Disability Supplements. *Am J Ment Retard* 2001; 106(3): 231–252.

Levitas AS, Hurley AD, Pary R. The mental status examination in patients with mental retardation and developmental disabilities. *Ment Health Aspects Dev Disabil* Jan/Feb/Mar 2001; 4(1): 1–16.

Lew M. Dialectical behavior therapy for adults who have intellectual disability. In *Psychotherapy for Individuals with Intellectual Disability.* Kingston, NY: NADD Press, 2011; 37–66.

Linehan MM. *Cognitive-Behavioral Treatment of Borderline Personality Disorder.* New York: Guilford Publications, 1993.

Long ES, Miltenberger RG. A review of behavioral and pharmacological treatments for habit disorders in individuals with mental retardation. *Journal of Behavior Therapy and Experimental Psychiatry* 1998; 29, 143–156.

Lowe K, Allen D, Jones E, et al. Challenging behaviors: Prevalence and topographies. *J Intellect Disabil Res* 2007; 51: 625–636.

Miller WR, Rollnick S. *Motivational Interviewing: Preparing People for Change.* New York: Guilford Press; 2002.

Romana MS. Cognitive-behavioral therapy. Treating individuals with dual diagnoses. *J Psychosoc Nurs,* 2003; 41(12): 30–35.

Royal College of Psychiatrists. *Diagnostic Criteria for Psychiatric Disorders for Use with Adults with Learning Disabilities/Mental Retardation (DC-LD).* London: Gaskell, 2001.

Sovner R. Limiting factors in the use of DSM-III criteria with mentally ill/mentally retarded persons. *Psychopharmacol Bull* 1986; 22(4): 1055–1059.

Szymanski L, and King BH. Assessment parameters for the assessment and treatment of children, adolescents, and adults with mental retardation and comorbid mental disorders. American Academy and Child and Adolescent Psychiatry Working Group and Quality Issues. *Journal of the American Academy of Children and Adolescents Psychiatry,* 1999, 38(12 Suppl), 5S–31S.

Unwin G, Deb S. Use of medication for the management of behavior problems among adults with intellectual disabilities: A clinician's consensus survey. *Am J Ment Retard* 2008; 113(1): 19–31.

Whitehouse RM, Tudway J, Look R, Kroese B. Adapting individual psychotherapy for adults with intellectual disabilities: A comparative review of the cognitive-behavioral and psychodynamic literature. *J Appl Res Intellect Disabil* 2006. 19: 55–65.

WHO. *International Classification of Diseases Tenth Revision, Guide for Mental Retardation.* World Health Organization, 1996. Available at http://www.who.int/mental_health/media/en/69.pdf. Access Date 05/18/11.

Wilkinson JE, Culpepper L, Cerreto M. Screening tests for adults with intellectual disabilities. *J Am Board Fam Med* 2007; 20: 402.

WPA. *Clinical Bulletin of the Developmental Disabilities Division. International Guide to Prescribing Psychotropic Medication for the Management of Problem Behaviours in Adults with Intellectual Disabilities.* World Psychiatry Association, Birmingham, UK(2010).

WPA. *Problem Behavior in Adults with Intellectual Disabilities: International Guide for Using Medication.* The World Psychiatric Association (WPA): Section on Psychiatry of Intellectual Disability (SPID) September 2008.

CHAPTER 29

ADDRESSING SUICIDE RISK IN COMMUNITY MENTAL HEALTH

DARCY HAAG GRANELLO

I n 2001, the Department of Health and Human Services (DHHS) issued the National Strategy for Suicide Prevention. Numerous public and private partners, including the Office of the Surgeon General, Substance Abuse Mental Health Services Administration (SAMHSA), the Centers for Disease Control (CDC), Department of Defense (DoD), and the National Institute of Mental Health (NIMH), developed the first-ever comprehensive and integrated public health approach to reducing suicide deaths and suicide attempts in the United States (DHHS, 2001). In 2003, the President's New Freedom Commission on Mental Health reiterated the importance of this strategy and called for the full implementation of the recommendations contained therein. More than a decade later, the original eleven goals outlined in the national strategy continue to provide an important structure for anyone working in community mental health. Divided into the three major categories of *awareness*, *intervention*, and *methodology*, the goals in the national strategy help focus suicide prevention efforts that involve millions of consumers of mental health as well as the professionals who work with them. This chapter uses the eleven goals in the national strategy to help organize the current research and best practices in suicide prevention and intervention in community mental health.

MAGNITUDE OF THE PROBLEM

Each year in the United States, more than 36,000 people take their own lives (Crosby, Han, Ortega, Parks, & Gfroerer, 2011). That equates to nearly 99 people a day, or a person lost to suicide every 14 minutes. In the United States, suicide is more than twice as common as homicide, and is now the tenth leading cause of death. Over the past decade, the suicide rate in America has been increasing. In 2008 (the latest year for which numbers are available), suicide rates increased 2.6% over the previous year, for a rate of 11.8 per 100,000 in the population, the highest rate in 15 years.

As alarming as these numbers are, focusing only on completed suicides belies the true magnitude of the problem. Each year, an estimated 1.1 million adults make a suicide attempt, translating to an attempt every 38 seconds. Greater still is the number of Americans who seriously consider suicide. In 2008, a national study of suicide risk found that 8.3 million American adults aged 18 or older (3.7% of the population) seriously considered suicide in the past year, and 2.3 million (1% of the population) made a suicide plan (Crosby et al., 2011). Among youth, 17% of high school students reported that they had seriously considered suicide in the past year, and more than 8% reported that they had actually attempted suicide during the same period, with 2.6% making an attempt that required medical attention (Eaton et al., 2006). A 2006 study of college students found that one in 10 said that they had "seriously considered suicide" during the past year (American College Health Association, 2007).

The effects of suicidal thoughts, attempts, and completions ripple outward beyond the individuals involved into the larger community. In addition to those who die by suicide each year, as many as 200,000 additional individuals are impacted by the loss of a loved one to suicide (Corso, Mercy, Simon, Finkelstein, & Miller, 2007). As many as 7% of the U.S. population (approximately 22 million people) state that they have been exposed to a suicide death within the last year, with 1.1% of the sample in a large national study stating that they have lost an immediate family member to suicide within the previous year (Crosby & Sacks, 2002).

There are also significant economic costs associated with suicide. The total lifetime costs of all self-inflicted injuries (attempts and deaths) occurring in just one year in the United States is approximately $33 billion, which includes $1 billion for medical treatment and $32 billion in lost productivity. Translated into cost per person, the average cost per case of suicide death is $1 million in lost productivity and $2,596 in medical costs. The average cost for each suicide attempt is $9,726 in lost productivity and $7,234 in medical costs (Corso et al., 2007).

Although all races, ages, and both genders are affected by suicide, some groups are at higher risk. Males are four times more likely than females to die by suicide, representing 78.8% of all suicide deaths. However, women are three times more likely than men to attempt suicide, with approximately 59 attempts for every completion (compared with eight attempts for every completion in men). Whites/Caucasians have suicide rates that are higher than those of any other racial or ethnic group. The Caucasian rate of 15.1 per 100,000 is higher than the rates for Hispanics (5.2 per 100,000), Blacks/African Americans (5.2 per 100,000), American Indians/Alaskan Natives (11.9 per 100,000), or Asian/Pacific Islanders (5.8 per 100,000) (Crosby et al., 2011).

Suicide risk differs by age. Among those aged 25 to 34, suicide is the second leading cause of death (behind accidents). Suicides represent the third leading cause of death among 15- to 24-years-olds (nearly 13% of all deaths annually). In addition, young people are significantly more likely to engage in suicide attempts. For every completed suicide in the 15 to 24 age group, it is estimated that there are up to 200 suicide attempts (Arias, Anderson, Kung, Murphy, & Kochanek 2003), compared with between two to four attempts for every completion in adults older than 65 (Miller, Segal, & Coolidge, 2000).

There are significant gender differences in suicide risk based on age. For example, suicide rates for women peak between the ages of 45 and 54. For men, suicide rates rise with age, with the highest rates occurring after age 65. Suicide rates for males over age 65 are approximately 40 per 100,000, compared with 6 per 100,000 for females. The highest suicide rate for any age group, however, is for Caucasian males over age 85. Their rate of nearly 70 per 100,000 makes this group, by far, the most likely of any demographic group to complete suicide (Granello & Granello, 2007).

NATIONAL STRATEGY GOAL AREA: AWARENESS

If the general public understands that suicide and suicidal behaviors can be prevented, and people are made aware of the roles individuals and groups can play in prevention, many lives can be saved.

—National Strategy for Suicide Prevention

GOAL #1: PROMOTE AWARENESS THAT SUICIDE IS A PUBLIC HEALTH PROBLEM THAT IS PREVENTABLE

In 1999, the Surgeon General issued a "Call to Action to Prevent Suicide," in which he acknowledged suicide as a major public health concern (U.S. Public Health Service, 1999). The World Health Organization declared suicide a "huge, but largely preventable public health problem" (World Health Organization, 2004). National and international campaigns have been launched to promote increased understanding and awareness of suicide. Underpinning these efforts is the widely held belief that promoting a better understanding of suicide risk and the importance of prevention and intervention among the general public can lead to a reduction in suicide deaths.

There have been significant efforts made over the past decade in moving toward a public-health approach to suicide. Increasingly, suicide is recognized as a product of the complex interaction of many different factors, both biological and environmental, spanning the socio-cultural, interpersonal, psychological, genetic, and neurological realms. As a result, there is increased understanding that suicide prevention is something that must be addressed using a population-based systems approach *in addition to* individually based intervention efforts (Center for Substance Abuse Treatment, 2008).

Strategies for Implementation of Goal #1

In community mental health, the goal of raising awareness is primarily done through education campaigns at the individual, group, and societal levels. There is evidence that Americans are often unaware of the options they have for effective mental health interventions, and in general, they do not have an adequate understanding of mental health or the preventable nature of suicide (U.S. Public Health Service, 1999).

Individual efforts. Education and information about a client's particular mental illness or disorder is recognized as one of the curative factors that helps clients improve in treatment (Yalom, 2000). By the same token, education and information about suicide can help "normalize" the topic of suicide and give clients permission to discuss this difficult topic, as well as the strong emotions that often accompany thoughts of suicide (Juhnke, Granello, & Granello, 2011).

Group efforts. Mental health offices, agencies, and hospitals can provide educational information to their clients and families. For example, posters and brochures that raise awareness about suicide crises as well as depression are available for free from many different sources, including the Suicide Prevention Resource Center (SPRC.org).

Community/societal efforts. Research demonstrates that giving members of the general public a list of information about suicide risk factors significantly improves people's ability to recognize if someone is suicidal, while simultaneously lowering the stigma associated with suicide

(Van Orden et al., 2006). Other strategies, such as posting the suicide hotline number, can be particularly effective. When seriously suicidal individuals call the suicide hotline, significant decreases in suicidality were found during the course of the telephone session, with continuing decreases in hopelessness and psychological pain in the following weeks (Gould, Kalafat, Munfakh, & Kleinman, 2007).

GOAL #2: DEVELOP BROAD-BASED SUPPORT FOR SUICIDE PREVENTION

During the last decade, suicide prevention has been recognized as a key element of a comprehensive mental health system (Center for Substance Abuse Treatment, 2008). There is increased understanding of the importance of a multidisciplinary approach. All human services professionals, not just mental health professionals, have an obligation to be better informed about mental health treatment resources in their communities and should encourage individuals to seek help from any source in which they have confidence (U.S. Public Health Service, 1999).

Unfortunately, research demonstrates that there is widespread variability in the education and training of mental health professionals in the area of suicide risk assessment and intervention, and even less training for professionals in the general healthcare field. The average amount of training in suicide in most graduate programs in behavioral healthcare is less than one hour (Granello & Granello, 2007), and fewer than 50% of pre-doctoral psychology interns say that their programs offer *any* formal education in suicide risk assessment or intervention (Dexter-Mazza & Freeman, 2003). In fact, most of the helping professions have no standardized requirements for working with suicidal clients during graduate training, and there are no standardized requirements for continuing education for professionals (Daniels & Walter, 2002).

Training for behavioral healthcare professionals alone, however, is clearly not sufficient. Physicians and others in the general medical field must be trained as well. More than 20% of *all individuals* who die by suicide have had contact with their primary physician in the *week* prior to their death. Among older adults, more than 75% visited their physician in the month prior to their suicide (National Research Council, 2002). Unfortunately, research has found that only about one-third of primary care physicians inquire about suicidal thoughts with patients demonstrating clear signs of depression and/or seeking antidepressant medication (Feldman et al., 2007). In another study, 47% of primary care physicians stated that at least one of their adolescent patients had a suicide attempt during the previous year, but only 23% of these physicians stated that they routinely screened their patients for suicide (Frankenfield, Keyl, & Gielen, 2000).

Strategies for Implementation of Goal #2

Because there are many paths to suicide, prevention must address psychological, biological, and social factors if it is to be effective. Collaboration across a broad spectrum of agencies, institutions, and groups—from schools, to faith-based organizations, to health care associations—is a way to ensure that prevention efforts are comprehensive.

Individual Efforts

Collaboration and consultation are the cornerstone of successful management of suicidal clients (Granello & Granello, 2007). Strong professional relationships between hospital and agency staff are critical to the successful outcome of suicidal emergencies, and these relationships are best managed when they are formed and nurtured outside of the context of the crisis. Taking time now to reach out and establish connections at the individual level can help ensure smoother transitions and better outcomes for suicidal individuals during crises. In addition, individuals can advocate for discussion and education about suicide in their respective practice environments, seeking out training at the individual or agency level.

Group Efforts

Education of all staff in agencies, hospitals, schools, and offices can help reinforce the message that suicide prevention is a shared responsibility. Relying on front-line behavioral health providers to recognize suicide risk means that many suicidal individuals will never be properly assessed for suicide. Relatively simple and cost-effective measures, such as hanging posters about suicide prevention in emergency room departments, can be highly effective. In fact, one study found that simply hanging a poster titled "Is your patient suicidal?" with a list of key risk factors and questions to ask (available from SPRC.org) significantly improved assessment of suicide risk by all types of providers, including physicians, residents, and nurses (Otto, 2011).

Community/Societal Efforts

To make suicide prevention efforts more effective and to make efficient use of resources, suicide prevention should be integrated into programs and activities that already exist and included in the agendas of pre-existing community-level groups. It is often possible to target several health or social problems with one intervention, particularly since some risk factors put population groups at risk for more than one problem at the same time. Therefore, an intervention that targets one or more risk or protective factors has the potential to effect change in more than one identified problem. For example, the suicide rate has risen steeply over the last two decades for African- American youth, a group with a high risk for other health and social problems. Programs focused on enhancing educational and occupational opportunities for African-American youth may contribute to feelings of hope and self-assurance, and as a byproduct reduce suicide. However, by consciously integrating program elements that address suicide prevention more directly (for example, encouraging help-seeking for emotional distress), a program may be even more effective overall (DHHS, 2001).

GOAL #3: DEVELOP AND IMPLEMENT STRATEGIES TO REDUCE THE STIGMA ASSOCIATED WITH BEING A CONSUMER OF MENTAL HEALTH, SUBSTANCE ABUSE, AND SUICIDE PREVENTION

Suicide is closely linked to mental illness and substance abuse, and effective interventions exist for both. More than 90% of individuals who die by suicide have a diagnosable mental illness and/or substance-use disorder (Granello & Granello, 2007), but the stigma associated with these disorders can prevent people from seeking the assistance they need. According to SAMHSA's 2006 National Survey on Drug Use and Health (NSDUH), of the 23.6 million people aged 12 or older in need of treatment for an illicit-drug-use or alcohol-use problem, only 2.5 million (fewer than 10%) received treatment at a specialty facility. In the same year, among the 24.9 million adults aged 18 or older reporting serious psychological distress (having a level of symptoms known to be indicative of a mental disorder), fewer than half, or 10.9 million (44.0%), received treatment for a mental health problem (Office of Applied Studies, 2007). Stigma for mental health and suicide is especially pronounced in rural areas and among certain cultural groups (Center for Substance Abuse Treatment, 2008).

Strategies for Implementation of Goal #3

Due to the historic bias and prejudice against those with mental illnesses, health care, mental health care, and substance-abuse treatment have traditionally been viewed as separate types of treatment, with behavioral healthcare and substance-abuse treatment receiving less funding and viewed as due, at least in part, to the "moral failings" of the individual (DHHS, 2001). Reducing stigma related to mental illness and substance abuse has great potential to increase the number of persons from all groups who receive appropriate treatment for mental disorders associated with suicide. Dispelling myths about mental illness, providing accurate knowledge to ensure more-informed consumers, and encouraging help-seeking by individuals experiencing mental health problems can all contribute toward positive outcomes of this goal.

Individual Efforts

Suicidal individuals suffer from internalized stigma, which can inhibit not only their willingness to seek treatment, but their level of involvement and participation in their treatment as well. Efforts to reduce stigma at the individual level, therefore, often are focused on empowerment and participation in treatment. Increased participation in the formulation of care plans and crisis plans, education and information about mental illness and suicide, peer-support and family involvement in treatment, and regular assessment of consumer satisfaction with services are all methods to help empower clients and reverse negative self-stigma (DHHS, 2001). Paying more attention to what clients and family members say about their experiences of discrimination, for example, in relation to work or housing, can allow mental health workers to deal more directly with the effects of stigma for their clients (Graham, Brohan, Kassam, & Lewis-Holmes, 2008).

Group Efforts

There is evidence that individuals who possess more information about mental illness are less stigmatizing than individuals who are misinformed about mental illness. Education campaigns and gatekeeper trainings of school staff, police departments, and other groups have been demonstrated to lessen stigma and improve help-seeking behaviors.

Community/Societal Efforts

Developing or supporting educational campaigns designed to help the public understand mental illness and suicide and to reduce stigma can have extremely positive effects. For example, as of April 2010, the Veteran's Administration (VA) reported nearly 7,000 rescues of actively suicidal veterans, which were directly attributed to seeing print ads, public service announcements

(PSAs), or promotional products. Additionally, referrals to VA mental health services increased. In Phoenix, Arizona, the VA reported a 234% increase in calls to the suicide hotline within 30 days of the launch of its public-awareness campaign (House Committee on Veteran's Affairs, 2010).

NATIONAL STRATEGY GOAL AREA: INTERVENTION

The close association between mental disorders, especially depression, and suicidal behaviors warrants ensuring that professionals are competent in applying the tools and techniques of diagnosis, treatment, management, and prevention to those mental disorders associated with suicidal behaviors.
—National Strategy for Suicide Prevention

GOAL #4: DEVELOP AND IMPLEMENT SUICIDE PREVENTION PROGRAMS

Because many suicide attempts and completions are the result of unrecognized and/or sub-clinically treated mental health and substance-abuse disorders, an important key to preventing many suicides is the ability to detect and intervene with people who are exhibiting signs of mental and emotional distress at the earliest possible occasion. Unfortunately, in the United States, most medical and social service systems are designed to respond only after a problem arises. Although the United States spends more on health care per individual than any other country in the world, only 1% of total health care expenditures are spent in prevention efforts (Granello & Granello, 2007). Many communities simply do not have adequate mental health care programs or resources available to provide effective primary prevention programs. However, it has become increasingly clear that in order to make significant progress in preventing suicides, we must challenge the current approach of responding only to crises or providing a minimal social safety net to the public.

A public-health approach to suicide prevention takes a long view. From a population perspective, prevention means providing people with the tools, skills, and knowledge they need to be healthy. According to the NIMH definition (1998), *prevention* includes not only interventions that occur before the initial onset of a disorder, "but also...interventions that prevent comorbidity, relapse, disability, and the consequences of severe illness...." Thus prevention is seen as spanning the full gamut of the health–illness continuum, with interventions ranging from primary prevention through recovery support (Center for Substance Abuse Treatment, 2008).

Although no specific tests can identify a person who is suicidal, specific risk and protective factors for suicide are known and can be identified. Protective factors include:

- Effective clinical care for mental, physical, and substance use disorders
- Easy access to a variety of clinical interventions and support for help-seeking
- Restricted access to highly lethal means of suicide
- Strong connections to family and community support
- Support through ongoing medical and mental health care relationships
- Skills in problem solving, conflict resolution, and nonviolent handling of disputes

- Cultural and religious beliefs that discourage suicide and support self-preservation (Suicide Prevention Resource Center, 2008).

According to SAMHSA, the two most significant issues related to the development and implementation of suicide prevention programs are (1) the adoption of an "upstream" approach that brings prevention to the people, with integrated services for prevention, assessment, diagnosis, and treatment; and (2) the identification and advancement of specific evidence-based programs to the specific cultural, community, and developmental norms of program participants (Center for Substance Abuse Treatment, 2008). Put simply, an upstream approach differs from the traditional model of mental health, by focusing not only on the people who are drowning, but moving upstream to keep people from falling into the river in the first place. By moving upstream and integrating care across disciplines, the toll taken by excess disability that arises when diagnosis and treatment come later along the health–illness continuum can be lowered.

Strategies for Implementation of Goal #4

The public-health approach provides a framework for developing prevention programs: clearly define the problem, identify risk and protective factors, develop and test interventions, implement programs that are based on local needs, and evaluate their effectiveness. Programs may be specific to one particular organization, such as a university or a community health center, or they may encompass an entire state. The integration of suicide prevention into existing service-based organizations provides opportunities to expand the numbers of individuals who may be reached by preventive interventions (DHHS, 2001).

Individual Efforts

Prevention efforts at the individual level are often targeted to individuals or small groups who may, without appropriate intervention, lack the necessary skills to manage crises. For example, teaching conflict-resolution or strategies for building positive relationships can help at-risk clients learn to cope with their problems before they escalate.

Group Efforts

Outreach prevention programs for families, schools, and other groups in the community can have positive and lasting effects. Most suicide prevention efforts are curriculum-based, with a focus on increasing awareness of the problem of suicide, identifying individuals at risk, and teaching referral techniques and resources. SPRC's registry of best practices highlights several education and gatekeeper training programs that have been demonstrated to be effective in suicide prevention, such as the Lifelines curriculum and Signs of Suicide (SOS) (SPRC, 2011).

Community/Societal Efforts

Universal prevention programs, such as depression screenings at local community events, fairs, or sports programs, can spread the message of prevention. Other examples include general suicide education, screening programs, crisis centers and hotlines, and gatekeeper training offered in the community.

GOAL #5. PROMOTE EFFORTS TO REDUCE
ACCESS TO LETHAL MEANS AND METHODS

Evidence from many countries and cultures demonstrates that limiting access to lethal means and methods of self-harm can be an effective strategy to prevent at least some suicides (Center for Substance Abuse Treatment, 2008). Referred to as "means restriction," this preventative approach is based on the belief that at least some suicidal acts are, in fact, impulsive, and a suicide may be prevented by limiting the individual's access to means. Suicide methods that have been successfully limited with means restriction include poisons and toxic fumes, prescription and over-the-counter medications, firearms, and bridges and tall buildings. Although a certain number of individuals who have their suicide thwarted through means restrictions will find alternative methods, it is clear that many will not. For example, a study of 515 people who were prevented from jumping from the Golden Gate Bridge found that 26 years later, 94% of the would-be suicides were either still alive or had died of natural causes. The study "confirmed previous observations that suicidal behavior is crisis-oriented and acute in nature. It concluded that if a suicidal person can be helped through his/her crises, one at a time, chances are extremely good that he/she won't die by suicide later" (Friend, 2003).

Several studies have shown that the mere presence of a firearm in a home significantly increases the risk of completed suicide. This holds true for the population as a whole and for every age group (Miller, Hemenway & Azrael, 2004). A national study found that the adjusted odds ratio for adult suicide by gun increased by a factor of 16 in homes with guns (Wiebe, 2003). In addition to efforts related to firearms, activities have been devoted to educating physicians and other prescribing and dispensing professionals about limiting prescriptions of potentially lethal medications to amounts that are non-lethal (Center for Substance Abuse Treatment, 2008).

Strategies for Implementation of Goal #5

Community mental health providers can advocate with local governments and institutions to help control and make safe the community environment (Granello & Granello, 2007). Many examples of means restriction must be handled at the community or state level, such as putting up barriers on overpasses or fencing along rail lines. Other strategies can be handled within particular environments, such as locking away dangerous chemicals in university labs. Still other examples of means restriction, such as limiting an individual's access to specific means, are handled with each client and his or her family.

Individual Efforts

Providing means restriction education to parents and families of potentially suicidal individuals is one of the most effective methods for suicide prevention. An SPRC evidence-based practice model for emergency room means-restriction education found that parents who received means restriction education following an emergency room visit for a child's suicide attempt were 27% more likely to restrict access to potentially lethal medications, 36% more likely to restrict access to or dispose of alcohol, and 63% more likely to restrict access to or dispose of firearms (Kruesi, 2009). Individualized means restriction education is designed to be brief and consists of three components: (1) informing the family when the client is not present that the client is at increased risk for suicide and why; (2) telling family they can reduce this risk by limiting the client's access to lethal means; and (3) educating the family and problem-solving with them about how to limit access to lethal means (SPRC, 2011). In spite of the relative simplicity of this approach, it is not universally employed in crisis situations. For example, one study of emergency department nurses found only 28% provided means restriction training to parents of children who had made a suicide attempt and only 18% worked in departments where such training was standard practice (Grossman, Dontes, Kruesi, Pennington, & Fendrich, 2003). Restricting access to guns is a critical component of suicide prevention. Locking guns away and keeping guns and ammunition in different locations can reduce the risk of death by up to 73% (Spielmann, 2011).

Group Efforts

Because it is impossible to limit all potential means for suicide from all environments, means restriction is often handled within subpopulations, based on potential risks that have been identified for that group. For example, after four suicide deaths by jumping from bridges by Cornell University students in 2010, the university engaged in a large-scale effort to install protective netting on all bridges around campus (Cornell University, 2011). Local surveillance of risk factors within specific groups can highlight the strategies necessary for means restriction.

Community/Societal Efforts

Educating the public is an important strategy for shaping behavior. Education and training programs that highlight the importance of gun safety or proper disposal of potentially dangerous medications can be important strategies in means restriction.

GOAL #6: IMPLEMENT TRAINING FOR RECOGNITION OF AT-RISK BEHAVIOR AND DELIVERY OF EFFECTIVE TREATMENT

Training members of the community to recognize risk factors and warning signs that place individuals at elevated risk for suicide and to learn effective strategies to intervene is typically done through gatekeeper training. "Gatekeepers" are any individuals who regularly come into contact with individuals or families in distress. Gatekeeper training has several inherent strengths, including the ability to adapt the training to the specific needs of a population, the ability to capitalize on existing relationships and systems by training multiple members of the same group, and the capacity to strengthen trainees' sense of control in situations in which they may have previously felt helpless. A comprehensive review of the existing research on the effects of gatekeeper training found positive impacts on the knowledge, skills, and attitudes of participants (Feister & Granello, 2011). Gatekeepers interact with people in the environments in which they live, work, and play, and they include (but are not limited to):

- Teachers and school staff
- School health personnel

- Clergy
- Police officers
- Correctional personnel
- Supervisors in occupational settings
- Natural community helpers
- Hospice and nursing home volunteers
- Primary healthcare providers
- Mental health care and substance-abuse treatment providers
- Emergency health care personnel
- Source: DHHS, 2001

Strategies for Implementation of Goal #6

Most suicidal people (more than 80% in some studies) tell someone else of their intent to kill themselves (Granello & Granello, 2007). However, they often tell peers or family members who do not know what to do to help. Afraid of making things worse or of breaking a confidence, these confidantes often remain silent. In fact, only 25% of adolescents say they would tell an adult if they knew a friend was suicidal (Juhnke et al., 2011). Gatekeeper training gives people the skills they need to recognize risk and intervene appropriately.

Individual Efforts

The knowledge, skills, and awareness that are part of gatekeeper training do not have to occur only in group settings in the community. These skills can be an important component of individualized treatment as well. Research has demonstrated that educating family members about how to understand, monitor, and intervene with family members at risk for suicide results in better management and treatment of those identified individuals (DHHS, 2001). Because the exact timing of suicidal behaviors is very difficult to predict, it is important that key members of the family unit and social support network are knowledgeable about potential risks for suicide and how to protect an individual from self-harm.

Group Efforts

Identifying groups who would benefit from gatekeeper training is an important component of community mental health interventions. For example, workers in respite houses or domestic violence shelters, attorneys working with families in divorce or conflict, and probation officers and workers in detention centers all could benefit from this type of training.

Community/Societal Efforts

Just like the first three goals in the national strategy focus on campaigns that educate the public and reduce stigma, this goal also can be appropriately addressed at the macro level. Having raised awareness that suicide is a problem that can be prevented, the next step is to teach people *how* to help prevent suicide by recognizing risk factors and warning signs and knowing what to do to intervene. Some of the most important aspects of implementing Goal #6 at the community level involve communication and marketing of existing effective community-level educational and support programs through collaboration with faith communities, mental health clinics, public health announcement providers, mass transit advertisers, and community service organizations (DHHS, 2001).

GOAL #7: DEVELOP AND PROMOTE EFFECTIVE CLINICAL AND PROFESSIONAL PRACTICES

GOAL #8: INCREASE ACCESS TO AND COMMUNITY LINKAGES WITH MENTAL HEALTH AND SUBSTANCE ABUSE SERVICES

Goals #7 and #8 of the National Suicide Prevention Strategy will be addressed together, as these are the two that essentially address the clinical implementation of intervention strategies for individuals at risk for suicide. Suicidal clients are some of the most difficult and challenging for mental health professionals, and developing and implementing strategies for working with these clients are critical to saving lives. There is a widely held belief among suicidologists that most suicidal individuals do not want to die, but simply cannot imagine continuing to live in their current state of psychological turmoil (Granello & Granello, 2007). In fact, suicidal crises are typically the result of a temporary, reversible, and ambivalent state, and interventions with suicidal clients are based on the premise that the suicidal crisis, if successfully navigated, need not be fatal (Granello, 2010a).

Individuals who receive appropriate treatment for mental disorders have the best likelihood of recovery (Bongar, 2002). Thus, it is critical that individuals with psychiatric disorders or who are at increased suicidal risk receive adequate assessment, treatment, and follow-up care. Assessing individuals to determine their level of suicide risk is one of the most difficult and challenging experiences a mental health professional can face. Accurate suicide risk assessment is essential to identify acute, modifiable, and treatable risk factors and to help clinicians recognize when clients need more specific interventions to help them manage their lives. Assessing a person for suicide risk always includes a comprehensive analysis of risk factors and warning signs. Risk factors can be biological, psychological, cognitive, and/or environmental/situational. There are over 75 identified suicide risk factors in the literature (Granello, 2010b). Among the most common are these:

Biopsychosocial

- Mental disorders, particularly mood disorders, schizophrenia, anxiety disorders, and certain personality disorders
- Alcohol and other substance-use disorders
- Hopelessness
- Impulsiveness and/or aggressiveness
- History of trauma or abuse
- Major physical illness
- Previous suicide attempt
- Family history of suicide

Environmental

- Job or financial loss
- Relational or social loss
- Easy access to lethal means
- Local clusters of suicide with a contagious influence

Sociocultural

- Lack of social support; sense of isolation
- Stigma of help-seeking behavior
- Barriers to accessing health care, especially mental health care and substance-abuse treatment
- Certain cultural and religious beliefs (for instance, the belief that suicide is a noble resolution of a personal dilemma)
- Exposure to (including through the media) and influence of others who have died by suicide

(*Source*: Suicide Prevention Resource Center, 2008)

Although there are ongoing attempts to develop evidence-based best practice models for assessment and intervention, at present, validated assessment and intervention strategies are limited. Dialectical behavior therapy (DBT) has the most empirical support among the evidence-based models, and it has been adapted for use with several different populations of suicidal individuals (SPRC, 2011). In general, working with clients in suicidal crisis includes many levels of care, including inpatient, short- and long-term outpatient, day treatment, and emergency intervention. Models and algorithms are available to assist clinicians in determining appropriate levels of care. These models vary, but generally include (a) conducting meaningful assessments, (b) developing treatment plans, (c) determining levels of care, (d) engaging in psychiatric evaluations for medications, (e) increasing access to treatment, (f) developing risk management plans, (g) managing clinician liability, and (h) assessing outcomes. (For more information on determining levels of care, see Bongar, 2002).

Interventions with suicidal clients are based on a two-tier approach. The first tier is short-term stabilization. Mental health professionals working with clients in suicidal crises use very specific acute management and crisis intervention strategies to keep clients alive and invested in counseling long enough to move to the core problems underlying their suicidality. The goal of the first tier of intervention is to prevent death or injury and restore the client to a state of equilibrium. The second tier of intervention addresses the client's underlying psychological vulnerability, mental disorders, stressors, and risk factors. However, it is not until clients are stabilized using crisis intervention strategies that the ongoing work of counseling can begin (Granello, 2010b).

Strategies for Implementation of Goals #7 and #8

Individual Efforts

One of the most important decisions any mental health professional can make is to seek out advanced training and education in suicide assessment and intervention. Almost all practicing mental health professionals will encounter a suicidal client during their careers, and most—as many as 71% in one study—will work with an individual who has made a suicide attempt (Rogers, Gueulette, Abbey-Hines, Carney, & Werth, 2001). In general, mental health professionals who experience a client suicide describe it as "the most profoundly disturbing event of their professional careers" (Hendin, Lipschitz, Maltsberger, Haas, & Wynecoop, 2000, p. 2022). There is evidence that even a single workshop can significantly alter a clinician's confidence and ability to work with suicidal clients. Six months after the completion of a continuing education workshop on empirically based assessment and treatment approaches to working with suicidal clients, 44% of practitioners reported feeling increased confidence in assessing suicide risk, 54% reported increased confidence in managing suicidal patients, 83% reported changing suicide care practices, and 66% reported changing their clinic policy (Oordt, Jobes, Fonseca, & Schmidt, 2009).

Group Efforts

Enhancing the quality of direct care of suicidal individuals is dependent on the extent to which community organizations and service delivery systems communicate with each other to facilitate the provision of mental health services to those in need, and the extent to which individuals at risk use these services. Because of the strong link between suicide and substance abuse as well as several mental disorders, such as schizophrenia, clients who are seen in specialty mental health and substance abuse treatment centers must be appropriately evaluated for suicide risk and given appropriate interventions (DHHS, 2001).

Community/Societal Efforts

Individuals at high risk for suicide due to mental health and substance abuse must receive prevention and treatment, but barriers to access can negatively affect outcomes. The elimination of health disparities and the improvement of the quality of life for all Americans are central goals for Healthy People 2010 (DHHS, 2000). Some of these health disparities are associated with differences of gender, race, or ethnicity; education; income; disability; geographic location; or sexual orientation. Many of these factors place individuals at increased risk for suicidal behaviors, because they limit access to mental health and substance abuse services (DHHS, 2001). Strategies to eliminate or reduce these barriers must be developed and implemented at community and state levels.

GOAL #9: IMPROVE REPORTING AND PORTRAYALS OF SUICIDAL BEHAVIOR, MENTAL ILLNESS, AND SUBSTANCE ABUSE IN THE ENTERTAINMENT AND NEWS MEDIA

The media has a powerful influence over the American psyche. With people connected to television, movies, Internet videos, and video games at an ever-increasing rate, there is greater concern about the role that the media plays in beliefs about mental illness and suicide. Approximately one-third of college students say that entertainment programming on television is their *primary source of information* about mental illness, and those who used television as their primary source of information were far more likely to hold negative views of people with mental illnesses (Granello, Pauley, & Carmichael, 1999).

There is also evidence that media coverage of suicide deaths can significantly influence "suicide contagion." The recognition of the role of the media began in the 1980s, after a suicide death by a man who jumped in front of a subway train in Vienna, Austria. Following his death, television reporters engaged in a series of dramatic and sensational stories of the suicide that culminated in a "reenactment" of the suicide on the evening news. Over the following weeks and months, there was a series of copycat suicides on the same subway tracks. It became clear that the news reporting itself was increasing the risk for suicide. An alternative media campaign was put into place, and within six months, subway suicides and non-fatal attempts dropped by more than 80%. Importantly, *all suicide deaths*, not just subway deaths, decreased significantly (Etzersdorfer, & Sonneck, 1998).

Because of the power of the media to impact suicide and suicide prevention, a protocol for media reporting has been developed by the American Foundation for Suicide Prevention (available at AFSP.org). Currently, no consensus recommendations have been formulated for entertainment media that specifically address the depiction of suicide and suicidal behaviors in the United States. In Australia, where such guidelines were developed and implemented, suicide rates declined 7% in the first year, nearly 20% in the four-year follow-up period, and subway suicides (a particular focus of the media guidelines) decreased by 75% (Pirkis et al., 2001).

Strategies for Implementation of Goal #9

Individual Efforts

Helping young people develop critical viewing skills can be an important protective factor for suicide. There is evidence that both educational programs and individualized discussions can help children and adolescents better decode the messages that they receive from the media. Direct interventions can help young people make sense of the way suicide and self-harm are depicted in the media and may be counteracted by accompanying messages of education and prevention (Bondora & Goodwin, 2005).

Group Efforts

Outreach efforts by community mental health professionals to media leaders could provide partnerships and strategies for appropriate and responsible depictions of suicide, mental illness, and substance use disorders within the local television markets.

Community/Societal Efforts

Given the substantial evidence for suicide contagion, a recommended suicide prevention strategy involves educating media professionals about contagion, in order to yield stories that minimize harm. Moreover, the media's positive role in educating the public about risks for suicide and shaping attitudes about suicide should be encouraged (DHHS, 2001).

NATIONAL STRATEGY GOAL AREA: METHODOLOGY

By advancing a comprehensive research agenda, industry and government, working together, can contribute significantly to the development of a knowledge base on the causes of suicide and the development of interventions aimed at prevention.

—National Strategy for Suicide Prevention

GOAL #10: PROMOTE AND SUPPORT RESEARCH ON SUICIDE AND SUICIDE PREVENTION

GOAL #11: IMPROVE AND EXPAND SURVEILLANCE SYSTEMS

Goals #10 and #11 of the National Suicide Prevention Strategy will be addressed together, as these two essentially address the management of data and research. The quantity and quality of research on suicide prevention, assessment, and intervention has increased dramatically over the last several decades, but there are still many questions remaining. The complexity of suicide risk, the confounding variables of culture and environment, and the comorbid role of mental illness and substance abuse, all make research into developing best-practice models particularly difficult.

At least part of the problem with the research is the lack of surveillance data. For example, there is no national registry of suicide attempts, making it difficult to determine even something as basic as how many Americans seek emergency room treatment following a suicide attempt each year. According to the national strategy report, "continued advancements in the prevention of suicidal behaviors can only come with solid support of a wide range of basic, clinical, and applied research endeavors designed to enhance understanding of the etiology, development, and expression of suicidal behaviors across the life span as well as those factors which enhance resiliency" (DHHS, 2001).

Strategies for Implementation of Goals #10 and #11

Mental health professionals have an important role to play in the collection of data and the implementation of research with suicidal clients. Effectiveness studies (or, what actually works in clinical practice) that occur within the community mental health system can offer practical and real-world complements to efficacy studies, which are often based on highly controlled laboratory situations that may have little applicability to practice (Granello & Granello, 2001).

Individual Efforts

Although research and data collection can seem daunting, keeping initial efforts manageable can help practitioners engage in research projects that are meaningful. Complex designs with multiple administrations and a large number of instruments may so overwhelm the clinician that they are never completed, or once completed, they are never statistically analyzed in a meaningful way (Granello & Granello, 2001).

Group Efforts

Agencies, hospitals, or programs who work with suicidal clients and their families already have a wealth of clinical data at their disposal, from client satisfaction surveys (demonstrated to be a critical for suicidal clients), to state-mandated reports and data, to clinician notes and reactions. An analysis of these data could be extremely useful to help identity gaps as well as areas of success.

Community/Societal Efforts

Without widespread data surveillance systems, it is difficult for any community or locale to accurately assess their population's risk and protective factors. Working together with state regulatory boards can be an important first step toward accurate data collection.

CONCLUSION

The magnitude of the impact of suicide makes suicide prevention a critical issue for anyone concerned with improving the mental health care of the nation. Crisis stabilization and hospitalizations, while critical to responding to imminent risk, are only part of the solution. A long-term vision for prevention and education at the individual, group, and societal levels, as well as a coordinated system of care for those at risk, may offer the best hope for reducing completed suicides. Everyone in the community mental health care system has a role to play, and the national strategy can offer a starting place for more active involvement in suicide prevention.

REFERENCES

American College Health Association (2007). *American College Health Association–National College Health Assessment: Reference Group Data Report—Fall 2006.* Baltimore, MD: ACHA.

Arias, E., Anderson, R. N., Kung, H. C., Murphy, S. L., & Kochanek, K. D. (2003). *Deaths: Final Data for 2001. National Vital Statistics Reports, 52(3).* Hyattsville, MD: National Center for Health Statistics.

Bondora, J. T., & Goodwin, J. L. (2005). The impact of suicidal content in popular media on the attitudes and behaviors of adolescents. *Praxis, 5,* 5–12.

Bongar, B. (2002). Risk management: Prevention and postvention. In B. Bongar (Ed.), *The Suicidal Patient: Clinical and Legal Standards of Care (2nd ed.),* pp. 213–261. Washington, DC: American Psychological Association.

Center for Substance Abuse Treatment. (2008). *Substance Abuse and Suicide Prevention: Evidence and Implications—A White Paper.* DHHS Pub. No. SMA-08-4352. Rockville, MD: Substance Abuse and Mental Health Services Administration.

Cornell University. (2011). Long-term means restriction for bridges. Available at www.cornell.edu. Accessed 10/5/12.

Corso, P. S., Mercy, J. A., Simon, T. R., Finkelstein, E. A., & Miller, T. R. (2007). Medical costs and productivity losses due to interpersonal violence and self-directed violence. *American Journal of Preventive Medicine, 32(6),* 474–482.

Crosby, A. E., & Sacks, J. J. (2002). Exposure to suicide: Incidence and association with suicidal ideation and behavior. *Suicide and Life-Threatening Behavior*, 32, 321–328.

Crosby, A. E., Han, B., Ortega, L. A. G., Parks, S. E., & Gfroerer, J. (2011). Suicidal thoughts and behaviors among adults aged ≥ 18 years—United States, 2008–2009. *Morbidity and Mortality Weekly Report*, 60(No. SS-13), 1–22.

Daniels, A. S., & Walter, D. A. (2002). Current issues in continuing education for contemporary behavioral health practice. *Administration and Policy in Mental Health*, 29(4/5), 359–376.

Dexter-Mazza, E. T., & Freeman, K. T. (2003). Graduate training and the treatment of suicidal clients: The students' perspective. *Suicide and Life Threatening Behavior*, 33(2), 211–218.

Eaton, D. K., Kann, L., Kinchen, S. A, Ross, J. G., Hawkins, J., & Harris W. A. (2006). Youth risk behavior surveillance—U.S. 2005. *Morbidity and Mortality Weekly Report*, 55(No. 2 SS-5), 1–108.

Etzersdorfer, E., & Sonneck, G. (1998). Preventing suicide by influencing mass-media reporting: The Viennese experience 1980–1996. *Archives of Suicide Research*, 4, 67–74.

Feister, K., & Granello, D. H. (2011). Assessing the Long-Term Effectiveness of Suicide Prevention Gatekeeper Training at a Large University. The Ohio State University. Unpublished manuscript.

Feldman, M. D., Franks, P., Duberstein, P. R., Vannoy, S., Epstein, R., & Kravitz, R. L. (2007). Let's not talk about it: Suicide inquiry in primary care. *Annals of Family Medicine*, 5(5), 412–418.

Frankenfield, D. L., Keyl, P. M., & Gielen, A. (2000). Adolescent patients—healthy or hurting? Missed opportunities to screen for suicide risk in the primary care setting. *Archives of Pediatric Adolescent Medicine*, 154(2), 162–168.

Friend, T. (2003). Jumpers: The fatal grandeur of the Golden Gate Bridge. *The New Yorker,* October 13.

Gould, M. S., Kalafat, J. Munfakh, J. L. H., & Kleinman, M. (2007). An evaluation of crisis hotline outcomes: Part 2: Suicidal callers. *Suicide and Life-Threatening Behavior*, 37(3), 338–352.

Graham, T., Brohan, E., Kassam, A., & Lewis-Holmes, E. (2008). Reducing stigma and discrimination: Candidate interventions. *International Journal of Mental Health Systems*, 2, 3. doi:10.1186/1752-4458-2-3

Granello, D. H., Pauley, P., & Carmichael, A. (1999). The relationship of the media to attitudes toward people with mental illness. *Journal of Humanistic Counseling, Education and Development*, 38, 98–110.

Granello, D. H., & Granello, P. F. (2001). Counseling outcome research: Making practical choices for real-world applications. In G. R. Walz & J. C. Bleuer (Eds.), *Assessment: Issues and Challenges for the Millennium*, pp. 163–172. Greensboro, NC: ERIC/CASS.

Granello, D. H., & Granello, P. F. (2007). *Suicide: An Essential Guide for Helping Professionals and Educators*. Boston: Allyn & Bacon.

Granello, D. H. (2010a). A suicide crisis intervention model with 25 practical strategies for implementation. *Journal of Mental Health Counseling*, 32(3), 218–235.

Granello, D. H. (2010b). The process of suicide risk assessment: Twelve core principles. *Journal of Counseling and Development*, 88, 363–371.

Grossman, J., Dontes, A., Kruesi, M. J. P., Pennington, J., & Fendrich, J. (2003). Emergency nurses' responses to a survey about mean restriction: An adolescent suicide prevention strategy. *Journal of the American Psychiatric Nurses Association*, 9(3), 77–85.

Hendin H., Lipschitz, A., Maltsberger, J. T., Haas, A. P., & Wynecoop, S. (2000). Therapists' reactions to patient's suicides. *American Journal of Psychiatry*, 157, 2022–2027.

House Committee on Veteran's Affairs. (July 14, 2010). Examining the Progress of Suicide Prevention Outreach Efforts at the U.S. Department of Veteran's Affairs. Available at http://archives.veterans.house.gov/hearings/transcript.aspx?newsid=2256. Accessed 10/5/2012.

Juhnke, G. A., Granello, D. H., & Granello, P. F. (2011). *Suicide, Self-Injury, and Violence in the Schools: Assessment, Prevention, and Intervention Strategies*. Los Angeles: Wiley.

Kruesi, M. (2009). Emergency Department "Means Restriction" Education. Idaho Suicide Prevention Research Project. Available at http://www.healthandwelfare.idaho.gov/Portals/0/Families/Suicide%20Prevention/Suicide%20Prevention%20Programs/EmergencyDeptRestrictionofMeansEducation-ISPRP-Brief.pdf. Accessed 10/5/2012.

Miller, J. S., Segal, D. L., & Coolidge, F. L. (2000). A comparison of suicidal thoughts and reasons for living among younger and older adults. *Death Studies*, 25, 257–265.

Miller, M., Hemenway, D., & Azrael, D. (2004). Firearms and suicide in the Northeast. *Trauma*, 57, 626–632.

National Institute of Mental Health (1998). *Priorities for Prevention Research at NIMH: A Report by the National Advisory Mental Health Council Workgroup on Mental Disorders Prevention Research* (NIH Publication No. 98–4321). Rockville, MD: National Institutes of Health.

National Research Council. (2002). *Reducing Suicide: A National Imperative*. Washington, DC: The National Academies Press.

Office of Applied Studies (2007). *Results from the 2006 National Survey on Drug Use and Health: National Findings*. NSDUH Series H-32, DHHS Publication No. (SMA) 07–4293. Rockville, MD: Substance Abuse and Mental Health Services Administration.

Oordt, M. S., Jobes, D. A., Fonseca, V. P., & Schmidt, S. M. (2009). Training mental health professionals to assess and manage suicidal behavior: Can provider confidence and practice behaviors be altered? *Suicide and Life-Threatening Behavior*, 39(1), 21–32.

Otto, M. A. (2011). Suicide Prevention Poster Improves ED Recognition, Management. Internal Medicine News Digital Network, available at http://www.internalmedicinenews.com/news/mental-health/single-article/suicide-prevention-poster-improves-ed-recognition-management/a5a96ba5c7.html.

NEW URL as of 10/5/2012:

http://www.skinandallergynews.com/views/insights-from-seminars/blog/suicide-prevention-poster-improves-ed-recognition-management/1f7f309f5fab52f2067ebc9319a4e153.html

Pirkis, J., Blood, R. W., Francis, C., Putnis, P., Burgess, P., Morley, B., et al. (2001). *The Media Monitoring Project: A Baseline Description of How the Australian Media Report and Portray Suicide and Mental Health and Illness*. Commonwealth of Australia, Canberra.

President's New Freedom Commission on Mental Health. (2003). *Achieving the Promise: Transforming Mental Health Care in America*. Rockville, MD: U.S. Department of Health and Human Services.

Rogers, J. R., Gueulette, C. M., Abbey-Hines, J., Carney, J. V., & Werth, J. L., Jr. (2001). Rational suicide: An empirical investigation of counselor attitudes. *Journal of Counseling and Development*, 79, 365–372.

Spielmann, G. L. (2011). Means Restriction. New York State Office of Mental Health. Available at http://www.omh.ny.gov/omhweb/savinglives/volume2/means_rest.html. Accessed 10/5/2012.

Suicide Prevention Resource Center (2008). Risk and Protective Factors for Suicide. From http://www.sprc.org/library/srisk.pdf. Accessed 10/5/2012.

Suicide Prevention Resource Center. (2011). Evidence-based programs. Available at http://www2.sprc.org/bpr/section-i-evidence-based-programs.

U.S. Department of Health and Human Services. (2000). *Healthy People 2010* (2nd ed.). Washington, DC: U.S. Government Printing Office.

U.S. Department of Health and Human Services. (2001). *National Strategy for Suicide Prevention: Goals and Objectives for Action*. Rockville, MD: U.S. Department of Health and Human Services.

U.S. Public Health Service (1999). *The Surgeon General's Call to Action to Prevent Suicide*. Rockville MD: U.S. Department of Health and Human Services.

Van Orden, K. A., Joiner, T. E., Jr., Hollar, D., Rudd, M. D., Mandrusiak, M., & Silverman, M. M. (2006). A test of the effectiveness of a list of suicide warning signs for the public. *Suicide and Life Threatening Behavior*, 36(3), 272–287.

Wiebe, D. J. (2003). Homicide and suicide risks associated with firearms in the home: A national case-control study. *Annals of Emergency Medicine,* 41(6), 771–782.

World Health Organization. (2004). Suicide Huge but Preventable Public Health Problem, Says WHO. Available online at http://www.who.int/mediacentre/news/releases/2004/pr61/en/index.html. Accessed 10/5/2012.

Yalom, I. (2000). *Theory and Practice of Group Psychotherapy* (4th ed.). New York: Basic Books.

CHAPTER 30

JAIL DIVERSION

Using the Sequential Intercept Model

MARK R. MUNETZ, PATRICIA A. GRIFFIN, AND KATHLEEN KEMP

ABSTRACT

Capital City, USA, is a medium-sized city in any state in the United States. Its downtown is active during the day, but at night it is dominated by the homeless, about half of whom appear to have a mental illness, a substance abuse problem, or both. The local police who work the downtown district are frustrated that so much of their time is spent addressing the needs of people with untreated mental illness. Its local hospitals have closed most of their inpatient psychiatric units, and the state hospital is 30 miles away and always full. The police feel there is no place to take people with mental illness who create a disturbance, so they frequently end up taking them to jail.

The sheriff in town is angry. He thinks his jail has turned into a mental hospital and his deputies are ill prepared to manage the screaming, irrational people who stream in day after day. His budget is increasingly consumed by psychiatric medication—and people who need to move to the state hospital for competency evaluations sit for days and often weeks in jail, awaiting an open hospital bed. He can't find psychiatrists willing to work in the jail, and it seems the professionals providing primary medical care and the mental health staff don't know how to coordinate care effectively.

The judges in town are frustrated. Every day they see defendants with obvious mental illness appearing in their courtroom—the same people again and again. The judges look for guidance from the mental health system but find it lacking. They order treatment as a condition of probation, but the probation officers don't seem to know what to do to get their probationers the help they need. Mental health staff rarely return the probation officers' phone calls; when they do, they cite Health Insurance Portability Accountability Act (HIPAA) and confidentiality as a reason they cannot share information.

The mental health staff are overloaded with cases, and the last thing they want to do is serve criminals with mental illness. They get angry when a judge tries to order treatment for someone whom the mental health professional has not assessed. They want to see motivated patients, not patients ordered into treatment by a judge who is untrained in mental health. People with mental illness who want help face long waiting lists and have little time with their doctor, nurse, counselor, or case manager. Many people with mental illness do not believe they are ill and don't want anything to do with the mental health system. Alcohol or street drugs provide more relief than psychiatric medication. The investigative reporter for the *Capital City Gazette* wants to know why the streets and the jail have become the new asylums for people with mental illness in her town.

THE CONTEXT

As deinstitutionalization has progressed and community mental health systems have developed, it has become increasingly clear that there is an over-representation of people with severe and persistent mental illness in our nation's jails and prisons (Steadman, Osher, Robbins, Case, & Samuels, 2009; Teplin, 1983, Telpin, 1984; Torrey et al., 1993). While it is tempting to refer to this as "transinstitutionalization," this is probably an oversimplification. The people with serious mental illness (SMI) in criminal justice institutions are not directly the same people who used to occupy long-term state hospital units (Prins, 2011).

For many years the mental health community turned a blind eye to this problem. In fact, many did not consider it a problem. That people with mental illness were no longer confined for long periods in psychiatric hospitals was considered a successful outcome of deinstitutionalization. If this meant that some people ended up committing crimes and subsequently going to jail, this was the consequence of the choices these individuals made and was seen as a larger consequence of normalizing mental illness. This let the mental health system off the hook. The incarceration of people for behavior directly or indirectly related to symptomatic mental illness, according to this line of thinking, was not the fault of the mental health system. Clinicians sometimes saw the arrest of their patients (clients) as a needed respite for the clinician from a challenging case. Rarely would the clinician follow the patient while he or she was incarcerated in a local jail awaiting trial or serving a short sentence; even more rarely would clinicians have any contact with patients serving sentences in state prisons.

Jail and prison administrators could rightly claim that it was not their business to address the needs of people with mental illness. However, ironically, since the 1976 U.S. Supreme Court decision in *Estelle v. Gamble*, prisons (and probably jails) are the only places in the United States where people have a Constitutional right to medical treatment, including mental health treatment. Furthermore, it is increasingly clear that jails and prisons need to attend to the discharge-planning needs of their inmates. The New York City case of *Brad H.* (*Brad H. v. City of New York*, 2000) established, at least in that jurisdiction, a responsibility on behalf of the correctional institution to conduct discharge planning with the local community mental health system (Barr, 2003).

Law enforcement was often caught in the middle of these situations. As first responders to people in a mental illness crisis, police officers were poorly prepared to deal with these situations, which at times led to tragic outcomes. More often, however, the police had few good options. They learned from experience that if they transported someone to a hospital, he often ended up back on the street very quickly, with no apparent improvement. If they took the person to jail, which at times seemed the only alternative, then they also found the justice system ill-prepared to handle the situation. The revolving door in and out of jail was often as fast as the door through the treatment system.

This is how many communities in America felt in the 1990s. Perhaps many still do today. It is clear that people with serious mental illness are over-represented in the criminal justice system. The prevalence of people with mental illness who are incarcerated in local jails is at least three times higher for men and almost six times higher for women relative to people with mental illness in the general population (National GAINS Center, 2004; Steadman et al., 2009; Teplin, 1990; Teplin, Abram, McClelland, 1996). No one can find this acceptable.

By the start of the twenty-first century, a number of novel efforts were taking place around the country to address what is often referred to as the problem of "criminalization of people with mental illness." These innovations included the Memphis Crisis Intervention Team model, specialized mental health dockets, specialized parole or probation officers, and reentry programs targeting individuals with serious mental illness. These programs all shared in common working across traditional boundaries, bringing people from the mental health system and people from the criminal justice systems together to work with their common clients. Often this work involved family members and other advocates, as well as people in recovery from a serious mental illness themselves.

As these specialized programs came to be known around the country, especially after the publication of the *Council of State Governments Consensus Project Report* in 2002 (Council of State Governments, 2002), many communities were interested in starting jail diversion programs. But where to start? There was no conceptual model to help a community to assess itself and determine where it might begin.

ORIGINS OF THE SEQUENTIAL INTERCEPT MODEL

The Sequential Intercept Model (SIM) was developed through collaborations between the National GAINS Center (Hank Steadman and Patty Griffin), the Summit County (Ohio) Alcohol, Drug Addiction and Mental Health Services (ADM) Board, and the Northeast Ohio Medical University (NEOMED, formerly known as the Northeastern Ohio Universities College of Medicine) (Mark Munetz) and the Ohio Department of Mental Health (ODMH). It is likely that the GAINS Center would have eventually developed a model like the SIM if these relationships had never developed, but arguably the SIM was developed and promulgated because of the public–academic partnerships at the local, state, and national levels.

In the late 1990s, Akron, Ohio, like many communities, was exploring ways to address the over-representation of people with mental illness in its local jail (Munetz, Grande, & Chambers, 2001; APA Bronze Achievement Award, 2003; Summit County [Ohio] Alcohol, Drug Addiction and Mental Health Services Board, 2003). Its county mental health system partnered with the Akron Police Department to develop a crisis intervention team (CIT) program and, with the Akron Municipal Court, to start a mental health court. To assist in the development of these programs and to address some other local systems issues, the Summit County ADM Board requested technical assistance from the GAINS Center. Patty Griffin provided the technical assistance consultation. In 2000, the Ohio Department of Mental Health—under the leadership of Mike Hogan—was developing a concept of statewide coordinating centers of excellence (CCoE). These centers were primarily based in a medical school or university with particular energy and expertise around a specific evidence-based practice. The CCoE would then be supported by the state to promote, disseminate, and support said practices statewide.

Essentially technical assistance centers, the concept was similar, at a state level, to what the GAINS Center had done nationally. Given the enthusiasm, in Summit County, for jail diversion alternatives like CIT and Mental Health Court, Summit County encouraged Dr. Hogan to designate it a center for jail diversion. Dr. Hogan consulted with Dr. Steadman and came to see the possibility of a "mini-GAINS Center" for the state. However, the Ohio Department of Mental Health was reluctant to support a center of excellence in jail diversion for three reasons (which on reflection are ironic): 1) they were unsure of the salience of the problem of criminalization of people with mental illness; 2) there were no clear evidence-based jail diversion practices; and 3) there was no conceptual model. The first concern, hard to fathom today, was real but overcome with the enthusiasm about jail diversion efforts like CIT that also helped address the second reservation. Ultimately, the Criminal Justice Coordinating Center of Excellence was established with a grant to the Summit County ADM Board, which contracted with Northeast Ohio Medical University (NEOMED) to operate the center. With funding of the center came a mandate from Dr. Hogan to develop a conceptual model.

THE SEQUENTIAL INTERCEPT MODEL

The Sequential Intercept Model is conceptually simple (Munetz & Griffin, 2006). People move from the community through the criminal justice system in a reasonably predictable, linear fashion, from arrest; to an initial hearing; to jail awaiting trial or adjudication of competence to stand trial; to release or reentry; and finally, to community supervision or support. Each of the these points through the justice system can be seen as an opportunity to intervene and "intercept" the person, moving them from the justice system to the treatment system; i.e., *diversion*.

Graphically, the model has been presented three ways: as a funnel, as a circle, and as a horizontal line. The funnel graphic makes the point that the earlier in the process an intervention occurs, the larger the number of individuals can be affected (see Figure 30.1). So Intercept 1 interventions (law enforcement/crisis services [e.g., a CIT program]) may divert more individuals than Intercept 3 interventions (e.g., a specialty mental health docket). The circular graphic makes the point that people can get caught in a revolving door and that intervention at any of the intercepts can stop or at least slow the door (see Figure 30.2). From this perspective, an intervention at any of the intercepts is likely to be helpful to some people. Finally, the horizontal graphic makes the point that movement through the system is in fact linear and predictable (see Figure 30.3).

The Sequential Intercept Model is based on the premise that, in an ideal world, the presence of people with mental disorders in the criminal justice system would be no greater than that of people from the same community without mental disorders. Fundamental to that premise is that people with mental illness who end up in the criminal justice system because of behavior resulting from untreated, symptomatic mental illness reflect a system failure. While the problem of the over-representation of people with mental illness in the justice system cannot be blamed entirely on a failed mental health system, at least part of the blame does belong there. Since the turn of this century, there has been a fraying of the mental health service systems in most parts of the United States. The Sequential Intercept Model encourages the system as a whole to examine its efforts.

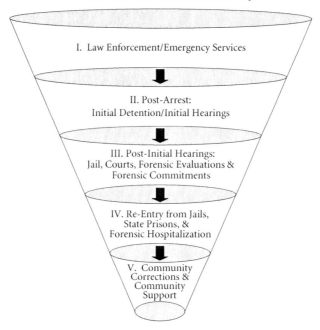

FIGURE 30.1 Sequential Intercepts

FIGURE 30.2 Sequential Intercept Model: A Circular View

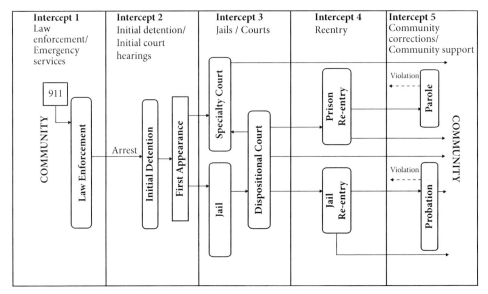

FIGURE 30.3 The Linear Model

There are many questions to be asked about how behavioral health efforts have contributed to the current crisis. How do individuals gain access to treatment? What barriers does the system put in place to remain in treatment? How does a system keep professionals adequately trained on evidence-based practices? While it would be easy to see this situation as a failure of the mental health system alone, it is more appropriate to view it as a community or total system failure. Efforts to address the needs of people with mental illness are complex and go beyond just the mental health system. The criminal justice system shares fault with the mental health system. Individuals with serious mental illness who enter the criminal justice system penetrate deeper into the system and often remain involved longer than people without mental illness (Ditton, 1999). The California Supreme Court rulings (*Coleman v. Schwarzenegger* [E.D. Cal. August 4, 2009]; *Plata v. Schwarzenegger* [N.D. Cal. August 4, 2009]) on the failings of the criminal justice system to provide adequate medical and mental health treatment, upheld by the U.S. Supreme Court (*Brown v. Plata*, 2011), demonstrate the limited tolerance of the mistreatment of a vulnerable population.

The problem of the over-representation of people with mental illness in the criminal justice system is a complex one with no single cause. In the same way, there is no single solution to this problem. A single new program or change in policy is not sufficient. The problem has to be approached systematically, at many levels, and as early as possible in the process. Steadman (2011) articulated the broader context of issues faced by the criminal justice and behavioral health systems that have led to the overrepresentation of individuals with serious mental illness in the criminal justice system. His argument stressed the importance of developing, modifying, or eliminating policies in order to prevent the unnecessary incarceration of individuals with serious mental illness by looking at the complicated system as a whole as well as its small moving parts. He further suggested that the four solutions proposed by the California Supreme Court to address the high numbers of people with mental illness in the state prison system (early release; diversion of technical parole violators to community-based sanctions or local jails; alternate sanctions for low-risk offenders; and increased community- and prison-based rehabilitation programming) focus on preventive or front-end efforts.

Ownership of the problem must be shared by the mental health, addiction, and criminal justice systems. Collaboration across these systems, rather than finger-pointing and blaming or simply ignoring each other, is key to creating effective solutions. This collaboration is necessarily interdisciplinary. Mental health and addiction professionals who work in the public sector, especially those who work with individuals with SMI, understand that to be effective they need to work in interdisciplinary teams. Mental health systems have been expanding the number of disciplines needed to work effectively beyond the traditional mental health disciplines (e.g., psychiatry, psychology, nursing, and social work) to include others viewed as critical in a recovery-oriented treatment system. These include, for example, supported employment and supported education specialists, housing specialists, and peer-support workers. Integrated dual disorders treatment (IDDT), an evidence-based treatment (Drake et al., 2001), is a team-based approach to integrating treatment of both serious mental illness and comorbid substance use disorders. While roughly half of the people with SMI in the community have a comorbid substance use disorder, 72% to 80% of justice-involved individuals with SMI have a co-occurring diagnosis (Abram & Teplin, 1991; Abram, Teplin, & McClelland, 2003). IDDT teams require representatives from the full array of mental health and chemical dependency disciplines as well as supported employment specialists, housing specialists, and peer support. In addition to behavioral health providers (mental health and addiction) working together, effective efforts at jail diversion require collaboration between behavioral health and criminal justice professionals. It has long been recognized that successful jail diversion requires "boundary spanners" (Steadman, 1992), individuals who are familiar with both mental health and criminal justice systems and cultures.

EVOLUTION OF THE MODEL—THE ULTIMATE INTERCEPT

At its inception, the Sequential Intercept Model assumed that the over-representation of people with mental illness in the criminal justice system was largely the result of symptomatic mental illness that directly resulted in behavior leading to criminal justice involvement. Thus, if more people with mental illness received effective treatment in the community, the problem would be diminished. Accordingly, Munetz and Griffin called an accessible mental health system the "*ultimate intercept:*" "An accessible, comprehensive, effective mental health system focused on the needs of individuals with serious and persistent mental disorders is undoubtedly the most effective means of preventing the criminalization of people with mental illness" (Munetz & Griffin, 2006).

We have argued that the most effective way to keep people with mental illness out of the justice system is by providing accessible, effective treatment services using treatment interventions for which there is evidence of efficacy and effectiveness. Recent research has examined the use of evidence-based practices as they specifically focus on justice-involved populations, including research on assertive community treatment (Morrissey & Meyer, 2008), integrated substance abuse and mental health treatment (Osher, 2006), and illness management and recovery (Mueser & MacKain, 2008). Furthermore, evidence-based intervention efforts are not limited to the mental health system. Skeem and colleagues (2006; 2011) identified community supervision approaches and probation officer characteristics that contribute to improved outcomes for individuals with SMI. Their research suggests that specialty mental health caseloads, probation officers with a "firm but fair" approach, and close working relationships between probation and behavioral health systems reduced recidivism rates for individuals with SMI.

It is also becoming increasingly evident that people with SMI who end up in the criminal justice system differ in important respects from people with SMI who do not. One example is the current debate as to what proportion of crimes committed by people with SMI involved in the criminal justice system are attributable to symptomatic illness (Peterson, Skeem, Hart, Vidal, & Keith, 2010; Skeem, Manchak, & Peterson, 2011). Recent studies suggest that we have overestimated the proportion of people with SMI who end up in the justice system because of untreated psychosis and underestimated the proportion who end up in the justice system because of additional risk factors including criminogenic influences (e.g., substance abuse, unemployment, criminal thinking, family dysfunction, antisocial peers), trauma, situational stress, and environmental factors. Peterson and colleagues (2010) found that only 7% of offenders with a mental illness committed crimes that were a direct result of psychosis (5%) or minor "survival" crimes related to poverty. Recent research advances reveal that treating mental illness alone may not be sufficient (Epperson et al, 2011; Fisher, Silver, & Wolff, 2006; Peterson et al., 2010; Skeem et al., 2011). An adequate mental health system is clearly necessary, though not sufficient, to effectively keeping people with SMI out of the criminal justice system. New evidence suggests that the mental health system as a whole needs to reconsider the goals of treatment— to go beyond mental illness and substance use needs and incorporate criminogenic needs that also contribute to recidivism. The mental health system has not traditionally addressed these risk and need factors in its population, not seeing that as its mission (Morgan, Fisher, Duan, Mandracchia, & Murray, 2010).

As the problem of over-representation of people with mental illness in the criminal justice system is better understood, it becomes increasingly clear that these criminogenic risk factors, in addition to the results of untreated, symptomatic mental illness, probably increase the risk that people with SMI will end up in the justice system. So, an accessible, effective mental health system, the "ultimate intercept," is still not the complete answer to the criminalization problem, unless that system includes expertise on the treatment of criminality. It has taken several decades to recognize that it is not effective to first treat mental illness and then substance dependence (or visa versa). They are more effectively treated simultaneously. It now appears that, to keep people with SMI out of the criminal justice system, treatment needs to be integrated in multiple areas. These include mental illness, substance dependence, trauma, situational stress, social disadvantages, and criminogenic risks (Epperson et al, 2011; Morgan et al., 2010).

Appelbaum (Daly, 2011) has suggested, as have Skeem and colleagues (2011), that we need to consider a paradigm shift. Commenting on the study by Peterson and associates (2010), Appelbaum (Daly, 2011) noted, "The new paradigm suggests that merely treating mental disorders may be insufficient to reduce criminality, including violence, unless specific criminogenic factors are addressed as well—for example, anger management and cognitive therapy for criminal cognitions." Epperson and colleagues (2011) suggest that mental health and criminal justice interventions must address a variety of factors that influence criminal behavior in an integrated and centralized format. The six modules of integrated treatment are medication adherence, criminogenic risk, addiction risk, trauma risk, stress risk, and social disadvantage risk. These modules parallel the research advances in risk assessment and risk management (for a complete review, see Epperson et al, 2011).

So perhaps the real "ultimate intercept" is a comprehensive, accessible, effective mental health and addiction system that is criminologically informed and working closely with criminal justice partners who understand the behavioral health needs of offenders.

BLUEPRINT OF USING THE SEQUENTIAL INTERCEPT MODEL FOR JUSTICE-INVOLVED CLIENTS IN THE COMMUNITY

The Sequential Intercept Model provides a working framework to help communities assess themselves and know where to begin to move forward with building a stronger, more effective system of behavioral health/criminal justice collaboration. The following intercept-by-intercept inventory of service-level action steps is based on the National GAINS Center's widely distributed brochure titled "Developing a Comprehensive Plan for Mental Health and Justice Collaboration: The Sequential Intercept Model" (available at http://gainscenter.samhsa. gov/pdfs/integrating/GAINS_Sequential_Intercept.pdf). Additional action steps have been added, based on work with counties and states across the country as they address the issue of over-representation of people with severe mental illness in their criminal justice systems. The first community inventory using the Sequential Intercept Model was developed by five southeastern counties in Pennsylvania (Bucks, Chester, Delaware, Montgomery, and Philadelphia) as they used the model as a tool to organize their work in a forensic task force charged with planning coordinated regional initiatives (Pennsylvania's Southeast Region Interagency Forensic Task Force, 2002).

INTERCEPT 1: LAW ENFORCEMENT AND EMERGENCY SERVICES

The first intercept reflects the pre-arrest period. Initial contacts may involve various agencies, including 911, mental health crisis response teams, homeless outreach services, Veterans' Affairs, and law enforcement. Experts estimate that 7% to 10% of patrol officer contacts involve individuals with mental health issues (Deane et al., 1999; Janik, 1992), and law enforcement plays an important role in the initial diversion of individuals with serious mental illness. Traditionally, law enforcement and mental health agencies have not coordinated responses to individuals in mental health crisis, such as developing cross-training program or committing to additional physical and personnel resources. However, recent attention to this intercept has resulted in the development of several models to address the needs of local systems. Mobile crisis teams responding with police, mental health workers hired by police to provide on-site or telephone consultation to officers, and specially trained police officers to respond to mental health crisis calls, are a few examples (Lamb, Weinberger, Decuir, 2002). One example of a police pre-arrest diversion program is the Crisis Intervention Team (CIT) model developed in Memphis, Tennessee (Memphis Police Crisis Intervention Team, 1999), and widely disseminated nationally and internationally (see http://www.cit.memphis.edu).

Service-Level Change Action Steps at Intercept 1

- 911: Train dispatchers to identify calls involving persons with mental illness, respond in ways that de-escalate crisis situations, and refer calls with appropriate information to designated, trained respondents.
- Police: Train officers to respond to calls where mental illness may be a factor; training should focus on strategies to de-escalate crisis situations and provide community alternatives to incarceration.
- Documentation: Document police contacts with persons with mental illness and outcomes of those contacts.
- Emergency/Crisis Response: Provide police-friendly drop-off at local hospital, crisis, or triage centers; integrate mental illness and substance abuse crisis services.
- Victims: Provide support services to assist in dealing with the stress of the situation and understand options for response.
- Follow Up: Provide service linkages and follow-up services to individuals who are not hospitalized and those leaving the hospital.
- Evaluation: Monitor and evaluate services through regular stakeholder meetings for continuous quality improvement.

INTERCEPT 2: INITIAL HEARINGS AND INITIAL DETENTION

Once an individual is formally arrested, post-arrest diversion may occur during initial hearings (e.g., bail hearings or arraignment) or initial detention (e.g., detention in local jail prior to adjudication). Individuals with SMI not diverted at pre-arrest may have a variety of summary, misdemeanor, or felony charges that will impact their ability to be considered for alternatives to prosecution or incarceration regardless of the presence of mental illness. Legal procedures vary significantly based on local and state systems, which makes efforts to address diversion at this phase complicated. Some communities have focused on screening for mental illness as an integral part of a standard medical intake procedure, while other jurisdictions have sought to coordinate treatment services in lieu of bail. Connecticut has a long-established statewide post-booking diversion program (Frisman, Sturges, Baranoski & Levinson, 2001). Dallas County, Texas (CMHS National GAINS Center, 2007), has an Intercept 2 diversion program that integrates fast electronic information-sharing and continuity of care of psychotropic medication and case management with diversion after arrest.

Service-Level Change Action Steps at Intercept 2

- Screening:
  - Screen for mental illness and substance use disorders at earliest opportunity
  - Initiate process that identifies those eligible for diversion or needing treatment in jail
  - Use validated, simple instrument or matching management information systems
  - Screen at initial detention, jail, or court by booking officers; pretrial services, prosecution, defense, judge/court staff; or service providers

- Screen for military service history or status; if present, link to Veterans Justice Outreach Specialist at nearest Veterans Affairs Medical Center
- Pretrial Diversion: Maximize opportunities for pretrial release and assist defendants with mental illness in complying with conditions of pretrial diversion
- Service Linkage: Link to comprehensive services, including care coordination, access to medication, integrated dual disorder treatment (IDDT—an evidence-based practice; Drake et al., 2001); as appropriate, prompt access to benefits, health care, and housing

INTERCEPT 3: JAILS AND COURTS

Once incarcerated, individuals with SMI often spend significantly longer time in jail compared with individuals charged with the same crimes but having no SMI (Axelson, 1987; McNiel, Binder, & Robinson, 2005). Diversion programs at Intercept 3 focus on alternatives to prosecution, alternatives to incarceration, and early-release programs. Problem-solving courts such as mental health courts and, more recently, veterans' courts have received widespread attention and press. Courts vary on whether participation in diversion programs at this intercept requires a pre- or post-adjudication plea, and eligibility criteria typically vary by jurisdiction. For example, having committed serious or violent felonies may exclude some individuals from eligibility. Additional efforts go beyond diversion to include the timely and accurate assessment and treatment of serious mental illness in the jail to reduce symptoms and increase treatment engagement prior to release. Efforts to coordinate between the local jail and behavioral health systems also serve to improve reentry at Intercept 4.

Service-Level Change Action Steps at Intercept 3

- Screening: Include diversion opportunities and need for treatment in jail with screening information from Intercept 2
- Court Coordination: Maximize potential for diversion in a mental health court or non-specialty court
- Service Linkage: Link to comprehensive services, including previous community care coordination and services, prompt access to psychotropic medication, IDDT as appropriate, and prompt access to benefits, health care, and housing
- Court Coordination: Monitor progress with scheduled appearances (typically directed by court); promote communication and information sharing between non-specialty courts and service providers by establishing clear policies and procedures
- Jail-based Services:
  - Provide services consistent with community and public health standards, including appropriate psychiatric medications
  - Coordinate care with community providers upon admission to jail and in preparation for release

INTERCEPT 4: REENTRY FROM JAILS, PRISONS, AND HOSPITALS

Continuity of care from jails and prisons into the community has received increased attention; partially due to class action litigations such as the successful *Brad H.* case (*Brad H. v.*

City of New York, 2000) against the New York City jail system for failing to provide adequate aftercare linkages for inmates with severe mental illness. Coordination of services between correctional institutions and community partners focus on identifying appropriate providers, establishing rapport through in-reach into jails, medication continuity, and housing as just a few of the important issues. The APIC model developed by Osher and colleagues (2003) offers a best practices approach to assess, plan, identify, and coordinate transition into the community.

Service-Level Change Action Steps at Intercept 4

- Assess clinical and social needs and public safety risks
- Develop Boundary Spanner position (e.g., discharge coordinator, transition planner) to systematically coordinate institutional care with community mental health and community service agencies
- Plan for treatment and services that address needs
    - GAINS Reentry Checklist outlines treatment plan and communicates it to community providers and supervision agencies—domains include prompt access to medication, mental health and health services, benefits, and housing
    - Identify required community and correctional programs responsible for post-release services; best practices include reach-in engagement and specialized case management teams
    - Coordinate transition plans to avoid gaps in care with community-based services with an emphasis on ensuring continuity in needed psychotropic medication from jail to community
    - Develop strategies to link and relink to public benefits, especially to health insurance such as Medical Assistance in order to facilitate continued access to treatment services
    - Work with client to ensure he/she is aware of aftercare appointments and required criminal justice obligations; Discuss transportation alternatives
- Incorporate Forensic Peer Specialists in reentry process in order to support the client's successful reintegration into the community

INTERCEPT 5: COMMUNITY CORRECTIONS AND COMMUNITY SUPPORT SERVICES

Individuals supervised in the community on federal, state, and local probation and parole represented over 5 million individuals in 2009 (Glaze & Bonczar, 2010). Conditions of probation and parole often mandate compliance with treatment; therefore, noncompliance poses a risk of revocation and reincarceration. As discussed previously, successful strategies require adaptation by both criminal justice and treatment providers to address all of the factors affecting recidivism. Research by Skeem and Louden has identified characteristics of successful probation approaches (2006) as well as individual criminogenic risk factors (2011) that impact outcomes of individuals with SMI.

Service-Level Change Action Steps at Intercept 5

- Screening: Screen all individuals under community supervision for mental illness and co-occurring substance use disorders; link to necessary services
- Maintain a Community of Care:
  - Connect individuals to employment, including supportive employment
  - Link to housing
  - Facilitate collaboration between community corrections and service providers to facilitate adherence to treatment conditions, address criminogenic needs and risk, and support individual's adjustment to the community
  - Establish policies and procedures that promote communication and information sharing
- Implement a Supervision Strategy:
  - Concentrate supervision immediately after release
  - Adjust strategies as needs change
  - Implement specialized caseloads
  - Implement cross-systems training
- Develop Graduated Responses and Modification of Conditions of Supervision:
  - Ensure a range of options for community corrections officers to reinforce positive behavioral and effectively address violations on noncompliance with conditions of release

CROSS INTERCEPTS

The GAINS Center identified several system-level approaches relevant across intercepts designed to facilitate successful outcomes for people with SMI who are involved in the criminal justice system:

- Encourage and support collaboration among stakeholders through:
  - Task forces
  - Joint projects
  - Blended and braided funding
  - Information sharing
  - Cross-training
- Make housing for persons with mental illness and criminal justice involvement a priority; remove constraints that exclude persons formerly incarcerated from housing or services
- Expand access to treatment; provide comprehensive and evidence-based services; integrate treatment of mental illness and substance use disorders
- Expand supportive services to sustain recovery efforts, such as supported housing, education and training, supportive employment, and forensic peer advocacy
- Ensure all systems and services are culturally competent, gender specific, and trauma informed—with specific interventions for women, men, and veterans

PRACTICAL APPLICATIONS OF THE SEQUENTIAL INTERCEPT MODEL

STATE, LOCAL, AND FEDERAL PLANNING

The Sequential Intercept Model is used for a variety of planning purposes at local, state, and federal levels. Pennsylvania has widely disseminated the model, especially to frame county annual plans for justice-related services. For instance, Allegheny County has used the model in their strategic planning (Cherna & Valentine, 2007), and a national conference on community alternatives to justice involvement for people with SMI. Another local example is the thoughtful way Beaver County has used the model to develop a broader range of criminal justice/behavioral health services and facilitate collaboration over time between their Criminal Justice Advisory Board and their county behavioral health system (see http://www.pacenterofexcellence.pitt.edu/documents/BeaverCoSIM_ForensicConf_12012011_Final.pdf).

A state planning guide addressing housing needs for justice-involved individuals with mental illness recently used the model to structure "how-to" information addressing the challenging issue of appropriate and accessible housing for this population (Diana T. Myers and Associates, Inc., 2010). Finally, the Pennsylvania Mental Health and Justice Center of Excellence organizes their technical assistance and website around the model (see http://www.pacenterofexcellence.pitt.edu/).

At the federal level, the U.S. Department of Veterans Affairs incorporates the Sequential Intercept Model in their policies outlining outreach, diversion, and services provided by the Veterans Health Administration facilities to veterans in the criminal justice system (see http://www.va.gov/vhapublications/ViewPublication.asp?pub_ID=2019).

CROSS-SYSTEMS MAPPING AND "TAKING ACTION FOR CHANGE" WORKSHOPS

Another real-world application of the Sequential Intercept Model is the Cross-Systems Mapping (CSM) workshop initially developed through the work of the National GAINS Center providing technical assistance during the SAMHSA jail diversion Knowledge and Development Application initiative (Steadman, et al, 1999). Seeing the practical utility, the Policy Research Associates, Inc., obtained a small-business-initiative grant to further develop the CSM workshops and create a facilitator training manual, workshop planning guide, and workshop curriculum (Vogel et al, 2007). The CSM consists of two separate workshops: the "Cross-Systems Mapping" workshop (Recently renamed "Sequential Intercept Mapping" by Policy Research Associates; see http://www.prainc.com/pdfs/training/fliersequentialinterceptmapping.pdf) and the "Taking Action for Change" workshop (see http://www.prainc.com/pdfs/training/fliertakingactionforchange.pdf). Each can be completed separately, but they are designed to benefit and build on each other. These workshops provide intensive technical assistance by facilitating cross-system collaboration, recording available services at each intercept, identifying gaps and opportunities, and developing action steps for each priority the local community wants to address (Policy Research Associates, 2007).

New Jersey, Florida, Virginia, and Pennsylvania are among the states with statewide initiatives providing the cross-systems mapping workshops to their counties in conjunction with state efforts to decrease the justice involvement of people with SMI. Virginia has mapped the most counties to date, as part of the work of the Commonwealth Consortium for Mental Health and Criminal Justice Transformation (see www.dbhds.virginia.gov/documents/Adm/091022Reinhard.pp). Pennsylvania has mapped over twenty-five counties through the work of the Mental Health and Justice Center of Excellence. Ohio is actively working to implement a similar statewide cross-systems mapping initiative.

CSM Facilitators—Successful CSM workshops require facilitators who provide an open forum to encourage local stakeholders to discuss challenging issues. A facilitator remains objective and encourages dialogue from all participants. They allow the priorities of the local community to remain at the forefront. The facilitators are also well versed in promising and best practices and national trends, and are familiar with various diversion programs throughout the country, which may provide a local community with some guidance. In addition, the facilitators, having gathered information about the local systems, recognize challenging issues that may arise during the workshop and affect the momentum of the group. Local leaders do not facilitate CSM workshops, so a more neutral and objective atmosphere is fostered. In order to become a CSM facilitator, each person must attend a train-the-trainer workshop conducted by Policy Research Associates. Two or more facilitators are assigned to each workshop.

Cross-System Mapping Participants—Cross-system interdisciplinary collaboration is a key feature of the CSM workshop. Participants should represent key players in behavioral health and criminal justice systems. The pre-planning period, discussed below, is used to confirm attendance from key stakeholders. The number of individuals attending the workshop varies significantly by location, but a recommended range based on previous experience is 30 to 45. It is important to engage both leaders and line staff in the CSM workshops from each of the intercepts. Behavioral health representatives may include directors of mental health/substance abuse (MH/SA) systems, MH/SA diversion program staff, local community treatment and case management programs, hospital emergency services, housing specialists, vocational training programs, and consumers. Criminal justice stakeholders include local law enforcement (sheriffs, local and state police, etc.), judges, court administration, probation/parole departments, jail diversion programs, pre-trial services, district attorney's office, and the public defender's office.

CSM Pre-Planning—The pre-planning phase utilizes a local representative(s) to identify potential participants, gather descriptive and specific data, coordinate workshop dates and location, send invitations, and maintain contact with stakeholders leading up to the workshop. The identified local representative(s) must have the time, motivation, and resources to coordinate the workshop and be the liaison between workshop facilitators and the local community for any planning issues. The facilitators provide a helpful pre-planning resource kit with detailed CSM information and examples (i.e., invitation, room set-up, etc).

CSM Workshop—The CSM workshop is a full day, using both presentation and interactive formats. The typical agenda for a workshop includes:

- Opening: Local leaders from both the behavioral health and criminal justice systems introduce and welcome participants and the workshop facilitators. The facilitators provide an overview of the workshop agenda, including the focus, goals, and tasks for the day. At each intercept, facilitators present promising practices using local and national examples to illustrate cross-system collaboration and diversion program efforts. Based on experience and research, facilitators also help lay out keys to success in developing, implementing, and maintaining diversion programs.

- Cross-Systems Mapping: The facilitators begin the mapping with an overview of the Sequential Intercept Model, and then turn to an intercept-by-intercept inventory of the local community, focused on individuals with mental health coming in contact with the criminal justice system. Visible to all participants, facilitators record information to provide a visual representation about the services available at each intercept. Facilitators pay close attention to how the services connect to each other, how they are accessed, and any relevant data. The process continues until all five intercepts have been mapped, the participants are satisfied that all of the relevant services/programs have been noted, and the facilitators have enough information to create a local systems map. Throughout the mapping process, gaps (e.g., obstacles such as Medicaid applications, lack of housing, etc.) and opportunities (e.g., new funding opportunities, previously unknown service availability, etc.) are recorded. The gaps are then used to help develop a list of priorities for change.

- Establishing Priorities: Following the successful completion of the local systems map, the conversation focuses on the future direction of the community and their priorities for change. The group collaborates to integrate priorities for change that has been identified at each intercept as the mapping progressed throughout the day. The priorities may focus on larger system-wide issues or more specific problems that the local community identifies as important. Participants are encouraged to lobby for priorities they feel are important to address. Each person then votes for his or her top two priorities. Facilitators add up the votes and finalize a list of the top five priorities identified by the group.

- Wrap-Up: Facilitators review the day's accomplishments, get feedback from participants about the process, and review the priorities the group process has generated. If the Taking Action for Change workshop is scheduled for the next day, facilitators will discuss how the newly established priorities will be used to develop action steps.

TAKING ACTION FOR CHANGE WORKSHOP

The Taking Action for Change (TAC) workshop is a half-day workshop designed to follow the CSM workshop. The TAC workshop builds on the momentum and creates concrete action steps for each of the top five priorities identified during the CSM. Ideally, the same individuals who participated in the CSM will return for the TAC workshop.

There are a few possible approaches to the TAC. Facilitators may break the larger group into small work groups to develop clearly defined and achievable action steps for each priority separately. The entire group then comes together for discussion and agreement on the action steps for each priority. If small groups are established, it is important to keep the cross-system collaboration spirit by having as much diversity in each small group as possible. The facilitators may also keep the larger group together to work together on a step-by-step action for each priority. With every action step, a community or facilitator point person is assigned to take responsibility for the task, and timelines are established.

CSM/TAC FINAL REPORT AND MAP

The final and most important product of the CSM workshop is the written report and Sequential Intercept map that incorporates all data obtained during the pre-planning phase and the workshop. The map is a visual representation of all the work currently being done in the local community and the relationships between those activities, represented by arrows connecting them. The final report includes:

- Introduction, background, and objectives to the Sequential Intercept Model and Cross-Systems Mapping
- Local community map and narrative of activities and programs at each intercept with as much specific data as possible (e.g., number of arrests, number of prison and hospital admissions, etc.)
- Top five priorities and Action Planning Matrix
- Summary of recommendations generated by CSM participants and facilitators
- Participant list with name, description, and contact information
- Appendices, which vary based on the local community and may include lists of local resources (e.g., housing, treatment programs, etc.), resources for cultural competence, and evidence-based practices

Several examples of reports and maps developed as the result of Cross-Systems Mapping workshops can be found at http://www.pacenterofexcellence.pitt.edu/mapping_Reports.html.

CSM workshops have occurred nationwide to facilitate understanding between behavioral health and criminal justice systems as well as generate diversion strategies that meet local need and fill gaps in services. These workshops can be conducted on either local or statewide levels in a variety of ways and can have significant impact on the creation, coordination, and provision of services in local communities for individuals with mental illness who contact the justice system.

FUTURE DIRECTIONS

Although many communities are interested in addressing the over-representation of people with mental illness in their local criminal justice system, the task can seem daunting, the various options confusing, and the challenges to collaboration across systems overwhelming. The Sequential Intercept Model provides a proven framework to facilitate jail diversion and collaboration between criminal justice and treatment systems that is easily adaptable to localities of varying sizes.

The field of jail diversion has grown significantly in the past twenty years. We expect to see continued growth in this area, although the current strained economic environment poses a real test to our efforts. Some localities and states have taken advantage, though, of this environment by implementing a variety of innovative cost-savings strategies that reduce the number of people with mental illness in the criminal justice system. To continue to move forward, it will be necessary in the future to pay close attention to the cross-intercept issues at the same time that each intercept is considered and addressed. In addition, recent work on the importance of addressing criminogenic risk in preventing recidivism underscores the need for behavioral health and criminal justice professions to work together, always including individuals in recovery in the process.

In closing, we leave you with the following quote, which guides our efforts in this area and provides encouragement in tackling the complexities and challenges of this work:

> I also saw how bringing disparate groups together—even those with conflicting missions—could often be effective.... The power of proximity—spending time side-by-side—had pulled us all to compromise in our efforts to help.... People, not programs, change people. The cooperation, respect, and collaboration we experienced gave us hope that we could make a difference.... (Perry & Szalavitz, 2006).

REFERENCES

Abram, K. M., & Teplin, L. A. (1991). Co-occurring disorders among mentally ill jail detainees: Implications for public policy. *American Psychologist, 46*(10), 1036–1045.

Abram, K. M., Teplin, L. A., & McClelland, G. M. (2003). Comorbidity of severe psychiatric disorders and substance use disorders among women in jail. *The American Journal of Psychiatry, 160*(5), 1007–1010.

Axelson, G. L. (1987). Psychotic vs. non-psychotic misdemeanants in a large county jail: An analysis of pre-trial treatment by the legal system. Doctoral dissertation. Fairfax, VA: George Mason University, Department of Psychology.

Barr, H. (2003). Transinstitutionalization in the courts: Brad H. *v. City of New York*, and the fight for discharge planning for people with psychiatric disabilities leaving Riker's Island. *Crime & Delinquency*, *49*(1), 97–123.

Brad H. *v. City of New York*, 185 Misc. 2d 420, 712 N.Y.S.2d 336 (Sup. Ct. 2000), 276 A.D.2d 440, 716 N.Y.S.2d 852 (App. Div. 2000).

Brown v. Plata, 131 S.Ct. 1910 (2011).

Cherna, M., & Valentine, P. (2007). Behavioral Health Justice-Related Services and Beyond in Allegheny County, Pennsylvania. Available at: http://www.alleghenycounty.us/uploadedFiles/DHS/Individual_and_Community_Health/Justice_Related_Services/JusticeRelatedServices.pdf. (October 7, 2012).

CMHS National GAINS Center. (2007). *Practical Advice on Jail Diversion: Ten Years of Learnings on Jail Diversion from the CMHS National GAINS Center.* Delmar, NY: Author.

Coleman v. Schwarzenegger, No. CIV S-90-0520 LKK JFM P, 2009 WL 2430820 (E.D. Cal. August 4, 2009).

Council of State Governments. *Criminal Justice/Mental Health Consensus Project.* New York, Council of State Governments, 2002.

Daly, R. (2011). Study examines relationship arrests, mental illness. *Psychiatric News, 46*(1), 9–10.

Deane, M. W., Steadman, H. J., Borum, R., Veysey, B. M., & Morrissey, J. P. (1999). Emerging partnerships between mental health and law enforcement. *Psychiatric Services, 50*(1), 99–101.

Ditton, P. M. (1999). *Mental Health and Treatment of Inmates and Probationers.* Bureau of Justice Statistics Special Report, U.S. Department of Justice, NCJ 17446.

Drake R. E., Essock, S. M., Shaner A, Carey, K. B., Minkoff, K., Kola, L., et al. (2001). Implementing dual diagnosis services for clients with severe mental illness. *Psychiatric Services, 52*(4), 469–476.

Epperson, M., Wolff, N., Morgan, R., Fisher, W., Frueh, B., & Huening, J. (2011). *The Next Generation of Behavioral Health and Criminal Justice Interventions: Improving Outcomes by Improving Interventions*. New Brunswick, NJ: Center for Behavioral Health Services and Criminal Justice Research.

Estelle v. Gamble, 429 U.S. 97, 1976.

Fisher, W. H., Silver, E. & Wolff, N. (2006). Beyond criminalization: Toward a criminologically informed framework for mental health policy and services research. *Administrative Policy Mental Health and Mental Health Services Research, 33,* 544–557.

Frisman, L., Sturges, G. E., Baranoski, M. V., & Levinson, M. (2001). Connecticut's criminal justice diversion program—A comprehensive community forensic mental health model. In *Forensic Mental Health: Working with Offenders with Mental Illness,* pp. 51–58. Kingston, NJ: Civic Research Institute; US.

Glaze, L. E., & Bonczar, T. P. (2010). *Probation and Parole in the United States, 2009.* U.S. Department of Justice, Office of Justice Programs, Bureau of Justice Statistics Bulletin. NCJ 231674.

Janik, J. (1992). Dealing with mentally ill offenders. *FBI Law Enforcement Bulletin, 61,* 22–26.

Lamb, R. L., Weinberger, L., & Decuir, W. J. (2002). The police and mental health. *Psychiatric Services, 53,* 1266–1271.

McNiel, D. E., Binder, R. L., & Robinson, J. C. (2005). Incarceration associated with homelessness, mental disorder, and co-occurring substance abuse. *Psychiatric Services, 56*(7), 840–846.

Memphis Police Crisis Intervention Team. (1999). Memphis, TN: Memphis Police Department.

Morgan, R. D., Fisher, W. H., Duan, N., Mandracchia, J. T., & Murray, D. (2010). Prevalence of criminal thinking among state prison inmates with serious mental illness. *Law & Human Behavior, 34*(4), 324–336.

Morrissey, J. & Meyer, P. (2008). *Extending Assertive Community Treatment to Criminal Justice Settings. Factsheet Series.* Delmar, NY: CMHS National GAINS Center.

Munetz, M. R., Grande, T. P., & Chambers, M. R. (2001). The incarceration of individuals with severe mental disorders. *Community Mental Health Journal, 37*(4), 361–372.

Munetz, M. R., & Griffin, P. A. (2006). Use of the Sequential Intercept Model as an approach to decriminalization of people with serious mental illness. *Psychiatric Services, 57*(4), 544–549.

Mueser, K. & MacKain, S. (2008). *Illness Management and Recovery in Criminal Justice. Factsheet Series.* Delmar, NY: CMHS National GAINS Center.

National GAINS Center for People with Co-Occurring Disorders in the Justice System (2004). *The Prevalence of Co-Occurring Mental Illness and Substance Use Disorders in Jails. Factsheet Series.* Delmar, NY: CMHS National GAINS Center.

Osher, F., Steadman, H. J., & Barr, H. (2003). A best practice approach to community reentry from jails for inmates with co-occurring disorders: The APIC model. *Crime & Delinquency, 49*(1), 79–96.

Osher, F. (2006). *Integrating Mental Health and Substance Abuse Services for Justice-Involved Persons with Co-Occurring Disorders.* Factsheet Series. Delmar NY: CMHS National GAINS Center.

Pennsylvania's Southeast Region Inter-Agency Forensic Task Force. (July 2002). *Final Report.* Harrisburg, PA: Office of Mental Health and Substance Abuse Services.

Perry, B. D. & Szalavitz, M. (2006). *The Boy Who Was Raised as a Dog and Other Stories from a Child Psychiatrist's Notebook: What Traumatized Children Can Teach Us About Loss, Love, and Healing.* Cambridge, MA: Basic Books.

Peterson, J., Skeem, J. L., Hart, E., Vidal, S., & Keith, F. (2010) Analyzing offense patterns as a function of mental illness to test the criminalization hypothesis. *Psychiatric Services, 61*(12), 1217–1222.

Plata v. Schwarzenegger, No. C01-1351 TEH, 2009 WL 2430820 (N.D. Cal. August 4, 2009).

Policy Research Associates, Inc. (2007). *Cross-Systems Mapping and Taking Action for Change.* Delmar, NY: Author.

Prins, S. J. (2011) Does transinstitutionalization explain the over-representation of people with serious mental illness in the criminal justice system? *Community Mental Health Journal, 47*, 716–722.

Skeem, J. L., & Louden, J. E. (2006). Toward evidence-based practice for probationers and parolees mandated to mental health treatment. *Psychiatric Services, 57*(3), 333–342.

Skeem, J. L., Manchak, S., & Peterson, J. K. (2011). Correctional policy for offenders with mental illness: Creating a new paradigm for recidivism reduction. *Law & Human Behavior, 35*(2), 110–126.

Steadman, H. J. (1992). Boundary spanners: A key component for the effective interactions of the justice and mental health systems. *Law & Human Behavior, 16*(1), 75–87.

Steadman, H. J., Deane, M. W., Morrissey, J. P., Westcott, M. L., Salasin, S., & Shapiro, S. (1999). A SAMHSA research initiative assessing the effectiveness of jail diversion programs for mentally ill persons. *Psychiatric Services, 50*(12), 1620–1623.

Steadman, H. J., Osher, F. C., Robbins, P. C., Case, B., & Samuels, S. (2009). Prevalence of serious mental illness among jail inmates. *Psychiatric Services, 60*(6), 761–765.

Steadman, H. J. (2011). Prison overcrowding in the context of the ACA. *Psychiatric Services, 62* (10) 1117.

Teplin, L. A. (1983). The criminalization of the mentally ill: Speculation in search of data. *Psychological Bulletin, 94*(1), 54–67.

Teplin, L. A. (1984). Criminalizing mental disorder: The comparative arrest rate of the mentally ill. *American Psychologist, 39*(7), 794–803.

Teplin, L. A. (1990). Detecting disorder: The treatment of mental illness among jail detainees. *Journal of Consulting and Clinical Psychology, 58*(2), 233–236.

Teplin, L. A., Abram, K. M., & McClelland, G. M. (1996). Prevalence of psychiatric disorders among incarcerated women. [Erratum appears in *Arch Gen Psychiatry* 1996 August; 53(8): 664]. *Archives of General Psychiatry, 53*(6), 505–512.

Torrey, E. F., Stieber, J., Ezekiel, J., Wolfe, S. E., Sharfstein, J., Noble, J. H., & Flynn, L. (1993). Criminalizing the seriously mentally ill: The abuse of jails as mental hospitals. *Innovations & Research, 2*, 11–14.

2003 APA Bronze Achievement Award. (2003). Summit County (Ohio) Alcohol, Drug Addiction, and Mental Health Services Board: A systematic approach to decriminalization of persons with mental illness. *Psychiatric Services, 54*, 1537–1538.

Vogel, W. M., Noether, C. D., & Steadman, H. J. (2007). Preparing communities for reentry of offenders with mental illness: The ACTION approach. *Journal of Offender Rehabilitation, 45,*(1/2), 167–188.

LEADERSHIP, ADMINISTRATION, MANAGEMENT

CHAPTER 31

NEW PROMISES

Specialized Dockets as Partnerships Between Treatment and the Criminal Justice System

ROBERT W. AHERN AND CHARLOTTE COLEMAN-EUFINGER

BACKGROUND

The mentally ill and substance abuse populations are frequently involved in the criminal justice system. The Los Angeles County jail, in a wing known as the Twin Towers, is the largest mental institution in the United States, housing 1,400 mentally ill patients (www.npr.org, retrieved October 3, 2011, p. 1). The Bureau of Justice Statistics noted that 56% of state prisoners and 45% of federal prisoners have current symptoms or a recent history of severe mental health problems (James & Glaze 2006). These trends in the United States are demonstrated in other regions of the world as well (Metzer, Gill, & Pettigrew 1994). Likewise, 53% of state prisoners and 45% of federal prisoners meet the criteria for drug abuse or dependency (Mumula & Karberg 2006). The *1997 Office of Justice Drug Court Report* notes, "For several decades, drug use has shaped our criminal justice system" (p. 5). Husak (2004) points out that alcohol is the substance most frequently connected to criminality, and it has been reported that 60% to 80% of people who break the law abuse recreational drugs (Hartwell (2004). Among those prisoners diagnosed with mental illness, 72% had a co-occurring substance abuse or dependency diagnosis. (Abram & Tepin, 1991). But our criminal justice system and prisons were not established to address, nor are they currently capable of addressing, the wide-ranging issues of mental illness and addiction. These vulnerable populations with the brain disorders of mental illness or addiction are also at risk in prison settings for abuse and maltreatment (*NIDA News,* May 2011, p. 1). The complex psychosocial treatment needs with concomitant legal issues calls for new methods to be established to attend to this set of realities.

SPECIALIZED DOCKETS

As a result of these concerns, mental health and drug courts, or *specialized dockets*, were begun in 1989 when a drug court was established in Miami-Dade County, Florida. Mental health courts began in the early 1980s in Indianapolis, Indiana. The assumption of such specialized dockets is that community partnerships would collaborate for continuity of care and bring about more efficacious treatment, symptom management, and a reduction of recidivism. Rather than just punishing the behavior of this population, treatment is provided under court monitoring. This includes intensive counseling, comprehensive wrap-around services, specialized treatment modalities, multi-agency treatment planning, and intensive monitoring by applying immediate sanctions. These new dockets (there are also prostitution dockets, domestic violence dockets, etc.) are not like the typical adversarial court in that a strength-oriented perspective is used as treatment is integrated with court compliance. Social services and enforcement work together to treat the mental illness or substance dependency that is at the root of this population's antisocial behavior. The Miami-Dade County report found that there was a lower rate of recidivism as well as a higher completion of probation requirements (Oetjen, Cohen, Tribble, & Suthahar 2003).

Hamilton County had the first specialized docket in Ohio, and the trend has spread throughout the state, to the point that the Ohio Supreme Court now has a Specialized Docket Section, which provides technical support in the planning and implementing of these programs. There are over 1,600 drugs courts currently operating in the United States (Wormer & Davis, 2008).

Also of note is that there are specialized dockets for both adults and adolescents. Adult drug courts can exist in Common Pleas, Municipal, and Juvenile Courts (Juvenile Courts have Family Dependency Courts that work with adults whose children have been removed due to their drug and/or alcohol dependency). There also are adolescent drug courts in many locations in the United States. As adult mental health courts are newer than adult drug courts, even more recent on the scene are adolescent mental health courts, which serve the needs of mentally ill who are in the juvenile justice system. Of note here is that probate courts, which function to provide safety to the mentally ill due to competency issues, are different from these specialized dockets because the probate system is not designed for those people who have broken the law. Specialized dockets provide judicially supervised treatment and are partnerships between substance abuse treatment services, mental health treatment services, the courts, prosecution, law enforcement, the defense bar, probation, child welfare and the recovery community. Thus, the courts mandate treatment for substance abuse or mental illness, and Marlowe, Festinger, Dugosh, Lee, and Benasutti (2007) report that there is no difference in the clinical outcomes between voluntary clients and those who are pressured by the court system to participate in treatment.

CASE STUDY: DRUG COURTS

John Doe is a 24-year-old European American male who was referred to the drug court coordinator for an assessment to determine his appropriateness for the program. He had four prior failed attempts at treatment, and reported that he had first smoked cocaine at the age of twelve, with his mother's then-boyfriend. This man also physically abused John Doe for the two years he was romantically involved with his mother. Raised in poverty by his mother, who was in and out of the criminal justice system due to her drug addiction, Mr. Doe has never met his father. He always had a close emotional bond with his mother (who began getting clean from her addiction issues when he was in his early twenties). Mr. Doe's drug use escalated so that by the time he was fifteen he met the criteria for polysubstance dependency. While he abused many drugs and alcohol, upon admission to the drug court program he reported that his drugs of choice were opiates and cocaine. He dropped out of high school at the age of 17, had various short-term jobs, but made most of his money by being a drug runner (delivering drugs for a dealer).

He contracted hepatitis C due to using dirty intravenous needles, and he had numerous girlfriends throughout his teen years and his twenties, which led to the girls' having both a miscarriage and an abortion. He currently is the father of a four-year-old son. His son's mother is incarcerated due to drug possession (she used opiates to self-medicate her untreated bipolar disorder). He and his son live together in a small apartment above a barbershop in a downtown urban location.

John Doe is an engaging young man who is intelligent and resourceful, with a desire to change the direction of his life. He is caring and musically gifted, but said that being "drug sick" (as a result of withdrawal) was so terrible that he has not been clean and sober for more than a few days since his mid-teens. He also complained of having depression and anxiety for the past ten years, which were self-medicated with street drugs but professionally untreated.

He was referred to drug court because the county Children's Services Agency had received a report that John Doe's son was seen walking alone at 10:30 p.m. in the streets near his apartment. An investigation was completed, and his son was taken into custody by the agency, alleging parental neglect. John Doe was then referred for a drug court assessment and was accepted into the program. He reported that he would do anything to get his son back, that he wanted to be a father that he never had, but that he could not tolerate the feelings of being "drug sick."

This program, a family dependency drug court, works to reunite families that have been affected due to parental drug or alcohol dependency. It is approximately a twelve-month program, with four approximate three-month distinct phases of treatment. The first phase includes weekly hearings with the judge; completion of detoxification; then beginning Intensive Outpatient Therapy (IOP) at the local treatment provider; three weekly drug screens; a weekly individual counseling session; seven Alcoholics Anonymous (AA) or Narcotics Anonymous (NA) meetings; and weekly work with his case manager to address psychosocial needs like health care (treatment of his hepatitis), employment, housing, etc. The Children's Services Agency arranged twice-a-week supervised visits with his son as well. The treatment court coordinator also met with Mr. Doe weekly, to oversee his multi-agency treatment with wrap-around services. He was also referred to a local psychiatrist for a medication assessment.

Because the drug court program was "strength based," the hearings were intended to be reward based. Applause, small rewards (movie rental certificates, gas vouchers, AA tokens, etc.) were given for compliance with court orders. The judge was trained in motivational interviewing and used these skills from the bench. Prior to each of the weekly hearings (there were thirty-five participants in drug court, in various phases of the program) an interdisciplinary case conference took place that included the judge, drug court coordinator, therapists from the local substance abuse treatment agency, representatives from the prosecutor's office, ongoing case worker from Children's Services, and the case manager.

John Doe had both success and clinical setbacks in Phase One of the program. While he did receive much praise for his involvement in therapy, he was not compliant with the required AA/NA meetings. He was given community service as a sanction, and as the compliance issues continued, he was given more graduated sanctions, an essay, and additional community service. The expected three months of Phase One took five and a half months, with multiple failed drug screens. This resulted in three weekend stays at the local county jail, with recovery homework assigned to be completed while incarcerated (reading a chapter a day of recovery-based books with a three-page essay on each chapter). While the psychiatrist and drug court team did not want to employ antidepressant medications until he had some time of being clean to assess his emotional stability, Mr. Doe did experience suicidal ideation (he had two prior attempts at suicide), and by the seventh week in the program it was decided to prescribe Mr. Doe medication for his affect disorder. Mr. Doe also asked a member of his 12-Step recovery group to be his sponsor, and this relationship became key to his future success.

At the end of five months the team discussed his compliance with court orders and treatment progress. Mr. Doe was asked to write a three-page essay on what he had learned in Phase One, which was read in court and which received applause, and he moved to Phase Two of the program. This phase continued with many of the Phase One requirements, but the hearings with the judge were moved to every other week and the intensive outpatient program was complete, so he began an aftercare program of a weekly three-hour group. During this phase his depression became more manageable and suicidal ideation abated, but symptoms of post-traumatic stress disorder (PTSD) emerged, related to the physical abuse he had experienced as a child. As a result, the treatment court coordinator made use of an evidence-informed treatment modality for trauma, Eye Movement Desensitization Reprocessing (EMDR). This work took ten sessions and was very helpful to Mr. Doe in that his PTSD was now managed quite well. Key to his recovery was this trauma-sensitive focus of the interagency treatment team and the court's focus on trauma issues that were very common in this specialized docket.

Of note is that, while each of the thirty-five participants in the drug court program had similar requirements in the four phases, the multi-agency treatment plan was tailored to meet the needs of each client. Also of note is that as the drug court program was planned, which was done in partnership with community agencies, it was decided that the treatment provided for the participants would only include evidence-informed services. An example here is that the Intensive Outpatient Program that the substance abuse agency provided used the Matrix model, an evidence-informed best practice developed by the University of California at Los Angeles (Rawson et al. 1995). A strength of this family drug court was the collaboration that took place within the community between key stakeholders. A quarterly meeting of key stakeholders took place; this was facilitated by the judge and included the executive director of the Mental Health and Recovery Board, the executive director of the Department of Child and Family Services, the sheriff, the prosecutor, and the lead attorney in the Defense Bar. Also of note is that a not-for-profit corporation was formed to support the family drug court. This organization, with trustees independent of the court staff, did fund-raising for the drug court, provided community awareness about the program, and worked with the media to communicate to the community the purposes and outcomes of this program. When Mr. Doe would receive an award for success in a hearing due to compliance with treatment and court orders, this was funded by the not-for-profit corporation.

Mr. Doe continued to do well in his supervised visits with his children. But six months into the program he had a relapse on heroin and almost died due to an overdose. He also lost his part-time job in food service at this time, was evicted from his apartment, and was involved in a misdemeanor assault (he was put on probation for this charge). As he was hospitalized for the overdose, the team worked in collaboration with him and decided that he would attend an inpatient residential program. His sanction was thus a clinical sanction (rather than a punitive judicial response like time in jail) in that he was ordered to attend inpatient care. The team sought treatment options, but due to fiscal restrictions and the assault charges there were many limitations on the alternatives available. After further searching, a facility was found and he was court-ordered and agreed to a thirty-day stay in a treatment center that would accept his Medicaid as partial funding (other funding came from the county Mental Health and Recovery Board). While in this treatment setting he was visited by the treatment court coordinator, who provided support to Mr. Doe, utilization review, and assisted in discharge planning.

Upon discharge from the inpatient program, he was integrated back into Phase Two of the program, but with higher accountability (more drug screens and increased supervision by the drug court coordinator) and increased treatment requirements. Because he came out of the program homeless, he was housed in a facility operated by the county Mental Health and Recovery Board that was designed for homeless clients who are in early recovery. This stable housing assisted him in socializing with pro-social peers, assisted him in searching for a job, and treatment staff closely monitored the facility. He also returned to his involvement with his sponsor and AA or NA groups.

What became integral for him during this time was being reunited with his mother. They had lost connection due to each of their addiction issues, but as she was now clean and sober for ten months and very active in twelve-step recovery. Their new healthy relationship galvanized his growth and his nascent recovery began to take a deeper meaning in Mr. Doe's life. They gathered around each other in their recovery journeys, and they each also grew closer to John's son, who continued in the care of the Children's Services Agency. More frequent visits with his son took place as he began to gain credibility with the treatment team.

The partnership of treatment and the courts was very important to John Doe. While prior treatment attempts had been unsuccessful, the intensive coordinated treatment, the accountability of the Court, along with his relationship with the judge from the bench, proved immeasurable in its importance. The comprehensive treatment provided to him assisted him in all aspects of his recovery. This holistic care, based on the community partnerships in the drug court, contributed to his success. While incarceration was used as a sanction while he was in the early phases, he began to be motivated by the praise and rewards that were also possible. He was treated with respect; he was supported; he was confronted. Throughout the program he kept his goals in mind: to get clean, to be in recovery, and to be reunited with his son.

In the final two phases of the drug court program, he continued to do his twelve-step work with his sponsor. His treatment plan for this time also included completing his General Education Development (GED) diploma and a twelve-week parenting class. Court staff and the counseling center where he received services collaboratively offered the parenting class. Again, an evidence-informed best practice was used, the Strengthening Families curriculum (Kumpfer, 2011). Visits with his son continued and now were unsupervised by the Children's Service Agency. Throughout the process John Doe received much positive reinforcement, which moved him in that the judge "caught me doing the right behavior." He was very active in Narcotics Anonymous meetings, chairing some meetings and developing deeply supportive sober relationships.

Mr. Doe continued to experience triggers to use drugs to alter his mood. But he used new coping methods that did not involve substances. He also struggled with obtaining viable employment. Due to his legal history he had difficulty obtaining work outside of food service, but the interagency team assisted him with obtaining volunteer work in addition to working in food service. He was aware that he would have to have both viable housing and income to be reunited with his son, who remained in foster care as he completed his treatment goals. At this point he attended individual counseling once a week, spoke with his sponsor daily, and went to five NA meetings weekly. He was only court-ordered to attend two NA meetings, but said that he was going to meetings now because he wanted to attend, not because he had to attend.

Of note is that the judge's interventions with him from the bench made use of the assumptions and language of twelve-step recovery. She reinforced living a day at a time. She discussed the first step of NA/AA with him from the bench, how his life was both unmanageable and that he was powerless to restore his life on his own. The interagency team also assisted him with twelve-step recovery, and during the latter half of his sixteen months in drug court he began incorporating recovery into his personality and everyday philosophy of life.

Near the end of his time in the drug court program, he was able to obtain a job as a forklift driver in a factory, a position with good pay and health insurance. As a result the judge approved that he find housing outside of the homeless facility in which he was living. He found a two-bedroom apartment, which met the requirements to be reunited with his son.

The first weekend in his new apartment, a knock came to his front door. When he answered the door, he discovered one of his old drug-using friends, high on crack cocaine and asking Mr. Doe to get high with him. For a moment Mr. Doe's cravings returned, the hunger for both the pleasure of getting high and the excitement of a drug dealer's life. But he thought about what he had learned from the judge, from his counselors, from his sponsor, and he refused to invite the person into his home. As soon as he asked this person to leave, he called his sponsor and they talked through what had taken place.

When he reported this at his next hearing, being in Phase Four he now only had a hearing every four weeks, he received applause and embraces from the judge and interagency team. He also began preparing his graduation essay, which he read in court to the interagency team at his next hearing. He reported that he had learned so much about himself and about recovery that gratitude was his primary feeling. After graduation, John Doe celebrated with the judge and team with cake and punch, and he received a graduation gift from the not-for-profit corporation that supports the drug court.

Within a few weeks his son left foster care and moved into his father's new apartment. Mr. Doe continued to attend three NA/AA meetings a week, and looked forward to sponsoring new people in recovery. He also attended individual counseling twice a month and worked through his deep shame and regret for all that he had done during his years of using drugs and alcohol. He had "a day at a time" of sober living ahead of him, and while it certainly would not always be easy, he could deal with life as a recovering person rather than as an active addict. Most of all, he prided himself on being the father to his son that he had never had.

OUTCOMES AND EFFICACY

While this case study illustrates a drug court case of an individual addicted to street drugs who also was diagnosed with dysthymia, the model has many similarities with other specialized dockets. Mental health courts, prostitution courts, domestic violence courts, all are multi-phased programs that are community partnerships. Of note is that there are specialized dockets for both adults and juveniles, with drug courts and mental health courts most common for the juvenile population. All include a coordination of court enforcement and psychotherapeutic programs.

Related to the above case study, empirical studies demonstrate considerable effectiveness. A meta-analysis of the literature (Belenko, Patapis, & French, 2005) compared the rates of recidivism of drug court graduates and those completing jail time and general probation. Over four years, the data demonstrated significant cost–benefit ratios. With reduced recidivism in the criminal justice system, the graduates not only saved the community the criminal justice costs, but also there was a decrease in future criminal activities, and a decrease in the use of Medicaid, mental health and recovery services, drug exposure of infants, and health problems.

Marlowe et al. (2007) write, "The effectiveness of drug courts is not a matter of conjecture. It is the product of decades of exhaustive scientific research . . . by 2006 the scientific community had concluded beyond a reasonable doubt from advanced statistical procedures that drug courts reduce criminal recidivism" (p. 1).

Positive clinical outcomes with drug courts have been demonstrated by Giacomazzi and Bell (2007, p. 309): "Our findings present ample evidence that the county drug court is experiencing considerable success. With only a few exceptions, the county drug court program, as implemented, is in compliance with benchmarks identified as a 'best practice for drug court operations.'" It has also been noted (Lutze & von Wormer 2007): "The overall success of drug courts to date is fully recognized and it is our hope that this trend will continue into further implementation" (p. 242). McNeil and Binder (2007) have reported that drug courts have much success in reducing both criminal behavior and violence of participants.

While mental health courts are newer and the research on outcomes is currently not as in-depth as drug courts, Herinckx et al. (2005) discovered the following trends. Overall crime by mental health court participants was reduced four times one year post-graduation from the program. Fifty-four percent of the participants, again one year after completion of the program, had no further arrests. Probation violations were reduced by 34%, and program graduates were 3.7 times less likely to re-offend.

CRITICISMS

In some communities, the public behavioral health system has capacity issues and struggles to meet the needs of their clients. And in some communities, the only way to access a higher level of care or more intense services is through specialized dockets, which tend to deal with the more challenging cases in a community. It is problematic, therefore, that one would have to enter the criminal justice system to access services. The solution here is to increase access for those needing more intense treatment *outside* of the criminal justice system,

Another criticism is that specialized dockets deepen rather than lessen a person's involvement with the criminal justice system. A "criminalization" of persons with mental illness or addictive behaviors could socialize individuals to antisocial norms of behavior. A judge and interagency team who take care to balance treatment with the social norms of the community and understanding of deviance can minimize this concern, especially if a strength-oriented perspective is frequently raised as a key assumption of how specialized dockets function.

Another criticism of specialized dockets is that treatment can be co-opted by the assumptions of criminal justice. With the leadership of the judge and treatment court coordinator, treatment can be seen as a function of the criminal justice system while steadfastly holding to the values of psychotherapy and counseling. There are some potential conflicts between the axiological world view of courts and treatment, but a cross-fertilization of ideas can take place, and the separate but connected realities of criminal justice and treatment can have a positive dynamic and further develop the program while better addressing the clinical needs of the participants.

A final critique is that legally, the considerable requirements of these intense and rather long programs are not necessarily the shortest routes through the criminal justice system. Some may prefer to go to jail rather than go to counseling and other types of treatment. Some may choose court sanctions over treatment as the path of least resistance. But the rewards of a life with managed mental health symptoms or a life of recovery from the devastating consequences of addiction offer much hope and promise.

CONCLUSION AND FUTURE DIRECTIONS

Substance dependency and mental illness are brain disorders. Our society has criminalized these brain disorders rather than treating them as a public health concern. Until we radically rethink the meaning of addiction and mental illness, and since they do frequently end up in the criminal justice system, drug and mental health courts are viable ways to provide treatment that is integrated with the court system. More humane treatment of these brain disorders is possible in the rapidly growing field of specialized dockets. To incarcerate a nonviolent person in many prisons is to put them at risk of being institutionalized to criminogenic ways of thinking and behaving. Many prisons have a paucity of treatment resources, and vulnerable populations can experience maltreatment.

Judges who initiate these specialized dockets have, therefore, developed problem-solving courts. As some clients are mentally ill and/or addicts who engage in criminal acts, and are not so much criminals who are mentally ill and/or addicts, a combination of treatment and enforcement is required. The marriage of the courts and treatment was long coming in that treatment providers have for years recommended group therapy or attendance at self-help meetings, only to discover that their recommendations were not heeded. With specialized dockets, treatment adherence is made more likely, and as people in society wrestle with being mentally ill, being an addict, or both, there is much promise for this new way of providing care.

REFERENCES

Abram, K., Teplin, L. (1991) Co-occurring disorders among mentally ill jail detainees. *American Psychologist,* 46(10): 1036–1045.

Belenko, S., Patapis, N., French, M. (2005). The Economic Benefits of Drug Treatment: A Critical Review of the Evidence for Policy Makers. Available at www.tresearch.org/resources/pubs_law.htm. Retrieved October 15, 2011.

Giacomazzi, A. & Bell, V. (2007). Drug court program monitoring: Lessons learned about program implementation and research methodology. *Criminal Justice Policy Review,* 18 (3): 294–312.

Hartwell, S. (2004). Comparisons of offenders with mental illness only and with offenders with dual diagnosis. *Psychiatric Services,* 55, 145–150.

Herinckx, H., Swart, S., Ama, S., Dolezal, C., & King, S. (2005). Rearrest and linkage to mental health services among clients of the Clark County Mental Health Court Program. *Psychiatric Services,* 56, 853–857.

Husak, D. (2004). The moral relevance of addiction. *Substance Use and Misuse,* 39, 399–436.

James, D., & Glaze, L. (2006). Mental health problems of prison and jail inmates. A Report of the Bureau of Justice Statistics. September.

Kumpfer, K. (Program Developer) (2011). *Strengthening Families for Parents and Youth 10–14.* Salt Lake City, Utah: University of Utah.

Lutze, F., & von Wormer, J. (2007). The nexus between drug and alcohol treatment program integrity and drug court effectiveness. *Criminal Justice Policy Review.* 18(3): 226–245.

Marlowe, D., Festinger, D., Dugosh, K., Lee, K., & Benasutti, K. (2007). Adapting judicial supervision to the risk level of drug offenders: Discharge and six-month outcomes from a perspective matching study. *Drug and Alcohol Dependency,* 88 (Suppl 2): S4–S13.

McNeil, D., Binder, R. (2007). Effectiveness of a mental health court in reducing criminal recidivism and violence. *American Journal of Psychiatry,* 164: 1395–1403.

Metzer, H., Gill, B., Pettigrew, M. (1994). *The Prevalence of Psychiatric Morbidity Among Adults Age 16–64 Living in Private Households in Great Britain.* London: Office of Population Censuses and Surveys.

Mumula, C., & Karberg, I. (2006). *Drug and Dependence: State and Federal Prisoners.* Washington, DC: Department of Justice, Office of Justice Programs, Bureau of Justice Statistics.

Oetjen, J., Cohen, J., Tribble, N., & Suthahar, J. (2003). The Sacramento dependency drug court: Development and outcomes. *Child Maltreatment,* 12(2): 161–171.

Rawson, R., Shoptaw, S., Obert, J., McCann, M., Hasson, A., Marinelli-Casey, P., et al. (1995). An intensive outpatient approach for cocaine abuse: The Matrix Model. *Journal of Substance Abuse Treatment,* 12(2): 117–127.

THE USE OF TECHNOLOGY IN A COMMUNITY MENTAL HEALTH SETTING

JESSICA LEVY AUSLANDER

A s technology advances, we will be continually faced with the issue of deciding what types of technology to incorporate into our personal and professional lives. We use technology to access information, facilitate communication, and improve efficiency on a daily basis. For those who work in the service of others, the use of technology raises unique professional, legal, and ethical questions. As various professional governing bodies struggle to establish best practices and guidelines, we must recognize that technology is constantly evolving, requiring us to periodically analyze and take responsibility for our own technology use. This chapter will address a few basic issues surrounding technology faced by new professionals in community mental health work, such as technology use by consumers, managing your digital reputation, technology-enhanced communication, and distance therapy.

Communication using phone, cell phone, email, or other Internet methods will be referred to as *distance communication*, and is not to be confused with *distance therapy*. Eysenbach (2001) defined a similar term, *e-health*, as "an emerging field in the intersection of medical informatics, public health and business, referring to health services and information delivered or enhanced through the Internet and related technologies. In a broader sense, the term characterizes not only a technical development, but also a state-of-mind, a way of thinking, an attitude, and a commitment for networked, global thinking, to improve health care locally, regionally, and worldwide by using information and communication technology." With the sophistication of information technology, the medical field has developed the electronic medical record (EMR) and other tools to facilitate communication between physicians and their patients, improve accuracy and efficiency of tasks such as documentation and ordering prescriptions or procedures, and enhance the flow of information both within and between medical networks and providers. This advancement in the medical field has the potential to enhance the interaction among physicians, psychiatrists, and community mental health providers to facilitate more effective communication and care for consumers.

TECHNOLOGY USE BY CONSUMERS

Studies of the use of the Internet by consumers of both medical and mental health services are becoming more common. There is an increasing body of literature that addresses the intersection of technology and healthcare. Trends include using the Internet to access information about diagnoses and treatment, using Internet-based methods to communicate with providers, and using the Internet to research the credentials and backgrounds of potential providers. Wald, Dube, and Anthony (2007) described a "triangulation" of the consumer, the provider and the Internet. This concept of triangulation emphasizes the extent to which technology can affect the dynamic between the consumer and provider. While there is a very real concern that the consumer is accessing incorrect information, this dynamic also provides an opportunity for the provider to work with the person to discuss the quality of information and help them be better informed about their treatment options. A person's ability to access information prior to their appointment and discuss it with their provider may help them feel more empowered and more like a partner in their care, presenting a shift in the perceived power of provider over the consumer. It is important to note that while the Internet in being used more and more by consumers, Sillence et al. found that the provider was still seen as the primary source of information (2007).

In 2006, Powell and Clarke found that 18 percent of all Internet users had accessed information related to mental health. This was higher among populations with a history of mental illness or who were currently experiencing symptoms. It is advisable for providers in the community mental health setting to be aware of the websites that are being accessed by consumers and their families. This can be accomplished by performing a variety of searches on diagnoses or symptoms using different search engines. In doing so, one can find thousands of websites that provide a wealth of information that may or may not be accurate. It is also easy to find online support groups, networks, and websites that even promote unhealthy lifestyles in connection to specific diagnoses. A strong example is the collection of websites, blogs, and online support groups that are referred to as "Pro-Ana" (pro-anorexia) and "Pro-Mia" (pro-bulimia). While some claim to be support networks for those suffering from an eating disorder, many state that it is a lifestyle choice that should be respected, not a diagnosis, and advise others on how to lose extreme amounts of weight and maintain drastically low body-weights. Other examples include "self help" websites that instruct readers how to sober up quickly or how to hide signs of alcohol and chemical dependence and abuse. One approach to assisting people in accessing correct information is to develop a list of websites that you or your agency leadership have evaluated and approved for distribution to consumers and their families. However, keep in mind that the Internet is fluid and pages are added, deleted, and changed every second, all over the world, so any list you provide should be rechecked on a regular basis to insure that the websites are still appropriate and the links are still functional.

Beckjord, et al. (2007) reported that in 2003, seven percent of Internet users had communicated with a health provider online; this number increased to 10 percent in 2005. They also found that those who had "more years of education, who lived in a metro area, who reported poorer health status, or who had a personal history of cancer" were more likely to have engaged in online communication with a healthcare provider this does not include telemedicine, which is addressed later in this chapter). This increase shows the need for providers to become aware of the progressing expectations of consumers and their families in regard to technologically enhanced communication, and to address issues of access and policy within their organizations.

Potential and current consumers and their families may also use the Internet to search for care providers. If your agency has a website, not only do you want to ensure that the information presented about you and your services is accurate, but you will want to advocate that it is accessible and appropriate for your audience. For example, many mental health-related websites are written by professionals with advanced degrees. While the information may be excellent, it may be above the reading level of the general public. Microsoft Word has the ability to analyze text and calculate the Flesch-Kincaid reading level. This metric applies a formula created by Rudolph Flesch and John P. Kincaid that incorporates the average number of words per sentence and syllables per word used in a text. The resulting score corresponds to the American academic grade levels 1–16 (first grade through collegiate postgraduate level). By enabling the "readability statistics" option, you can determine the reading-grade level of your text. To do this in Microsoft Word, open the spelling and grammar check function, click "Options," then click "Show readability statistics." Most newspapers are at the high-school level (9–12), but, depending on the population served, it may be better to have text at a lower reading level. Keep in mind that specific words can advance the reading level, so it may be helpful to analyze the text with and without technical terms, such as the names of diagnoses or medications. Another aspect of website accessibility involves user options that allow consumers to increase or decrease font sizes or disable graphics (a "text-only" option). It can be helpful to have a section of your website designed for consumers and their families, and another area designed for other stakeholders.

YOUR DIGITAL FOOTPRINT

Those who work in the service of others in either public or private settings and who are licensed or credentialed must hold themselves to a higher standard of ethical scrutiny. It is the responsibility of the individual to be vigilant in protecting his or her reputation both online and offline. Greysen, Kind, and Chretien (2010) discussed the impact of an individual's "digital footprint" on their own professional reputation, as well as how it could impact their professional community as a whole. Regulatory bodies throughout the world and a myriad of professions struggle with defining appropriate Internet use for their professionals. Consequences of questionable technology use or inappropriate material posted on social media sites can range from loss of a job, to loss or suspension of one's license, even to legal action. These actions can also have a ripple effect and tarnish the reputation of the organization or profession with which the individual in question was affiliated. Therefore, it is vital that professionals be vigilant in creating and maintaining a positive online presence.

There are no universally adopted standards for the non-clinical use of technology in the professional setting. Always refer to your profession's code of ethics and any policies put in place by your agency. While there are companies who specialize in online "reputation management," there are several additional things professionals can do to protect themselves in terms of their web presence, communication methods, and the use of personal electronic devices. It is important to keep in mind that everything posted or published on the Internet is considered permanent; even though it may not be actively online, it can still be retrieved electronically. The best way to maintain a positive online presence is to be very conservative about what you post and to constantly monitor what is posted about you. For those who are very active online, an initial audit of online activity can be daunting. A quick way to begin is to enter your name into a search engine and go through as many results as you can. Repeat this with variations of your name (and maiden name if applicable), and with different search engines. This should be done on a regular basis to catch any obvious errors or misrepresentations. It is also helpful to pay attention to search results that do not directly apply to you. If someone has the same or similar name as you and they have a less-than-appealing web presence, educate yourself so that you can be prepared to explain the coincidence to others.

Another benefit to conducting regular web searches on your own name is to determine what information has been made public about you. Many websites now exist that allow consumers to rate their providers or choose potential providers from a public directory. The information provided in these unsolicited directories is often incorrect and can cause frustration for potential consumers and their families. Other sites, such as www.whitepages.com, specialize in publishing personal information that can include full name, address, phone numbers, email addresses, and even family members' information. If you do find information published about you that is incorrect, contact the site administrator immediately to have it corrected or removed.

Many licensing boards and professional organizations provide online directories of their members to promote the profession or provide transparency to the public regarding the status of providers' licenses. Check with any applicable boards' websites to determine how your information is presented online and to ensure that it is accurate. If you have any former employers who list staff on their websites, also ensure that your information has been removed from their site if you no longer have a professional relationship.

One of the most controversial aspects of professional web presence is the use of social networking. While many companies have policies that prohibit employees from accessing social networking sites during work hours, others, such as some public school districts, have prohibited their employees from holding accounts on sites like Facebook to prevent inappropriate social interaction or the portrayal of a negative image of the organization. If you choose to engage in social media, review the privacy policies and your personal account settings on a regular basis. If your personal page includes photos, make sure they are tasteful and ones that you would want other professionals or clients to see. Even if you have strict privacy settings, it is always possible for someone who has approved access to your page to show it to another individual who is not on your personal network.

While universities and organizations provide their students and employees with a standardized email address, most people have a personal email address. The personal email address should not be used as a primary method of communication with consumers, as it is probably not protected or encrypted. Many organizations have developed policies restricting employees from accessing personal email accounts at the workplace due to security concerns. While it is wise to have a secondary email account as a backup, if it will be used for professional purposes at any point, choose an email address and carrier that sounds professional and legitimate. This is particularly crucial when initially applying for positions if your university email address will expire shortly after graduation. A typical acceptable format is firstname.lastname@domain.com or firstinitial.lastname@domain.com. Avoid nicknames, references to hobbies, etc., in your email address. When choosing your domain provider, research security features, document-download capability, and the use of advertising.

As mobile phone technology advances, more and more users are upgrading to "smartphone" devices that have voice, text, and web capabilities. It is important to keep in mind that communication using cell phones is not considered secure, as they can be easily overheard by others and the signals picked up by other phones and devices. These devices are also designed to be replaced every one to three years, so it is not advisable to store important data directly on the phones; rather, consider them access points to more reliable sources. Be sure that your phone is locked with at least one password in case it is picked up by another person, and always be mindful of your ringer and notification settings while in the workplace. Many smartphones allow users to set up a "work" profile where you can set a generic ringtone and not have personal application icons displayed on the screen.

As smartphone technology advances, so does its potential as a therapy-enhancing tool. Consumers who use smartphones could use them to track appointments, save key contacts in the event of crisis or emergency, and send and receive email and other forms of electronic messaging. Providers can use this opportunity to reinforce the work being done together in the office by sending handouts or reminders, or checking in with the consumer between sessions. Users of smartphones and similar electronic devices also have access to thousands of applications (commonly referred to as "apps") to expand their device's capabilities. A quick search for mental health applications will lead the user to thousands of possible choices (free or for a small fee) that serve as references, self-tests, and apps designed specifically to support certain diagnoses. Consumers can download entire workbooks written by experts, or track daily behaviors or moods. The quality of these varies, so it may be helpful to discuss this with a consumer or family member if they use this technology.

TECHNOLOGY-ENHANCED COMMUNICATION

One of the most common uses of technology is to facilitate communication. Phones, cell phones, and email have become part of our daily lives, both personally and professionally. As Kane and Sands (1998) emphasized in a paper written for the American Medical Informatics Association, technology-enhanced communication should improve a caregiver's relationship to a client, not make things confusing or complicated. AMIA also recognized that it would not be realistic to set universal recommendations, as every care organization is unique. As a new professional entering a community mental health agency, you should familiarize yourself with your agency's policies regarding the use of phone, email, and other distance communication technologies with clients and professionals from other agencies. If your organization does not have any such policies, advocate that this area be explored and written policies created to protect yourself and your clients. Policies regarding communication methods should also be communicated in your professional-disclosure statement.

Factors to consider in creating your communication policy can include:

- If contacted by a professional from another agency by phone or email, how will these requests be handled, and how will confidentiality be maintained?
- Does my organization's technology infrastructure have the necessary security features in place?
- Does my email have a disclaimer on the bottom addressing confidentiality and an emergency plan?

- Does my voicemail clearly state the hours I am available by phone, and what to do in my absence or in case of emergency?
- How will I handle phone calls from clients between office visits if they are calling for reasons other than scheduling an appointment?
- How will I handle emails from clients?
- Will I allow my cell phone number to be given out, or is there an agency cell phone for after-hours use?
- Does my agency have legal counsel available if I have questions?

DISTANCE THERAPY

The terms *distance therapy*, *distance counseling*, and *telemedicine* all refer to providing treatment or interventions using technology when not face-to-face with the consumer. For the purposes of including all disciplines in this chapter, these will be generally referred to as *distance care*. This should not be confused with computer-assisted therapies, which use computer technology to either complement traditional therapy to enhance efficacy or are used with little interaction with a therapist to reduce therapist time (Wright et al., 2002, 2005).

While it is easy to think of anything involving technology as modern and advanced, the concept of distance care is not a new one. Wootton (2001) noted an early example of doctor–patient communication using ship-to-shore radio to give medical advice to captains at sea. In 1958, the first American suicide prevention telephone hotline was created at the Los Angeles Suicide Prevention Center (Spencer-Thomas & Jahn, 2012). As communication technology has advanced, so has the number of ways it can be used to facilitate medical and mental health care.

There are both benefits and disadvantages to engaging in distance care that have been documented across professions. One of the primary advantages is that it can provide access to care for traditionally underserved populations (Riemer-Reiss, 2000). The United States Department of Health and Human Services (HHS), through their Health Resources and Services Administration, provides an online directory of Health Professional Shortage Areas (HPSA) (http://hpsafind.hrsa.gov/HPSASearch.aspx). This directory is updated daily and provides information about shortages in primary medical care, dental care, or mental health care by state and county, including island territories. For example, as of December 14, 2011, they estimated 88.9 million people living in Mental Health HPSAs. Using a ratio of one mental health practitioner per 10,000 people, it is estimated that 5,818 additional practitioners would be needed to meet the current need.

Providing access to underserved populations is not just about spanning a geographical distance. Other barriers to accessing care that could be addressed by distance care include persons suffering from severe physical or mental illness who are not comfortable or able to leave their homes to attend regular appointments in an office setting. Others may not be comfortable with face-to-face social interaction, or would benefit more from using the written word via email, chat, or other Web-based communication methods than speaking. Stigma is another barrier to accessing care that could be greatly reduced by distance methods. If an individual is concerned about the stigma associated with attending appointments at a mental health agency, that person may be more comfortable accessing the care they need in the privacy of their home.

Another benefit of distance care is that it can be cost-effective for both the consumer and the provider. Medicaid covers telemedicine and telehealth services, and over the past few years, several states have passed legislation to require that these services be covered by private insurers as well. This allows providers to be reimbursed just as they would be for providing traditional office care, but with less administrative cost. Also, the consumer does not have the expense of transportation or extra time spent commuting and waiting at an office.

While distance care can provide many benefits for consumers and their caregivers, there are also some risks. Distance care is not appropriate for every consumer, and a professional trained in distance methods should appropriately screen and provide a distance-specific disclosure statement educating consumers of the benefits and potential risks. Risks can vary by distance method used. For example, if conducting a counseling session on the phone, both the counselor and the consumer need to be aware of the absence of nonverbal cues. Other risks include security (and therefore confidentiality) issues, and reliability of the technological infrastructure used.

The primary barrier to accessing distance care is a lack of resources. While distance care can be very beneficial to serving a rural population, there must first be the technological infrastructure to support the methods used. While a provider may prefer to use video conferencing, it may not be possible if the consumer is in a remote area that does not have high-speed Internet access, or if they do not have access to a computer that can support such a technology.

Another major resource that is lacking is the provider. Providing distance care is not as simple as just using a phone or computer instead of being in the same room with a person. Individual professions have developed or are in the process of developing policies and credentials for providing distance care. These address the legal issues (for example: if you are licensed in one state, can you provide services to someone in a different state?), the ethical concerns, and the best practices in adapting service provision to distance methods. Vitacca et al. (2009) developed the following core competencies (Table 32.1) in implementing telemedicine or other e-health services.

Anyone providing distance care must first hold a clinical license in their field, but some professions have developed additional training and credentials for those looking to expand their scope of practice. For physicians, this varies by state, as more are starting to recognize the need for services. This has already been recognized at the national level; in 2011, the Centers for Medicare and Medicaid Services made providing telemedicine services to rural area hospitals easier by removing the rule that required that physicians providing telemedicine services must be credentialed by the receiving hospital (Lowes, 2011). This makes it easier for experts from larger hospital systems to provide consultation to smaller hospitals that may not have access to highly specialized providers. The American Medical Association (AMA) Code of Medical Ethics also addressed the practice of physicians' contributing to health-related websites in Code 5.027–Use of Health-Related Online Sites (AMA, 2003).

Regarding the use of email to communicate with patients, the AMA incorporated Opinion 5.026–The Use of Electronic Mail into the AMA Code of Medical Ethics (2002). The AMA supports the use of email to enhance the physician–patient relationship, but outlined a series of precautions that should be taken when engaging in email communication (Table 32.2).

They also established specific guidelines for physicians using email for patient and practice related communications, as well as a separate list to address administrative concerns (see Tables 32.3 and 32.4).

Table 32.1 Core Competencies to Implement E-Health and Telemedicine

Patient-centred care	Interviewing and communicating effectively
	Assisting behavior change
	Supporting self-management
	Using a proactive approach
Partnering	Partnering with patients
	Partnering with other providers
	Partnering with communities
Quality improvement	Measuring care delivery and outcomes
	Learning and adapting to change
	Translating evidence into practice
Information and communication Technology	Designing and using patient registries
	Using computers
	Communicating with partners
Public health perspective	Providing population-based care
	Systems thinking
	Working across the disease continuum
	Working in primary care-led systems

Vitacca, M., Mazzu, M., and Scalvini, S. (2009). Socio-technical and organizational challenges to wider e-Health implementation. *Chronic Respiratory Disease* 6:91–97. doi:10.1177/1479972309102805

Table 32.2 AMA Code of Medical Ethics, Opinion 5.026

(1) E-mail correspondence should not be used to establish a patient–physician relationship. Rather, e-mail should supplement other, more personal, encounters.

(2) When using e-mail communication, physicians hold the same ethical responsibilities to their patients as they do during other encounters. Whenever communicating medical information, physicians must present the information in a manner that meets professional standards. To this end, specialty societies can provide specific guidance as to the appropriateness of offering specialty care or advice through e-mail communication.

(3) Physicians should engage in e-mail communication with proper notification of e-mail's inherent limitations. Such notice should include information regarding potential breaches of privacy and confidentiality, difficulties in validating the identity of the parties, and delays in responses. Patients should have the opportunity to accept these limitations prior to the communication of privileged information. Disclaimers alone cannot absolve physicians of the ethical responsibility to protect patients' interests.

(4) Proper notification of e-mail's inherent limitations can be communicated during a prior patient encounter or in the initial e-mail communication with a patient. This is similar to checking with a patient about the privacy or security of a particular fax machine prior to faxing sensitive medical information. If a patient initiates e-mail communication, the physician's initial response should include information regarding the limitations of e-mail and ask for the patient's consent to continue the e-mail conversation. Medical advice or information specific to the patient's condition should not be transmitted prior to obtaining the patient's authorization. (I, IV, VI, VIII) (Opinion 5.026, AMA Code of Ethics, 2002).

The American Counseling Association Code of Ethics addresses similar aspects of technology use, but covers a wider base of technological applications and their uses (Table 32.5).

Professional counselors, social workers, couple and family therapists, psychologists, psychiatrists, and other independently licensed mental health care providers can attend specialized training and obtain the Distance Credentialed Counselor (DCC) credential, which is recognized by the National Board for Certified Counselors (NBCC). This is a five-year credential that must be maintained through continuing education. As this is a rapidly evolving field, it is predicted that other professions will develop distance-specific guidelines and credentials. Professional organizations and journals are developing to specifically address the intersection of health, mental health, and technology, such as the International Society for Mental Health Online (ISMHO), an interdisciplinary, international organization for mental health professionals.

As the fields of health and mental health expand, it is expected that technology will continue to enhance and facilitate professional growth and consumer access to services. At the least, in order to meet or anticipate the needs of current and future consumers, providers will need to incorporate technology-related topics into their professional development and continuing-education

Table 32.3 AMA Communication Guidelines When Using Email

1. Establish turnaround time for messages. Exercise caution when using e-mail for urgent matters.
2. Inform patient about privacy issues.
3. Patients should know who besides addressee processes messages during addressee's usual business hours and during addressee's vacation or illness.
4. Whenever possible and appropriate, physicians should retain electronic and/or paper copies of e-mails communications with patients.
5. Establish types of transactions (prescription refill, appointment scheduling, etc.) and sensitivity of subject matter (HIV, mental health, etc.) permitted over e-mail.
6. Instruct patients to put the category of transaction in the subject line of the message for filtering: prescription, appointment, medical advice, billing question.
7. Request that patients put their name and patient identification number in the body of the message.
8. Configure automatic reply to acknowledge receipt of messages.
9. Send a new message to inform patient of completion of request.
10. Request that patients use autoreply feature to acknowledge reading clinicians message.
11. Develop archival and retrieval mechanisms.
12. Maintain a mailing list of patients, but do not send group mailings where recipients are visible to each other. Use blind copy feature in software.
13. Avoid anger, sarcasm, harsh criticism, and libelous references to third parties in messages.
14. Append a standard block of text to the end of e-mail messages to patients, which contains the physician's full name, contact information, and reminders about security and the importance of alternative forms of communication for emergencies.
15. Explain to patients that their messages should be concise.
16. When e-mail messages become too lengthy or the correspondence is prolonged, notify patients to come in to discuss or call them.
17. Remind patients when they do not adhere to the guidelines.
18. For patients who repeatedly do not adhere to the guidelines, it is acceptable to terminate the e-mail relationship.

Table 32.4 AMA Guidelines for Using Email for Administrative Concerns

1. Develop a patient–clinician agreement for the informed consent for the use of e-mail. This should be discussed with and signed by the patient and documented in the medical record. Provide patients with a copy of the agreement. Agreement should contain the following:
2. Terms in communication guidelines (stated above).
3. Provide instructions for when and how to convert to phone calls and office visits.
4. Describe security mechanisms in place.
5. Hold harmless the health care institution for information loss due to technical failures.
6. Waive encryption requirement, if any, at patient's insistence.
7. Describe security mechanisms in place including:
8. Using a password-protected screen saver for all desktop workstations in the office, hospital, and at home.
9. Never forwarding patient-identifiable information to a third party without the patient's express permission.
10. Never using patient's e-mail address in a marketing scheme.
11. Not sharing professional e-mail accounts with family members.
12. Not using unencrypted wireless communications with patient-identifiable information.
13. Double-checking all "To" fields prior to sending messages.
14. Perform at least weekly backups of e-mail onto long-term storage. Define long-term as the term applicable to paper records.
15. Commit policy decisions to writing and electronic form.

Table 32.5 From the American Counseling Association (ACA) Code of Ethics, Relating to Technology

A.12. Technology Applications

A.12.a. Benefits and Limitations

Counselors inform clients of the benefits and limitations of using information technology applications in the counseling process and in business/ billing procedures. Such technologies include but are not limited to computer hardware and software, telephones, the World Wide Web, the Internet, online assessment instruments, and other communication devices.

A.12.b. Technology-Assisted Services

When providing technology-assisted distance counseling services, counselors determine that clients are intellectually, emotionally, and physically capable of using the application and that the application is appropriate for the needs of clients.

A.12.c. Inappropriate Services

When technology-assisted distance counseling services are deemed inappropriate by the counselor or client, counselors consider delivering services face to face.

A.12.d. Access

Counselors provide reasonable access to computer applications when providing technology-assisted distance counseling services.

A.12.e. Laws and Statutes

Counselors ensure that the use of technology does not violate the laws of any local, state, national, or international entity, and observe all relevant statutes.

A.12.f. Assistance

Counselors seek business, legal, and technical assistance when using technology applications, particularly when the use of such applications crosses state or national boundaries.

(continued)

Table 32.5 Continued

A.12.g. Technology and Informed Consent

As part of the process of establishing informed consent, counselors do the following:

1. Address issues related to the difficulty of maintaining the confidentiality of electronically transmitted communications.
2. Inform clients of all colleagues, supervisors, and employees, such as informational technology (IT) administrators, who might have authorized or unauthorized access to electronic transmissions.
3. Urge clients to be aware of all authorized or unauthorized users, including family members and fellow employees who might have access to any technology clients may use in the counseling process.
4. Inform clients of pertinent legal rights and limitations governing the practice of a profession over state lines or international boundaries.
5. Use encrypted Web sites and e-mail communications to help ensure confidentiality when possible.
6. When the use of encryption is not possible, counselors notify clients of this fact and limit electronic transmissions to general communications that are not client-specific.7. Inform clients if and for how long archival storage of transaction records is maintained.8. Discuss the possibility of technology failure and alternate methods of service delivery.9. Inform clients of emergency procedures, such as calling 911 or a local crisis hotline, when the counselor is not available.10. Discuss time zone differences, local customs, and cultural or language differences that might impact service delivery.11. Inform clients when technology assisted distance counseling services are not covered by insurance. (*See A.2.*)

A.12.h. Sites on the World Wide Web

Counselors maintaining sites on the World Wide Web (the Internet) do the following:

1. Regularly check that electronic links are working and professionally appropriate.
2. Establish ways clients can contact the counselor in case of technology failure.
3. Provide electronic links to relevant state licensure and professional certification boards to protect consumer rights and facilitate addressing ethical concerns.
4. Establish a method for verifying client identity.
5. Obtain the written consent of the legal guardian or other authorized legal representative prior to rendering services in the event the client is a minor child, an adult who is legally incompetent, or an adult incapable of giving informed consent.
6. Strive to provide a site that is accessible to persons with disabilities.
7. Strive to provide translation capabilities for clients who have a different primary language while also addressing the imperfect nature of such translations.
8. Assist clients in determining the validity and reliability of information found on the World Wide Web and other technology applications.

---

regimens. The challenge will be to go beyond simply learning what others have already done with technology; providers must explore new ways to use technology in the practice of mental health. Technology, used in line with a profession's code of ethics or adopted professional standards, can be a powerful tool for facilitating interdisciplinary collaboration among other professionals, community members, and consumers. Mental health providers can also serve as advocates for consumers on issues of public policy related to access, standards, and regulation, as society will also continue to struggle with the questions raised by technology's rapid progress.

CONCLUSION

This chapter provided a brief overview of different aspects of technology and its impact on mental health care providers and consumers. It is important to make the distinction between the use of technology to enhance current practices (distance communication) and the use of technology to provide services (distance therapy or distance care). As technology progresses, it is vital for the mental health professional to remain vigilant about their own digital footprint as well as how advancements impact the lives of consumers and their families. It is also imperative that professionals remain current with the changes in their field's codes of ethics or professional standards as well as with any local laws in regard to the use of technology with consumers and the general public. By staying current with emerging technologies, mental health professionals can also find opportunities to revolutionize how we collaborate with each other and deliver services to those in need, and likely underserved.

REFERENCES

American Counseling Association Code of Ethics (2005). Available at http://www.counseling.org/Resources/CodeOfEthics/TP/Home/CT2.aspx. Accessed December 30, 2012.

American Medical Association. (2003). Ethical Guidelines for the Use of Electronic Mail between Patients and Physicians, adopted December 2002, *American Journal of Bioethics. 3*(3). Doi: 10.1162:152651603322874780

Beckjord, E.B., Finney, L., Squiers, L., Arora, N.K., Volckmann, L., Moser, R.P., and Hesse, B. (2007). Use of the Internet to communicate with health care providers in the United States: Estimates from the 2003 and 2005 Health Information National Trends Surveys (HINTS). *Journal of Medical Internet Research* July–September: 9(3):e20. doi: 10/2196/jmir.9.3.e20.

Eysenbach, G. (2001). What is e-health? *Journal of Medical Internet Research* 3(2):e20. doi:10.2196/jmir.3.2.e20.

Greysen, S.R., Kind, T. and Chretien, K.C. (2010). Online professionalism and the mirror of social media. *Journal of General Internal Medicine* 25(11):122–1229. doi: 10.1007/s11606-010-1447-1.

KaneB., and Sands D.Z. (1998). Guidelines for the clinical use of electronic mail with patients. The AMIA Internet working group, task force on guidelines for the use of clinic–patient electronic mail. *Journal of the American Medical Information Association* 5(1):104–111.

Lowes, R . (2011). CMS removes credentialing barrier to telemedicine. *Medscape Medical News*. May 3. Accessed December 30, 2011, at http://www.medscape.com/viewarticle/742028.

Powell, J., and Clarke, A. (2006). Internet information-seeking in mental health: Population survey. *The British Journal of Psychiatry* 189:273–277. doi: 10.1192/bjp/bp.105.01731.

Riemer-Reiss, M.L. (2000). Utilizing distance technology for mental health counseling. *Journal of Mental Health Counseling* 22(3) July: 189–203.

Sillence, E., Briggs, P., Harris, P.R., and Fishwick, L. (2007). How do patients evaluate and make use of online health information? *Social Science and Medicine* 64(9) May: 1853–1862. doi: 10.1016/j.socscimed.2007.01.012.

Spencer-Thomas, S., and Jahn, D. (2012) Tracking a movement: U.S. milestones in suicide prevention. *Suicide and Life-Threatening Behavior. 42*(1), 78–85.

Vitacca, M., Mazzu, M., and Scalvini, S. (2009). Socio-technical and organizational challenges to wider e-Health implementation. *Chronic Respiratory Disease* 6:91–97. doi:10.1177/1479972309102805.

Wald, H.S., Dube, C.E., and Anthony, D.C. (2007). Untangling the Web—The impact of Internet use on health care and the physician–patient relationship. *Patient Education and Counseling* 68(3) November: 218–224. doi: 10.1016/j.pec.2007.05.016.

Wootton, R. (2001). Telemedicine: Clinical review. *British Medical Journal* 323:557–560.

Wright, J., Wright, A.S., Salmon, P., Beck, A.T., Kuykendall, J., Goldsmith, L.J, et al. (2002). Development and initial testing of a multimedia program for computer-assisted cognitive therapy. *American Journal of Psychotherapy* 56(1):76–86.

Wright, J., Wright, A.S., Albano, A.M., Basco, M.R., Goldsmith, L.J., Raffield, T., et al. (2005). Computer-assisted cognitive therapy for depression: Maintaining efficacy while reducing therapy time. *American Journal of Psychiatry* 162:1158–1164. doi: 10.1176/appi.ajp.162.6.1158.

CHAPTER 33

ESTABLISHING A COMPREHENSIVE, CONTINUOUS, INTEGRATED SYSTEM OF CARE FOR PERSONS WITH CO-OCCURRING CONDITIONS

KENNETH R. YEAGER AND KENNETH MINKOFF

INTRODUCTION

The term *co-occurring conditions* in this chapter is used to refer to people of any age with any combination of any mental health and any substance use or addictive problem, including gambling, Internet porn, sex, shopping, or nicotine dependence. Kohn, Saxena, Levav, and Laraceno (2004) reported a high prevalence of co-occurring conditions worldwide, with as many as seven to ten million persons in the United States suffering from combined mental illness and substance use disorder (DHHS, 2003). While definitions vary, the term *severe and persistent mental illness* generally includes the conditions of: schizophrenia, bipolar disorder, severe and recurrent depression, post-traumatic stress disorder, and other associated anxiety conditions, including severe obsessive-compulsive disorder. Substance use conditions include alcohol, cannabis, cocaine, opiate, amphetamine, and sedative hypnotic use and dependence, as abuse of these mood-altering substances may adversely affect the functioning, stability, and behaviors of those with severe and persistent mental illness.

Two decades of research in a wide variety of settings, and with a variety of populations ranging from adolescents and families involved within the court system (e.g., criminal justice or child protection) to adult populations with severe and persistent mental illness, has demonstrated a need to develop approaches to care that integrate both mental health and substance-use conditions. Increasingly, researchers and care providers are recognizing individuals with co-occurring conditions as a population with higher costs and poorer outcomes within multiple domains of care. In a 2002 report to Congress, the Substance Abuse and Mental Health Services

Administration (SAMHSA) acknowledged that "dual diagnosis is an expectation, rather than an exception" in all settings (Kohn et al., 2004).

In recent years, it has been increasingly clear that the issues and experiences of persons with co-occurring mental health and substance-use disorder conditions are relevant to multiple other types of issues and conditions, and that the strategies that have been learned for mental health and substance-use disorders apply to all types of complex needs among persons seeking care. Thus, we need to consider the problems faced by individuals with combinations of health and behavioral health conditions, behavioral health and developmental disability/brain injury/cognitive disabilities, trauma with all types of conditions, as well as co-occurring "social conditions" such as homelessness, criminal-justice involvement, child welfare issues, unemployment/disability, and so on. In this chapter, we propose a general systems approach. While we mostly focus on co-occurring mental health/substance abuse, this approach can be, and is being applied, to systems, programs, families, and individuals addressing all types of overlapping and complex needs.

ESTIMATES OF THE PROBLEM

Numerous studies have demonstrated a strong link between mental illness and substance-use conditions. The question of the current prevalence of the problem is also well understood. According to National Health Survey Data in 2009, there were an estimated 45.1 million adults aged 18 or older in the United States with "any mental illness" in the past year. This represents 19.9% of all adults in this country. Among adults aged 18 or older in 2009, the percentage having serious mental illness (SMI) in the past year was 4.8% (11.0 million adults) (SAMHSA, 2010, p. 9).

Within the 45.1 million adults aged 18 or older with any mental illness in the past year, 19.7% (8.9 million adults) met criteria for substance dependence or abuse in that period, compared with 6.5% (11.9 million adults) among those who did not have mental illness in the past year. Of the 11.0 million adults aged 18 or older with SMI in the past year, 25.7% also had past-year substance dependence or abuse compared with 6.5% of adults who did not have mental illness (SAMSHA 2010, p. 33).

Compounding this already prominent public health issue is the fact that many with severe mental illness and substance-use conditions remain untreated. Estimations of this lack of treatment have been documented in as many as 37 studies examining service utilization. The most frequently referenced percentage associated with schizophrenia was 32.2%. Depression demonstrated a 53.6% treatment gap. Dysthymia demonstrated a 56.0% treatment gap; bipolar disorder demonstrated a 50.2% treatment gap; and generalized anxiety disorder demonstrated a 57.5% treatment gap, with the average gap between onset of symptoms and active treatment estimated to be as high as 30 years. Obsessive-compulsive disorder demonstrated a 57.3% treatment gap. Furthermore, alcohol abuse and dependence presented the most significant treatment gap, with an estimated 78.1% gap. While the estrangement between prevalence of conditions and the number of those receiving treatment varies greatly around the world, it can be assumed that the numbers may be even higher than suspected, as gathering data from community-based data programming, including data from developing countries, where services are few and far between, may even raise the level of this already enormous treatment gap (Kohn et al., 2004).

The landmark study "Comorbidity of mental conditions with alcohol and other drug abuse: Results from the Epidemiological Catchment Area (ECA) Study" (Regier et al., 1990) highlighted the prevalence of comorbid mental illness and substance-use conditions in the United States. This study indicated that 47% of persons with active schizophrenia have experienced an active substance-use disorder in their lifetime, with 34% reporting an alcohol use disorder and approximately 28% reporting use of other drugs; specifically cannabis and cocaine as frequently referenced as drugs of choice. Persons with active mood conditions demonstrated a 32% lifetime prevalence of comorbid substance-use disorder, with bipolar conditions occurring at nearly twice the rate of major depression: 57% versus 27%. Within this population, alcohol was reported to be the most frequently abused substance. Within the bipolar disorder population, abuse of drugs remained second to alcohol. Commonly abused drugs included cannabis, cocaine, and amphetamine. Within the population suffering with anxiety conditions, approximately 15% reported co-occurring substance-use disorder. Within this population, persons with generalized anxiety disorder reported the highest rates, at 21%, those with post-traumatic stress disorder (PTSD) reporting 18%, and those with social phobia reporting 17% prevalence of co-occurring substance-use conditions (Regier, et al., 1990; Strakowski and DelBello, 2000; Cassidy et al., 2001; Winokur et al., 1995). Additionally, Kessler and Wang (2008) reported that among the 17.1 million adults aged 18 or older with "past-year any mental illness" who reported receiving mental health services in the previous year, 55.2% received one type of care (inpatient, outpatient, or prescription medication), 39.9% received two types of care, while only 4.9% received all three types of care.

CHALLENGES WITHIN THE TREATMENT PROCESS

Questions related to addressing both mental illness and substance abuse are complex. Compared with substance-use conditions alone, persons with severe and persistent mental illness have impairments that obstruct thinking, leading to cognitive deficits, low motivation to change, and poor social skills. As those with comorbid illness are more difficult to engage in treatment, they are likely to make slower progress and have higher dropout rates; additionally, they are likely to experience greater social challenges such as prominent lack of support systems, economic challenges, and housing difficulties. This population challenges the clinician's therapeutic skills in both the establishment of working relationships and the development and implementation of a clearly outlined plan of care that is not only effective but is agreed upon by both the clinician and the client (Mueser, 2005; Linszen et al., 1994; Pages et al., 1998).

To optimize effectiveness, the plan should address the individual's personality, environment, physical and mental factors, and financial, legal, emotional, and spiritual strengths and challenges. When optimally effective, the treatment plan should engage the person, clinician, and others within the person's day-to-day environment who can support implementation of the treatment plan. In doing so, the plan should be based on a mutually agreed-upon goal or outcome that works toward solutions that capitalize on the individual strengths of the person in a manner that preserves or restores his or her natural dignity (Dejong & Berg, 2002; Saleebey, 2002; Yeager, 2002).

Current evidence suggests reorganizing care around the individual with teams that are accountable to each other and to consumers, and that are supported by information systems that guide and drive improvement, have the potential to eliminate waste, reduce medical errors, and improve outcomes—at lower total cost. Such accountability was notably absent when the managed care movement was growing in the 1990s, giving rise to concerns that financial incentives were undermining rather than enhancing quality of care (Robinow, 2010).

Accomplishing this requires changing the incentives upon which the health care system is built. The fee-for-service payment that currently typifies the U.S. health system emphasizes the provision of health services by individual providers rather than coordinated teams of providers who collaborate to address individuals' needs. Within an accountable care organization, payer sources will be monitoring a number of outcome indicators to determine the overall effectiveness of care provided, which will in the long term determine levels of reimbursement for the organization (Guterman, Schoenbaum, Davis, et al., 2011). Thus, care providers will be challenged directly to demonstrate positive outcomes in a manner that will drive future reimbursement. Within this challenging environment, mental health professionals providing direct care are finding the combination of crisis intervention with brief solution-focused approaches is effective in producing positive outcomes while meeting the rigorous demands of accountable care organizations.

The emergence of managed care drove market shifts from inpatient to outpatient therapy approaches in the past 25 years. Currently, the movement is to minimize inpatient hospitalization, establishing patient care within a medical home that will provide a holistic approach within an outpatient setting. This shift in care environment has led many to consider application of innovative approaches to mental health care. The focus has been placed on the individual and how the system of care can interact with the individual in ways that lead to effective outcomes within a cost contained framework (O'Hanlon & Weiner-Davis, 2003; Pinkerton, 1996).

Historically, individuals with co-occurring conditions have not been well served in either mental health, substance abuse, or rehabilitation settings or systems. Efforts to refer persons with co-occurring conditions to specialized programming or "parallel" substance abuse and mental health programming have been consistently challenged to meet the need of the populations. As a result of difficulties associated with coordination of parallel mental health rehabilitation and substance-abuse services, providing for this complex population has proven to be difficult. Yet there has been increasing research in the development of successful treatment approaches for individuals with co-occurring conditions, and this research has progressed from examining specialized programs to beginning to explore the specific intervention strategies within individual programs.

APPROACHES TO CO-OCCURRING CONDITIONS

Building on these findings, Minkoff (2000) and Minkoff and Cline (2004, 2005) have elaborated the comprehensive, continuous, integrated system of care approach for system design and transformation. Simply put, within this approach, all programs and clinicians become co-occurring-disorder–capable. This requires a systemic change to assure the system is designed to support a structure where each component of programming has an organized set of instructions that provide matched interventions to the co-occurring population served. This matching of care is supported by evidence-based approaches to care placed within the context of an integrated care model of service that provides not only common language but also a common treatment philosophy that makes sense from the perspectives of both mental health and addiction. Within this model of care, each principle is tied to specific intervention strategies to be applied by any clinician with any population, in any setting. When tied together, these principles provide a set of practice guidelines for assessment, treatment rehabilitation, and psychopharma-cology. (Full information can be found at www.ziapartners.com.)

This approach emphasizing the development of co-occurring capability within the field of psychiatric rehabilitation is philosophically consistent, mainly requiring the integration of existing rehabilitation approaches to include relevant attention to substance-related choices, decisions, skills, and disorder management. This integrated model of service delivery builds on best practice findings within a clinical conceptual framework of empathic, hopeful, integrated, strength-based community-based learning relationships in which persons with complex prob-lems are assisted to identify attainable, measurable, clinician- and client-agreed-upon goals to work their way through the stages of change while learning how to make better choices that support the advancement of their treatment incrementally and to support implementation of treatment based skills into day-to-day activities.

At a minimum, staff working with individuals with co-occurring mental health and sub-stance-use conditions should be able to implement the following activities:

1. Welcome the client into an empathic, hopeful, strength-based, and integrated bi-directional approach for recovery.
2. Screen for the presence of comorbidity, and arrange appropriate follow-up evaluation and/or intervention for individuals who screen positively.
3. Identify acute risk issues and know how to help the person remain or become safe.
4. Obtain a comprehensive bidirectional assessment of the co-occurring conditions and understand the content of the assessment to facilitate the development of recommenda-tions for care.
5. Support adherence to these recommendations with the client.
6. Identify stage of change for each problem presented by the client.
7. Encourage the client in individual, group motivational, and/or educational interven-tion to facilitate better choices regarding co-occurring conditions using person cen-tered goals to guide the recovery process.
8. Provide specific skills training to assist the client in managing co-occurring conditions and related difficulties (e.g., asking for help and assuming greater levels of responsibility for the recovery process).
9. Provide assistance with accessing resources to support treatment of co-occurring disorders.
10. Assist the client in their interface with community resources to support her/his co-occurring needs.
11. Collaborate with involved care providers to insure that the client receives an integrated message.
12. Modify skills training to accommodate the clients' cognitive, emotional, and social impairments.
13. Identify methods to reward incremental progress in decisions and skill acquisition.
14. Provide specific rehabilitation services (e.g., vocational rehabilitation, individualized placement, and support to individuals with co-occurring conditions) as a means of developing hope and capacity to achieve a stable functional outcome.
15. Educate the client regarding how to participate in recovery programming, including the appropriateness of taking prescribed medication while participating in 12-Step or other addiction recovery self-help meetings.

CONCEPTUAL FRAMEWORK OF BEHAVIORAL HEALTH INTEGRATION

Historically, and perhaps currently within some states and programs, the idea was that mental health systems funded mental health programs with mental health funds to provide mental health services to individuals with mental health needs. At the same time, the substance-abuse system funded substance-abuse programs with substance-abuse funds to provide substance-use disorder services to individuals with substance abuse or dependence issues. Within these systems, individuals with co-occurring conditions were experienced as "misfits," and services for both problems could occur primarily only through parallel or sequential treatment involving multiple systems, programs, and funding streams, and the individual (or family) was responsible for figuring out how to integrate the multiple services needed on his or her own. In this context, research supporting the development of "integrated treatment or recovery services" was built on the creation of specialized program models for this population, and the evaluation of those program models was conducted through a steady accumulation of research efforts. The result is a variety of evidence-based (to varying degrees) specialized "integrated programs" for this population. Some of the better known examples of "integrated programs" are Integrated Dual Disorder Treatment (IDDT) teams as described in the SAMHSA IDDT Toolkit (Drake et al., 2001), the Modified Therapeutic Community, described by Sacks and others (Sacks et al., 1999), and Treatment Improvement Protocol (TIP-42) TIP a recognized set of evidence-based guidelines for substance-use clinicians to assist in working with co-occurring client populations (CSAT, 2005).

Because these specially developed programs existed in a context that was not an integrated system, there has been a growing and evolving assumption that the only "integrated program" could be a specialized program providing specialized interventions for persons with co-occurring conditions that were somehow to be maintained outside of mainstream treatment services. Yet, more and more programs are recognizing the need for some form of integrated services within the framework of integrated programming. These include interventions for individuals and families with co-occurring conditions, because of the prevalence of poor outcomes associated with this population.

To make heads or tails of the concept of *integrated care* it is important to begin by examining the term itself. When broadly defined, *integration* within the term *integrated care* always includes two components. First is an organizational function, and second is a client/family interface component.

Within the organizational function level, Cline (2005) indicated that "integration" refers to those activities at the level of any behavioral health organization to develop a structure within the organization that supports an interwoven approach to both mental health and substance-use conditions that is articulated in a coherent manner that supports the organization's mission and supports the population of individuals and families with co-occurring conditions.

At the client family interface, integration refers to any mechanism by which appropriately matched interventions for both mental health and substance-use issues or conditions are combined in the context of a clinical relationship with an individual clinician or clinical team so that the client or family experiences the intervention as a person-centered or family-centered integrated experience rather than as a disjointed or disconnected process.

PRINCIPLES OF SUCCESSFUL TREATMENT

PRINCIPLE #1: CO-OCCURRING CONDITIONS AND ISSUES ARE AN EXPECTATION, NOT AN EXCEPTION

This expectation must be incorporated in a welcoming manner and is a key clinical component that begins the moment the client makes initial contact. These welcoming functions promote access to care and are the first step in providing accurate screening and identification of individuals and families with co-occurring conditions and issues. Structured interviews seek to explore the individual's experience from a "desire to know and understand" basis, and by doing so, this inquisitive nature demonstrated by the caregiver establishes a rapport with the client and serves as the foundation for information gathering that examines all aspects of the client's presenting problem.

PRINCIPLE #2: THE FOUNDATION OF A RECOVERY PARTNERSHIP IS AN EMPATHIC, HOPEFUL, INTEGRATED STRENGTH-BASED RELATIONSHIP

Within the working partnership between the client and caregivers, integrated longitudinal strengths-based assessment, intervention, support, and continuity of care promote a step-by-step community-based learning approach for each issue or condition. Within this approach, clients and caregivers explore the dimensions of the illness in an effort to understand what works and what doesn't work. It is a simplistic yet complex effort that involves an honest exploration that results in building upon what works and learning to discard what doesn't work. All too often, persons with co-occurring conditions who relapse have been asked to leave treatment because their use of mood-altering substances has "violated" program rules. In this new strengths based approach, however, empathy is the mantra. When individuals with mental illness and substance conditions are not following recommendations, they are doing their job. Yes that's right…*they are doing their job*! It is the job of the professional to understand their job, to join them in it, and to help them make it better. This is a very different approach. It is approach of seeking to understand, not to blame. The job of the professional is to assist the client in coming to terms with the painful reality of having both mental illness and a substance disorder. The client really would rather not have either, yet they are required to build an identity that involves making an active effort toward recovery for both illnesses. This is a difficult task that requires empathy and understanding from the professional.

A funny thing happens when the professional begins seeking to understand the work of the client. It is called hope, and this is really a five-step process that begins with: (1) establishing a goal of a happy life. That's a goal that nearly everyone can agree with. When the caregivers (2) genuinely empathize with the client's "current reality," the life they are living, and acknowledge the despair the clients are experiencing, it functions to (3) establish a legitimacy of the need to ask for help, at times extensive help. This is not an easy task. When clients understand the appropriateness of asking for help, a balanced working relationship is established that naturally leads to (4) identifying and establishing realistic, attainable, and measurable goals that function as steps of success and progress. Finally, as clients experience success, celebrations of success provide the opportunity to (5) foster a hopeful vision of pride and dignity to counter self-stigmatization.

PRINCIPLE #3: ALL PEOPLE WITH CO-OCCURRING CONDITIONS AND ISSUES ARE NOT THE SAME, SO DIFFERENT PARTS OF THE SYSTEM HAVE A RESPONSIBILITY TO PROVIDE CO-OCCURRING CAPABLE SERVICES FOR DIFFERENT POPULATIONS

The four-quadrant model is primarily used for systems mapping, but it has been applied to co-occurring behavioral health/developmental disabilities. In this system-mapping process, each "subsystem" is responsible for integrated care for its own cohort of clients, and other "subsystems" function as helpful partners to support integrated capability development. Thus, the mental health system is responsible for integrated care for severe mental illness and severely emotionally disturbed children. With support for other co-occurring conditions that are less severe from other "subsystem" care providers who assume responsibility for addiction services. In turn, the highly acute substance-use disorder care provider assumes primary responsibility for treatment of substance-related issues, while mental health partners address lower severity mental health issues. Hence each system helps the other build internal capacity through consultation, education, in-reach, and support so more people get what they need through a "single door" of access to services.

PRINCIPLE #4: WHEN CO-OCCURRING CONDITIONS AND ISSUES CO-EXIST, EACH CONDITION OR ISSUE IS CONSIDERED PRIMARY

The best-practice intervention is integrated dual or multiple primary treatment, in which each condition or issue receives appropriately matched intervention at the same time. This requires a different approach to mental health and substance-use conditions within a model that seeks to match equally the need of the individual with interventions that function as a balanced approach to stabilization of mood and substance withdrawal. The reality is that health, substance-use disorder, and mental health symptoms overlap and manifest across the individual. There is no such thing as good physical health without good mental health; additionally there is no such thing as "recovery" from addiction when mental health issues remain unaddressed. And finally, there is no mental health recovery when the individual is attempting to self-medicate symptoms of mental illness with mood-altering substances. For true recovery to begin, all systems must be addressed concurrently; this leads us to Principle #5.

PRINCIPLE #5: PARALLEL PRIMARY RECOVERY PROCESSES, INVOLVES MOVING THROUGH STAGES OF CHANGE AND PHASES OF RECOVERY FOR EACH CO-OCCURRING CONDITION OR ISSUE

Recovery applies not just to mental health, physical health, and addiction. Recovery applies to all types of chronic incurable conditions, such as trauma, physical disability, incarceration, homelessness, etc. In this sense, "recovery" is not recovery from the condition, but recovery of the human being who has the condition, so a person with one or more chronic incurable conditions recovers a sense of pride, self worth, hope, dignity, and meaning, even though the conditions may persist, the risk of relapse may persist, the need for services may persist, and the stigma, symptoms, and disability may persist. This requires approaching healing within stepwise phases of recovery in which change is considered in reference to issue-specific not person-specific frames of reference; thus, as new issues present, individuals are challenged to work through the stages of change with each new issue. When we are asked, "What stage of change is a person in?" the correct answer is, "For which issue?"

Phase 1: Acute Stabilization

This phase involves actions required to stabilize symptoms associated with active substance abuse or acute psychiatric symptoms or other immediate risks.

Phase 2: Engagement/Motivation Enhancement

This phase involves assisting the individual in moving through the stages of change (Bellack & DiClemente, 1999).

- Pre-contemplation: You may think this is an issue, but I don't and even if I do I don't want to deal with it so don't bug me.
- Contemplation: I'm willing to think with you, and consider if I want to change, but have on interest in changing, at least for now.
- Preparation: I'm ready to start changing but haven't yet started, and I need some help to know how to begin.
- Early Action: I've begun to make some changes, and need some help to continue, but I'm not committed to maintenance or to following all of your recommendations.
- Late Action: I'm working toward maintenance, but I haven't gotten there, and need some help to get there.
- Maintenance: I'm stable and trying to stay that way, as life continues to throw challenges in my path.

It is important to note that stage of change is issue specific, not person specific.

Phase 3: prolonged stabilization

Prolonged stabilization entails working to achieve maintenance and to support ongoing recovery through active and aggressive actions to prevent relapse; this speaks to the level of sustainable recovery efforts developed during the treatment process.

Phase 4: rehabilitation

Rehabilitation requires active engagement in recovery activities on a daily basis leading to personal growth and learning over time; this is not a project or process that is ever completed. Rather, it is a repetitive process of growth, self-definition, and change.

One final note prior to leaving Principle #5: it is essential that, for each condition or issue, interventions and outcomes be matched to the stage of change and the phase of recovery for optimal outcome. Recovery is a process that is never really complete. As individuals continue their lives, they continue to experience life challenges and will be challenged to work through each phase and stage of change.

PRINCIPLE #6: PROGRESS OCCURS THROUGH ADEQUATELY SUPPORTED, ADEQUATELY REWARDED SKILL-BASED LEARNING FOR EACH CO-OCCURRING CONDITION AND ISSUE

Skill-based learning involves obtaining an accurate history for the individual seeking treatment. Based on the assessment, treatment providers work with persons with co-occurring conditions to develop an accurate set of recommendations that are patient-centered, and thus more likely to engage the patient in developing new skills to support the recovery process. For any issue individuals have, there is a need to help them develop the skill sets needed to succeed. The more challenged the individual, the more and smaller are the steps that will be required; each step should be accompanied by bigger rounds of applause. Such skills as self-management, self-responsibility and asking for help are key and necessary skills that can be acquired and practiced. There are increasing numbers of skill manuals available for co-occurring teaching, such as: *Seeking Safety: A Treatment Manual for PTSD and Substance Abuse* (Najavits 2001), *Overcoming Addictions: Skills Training for People with Schizophrenia* (Roberts et al., 1999), *Behavioral Treatment for Substance Abuse in People with Serious and Persistent Mental Illness: A Handbook for Mental Health Professionals* (Bellack, Bennet, & Gearon, 2007) and *Social Skills Training for Schizophrenia: A Step-by-Step Guide,* 2nd edition (Bellack et al., 2004).

PRINCIPLE #7: RECOVERY PLANS, INTERVENTIONS AND OUTCOMES MUST BE INDIVIDUALIZED; THERE IS NO SINGLE "CORRECT" CO-OCCURRING PROGRAM OR INTERVENTION FOR EVERYONE

For each person, integrated treatment interventions and treatment outcomes must be tailored to the person's goals, specific diagnosis, conditions, and issues, phase of recovery, stages of changes, strengths, skills, and available support for each condition. The recovery plan is a blueprint for progress designed to meet the individual needs of the person with co-occurring conditions as he or she progresses. The recovery plan begins with the assessment process. Quantifiable processes and goals are established and agreed on with input from the individual, his or her family, and all members of the treatment team. The recovery plan is then implemented, assessed, revised, and implemented again, until the agreed-upon goals are completed. The goals in the recovery plan are broad statements that are reflective of the overall desired outcome; the objectives of the recovery plan are statements of targeted observable and measurable changes to support recovery efforts (see Fig. 33.1).

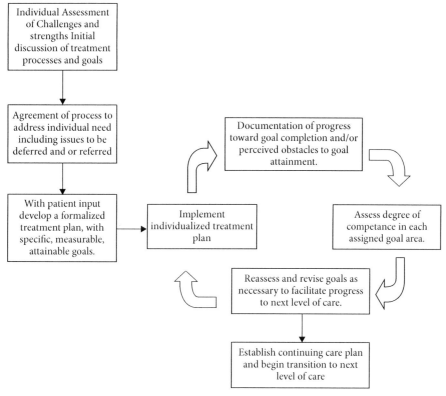

Figure 33.1

Recovery plans are like a good roadmap. They should be clear, list who will do what and when, and what the expected outcome will be. Recovery plans should also include staff efforts demonstrating a team approach to the recovery process. Interventions can range from medication treatments, to homework assignments, to linkages in the community, to housing plans, and any number of methods used to stabilize whatever co-occurring condition is being addressed. All interventions should be reflective of the interdisciplinary team approach: listing the type and frequency of interventions, the name of the person responsible for completion of the task, and a target date for completion. The recovery plan becomes a contract between persons with co-occurring disorders and caregivers, outlining specific processes and responsibilities for care. The plan should follow a logical progression from assessment, to intervention, to staff reassessment, and progress naturally to discharge planning. Effective recovery plans should meet the following qualifications:

- Is the plan reasonable?
- Is the plan person-centered?
- Will the plan facilitate the desired behavioral change?
- Is the plan attainable? The last thing an individual in early recovery needs is to be set up to fail by a plan that reaches beyond his or her ability.
- Are the goals clearly stated and free from ambiguity so the individual, family members, and other staff can understand them?

- Is the plan measurable? Does the plan clearly outline the who, what, when, and where of the care process?
- Is the plan sustainable? That is, does the plan support the person's need for the level and length of care being provided?

HOW TO IMPLEMENT A COMPREHENSIVE, CONTINUOUS, INTEGRATED SYSTEM OF CARE MODEL

So how does one go about establishing a comprehensive, continuous, integrated system of care (CCISC)? To begin this process, it is important to revisit one component of the system: that it is a system of care that is welcoming to the individual in need of treatment for psychiatric and substance-use conditions. This component is a welcoming component.

"Welcoming" at a system level implies that every level of the system—program, clinical practice, clinician competence and training, as well as outcome evaluation—is based on accepting the individuals with co-occurring conditions. Instead of assessing why the individual has returned to the center, or what failed in their treatment, or blaming the victim of the illness, people are welcomed back with the attitude of, "Great, you were able to implement your plan of care for six and a half months!" Not a viewpoint that echoes failure by asking, "Did you go to meetings? Call your sponsor? What did you fail to do that led to your relapse?" (Minkoff & Cline, 2004). Welcoming is extremely important for those immediately served and for those not immediately able to access services, as this serves to communicate a sincere desire to engage the individual in care as soon as possible. It is the beginning of an empathic and hopeful connection that is the first step in assisting this person in getting the help they need.

Welcoming is more than just an attitude. The welcoming aspect is written into policy; anchored in clinical language and programming standards. It is defined as both a clinical practice expectation and a policy requirement. Welcoming is embedded in systemic continuous quality improvement as well as outcome evaluation processes for evaluating the program. Additionally, welcoming is completely intertwined with the implementation of cultural competency and welcoming is defined as a practice that is independent of resource availability or programming eligibility. At times "welcoming" is defined as "no wrong door for entering treatment," or "no wrong reason for seeking care." The process has been described as a step-wise progression of implementation, which is outlined below:

1. Identify and empower a decision-making structure that is appropriately positioned within the service infrastructure: Frequently, systems of care are fragmented because of funding sources. Service providers work to stake out their territory and to define the scope of services offered by a particular group or agency. At times this will happen within a particular city or at the county level. At times this will be identified at a state or district level. Whatever the case, the decision making structure has to be defined as the system of care that will be the scope of the project. Once the scope of the project is defined, all program managers around the table are tasked with the power to change their own system, and only their system. It is necessary to have all on the same page moving in the same direction toward a comprehensive, continuous, integrated system of care, but it is not necessary for the system to have a uniform or merged structure. In

most systems of care, an overarching structure that brings each subsystem to the table in a common effort is necessary. However, the actual implementation of change will occur in the policies and procedures of each subsystem separately.

2. Develop a document that defines *consensus* on the CCISC model and set of implementation activities with identified priorities and incentives for clinical practice implementation within existing funding streams and existing funding constraints: These "charter documents" provide the basic structure and describe the co-occurring disorder problem (high volume, poor outcome, high costs, and poorly served populations) and describe the implementation of CCISC. The next task for development of the charter documents is to outline a set of implementation activities for each participating subsystem agency or program, usually over a year-long period. Within this process, most charters identify key elements that all stakeholders can agree upon as important to address within the first year. Most charters are developed in a manner that provides the opportunity for participants to vote on key components for of the system for the first year. The charter document may or may not be signed, but it is generally identified as requiring a sustained voluntary effort on the part of all involved. The carrot for participation is generally some incentive provided by the system, which can be in the form of financial support that is frequently an opportunity to inform or shape policy through education or research to support policy development and to later develop new programming through system supported training and/or technical assistance.

3. Identify the CCISC process as a systemic continuous quality improvement initiative, and welcoming as one of the objectives or indicators for the outcome of this process. By integrating quality indicators into the charter as outcome tools, the system becomes responsible to share data in a manner that sets the stage for cooperative exchanges of best practices toward key indicators of care. For example, if the indicator is access to care, cooperating agencies can explore and share processes for removing barriers to services. One of the components of the program is for participating agencies to develop performance indicators in relation to priority activities. By doing so, all priority activities of the charter are incorporated into routine quality improvement (QI) audit measures. This facilitates observation and accountability for the system in moving toward accomplishment of all of the key goals of the charter.

4. Identify those with co-occurring disorders as a system priority population and write a formal welcoming policy that defines the expectation that all components of the system will themselves develop formal processes to welcome individuals with co-occurring conditions into treatment. While this seems simplistic and relatively easily accomplished, it is more of a process than an event. The time frame for adoption and actual implantation of the formal welcoming policy usually occurs well into the first year of system operations. This is the result of the need to establish the clinical infrastructure necessary to make the welcoming policy implantation a reality. While this may seem like a top-down policy implementation, it really is not. This is more of an integrated process requiring efforts from both the top and the bottom to make this policy a reality. It can be tracked through the aforementioned quality improvement structure with measures such as a live person answering the phone twenty-four hours. In this day of automated telephone systems, it is both a surprise and treat to find a person rather than a machine answering the call, and nothing is more important than a live voice being there when someone reaches out for help. This is the foundation of a truly welcoming system of care.

5. Establish welcoming as a priority program standard for implementation of co-occurring capability, by charter definition, and incorporate implementation of welcoming into a continuous quality improvement (CQI) action plan that each participating program is required to develop. Expectations are a part of all charters; this one is no different. Within the charter there is to be an expectation that all programs will begin to move at their own pace toward establishment of co-occurring capability. Within this CQI action plan is a clearly outlined set of measurements to determine a welcoming process, including the presence of a welcoming policy. A written and clearly articulated mission statement or vision statement, welcoming orientation materials, a physical plant assessment for welcoming accommodations, welcoming orientation for staff of each program, and processes such as "the telephone will always be answered by a human not a machine" approach. Each program is provided the flexibility to develop its own plan for quality management, but each quality management plan is expected to be reflective of the priorities documented in the charter. Other CQI focuses should examine the application of evidence-based practices and best practices. In all, the CQI mission is to monitor system change activities and to assure that system policy development is aligned with the existing program level action planning to build welcoming and other priorities contained within the charter document.

6. Each program defines and implements welcoming clinical practices and procedures for clients with co-occurring conditions that are particularly challenging. The translation from policy to reality is frequently difficult. This is a process that usually requires technical assistance to implement a change in clinical behavior. For example, the implementation of a welcoming process can be as simple as customer service training for staff around how to engage and interact with dual-diagnosis populations. Yet at times this is more difficult, such as when addressing the difficult client who arrives at the facility intoxicated and is demanding services. This requires a welcoming skill that incorporates risk assessment as well as limit setting in a way that the client is not made to feel unwelcome. It is the integration of such activities that requires practice and role playing with staff to translate a policy into clinical practice.

7. There is a systematic training plan that creates an expectation that all programs expect their clinicians to develop competency in "welcoming" and provides continuous onsite training and supervisory support to implement this competency over time for all staff. While training and competency development are core elements to development of CCISC it is important to implement any form of effective system change, this type of training cannot occur "in a vacuum," as this type of competency development requires onsite training where the competency is tied not only to acquiring new skills but also to attitudinal changes. This will not occur in a single training session or a series of "staff retreats." Rather, this process is one that is verbalized by administration and leadership, modeled and reinforced at all levels of the organization. It is a good idea to develop a trainer cadre in which participants who function as trainers are also functioning in the role of system change agents and are opinion leaders whose job it is to define and assist the system in the translation of policy into day-to-day front-line application skills, providing feedback to the system both when policies are not upheld, but more importantly when the system is not supporting the clinician in fulfilling the expectations of the organization policy.

8. Development and implementation of recovery-oriented co-occurring capable practice guidelines: CCISC implementation requires system-wide transformation of clinical practice in accordance with the above principles. This can be realized through dissemination and incremental developmental implementation of Quality Improvement or Improvement Sciences processes focusing on building a clinical consensus around best practices. The clinical consensus should begin with assessment and progress through treatment intervention, rehabilitation, program matching psychopharmacology and program outcomes. Obtaining input from and building consensus with clinicians prior to final dissemination of practice guidelines is highly recommended. (There are existing documents available to facilitate this process at www.bhrm.org.) Quality improvement processes can be used to monitor clinical processes and to facilitate welcoming, access and identification of those with co-occurring disorders. This monitoring process is critical to establishing and promoting empathic, hopeful, integrated, continuous relationships needed to fuel a highly successful and accountable co-occurring disorder program.

9. Facilitation of welcoming, providing access to services that includes integrated screening to facilitate the identification of multiple co-occurring conditions: This step requires an improvement science partnership that: (1) addresses welcoming and "no wrong door" access in all programs; (2) eliminates arbitrary barriers to initial access and evaluation; and (3) improves clinical and administrative practices of screening, clinical documentation, event reporting, and appropriate next step intervention for individuals and families with co-occurring conditions.

10. Implementation and documentation of integrated services: Integrated treatment relationships are a vital component of CCISC. Implementation requires creating an improvement science process in which clinicians and managers work in partnership on the process of developing and documenting and integrated treatment or recovery plan in which the client or family is assisted to make progress toward hopeful goals by following issue specific and stage specific recommendations for each issue simultaneously. This expectation must be supported by clear definition of the expected "scope of practice" for singly licensed clinicians regarding co-occurring disorders, and incorporated into standards of practices for reimbursable clinical interventions—in both mental health and substance settings—for individuals who have co-occurring conditions.

11. Development of recovery-oriented co-occurring competencies for all clinicians: Creating the expectation that all clinicians can make progress toward developing universal competency, including attitudes and values, as well as knowledge and skills, is a significant characteristic of the CCISC process. Available competency lists for co-occurring conditions, such as the 12 Steps for Clinicians, can be used as a reference for beginning a process of consensus-building regarding the competencies. Mechanisms can be developed to establish competencies in existing human resource policies and job descriptions, to incorporate them into personnel evaluation, credentialing, and licensure, and to measure and support clinician attainment of competency. (For more on competency self-assessment tools, see CODECAT-EZ, ZiaPartners, 2009, at http://www.ziapartners.com/tools-2/tools-codecat-ez/.)

12. Implementation of a change agent team: In the CCISC Improvement Science process, both capability development and clinician competence development occur through a

top-down, bottom-up partnership, in which front-line clinician and consumer/family change agents in each program work in partnership with leadership to effect the change. Furthermore, the change agents in a system ideally become an empowered team to represent the principles and values of front-line service delivery and service recipients in the system planning and implementation process.

13. Development of a plan for a comprehensive program array. The CCISC model requires development of a strategic plan in which each existing program begins to define and implement a specific role or arena of competency with regard to provision of recovery-oriented co-occurring capable services for people with co-occurring conditions, within the context of available resources. This plan should also identify system gaps that require longer range planning and/or additional resources to address and identify strategies for filling those gaps.

Four important areas must be addressed in each CCISC process:

    a. *Evidence-based practice:* there needs to be a specific plan for identification of any evidence-based best practice for any mental illness (e.g., Individualized Placement and Support for vocational rehabilitation) or substance disorder (e.g., buprenorphine maintenance), or an evidence-based best practice program model for a particular co-occurring disorder population (e.g., Integrated Dual Disorder Treatment for SPMI adults in continuing mental health care) that may be needed but not yet be present in the system, and planning for the most efficient methods to promote implementation in such a way that facilitates access to co-occurring clients that might be appropriately matched to that intervention.

    b. *Peer dual-recovery supports:* The system can identify at least one dual recovery self-help program (e.g., Dual Recovery Anonymous) and establish a plan to facilitate the creation of these groups throughout the system. The system can also facilitate the development of other peer supports such as recovery coaching, peer outreach, and peer counseling.

    c. *Residential supports and services:* The system should begin to plan for a comprehensive range of programs that address a variety of residential needs, building initially upon the availability of existing resources through redesigning those services with the recognition that co-occurring conditions are an expectation. The range of programs should include

        i.   Addiction residential treatment (e.g., modified therapeutic community programs)

        ii. Abstinence-mandated (dry) supported housing for individuals with psychiatric disabilities

        iii. Abstinence-encouraged (damp) supported housing for individuals with psychiatric disabilities

        iv. Consumer-choice (wet) supported housing for individuals with psychiatric disabilities at risk for homelessness.

    d. *Continuum of levels of care:* All categories of service should be available in a range of levels of care, including outpatient services of various levels of intensity; intensive outpatient or day treatment, residential treatment, hospital diversion programming, and hospitalization. This can often be operationalized in managed care payment arrangements and may involve more sophisticated level of care assessment capacity.

CCISC implementation is an ongoing quality improvement process that encourages the development of a plan that includes attention to each of these areas in a comprehensive service array.

CONCLUSION

This chapter has reviewed processes for implementation of system-wide integrated programming for persons with co-occurring conditions. It has discussed and illustrated many methods and approaches that can be applied to address the challenges faced by care providers addressing co-occurring conditions. Some of the concepts contained in this chapter will not stand up to the scrutiny and science applied to evidence-based practice (e.g., welcoming), yet one can hardly argue that a system approach that welcomes rather than placing blame is a much more effective approach. This type of intervention is best described as a service delivery standard. Let's not forget that standards for care and service are ranked along with best practices when building effective treatment approaches. All of the best practices in the world will be less effective if delivered in a system that is not welcoming to the population it is designed to serve. Additionally, CCISC is an approach that can be applied within the general programming of any system. It has been recognized as an effective approach that has been found to demonstrate early success within a variety of systems. While it is clear that more evaluation is needed to meet the gold standard of "evidence-based" practice, it certainly can and should be considered an evidence-informed approach to the treatment and management of co-occurring conditions. I don't recall exactly when I first heard or read Dr. Paul Batalden's observation, "Every system is perfectly designed to get the results it gets," but it was an eye-opening experience. When thinking about the need to transform systems to address the ever-growing need to treat co-occurring conditions, we would strongly suggest that you ask yourselves: "Are we happy with the results our program is getting? Is the design of our program leading to the results we are getting?" and finally, "What can we do to improve the results we are getting?" If you think CCISC would help, we are here to help.

REFERENCES

Bellack, A.S., & DiClemente, C.C. (1999). Treating substance abuse among patients with schizophrenia. *Psychiatric Services* 50:75–80.

Bellack, A.S., Mueser, K.T., Gingerich, S., &Agrest, J. (2004). *Social Skills Training for Schizophrenia: A Step-by-Step Guide (2nd ed.)*. New York: Guilford Press.

Bellack, A.S., Bennet, M.E., & Gearon, J.S. (2007). *Behavioral Treatment for Substance Abuse in People with Serious and Persistent Mental Illness: A Handbook for Mental Health Professionals*. New York: Taylor and Francis.

Cassidy, F., Ahearn, E.P., &Carroll, B.J. (2001): Substance abuse in bipolar disorder. *Bipolar Disorder* 3:181–188.

Center for Substance Abuse Treatment. (2005). *Substance Abuse Treatment for Persons with Co-Occurring Disorders.* Treatment Improvement Protocol (TIP) Series 42. DHHS Publication No. (SMA) 05-3922. Rockville, MD: Substance Abuse and Mental Health Services Administration.

Cline, C.A. (2005). Personal communication.

Dejong, P., & Berg, I. (2002). *Interviewing for solutions (2nd ed.).* Belmont, CA: Brooks/Cole.

Drake, R.E., Essock, S.M., et al. (2001). Implementing dual diagnosis services for clients with severe mental illness. *Psychiatric Services* 54(4):469–476.

Guterman, S., Schoenbaum, S.C., Davis, K., Schoen, M.S., Audet, A.J., Stremikis, K., et al. (2011). *High Performance Accountable Care: Building on Success and Learning from Experience.* The Commonwealth Fund. Pub no 1494. Available at http://www.commonwealthfund.org/ (accessed 11/11/2011).

Kessler, R.C., & Wang, P.S., (2008). The descriptive epidemiology of commonly occurring mental disorders in the United States. *Annual Review of Public Health* 29:115–129.

Kohn R., Saxena, S., Levav, I., & Saraceno, B. (2004). The treatment gap in mental health care. *Bulletin of the World Health Organization* 2004;82(11):858.

Linszen, D.H., Dingemans, P.M., & Lenior, M.E. (1994). Cannabis abuse and the course of recent-onset schizophrenic conditions. *Archive of General Psychiatry* 51(4):273.

Minkoff, K., & Cline, C. (2004). Changing the world: the design and implementation of comprehensive continuous integrated systems of care for individuals with co-occurring disorders. *Psychiat Clin N Am.* 2004;27:727–743.

Minkoff, K., & Cline, C. (2005). Developing welcoming systems for individuals with co-occurring disorders: The role of the comprehensive continuous integrated system of care model. *J Dual Diagnosis.* 2005;1:63–89.

Mueser, K. (2005). Psychosocial interventions for adults with severe mental illnesses and co-occurring substance use conditions: A review of specific interventions. *Journal of Dual Diagnosis* 1:57.

Najavits, L. (2001). *Seeking Safety: A Treatment Manual for PTSD and Substance Abuse.* New York: Guilford Press.

New Freedom Commission on Mental Health. (2003). *Achieving the Promise: Transforming Mental Health Care in America.* DHHS, Final Report, Publication no. SMA-03-3832. Rockville, MD.

O'Hanlon, W., & Weiner-Davis, M. (2003). *In Search of Solutions: A New Direction in Psychotherapy (rev. ed.).* New York: W.W. Norton.

Pages, K.P., Russo, J.E., Wingerson, D.K., Ries, R.K., Roy-Byrne, P.P., & Cowley D.S. (1998). Predictors and outcome of discharge against medical advice from the psychiatric units of a general hospital. *Psychiatric Services* 49(9):1187.

Pinkerton, R. (1996).The interaction between brief and very brief psychotherapy: Allowing for flexible time limits on individual counseling services. *Professional Psychology: Research & Practice* 21:315.

Regier, D.A., Farmer, M.E., Rae, D.S., Locke, B.Z., Keith, S.J., Judd, L.L., et al. (1990). Comorbidity of mental conditions with alcohol and other drug abuse. Results from the Epidemiological Catchment Area (ECA) Study. *Journal of the American Medical Association* 264(19):2511.

Roberts, L.J., Eckman, T.A., & Shaner, A. (1999). *Overcoming Addictions: Skills Training for People with Schizophrenia.* New York: W.W. Norton.

Robinow, A. (2010). *The Potential of Global Payment: Insights from the Field.* The Commonwealth Fund, February 2010. Available at http://www.commonwealthfund.org/Publications/Fund-Reports/2010/Feb/The-Potential-of-Global-Payment-Insights-from-the-Field.aspx#citation   (accessed 11/11/2010).

Sacks, S., Sacks J.Y., & DeLeon, G. (1999). Treatment for MICAs: Design and implementation of the modified Therapeutic Community. *Journal of Psychoactive Drugs* 31:19–30.

Saleebey, D. (2002). *Strengths Perspective in Social Work Practice (3rd ed.).* Toronto: Allyn & Bacon.

Strakowski, S.M., & DelBello, M.P. (2000) Substance abuse and bipolar affective disorder. *Journal of Nervous Mental Conditions* 182:349–352.

Substance Abuse and Mental Health Services Administration. (2010). *Results from the 2009 National Survey on Drug Use and Health: Mental Health Findings.* Office of Applied Studies, NSDUH Series H-39, HHS Publication No. SMA 10-4609. Rockville, MD: SAMHSA.

SAMHSA. Position statement on use of block grant funds to treat people with co-occurring disorders. 2000

Winokur, G., Coryell, W., Akiskal, H.S., Maser, J.D., Keller, M.B., Endicott, J., et al. (1995). Alcoholism in manic-depressive (bipolar) illness: Familial illness, course of illness, and the primary-secondary distinction. *American Journal of Psychiatry* 152:365–372.

Yeager, K.R. (2002). Crisis intervention with mentally ill chemical abusers: Application of brief solution-focused therapy and strengths perspective. *Brief Treatment and Crisis Intervention* Fall 2002;2(3):197–216.

TRANSFORMATIONAL LEADERSHIP IN MENTAL HEALTH

DALE SVENDSEN, MICHAEL HOGAN, AND JUDY WORTHAM-WOOD

LEADERSHIP OF MENTAL HEALTH ORGANIZATIONS

Any organization requires leadership. Certainly mental health organizations are no different. Despite this, very little has been published about the special needs and challenges associated with leading mental health programs, agencies, or systems. But this is in a way counterintuitive. How can it be that there is not more instructive material available to guide those of us who are interested in this work?

Perhaps one answer is that, in the past, leaders of mental health organizations rose "through the ranks" directly from clinical positions and did not have management training to bring to this new level of work. Another possibility is that the universe of mental health organizations is relatively small, and not connected to the mainstream of organizational leadership in the business world. Leaders of mental health organizations did have significant training, but it was within a clinical discipline. And while some clinical training (e.g., in group work) is very relevant to filling leadership roles, there is more to it. We would add that mental health leadership duties nearly always used to be performed by psychiatrists who, since the middle of the nineteenth century, learned their trade as superintendents of state hospitals. But since the early 1970s, psychiatrists have moved away from such roles. In the 1960s and 1970s, most directors of State Mental Health Agencies (SMHAs) were physicians. By 2011, only three SMHA directors were physicians. State leadership roles tend now to be occupied by individuals with diverse backgrounds, with training in not only the clinical disciplines, but also management and law.

Actually, there is a vast literature on management and leadership. But most of it is focused on the business world. Much of this work may be relevant, but the mission and methods of leading mental health organizations are not exactly the same as those involved in operating a business. There has also been much written about leadership in health care, and training programs in hospital, health care, and public health abound. But as we said, mental health organizations are not the same. We will apply case histories in this chapter to illustrate some special aspects of leadership in mental health.

There is a view in some circles that a good manager can lead any kind of organization. But we believe that, at least for mental health organizations, this is not true—or at least not exactly true. For example, Gabarro (1987) studied the transition of general managers taking on new jobs, examining patterns of "taking charge" and success factors. One of his findings was that managers coming from a different field and taking over organizations needing a "turn-around" did not do as well as those who had specific experience in the industry.

A more recent study by Anthony and Huckshorn (2008) reported on leadership factors of mental health organizations and systems. Their methodology was first to review the leadership literature generally, but then to interview a large number of individuals identified as leaders in the field, in search of common patterns. Their study yielded eight principles of mental health leadership, summarized in Table 34.1 below.

Table 34.1 Principles of Mental Health Leadership

1. Leaders communicate a shared vision
2. Centralize by mission and decentralize by operations
3. Create an organizational culture that identifies and tries to live by key values
4. Create an organizational structure and culture that empowers their employees and themselves
5. Ensure that staff are trained in human technology that can translate vision into reality
6. Relate constructively to employees
7. Access and use information to make change a constant ingredient of their organization
8. Build their organization around exemplary performers

Anthony and Huckshorn, 2008.

In another discussion of mental health leadership, Brown, Isett, and Hogan (2010) discussed "stewardship"—a proxy for leadership—in mental health policy. They concluded that stewardship requires trust, wisdom, and a place to exercise leverage, or an "institutional home." This view reflects their observation that government responsibility for mental health care has become diffuse, with many agencies at many levels of government having some level responsibility. They also noted that the ingredients of good stewardship/leadership include authority, analysis, and advocacy.

Both of these papers on leadership in mental health identify aspects of leadership that seem intuitive. They focus on common-sense principles, on mission and vision, and emphasize the proactive nature of leadership work. Schwartz (1989) points out that learning to be an administrator bears a resemblance to learning to be a parent. It takes supervised experience, just like being a parent requires having had decent parenting. In other words, good mentoring is necessary for creating skilled mental health administrators.

One critical element often missing in the literature is the notion of teamwork. In our view and experience, *work carried out by teams* is perhaps the most significant aspect of leadership in mental health. Vandiver and Corcoran (2012) discuss leadership and working in teams within the framework of "quality management and program evaluation" in the organization. This can be found in Chapter 36 in this volume. Burti et al. (2012) in Chapter 6 in this volume focuses on "the community team acting as a whole with all the workers involved in the case in the various phases of the treatment plan." It is our belief that teamwork is needed at all levels in mental health care and administration; the clinical, the consumer and family perspective and the management and administrative leadership levels.

OUR LEADERSHIP EXPERIENCE

In our case discussions, we offer the leadership experience we had working together in administration in the state of Ohio. *Transformational leadership* was first defined in the business literature by James Macgregor Burns in his book *Leadership,* in 1978. Burns said, "The function of leadership is to engage followers, not merely to activate them, to commingle needs and aspirations and goals in a common enterprise…." We believe our experiences will serve as an example of transformational leadership as it applies to mental health.

Our shared experience as part of a state mental health leadership team took place over a decade and a half (1991–2007). Our roles were as director (Mike), medical director (Dale) and deputy director for policy and programs (Judy) in the Ohio Department of Mental Health (ODMH). Mike and Dale worked together for this entire period, and Judy served with us for most of the last 10 years. Our belief from this experience is that successful leadership of mental health organizations is not well-suited to a "Lone Ranger" model—a single leader. Rather, we believe leadership of mental health organizations is a "team sport." This has many implications: finding a shared direction when team members have different styles and roles; blending diverse perspectives and points of view, and balancing different responsibilities. Mental health agencies and organizations of any size are complex and challenging. Leadership teams, like treatment teams in the clinical setting, have differing perspectives that must be considered. Clinical knowledge and leadership that reflects the core healing role of the organization, general management, and the consumer and family perspectives must all be considered and involved in the leadership process as distinct important points of view.

Figure 34.1 is an oversimplification, but it illustrates the merger of various stakeholders with important principles, timing, and hoped-for outcomes. Usually more roles and perspectives than these three core roles are involved. On the "clinical side" of a mental health organization—like on a multidisciplinary team—the different mental health disciplines often have a role. Quality assurance and improvement and program development have clinical aspects. And management and administration in mental health also has many components: budget and fiscal management,

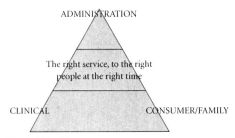

FIGURE 34.1 Leadership in Mental Health

human resources, facilities engineering, and information technology, for example. We do not believe that there is a single or "right" way to organize a mental health agency. But we do believe that mental health organizations inherently involve team leadership, and that the three perspectives of clinical, overall management, and the consumer perspective should all be reflected in mental health leadership teams.

LEADERSHIP CHALLENGES

We were fortunate to be at the helm of ODMH for a considerable period—especially since the average tenure of SMHA directors (like that of other state agency leaders and big-city school superintendents) is two and a half to three years. This long perspective meant that we were at the helm long enough to deal with very different challenges that confronted our organization. We will describe experiences with leadership under different circumstances. First, there was the challenge of leading during a tumultuous period of externally directed change—like the period of health care reform that we are now in. This might be described as *leadership during stormy times.* Whether the external challenge is changes in funding, major policy shifts, or other mandates imposed on the mental health organization, people in the organization look to their leaders in stormy times. They want reassurance and support, but mostly, they want to know that there is a direction for change that can address the challenges and lead to organizational success—and possibly to greater stability after the changes have been confronted. We will describe challenges for team leadership that we confronted during stormy times of change.

A very different set of leadership challenges arises when, so to speak, *the seas are calm.* These are times of relative stability in the external environment: funding levels, policies, and mandates are somewhat stable. Perhaps some may feel that it is unlikely we will ever face calm seas in mental health care—but all things are relative. After emerging from a period of tumultuous change into relative stability, very different challenges for leadership will start to emerge. What is our direction and vision when it is not being set for us? What will challenge us when things are going relatively smoothly?

LEADERSHIP DURING STORMY TIMES

The early phase of our experience at ODMH was during the tenure of George Voinovich as Governor of Ohio (1991–1999). The "storm" during this period resulted from legislation (Ohio's Mental Health Act of 1988; Am. Sub. H.B. 256) that virtually turned the mental health system upside down. From a state-dominated system in which hospital care was the dominant model, the Mental Health Act envisioned a community managed system, with local mental health authorities (county based boards) responsible financially and clinically for care. The engine of change embedded in the law was giving the boards phased-in responsibility for the state hospital funds used to care for their residents and thus creating incentives to use inpatient care frugally. Implementing the law required us to deal with mandated change in an uncertain environment (e.g. budget constraints negated all of the fiscal models that had been used to plan for the law). In this tumultuous period, flexible leadership and coping with both downsizing and growth were needed for success.

Aside from the challenges of mandated change from hospital to community care and state control to local auspices, this period was stressful because of funding challenges. The legislation's feasibility was based on a projection of healthy funding increases—that would be sufficient to build new community services (especially for people with significant disabilities transitioning from hospital to community), allow for adequate care in hospitals while they were downsized, and finally to expand needed care in communities that had not used much hospital care. The goal of funding equity had been critical to securing support for the legislation from these counties—many rural or suburban and far from hospitals—because they had little to gain from resources tied to reducing hospital use.

Of course, debating issues like this was one thing, and having enough money to fund the good intentions was something else—especially since the recession of 1991–1992 reduced state revenue growth to drips, rather than the flood needed to meet mental health expectations. The pressure rapidly increased to downsize/close hospitals at a precipitous rate, to meet community expectations. The team leadership challenge we faced was how to weather this storm. The legislation could not succeed without a movement to community care. Support for reform required expanded resources to all communities, not just those reducing hospital care. And the quality of hospital care threatened to crash if downsizing was precipitous. The question confronting us was what strategies would get us through these challenges.

CASE STUDY: LEADING THROUGH ADVERSITY

The Mental Health Act of 1988 created mounting pressure to quickly downsize and close hospitals and move care and fiscal resources from state hospitals to community boards and agencies. Despite the fairly recent deinstitutionalization experiences of the 1960s and 1970s, when patients were rapidly discharged to nursing homes and inadequate community services, the promise of the new law led many to push for immediate, rapid change, ignoring the lessons of deinstitutionalization. It was inevitable that change was going to take place, but leadership was needed for a shared vision that embraced quality care, safety, and the hope for recovery. We needed a plan and a process to move ahead.

The response to these challenges required leadership on several fronts. First, while community placement and hospital downsizing were necessary, there was no plan or agreement on the desired role of hospitals—if any. Second, rapid downsizing threatened to demoralize staff, create labor conflict, and undermine the quality of care. The combination of incentives with reduced budget allocations (a result of the recession of 1991–1992) led for calls to accelerate hospital downsizing and closures to provide "promised" funding for community care.

A first response to these challenges, early in 1991, was, ironically, to slow down the pace of hospital staff reductions. This had two purposes—first to keep the quality of hospital care from "crashing," which would have threatened reforms just as they were beginning, and second to focus attention on the shared dimensions of reform—e.g., on some commitment to hospital staff, and on sufficient budgets. This was a subtle "reframing" of the problem—not a reversal of direction, but a message that viable solutions and plans for hospital care and the pace of downsizing were needed.

The strategy eventually worked, but it was messy—as strategies in a conflicting environment often are. Stakeholders on the community side of the system—especially boards and providers—clamored for action. The demand for solutions allowed us to create Inpatient Futures, a task force (ODMH, boards, providers, families, and consumers) empowered to develop a vision for future hospital and community care. Without slowing down the pace and educating about unintended consequences, community stakeholders would not have agreed to such a "planning" exercise. They wanted action. But if planning and compromise were needed to speed up the action, they would participate. The "Inpatient Futures" group developed a proposed mission for future inpatient care (a focus, as in the rest of health care, on acute-care, stabilization, and short-stay treatment) and recommended next steps. Regional stakeholders groups would plan for the future of each hospital (anticipated capacity, within broad state parameters and the agreed mission, as well as options for downsizing, merger, or closure). The regional groups would include hospital labor representatives, giving staff a voice, and leading commitments to employ former hospital staff to run some of the new community services in each region.

Reframing the "hospital problem" from a rapid "win-lose" proposition to a shared "win-win" (or at least, "win–not lose") approach produced a viable strategy for implementing the Mental Health Act, but it was not without its problems. The local boards that had never used hospitals much—but anticipated getting significant new resources—would have their hopes deferred. With limited resources, we directed funds from downsizing primarily to the communities that were in a position to bring their residents home. The low-use boards, upset by the change, filed a lawsuit that would not be settled for several years, until it was clear that downsizing would eventually produce significant savings. The Inpatient Futures effort worked, validating one strategic response that leadership teams may find useful in periods of intense, short-term conflict: reframing the problem from an immediate unsolvable tension to a longer-range shared solution with elements of a "win-win" approach.

Finding a solution to community funding problems and developing a long-range vision of a (reduced) hospital role was not enough to insure the quality of hospital care. Leadership and staff morale was improved somewhat, but the hospitals were still vulnerable and buffeted. In short, Ohio's state hospitals were not in good shape. The National Alliance for the Mentally Ill (NAMI) (Torrey, Erdman, Wolfe, & Flynn, 1990) sponsored report "Care of the Seriously Mentally Ill: A Rating of State Programs" had found the quality of care in Ohio's state hospitals poor, especially the quality of the medical staff. "Too much idleness for patients and staff and not enough therapeutic activities at State Hospitals" was another view expressed by the task force appointed by newly elected Governor George Voinovich to evaluate state agencies. A response to the governor and a viable role and vision for the hospitals was required.

We initiated a process to improve care in our state hospitals, places that were our direct responsibility. If we demonstrated quality care here, we believed we could credibly assert leadership for a quality-of-care agenda in community agencies. Perhaps a focus on clinical quality could also counterbalance the local desire for more money, quickly. Our state hospital approach began with a plan to focus on the quality of care through best practices and empowering medical and clinical staff. We engaged the hospital CEOs in a combined leadership role with medical directors while also empowering other clinical leadership. Believing that clinical quality begins with leadership, we focused on the recruitment of medical staff, via affiliations with medical school departments of psychiatry. Collaboration included creating a "Professor of Public Psychiatry" (Svendsen et al., 2005) in each medical school, charged with collaborating with the public system.

We focused on best-practices initiatives, beginning with a $1 million/year state appropriation to bring the newly available drug clozapine to hospitalized patients. The $1 million was enough to provided clozapine for 400 long-stay (average length of stay was four years) hospitalized persons with schizophrenia, for whom previous treatments had not provided adequate relief for them to leave the hospitals. Jointly with our clinical leadership, we developed treatment guidelines for clozapine, and all staff monitored outcomes and side effects closely. Psychologists utilized the Brief Psychiatric Rating Scale (BPRS) to assess response and outcomes. Together we learned the benefits of psychosocial interventions when we discovered, for example, that not one person initially started on clozapine was discharged in the first six months. This was not because people were not improving, but because extensive habilitation was required to recover from such prolonged and serious illness and the effects of institutionalization. We also learned that when patients were discharged on clozapine, with community supports, readmission was rare, and community functioning was adequate. While outcomes for patients were the most important results of these efforts, the focus on quality improved staff focus and morale.

We responded to the Governor's Task Force criticism of excessive idleness by staff and patients and a lack of therapeutic activities by creating the Therapeutic Activities and Recovery Process initiative (TARP). We brought clinical staff from all hospitals together for the first time in memory to share their best programming. Immediately hospitals learned from each other and began benchmarking clinical approaches, and sharing continued afterwards as well. We shared clinical accomplishments and best-practices approaches in our hospitals and invited community agency partners to learn what our hospitals were doing via a TARP newsletter and a "Clozapine Next Steps" conference. Hospital morale improved, clinical teams became energized and felt valued, and community leaders, advocates, and providers took note. Hospitalized patients improved and were discharged in record numbers through the combination of expanded community services, improved treatment, and incentives to avoid hospitalization. The hospital population declined, from 2,800 in 1991, to 1,200 by 2000.

We then began a process to reengineer our hospital system to be more efficient and clinically effective (Buckley, Svendsen, et al., 1999.) The process was highlighted by periodic "reengineering retreats" over a three-year period. Hospital reengineering was also a "reframing" effort, directed this time at hospital leadership and staff. The focus was to shift energies away from reacting to externally imposed downsizing and toward an active role in competing for resources based on the quality and price of services. This focus was assisted by a statewide quality improvement initiative championed by Governor Voinovich. Quality Services Through Partnership, or QSTP, was an effort to bring the quality-improvement message of Deming (1993) to state government. Given the emphasis on quality improvement that the hospitals had learned via the

Joint Commission's accreditation emphasis on quality, state hospitals became among the most successful adopters in state government of quality management practices.

We engaged community boards, agencies, clinicians, political leaders, consumers, and families to join our central office and hospital leadership in the process. We began with an emphasis on streamlining administration to maximize the resources available for clinical care. This was an effort that hospitals could agree on. The closure of some hospitals and administrative consolidation of others resulted in a move from 14 separate hospitals to nine inpatient sites managed as five hospital systems. The savings from hospital downsizing plus closures were sufficient to persuade the boards to settle the funding lawsuit with a mediated agreement. We then improved clinical services by identifying key clinical functions and creating four service lines to improve the quality of our care. Our service lines included: 1) Forensic Services; 2) Intensive and Specialized Services for acute care of people newly admitted and for those with longer stays but high acuteness, such as those with dual diagnoses; 3) Family and Children, focusing on the needs of patient's family members; and 4) Community Support Network, the outpatient services provided by hospital-employed community staff. The "product-line" approach enabled us to focus and use data to improve efficiency in care and measure outcomes. Each product line was led by a hospital CEO and medical director with other clinical disciplines from each hospital site. We thus had a matrix system with hospital systems running clinical care at their site(s) but product lines providing administrative and best-practice guidance. The principles of mental health leadership later described by Anthony and Huckshorn (2008) were exemplified. We developed a shared vision and a culture to live by this vision; we were united by mission but decentralized by operations; there was leadership at many levels by professionals from many disciplines; staff at all levels were trained and empowered; and exemplary performers were recognized and became leaders. Data and information were used to change and guide development. Team leadership at the state level was matched or exceeded by team leadership in each hospital system. Care, efficiency, and staff morale improved. Patient and family satisfaction were frequently measured and showed improvement. Hospitals passed Medicare and JCAHO surveys with impressive scores. Also in contrast to the 1990 NAMI evaluation of state mental health systems when state hospitals were singled out for the poor quality of care, the 2006 NAMI report ranked Ohio's mental health system as the best in the country, and the quality of care in hospitals was not even mentioned.

TRANSITIONAL LEADERSHIP: SETTING THE STAGE FOR FUTURE DEVELOPMENTS

Two major "getting ready," or transitional, predisposing efforts had begun during the stormy times that set the stage for future developments. The first and foremost of these was bringing the system together around a vision of *recovery*. The second was a focus on leadership development and becoming a learning organization and sharing leadership with community stakeholders. We will describe these two transitional efforts below.

CASE STUDY: LEADERSHIP IN A TIME OF TRANSITION: ESTABLISHING A RECOVERY FOUNDATION

As the Inpatient Futures process established a direction for structural change, and the focus and mission of inpatient care were shaped by the reengineering efforts, unifying themes for community care were needed. A shared goal that went beyond getting people out of hospitals and into communities was needed. Ohio's mental health system enjoyed a good foundation of "basic" services. The state had enthusiastically embraced the Community Mental Health Center (CMHC) program, so a network of CMHCs/clinics had long existed. The major services innovations promoted by Pam Hyde and Marti Knisely (the architects of the 1988 Mental Health Act) had been strengths-based case management (Rapp and Goscha, 2006) and supported housing termed "housing as housing." These models were adaptive in that they provided more flexibility and structure than traditional clinic services for people with long hospital stays, without imposing new institutional structures or unsustainable costs. Ohio had also developed a network of Consumer Operated Services, providing peer-directed alternatives on a modest scale in many communities.

This basic array of services (clinical, case management, housing) was both common-sense and functional. But by the 1990s, more focus and inspiration were needed. William Anthony's paper (1993) proposing "recovery" as the organizing principle for community support provided a springboard to position this emerging paradigm as an organizing and motivating vision. But "recovery" did not have a foothold in Ohio, except as a concept in the addiction system—a partner/competitor. People were not ready to embrace a concept viewed as the property of addiction treatment.

Leadership to develop "mental health recovery" as a theme for Ohio was provided by Wilma Townsend, head of the Community Support/Consumer Services office in ODMH. A social worker with the instincts of a community organizer, Wilma designed a multistage "bottom-up and top-down" change process to make recovery a central theme in Ohio's mental health system. The first stage was launched in April 1994, when ODMH convened a "recovery dialogue" to explore the new concept's relevance for Ohio. National and state leaders spent two days exploring recovery. The conversation planted a seed that needed to be nurtured. The second stage was to conduct recovery dialogues in every region of Ohio. ODMH leaders participated with board and agency staff, families, and consumers. Each dialogue, conducted in the late afternoon or evening to facilitate participation, began with a local individual describing their personal recovery journey, and guided inquiry into the meaning of their experiences. Then participants broke into smaller groups to brainstorm ways to advance recovery.

The themes and energy from the regional recovery dialogues were used to launch three rounds of competitive, mid-sized (e.g., $100,000/year per funded project) recovery demonstrations. Each project was "owned" and operated by a local consumer group, with the sponsorship and support of the board. The solicitation was open-ended; communities could propose alternatives that in their view best advanced a recovery vision. Borrowing from Jean Campbell's Well Being Project

(1993), each project included a participant driven evaluation project, mentored and overseen by a university faculty member. A learning community process supported the demonstration projects. Papers from the evaluation (e.g., Bullock, Ensing, & Alloy and Young & Bullock at the University of Toledo and Wishnick and Stefan et al. at the University of Cincinnati published in 1998–1999) added to the conceptual and evidence base of the emerging recovery concept.

The Department's Community Support Program (CSP) Advisory Committee took the lead in synthesizing the themes that emerged from this multistage innovation (Beale & Lambric, 1995). It was useful to have this diverse group of advisors work on a "real" project, and to balance concerns developed by staff. In 2000 recovery learning was synthesized in *Emerging Best Practices in Mental Health Recovery* which became a widely cited resource in the United States and the United Kingdom.

The effort to develop a recovery framework for Ohio illustrates several aspects of change management. First, the leadership in the effort came from senior staff (principally CSP leader Wilma Townsend and Evaluation/Research Director Dee Roth) at a time when the top leadership team of ODMH was caught up in the challenges of implementing the Mental Health Act. With the support of the top leadership team, these staff entrepreneurs were not caught up in the challenges of hospital downsizing, funding lawsuits, and the like. But they were dedicated and competent to lead an initiative that started small but would become a state and national vision. By that time the system would become calmer, the resource of recovery would be well enough developed to become a strategic imperative.

CASE EXAMPLE: LEADERSHIP IN A TIME OF TRANSITION: LEADERSHIP TRAINING

In the mid-1990s, our ODMH leadership team engaged the expertise of the Ohio State University School of Public Administration faculty to assist us with our work. They joined our leadership team at times and helped us develop processes and to engage many throughout our organization in learning projects. The theoretical model and the coursework first involved the use of the text *The Fifth Discipline: The Art and Practice of the Learning Organization* (2000), by Peter Senge, a senior lecturer at the Massachusetts Institute of Technology. The goal of this approach is for the organization to become a "learning organization," a term used to describe an organization that facilitates the learning of its members and continuously transforms itself. The consultation and the model assisted a cultural change process. It emphasized group problem-solving using systems thinking to become a learning organization.

Our public administration consultants provided classes for enrollees with homework and applications provided from within our mental health organization and system. People were educated in the Senge's five main disciplines: systems thinking, personal mastery, mental models, shared vision, and team learning. These theories and methods helped us foster aspiration, improve reflective conversation, and better approach and understand complexity.

As a learning organization we also engaged with our consultants and often on our own in other management and organizational models and approaches. Our consultants provided Myers-Briggs testing for personal styles and how these might work with others on the team. One specific course for interested staff included the use of data to make decisions. Another embraced the Steven Covey book *The Seven Habits of Highly Effective People* (1989). A third approach, following Margaret Wheatley's **Leadership and the New Science: Discovering Order in a Chaotic World** (1999), focused on the value of personal relationships in leadership, change, and becoming a "self organizing" organization. Participation was voluntary, but many leaders and managers at different levels participated, and our entire mental health department became more of a learning organization.

Our university consultants worked regularly with our leadership team for an initial time period, but after a two- to three-year period, consultation ceased. However, the approaches we learned were continued; for example, the Leadership Team continued to have quarterly retreats to review, anticipate, and set direction.

Our mental health department also provided funding to bring university-based mental health leadership programs to mental health leaders throughout the local and community system. Mental Health Leadership Programs (2005) included the Ohio State University Leadership 2000+ Academy and the Case Western Reserve Mental Health Executive Leadership Program (MHELP). Each enrolled mental health leaders for monthly full-day or more learning opportunities over an academic year. Class work focused on issues such as finance and marketing in health care, performance improvement and quality strategies, updates on legal issues in mental health care, value-based management and leadership, public policy and legislative issues, strategic thinking and planning, finance, marketing, evidence-based practices- and consumer/recovery-focused care.

One of the measurable outcomes of these leadership efforts was familiarity with business planning and the requirement that all who received technical assistance grants from ODMH would submit a business plan. This aligned our processes and encouraged reflection and careful planning and evaluation of mental health programs throughout our state. Another example is the shared leadership that developed as both state and community partnerships came together. One example is the program known as Solutions to Ohio's Quality and Compliance, popularly termed SOQIC. This multi-stakeholder effort created and implemented a set of standardized documentation treatment forms for Ohio's mental health system. Another example of shared leadership is described in the next section of this chapter in the case example "Recovery Efforts Provide Direction."

LEADERSHIP WHEN THE SEAS ARE (TOO) CALM

The third major phase of our leadership experience followed the period of structural change implementing comprehensive reform legislation. This period paralleled the administration of Ohio Governor Bob Taft (1999–2007). The transition from hospital care and a state-centered system had been largely completed. The hospital system had shrunk from 16 facilities to five hospitals providing care at nine sites, and from roughly 2,800 inpatients to about 1,200. The mission of the hospitals had shifted to acute and high-urgency care; resources were relatively stable; and the quality of care was improved. Community care had been greatly expanded, and most local systems had adapted to the dimensions of change that had been thrust on them (responsibility for serving people with the most serious illnesses; careful management of hospital utilization).

No major external challenges confronted the system during this period. Funding was tight, but manageable. Healthcare reform was a decade away. The trend toward Medicaid managed care that swept up many states largely passed Ohio by, except for a failed effort to gain control of and manage Medicaid inpatient psychiatric care. Litigation by the county boards related to implementation of the Mental Health Act of 1988 had been resolved with successful hospital downsizing and cost control.

Viewed strategically, the major challenges in this period were not primarily of external origin. Rather, the major issue was to create an agenda that would bring people together in the absence of a dominant threat. The transitional predisposing efforts of a vision for recovery and a focus on leadership development had begun. The major themes during this time revolved around expanding a vision of recovery. Team approaches and shared management approaches were our methods. Clinically, our focus was on developing a clinical quality agenda, paying attention to outcomes and quality improvement, and bringing evidence-based mental health practices to our hospital and community system.

CASE EXAMPLE: RECOVERY EFFORTS PROVIDE DIRECTION

During this relatively calm period, we were able to focus more explicitly on installing a vision of recovery as a foundation for the mental health system. The work done in the recovery demonstration projects and documented in *Emerging Best Practices in Mental Health Recovery* was ready for the mainstream. This was validated when the President's New Freedom Commission on Mental Health focused on recovery in their Final Report (2003). *Emerging Best Practices* outlined nine essential components of recovery (clinical care, family support, peer support and relationships, work and meaningful activity, power and control, stigma, community involvement, access to resources, and education) and four stages that many people in recovery would experience (moving from being Dependent and Unaware to Aware but Dependent, to Aware and Independent, and finally to Aware and Interdependent). The dissemination process included a statewide Recovery Conference, followed by numerous local recovery conferences, presentations with consumers sharing their experiences and recovery journeys at board meetings, and consumer organization meetings.

ODMH also used its leadership staff to reinforce the recovery and resiliency practice and policy. The area directors functioned as regional "account managers" with community mental health key stakeholders; i.e., community mental health boards, community mental health agencies, consumers and family members, as well as other constituencies. Leaders in staff roles also exercised leadership, especially the Consumer Services Office, who provided comprehensive leadership and partnership with consumers, family members, and their respective associations.

The culture of ODMH as a learning organization assisted the dissemination of recovery principles. Team members sought new learning to become empowered with theory, knowledge, and tools to support dynamic system change. Employing staff retreats, referred to as "advances," theoretical approaches, including the work of Margaret Wheatley and Peter Senge, provided supplemental learning and leadership tools. This information supported change as a constant ingredient in the organization. ODMH strived to become a "leader-full" organization.

Recovery Centers

Recovery in practice at local levels was best exemplified by the developing Recovery Centers throughout Ohio. Several of the Recovery Centers had emerged or grown as a result of the recovery demonstration grants. Others were funded by county boards. Recovery Centers were local programs governed predominantly by a consumer board. They provided peer support, consumer-operated services such as transportation, housing and employment, and opportunities for consumer empowerment and hope. Recovery Centers were a self-directed alternative, building on consumer-operated services, which had existed in Ohio since the 1980s.

As the demand for consumer-operated services increased, ODMH redirected community capital project funds, which had previously been used only for treatment facilities and housing, to support Recovery Centers. Consumer-operated services (COS) have been described as "peer-run service agencies that encourage and support persons with mental illness who have been underserved and require assistance to obtain vital services through peer advocacy." The local models for recovery centers and consumer-operated services varied, from a small organization providing peer support or a drop-in center, to a fully staffed consumer recovery center providing a full range of consumer services, including housing and employment. Some examples include The Main Place, in Newark, Ohio; and The Thomas M. Wernert Center in Toledo.

Glenn Hopkins, executive director of The Main Place, developed a toolkit, *Poverty: Breaking the Trend, Livin' the Dream—A Guide to Overcoming Mental Illness and Poverty*. Hopkins states that the "toolkit is a starting point and reference for thinking about the impact of poverty on your life, a learning tool, a teaching tool, and as a stepping-stone to enhance your recovery" (Hopkins, Voelkle, and Bauman, 2009). The curriculum and training material enabled consumer-operated service centers to share practices for program development in other communities. Ohio's Consumer-Operated Services grew from two drop-in centers to over 60 during the past three decades.

We also found that community recovery practices needed additional support. ODMH did not have the staff to provide this, but enthusiastic, mission-driven organizations would provide this with modest support. We developed a range of "extenders" to highlight and disseminate new practices. These included the Consumer Recovery Network, a project to promote use of Wellness Recovery Action Plans (WRAP), a cultural competence initiative led by Multi-ethnic Advocates for Cultural Competence (MACC), a Housing Initiative, and a project to support Advance Directives. There was a natural synergy between recovery as a concept and value and these allied technical assistance entities that helped make recovery an integrated and mainstream activity.

CASE EXAMPLE: EVIDENCE-BASED PRACTICES (EBPS) IMPROVE CLINICAL CARE

The recovery paradigm inspired and motivated many people in the system, including many clinicians, but it spoke most directly to consumers. Activities to organize and motivate clinicians and providers were also needed. A clinical quality agenda based on goals of recovery for adults and resiliency for children and adolescents became our project during these calm times, focusing on quality improvement, outcomes measurement, and evidence-based practices. Our evidence-based practice initiatives were especially successful, and many of them continue as important and viable tools.

By the late 1990s, evidence-based practices were fast becoming the approach in all of medicine and community mental health was no exception. Structural reform, such as had occurred in Ohio, was found to be helpful and perhaps necessary but by itself did not improve outcomes for consumers (Morrissey et al., 1994; Bickman et al., 2000). Mental health services research, however, was demonstrating improved outcomes for individuals using multidisciplinary interventions like Assertive Community Treatment and Supported Employment. Bob Drake had worked with colleagues in New Hampshire to create a partnership with providers to test and support these evidence-based practices, and Scott Henggler had developed the Family Services Research Center at the Medical University of South Carolina to support and study implementation of evidence-based children's services in community settings. Fidelity to the model was essential for successful outcomes, and training of multidisciplinary staff was essential. However, sending hundreds of clinicians to New Hampshire or South Carolina was not going to work. Also, the EBP "movement" was stirring up some reactions. For example, critics wondered about good approaches that the researchers had not yet validated. We needed an approach for Ohio—one that would install the proven best-practice models but one also that would help providers modify and improve their own programs, and one that would be broad enough to support different strategies.

For people with serious mental illnesses, such as schizophrenia, the evidence-based practices were usually multidisciplinary team approaches such as Assertive Community Treatment. By their very nature they were complex, and they required fidelity to the model to be effective. Adopting agencies needed to see a benefit from installing them—such as financial savings or reduced hospitalizations. EBPs needed to be salient to a significant portion of the serious mental illness (SMI) population. "Requiring and mandating" was not considered a doable option, so we needed a method to "encourage and promote." The shared vision to get there became our "Quality Agenda," which was defined as achieving recovery and resilience through evidence-based practices while measuring outcomes and promoting quality improvement.

After consultation with Robert Drake and others from New Hampshire (Drake et al., 2001), we began with the Integrated Dual Diagnosis Treatment (IDDT) model for co-occurring mental illness and substance use disorders. ODMH partnered with the Ohio Department of Alcohol and Drug Addiction Services and together funded the Case Western Reserve University Departments of Psychiatry and Social Work to offer the IDDT model to community providers and state hospitals. Bob Drake and his colleagues would guide the initial development of the Coordinating Centers of Excellence, referred to for short as the CCOE. The Coordinating Centers would provide free consultation and technical assistance, including initial assessment of the risks and benefits of adopting the EBP, initial training of staff, ongoing education, evaluation tools, and consultative supports. By 2007, over 60 agencies in Ohio were employing IDDT, reaching persons with a co-occurring mental illness and substance use disorder.

ODMH did not have the expertise or the resources to bring evidence-based practices to community providers. However, by building on the success of the IDDT partnership, typically with university and/or community partners, other salient coordinating centers of excellence (CCOEs) were developed, and most flourished. All CCOEs developed skills at consulting and providing technical assistance to agencies about EBPs. These included extensive consultation with leadership and staff in the getting-ready or predisposing-factors phase, when an agency considers whether to proceed with adopting an EBP into its structure and evaluates its likelihood for success. CCOEs also provided training and technical assistance with the implementation phase, as well as assistance in reinforcing and sustaining success over time. Many CCOEs included not only clinical and administrative partners, but consumer partners as well.

For most EBPs, fidelity measurement and evaluation was a frequent component of the CCOE technical assistance process. Adoption and implementation of EBPs was studied by an ODMH research initiative, The Innovation Diffusion and Adoption Research Project (IDARP), described by Panzano and Roth in 2006.

Ohio Coordinating Center of Excellence initiatives proved to be quite successful. They began in 2000, and most are still thriving today. The CCOE strategy was highlighted in the 2006 NAMI **Grading the States** report as "impressive"; and "other states would do well to take notice of Ohio's approach." The list of Ohio's CCOEs included:

Integrated Dual Diagnosis Treatment (IDDT)

Supported Employment (SE)

Cluster-based Planning Alliance (Clusters)

The Ohio Medication Algorithm Project (OMAP) (This CCOE was discontinued.)

Multi-Systemic Therapy (MST)

Mental Illness/Mental Retardation (MI/MR, and now Mental Illness/Developmental Disability [MI/DD])

Wellness Management and Recovery (WMR)

Assertive Community Treatment (ACT)

Advanced Directives (initially in partnership with the ODMH Office of Consumer Services and later outsourced to the State Consumer Advocacy organization)

Criminal Justice CCOE (CJ CCOE)

REFLECTIONS ON TRANSFORMATIONAL LEADERSHIP

In reflecting back on our shared leadership experiences over many years, several major principles and lessons come to mind. It should be said that we did not begin with a focus on the term *transformational leadership* of the mental health system—but in retrospect, the concepts and approaches do fit. We did, however, begin our work together with the transformative task of implementing the Mental Health Act of 1988—to move mental health services and funding from a centralized authority to shared responsibility with local authorities, while safeguarding or improving clinical quality and consumer outcomes. Our next transformational task was guided by a shared vision of recovery for those experiencing a mental illness. We believe our case examples describe our transformational approaches.

The function of transformational leadership, according to Burns (1978), "is to engage followers, not merely to activate them, to commingle needs and aspirations and goals in a common enterprise…of both leaders and followers." Clearly this is what Mike Hogan did from the beginning. He came into his leadership role with the clear goal of implementing the Mental Health Act of 1988. This was the stated mission also for Dale when he was hired as medical director; as well as to focus on improving clinical care, beginning in the hospitals. Mike accepted this challenge and shared his vision for implementation and engaged many, including a leadership team, to adapt (i.e., reframe as needed) and to adopt this vision and its specific goals. Later, with a vision of recovery from mental illness, Judy Wortham Wood took a major lead in focusing the system on recovery while working with others on the leadership team. Together with Mike, we shared the transforming message and implementation strategies throughout the organization and with other leaders and followers in the state to bring the shared visions into reality.

How well did Ohio do during our leadership time in transforming its mental health system? Two things come to mind.

- The best outside evaluation of our efforts was described in the 2006 National Alliance on Mental Illness evaluation of state mental health care systems. Ohio received an A grade in information access, a B in infrastructure, a B in services, and a B for recovery supports. Ohio received recognition for recent innovations in consumer and family roles in the system, impressive implementation of EBPs and criminal justice system initiatives and strong state-level leadership in various branches of government. Overall, Ohio received a grade of a high B, which was one of the two best grades for state mental health systems.
- A second accolade was that Mike Hogan was chosen to lead President Bush's New Freedom Commission on Mental Health. Its 2003 report, *Achieving the Promise: Transforming Mental Health Care in America*, describes a strategy for mental health care transformation to ensure services and supports that actively facilitate recovery and build resilience. The report identified six goals of transformation and showcased model programs to illustrate these goals. The Mental Health Commission report has similarities to many of the approaches we had been doing in Ohio.

Some of the principles that guided us through rough, transitional, and calm times are stated below. We believe our case histories provide examples of these principles.

- Keep your eye on the star.
- "Taking care of business" is job one. Managing the mental health department with its clinical care, regulatory compliance, and funding must be done first and done well. To demonstrate this, Mike Hogan shared his mom's rule: "clean up your room before you go out and play."
- Share the vision and develop it further with others.
- When the problem seems impossible to resolve, try reframing the issues.

- Mental health leadership is a team sport.
- Mental health leadership focus includes consumer, clinical, and administrative perspectives.
- "Do the right thing": A value-based approach leads to trust.
- You can't do just one thing. Change takes action on many fronts at the same time.
- Lead, follow, or get out of the way.
- Seek outside consultation to assist. Examples include university assistance in leadership training and evidence-based practice assistance.
- Partner with your best resources. Examples include consumers to help establish recovery or universities to assist with implementing evidence-based practices.
- Schedule time to consider, gather input, and set direction. Hold large retreats to seek input and set strategic direction; and quarterly leadership team retreats to evaluate, consider, and define new directions.

REFERENCES

Anthony, W. A. (1993). Recovery from mental illness: The guiding vision of the mental health service system in the 1990s. *Psychosocial Rehabilitation Journal* 16(4), 11–23.

Anthony, W. A., and Huckshorn, K. A. (2008). *Principled Leadership in Mental Health Systems and Programs.* Center for Psychiatric Rehabilitation, Boston University.

Beale, V., andLambric, T. (1995). A Report by the Community Support Program (CSP) Advisory Committee: *The Recovery Concept: Implementation in the Mental Health System*, August.

Bickman, L., Lambert, E. W., Andrade, A. R., and Penaloza, R. V. (2000). The Fort Bragg continuum of care for children and adolescents: Mental health outcomes over five years. *Journal of Consulting and Clinical Psychology* 68(4) August, 710–716.

Brown, L. D., Isett, K. R., and Hogan, M. F. (2010). Stewardship in mental health policy: Inspiration, influence, institution? *Journal of Health Politics, Policy and Law* 3(35), 389–406.

Bullock, W. A., Ensing, D. S., and Alloy, V. (1999). Consumer leadership education: Evaluation of a program to promote recovery in persons with psychiatric disabilities. *New Research in Mental Health,* Ohio Department of Mental Health website, Vol. 14, 1998–1999, at http://mentalhealth.ohio.gov/what-we-do/promote/research-and-evaluation/publications/new-research-in-mental-health.shtml.

Burns, J. M. (1978). *Leadership.* New York: Harper & Row.

Burti, L., Berti, L., Canova, E., Fornari, M., and Pavani, D. An approach to interdisciplinary mental health work in South-Verona, Italy. This volume—Chapter 6.

Buckley, P., Svendsen, D., Hogan, M., Herndon, S (1999). Managed care in public mental health systems: The Ohio Initiative. *Journal of Practical Psychiatry and Behavioral Health* 5(1), 44–46.

Campbell, J. (1993). The Well-Being Project: Mental Health Clients Speak for Themselves. Paper presented at the annual conference of Mental Health Services Research and Evaluation, Arlington, VA.

Covey, S. R. (1989). *The Seven Habits of Highly Effective People.* Turtleback Books.

Deming, W. E. (1993). *The New Economics for Industry, Government and Education.* Cambridge, MA: Massachusetts Institute of Technology Center for Advanced Engineering Study.

Drake, R.E., Goldman, H. H., Leff, H. S., Lehman, A. F., Dixon, L., Mueser, K. T., and Torrey, W. C. (2001). Implementing evidence-based practices in routine mental health service settings. *Psychiatric Services, 52,* 179–182.

Gabarro, J. (1987). *The Dynamics of Taking Charge*. Boston: Harvard Business School Press.

Henggler, S., Melton, G., Brondino, M., Sherer, D., & Henley, J. (1997). Multisystemic therapy with violent and chronic juvenile offenders and their families: The role of treatment fidelity in successful dissemination. *Journal of Consulting and Clinical Psychology*, 65(5), 821–833.

Hopkins, G., Voelkel, R., and Bauman, G. (2009). Poverty: Breaking the Trend, Livin' the Dream—A Guide to Overcoming Mental Illness and Poverty. Grant number 5U79SM057460–04 from the Substance Abuse and Mental Health Services Administration (SAMHSA).

Mental Health Leadership Programs, in ODMH Quality Matters Newsletter: *Connecting Through Clinical Quality, Recovery and Resiliency* (May 2005), http://dmhext01.mh.state.oh.us/dmh/news-letter/qualitymatters.nsf/content/7C803B3C9FBD9AD485256FD6004C6E43?OpenDocument#10.%20Mental%20health%20leadership%20prog.

Morrissey, J. P., Calloway, M., Bartko, W.T., Ridgely, M. S., Goldman, H. H., and Paulson, R. I. (1994). Local mental health authorities and service system change: Evidence from the Robert Wood Johnson program on chronic mental illness. *The Milbank Quarterly* 72(1), 49–80.

National Alliance on Mental Illness. (2006). *Grading the States: A Report on America's Health Care System for Serious Mental Illness*. Arlington, VA: Author.

Panzano, P. and Roth, D. (2006). The decision to adopt evidence-based and other innovative mental health practices: Risky business? *Psychiatric Services* 57, 1153–1161.

The President's New Freedom Commission on Mental Health (2003): *Achieving the Promise: Transforming Mental Health Care in America, Final Report*, Rockville, MD: DHHS Pub. No. SMA-03–3832.

Rapp, C. A., and Goscha, R. J. (2006). *The Strengths Model: Case Management with People with Psychiatric Disabilities*. New York: Oxford University Press.

ResiliencyWorkgroup, Program and Policy Development . (2006). Ohio Department of Mental Health, Version 1, July 2006.

Schwartz, D. A. (1989). A Précis of Administration. *Community Mental Health Journal* 25(3), 229–244.

Senge, Peter M. (1990). *The Fifth Discipline*. Doubleday/Currency.

Svendsen, D. P., Cutler, D. L., Ronis, R. J., Herman, L. C., Morrison, A., Smith, M. K., et al. (2005). The Professor of Public Psychiatry model in Ohio: The impact on training, program innovation, and the quality of mental health care. *Community Mental Health Journal* 41(6), 775–784, December.

Torrey, E. F., Erdman, K., Wolfe, S. M., and Flynn, L. (1990). *Care of the Seriously Mentally Ill: A Rating of State Programs*. Washington, DC: Public Citizen Health Research Group and National Alliance for the Mentally Ill.

Townsend, W., Boyd, S., Griffin, G., andHicks, P. L. (2000). *Emerging Best Practices in Mental Health Recovery*. Columbus, OH: The Ohio Department of Mental Health.

Townsend, W., and O'Brien, J. (2009). Phase One: Gathering and Analysis of Current COS and Peer Support Services. December 31, 2009.

Wheatley, M. (1999). *Leadership and the New Science: Discovering Order in a Chaotic World*. San Francisco: Barret-Koehler Publishers.

Wishnick, H. M., Steffen, J. M., Ensfield, L. B., Krzton, K. M., Wilder-Willis, K. E., Yangarber-Hicks, N. I., et al. (1999). Researching Recovery: The Hamilton County Recovery Initiative Research Team, Ohio Department of Mental Health. *New Research in Mental Health* 14, @ http://mentalhealth.ohio.gov/what-we-do/promote/research-and-evaluation/publications/new-research-in-mental-health.shtml.

Young, S.L., and Bullock, W. A. (1999). Development and evaluation of a recovery enhancement group for mental health consumers. *New Research in Mental Health, Ohio Department of Mental Health* 14, http://mentalhealth.ohio.gov/what-we-do/promote/research-and-evaluation/publications/new-research-in-mental-health.shtml.

CHAPTER 35

PSYCHIATRIC RISK MANAGEMENT

Efforts to Reduce Unforeseen Outcomes

LESLIE A. WINTERS, GREGORY B. TEAGUE, AND
KENNETH R. YEAGER

As part of our daily living, each one of us takes on risk. All of our daily activities involve a certain amount of risk. Just in driving to work, we could be hit by another car and injured, but most of us are willing to assume that risk. We make decisions on the level of risk we consider acceptable and act accordingly. At times, if we cannot control the level of risk involved in our activity, we may have the option of deciding whether or not to forgo that activity—for example, deciding not to have evening appointments if we would be the only mental health professional on the premises. But there are risks inherent in many professional activities we cannot forgo.

As a mental health professional, not only are you exposed to the risks you decide to undertake, but you are also exposed to those risks your clients decide to undertake, such as their not taking their prescribed medication despite the resulting delusional thoughts. Controlling both types of risks can be a challenge, and the consequences can have a significant impact, not only (and most importantly) on the well-being of the client, but also on you and other professionals involved in treatment.

This chapter is intended to identify a range of approaches to manage those risks. We will identify approaches to risk management in three general categories: first, we will describe considerations for development of a general crisis management plan, focusing on aspects of facilities and operations that may raise or lower risks for patients. Next, we will highlight clinical strategies within treatment that reduce the risk that patients will pose a danger to themselves or others. Last, we will identify additional strategies for reducing risk to either patients or professionals. We will close the chapter with a brief list of best practice take-away points, followed by references and other resources, grouped by topic.

CRISIS MANAGEMENT PLAN

In this day and age of reduced mental health services, it is more likely than ever that the community mental health professional will have to deal with a patient in crisis. Without planning for the management of patients in crisis, it is more likely that there will be an unexpected or adverse patient outcome. Couple the professional desire to avoid unexpected outcomes with the propensity of the members of our society to try to hold someone else accountable for all bad outcomes, and it is in everyone's interest to do as much as possible to avoid the adverse outcome. Again, we do that by attempting to manage our risk. Whether you have a one-person clinic or manage a community-wide crisis center, it is important for all mental health professionals to have a crisis management plan for their facility and their patients.

There are three main components to a good crisis management plan. They are recognition of the risks, management of the risks, and responding appropriately to incidents. The first component of the plan involves recognition and analysis of potential risks, which can involve a multitude of pathways such as the risks to the patient, the risks to the family, or the risks to the clinician and staff. Once the risks have been clearly specified and analyzed, the second component comes into play, in the development of a plan to manage each of them by either eliminating or controlling the risk. The third component is the development of a plan to respond to each type of situation should it occur. If these three components are developed in detail prior to a crisis, clinicians will know how to recognize and respond to a situation if it occurs. A timely and appropriate response will be more likely—and avoiding the bad outcome will also be more likely. Following is a description of each component of the crisis management plan in more detail.

RISK ASSESSMENT

Whether a sole practitioner or the member of a team from a larger facility, clinicians should consider the risks they face with their particular patient population. It is important to consider risks associated with both the stable patient and the patient in crisis, as the same patient may need to be assisted in both states. A multidisciplinary approach to risk assessment will result in the broadest recognition of the potential risks.

Facilities

Begin with an assessment of the facilities in which you are treating the patient. Do a walk-through of the facility and consider the risks to the patients, visitors, and staff. For example, consider where the doors are in relationship to the location of the treatment team member. Will the clinician always be able to get away from the patient? If the patient will be left alone in the treatment room, look at all the ways the patient might injure themselves. Are there hanging points? Are there items the patient could use to wrap around their neck such as a telephone cord, sheet, or trash bag? It is important to look high and low, as the patient can sit on the floor and use a waist-high handrail as a hanging point. What medications are kept in the area? Can the patient get to them? Are there tools kept in the area that could be used as a weapon? Are the windows locked? If the patient tried, could they jump out of the window? Would it break away?

While many of these types of questions seem rather basic, we often work in an environment without really noticing all of the risks. It takes a conscious assessment to try to determine the risk factors associated with a facility. Consider an annual walk-through with the safety, quality, risk management, facilities, and housekeeping staff. In a small office, bring in all of the staff and maybe the property manager. Consider asking the police or a regular contractor to assist in providing those additional eyes. Try to think like a patient in crisis. Look for ways to hurt yourself or someone else. That will help you find your facility's risk points.

Don't forget to consider family waiting areas. In times of crisis, the family can be extremely agitated. If a family member becomes violent or agitated, is there a way to protect the staff? Are there items that might become weapons? Are there ways to keep the patient and the family separated if need be?

In addition to looking for facility issues that might pose a risk, look at the facility with the outlook of whether the environment might over-stimulate a patient. Are there ways to create a more calming environment for the patients and families?

A single facility assessment, however comprehensive, is insufficient. The assessment needs to be repeated regularly, particularly in conjunction with all construction projects or changes in the use of the space. Over time, new items can be brought into an area without anyone thinking about the hazards. Likewise, spaces can be given new uses without a risk assessment. A regular program of reassessment will avoid creating new problems.

Once the facility assessment is done, the decision can be made to either eliminate the danger or manage the risk. It is important to note that it is not always cost-effective or physically possible to eliminate all facility risks. For example, equipment that poses a danger may be needed for operational purposes. However, many risks may still be managed. For example, the risk that cannot be eliminated but can be managed is by using additional staffing to control the activity in an area. There may be many doors that cannot be secured, but can the reception desk be placed near the doors? If an internal courtyard is used for patients, is there a way to prevent patio furniture from being used as a ladder to scale the walls? Another simple fix might be to lock an area, eliminating patient and family access.

Operations

Once you have finished a facility assessment, it is time to consider the risks associated with your operations. For example, the sole practitioner will most certainly need to meet with patients in crisis. Since that is the nature of the services provided, the risks associated with that type of situation cannot be eliminated. In a community mental health facility, there will often be patients in crisis who are awaiting transfer to another mental health facility. These types of operational risks have to be recognized so that a plan can be developed on how to manage the risk. What steps can be taken to minimize the safety risks for the staff, the patients and the public? Does it make sense to take patients out of the facility even if for therapeutic reasons? Is the screening of visitors for contraband appropriate? Should a patient be placed in a gown? What should the staffing ratio be? Look at all aspects of the operation and develop a list of potentially risky situations. Again, using a multidisciplinary team is the best way to do an operational assessment.

Part of the operations plan should include knowing how to address legal issues when they arise. Staff should be familiar with the local commitment procedures, duty-to-warn requirements, and how guardianships are obtained. The facility should have specific guidelines on how those issues will be addressed within the particular facility, as well as how staff will be kept current on the issues. Expectations about communication and documentation should also be clearly defined we will discuss these topics in more detail below).

Policies should be developed to formalize the relationship between the patients, families, and staff. The relationship between the mental health clinician and the patient is not evenly balanced. The clinician is typically seen as being in a position of power. Additionally, the patient may have cognitive issues that impact their perception of their relationship with the clinician. For those reasons, the relationship between the clinicians and the patients and their families should always be strictly professional—within, of course, the context of an appropriate and effective working or therapeutic alliance. The policies should set boundaries on the relationships such as prohibiting fraternization outside of the workplace. They should also restrict social networking (communicating on Facebook, Twitter, and such sites), calling, or emailing outside of the clinical relationship. The type of gifts that may be accepted, if any, should be spelled out. As part of the operational plan, there should be consideration given to how patients will be addressed. Will patients always be called by their last name? Using a first name may be seen as inconsistent with a professional relationship in that setting and may be misinterpreted. Some staff may have the tendency to touch patients. Normally that would not be permitted, but there are times when your facility might find it acceptable. Those guidelines should be spelled out for both clinicians and staff. By thinking about these issues in advance, mental health providers may avoid making a mistake in a crisis.

Not only is fraternization a concern, but the policies should advise staff on ways to deal with the patient who is sexually preoccupied. All clinicians and staff need to have awareness of such propensities, and have support for the staff who have to care for those patients, such as a two-person team or an open setting when dealing with those patients. Likewise, if your facility has inpatient beds, how will those patients be kept from preying on another patient?

THE MANAGEMENT PLAN

Once the team has thought through the risks associated with both their facilities and their operations, it is time to develop a plan to manage the risks. The management plan should take into consideration capital improvement projects, policies, and staffing. In a separate section below, we discuss a number of approaches that can be built into both the general way of providing clinical services, and more particularly, a specific patient's treatment plan; these may reduce the likelihood that a crisis situation may arise in the first place. Things such as scheduling might be part of the management plan. For example, if you know you are seeing a patient who has a dual diagnosis of autism and bipolar disorder, who regularly strikes out at staff, can that patient be scheduled at times when there is less commotion in the facility, when there are more staff in the facility, or when a specialist is in the facility?

In terms of the facilities, begin by looking at the easiest things to fix, such as removing items from the patient areas and securing dangerous items in non-patient areas. Address minor facility issues such as removing hooks, changing door knobs, eliminating beds with cords. If housekeeping carts contain chemicals, can they be locked away? Can the cleaning crew switch to cleaning products that are not hazardous if they are ingested or thrown in someone's eye? Develop a plan for addressing major facility issues over time as the budget reasonably allows. If fixes are not readily available or apparent, consult with other facilities to see what they might have developed.

If a facility has a large number of exit points, and escape is a risk, you may not be able to eliminate all of the risks associated with the doors without creating a fire-safety hazard. In cases like that you must consider staffing patterns. When risk factors cannot be eliminated, staffing must be increased to control the risk.

Policies need to be developed to teach staff how to monitor the situation. For example, how often should your staff do safety rounds? If a patient has to be given a dangerous item, such as a razor that is needed for shaving, what is the policy for monitoring its use? How will the staff remember to secure the item following the patient's use of it? The policy should address how these situations will be handled. Once the policy has been implemented, routine checks should be done to monitor compliance with the policy. There should also be a way for staff to report violations or lapses in policy enforcement. In the event of a serious lapse or one resulting in an injury, an analysis should be conducted to determine why the policy failed.

Part of the management plan should also include consideration of how outside resources will be utilized for support. When will police or security be called to assist with a patient situation? Do the local police understand the nature of your operations and the layout of your facilities? This type of information could be crucial in a crisis situation. Likewise, are internal resources available to call for assistance? Does the reception desk have a panic alarm? Is there an overhead paging system?

The team should understand what type of police support is available to support them in the event of a crisis. Many cities have police teams that are specifically trained in managing critical incidents with mental health patients. Other cities use teams of social workers to assist the police. The type of system provided in your city should influence your plan on how to manage a patient in crisis. Consider inviting your critical incident responders to your facility for a dialogue on your needs. Those relationships can be of value in a crisis situation.

One often overlooked component of the management plan is how to include all staff in the management of the patient. For example, at a facility that boards patients, how will all staff know someone is a patient and should not be allowed to leave? Do the patients wear any specific type of gown that would identify them as someone who may not leave? Are the patient's critical issues identified as part of the shift report? Does the dietary technician know the patient shouldn't be given silverware? It is helpful if the entire unit or office has the same understanding regarding a patient crisis. You don't want a nurse to stand by while the patient walks out the door just because she lacks the knowledge that the patient must not leave.

Developing patient-specific crisis plans is an excellent way to avoid an adverse outcome. The entire treatment team should consider the potential crisis issues and develop a plan to manage the risk. These plans may be very different depending on the type of crisis being addressed. Is staff trying to prevent a suicide, to prevent someone from swallowing a foreign object, or to prevent a patient from assaulting another patient? A different type of plan would be needed for each of these situations.

The operational plans should consider ways to avoid a situation from escalating. Have staff been trained in verbal interventions to de-escalate aggressive or other dangerous behavior? Some situations may require medicating the patient. Is there a medication plan for the patient in crisis that can be executed quickly? Are the medications available in a location where staff can get to them? How will the medication orders be obtained from the physician? If the mental health facility doesn't have a physician on staff at all times, the team should consider the ability to obtain medication orders to address crisis situations. In determining what can be done with standing orders, it is important to consider the state licensing regulations. Some states do not allow nurses to administer medication using a standing order.

Even if staff are well trained in de-escalation, in an extreme situation it still may be necessary to restrain the patient temporarily, or to take the patient to the floor. This can involve the risk of physical injury for both the patient and the staff. The operational plan should include training on the rules regarding restraint. Facilities that are covered by the Center for Medicare and Medicaid Services (CMS) guidelines must know how to comply with the CMS rules on restraint. The plan should also include how staff will be trained to execute a takedown. That training should include simulation of crisis situations. It should also include refresher training. Consideration must also be given to where a patient will be placed following physical restraint. If they are still violent, is there a location to seclude them? Is that area free of items that could injure the patient? While a crisis facility may have regular seclusion rooms, what is available in the small clinic setting? If there isn't an appropriate room, then training has to be provided so that staff recognize a patient who is escalating and know how to either get help or get the patient to a crisis center.

For patients who are known to have a propensity to violence, it is important to gather as much information as possible about their home life, the places they frequent, and the names and numbers of friends and family. A patient may walk out of a facility but still be willing to answer their cell phone and talk to a clinician about their status. All of this information may prove useful when trying to determine whether the patient is in danger or whether there is a threat to another person. Having family involved in the treatment plan, and obtaining appropriate releases allowing you to contact family and friends, will give the clinician the tools to make an appropriate assessment of the danger. The operational plan should set out mechanisms for gathering this information in a standardized manner.

RESPONDING TO A CRISIS

Despite planning to avoid crisis situations, they will occur. The nature of mental health care treatment is that providers will have to deal with patients and families in a crisis situation. A patient may come in for treatment who is known to be chronically suicidal, but now has a plan to carry out their ideations. Or a patient may be having a psychotic episode. Prior to this happening, the facility and operational evaluations should have been completed, and the management plan developed, so staff should know the risks they are facing and how to respond. At this point it should be a matter of implementing the plans that were developed. If clinicians and staff have been trained on the operational plan, they should be able to execute the plan without an issue.

Each person on the response team should know their role. That should include an understanding of what they can do to safely manage the crisis within the scope of their license. Staff needs to understand that they may not exceed the scope of their license, even in a crisis situation.

One way to know a facility is ready to manage the crisis situation is to have practice drills simulating the crisis. Create a scenario to which staff must respond. Have a staff member play the part of the patient in crisis. Once the mock scenario has been completed, and the crisis resolved, the entire team should evaluate their performance. Adjust the response plan as needed.

There is no better way to learn where you need to improve your crisis management plan than to review a real crisis incident. Any time a patient has a crisis and it results in an adverse outcome for the patient or an injury to staff, a team should be put together to assess what went wrong. In a no-blaming environment, the team should be able to look for the root causes of the incident. They should begin by interviewing the staff involved and look at the physical area where the incident occurred; then begin mapping a timeline of the event. Once the timeline has been established, look at each piece of the timeline and determine where there was a failure in the system. For each of those incidences or occurrences, ask why the system failed. Then ask why again. Only when you cannot ask why again do you have the root cause of that inappropriate act. Once the causes of the failure are determined, put together an action plan to remedy the problems. The action items should be measurable. The outcomes should be reviewed after implementation to ensure they are working to prevent future problems.

Normally in healthcare we have put in place multiple barriers to prevent a problem from happening. We also have a highly trained staff capable of preventing breakdowns in our processes from occurring. When doing a root-cause analysis, don't look just at individual failures but also review your systems for failure. James Reason developed what is known as the "Swiss cheese model." He explained his model, saying most entities have put barriers in place to prevent bad outcomes. The barriers can include such things as policies, automated equipment, staffing models, or facility design changes. Any one of those barriers might stop the bad outcome from happening. It is only when there is a breakdown in multiple barriers, or the holes in the Swiss cheese line up, that something bad can happen (Reason, 2000). When we review an incident to look at the root causes, we have to consider what happened to allow our multiple barrier breakdown. Do we have staffing issues; is the environment overly chaotic; are the appropriate records unavailable on a timely basis; do the staff not have orders when they need them; have we not trained staff on managing the patient in crisis? All of these types of system issues need to be reviewed. A practice is always safer when the clinicians involved acknowledge the potential for errors and build in error-reduction strategies.

CLINICAL APPROACHES TO REDUCING RISK

In the foregoing section we have presented a generally external and objectifying view of patients. Despite recent advances in articulating concepts and practices in the context of recovery as a guiding principle for mental health care (e.g., see http://partnersforrecovery.samhsa.gov/), some contingencies require consideration of strategies for strictly exogenous management. However, even in acute care settings, most patients are not in crisis most of the time, and strategies for treatment may be applied that involve engaging patients and families in such a way that they become active participants in reducing the risk that patients will harm themselves or others. Retrospective reports from patients following crisis events underscore the degree to which patients experience themselves as out of control, and coercive interventions exacerbate this phenomenon (e.g., see Substance Abuse and Mental Health Services Administration, 2005). In this section we highlight some key approaches that empower the patient with greater control over situations and their own behavior.

SHARED DECISION-MAKING

It is now generally accepted by practitioners in general healthcare that decisions about medical treatment are made with some degree of collaboration between doctors and patients.

Incorporation of patient preferences in treatment plans is a recognized component of evidence-based medicine (Drake et al., 2003). Partly because of cognitive impairment that can follow from some mental disorders, and partly because of more generalized stigma, this recognition has come more slowly in the treatment of psychiatric conditions.

Nonetheless, shared decision-making is increasingly recognized as a potentially powerful component of the treatment planning process in mental health. A Substance Abuse and Mental Health Services Administration publication (SAMHSA, 2010) provides a guide to current knowledge and practice. By engaging patients in determining their care, clinicians gain access to relevant information; patients' unique balance of preferences and needs is taken into account, yielding a treatment plan for which they can feel a sense of increased responsibility; and patient–provider relationships can be strengthened.

When families are available, they too should be involved—necessarily with minors, but more generally in view of potential impairments to a patient's decisional capacity. When determining the treatment plan for a patient, whether the patient is in a crisis situation or not, it is imperative that clinicians try to obtain the input of family members. The family can serve as eyes and ears for the treatment team, providing valuable information to assist the clinician in determining the patient's safety and the potential risk to others. Family input should be solicited. If a patient refuses to allow a clinician to consult with family or friends, the clinician must consider what, if anything, the patient is not sharing with the treatment team. A patient may not be safe to go home if the patient will not allow the clinician to talk to their family. At the very least, the patient's behavior is a reason to reassess the situation to insure the appropriateness of the clinical decision.

If a family member is concerned about their safety, those concerns should be considered. In these times of scarce resources, it may be easier to allow the patient to continue in outpatient therapy despite the family's fears for their own safety, but that may or may not be the best decision. If a clinician learns of family safety concerns, the patient's medical record should indicate that those concerns were heard and analyzed. The clinician should attempt to obtain as much information as possible about the behaviors that have made the family feel unsafe. The courts have held clinicians responsible for the injuries to third parties when they have not appropriately responded to the family's fears. The clinician should document the protective factors that lead the clinician to feel the family was safe in spite of their fears. If the clinician agrees with the family, they need to document the steps taken to protect the family from the patient, including any obstacles they encountered. For example, if the patient refused to be admitted to a hospital, did they try to commit the patient through the probate courts? If the decision is made that a patient won't be admitted to a psychiatric hospital, what is the plan to manage the patient on an outpatient basis? What are the factors that are going to make that plan successful? Is the family in agreement with the plan? All of those points must be considered and documented.

A shared decision-making model can help a clinician provide better-quality care for the patient as well as reduce the risk of a malpractice claim in the event of an adverse outcome. Allowing the patient and family to have input into the care plan fosters a sense of trust and satisfaction. It can also lead to better outcomes. If the family has agreed with the physician on the course of treatment, they are less likely to bring a suit against the provider if there is an adverse outcome.

PSYCHIATRIC ADVANCE DIRECTIVES

One way to involve the patient in the shared decision-making model is to work with the patient to complete a mental health care advance directive. Laws authorizing these documents have been passed in almost every state. (See the National Resource Center on Psychiatric Advance Directives [NRC-PAD] at www.ncr-pad.org for state-by-state information, as well as general help in developing and using advance directives.) It was the intention of the mental health advocates who pushed for passage of these laws that psychiatric advance directives would be used as a résumé of sorts, outlining the patient's complete history and providing guidance on which medications and treatments would work best in a crisis situation. The document can also outline which medications have resulted in an adverse reaction and what treatments the patient is not willing to undergo. The document can be kept on file with providers and family. In the event of a crisis, the treating physicians then know exactly what the patient wants. They understand what they are authorized to do and can work out the appropriate treatment plan.

The documents need to be completed while the patient has the capacity to make decisions. If an outpatient provider is working with a patient on the completion of a psychiatric advance directive, the clinician should include documentation that the patient had capacity at the time of completion of the document. This will eliminate future problems, because when it actually needs to be used, the patient won't have the capacity to sign a legal document.

When advocates pushed for the passage of the laws to authorize psychiatric advance directives, they envisioned all mental health patients having one. In reality, very few have been completed. Studies have found patients are more likely to complete them if they are given guidance on how to complete them in a structured setting and, again, have indicated they are a good format for decision-making discussions between the patient and the provider.

BEHAVIOR THERAPY

The evidence for two common approaches to reducing seclusion and restraint—regulatory imperatives and staff training in verbal de-escalation—shows that, although use of seclusion and restraint has indeed declined, the incidence of violent behavior among inpatients and of staff injuries has not. On the basis of social learning theory, Robert Liberman (2011) argues that the social interaction involved in the verbal interventions designed to calm patients down has the inadvertent effect of reinforcing the original aggressive and otherwise dangerous behavior. A more effective alternative, therefore, would be to include as a treatment, behavior therapies that reinforce other positive behavior.

Interventions based on behavioral learning principles are applied within a behavior analytic framework. Antecedents to dangerous behavior in both the environment and the individual are analyzed and monitored over time as potential causal factors. Interventions that address the individual situation are then applied, and their effectiveness in shaping the desired behavior is tracked closely over time to guide decisions about continuation or change of treatment strategies. Such alternative interventions may include social skills training, which can entail teaching appropriate interactions with others; social learning modalities involving positive reinforcement of adaptive behavior, including token economies or credit incentive systems; positive programming or activity scheduling; or "time out" from situations that reinforce aggressive behavior.

These approaches to reducing the risk of aggression, destructive behavior, and self-injury using behavior therapy are not alternatives to traditional pharmacotherapy but are provided in conjunction with it. They also require substantial training, ongoing supervision and monitoring, and administrative support. However, facility- or program-wide as well as patient-specific interventions of this type can substantially reduce the risk of patients' exhibiting the kind of behaviors that put themselves or others at risk and invoke coercive interventions.

OTHER APPROACHES TO REDUCING RISK OF ADVERSE OUTCOMES

DUTY TO WARN

Most states have passed legislation codifying the "duty to warn" obligation. While state laws may vary, the majority follow some of the most publicized cases. The *Tarasoff* case is the most commonly cited case. In *Tarasoff,* the court looked at whether an injury to a third party was foreseeable. While they believed there normally is no duty to control the behavior of another, in the case of a mental health provider they found a special relationship that supported an affirmative duty. The court recognized that the clinician would not always make the correct decision regarding the actuality of the patient's carrying out a violent act, but felt a few warnings about potential threats that did not come to pass was a small price to pay for the safety of individuals.

A mental health provider who has a patient who presents a danger to another person must make a decision on how to respond. The clinician has an obligation to both the patient and the potential victim. The obligation to the patient is to keep their confidence. By warning the potential victim, that patient–physician confidentiality is broken, so it must only be done in the most extreme circumstances. It is up to the clinician to determine whether an actual threat exists and whether the patient has the means to carry out that threat. If the patient has no means to carry out the threat, there is no danger, and the duty to warn would not apply.

It is important to know your state law on duty to warn. The varying state positions include: saying a physician has a duty to warn an identifiable victim of a patient's violent intentions; saying the duty to warn expands to an entire identifiable group of potential victims; saying that duty to warn exists even if the threat isn't explicit; saying the practitioner has a duty to take reasonable steps to avoid the violence from happening; imposing no specific duty to warn but saying it is more factually based; and finally, in some states they have not acknowledged the duty to warn but have allowed a waiver of the patient confidentiality. You can see there are various options, all requiring different actions on the part of the clinician; thus a clinician must understand the rules of their state or risk violating patient confidentiality.

CORROBORATING SOURCE MATERIAL

Many mental health patients see multiple providers. Some have had multiple inpatient admissions in a variety of hospitals. When making decisions on the appropriate treatment plan for a patient in crisis, it is important that the clinician have as complete a picture of the patient's diagnosis and treatment history as possible. To gather that information, the clinician should attempt to secure as much of the patient's treatment history as they can. The patient may not have all of this information or may not be willing to share the information. Family members may have treatment information that they can share. That information can then be discussed with the patient. If possible, the medical records from outside entities should be obtained. Calls should be made to other providers to gather their input into the current situation. By gathering all of this information about the patient, the clinician can make the best possible decision on a treatment course. Additionally, it is much harder to say the clinician failed to meet the standard of care relative to their diagnosis and treatment plan when they took the time to gather a complete picture of the patient's condition.

At times a patient who is relatively unknown to the clinician will present in crisis. In those cases, it is particularly important to reach out to other providers to provide clinical information on the patient's history of treatment and symptoms. Those providers may have information that would be critical to the decision-making process.

DOCUMENTATION

A key to the appropriate management of risk is appropriate documentation of the clinical decision-making process. As workloads continue to increase, it is easy to let this part of the practice lapse; but whenever there is a bad outcome, good documentation in the record will be what protects the clinician from liability. This is especially true in the mental health field. There are no laboratory tests or physical procedures that can determine what is going on in the patient's mind. This is also a field where patients will regularly withhold information from the clinician or try to fool them about their diagnosis. On top of that, even when the clinician has a clear picture of the patient's clinical picture, the patient's mental state may change the moment the patient leaves the office and encounters the stresses of everyday life.

It is known that not all clinicians are going to make the correct decision on whether to allow a patient to continue as an outpatient or to require admission. In some instances, the incorrect decision will result in the death of a patient. One of the biggest mistakes a clinician can make is failing to document their clinical decision-making on how they got from the patient with a suicidal plan to a patient who was safe to continue as an outpatient. There should be documentation of a full investigation of the patient's current suicide plan and past attempts at suicide. Also, document information on why the patient may have thought about committing suicide but decided against it. Document all of the known protective factors such as family support or a strong religious belief. Finally, document the safety plan that will allow the patient to continue as an outpatient. Were any items in the home environment secured? Did the family take a protective role?

While lawsuits against psychiatrists and other mental health professionals are not that common, they do occur. Suicides are the most common reason for a lawsuit. Irwin Perr stated that it is only in psychiatry that a physician is held responsible for the actions of their patient. While suicide can be considered an adverse outcome, or an inappropriate result of treatment, a suicide alone does not mean the mental health professional was negligent in their treatment of the patient. A treatment outcome can never be guaranteed, nor can all suicides be predicted (Perr, 1965).

A malpractice lawsuit is often avoided if the medical record indicates the clinician was thorough in their assessment. If a clinician thoroughly assessed the situation, and documented a logical decision-making process, even if the clinician made the wrong decision, many malpractice lawyers won't even take the patient's case. If the case does go to trial, the jury is going to try to determine whether the suicide could have been foreseen. The clinician isn't going to be held to the standard of absolute knowledge of what the patient might do, but rather, to the standard of having performed and documented a thorough assessment and then reached a logical clinical plan based on that assessment.

Documentation should always be done contemporaneously with the care being provided, whether it is an office visit or a phone call. At the very least, the documentation should be done on the same day. If it isn't documented in a timely fashion, it shouldn't be done at all. Documentation after the fact is not viewed favorably by juries, but rather, is looked at as an attempt to protect the clinician.

The old saying that "if it isn't documented it wasn't done" still holds true. If you don't document your assessment or the rationale for why you decided on a course of action, the jury isn't likely to believe you actually did the assessment or thought about the course of action. In a *Journal of Psychiatric Practice* article by plaintiff's counsel Simpson and Stacy, they wrote, "There is always information that a physician felt compelled to enter into the chart that was far less critical than a dialogue regarding suicide. Since suicide is one of the worst possible outcomes for a psychiatric patient, most juries conclude that if a psychiatrist actually conducted a suicide assessment, he or she surely would have documented it" (Simpson and Stacey, 2004). They also stated that they believed good documentation improved the quality of care the patient received. They felt having to document the assessment forced the clinician to review their thought process, both considering the thoroughness of the assessment and the validity of their clinical formulation of a treatment plan.

Assessments are particularly important any time there is going to be a change in the level of care the patient is receiving or the level of observation the patient is under. These are times that are stressful for the patient, and the impact of that stress on the patient needs to be considered. The documentation should include information on the patient's plan to deal with the stress. Documentation of the decision-making process is particularly important whenever the level of patient risk is going to increase as a result of the decision. Document the clinical benefits of the decision to give the patient continuing or additional freedom.

Patient autonomy has to be respected. As noted earlier, it is recognized that patients should have the right to make decisions about the care they receive. At times this will mean that a patient will decide not to follow the recommendations of the treatment provider. Patient non-adherence should be documented in the medical record; such documentation can provide a defense against a malpractice suit.

The documented medical record also serves to provide a historical guideline for other caregivers in your absence. It can assist an outside provider, such as an emergency physician. It gives them guidance on medications and treatments that have or have not worked. It can provide a complete history of the patient's past treatment record, often conveying better information than the patient is willing or able to share. In the event of an emergency situation or when another physician is covering for you, it is less likely that key information will be overlooked. Again, this leads to better patient outcomes and less risk for the mental health provider.

STANDARDIZED HANDOFF COMMUNICATIONS

Almost every adverse outcome involves a communication failure. According to the most recent reports of the Joint Commission on Healthcare Accreditation, a national accrediting body for hospital facilities, 82 percent of reported sentinel events involved a communication failure. In fact, for the last three years reported, communication has been one of the top three root causes in suicide events. It has been the only consistent root cause in suicide events. (Joint Commission, 2011). Thus, to manage risk, mental health professionals must manage the communications between the team members.

Each time the care of the patient transfers from one individual to another, there should be a transfer of the pertinent information relating to the patient's care plan, commonly known as a "handoff." The handoff communication or report tells the new caregiver what went on while the current team member was providing care and gives them an idea of their responsibility in the care of the patient. It gives the entire care team a shared picture of the patient's condition and the critical issues to be addressed. Failures in either the oral or written handoff communication can lead both to knowledge gaps within the team and medical injuries.

Gaps in the handoff process can lead to situations where providers don't have the information they need to make the correct decisions for patients. Studies have shown that where there is a knowledge gap there may be a delay in care. Alternatively, a provider may make an intelligent guess at the appropriate treatment. Either of these options can lead to a bad outcome.

Each member of the treatment team will gather slightly different information from the patient. The patient may deny suicidal thoughts to one member of the team and then clearly declare a plan to commit suicide to another member of the team. For that reason, it is important to have a standardized communication tool for handoffs between staff members. For something as important as a suicidal plan, there should be specific ways the information is to be communicated to the team. The situation where one clinician thought they told another of a plan, as they usually tell them, serves no one well in the event of a bad outcome. Nor does the belief that everyone will read what you documented.

By standardizing the handoff process, the clinician will develop the habit of addressing the key diagnostic and treatment elements every time. By doing this they are less likely to miss an element. The handoff becomes a checklist. This standardization not only includes the use of commonly understood terminology but also includes communication in a format that is legible

It has been determined that checklists or templates are highly effective communication tools. They establish a standardized way of communicating that is followed each and every time. They are particularly helpful at the time of a handoff. Atul Gawande, the best-selling author of *The Checklist Manifesto*, talks about how complicated medicine has become and how easy it is for a clinician to forget a step in a process while under stress. He advocates using checklists as a way to "hardwire" a process for a clinician or a team of clinicians. He believes we can improve outcomes if we do so (Gawande, 2009). While these tools are not regularly utilized in the mental health field at this time, they are very useful tools that should be considered. Each facility would develop a checklist that would list each of the steps in a process and indicate who is responsible for each step. Required fields of information would be included in the template.

In highly specialized fields such as aviation, which has been compared to medicine in terms of having highly skilled individuals involved in stressful situations where they have the life of other individuals in their care, the skills needed to improve communications are guided by checklists, and the processes are practiced. Every member of the team is encouraged to speak up in the event they see the potential for an error or bad outcome. In fact, the team leader is required to tell the team it is their obligation to speak out if there is a safety or process issue. Using these methods, system errors are detected and either prevented or mitigated by staff. By using these guidelines, aviation has been able to reduce its errors. Recently, these same skills have been implemented in medical facilities as a way to reduce errors.

This type of training could be very helpful in a treatment team setting, as each member of the team would be required to state their agreement with the plan and to raise any safety issues that were not being adequately addressed. This type of environment would reduce the instances where only one member of the team knew the information provided by the patient. It would also be a useful tool for recognizing issues that might have been left unresolved at the time of discharge.

Not only is team communication important, but clinician to patient communication is critical. Skills must be developed to provide information to patients and families in a way that they understand. Issues with "medical literacy," the ability to understand complicated medical information, need to be considered. The cognitive difficulties of the patient need to be considered when deciding the appropriate terminology to be used. The stressfulness of the situation is another factor to be considered. Patients understand less of what we say to them when they are in a stressful situation. Some studies say they only retain 10 to 15 percent of what is said to them. If there are concerns about a patient's understanding of information, bring in an additional family member or use handouts. The teaching tools are a good way to assist the clinician in getting the information across to the patient. The "teach back" method is another option. Using that method, the clinician gives the patient the necessary information and then asks the patient to repeat the information back to them, thus showing an understanding of what they have been told.

By doing the risk-management planning set out in this chapter and following some of the other suggestions, your community health facility, whether large or small, will provide better care for your patients, will be a safer place for staff to work, and will have fewer legal problems. Many of these steps are easy to implement; they just take a little time and planning. Make good risk management a priority for your organization. Develop good habits, and things will go better when your patients are in a crisis.

BEST-PRACTICE TAKEAWAYS

1. Good risk management is all about the avoidance of risks. This starts with the analysis of potential risks and continues with plans to mitigate the chance of specific risky events' occurring, including incorporation of behavioral management strategies into individual treatment plans.

2. Prior to a crisis, engage patients and their families in their care plan. Make sure there is shared decision-making about care plans, as well as the use of advance directives for potential crisis situations. Where aggressive or other intolerable behavior is anticipated, the care plan should include behavioral interventions to reduce the probability of occurrence.

3. Make sure you listen to the patient and their family. Consider the information they are giving you before you fully develop your care plan. Likewise, heed their concerns before deciding to discharge a patient or allowing a patient to remain at home.

4. Each facility should have a crisis management plan. The plan should include an environmental assessment of your facilities.

5. Not all crises can be avoided all of the time, so each risk management plan should have a plan for responding to a crisis, including the names of those involved in the response team and each member's role.

6. Make sure staff is trained on verbal de-escalation. Have a policy for physical intervention and the use of pro re nata (PRN) medication, should those become necessary. Train the staff on the policy and the process. Simulation of events can help staff develop their skills.

7. Tabletop drills help the response team prepare to respond. The drills also point out flaws in the response plan that can be corrected prior to a real-life crisis.

8. Engage the police and other ancillary responders in your planning process.

9. Team communication is critical when caring for the mental health patient. Everyone on the care team should have input into the care plan. The team should discuss the plan of care and coordinate information that may have been given to just one member of the team. Work out any concerns that any member of the team might have.

10. Good documentation is critical to the avoidance of liability. Make sure your assessments are completely documented. Document your clinical decision-making process.

11. If a crisis occurs, don't forget about the needs of the patient, family, and staff. If a patient has been harmed as a result of a staff error, apologize. Don't go into a hunker-down mode, avoiding the patient or family. Share information on what happened and how you are going to fix the problem. Engage the family in the corrective plan as appropriate.

REFERENCES

American Psychiatric Association, American Psychiatric Nurses Association, and the National Association for Psychiatric Health Systems (APA, APNA, and NAPHS). *Learning from Each Other: Success Stories and Ideas for Reducing Restraint/Seclusion in Behavioral Health.* Arlington, VA, and Washington, DC: APA, APNA, and NAPHS; 2003. Available at http://www.naphs.org/rscampaign/ Learning.pdf. Accessed December 19, 2011.

American Society for Healthcare Risk Management (ASHRM). *Risk Management Pearls for Physicians*, 2003. Available through the American Hospital Association Online Bookstore at www.ahaonline-store.com

APA, APNA, and NAPHS. Appendix [contains sample forms & checklists]. In *Learning from Each Other: Success Stories and Ideas for Reducing Restraint/Seclusion in Behavioral Health.* Arlington, VA, and Washington, DC: APA, APNA, and NAPHS. Available at https://www.naphs.org/rscam-paign/Appendix.pdf. Accessed December 19, 2011.

Arora, V, Johnson, J, et al. Communication failures in patient sign-out and suggestions for improvement: A critical incident analysis. *Quality and Safety in Health Care*, 14: 401–407, 2005.

ASHRM . *Risk Management Pearls of Psychiatric Care Across the Continuum*, 2005 available through the American Hospital Association Online Bookstore at www.ahaonlinestore.com.

Borum R : Police perspectives on responding to mentally ill people in crisis: Perceptions of program effectiveness, *Behavioral Sciences and the Law*, 16: 393–405, 1998.

Chacko, V, Varvarelis, N, et al. An IBM Lotus Domino application for ensuring patient safety and enhancing resident supervision in hand-off communications. Annual Symposium Proceedings Archives (AMIA). American Medical Informations Association, 874, 2006.

Deane, S, et al. Emerging partnerships between mental health and law enforcement. *Psychiatric Services,* 50, 99–101, 1999.

Drake RE, Rosenberg SD, Teague GB, Bartels SJ, Torrey WC. Fundamental principles of evidence-based medicine applied to mental health care. In *Evidence-Based Practices in Mental Health, Special Issue. Psychiatric Clinics of North America,* 26: 811–820, 2003.

Gammon TE and Hulston JK. The duty of mental health care providers to restrain their patients or warn third parties. *Missouri Law Review,* 60, 750–797, 1995.

Gawande A. *The Checklist Manifesto: How to Get Things Right.* Metropolitan Books, Henry Holt and Co., New York, 2009.

Gutheil Tand Gabbard G. The concept of boundaries in clinical practice: Theoretical and risk management dimensions. *The American Journal of Psychiatry,* 150(2), 188–196, 1993.

JointCommission, The. *Sentinel Events: Evaluating Cause and Planning Improvement,* 2nd ed. 1998, The Joint Commission on Accreditation of Healthcare Organizations, One Renaissance Blvd, Oakbrook Terrace, IL. www.jointcommission.org.

Joint Commission, The. *Sentinel Event Data, Root Causes,* 2011. The Joint Commission on Accreditation of Healthcare Organizations, One Renaissance Blvd, Oakbrook Terrace, IL, www.jointcommission.org

Knoll J and Gerbasi J. Psychiatric malpractice case analysis: Striving for objectivity. *Journal of the American Academy of Psychiatry and the Law,* 34: 215, 2006.

Leape L. Error in medicine. *Journal of the American Medical Association,* 272: 1851–1857, 1994.

Lewis M. Duty to warn versus duty to maintain confidentiality: Conflicting demands on mental health professionals. *Suffolk University Law Review,* 20, 579–615, 1986.

Liberman RP. Commentary: Interventions based on learning principles can supplant seclusion and restraint. *Journal of the American Academy of Psychiatry and the Law,* 39: 480–495, 2011.

Marder R. and Sheff R. *The Step by Step Guide to Failure Modes and Effects Analysis,* Opus Communications, Inc., Denver, Colorado, 2002.

National Resource Center on Psychiatric Advance Directives. *Psychiatric Advance Directives: Health and Legal Professionals.* Available at http://www.nrc-pad.org/content/view/286/85/, where you may also see three commentaries on this article. (Accessed December 19, 2011.)

Perr I N. Liability of hospital and psychiatrist in suicide. *American Journal of Psychiatry,* 122(6): 631–638, 1965.

Rachlin S. Double jeopardy: Suicide and malpractice. *General Hospital Psychiatry,* 6, 302–307, 1984.

Reason J. Human Error: Models and management. *British Medical Journal,* 320: 768, March 2000.

Recupero PR, Price M, Garvey KA, Daly B, Xavier SL. Restraint and seclusion in psychiatric treatment settings: Regulation, case law, and risk management. *Journal of the American Academy of Psychiatry and the Law,* 39: 465–476, 2011.

SAMHSA. *Practice Guidelines: Core Elements for Responding to Mental Health Crises.* HHS Pub. No. SMA-09-4427. Rockville, MD: Center for Mental Health Services, Substance Abuse and Mental Health Services Administration, 2009. Available at http://store.samhsa.gov/shin/content/SMA09-4427/SMA09-4427.pdf (Accessed December 19, 2011).

SAMSHA. *Roadmap to Seclusion and Restraint Free Mental Health Services.* DHHS Pub. No. (SMA) 05-4055. Rockville, MD: Center for Mental Health Services, 2005. http://store.samhsa.gov/shin/content/SMA06-4055/SMA06-4055-A.pdf

SAMSHA. *Shared Decision-Making in Mental Health Care: Practice, Research, and Future Directions.* HHS Publication No. SMA-09-4371. Rockville, MD: Center for Mental Health Services, Substance Abuse and Mental Health Services Administration, 2010. Available at http://store.samhsa.gov/shin/content//SMA09-4371/SMA09-4371.pdf.

Shea, S. *The Practical Art of Suicide Assessment: A Guide for Mental Health Professionals and Substance Abuse Counselors.* New York: John Wiley and Sons, 2002.

Simpson S and Stacy M. Avoiding the malpractice snare: Documenting suicide risk assessment. *Journal of Psychiatric Practice*, 10: 3, 185–189, May 2004.

Solet D, Norvell JM, et al. *Lost in Translation: Challenges and Opportunities in Physician-to-Physician Communication During Patient Handoffs*. Academic Medicine, 80(12), 1094–1099, 2005.

Substance Abuse and Mental Health Services Administration (SAMSHA), Leaving-The-Door-Open-Alternatives-to-Seclusion-and-Restraint, HHS Publication No. SMA10-4508. Rockville, MD: Center for Mental Health Services, Substance Abuse and Mental Health Services Administration, 2010. Available at http://store.samhsa.gov/product/Leaving-The-Door-Open-Alternatives-to-Seclusion-and-Restraint-DVD-/SMA10-4508.

SwansonJW, McCrary S, Swartz MS, Elbogen EB, Van Dorn RA. Superseding psychiatric advance directives: Ethical and legal considerations. *Journal of the American Academy of Psychiatry and the Law,* 34: 385–394, 2006. Also available at the National Resource Center on Psychiatric Advance Directives; http://www.nrc-pad.org/

Swanson JW, Swartz MS, Hannon MJ, Elbogen EB, Wagner HR, McCauley BJ, et al. Psychiatric advance directives: A survey of persons with schizophrenia, family members, and treatment providers. *International Journal of Forensic Mental Health*, 2: 73–86, 2003.

Tarasoff v Regents of University of California, 551 P.2nd 334 (Cal, 1976).

University Health Consortium. *Medical Legal Survival: A Risk Management Guide for Physicians*, 2001. University Health Consortium, 2001 Spring Road, Suite 700, Oak Brook, IL.

Vincent C, Taylor-Adams S, Chapman E, et al. How to investigate and analyze clinical incidents: Clinical Risk Unit and Association of Litigation and Risk Management Protocol. *British Medical Journal*, 320: 777, 2000.

VincentC, Taylor-Adams S, et al. Framework for analyzing risk and safety in clinical medicine. *British Medical Journal,* 316, 1154, 1998.

What are psychiatric advance directives? Where did they come from? Excerpted from Swanson, J., et al, Psychiatric advance directives: A survey of persons with schizophrenia, family members and treatment providers; International Journal of Forensic Mental Health, 2, 73–86, 2003, available at the National Resource Center on Psychiatric Advance Directives, http://www.nrc-pad.org/images/stories/PDFs/pads%20background.pdf (Accessed December 19, 2011).

Wiff-Miron R, Lewenholl I, et al. From Aviation to Medicine: Applying Concepts of Aviation Safety to Risk Management in Ambulatory Care. *Quality and Safety in Healthcare*, 12(1), 35–39, 2003.

CHAPTER 36

QUALITY MANAGEMENT AND PROGRAM EVALUATION

VIKKI L. VANDIVER AND KEVIN CORCORAN

INTRODUCTION

Behavioral health care organizations have changed significantly over the last three decades. Fueling this change has been the expectation that organizations will increasingly deliver and evaluate the impact of evidence-based services. Oregon, for example, has a state statute mandating evidence-based practices in most social service agencies, including corrections, mental health, child welfare, and other areas. A determining force in being able to deliver effective services hinges on three core interconnected administrative components: *quality management,* via the use of *interdisciplinary teams,* which use *program evaluation* for determining quality at the agency and individual level of services. This chapter will review these components and delineate a practical approach to evaluating programs in order to manage their quality.

QUALITY MANAGEMENT

When we talk about "quality management" in behavioral healthcare settings, we are addressing a wide range of issues and concerns. There are numerous factors involved in quality management. Chief among them are how we define programs and change (theory), the codes of conduct (principles), and character (leaders and leadership). Additionally, quality management seems most likely to succeed with the formation of competent interdisciplinary teams, program evaluation, and measurement tools used to evaluate the magnitude of quality, including at the agency and individual systems levels. This section begins with an overview of theory, principles, and characteristics of leaders and leadership. Additional information is provided on an example of macro-level best practice, learning collaboratives, and the use of benchmarking to monitor best practices. We will then delineate practical program evaluation and measurement to help assure quality.

FROM THEORY TO PRACTICE

A useful and classic theory for understanding how quality management influences organizational change is *force-field analysis* (Lewis, Goodman, & Fandt, 2004). It is defined as a "systematic step-by-step process for examining pressures that support or resist proposed change" (pp. 357–358). This framework is based on the assumption that just introducing a change does not guarantee that the change will be successful. Therefore, in order to support the successful change that is necessary to integrate and evaluate evidence-based interventions into mental health practice, force-field analysis suggests four steps. These are: 1) create a shared vision, 2) communicate and share information, 3) empower others to act on the vision, and 4) evaluate the results (Vandiver, 2008, p. 384).

- Creating a shared vision: The very act of developing a vision helps bring awareness of the need for change and prompts discussion about forces supporting and resisting change efforts—referred to as "unfreezing." Often organizations are "frozen" into safe and predictable ways of functioning or performing. When all stakeholders can be involved in setting a new vision, participants are more likely to work toward successful change and thus unfreeze themselves from the old way.
- Communication: Sharing information is a key strategy that helps gain staff support while also helping them learn. Research suggests that new behaviors are more readily learned when delivered using a variety of formats, such as verbal, written, and non-verbal messages. Therefore, a manager needs to discuss changes with the staff and continually circulate minutes and memos, and role-model the desired goals.
- Empower employees: Management literature now recognizes employee empowerment as a critical variable in a healthy organization. From a management perspective, *empowerment* is defined as "the interaction of the leader giving away or sharing power with those who use it to become involved and committed to high-quality performance" (Lewis, Goodman, & Fandt, 2004, p. 599). Successful organizational change can be credited to employees who have felt empowered and strengthened in the process of change. Their development is encouraged at two levels, individual and organizational. Individual development includes anything that helps an individual learn how to adapt and change, such as mentoring from supervisors and attaining more education. Organizational development refers to teaching people to interact successfully with others in the organization such as group and team training. Thus, by improving the lives of employees, the organization is improved.
- Evaluate: Similar to outcome measures for client change, managers also need to measure and evaluate the need for change (i.e., needs assessment) and whether the change has had the intended effects. Evaluation methods can be designed by both managers and employees, who can also set the outcome criteria.

PRINCIPLES OF QUALITY MANAGEMENT

Principles are useful guideposts for staying focused on the values and direction of an organization's mission. Using meta-analyses of management literature, Terry (2003) identifies three core principles of effective quality management: *authenticity*, *service to others* and *shared power*—all of which speak to the character of a leader. In other words, quality management requires leaders whose intention is to effect positive, sweeping, measurable, and memorable improvements in mental health care (Terry, 2003). Wheatley (1999) describes the principles of *relevance* and *participation*. The principle of relevance refers to starting where people are and with what is meaningful to them. The principle of participation refers to eliciting participation by staff, community, clients, and family members.

All of these principles are important for quality management because they involve a multistage process that mobilizes people and resources for a common purpose. These principles have excellent relevance to management because they help promote ownership in the organization while also fostering active learning by all participants—a feature that will be discussed later, in the section "Learning Collaboratives."

CHARACTERISTICS OF QUALITY MANAGEMENT: PERSON, PROCESS, AND PRACTICES

When we use the term "quality management," three features come to mind: person (leader), process (leadership), and practices (learning collaboratives for best practices and evaluation). Quality management involves a leader or manager who provides a certain kind of management style—quality. But quality management also refers to a process—an organization that engages in quality management practices typically has strong leadership. Quality management occurs through the process of strong leadership in which quality of care is focused on improving methods for assessing quality, concern about the effects of incentives in managed care contracts (i.e., under treatment), restricted access, and meeting the growing demand performance and fiscal accountability identified by federal, state and county governments (Chavez & Barry, 1998). Strong leaders who exhibit strong and participatory leadership skills have an easier time of bringing about organizational change that incorporates the use and evaluation of best practices.

THE PERSON GUIDING QUALITY MANAGEMENT: THE LEADER

There has been an increased expectation that mental health leaders will develop new skills and relationships to deal with a changing mental health environment. The expected model for chief executive officers has become more that of a collaborative manager who values diversity and participatory management and less that of a professional manager who is hierarchal and uses a top-down decision-making style. The leaders in today's behavioral health environment must be ready to embrace change, encourage dialogue, use participatory decision making, instill a team-oriented culture, use and evaluate evidence-based approaches, and be able to build management teams that know how to execute the organizations mission and values. Additionally, they must have the requisite business acumen and professional skills to be effective—meaning understanding financial statements, demonstrating policy-making skills, and being able to manage individual, team, and a variety of in-house and community relationships.

A central responsibility of a leader is to help the organization and or community develop its vision and then assist in developing a flexible, strategic plan for how to get there. In essence, before mental health clinicians can be successful with clients, agency leaders must first be successful with the community. Quality management recognizes the power of communities to aid in the healing, health, and mental health of individuals and their families. Leaders within the field of mental health are only now beginning to embrace the benefits of broad community involvement (Vandiver, 2008).

Terry (2003) describes the characteristics of leaders engaged in quality management. Leaders provide quality management using five core strategies. *First*, they lead by fiscal example. They commit at least five percent of mental health program budgets to research and evaluation. *Second*, leaders welcome scrutiny. They invite outside reviewers or evaluators to evaluate existing clinical and organizational practices to see if their policies and programs are supporting their mission and values. *Third*, leaders are active, not passive. They acknowledge and support mental health programs that demonstrate effectiveness. *Fourth,* leaders are teachers. They offer to speak to local health and mental health care organizations, business clubs, and fraternal organizations about the value of community partnerships and relationships. *Fifth* and last, leaders are collaborators for community change. They commit to working outside the mental health profession to bring together politicians and business and community leaders to create partnerships that promote community change for health and mental health (pp. 162–167).

Leaders who demonstrate quality management utilize many approaches. Perhaps we can learn from other industries, such as Google, which recently conducted a large-scale survey to learn how to "build better bosses." In 2009, in a bold project titled "Project Oxygen," Google statisticians gathered more than 10,000 observations about managers across more than 100 variables ranging from performance reviews to feedback surveys. Manager interview protocols were developed followed by in-person interviews. Finally, the analyzed data produced more than 400 pages of interview notes.

What did Google management learn about what employees valued? Their effort produced a report titled *Eight Habits of Highly Effective (Google) Managers* (Bryant, 2011). In priority ranking, these habits are:

> 1) Be a good coach, 2) empower your team, 3) express interest in team members' success and personal well-being, 4) don't be a sissy: be productive and results-oriented, 5) be a good communicator and listen to your team, 6) help your employees with career development, 7) have a clear vision and strategy for the team, and 8) have key technical skills so you can help advise the team. Basically, what employees valued most were even-keeled bosses who made time for one-on-one meetings, who helped people puzzle through problems by asking questions, not dictating answers and who took an interest in employees' lives and careers. (Bryant, 2011, p. 1)

What makes this information practical is that it was developed in the context of the company, not through an independent, stand-alone leadership training seminar brought in to tell people how to do it. Also, what matters here is that the information emerged from within the company and therefore earned more credibility at feedback sessions to employees and managers. What Google discovered is that managers had a much greater impact on employees' performance and how they felt about their job than any other factor. So what can behavioral mental health care organizations take away from this exercise? Have time for employees and be consistent with them.

THE PROCESS OF QUALITY MANAGEMENT: LEADERSHIP

If leaders are the WHO of quality management, then leadership is the WHAT and the WHERE. In other words, leadership (the what) is the process of what happens when an individual or group of individuals (the who) guide the organization toward its stated goals and mission (the where). Let's look at examples of effective leadership. "Strategies" will describe "the what" and later, "learning collaboratives" describe "the where."

Strategies for Effective Leadership

Castro and colleagues (1999) identified seven factors linked with competent leadership. These included: 1) garnering support for a program from the local community and funding agency, 2) strengthening staff morale and commitment to program goals, 3) maintaining fidelity in program implementation when necessary, 4) identifying serendipitous developments that can be added to the program evaluation data to aid in documenting program development and effectiveness, 5) meeting regularly with staff to assess program activities, 6) engaging in problem solving, and 7) planning for future activities and program growth (pp. 138–145).

Effective leadership, in part, models the behaviors that are expected at the clinical care level. As described in the IOM Report *Improving the Quality of Healthcare for Mental and Substance-Use Conditions* (IOM, 2006)—The Robert Wood Johnson Foundations Initiative on Depression in Primary Care, leadership was one of six component interventions to overcome barriers to the delivery of effective care for depression in primary care settings. Teams of primary care, mental health, and senior administrative personnel were responsible for securing needed resources, representing stakeholder interests, promoting adherence to practice standards, settings goals for key process measures and outcomes, and encouraging sustained efforts at continuous quality improvement.

Effective leadership is well known to be a critical process factor in shaping organizational culture (IOM, 2006). In other words, what are the *formal* and *informal* values, rules and guidelines that influence the practices of managers and staff? In this case, "formal" refers to written policy and procedures documents that endorse and specify organizational values (mission statements) and actions. "Informal" refers to the social interactions among and between staff and leaders—which are often the most potent form of communication about policies. Both of these elements create what is commonly referred to as the "organizational culture." One way to test whether leadership is promoting a healthy organizational culture is to examine whether the formal policies (e.g., policies and procedures manual) match the informal values and practices of the agency and staff. For example, if recovery and client-centered care are priority goals, practices, and philosophies of the staff and clients, does leadership provide the resources and support for these priorities?

Leadership can help promote a healthy organizational culture by providing transparency. Transparency in leadership, according to the Institute of Medicine's *Crossing the Quality Chasm* (IOM, 2001), refers to a process in which the mental health care system provides information describing the system's performance on safety, evidence-based practice, and patient satisfaction (p. 8). This information is available not only to staff but to clients, patients, and their families. By availing themselves of it, staff and stakeholders can truly make informed decisions when choosing a health plan, hospital, agency, and provider.

Evidence-Based and Best Practices

Effective leadership is also characterized by ensuring the existence of a quality measurement and reporting infrastructure that is responsive to the agency. Much of our knowledge base of what works (e.g., evidence-based and/or best practices) in community mental health care settings has been initially fielded and tested in health care settings. Let's look at one best-practice approach that is used in behavioral health care settings: the learning collaborative.

Learning Collaboratives

Learning Collaboratives constitute the "where" of quality management and have been used extensively to promote quality improvement in healthcare in areas such as improving chronic illness care (Cretin, Shortell, & Keeler, 2004), treatment of depression (Solberg, Fischer, & Wei, 2001), general community health (Shortell, Zukoski, & Alexander, 2002) and asthma care (Schonlau, Mangione-Smith, & Chan, 2005). They involve five activities: 1) the use of cross-discipline and inter-organizational teams, 2) working on a specific problem, 3) supporting leadership by evidence, 4) providing faculty experts, and 5) utilizing project management coaches to modify and or improve specific practices (Cretin, Shortell, & Keeler, 2004). A central goal of a learning collaborative is to grow a culture of quality in which systematic implementation of research findings can be adapted to local conditions. These approaches are designed to simultaneously solve business problems, guide quality improvement, provide training to staff, and build a foundation for longer-term change (Dückers, Spreeuwenberg, Cordula, & Groenewegen, 2009).

Learning collaboratives can range in size from three to 20 units with staff teams or organizations. Bringing these groups together is referred to as "learning sessions," and these may spread over the lifetime of a project. Learning sessions can range from three two-day meetings over 12 months to eight to ten 1- or 2-day meetings. Between sessions, the groups implement their action steps and collect data. Technology, such as webinars and video conferencing, can be used to enable group meetings with long-distance stakeholders. Problems may be identified in advance or jointly defined. These same problems are best solved when various stakeholders identify and agree to a mutual or shared solution, rather than a series of connected problem areas. Finally, the projects with the most success are those where there is an existing evidence base in the literature and thus, readily available data.

How they Work

Dougherty (2007) provides a practical description of a learning collaborative. They work like this: Collaboratives start with an analysis of where your organization is now. The first goal is usually to "improve performance," which occurs through a series of focused short-term interventions and improvement methods nested within a long-term goal. Next, groups of various staff members from different settings work together to define action-oriented, specific project aims, measures, and interventions. One method that has extensive testing in the field of addiction treatment is Plan-Do-Study-Act (PDSA) method. Common questions that emerge from this method are: "What are we trying to accomplish?" "How will we know that a change is an improvement?" and "What changes can we make that will result in an improvement?" This is an incremental approach to quality improvement that translates research into practice through the systematic implementation of research findings into local conditions. Barriers are identified and data are used to drive systematic improvement. Ultimately, learning collaboratives are data-based change processes that focus on quality improvement of some kind.

Examples of Learning Collaboratives

Examples of mental health and substance abuse–related collaboratives include the Robert Wood Johnson Foundation Depression and Primary Care Initiative, the California Institute for Mental Health's California Learning Collaborative, and the Massachusetts Department of Mental Health's Readmission Collaborative. The Substance Abuse and Mental Health Services Administration (SAMHSA)–Center for Mental Health Services (CMHS) has recently awarded several large grants to states to conduct learning collaboratives (SAMHSA, 2009). Examples of learning collaboratives can be seen in efforts to improve services for children. Dougherty (2007) describes a mental health collaborative that was formed to improve access to services through first-intake appointments for children requiring care for mental health conditions. The collaboratives consisted of the New York City Department of Health and Mental Hygiene, Mount Sinai School of Medicine, and the New York State Office of Mental Health. Another example of a learning collaborative for children and mental health is taken from the Mississippi State Department of Health/Child Mental Health Initiative–Pine Belt System of Care project (Jackson, Mississippi). The state was awarded a six-year (2006–2012), multimillion-dollar grant to establish a system of coordinated, individualized care for children affected by severe emotional disturbance (SED) or co-occurring SED and substance misuse. The project is sponsored by three Mississippi organizations, is based on work set by the Center's Children's Mental Health Initiative and other systems of care initiative—all of which have solid track records—to ensure its successful completion. Its primary aim is to establish a local system of care of underserved families and youth and to serve as a national model for systems of care in rural areas.

What makes a Successful Learning Collaborative?

Øvretveit and colleagues (2002) have listed four factors shown to be important to a collaborative success: 1) projects need to be practical and relevant to the organization and stakeholders; 2) senior managers are involved and supportive; 3) objectives are relevant, reasonable and measurable; and 4) there is a plan to infuse and spread the findings among the staff and throughout the stakeholder organizations. Dougherty (2007) reminds us that, ultimately, learning collaboratives are data- and information-guided ways to simultaneously solve mutually agreed upon business problems (e.g., children's lack of access to mental health services through the intake process), provide training to staff, and build a foundation for longer-term change.

BENCHMARKING AS A STRATEGY FOR IMPROVING PERFORMANCE THROUGH BEST PRACTICES

Benchmarking is a systematic process involving the search, introduction, and implementation of best practices. Although originally used in management, the concept of benchmarking is now a common practice in behavioral healthcare quality management circles. Owen (2007) describes benchmarking as:

> the search for best practices that can be applied with a view to achieving improved performance.
> It is a systematic and continuous process of measuring and comparing an organization's business

processes against those of leaders anywhere in the world, to gain information which will help drive continuous improvement (p. 180).

Benchmarks attempt to answer the following questions: Who is doing the best? How do they do it? How well are we doing relative to the best? How good do we want to be, relative to the best? Benchmarking generally includes the following stages:

1) Identification of the area of operation to be benchmarked;
2) Identification of best practice in selected organizations or sections of organizations;
3) Collection and analysis to determine the common characteristics of this practice;
4) Development of best-practice indicators and levels to be achieved on these indicators;
5) Communication of best-practice indicators internally and gaining of acceptance;
6) Development and implementation of plans to achieve these levels;
7) Progress monitoring; and
8) Full integration of practice into the functioning of the organization

It should be noted that Stages 1–4 are the first steps in establishing benchmarks, whereas Stages 5–8 apply the benchmarks to operations of the organization. Ultimately, any organization that is using learning collaboratives to implement process change or evaluate outcomes of evidence-based practice interventions, bench marking is one strategy that leadership will probably want to utilize.

INTERDISCIPLINARY TEAMS

As mentioned previously, learning collaboratives as well as other models of care recommended by the Institute of Medicine (2006), like the "chronic care model" (Wagner, 1998), will require professionals to shift from solo practice roles to interdisciplinary roles. Along with this shift will come an expansion of old tasks and acquisition of new tasks and skills (Gilbody, Whitty, Grimshaw, & Thomas, 2003). One method for addressing these changes is for management to support the training and structuring of interdisciplinary team models of caregiving.

We will begin with this assumption: Quality management could not exist without staff to manage, and the best staff arrangements are those that exist in an interdisciplinary team configuration. But what is an interdisciplinary team?

Definitions

Interdisciplinary work is now considered a mainstay of behavioral health care organizations. The term *interdisciplinary* refers to a systematic process of developing the ability to analyze and synthesize from the perspective of various disciplines (e.g., psychiatry, public health, social work). Its goal is to recognize and integrate the relationships between all the individual elements, synthesize and link disciplinary knowledge, and put it within a larger systemic framework. In other words, specialists may work interactively with non-specialists to study a problem, integrate their multiple viewpoints, and make recommendations to solve a specific individual, family, community, or organizational issue. Other terms that are used simultaneously to refer to this approach are *multidisciplinary* and *transdisciplinary*. Interdisciplinary differs from multidisciplinary and transdisciplinary approaches in that multidisciplinary approaches are where several disciplines are brought together with no systematic attempt to collectively integrate or synthesize the information. A transdisciplinary approach operates from the assumption that, regardless of ones' discipline, all knowledge is valuable and that dividing issues up by discipline is neither helpful nor practical for solving real world issues. As the "trans-" prefix implies, transdisciplinary approaches go beyond disciplinary divisions. In other words, problems and solutions are drawn from many disciplines in order to build understanding, content, and methodology (Cohen & Bailey, 1997; Sellamna, 2011).

Interdisciplinary work generally begins when specialists contribute their experience and disciplinary knowledge of concepts, methods, and tools, working interactively with other specialists in a team to study the problem and make recommendations to solve it. These specialists come together to form the interdisciplinary team. Cohen and Bailey (1997) define a *team* as:

> a collection of individuals who are interdependent in their tasks, who share responsibility for outcomes, who see themselves and who are seen by others as an intact social entity embedded in one or more larger social systems (e.g., mental health organization) and who manage their relationships across organizational boundaries (p. 2).

A team usually consists of at least two individuals who have specific roles, perform independent tasks, are adaptable, and share a common goal (Cohen & Bailey, 1997).

An example of an interdisciplinary team at work would be when a psychiatrist, social worker, public health nurse, and dentist work together to research key problems in supporting oral health for mental health clients with dental diseases and then provide a drop-in "Health and Wellness" class weekly at the local community mental health agency. The class may be staffed by dental technicians, run by the public health nurse, and coordinated by the social worker, with medications managed by the psychiatrist.

Steps for Establishing a Team

Behavioral healthcare organizations utilize teams that are suited to its own needs. There are three steps that any one team must establish from the get-go. *First*, establish the aim. What is the team trying to accomplish? *Second,* consider the system that the aim is addressing. What will tell us if the change represents an improvement in the system? *Third,* create an inclusive team that represents different parts of the intended change process. Who is needed from different parts of the organization—from managers to front-line workers—who can promote change toward improvement? (Institute for Healthcare Improvement, 2011).

Strategies for Interdisciplinary Work

There are four tenets of interdisciplinary work: 1) complex problems require an interdisciplinary approach; 2) teams require shared objectives; 3) teamwork involves both individual and collective activities; and 4) teamwork involves understanding the value systems of other disciplines (Sellamna, 2011). Let's explore some of these tenets in more detail as they relate to quality management and, later, program evaluation.

- Tenet 1: Complex problems require an interdisciplinary approach.

Many of the individual and systemic issues that clients and organizations face can only be studied and solved through cooperation between several disciplinary competencies. Fiscal managers (e.g., MBAs or CPAs) need to have an understanding of counseling staff's (e.g., LPCs, MSWs) clinical and time demands in order to develop realistic performance measures. One example of a complex problem is the many clients who experience the symptoms of mental illness complicated by severe health issues (e.g., untreated diabetes). These individuals may require multiple community contacts by outreach staff just to engage in services. Without an understanding of the time needed for outreach services, fiscal management could create restrictive, office-based performance indicators that have little relevance to real-time activities that constitute the work world of staff. Quality management includes opportunities for different disciplines in different departments to strategize together on mutually complex problems that are the responsibility of the agency as a whole.

- Tenet 2: Teams require shared objectives.

Part of what constitutes quality management is the notion of shared values. In all teams, it is important to have commonly agreed-upon objectives. These values should be formulated in a way that appeals to and includes all the disciplines present in the team and at which the "bigger picture" is made explicit (Sellamna, 2011). Although an interdisciplinary team may be given specific guidelines about their department's or unit's objectives, they will still need an opportunity to discuss different disciplinary viewpoints, and come to a common definition of the purpose of the team's activity and the specific outputs expected from the team. Once a common understanding is established, the team can go on to find common ground through a definition of the central issues, goals, or problems. The various viewpoints have the benefit of providing different views about the problem and different approaches to the issues. For example, mental health case managers may advocate that clients have the right to refuse medication without fear of being hospitalized against their will, whereas the medical team may strongly feel that certain clients are a danger to themselves and society without their medication, and should be hospitalized against their will if necessary. If the two sets of providers, along with the client, find a common point of understanding, such as "choice" or "client rights," then the team can better operate with shared objectives rather than competing objectives.

- Tenet 3: Teamwork involves both individual and collective activities.

Key strategies for working in interdisciplinary teams include identifying and acknowledging disciplinary contributions, individual capabilities, and variation in tasks. The goal is to find the right balance between collective and individual activities. Certain activities best done in teams are to produce ideas, exchange experiences, communicate information, and make decisions. Activities best done by individuals include gathering information, elaborating on ideas, implementing a team plan, and formulating or writing reports. For example, an interdisciplinary team may collectively agree that in-home visits are vital to the support of at-risk, medically fragile mental health consumers living independently. It is, however, the psychiatric nurse practitioner who is deemed the most appropriate person to conduct these home visits, due to the specialty health care background he possesses.

- Tenet 4: Understanding the value systems of other disciplines.

Behavioral health care organizations are composed of a rich array of staff, clinicians, and professionals. Each of these individuals emerges from different disciplines with different knowledge constructs and values. In other words, they have different concept "maps" about what they need to do. By understanding these different concepts, they can then understand and appreciate what other disciplines can offer and how they can contribute to the goals of the program, understand the specific language of their colleagues and better communicate with them and see the similarities and differences with their own specific discipline. For example, team building exercises could include a review of each discipline's professional code of ethics. Psychologists, nurses, psychiatrists, social workers, and counselors all operate under a code of ethics specific to their discipline. These guidelines typically influence the value base of the person's profession, which is often reflected in their practice style. By understanding your colleague's code of ethics, you may have a better glimpse into their practice style.

What makes a Successful Team?

In order for interdisciplinary teams to be effective, actions must be taken by both management and employees. Let's first look at the role of management. Two key management actions are needed: 1) support and active involvement by top management and 2) training in the practice of collaborative practice behaviors. Executives have to communicate a vision or key values and provide strong organizational support that stimulates employees' willingness to change from old-practice models (i.e., solo) to team-practice models (Mills & Weeks, 2004). In order for staff to have the requisite skills to engage in interdisciplinary teams, it will be necessary for management to provide training and development in collaborative practice behaviors, such as effective communication and conflict resolution (IOM, 2006, p. 242). Collaboration is enhanced by a shared understanding of agreed-upon collective goals and new individual roles (IOM, 2006, p. 242). In addition, new communication patterns and changes in roles can be uncomfortable for behavioral healthcare professionals. It is common for staff to experience role confusion and conflict when asked to work in personnel arrangements they are unfamiliar with. Active training and support in the skills necessary for interdisciplinary work from management can help reduce these conflicts.

Employees also play a key role in how effective their teams will be. If organizational improvement often hinges on the effectiveness of its interdisciplinary teams, how do we constitute effective teams? The Institute for Healthcare Improvement (IHI, 2011) identifies three different kinds of employees that represent different kinds of expertise within the organization: *system leadership*, *technical leadership* and *day-to-day leadership*. An effective team will have a system's leader who has enough authority to be able to cut through bureaucratic obstacles when a plan is devised and who can allocate the time and resources to achieve the aim identified by the team. A person who represents clinical technical leadership will provide credibility when it comes to knowing the subject matter intimately and can help devise methods for determining what to measure, selecting effective measurement tools, providing guidance on data collection and most critically, interpretation and display of data. A day-to-day leader can be a central player in the team in that they understand all the ins and outs of the system but also know the downstream impact of identified aims and changes in the system. Having the ability to work seamlessly and diplomatically among disparate groups also helps a lot. One example of this model is illustrated below:

> *Example 1:* Reducing waiting lists for intake appointments referred by Crisis Clinic.
> *Aim:* Our clinic will improve the intake appointment time from one week to same day for all referrals sent to clinic from Crisis Team.
> *Team:* Leader, M.D., Psychiatrist and Medical Director in charge of admissions and referrals for clinic;
> *Technical Expert,* MSW (Master's Level Clinician)—understands process and delays related to calls, scheduling, computer referrals, and intake information and scheduling of on-call staff to cover intake schedule;
> *Day-to-Day Leader,* PNP (Psychiatric Nurse Practitioner), Manager of the clinic, who coordinates all referrals;
> *Additional Team Members,* front-line desk staff, on-call staff, scheduler.

PROGRAM EVALUATION: WHAT IS IT AND WHY SHOULD WE CARE?

Once an organization has instituted a robust interdisciplinary team approach to client care, a natural next step would be to determine if the services provided are needed and which ones are effective. This is where program evaluation becomes the tool of quality management. It is systematic assessment, using as valid and reliable scientific research methods as possible, that examines the processes, outcomes, or performance of an organization and/or monitors change for groups of clients (Grinnell, Unrau, & Gabor, 2011). The purpose of program evaluation is to "improve efficiencies, effectiveness and the experience of services" (Grinnell, Unrau, & Gabor, 2011; p. 522). A central theme of any program evaluation is its accountability to stakeholders groups (Posavac & Carey, 2007). It is guided by a set of philosophies and methods that aim to determine "what works" and report back its findings to various stakeholders—for example, clients, professional groups or organizations, funding bodies, and regulatory agencies. Clients value assurances that services offered are effective; professionals appreciate understanding what works for different client problems and groups; funding bodies demand accountability that allocated funds result in effective outcomes; and regulatory agencies monitor agency or program compliance with legal mandates (Bamberger, Rugh, & Mabry, 2007).

Guiding Principles for Evaluators

Program evaluation is often conducted within the context of the needs of individuals and communities or organizations. Owen (2007) reminds us of the sensitive role that evaluators assume when they are asked to assess an organization's or team's performance. He notes that the evaluator can be regarded as an outsider or insider relative to the "client" (organization), and the evaluative contributions might include that of consultant, educator, or change agent. Without clear, guiding principles, these roles can lead to conflict between the evaluator and management or between evaluator and program provider. The reputation and career of the evaluator depend on providing accurate and candid information, while a program manager's career may be bound up with the provision of successful programs, free of conflict or negative impact.

To help guide program evaluators, Owen (2007) has listed five principles endorsed by the American Evaluation Association that can serve as codes of behavior. These are summarized below:

- **Principle of Systematic Inquiry**: Evaluators conduct systematic, data-based inquiries about whatever is being evaluated (p. 156). They utilize the highest level of technical standards in order to increase the accuracy and credibility of the evaluative information they produce.
- **Principle of Competence**: Evaluators provide competent performance to stakeholders (pp. 156–157). Evaluators should practice within the limits of their profession and expertise, provide the highest level of performance in the evaluation, and actively engage in continuing professional development to upgrade skills and expertise.
- **Principle of Integrity and Honesty:** Evaluators ensure the honesty and integrity of the entire evaluation process (p. 157). Evaluators should negotiate honestly with clients and all stakeholders regarding costs, tasks, and limitations of methodology and make explicit any conflicts of interest or disclose roles or relationships that would compromise findings, as well as communicate concerns in a forthright manner.
- **Principle of Respect for People:** Evaluators respect the security, dignity, and self-worth of the respondents, program participants, clients, and other stakeholders with whom they interact (p. 158). Evaluators should attempt to foster the social equity of the evaluation such that those who gave to the process receive some benefits in return, and in the event that negative results are found, the information is shared in a manner that respects the stakeholders' dignity and self-worth while still communicating the truthfulness of the findings.
- **Principle of Responsibility for General and Public Welfare:** Evaluators articulate and take into account the diversity of interests and values that may be related to the general and public welfare (p. 159). Evaluators have the responsibility of considering, not only immediate outcomes for the agency, but how the findings are related to broader assumptions, implications, and potential side effects, and therefore, in the spirit of transparency, make available access to evaluative information by stakeholders impacted by results.

Types of Program Evaluation

Kettner and colleagues (2008) describe four common types of program evaluations that are seen in community mental health organizations. These are (1) *needs assessments*, 2) *process evaluations*, 3) *outcome evaluations,* and 4) *cost-efficiency/effectiveness evaluations* which are also known as *cost/benefit analyses*.

Needs Assessments

Two of the initial questions asked in quality management are "What are the needs of a community?" and "Are current services still needed?" A needs assessment is an evaluation whose aim is to determine the nature, scope, and locale of a particular problem, and propose practical solutions to the problem (Hatry, Cowan, Weiner, & Lampkin, 2003). Specific needs assessment questions include examining demographics (e.g., describe characteristics or profile of people to be served), history of problem (e.g., what has worked in the past), demand for services (e.g., describes needs and service gaps of targeted clientele), and strengths (e.g., identify assets of community).

An example of a need assessment is an approach called a "context evaluation." The purpose of a context evaluation is to develop a program rationale through the analysis of unmet needs and unused opportunities. This approach describes discrepancies between what is and what is desired. The strengths are that the program's effectiveness is enhanced when the conceptual basis for the program (e.g., free medication for impoverished clients) is perceived needs; in other words, the program's values match its approach. The limitation is that the target audience may fail to recognize or express needs. A sample question from an input evaluation would be: "What are the needs of low-income mental health clients who do not have access to health insurance for medication?"

Process Evaluations

Process evaluations facilitate quality management as it evaluates what is happening in a program or set or services. Its aim includes describing the nature of services (e.g., type, frequency, duration) of real-time program operations and client service activities. In other words, process evaluations try to determine what is actually done in the service delivery in order for it to be replicated by others and elsewhere. If we are not doing the service, program, or intervention correctly, then if there is any quality, it is pure luck; quality management does not want to hear "it didn't work because we didn't do it right!" There wouldn't be much quality in that, and, if anything, it would be quality mismanagement.

Specific process questions include examining program structures (organizational structure of communication and decision making), program supports (what supports exist for workers to do their jobs), client service delivery (what do workers do and how often?), decision making (who makes decisions and how documented?), program integrity (determine fidelity to original blueprint and how closely it is being followed), and lastly, compliance (does program adhere to internal and external standards established by the administration, funders, and external bodies such as government or accrediting bodies?).

An example of a process evaluation is an "input evaluation." The purpose of an input evaluation is to identify and assess program capabilities. This approach describes strong and weak points of strategies for achieving program or agency objectives. The strengths are that it provides useful information to guide program strategy and design. The limitations are that the approach can be complex and frustrating if priorities and aims are not set at the beginning and followed. A sample question from an input evaluation would be: "Are case management in-home visits or in-office appointments more appropriate for the target population the agency works with?"

Outcomes Evaluations

Outcomes evaluations are a third type of evaluation whose aim is to determine the amount and direction of change experienced by clients or participants during or after the receipt of an agency's services (Lampkin & Hatry, 2003). Awkward as it sounds, the area is *outcomes*, plural, as few program or clinicians have a single outcome. Some specific outcomes questions examine program integrity (are benchmarks being met and goals achieved?), program effects (are clients better off after having received services than before, not worse?), differential effects (does one group benefit over the other and if so, how and why?), causality (what's the evidence for effectiveness?), and lastly, satisfaction (e.g., client and stakeholder satisfaction with services).

An example of an outcomes evaluation is an approach called "impact evaluation." The purpose of an impact evaluation is to describe direct and indirect program or agency effects or results. This approach addresses the impact of a program on the program recipient. The strengths are that it tests the usefulness or success of a program in ameliorating a particular problem or issue. Limitations include the fact that it is difficult to establish causality using scientific methods of evaluation. A sample question from an impact evaluation would be: "Are participants able to improve their communication skills with family members after participating in a Youth Only Rap Group?"

Cost-Efficiency/Effectiveness Evaluations

Cost-efficiency/effectiveness evaluations are a fourth type of evaluation, whose aim is to demonstrate fiscal accountability of costs associated with providing services to specific populations (Newmann, 2005). Specific cost-efficiency/effectiveness questions include examining unit costs (average cost per client, per unit of service—such as intake, intervention and follow-up), cost distributions (such as percentage of costs for direct and indirect services such as therapy and administration), and cost reduction/recovery (can costs be reduced or recovered without loss of quality?).

An example of a cost-efficiency/effectiveness evaluation is an approach called "cost–benefit evaluation." The purpose of a cost–benefit evaluation is to describe the economic efficiency of a program regarding actual or anticipated costs and known or expected benefits. This approach compares program costs and program outcomes in terms of fiscal amounts. The strengths are that it is useful for convincing policy makers, funders, and regulatory decision makers that dollar benefits justify the program costs. Limitations include difficulty in quantifying multiple outcomes in monetary terms and expressing costs and benefits in terms of common program denominators. A sample question from a cost–benefit evaluation would be: "What was the total estimated savings to society as a result of client diversion from prison to state hospital settings?"

HOW TO MEASURE BEHAVIORAL HEALTHCARE QUALITY MANAGEMENT

Overview

"Quality management," as defined here, is a complex interaction of person, process, and practice to select the best evidence-based interventions. As applied here, program evaluations in general, and benchmarking in particular, are the organization's effort to provide systematic and continuous feedback about what seems to work with the particular agency, the particular clinician, and the agency's particular clients. As such, measurement is useful at the agency, program, and individual client levels. It includes needs assessments, process evaluation, outcomes assessment, and cost/effectiveness analysis, all with the purpose of managing quality to assure more effectiveness. Emphasis here will be given to the individual-client levels of measurement and process measures.

At the individual-client level, use of an evidence-based practice does not ensure effective outcomes. Clients are different in many ways, including their motivation to change and resources to facilitate change. Similarly, clinicians are humans with varying degrees of talent and training; they even seem to vary day to day over the course of a career. No two are the same, and no one stays the same. Therefore, continuous assessment ascertains what seems to work, and it is important feedback to the individual clinician and the organization. Similarly, in spite of the uniformity of evidence-based practice (EBP), its applications vary from setting to setting, from clinician to clinician, and from client to client. While EBPs tend to be more standardized in the application, they are not cookbook recipes but should be adopted to fit the form to the client's fuss.

In so doing, the agency needs continuous measures to ascertain if the client outcomes are as desired and designed by the evidence-based practice. Measurements allow the clinician and agency to determine if positive outcomes are being obtained, either by obtaining specific goals or the reduction in mental health symptomatology. Most mental health systems that strive for improvement often find themselves relying on various kinds of measures to observe change in behavioral healthcare. There are different measurement tools for whether the quality management is assessing the need, the process, outcomes, or cost/effectiveness.

Outcomes measures are from the perspective of the client or patient and determine how the system is performing as well as the impact on the client's problem. For example, at the system level, "access" is a critical measure of quality. Simply stated, the best program is of limited value if it is inaccessible for whatever reason: location, transportation, hours of operation, allied services, and so on. One access measure that clients find critical is time. This is in terms of the number of days between calling for a mental health appointment and being seen for the appointment. It also includes how much time is spent in the waiting room in advance of a scheduled appointment; few clients/consumers like being kept waiting.

Using measures of the client's progress over the course of treatment provides continuous feedback of the client outcomes and the clinician's performance. These measurement tools may be used to compare a client's progress over the course of the treatment by comparing changes in his or her scores. Alternatively, client scores may be compared with norms to determine if their scores are similar to, or distinguishable from, clinical samples and the general population. Outcome measures are best when they are short, rapidly completed, and quickly scored in order not to interfere with the limited time available for each individual client. One resource describing over 600 rapid-assessment instruments for problems of individuals, couples, families, and children is Fischer and Corcoran (2007). Using a rapid assessment tool at the beginning, middle, and end of a program or treatment provides persuasive evidence of client change and, to a lesser degree, clinician effectiveness.

Process measures are useful at the system level to determine if the public health needs are being met or are in need of particular services that are currently missing. The needs may be anything ranging from transportation, to hospital beds, to treatment programs for marginalized populations such as immigrants, teen moms, the unemployed; and the list continues.

Additionally, process measures enable the organization to determine whether specific parts or steps in the system are performing as planned. One example is staffing. Continuous assessment is necessary to determine how many clinicians and support staff members are available each day to see the number of clients requesting services, which itself varies from day to day and over the course of a year. At the clinician level, process measures facilitate determining if the treatment complies with the evidence-based practice procedures. These measures are known as a "fidelity checklist." A fidelity checklist enumerates the critical components of the program and describes them so others can determine if they are true to the program they are trying to replicate, whether with a new client population or a new setting. They typically accompany evidence-based practice manuals or are published separately (Smock, Trepper, Wetchler, McCollum, Ray, & Pierce, 2008).

Balancing measures are from the perspective of looking at a system from different directions or locations to determine if changes in one part of the system caused unintended consequences in another part. One example is involuntary admissions. The quality management issue might well be whether admissions to long-term units are going up as a consequence of diverting mentally ill people from jail and into diversion programs that provide indefinite hospital stays. While a hospital is sometimes a preferable facility for treating mental illness, it comes at a cost, and quality management is needed to correct any adverse impact. Similarly, do drug courts result in less use of treatment and more reliance on crime, punishment, and restitution? And if so, how is the quality of services managed? One common example of the concern for balancing measures is putting the desired "speed bumps" in streets of neighborhoods with children, until there is a need for ambulances as the neighbors get old; slowing traffic down is good for children and bad for someone with a heart attack.

LIMITATIONS IN MEASUREMENT

"You can't improve what you can't measure" is a common maxim in behavioral healthcare, which was heralded nearly four decades ago (Hudson, 1978). Measuring the quality of care provided by individuals, organizations, and health plans and reporting the results is linked both conceptually and empirically to reductions in variations in care and increases in the delivery of effective health care.

Uses of measurement in practice, whether at the individual client and clinician level, are not without limitations. First of all, there is no general agreement in behavioral healthcare about which measures to use. In health care, there is a consensus that blood pressure, temperature, pain, and problems with intake or output are indicators of health concerns and are routinely ascertained using standardized assessment procedures. The behavioral healthcare industry does not have such uniform indicators of mental health or mental health condition. Indeed, depression and anxiety are related to many if not most mental health conditions, although there is no agreement on the best assessment procedures.

Moreover, limitations in measurement are just not an agency-specific challenge or due to lack of instruments, but also due to the separation of mental illness and substance use from physical health care. The whole behavioral healthcare industry is challenged. For example, the National Healthcare Quality Report (AHRQ, 2003) identified mental illness as a clinical area lacking broadly accepted and widely used measures of quality. They found that, of 107 measures of the effectiveness of health care, only seven addressed mental health: three were for the treatment of depression in adults, one for suicide, and three for management of delirium and confusion in nursing homes. None addressed the quality of care for substance-use problems and illnesses. And yet compendiums reprinting hundreds of measurement tools are available (e.g., Corcoran & Fischer, 2014) and have been for over 30 years. The big issues are lack of quality measurement and reporting infrastructure; so what can management do about this? One source of answers is the Institute on Medicine report *Improving the Quality of Healthcare for Mental and*

Substance Use Conditions (IOM, 2006). This stellar report advances eight functions for effective measurement of quality:

1. Effectively measuring quality and reporting results to providers, consumers and over-sight organizations requires structures, resources and expertise to perform several related functions:
2. Conceptualizing the aspects of care to be measured
3. Translating the quality of care measurement concepts into performance measure specifications
4. Pilot testing the performance measure specifications to determine their validity, reliability, feasibility and cost
5. Ensuring calculation of the performance measures and their submission to a performance measures repository
6. Auditing to ensure that the performance measures have been calculated accurately and in accordance with specifications
7. Analyzing and displaying the performance measures in a format or formats suitable for understanding by multiple intended audiences such as consumers, health care delivery entities, purchasers and quality oversight organizations
8. Maintaining the effectiveness of individual performance measures and performance measure sets and policies over time (p. 181).

These functions require a coordinated approach that maximizes the efficiency and effectiveness of various efforts. These useful and government-endorsed guidelines are delineated in detail, and yet in summary, measurement instruments should be selected judiciously as performance measures of quality. Examples of quality performance measures include reducing the waiting list time for the crisis center and increasing client service satisfaction.

In spite of the limitations of measurement, remembering that scores are merely *estimates*, numerous instruments exist for almost every client problem and agency or program goal. The biggest problem remains what it has been for decades—clinicians simply don't use them! In order for program evaluation to actually be a tool of quality management, the task remains how to get instruments to be used *routinely*. Without measurement tools, there are no program evaluations, and in turn, quality is not managed.

FUTURE DIRECTIONS

So far we have illustrated how quality management is a function of leadership, "teamship," and the use of program evaluation as a tool for assessing quality. Program evaluation is taking a more front-and-center role in the interdisciplinary movement toward evidence-based practice in behavioral health care organizations (Mullen, Bellamy, & Bledsoe, 2005). Why? One way to explain this movement is what appears to be a future trend toward an increase in governmental audits and program reviews. Given the increasing climate of distrust shared by taxpayers and certain political affiliates toward any form of government-supported services (think Social Security and Medicaid), program administrators will be increasingly asked by funders and or politicians to provide more data and "proof" that their programs are working. This will require more standardized evaluation techniques, a differently trained workforce, and a management team that is both nimble and ready to provide critical data. Program evaluation will no longer be considered either a luxury or a nuisance, but a necessary prerequisite to the acquisition of (renewed) funding. Behavioral healthcare organizations must be prepared to rise to these new expectations, and they themselves set the standard for what is quality.

REFERENCES

Agency for Healthcare Research and Quality (AHRQ). (2003). *National Healthcare Quality Report*. Rockville, MD: U.S. Department of Health and Human Services.

Bamberger, M. J., Rugh, J., & Mabry, L. (2007). *Real World Evaluation: Working under Budget, Time, Data, and Political Constraints*. Thousand Oaks, CA: Sage.

Bryant, A. (2011). The quest to build a better boss. *New York Times* (pp. 1, 7), Sunday, March 13.

Castro, F., Cota, M., & Vega, S. (1999). Health promotion in Latino populations: A sociocultural model for program planning, development and evaluation. In R. Huff & M. Kline (Eds.), *Promoting Health in Multicultural Populations: A Handbook for Practitioners*. (pp. 131–167). Thousand Oaks, CA: Sage.

Chavez, N., & Barry, C. T. (1998). *Contracting for Managed Substance Abuse and Mental Health Services: A Guide for Public Purchasers*. Technical Assistance Publication (TAP) Series 22. Department of Health and Human Services—Substance Abuse and Mental Health Services (SAMHSA). Rockville, MD: DHHS [Online]. Retrieved March 11, 2011, from www.samhsa.gov/products/manuals/taps/22b.htm.

Cohen, S. G., & Bailey, D. E. (1997). What makes teams work: Group effectiveness research from the shop floor to the executive suite. *Journal of Management, 23*, 239–290.

Corcoran, K., & Fischer, J. (2014). *Measures for Clinical Practice and Research: A Sourcebook* (5th ed., 2 vols.). New York: Oxford University Press.

Cretin, S., Shortell, S. M., & Keeler, E. B. (2004). An evaluation of collaborative interventions to improve chronic illness care: Framework and study design. *Evaluation Review, 28*(1): 28–51.

Dougherty, R. H. (2007). Improving quality step by step. *Behavioral Healthcare, 27*(9): 36–39

Dückers, M. L, Spreeuwenberg, P., Cordula, W., & Groenewegen, P. P. (2009). Exploring the black box of quality improvement collaboratives: Modeling relations between conditions, applied changes and outcomes. *Implementation Science, 4*(74): 1–12. doi: 10.1186/1748-5908-4-74

Gilbody, S., Whitty, P., Grimshaw, J., & Thomas, R. (2003). Educational and organizational interventions to improve the management of depression in primary care: A systematic review. *Journal of American Medical Association, 289*(23): 3145–3151.

Grinnell, R., Unrau, Y., & Gabor, P. (2011). Program evaluation. In R. M. Grinnell & Y. A. Unrau (Eds.) *Social Work Research and Evaluation: Foundations of Evidence-Based Practice* (9th ed., pp. 521–529). New York: Oxford University Press.

Hatry, H. P., Cowan, J., Weiner, K., & Lampkin, L. M. (2003). *Developing Community-Wide Outcome Indicators for Specific Services*. Washington, DC: Urban Institute.

Hudson, W. W. (1978). First axioms of treatment. *Social Work, 23*, 65–66.

Institute for Healthcare Improvement (IHI) (2011). Forming the Team. [Online]. Retrieved February 5, 2011, from http://www.ihi.org.IHI/Topics/ImprovementMethods/HowToImprove/Formingtheteam.

Institute of Medicine (IOM). (2001). *Crossing the Quality Chasm: A New Health System for the Twenty-first Century*. Washington, DC: The National Academies Press.

IOM. (2006). *Improving the Quality of Healthcare for Mental and Substance Use Conditions.* Quality Chasm Series. Washington, DC: The National Academies Press.

Kettner, P. K., Moroney, R. K., & Martin, L. L. (2008). *Designing and Managing Programs: An Effectiveness-Based Approach* (3rd ed.). Thousand Oaks, CA: Sage.

Lampkin, L. M. & Hatry, H. P. (2003). *Key Steps in Outcome Management.* Washington, DC: Urban Institute.

Lewis, P., Goodman, S., & Fandt, P. (2004). *Management Challenges for Tomorrow's Leaders.* Mason, OH: Thomson Publishing.

Mills, P. D., & Weeks, W. B. (2004). Characteristics of successful quality improvement teams: Lessons from five collaborative projects in VHA. *Joint Commission Journal on Quality and Safety, 30,* 152–162.

Mullen, E. J., Bellamy, J. L., & Bledsoe, S. E. (2005). Implementing evidence-based social work practice. In P. Sommerfeld (Ed.), *Evidence-Based Social Work: Towards a New Professionalism?* (pp. 149–172). Berlin: Peter Lang.

Newmann, J. P. (2005). *Using Cost-Effectiveness Analysis to Improve Health Care.* New York: Oxford University Press.

Øvretveit, J., Bate, P., Cleary, P., Cretin, S., Gustafson, D., McInnes, K., et al. (2002). Quality collaboratives: Lessons from research. *Quality and Safety in Health Care, 11,* 345–351.

Owen, J. (2007). *Program Evaluation: Forms and Approaches* (3rd ed.). New York: Guilford Press.

Posavac, E. J., & Carey, R. G. (2007). *Program Evaluation: Methods and Case Studies* (7th ed.). Englewood Cliffs, NJ: Prentice-Hall.

Schonlau, M., Mangione-Smith, R., & Chan, K. S. (2005). Evaluation of a quality improvement collaborative in asthma care: Does it improve processes and outcomes of care? *Annals of Family Medicine, 3*(3): 200–208.

Sellamna, N. (2011). Interdisciplinary teams: Key concepts. In R. Hawkins (Ed.), *Learning Resources for Capacity Building.* Wageningen, The Netherlands: International Centre for Development Oriented Research—Agriculture (ICRA) [Online]. Retrieved March 30, 2011, from http://www. Icra-edu. org/objects/anglolearn/interdisciplinary_Teams-Key_Concepts.

Shortell, S. M., Zukoski, A. P., & Alexander, J. A. (2002). Evaluating partnerships for community health improvement: Tracking the footprints. *Journal of Health Policy Law, 27*(1): 49–91.

Smock, S. A., Trepper, T. S., Wetchler, J. L., McCollum, E. E., Ray, R., & Pierce, K. (2008). Solution-focused group therapy for level 1 substance abusers. *Journal of Marital and Family Therapy, 34,* 107–120.

Solberg, L., Fischer, L., & Wei, F. (2001). A CQI intervention to change the care of depression: A controlled study. *Effective Clinical Practice, 4*(6): 239–249.

Substance Abuse and Mental Health Services Administration (SAMHSA) (2009). *Grant Awards by State, FY 2009: Discretionary Funds in Detail*: Grantee: Center for Mental Health Services (CMHS) Mississippi State Department of Health, Jackson, Mississippi, SM057025 [Online]. Retrieved March 24, 2011, from http://www.samhsa.gov/StateSummaries/detail/2009/MS.aspx.

Terry, P. (2003). Leadership and achieving a vision: How does a profession lead a nation? *American Journal of Health Promotion, 18*(2): 162–167.

Vandiver, V (2008). *Integrating Health Promotion and Mental Health: An Introduction to Polices, Principles and Practices.* New York: Oxford University Press.

Wagner, E. H. (1998). Chronic disease management: What will it take to improve care for chronic illness? *Effective Clinical Practice, 1*(1): 2–4.

Wheatley, M. (1999). *Leadership and the New Sciences: Discovering Order in the Chaotic World.* San Francisco, CA: Berrett-Koehler.

A SOCIAL SYSTEMS PERSPECTIVE ON LEADERSHIP IN SYSTEMS OF CARE

PHILIP CASS, GRAYCE M. SILLS, AND LAURA WEISEL

This book is filled with information about a wide variety of best practices thought to be useful in the work of community mental health. However, a central issue remains. How does one work from this plethora of information to implementation of new practices and ideas in the workplace?

Numerous case examples have been provided to richly illustrate the benefits of the many practices described. We have been given the benefit of the described experience of system changes at the state level in Chapter 34, "Transformational Leadership in Mental Health" (Svendsen, Hogan, Wortham-Wood). We have been enlightened by the excellent work in the chapter "Psychiatric Risk Management: Efforts to Reduce Unseen Outcomes (Winters, Teague & Yeager). The chapter on trauma-informed care and treatment brings to the cutting edge of contemporary understanding the phenomena we treat under the rubric of mental health care. The two chapters presenting differing perspectives on medication management give us some insight into the complexity of this critical element of treatment. So in a sense this text has provided a library of rich and varied musical compositions but has yet to address how that music comes to life in a real-world performance.

What follows in this final chapter is an effort to explicate some additional answers to the question of how these best practices can be brought to life in the milieu of community treatment and care. How can we move beyond best practices, co-creating innovation and the future of community mental health? Can we make the music come to life—as a soloist, an ensemble, or a full-throated orchestra in collaboration with each other, the conductor, and the composer?

The argument made here is that leaders must have a clear sense of purpose, an enlightened understanding of one's own sense of self and being. That is thought to be necessary, but not sufficient, to lead sustainable changes within systems. One must also have a systems view/perspective that leads one automatically to veer from blame-and-shame attributions as the source of problems but rather to a broad examination of multiple perspectives on the problem or issue at hand.

In this chapter, we present practices that augur well for a future that will require the best efforts from all the participants in the process to engage with one another in ways that may be new and unfamiliar. As we know, comfort lies in the familiar. We hope this chapter may create some discomfort *and* that on the way you find new and energizing ways to create and sustain system-change.

THE BLIND SPOT OF OUR TIMES

"The blind spot of our times," is a phrase that Otto Scharmer coined in his book *Theory U—Leading from the Future as It Emerges* (Scharmer, 2009b). There is a plethora of leadership literature that helps us understand the importance of clearly defining and measuring the results we are trying to achieve. There is even more literature written about the processes needed to achieve those results. However, there is a third dimension required in the equation that describes social reality, and that is the dimension of "who." It is this inner place from which leaders operate that Scharmer defines as the *blind spot* of our times. How we pay attention affects how things emerge, or as Scharmer said, "I pay attention this way, therefore things emerge that way" (Scharmer, 2009b, p. 228). Using the formula r = f(a), where "r" is social reality and "a" is awareness, awareness becomes the key intervention point in work designed to shift social reality (Scharmer, 2010).

All one needs to do for this to become obvious is to do an inventory of the people whom we hold in the greatest esteem. These may be people we directly know (a favorite teacher, professor, parent, grandparent, mentor, supervisor, etc.) or people about whom we've read (Gandhi, Martin Luther King, Abraham Lincoln, the Dalai Lama, etc.). When we ask ourselves, "What was it about these people that made a difference in me and in the lives of others?" we discover that these people seem to operate more consistently than most from their highest possibility. Those operating from this highest possibility almost always seem to have characteristics that include large ego/no ego, personal power/personal humility, self awareness/awareness of others, knowing/not knowing, the capacity to be present/the capacity to suspend, wanting/not wanting. Somehow, the individuals whom we hold in great esteem developed the capacity to hold, work with, and transcend the great paradoxes of life in a way that makes a difference in people's lives. And, somehow we discover ourselves in them, and they simultaneously embody us within themselves. They are transcendent leaders. Transcendent leaders go beyond transformation (changing structures, appearance, or character) and invite us to be our highest possibility.

Is this capacity to transcend (exceed the usual limits) really the key element in leadership? What makes this characteristic of transcendence the "road less traveled?" Again, in his book *Theory U,* Scharmer (2009) posits the notion that this is related to three different internal voices that we carry with us:

- The Voice of Judgment, which shuts down our capacity to operate with an Open Mind
- The Voice of Cynicism, which shuts down our capacity to operate with an Open Heart
- The Voice of Fear, which shuts down our capacity to operate with an Open Will (Scharmer, 2009a, p. 42).

In a world where we live day to day with a Congress that is stuck, an economic world order that is stuck, organizations and systems (both for profit and not-for-profit) that are stuck, and even personal relationships that are stuck, what are the necessary practices that transcendent formational leaders need to be engaging in? Perhaps what is even more important is what are the collective transcendent practices that groups of committed people can engage in that will make a difference? Albert Einstein suggested that "the world we have made as a result of the level of thinking we have done thus far creates problems we cannot solve with the same level of thinking which created them." What are the individual and collective practices that develop higher-order consciousness in individuals and in groups? We will come back to these questions and some possible directions after we first explore two worldviews: the machine worldview and the living systems worldview.

TWO WORLD VIEWS: MECHANISTIC AND LIVING SYSTEMS

Wheatley (2006) laid out the tremendous influence that Newtonian thinking has played in almost all of our current organizations. Since the days of Newton and Descartes, we have seen the world, including ourselves and all of our organizations, as a "vast and complex machine that had been entrusted to our care" (Wheatley, 2006. p. 30). Newton and Descartes' world is linear, can be objectively measured, and the whole understood by summing its parts.

We have been taught that if we can understand an organization and all of its parts through measurement, then we can understand its ultimate laws and can control it. This view, along with the early interpretation of Darwin's theory of evolution, is based on "survival of the fittest" as opposed to the more contemporary understanding of the "survival of fit." This belief has given rise to much of our economic theory, organizational theory, and leadership theory. Hierarchy (there are people who know and people who don't know) and bureaucracy (a way that is thought to control resources and decision making) are some of its manifestations. While both Newtonian and Darwinian theory have been helpful in many ways, these theories don't always serve us well in a world that is populated by human beings who do not behave by these same laws. As living beings we behave in a "living systems" kind of way. It also stands to reason that anything developed by humans will look like, behave like, and adhere to principles aligned with living systems and not aligned with machines. Organizations, built by human beings that are based on mechanistic principles to do things, are not "human" by their nature. Yet our organizations inescapably are living systems and incur great challenges when constantly confronted by mechanistic principles.

It should be no surprise that social media have become central to how we operate in today's world. Social media are made up of some of these same characteristics (cells connected into networks) that are the building blocks of humans. What social media do is make visible already connected but invisible networks of human beings. These same kinds of networks are the building blocks of our human-made organizations and frequently go unseen. Nonetheless, they are there, operating within all organizations. We may think that we are leading our organizations in accordance with the structure, policies, and procedures that are documented in a manual, but that is seldom what is really going on throughout the organization. When we attempt to lead our organizations as though they are machines, we then can observe what goes on in behavioral healthcare organizations and in most organizations in general.

So, what appear to be the principles of living systems and the principles that can grow and sustain innovation and transformation, and reflect a real responsiveness to the people in organizations and communities? Margaret Wheatley and Myron Kellner-Rogers (Wheatley & Kellner-Rogers, 1999, p. 2) shed some light on this when they articulate the following:

- A living system only accepts its own solutions (we only accept those things we are a part of creating).
- A living system only pays attention to that which is meaningful to it here and now.
- In all nature, including ourselves, there is constant change without change management.
- Nature seeks diversity—new relationships open to new possibilities. It is not survival of the fittest but everything that is fit—as many species as possible. Diversity increases our chances of survival.
- Tinkering opens up to what is possible; here and now—nature is not intent on finding perfect solutions, but rather those that are workable.
- A living system cannot be steered or controlled; a living system can only be teased, nudged, and titillated.
- A system changes identity when its perception of itself changes.
- All the answers do not exist "out there." Sometimes we must experiment to find out what works.
- Who we are together is always different and more than who we are alone. The range of creative expression increases as we join others. New relationships create new capacities.
- Human beings are capable of self-organizing, given the right conditions.
- The act of self-organizing shifts an organization's work and culture to a higher order.

Here are some questions to consider if the future of behavioral healthcare lies in shifting the work and culture to a higher order.

- Based upon these characteristics of a living system, what are the individual and collective leadership practices needed to effectively lead and transform behavioral healthcare organizations/communities into a living systems framework?
- What are the individual and collective practices that develop higher-order consciousness in individuals and groups?
- Can these practices, i.e., the individual and collective practices, address the "who" in transformational/transcendent leadership?

LEADERSHIP TOOLS FOR WORKING WITH LIVING SYSTEMS

Beck and Cowan's work on spiral dynamics (1996), which built upon the earlier work of Clare Graves (Cowan and Todorovic, 2005), suggested that there is a sequencing of stages of consciousness that is the result of the interaction between the human being and the environment in which they exist. Graves once said, "The development of the human being is an unfolding or emergent process marked by the progressive subordination of older behavioral systems to newer, higher order systems. Clearly we have a powerful and dynamic mind, one that can recalibrate itself."

In view of the challenges and the opportunities in transforming behavioral healthcare and the leadership needed to both develop and co-create a viable future for behavioral health, are there practices that can assist leaders in all sectors of the behavioral healthcare system in the development of higher-order consciousness? We believe there are practices that do create the inner capacity for higher-order consciousness and hence move toward the ability to see a new, emerging, and different view of what it will take to "lead for the future as it emerges" (Scharmer, 2009b). What follows is a presentation of a few, if not all, of the useful practices and guides to a higher-order future.

INDIVIDUAL AND COLLECTIVE PRACTICES THAT FOCUS TRANSFORMATIONAL LEADERS AND INNOVATE TRANSFORMATIONAL CHANGE WITHIN HUMAN NETWORKS

First, as West meets East, ancient practices like mindfulness meditation are being subjected to the scrutiny of scientific inquiry and passing with flying colors (Williams and Zylowska, 2009). Individuals who consistently practice mindfulness meditation will attest to the long-term impact on their lives of "meeting their mind" every day. Developing the capacity to rest one's mind on the breath and to see yourself and others in a larger context is available to us all. While the world is in constant flux, humans can personally practice slowing down, breathing with consciousness, taking the time to see the world more clearly, and make decisions from a cultivated inner space. Practicing mindfulness meditation shifts the place of awareness (the intervention point) of the person (the "who") as leader as the intervener.

Mindfulness meditation is only one form of reflective practice. Tai chi, yoga, qigong, and the various martial arts are all gifts from the East that one can decide to learn and practice. Many people from many cultures have developed other reflective practices, including the practice of regular journaling. It was the practice of many of our grandparents to sit in prayer, say the rosary, or go to a place of worship on a daily basis. Harry Truman was known for his morning walks, and when you dig into the lives of the world's most revered leaders, you almost always find that they engaged in some form of regular personal reflective practice.

The point is, we can develop various forms of reflective practice or contemplation that can aid in the development of our own levels of consciousness that have a direct effect on leadership and therefore impact the people and organizations where we are charged with leadership. It is suggested here that learning and adopting a form of personal reflective practice may be a requirement for those espousing to be transcendent leaders. Brian Arthur (1999), the legendary leader of the Hanover Insurance Company, is noted to have said, "The success of an intervention depends on the interior condition of the intervener."

What are some collective practices that can aid in shifting the consciousness of groups of people (families, organizations, communities) that are living systems?

Over the past twenty years or so numerous dialogic processes have been developed and named that have their own ancient roots. These processes are being convened individually and together under the mantle of "participatory leadership" and include: Circle, World Café, Open Space, and Appreciative Inquiry. Each of these processes has an author, and an overview will be offered below.

Within the past fifteen years, leaders such as Toke Moeller and Monica Nissen from Denmark, along with numerous others, have brought these four practices together and offer them as "The Art of Hosting Conversations that Matter," which they also refer to as "The Art of Participatory Leadership" (see "Art of Hosting," www.artofhosting.org). They have demonstrated this practice in places as diverse as the European Commission; Columbus, Ohio; a village in Africa; Australia; New Zealand,; Japan; across Europe; Canada; the United States; South America; and Mexico.

Weisel (2011) and others have brought these processes into learning, multidisciplinary education settings, and professional development as "participatory learning." Together, these practices set a framework for building individuals and professionals who can respectfully work together on teams, organizations, advisory boards, learning communities, and in the development of social capital skills such as collaboration, problem solving, advocacy, leadership development, listening skills, creativity, and creating innovations.

In the context of organizations, Cass (Wheatley and Frieze, 2011) implemented these four "human technologies" as both an operating system for four non-profit medical organizations and in work with a statewide task force in the state of Ohio to redesign and create an innovative framework for transforming youth psychiatric service delivery.

CIRCLE

Baldwin and Linnea (Baldwin, 1998; Baldwin and Linnea, 2010) have been practicing, teaching, and writing about the ancient practice of "the Circle" for individuals and groups all over the world. The circle is an ancient form of meeting that has brought human beings together in conversations of respect for centuries. For many cultures, circles are part of their foundation. "What transforms a meeting into a Circle is the willingness of people to shift from informal socializing or opinionated discussion not a receptive attitude of thoughtful speaking and deep listening" (Nissen, Moeller, Cass, and Weisel, 2011).

WORLD CAFÉ

Juanita Brown and David Issacs have worked together in the development and evolution of a process called "the World Café" (2005). Café is a "method for creating a living network of collaborative dialogue around questions that matter in real life situations" (Nissen, Moeller, Cass, and Weisel, 2011). Café is a metaphor for how individuals, families, and communities have come together to share experiences, solve problems, and find common ground.

Café has a set of operating principles, assumptions, and etiquette for how to engage a group of individuals in gathering around tables and addressing questions that can both drive meaningful conversations and build on the shared experiences and ideas of everyone in the group. Multiple café tables, with four members per table, address a common question. The richness of these conversations is derived from the initial conversation and the hybrid of the conversations as participants move from one café table to another.

OPEN SPACE

The goal of "open space technology" is "to create time and space for people to engage deeply and creatively around issues of concern to them" (Nissen, Moller, Cass, and Weisel, 2011). The agenda is set by the individuals who have the desire and power to see the meeting as a tool to engage in conversations that are on topics related to a common issue. Open Space meetings result in transformative experiences for individuals and groups involved. Open Space is a simple and powerful way to catalyze effective dialogue and invite organizations to thrive in times of change (Nissen, Moeller, Cass, and Weisel, 2011).

Open Space operates with a set of principles and one law that clearly define the process. They work together to support an individual's passion around a matter of importance to them. The process of Open Space is an excellent framework for groups engaged in co-creating a strategic direction, conflict resolution, community planning, inclusion of multi-stakeholders, collaboration, and deep learning about issues and perspectives of multi-stakeholders.

APPRECIATIVE INQUIRY

Cooperrider developed "appreciative inquiry" in 1985 as a strategy for intentional change (Cooperrider and Whitney, 2005). Rather than looking at "what is," Appreciative Inquiry seeks to pursue possibilities by looking at "what could be." Appreciative Inquiry works with a "4-D" process:

1. Discover the "best of what is"—they identified where the company's processes worked perfectly.
2. Dream "what might be"—they envisioned processes that would work perfectly all the time.
3. Design "what should be"—they defined and prioritized the elements of perfect processes.
4. Create a Destiny based on "what will be"—they participated in the creation of the design.

Appreciative Inquiry is based on several guiding principles, including that a positive focus tends to deliver a positive effect. This principle of accentuating the positive goes beyond conventional business wisdom, which says the best way to overcome a major challenge is to focus on what you're doing poorly and determine how to improve (Kinni, 2003).

Some derivatives of these, such as the Pro-Action Café and the Story Harvest Process, have emerged as people have been working with these processes on a massive scale around the globe. These practices are being used by couples, in families, in meetings both large and small, in very large group settings, within organizations, and even within in whole communities. Using these processes as a framework for gathering groups of individuals together has been exploding all over the world because of the hunger within people to be in more meaningful relationships with each other. These collective practices can be taught and learned by all of us. However, like the individual reflective practices written about earlier, these, too, take discipline and practice, and are the most effective when hosted by people who have developed their own cultivated inner space.

Several pathways exist for developing one's capacity to cultivate their inner space. One such is The Presencing Institute, formed by C. Otto Scharmer (www.presencinginstitute.com) and his colleagues at MIT. They have developed practices such as learning journeys, sensing interviews, and solo experiences in nature that facilitate individuals' moving away from their own self (as the sole reference point) to walking in another's shoes and beyond that to sensing from the whole what is wanting to happen in the future.

Others, including Block (Block, 2009) and again Wheatley (Wheatley, 2006) have been encouraging all of us to seek our answers in community. All of this does suggest that the transcendent leader may need to shift from being the *lone wolf* to being the *host* of the intelligence that already exists within his/her organization.

STORIES OF TRANSFORMATION

Like the practices that transcendent leaders utilize (previously described in this chapter) that are cultivated over time, transformation itself may sometimes appear to happen overnight, or subtly show over a prolonged period of time; the following stories tell us about several "root system" developments and some that are starting to show flowers.

SHIFT THE QUALITY OF CIVIL DIALOGUE IN A COMMUNITY

In 2005, in a Midwestern city, 36 leaders were trained in the "Art of Hosting Conversations that Matter." This initiative began with a long-term purpose by a small group of people to shift the quality of civic dialogue in their community. As of this writing, the small initiative has now grown into a major movement with over 600 trained individuals.

The process of hosting meaningful conversations has become part of the culture of a major university that is seated in that community, and is now being incorporated into numerous organizations including the Health Department, food bank, organizations serving people who are homeless, the Medical Association and free clinic, physicians' offices, the State Board of Regents, the Community Shelter Board, a child advocacy agency, city government, medical practices, the Chamber of Commerce, United Way, behavioral healthcare leadership development, the state Psychological Association, an MBA program for nonprofit leadership, and many more. In these settings and more, it is easy to find all types of meetings being held that are consciously hosted using the processes of Circle, World Café, Open Space, and Appreciative Inquiry.

A not-for-profit organization is finding great success with system changes in the delivery of primary healthcare. By simply instigating conversations that matter through good invitations to participate in conversations, this organization that holds no actual power—government authority, sanction by business, or legal authority—is being highly successful in creating significant systemic changes related to creating patient-centered medical homes. The not-for-profit organization was influenced by a set of ten public dialogues or assemblies on sustainable health hosted by a small group of committed citizens using the technologies comprised in The Art of Hosting along with key elements from Theory U (Scharmer, 2009). In *Walk Out/Walk On,* authors Margaret Wheatley and Deborah Frieze (2011) offer a complete story of this ongoing transformation.

CHILD AND ADOLESCENT PSYCHIATRIC
CARE IN THE STATE OF OHIO

Similar to almost every state in the United States, Ohio has only a small portion of the child and adolescent psychiatrists needed to serve the needs of its citizens. The Ohio Department of Mental Health first commissioned a study to document this problem. One of the recommendations from that study was that a multi-stakeholder task force be established to investigate this issue more thoroughly and to deliver a set of recommendations to the director and to the governor on how to improve on this situation. A core team was selected to develop the question that was to be directed to the task force. The core team's question was, "What is required to increase access to child and adolescent psychiatric services across the State of Ohio?" The multi-stakeholder task force, comprising 25 volunteers, reflected the diversity of perspectives represented in this issue and included professionals as well as families of children and adolescents with psychiatric problems. The director of the Ohio Department of Mental Health appointed a chairperson for the task force. The chairperson proposed to use a "Change Lab" process based on the Theory U work of Otto Scharmer (2009a).

The Change Lab engaged all 25 task force members to first complete a review of the literature on increasing access to child and adolescent psychiatry services. Once steeped in the information from this literature review and from their own personal experiences, task force members were trained to do "sensing interviews" (Scharmer, 2009). These are two-hour in-depth interviews, are designed to help the interviewer and the interviewee get beyond what is on the surface of the issue, and help to develop a deeper understanding of the issue from a larger systemic and worldview. Sensing interviews are typically done in the context of the interviewee so that the entire experience of the interviewee can be taken in and the interviewer has a better context for understanding the issue from the interviewee's perspective. Sensing interviews took place with families, children, judges, mental health professionals, general healthcare professionals, directors of programs related to providing services to children with mental health challenges, child welfare professionals, along with many others who participated across the state of Ohio. All twenty-five task force members conducted at least two of sensing interviews. Once the interview process was completed, the task force met for a two-day residential retreat.

At the residential retreat, task force members spent time re-hearing the *voices* (what they actually heard) in the interviews and participated in some solo time in nature to reflect on what they were sensing *was wanting to happen*. Following the solo time, they did some "modeling" (rapid prototyping) using modeling clay, pipe cleaners, and other objects to quickly build three-dimensional models of what a future system of child and adolescent care could look like. Out of this rapid prototyping, three models emerged:

- A more holistic and integrated delivery system of care
- A more integrated funding system for care
- A model of a new advocacy effort to support children and adolescents and their families who struggle with these issues.

Following the retreat, the core team reconvened and wrote a draft report for the whole task force to review. Once the task force members made their changes, the report was finalized and sent to the director of the Ohio Department of Mental Health and to the governor. The report was finished just at the time when the governorship was changing hands in Ohio, so the report had to be reintroduced in a new administration. A number of changes have been reported as a result of this work.

Because of the task force's work and recommendations, the integrated model of care became the main emphasis for mental health system reform, not just for the child and adolescent system but for the whole system of behavioral healthcare. At this time, the integrated model for child and adolescent psychiatric care is being experimented in a number of settings across Ohio. One interesting outcome of the task force's work is a collaborative project of all three Children's Hospitals in Ohio. From the task force study it became clear that it was not useful to spend an inordinate amount of resources trying to recruit more child and adolescent psychiatrists, but that the existing talent could be used more effectively in an integrated way. This collaboration has resulted in a 1-877-PSY-OHIO phone number that assures any pediatrician or family practice physician in Ohio of a child and adolescent psychiatric consult within thirty minutes, 24/7. This represents both innovation and transformative change!

REPURPOSING A 119-YEAR-OLD COUNTY MEDICAL SOCIETY

Similar to most trade associations, the Columbus Medical Association (CMA) has, for 119 years, worked very hard to meet the needs of physicians of all specialties residing in Columbus, Ohio. This particular medical society has a long and proud history of being entrepreneurial in meeting both the physician community's and public's needs. Historically, the medical society's core task has been to physically bring physicians together so that physicians experienced being part of a physicians' community. This sense of community had many and different benefits to its members over time. Through needs surveys and good intuition, the staff of the medical society was able to provide both professional and social functions that had resulted in reasonable membership numbers as well as revenue from sponsors and advertisers wanting to gain the attention of physicians. However, when the CMA took a closer look, an awareness developed that signaled that this trade association model was no longer sustainable.

Rather than trying to tinker with a formula for trade associations that has been used for a very long time, the CMA's board of directors asked a more fundamental question: "What would be the purpose, functions and structure of an organization that supported physician's highest aspirations?" The CMA board of directors even went as far as to question the need for the existence of a local medical society in the twenty-first century; a brave question indeed.

As with the earlier example, the CMA board chose to use a Theory U Change Lab approach to its strategic planning. The board and staff first reviewed the literature on what was happening in the world of medical societies and other trade organizations. In their review of the literature they discovered that they were as contemporary in their thinking and in their offerings as anything they could find in the literature.

Board members and staff were then trained to do the sensing interviews. It was decided that 50 demographically well-stratified interviews would be needed to "sense the whole" of the physician community in Columbus. These are two-hour intense interviews. An important question was whether they could succeed in attracting 50 physicians to sit for two hours and be interviewed. When the invitation was sent out to the membership, 150 physicians indicated a willingness to be interviewed. This response alone was valuable information that suggested that there was some unmet need that this process was tapping into. Staff and board members conducted fifty interviews (the board is composed entirely of physicians), yielding the following generalized results.

- *Connectivity*: Physicians feel very disconnected from each other—there is no sense of a community of physicians any more.
- *Dissatisfaction*: Physicians are not feeling satisfied with how they are being required to practice medicine, which is leading to depression and other health risks.
- *Respect*: Many physicians are feeling a lack of respect from places such as insurance companies, the institutions they work for, and sometimes from their patients as well.
- *Generational Differences*: There are significant differences between how older physicians were trained and view the practice of medicine and the way younger physicians are trained and view their practices.
- *Fragmentation*: Just as patients often feel the effects of a fragmented health care system, so, too, do physicians; and things like making referrals to colleagues can be very challenging.
- *Health Literacy*: Physicians often feel frustrated with the lack of patient compliance with treatment regimens and the influence of drug advertising.
- *Machine Health*: Physicians are increasingly feeling like pieces and parts (cogs in a wheel) of the machine called "health care." This they weren't trained to be.

In looking at the results from these interviews, the board and staff asked themselves what a local medical society could do to help physicians deal with these very negative experiences that physicians were having.

At the planning retreat, based upon a literature review and the physician interviews, the board and staff created three-dimensional models of what a future local medical society could look like. Three models emerged. Staff then took the models and built a single hybrid model. This model was then tested with the board. Additional details were added, and the model was tested by focus groups of physicians. After several focus groups, some additional changes were made to the model and a business plan was developed and subsequently approved by that fundamentally repurposed CMA.

The new CMA's purpose is "to create the conditions for connecting, convening and operationalizing the physician's highest aspirations to improve the health and healing of physicians, individuals and the community" (CMA Strategic Plan, 2011). Getting into the details of the new CMA is not the task of this chapter, but the outcome of transforming and innovating an organization is the purpose of this chapter. Based on the organization's work with Theory U and the change lab, the new model included a new future for how physicians and patients/clients work together. Using a private social media technology a twenty-first century, model includes developing a medical community with physicians positioned at the center of the community. The social media will also include space for physicians to communicate with other physicians about issues that are critical to their practice, and a new way to be in community with their co-workers and patients. As one physician said, "this is a community of physicians with their patients" (CMA, 2011). Results already starting to emerge:

- Six physicians came together for a discussion on Accountable Care Organizations that resulted in a webinar for the whole membership.

- Four physicians came together to discuss physician wellness, which led to the creation of a physician wellness column in the monthly newsletter, made up of tips for wellness by their own colleagues.
- A summit was called at which 36 physicians explored how to improve the referral relationship between primary care physicians and specialists, with a set of principles as the product of that discussion.
- Twelve physicians are exploring whether it is time to develop a local leadership academy for members.

The Columbus Medical Association is now an organization about physicians taking responsibility for their own futures, supported by technology.

A CALL TO ACTION

A recently published article was titled "It's Time for the Heroes to Go Home" (Frieze and Wheatley, 2011). The authors argue that the world is just too complex for the hero model of leadership to hold any possibility of working in the modern world in which we live.

> There are no simple answers, and no single individual can possibly know what to do. Not even the strongest of leaders can deliver on the promise of stability and security. But we seldom acknowledge these complex realities. Instead, when things go wrong, we fire the flawed leader and begin searching for the next (more perfect) one. (Wheatley and Frieze, 2006b, pg. 27)

Perhaps it is time for the heroes to go home. In a world that has always been connected but now realizes it (i.e., using the Internet and social media for easy connections to information and people), perhaps the concept of a leader as host needs to emerge. Host what? That is the question. Most leaders have secretly wished that they could unload these unreasonable expectations. The culture of organizations and the training of leaders has not offered existing leaders the skills or knowledge needed to engage their entire workforce differently in helping to solve the tough problems like service delivery in today's new reality of politics and financial support for community-based services. Learning how to "host" the intelligence of the entire organization may be the most important thing a leader can do today. Servant leadership has gained a great following based on the writing of Greenleaf (2002). Perhaps *hosting* includes the skills servant leaders need to carry this concept to fruition.

Individuals who are being asked to lead multidisciplinary, integrated approaches in health care, or any other field, must be purposefully educated in the skills necessary to support these approaches, because the old command and control leadership practices seldom work in today's world. Individuals with a new set of hosting skills need to be involved. Such an individual needs to be someone who sees the importance of every person in the group and who knows, very clearly, the processes needed to help the group realize its potential. These hosting skills are the skills referred to earlier in this chapter about collective practices (Circle, World Café, Open Space, and Appreciative Inquiry, etc.).

However, while collective practices are beneficial and powerful in and of themselves, this same set of hosting knowledge and skills can also be used in ways that are not beneficial to an organization or to society at large. As one person recently put it, "networks and collective intelligence is not benign" (Nissen, Moeller, and Cass (2011). This is where individual consciousness practice becomes critically important for leaders. When a person establishes a habit, a practice, of meeting themselves every day, it doesn't take long for that person to realize that they are only part of a much bigger picture. It is from that realization that consciousness and conscience begins to diminish the shadows (i.e., negative aspects) in people and organizations and where the light of highest aspirations can be realized. It is necessary for leaders to develop personal and collective practices in order to serve as leaders in a world that so desperately needs these kinds of leaders.

Finally, and perhaps as important as anything shared in this chapter, the transcendent leaders of today need people who support their courage, their humanness, and who participate with them in continuing to co-learn. This notion of leader as host is a work in progress. If done correctly, it will always be a work in progress *because that is the nature of things*, i.e., always emerging. We can refer these as "communities of practice": places where people continue to learn together and practice their practices in real relationships. After all, it is these relationships and continuous lessons that may well be the bottom line anyway. It is always about relationships.

"In the end, it is the reality of personal relationships that saves everything," said Thomas Merton (Forest, 1991).

REFERENCES

Art of Hosting website. See www.artofhosting.org.

Arthur, B. (1999). *From a Conversation with Michael Jung, Peter Senge, and Otto Scharmer. Dialogue on Leadership*. Presencing Institute website: www.presencing.com/presencing/dol/about.shtml.

Baldwin, C. (1998). *Calling the Circle: The First and Future Culture*. New York: Bantam Books.

Baldwin, C., & Linnea, A. (2010). *The Circle Way: A Leader in Every Chair*. San Francisco: Barrett-Koehler Publishers.

Beck, D. E., & Cowan, C. (1996). *Spiral Dynamics: Mastering Values, Leadership and Change*. Cambridge, MA: Blackwell.

Block, P. (2009). *Community: The Structure of Belonging*. San Francisco: Barrett-Kohler Publishers.

Brown, J., & Issacs, D. (2005). *The World Café*. San Francisco: Barrett-Koehler Publishers.

CMA—Columbus Medical Association Strategic Plan. (2011). Graves, C. Human nature prepares for momentous leap. *The Futurist*. April 1974, 72–87.

Cooperrider, D., & Whitney, D. (2005). *Appreciative Inquiry: A Positive Revolution in Change*. San Francisco: Barrett-Kohler Publishers.

Cowan, C., & Todorovic, N. (2005). *The Never-Ending Quest: Clare W. Graves Explores Human Nature*. Santa Barbara, CA: ECLET Publishing.

Greenleaf, R. (2002). *Servant Leadership: A Journey into the Nature of Legitimate Power and Greatness*. Mahwah, NJ: Paulist Press.

Frieze, D., & Wheatley, M. (2011). It's time for the heroes to go home. *Leader to Leader, 62*, 27–32.

Forest, J. (1991). *Living with Wisdom: The Life of Thomas Merton*. New York: Orbis Books.

Kinni, T. (2003). *The Art of Appreciative Inquiry*. Harvard Management Update, Vol. 8, No. 8, August 2003. http://hbswk.hbs.edu/archive/3684.html accessed December 2, 2011.

Nissen, M., Moeller, T., Cass, P., & Weisel, L. (2011). *Leading Transformation Across Collaborative and Hierarchial Cultures*. Mennorode, Netherlands: ALIA Institute.

Nissen, M., Moeller, T., & Cass, P. (2011). *Art of Hosting*. Bisbane, Australia.

Owen, H. (2008). *Open Space Technology: A User's Guide*. San Francisco: Barrett-Kohler Publishers.

Scharmer, C. O. (2009a). *Theory U: Leading from the Future as It Emerges*. San Francisco: Barrett-Kohler Publishers.

Scharmer, C. O. (2009b). Executive Summary. *Theory U; Leading from the Future as It Emerges*. Available at www.presencing.com. Accessed December 7, 2011.

Scharmer, C. O. (2010). Theory U Master Class. Lecture notes.

Weisel, L. (2011). *PowerPath to Education and Employment*. Columbus, OH: The TLP Group.

Wheatley, M., & Kellner-Rogers, M. (1999). *A Simpler Way*. San Francisco: Berrett- Kohler Publishers.

Wheatley, M. J., & Kellner-Rogers, M. (1998). Bringing life to organizational change. *Journal for Strategic Performance Measurement*. April/May 1998. http://www.margaretwheatley.com/articles/life.html. Accessed December 10, 2011.

Wheatley, M. (2006). *Leadership and the New Science: Discovering Order in a Chaotic World*. San Francisco: Barrett-Kohler Publishers.

Wheatley, M., & Frieze, D. (2011). *Walk Out/Walk On*. San Francisco: Barrett-Kohler Publishers.

Williams, J., & Zylowska, L. (2009). *Mindfulness Bibliography*. Los Angeles: Awareness Research Center, UCLA Semel Institute.

DIRECTORY OF INTERNET RESOURCES

American Association of Community Psychiatrists The professional organization dedicated to public and community psychiatrists. They offer publications, conferences and training. www.communitypsychiatry.org

American Association of Suicidology was founded in 1968 as an organization for all those who work in suicide intervention, prevention, or who have been affected by suicide. The organization supports research and provides resources, training, and an annual conference. <http://www.suicidology.org>

American Case Management Association is an organization for hospital case management professionals. ACMA offers resources, certification, conferences and career networking. http://www.acmaweb.org/

American Foundation for Suicide Prevention supports research into suicide prevention, educational campaigns, demonstration projects and policy work. AFSP is growing a network of community based chapters and organizes grassroots campaigns to advocate for state and federal legislation to advance suicide prevention. <http://www.afsp.org>.

American Counseling Association was founded in 1952 as the national organization for professional counselors. ACA provides resources, publications, conferences and policy advocacy. www.counseling.org

American Distance Counseling Assocation a professional organization that advocates for safe online education and mental health treatment. ACDA provides resources and support for distance counselors. http://adca-online.org/index.html

American Psychiatric Association was founded in 1844 and is the world's largest organization dedicated to psychiatry. APA supports research, education, advancement of the field, and provides publications, resources and a charitable division. www.psychiatry.org

American Psychiatric Nurses Association the professional organization dedicated to the advancement of psychiatric mental health nursing. APNA provides resources, continuing education opportunities, networking and publications. www.apna.org

American Psychological Association is the largest organization representing the field of psychology in the world. APA provides resources, publications, policy advocacy, career networking and supports education and research. www.apa.org

American Telemedicine Assocation is the leading international resource for advancing the use of remote medical technology. ATA advocates for public policy, and provides continuing education, meetings, and training program accreditation. www.americantelemed.org

Annapolis Coalition The mission of the Annapolis Coalition is to improve the quality of life of individuals and communities by strengthening the effectiveness of all who work to prevent, treat, and support recovery from mental and substance use conditions. The AC provides resources and assistance to non-profit organizations as well as state and federal agencies. www.annapoliscoalition.org

Assertive Community Treatment Association This site offers much information about the ACT model including fidelity standards, annual conference proceedings and a bibliography. http://www.actassociation.org/.

Assertive Community Treatment (ACT) Evidence-based practices (EBP) kit. This is a "how to" manual for providers interested in implementing this evidence-based practice. http://store.samhsa.gov/product/Assertive-Community-Treatment-ACT-Evidence-Based-Practices-EBP-KIT/SMA08–4345

Association for Academic Psychiatry is focused on education in psychiatry from medical school through lifelong learning for medical professionals. www.academicpsychiatry.org

Association of American Medical Colleges provides leadership and publications for the academic medical community. www.aamc.org

Behavioral Healthcare A news journal that provides contemporary articles on all matters of behavioral healthcare http://www.behavioral.net

Business Dictionary www.businessdictionary.com

Case Management Society of America is the professional organization for Case Managers in the healthcare fields. http://www.cmsa.org/

Center for Evidence Based Practices at Case Western Reserve University provides consultation, training and evaluation for service innovations that improve the quality of life for people with mental illness or co-occurring disorders. www.centerforebp.case.edu

Center for Psychiatric Rehabilitation Boston University provides research, training and service dedicated to improving the lives of persons with psychiatric disabilities. www.bu.edu/cpr/

Centers of Excellence in Ohio, Pennsylvania, and Florida The goal of the Ohio Criminal Justice Coordinating Center of Excellence is for each county in the State to develop an array of programs that will divert people with mental disorders from jail and keep people with mental disorders in treatment through the utilization of the Sequential Intercept Model. http://cjcccoe.neomed.edu/

Child Trauma Academy is a non-profit organization that works to improve the lives of high-risk children through service, research and education. http://www.childtrauma.org/

CIT International is a non-profit organization whose purpose is to facilitate understanding, development and implementation of Crisis Intervention Teams. http://www.citinternational.org

Coming Off Medications provides information about psychiatric medication and the withdrawal process. www.comingoff.com

Council of State Governments Criminal Justice/Mental Health Consensus Report national nonpartisan effort to bring together state leaders for vigorous and collaborative dialog to initiate innovative changes supported by research and public policy. CSG, in collaboration with local, state, and federal stakeholders, created the Criminal Justice/Mental Health Consensus Project Report, a document designed to make specific recommendations to improve the criminal justice system's response to people with mental illness. http://consensusproject.org/

The Criminal Justice, Mental Health, and Substance Abuse Technical Assistance Center at the University of South Florida, Florida Mental Health Institute, provides technical assistance to counties in preparing a grant application, assists applicant counties in projecting the effect of the proposed intervention on the population of the county detention facility, disseminate and share evidence-based and best practices among grantees and statewide, acts as a clearinghouse for information and resources related to criminal justice, juvenile justice, mental health, and substance abuse. http://www.floridatac.org/

Dartmouth IPS Supported Employment Center provides resources about Individual Placement and Support (IPS) supported employment. www.dartmouth.edu/~ips

EASA Early Assessment & Support Alliance provides information and support to young people in Oregon who are experiencing symptoms of psychosis for the first time. http://www.eastcommunity.org

Florida CIT http://www.floridacit.org/

Georgia Mental Health Consumer Network is a non-profit organization founded by consumers of state services for mental health, developmental disabilities and addictive diseases. http://www.gmhcn.org/

Georgia Certified Peer Specialist Project implements peer support services, Assertive Community Treatment Teams, Community Support Individuals and other services to assist peers in their recovery journeys. www.gacps.org

Harm Reduction Guide To Coming Off Psychiatric Drugs, by Will Hall, published by Icarus Project and Freedom Center, 2007 www.willhall.net/comingoffmeds

Health Resources and Service Administration (HRSA) Health Professionals Shortage Area Directory http://hpsafind.hrsa.gov/HPSASearch.aspx

The Icarus Project is a network of people living with or affected by experiences that are often diagnosed or labeled as psychiatric conditions. www.theicarusproject.net

Institute for Healthcare Improvement A web based resource that provides a series of modules and white papers discussing health care improvement and patient care. http://www.ihi.org

Institute of Medicine of the National Academies is an independent, non-profit organization that works outside of the government to provide unbiased and authoritative advice to decision makers and the public. www.iom.edu

International Critical Incident Stress Foundation provides leadership, education, training, consultation and support services in comprehensive crisis intervention and disaster behavioral health services to the emergency response professions, other organizations and communities worldwide. http://www.icisf.org

International Early Psychosis Association is an international network for the study and treatment of early psychosis. http://www.iepa.org.au

International Society for Mental Health Online is an international community that explores and promotes mental health in the digitial age. https://www.ismho.org/home.asp

The Judge David L. Bazelon Center for Mental Health Law a national organization with a longitudinal history of effective legal and social advocacy opposing involuntary civil commitment based on individual rights to liberty and access to treatment in the least restrictive environment necessary. http://bazelon.org

Justice Center A project of the Council of State Governments, the Center is a national nonprofit agency designed to help improve the response to individuals with mental illness who come in contact with the criminal justice system by providing technical assistance, information dissemination of new research, program, and policy developments in the field, and educational presentations pertaining to mental health and criminal justice. The Center promotes data informed practices to create practical solutions to address public safety and cross-systems issues at the local, state, and federal level. http://www.justicecenter.csg.org/

Liaison Committee on Medical Education The Liaison Committee on Medical Education (LCME) is the nationally recognized accrediting authority for medical education programs leading to the MD degree in the United States and Canada. The LCME is sponsored by the Association of American Medical Colleges and the American Medical Association. www.lcme.org

Madness Radio www.madnessradio.net

Medicaid and Telemedicine http://www.medicaid.gov/Medicaid-CHIP-Program-Information/By-Topics/Delivery-Systems/Telemedicine.html

Mental Health First Aid a collaborative education program that helps the public identify, understand, and respond to signs of mental illnesses and substance use disorders. Mental Health First Aid USA is managed, operated, and disseminated by three national authorities—the National Council for Community Behavioral Healthcare, the Maryland Department of Health and Mental Hygiene, and the Missouri Department of Mental Health. http://www.mentalhealthfirstaid.org/cs/program_overview/

Mental Health A Report of the Surgeon General, reports on the scientific research along the continuum of mental health and mental illness across the lifespan. Addresses treatment, administration and policy, costs, consumers, privacy and confidentiality, ethics and values, and future visions. http://www.surgeongeneral.gov/library/mentalhealth

Mental Help A quick resource providing tips on how to address a wide variety of mental health challenges. This site also provides the opportunity to chat online with a psychiatrist. http://mentalhelp.net/

National Alliance on Mental Illness (NAMI) a national organization with state and affiliated local chapters providing advocacy, education, and support for individuals and family members including a succinct primer on mandated treatment options for many states. http://www.nami.org

National Association of Case Management This site provides case managers, service coordinators, supervisors, and program administrators with an opportunity for professional growth and for the promotion of case management. http://www.yournacm.com/

NAMI CIT Resource Center http://www.nami.org/template.cfm?section=CIT2

The National Archives (Veterans' Service Records) This site provides the opportunity to request military service records, research using military records, and the opportunity to browse WWII photos and many other resources online. www.archives.gov/veterans

National Association of Addiction Treatment Providers has assumed a strong leadership role on behalf of treatment providers in areas such as treatment standards, education, research, and advocacy of legislative, regulatory and reimbursement positions supported by the field. www.naatp.org

National Association of Social Workers This site provides resources, and guides for social workers, it is designed to facilitate professional growth and development of NASW members. www.socialworkers.org

National Association of State Mental Health Program Directors This organization provides national representation and advocacy for state mental health agencies and their directors and supports effective stewardship of state mental health systems. http://www.nasmhpd.org/

The National Association of County Veteran Service Officers This site is a one-stop shop for county veteran service officers assisting with linking with resources, documents forma and to keep providers informed of changes in legislation impacting veteran services. www.nacvso.org

The National Board for Certified Counselors This resources provides information on certification, advocacy efforts updates for the profession as well as resources for certification and career advancement. www.nbcc.org

National Collaborating Centre for Mental Health The National Collaborating Centre for Mental Health (NCCMH) is one of four centres established by the National Institute for Health and Clinical Excellence (NICE) to develop guidance on the appropriate treatment and care of people with specific diseases and conditions within the NHS in England and Wales. It provides guidelines, updates of events, and publications of interest. www.nccmh.org.uk

National Institute for Health and Clinical Excellence This site provides guidance for improving quality of care through access to quality standards, practice guidelines and educational links. www.nice.org.uk

National Institute of Mental Health (NIMH) Provides links to health topics research and funding as well as clinical resources on a variety of mental health topics, treatments and research. www.nimh.nih.gov

The National Center for PTSD Provides sites to veteran services, education and support, benefits and services and well as information on a variety of health and well-being topics. http://www.ptsd.va.gov/

The National Center for Trauma-Informed Care SAMHSA's National Center for Trauma-Informed Care (NCTIC) is a technical assistance center dedicated to building awareness of trauma-informed care and promoting the implementation of trauma-informed practices in programs and services. http://www.samhsa.gov/nctic/

National Child Traumatic Stress Network Provides forums for parents, care givers, families, professionals and educators on issues of traumatic stress in children including treatment services, a variety of support networks, education on a variety of trauma topics. http://www.nctsn.org/

The National Reentry Resource Center A project of the Council of State Governments, was established by the Second Chance Act (Public Law 110–199) to provide education, training, and technical assistance to state, local, tribes, territories, nonprofit agencies, and correctional institutions working on prisoner reentry. http://www.nationalreentryresourcecenter.org

New Research in Mental Health http://mentalhealth.ohio.gov/what-we-do/promote/research-and-evaluation/publications/new-research-in-mental-health.shtml

Ohio's Coordinating Centers of Excellence Provides resources for a variety of professionals promoting jail diversion alternatives for people with mental disorders. It provides information on crisis intervention teams, jail diversion research and links to a variety of resources designed to promote jail diversion. http://www.mh.state.oh.us/what-we-do/promote/coordinating-centers-of-excellence.shtml

Ohio Criminal Justice Coordinating Center of Excellence http://cjccoe.neoucom.edu/

Orygen Early Psychosis Prevention and Intervention Center (EPPIC) This website is a training and education resource for early psychosis clinicians and researchers. http://www.eppic.org.au

Peer Support and Wellness Center http://www.gmhcn.org/wellnesscenter/

Permanent Supportive Housing Evidence-Based Practices (EBP) Kit http://store.samhsa.gov/product/SMA10–4510?WT.ac=AD20100918HP_SMA10–4510

The Pennsylvania Mental Health and Justice Center of Excellence is a collaborative effort of Drexel University and the University of Pittsburgh to work with Pennsylvania communities to reduce the involvement of people with serious mental illness and often co-occurring substance use disorders in the criminal justice system. The Center uses the Sequential Intercept Model to identify points of interception for diversion, implement programs, provide information to promote use of evidence-based practices, and serve as a resource for technical assistance and training. http://www.pacenterofexcellence.pitt.edu/index.html

Portland Hearing Voices Portland Hearing Voices is a community group to promote mental diversity. We create public education, discussion groups, training, and community support related to hearing voices, seeing visions, and having unusual beliefs and sensory experiences often labeled as psychosis, bipolar, mania, paranoia, schizophrenia, and other mental disorders www.portlandhearingvoices.net

President's New Freedom Commission on Mental Health http://store.samhsa.gov/product/Achieving-the-Promise-Transforming-Mental-Health-Care-in-America-Executive-Summary/SMA03–3831

Project GREAT webpage hosted by the Department of Psychiatry and Health Behavior of Georgia Health Sciences University—includes links to Project GREAT publications and resources for consumers and practitioners. Available: http://www.georgiahealth.edu/medicine/psychiatry/projectgreat.html

Recovery to Practice Resources Center for Behavioral Health Professionals—Webpage provides practitioners with information about recovery and recovery-oriented practice. Information available: http://www2.dsgonline.com/rtp/resources.html

The Royal College of Psychiatrists Provides resources and links for psychiatrist in the UK, including fact sheets, resources and tools, support services and career development for those practicing psychiatry. www.rcpsych.ac.uk

The Schizophrenia Patient Outcome Research Team (PORT) treatment recommendations for schizophrenia. Available: http://www.state.sc.us/dmh/clinical/port.htm

Substance Abuse and Mental Health Services Administration (SAMHSA) Provides links to research education, publications, grant information and strategic initiatives. It is devoted to providing information to assist persons to act on knowledge to promote mental wellness www.samhsa.gov

SAMHSA's GAINS Center for Behavioral Health and Justice System Transformation A nationally recognized center that addresses system- and service-level issues for individuals with co-occurring disorders involved in the criminal justice system with an emphasis on evidence-based practices. http://gainscenter.samhsa.gov/. For a complete explanation of terms and components of the criminal justice system, see the National GAINS Center monograph "Working with People with Mental illness Involved in the Criminal Justice System: What Mental Health Service Providers Need to Know." http://gainscenter.samhsa.gov/pdfs/jail_diversion/Massaro.pdf

Temple University Collaborative on Community Inclusion of Individuals with Psychiatric Disabilities is a National Rehabilitation Research and Training Center, Funded by the National Institute on Disability and Rehabilitation Research. www.tucollaborative.org

The Texas Medication Algorithm Project for Schizophrenia Available: http://schizophreniabulletin. oxfordjournals.org/content/30/3/627.full.pdf

Trauma Informed Care Resources is a page of resources compiled by The Anna Insititute. http://www. theannainstitute.org/TIC-RESOURCES.html

Trauma Informed Webliography http://theacademy.sdsu.edu/programs/BHETA/trauma_informed_ webliography.pdf

Treatment Advocacy Center (TAC) a national organization with a longitudinal history of policy and social advocacy for advancement of individual and public mental health interventions including involuntary civil commitment. http://www.treatmentadvocacycenter.org/

United Nations Enable The Convention in Brief http://www.un.org/disabilities/default.asp?navid= 13&pid=162

The United States Department of Veterans Affairs www.va.gov

University of Kansas School of Social Welfare Office of Mental Health Research and Training http:// www.socwel.ku.edu/mentalhealth/projects/promising/supporthousing.shtml

University of Memphis CIT Center http://cit.memphis.edu

University of Verona Department of Public Health and Community Medicine Section of Psychiatry and Clinical Psychology http://www.psychiatry.univr.it/

Vet Center Readjustment Counseling Services www.vetcenter.va.gov

Wellness Recovery Action Plans-Mary Ellen Copland www.mentalhealthrecovery.com/

ZiaPartners, Inc www.ziapartners.com

GLOSSARY

ALLOPATHIC the term used by alternative medicine advocates to refer to the practice of conventional medicine, which uses pharmacological or physical interventions.

ASSERTIVE OUTREACH involves frequent visits to consumers in their home or other community settings to offer services and supports, rather than waiting in an office for consumers to show up for services.

BOUNDARY SPANNING Collaborative professional teamwork that attempts to engage and employ the combined talents of individuals who previously operated independently due perceived systemic, cultural, or institutional divisions

CASE MANAGEMENT A collaborative process of assessment, planning, facilitation, and advocacy for options and services to meet an individual's holistic needs through communication and available resources to promote quality, cost-effective outcomes.

CERTIFIED PEER SPECIALIST a person in recovery from a serious mental illness who has completed training in how to offer self-help and other supports to their peers.

CIVIL COMMITMENT as defined by state law, the civil process for admitting (usually involuntarily) someone to inpatient or outpatient psychiatric treatment.

CLEAR AND CONVINCING EVIDENCE the median of three legal standards by which evidence is established with at least 75 percent judicial certainty. The standard is applied to civil commitment and other circumstances to which civil liberties and individual freedoms are determined. "Clear and convincing evidence" compares to standards of "preponderance of the evidence"—51 percent certainty (more likely than not) and "beyond a reasonable doubt"—90 to 95 percent certainty. The "clear and convincing evidence" standard specifically weighs "the individual's interest in not being involuntarily confined indefinitely and the state's interest in committing the emotionally disturbed [person]."

CLIENT-CENTERED APPROACH insures that treatment is designed to address the unique strengths and needs of the individual served.

COGNITIVE BEHAVIORAL THERAPY (CBT) CBT is a type of talk therapy that focuses on changing faulty thought processes to bring about improvement in negative emotions and dysfunctional behaviors.

COLLABORATIVE CARE sharing of mental health and medical care information between medical and mental health care settings so that care may be coordinated. It involves working with the consumer and all others involved in their care and treatment toward the achievement of a mutually agreed-upon goal or goals: "Nothing about me without me!"

COMMUNITY INTEGRATION involves the opportunity for a patient to live, learn, work, and socialize in natural community settings with others who may or may not have a disability.

COMORBIDITY The occurrence of a mental disorder and another disorder in the same individual at the same time. Examples include: a mental disorder and a physical disorder; a mental disorder and a substance-use disorder; a mental disorder and a developmental disability disorder.

CONTINUITY OF CARE while hospital psychiatry is based on individual episodes of care, community psychiatry is based on the ongoing responsibility toward the individual patients in their charge. The structure of the service and programs, the organization of community teams, and the style of intervention aim at maintaining a continuous relationship. This reinforces the therapeutic relationship and ideally transforms it into a therapeutic alliance, which is usually difficult to establish in the public system and with the most severely ill patients.

CRISIS An acute disruption of psychological homeostasis in which one's usual coping mechanisms fail and there is evidence of distress and functional impairment. It is the subjective reaction to a stressful life experience that compromises the individual's stability and their ability to cope or function.

CRISIS EVENT A subjective response to external stimuli involving stress or a traumatic life event, or series of events, that are perceived by the person as hazardous, threatening, or extremely upsetting, which is not resolved by using the person's inherent coping mechanisms.

CRISIS INTERVENTION TEAM (CIT) A police-based mental health response model designed to pair specially trained law enforcement officers to assist individuals experiencing a mental health crisis.

CULTURAL COMPETENCE the ability to interact effectively with people of different cultures, values. and belief systems.

DD214 Department of Defense Form 214 is a "Certificate of Release or Discharge from Active Duty" that is given to a military veteran upon being discharged from active duty with the military. The document verifies a veteran's rank, time of service, dates of service, awards, military occupation, and the character of his service.

DEINSTITUTIONALIZATION refers to the movement of persons with severe mental illness from large institutions into the community, and the full or partial closures of these institutions. This change has been credited to the development of chlorpromazine (Thorazine), the first effective antipsychotic medication.

DISCRIMINATION the prejudicial treatment of an individual based on their membership in a specific group.

DUAL DIAGNOSIS a term commonly used to describe a combination of an alcohol or substance-use disorder and a mental disorder.

DURATION OF UNTREATED PSYCHOSIS (DUP) The period of time during which an individual who is experiencing psychosis first receives treatment from a mental health clinician.

EARLY INTERVENTION Specialized treatment provided during the at-risk period or prodromal state or the first episode of acute psychosis.

EARLY PSYCHOSIS Refers to a stage of illness that is considered either an at-risk stage of developing a major psychotic disorder or the first episode of a major psychotic disorder.

ETHNOCENTRISM the belief that one's own cultural or ethnic group is central; evaluating all other groups in relation to one's own culture.

EVIDENCE-BASED PRACTICE (EBP) an intervention that has been empirically researched using randomized controlled trials and has been found to consistently produce positive outcomes.

FACILITATOR A person designated to provide support and guidance to the person with mental illness to ensure that s/he actively participates in the service planning process, that the interdisciplinary team understands her/his perspective about all components of the plan, and that the person understands the team's perspective.

FAMILY-AIDED COMMUNITY TREATMENT (FACT) FACT integrates all the treatment components for a person with a psychotic condition into one coordinated system. The treatment includes:

community-based counseling and case management, employment and education support, medication management, occupational therapy, and family support and counseling. This integration of all the components, including family support, reduces the likelihood of contradictions, collusion, and disagreements among those who are invested in the recovery of the individual (McFarlane, Stastny, & Deakins, 1992).

FIRST EPISODE OF PSYCHOSIS The term is used to denote the first onset of full acute psychotic symptom(s). It may not be clear what the specific diagnosis is during this period; the individual is distressed or impaired by the clear presence of the symptoms, is modifying their behavior based on psychotic symptoms, and is unable to engage in active reality-testing.

FIRST RESPONDER A public safety professional initially dispatched to or arriving at the scene of a crisis or emergency; oftentimes a police officer, firefighter, or paramedic.

GRASS ROOTS A movement or action of and by the ordinary people, as distinct from a movement instigated and led by the active leadership of a party or organization.

GROUP PSYCHOTHERAPY a time-limited process, with the therapist's role and group process derived from a specific theoretical approach (dynamic, supportive, or specialized focus).

HEALTH HOME A provider or team of health professionals who provide integrated health care for an individual. In a Health Home, all providers coordinate treatment based on shared information.

HOMEOSTASIS A natural state of equilibrium that all people seek. An individual is more amenable to intervention when in a state of disequilibrium caused by an acute event.

HOPE Hope is the catalyst of the recovery process. Recovery provides the essential and motivating message of a better future, that people can and do overcome the barriers and obstacles that confront them. Hope is an internal state; but it can be fostered by peers, families, friends, providers, and others.

INTERDISCIPLINARY TEAM a group of professionals representing various clinical specialties who contribute their individual expertise to the treatment of mutual clients.

INTERPROFESSIONAL working with individuals of other professions while maintaining a climate of mutual respect and shared values.

ITALIAN PSYCHIATRIC REFORM This reform was passed in 1978 when a small, but very active, radical party issued a national referendum to repeal the existing mental health law that supported the system of the state mental hospitals. The government quickly summoned a commission to draw up a new law, which incorporated a number of the ideas and treatment modalities developed in the previous two decades by the deinstitutionalization movement, whose most famous representative was Dr. Franco Basaglia.

MANAGED CARE Any arrangement for health care in which an organization, such as an HMO, another type of healthcare mental healthcare network, or an insurance company, acts as an intermediary between the person seeking care and the care provider.

MEDICAL MODEL a Western approach to health care that focuses on symptom-reduction through the use of medication.

MICRO-AGGRESSION brief and commonplace daily verbal, behavioral, or environmental indignities, whether intentional or unintentional, that communicate hostile, derogatory, or negative racial slights and insults toward people of other races.

MICRO-INSULTS communications that convey rudeness or insensitivity and demean a person's racial heritage or identity.

MONOCULTURALISM actively preserving a culture; excluding external influences.

MULTICULTURALISM the appreciation, acceptance, or promotion of multiple cultures.

MULTIDISCIPLINARY TEAM a group of professionals representing various clinical specialties working independently with a mutual client. Little communication and coordination occurs among the team members.

NORMALIZATION a principle insuring that people with psychiatric disabilities have the opportunity to participate in life activities that are as close as possible to what society typically offers to all its citizens.

NATIONAL ASSOCIATION OF STATE MENTAL HEALTH PROGRAM DIRECTORS (NASMHPD) member organization representing state executives responsible for the $36.7 billion public mental health service delivery system serving 6.8 million people annually in all 50 states, four territories, and the District of Columbia. NASMHPD operates under a cooperative agreement with the National Governors' Association.

NATIONAL MENTAL HEALTH ACT OF 1946 signed into law by President Harry S Truman, this created a significant amount of funding for psychiatric research and education, leading to the founding of the National Institute of Mental Health (NIMH) in 1949.

OSTEOPATHIC MEDICINE a branch of medicine with a historical emphasis on primary care and holistic health.

PATIENT PROTECTION AND AFFORDABLE CARE ACT OF MARCH 2010 signed into law in March 2010, it reformed specific aspects of the private health insurance industry and public health insurance programs. Features include mandatory insurance, increased coverage of preexisting conditions, and increased access to health insurance to previously uninsured Americans.

PEER a self-disclosed consumer of mental health service with lived experience with mental illness who works in service settings as an equal with non-consumer employee-colleagues.

PEER SUPPORT Mental health consumers providing support to peers in order to promote wellness and bolster skills needed to work toward recovery.

PERSON-CENTERED APPROACH A non-directive approach to being with another; which believes in the other's potential and ability to make the right choices for himself or her self, regardless of the clinician's own values, beliefs, and ideas.

PREJUDICE making a judgment or assumption about someone or something before acquiring accurate information.

PRESIDENT'S NEW FREEDOM COMMISSION ON MENTAL HEALTH (2003) the first Presidential Commission (President George W. Bush) on mental health convened since the Carter administration, it was charged with assessing the state of mental health care in the United States. The Commission made sweeping recommendations and called for fundamental transformation of mental health services.

PROGRAM EVALUATION a form of appraisal, using valid and reliable research methods, that examines the processes and outcomes of an organization or program.

PSYCHIATRIC ADVANCE DIRECTIVE a legal instrument developed by a competent person defining specific instructions and preferences regarding recovery and future mental health treatment.

PSYCHIATRIC REHABILITATION Mental health service that focuses on developing skills and supports needed to function in a specific residential, vocational, educational, or social role of the individual's choice.

QUALITY MANAGEMENT a multidimensional concept that generally refers to leaders and leadership who demonstrate an array of characteristics such as accessibility, assurance, communication, competence, courtesy, durability, humaneness, performance, security, reliability, responsiveness, and tangibles.

RECOVERY A process of change through which individuals improve their health and wellness, live a self-directed life, and strive to reach their full potential. Through the Recovery Support Strategic Initiative, the Substance Abuse and Mental Health Services Administration (SAMHSA) also has delineated four major dimensions that support a life in recovery:

Health: Overcoming or managing one's disease(s) as well as living in a physically and emotionally healthy way.

Home: A stable and safe place to live.

Purpose: Meaningful daily activities, such as a job, school, voluntarism, family caretaking, or creative endeavors; and the independence, income, and resources to participate in society.

Community: Relationships and social networks that provide support, friendship, love, and hope. (SAMHSA, 2011)

REHABILITATION MODEL an approach to health care that focuses on developing adaptive functioning through skills training and environmental supports.

SERVICE-CONNECTED DISABILITY an injury or illness that was incurred or aggravated during active military service.

SHARED DECISION-MAKING an approach to treatment planning that promotes the consumer's role in the process through discussion of intervention options and their personal values and preferences related to these options.

SOCIOECONOMIC STATUS (SES) a sociological measure of a person or family's economic position in relation to others, factoring in income, education, and occupation. Typically sorted into high, middle, and low SES.

STEPPED CARE Monitoring physical and mental symptoms in order to inform adjustments to services to either a higher or lower intensity, as needed.

STIGMA Refers to a cluster of negative attitudes and beliefs that motivate the general public to fear, reject, avoid, and discriminate against people with mental illness.

THERAPEUTIC CASE MANAGER the worker in charge of a patient acts as the principal therapist and case manager at the same time. He has his own decision power when there is no time to consult the team, but can also count on all the other members of the team and on other health and social agencies in the area where he can refer his patient. In some systems, instead of a formal referral, the worker in charge prefers to accompany his patient to the colleague or other agency if necessary, so acting as a guide and mentor.

TOKENISM the practice of making only a symbolic effort to include an individual to prevent criticism or give the appearance of equal treatment, involvement, or participation.

TRANSDISCIPLINARY TEAM A group of professionals from various backgrounds who may work collaboratively and across disciplinary boundaries to offer knowledge and skills to mutual clients. A great deal of information-sharing and coordination occurs among the team members.

TRAUMA the experience of violence and victimization, including sexual abuse, physical abuse, severe neglect, loss, domestic violence and/or the witnessing of violence, terrorism, disasters, and natural disasters.

TRAUMA-INFORMED CARE care that is organized around a contemporary, comprehensive understanding of the impact of trauma that emphasizes strengths and safety, and focuses on skill development for individuals to rebuild a sense of personal control over their life.

TREATMENT MALL a physical entity, usually in a central location, offering a variety of services and resources with the aim of enhancing recovery.

QUALITY MANAGEMENT a multidimensional concept that generally refers to leaders and leadership who demonstrate an array of characteristics such as accessibility, assurance, communication, competence, courtesy, durability, humaneness, performance, security, reliability, responsiveness, and tangibles.

WAIVERS Vehicles states can use to test new or existing ways to deliver and pay for health care services in Medicaid.

VBA The Veteran Benefits Administration is the agency of the Department of Veteran Affairs that administers access to and distribution of benefits to veterans or qualifying family members.

VETERAN SERVICE OFFICER (VSO) a person trained to assist a veteran accessing benefits. The VSO will have knowledge of the various benefits and agencies that offer assistance to veterans and will know the process to apply for these benefits.

VETERANS HEALTH ADMINISTRATION (VHA) The Veterans Health Administration is the agency of the Department of Veteran Affairs that provides healthcare for qualifying military veterans.

INDEX